HUMAN RESOURCE MANAGEMENT
INDUSTRIAL RELATION
LABOUR WELFARE

For

UGC-NET/SET

(Competitive Examinations)

(IBPS Specialist officer, Management Trainee-SAIL, ONGC, GAIL, MSEB, HPCL, MOIL, BHEL)

Mr. Nilesh S. Ugemuge

UGC-NET(HRM), UGC-NET(IR), SET(SW), PGDHRM, MIRPM, MSW
M.Sc.(Phy.), MA(Eco.), MA(Pub. Administration), B.Ed.
Assistant Professor
Priyadarshini College of Engineering,
Nagpur (Maharashtra).

Er. Moreshwar N. Kudkilwar

B.E.(Fire), LLB, PGDIS, MIRPM
Sr. Fire Officer
Neelam Process Complex
ONGC, Bombay High, **Mumbai.**

Forwarded by

Arunkumar S. Sutaria, IAS

Revenue Inspection Commissioner & Ex-officio Secretary to Government, Revenue Department, Sachivalaya, Gandhinagar, **Govt. of Gujarat**.

Himalaya Publishing House

MUMBAI • DELHI • NAGPUR • BANGALORE • HYDERABAD • CHENNAI • PUNE • LUCKNOW
AhMEDABAD • ERNAKULAM • BHUBANESWAR • INDORE • KOLKATA • GUWAHATI

First Edition : 2013

Published by : Mrs. Meena Pandey
for **HIMALAYA PUBLISHING HOUSE PVT. LTD.,**
"Ramdoot", Dr. Bhalerao Marg, Girgaon, Mumbai - 400 004.
Phones: 23860170, 23863863, Fax: 022-23877178.
Email: himpub@vsnl.com Website: www.himpub.com

Branch Offices:

New Delhi : "Pooja Apartments", 4-B, Murari Lal Street, Ansari Road, Darya Ganj, New Delhi-110 002. Phones: 23270392, 23278631, Fax: 011-23256286

Nagpur : Kundanlal Chandak Industrial Estate, Ghat Road, Nagpur - 440 018. Phones: 2738731, 3296733 Telefax: 0712-2721216.

Bengaluru : No. 16/1 (Old 12/1), 1st Floor, Next to Hotel Highlands, Madhava Nagar, Race Course Road, Bengaluru - 560 001. Phones: 22281541, 22385461, Telefax: 080-22286611.

Hyderabad : No. 3-4-184, Lingampally, Besides Raghavendra Swamy Matham,Kachiguda, Hyderabad - 500 027. Phones: 040-27560041, 27550139.

Chennai : No. 85/50, Bazullah Road, T. Nagar, Chennai - 600 017. Phones: 044-32463737, 42124860.

Pune : First Floor, "Laksha" Apartment, No. 527, Mehunpura, Shaniwarpeth, (Near Prabhat Theatre), Pune - 411 030. Phones: 020-24496323, 24496333.

Lucknow : House No. 731, Shekhupura Colony, Near B.D. Convent School, Vikas Nagar, Aliganj, Lucknow - 226022. Mob: 09307501549.

Ahmedabad : 114, "SHAIL",1st Floor, Opp. Madhu Sudan House, C.G.Road, Navrang Pura, Ahmedabad - 380 009. Phone: 079-26560126.

Ernakulam : 39/176 (New No: 60/251) 1ST Floor,Karikkamuri Road,Ernakulam, Kochi - 682011, Kerala. Tel : (91) (0484) 2378012, 2378016.

Bhubaneswar : 5 Station Square, Bhubaneswar (Orissa) - 751 001. Phone: 0674-2532129,9338746007.

Indore : Kesardeep Avenue Extension, 73 Narayan Bagh, Flat No. 302, IIIrd Floor, Near Humpty Dumpty School, Narayan Bagh, Indore (M.P.).

Kolkata : 108/4, Beliaghata Main Road, Near ID Hospital, Opp. SBI Bank, Kolkata - 700 010. Phone: 033-32449649.

Guwahati : House No. 15, Behind Pragjyotish College Near Sharma Printing Press, P.O. Bharalumukh, Guwahati-781 009 (Assam). Mobile: 09883055590/36.

Printed at : Geetanjali Press Pvt. Ltd., Nagpur on behalf of H.P.H.

Dedicated To

Our Beloved

Parents

सत्यमेव जयते

Shri. Arun Kumar S. Sutaria, IAS

Revenue Inspection Commissioner & Ex-officio Secretary to Government, Revenue Department, Sachivalaya, Gandhinagar

FORWARD

I am delighted to write the foreword to the first edition of Human Resource Management Industrial Relation and Labour Welfare for UGC-NET/SET and other competitive examination by Prof. Nilesh S. Ugemuge & Er. Moreshwar N. Kudkilwar for several reasons.

It is truly an excellent, complete study material for the UGC-NET/SET in HRM/IR/LW. This book includes comprehensive concepts about every topics and objective question answer for the detail preparation. Indeed, it makes the reader easy and cognizable.

Prof. Nilesh S. Ugemuge and Er. Moreshwar N. Kudkilwar are unusual and unique blend of talent which make them an excellent textbook auther.They are academically well trained and recognized HRM scholar. In addition they have adequate academic and industry experience.

Therefore in view of the above, I would like to foreword this book for the aspirants of UGC-NET/SLET in Human Resource Management. In particular, this book will be useful to students of HRM, IR & LW.

(Shri. Arun Kumar S. Sutaria, IAS)

PREFACE

The idea come and crop up to bring this master piece in the form of text book only for those thousands and lakhs of students who are in search of their attainment and achievement of goal in the field of Human Resource Management. The aim of this project is to provide a textbook distinctly covering the basics and intricacies of the topics laid down into the content of this book.

While preparing for competitive examinations adequate and legible study material is required this can give elaborate idea about the topic in short period of time. An attempt is being made to bring this all requirements of the readers at one platform at the same time in form of this book. This book provide the extensive material in the form of more than two thousand objective type question for the aspirants of various competitive examination in the field of HRM and allied subjects like Industrial Relation, Labour Welfare etc.

Also an attempt has been made to cover wide spectrum of contents with illustrations and associated objective type questions followed by their answers. Each section of chapter begins with an outline of contents and learning objectives.

In preparing this edition, a sincere effort has been made towards the clarity in explanation and legibility of the words. Keeping in view the extensive practice to answer objective questions large number of associated objective type questions on respective topics is incorporated.

We wish to express our heartfelt gratitude to our family member and colleagues of Department for their constant support and encouragement during this project. We would like to express our heartfelt thanks to the Management of LTJSS, Principal Dr. M. P. Singh and Dr. R. V. Kshirsagar, Vice Principal and Dean Faculty of Engineering, RTM Nagpur University, for their encouragement. We would also like to express our gratitude to all those who helped us, in every way in our endeavor.

An untiring help rendered by Mr. **Gokulji Pandey** is sincerely acknowledged. We wish to particularly thank the entire team of Himalaya Publishing House for their continuous help of all kind.

We are grateful to and in particular thank the Himalaya Publishing House for their constant support in all kind.

Constructive criticism and suggestions will be most welcome.

Nilesh S.Ugemuge

nilesh_pce@hotmail.com

Moreshwar N. Kudkilwar

mkudkilwar@gmail.com

ACKNOWLEDGEMENTS

A large number of works were consulted while preparing the present book. The authors do not claim originality in content or presentation of the material included in this book. The authors record here their indebtedness to the authors of those original works from where much of the information is liberally drawn.

We offer our thanks to Gokulji Pandey and team of Himalaya Publication for constant support during entire work and giving the opportunity to publish this book.

I also thanks to editorial staff of HPH for designing and arranging text in an appropriate manner.

CONTENTS

UNIT - I

SCHOOLS OF MANAGEMENT THOUGHT

1.1. EARLY CONTRIBUTION

- *Adam Smith:* Explained the concept and consequences of division of labour.
- *Turgot:* Explained the importance of direction and control.
- Before the systematic study of Management up to 19th Century, the concept of organization and administration existed in ***Egypt*** in 1300 BC.
- Confucius suggested proper public administration and admonitions to choose honest, unselfish and capable ***public officer***.
- ***Kautilya*** offered sound principles of state of administration in 320 B.C.
- ***Roman Catholic Church*** introduced the concept of ***staff personnel*** in church administration.
- In the field of business organization some stray contributions have come from ***Robert Owen, James Watt, Charles Babbage and Henry town*** and these contribution stimulated ***systematic study of management***.
- Evolution of Management can be categorize into three parts:
  1. **Early classical approaches:** Scientific management, administrative management and bureaucracy.
  2. **Neo-classical approaches:** Human relations movement and behavioural approach.
  3. **Modern approaches:** Quantitative approach, Systems approach and Contingency approach.

1.2. CLASSICAL SCHOOLS OF MANAGEMENT

- First schools of management thought, the ***classical school of management***, developed during the Industrial Revolution when new problems related to the factory system began to appear.
- It was difficult for managers to train employees or deal with increased labor dissatisfaction, so they began to test solutions.
- This school of thought is made up of two branches:
  - o Scientific school
  - o Administrative school

1.2.1. Scientific school(Scientific management)

- ***Frederick Wilson Taylor:*** **Father of Scientific management** introduces concept of scientific management.
- ***Scientific management focused on the productivity of individuals.***
- The classical scientific school arose because of the need to increase productivity and efficiency.

- The emphasis was on trying to find the best way to get the most work done by examining how the work process was actually accomplished and by scrutinizing the skills of the workforce.
- Scientific management was introduced in an attempt to create a mental revolution in the workplace.
- **It is the systematic study of work methods in order to improve efficiency.**
- ***Frederick W. Taylor*** was its main proponent. Other major contributors were ***Frank Gilbreth, Lillian Gilbreth, and Henry Gantt***.
- **The basic ideas regarding scientific management development are developing new standard methods for doing each job.**
- Selecting, training, and developing workers instead of allowing them to choose their own tasks and train themselves.
- Developing a spirit of cooperation between workers and management to ensure that work is carried out in accordance with devised procedures. Dividing work between workers and management in almost equal shares, with each group taking over the work for which it is best fitted.
- **Scientific management gave to work design encouraged managers to seek that *"one best way"* of doing a job.**

Principles of Scientific management

- Calls for the application of the scientific method to work in order to determine the best method for accomplishing each task.
- Workers should be scientifically selected based on their qualifications and trained to perform their jobs in the optimal manner.
- **Genuine cooperation between workers and management based on mutual self-interest.**
- Management should take complete responsibility for planning the work and that workers' primary responsibility should be implementing management's plans.
- It has contributed to the study of management and organizations in many areas, including human resource management and industrial engineering.

Steps in Scientific Management

Step-I : Develop a science for each element of the job to replace old rule of thumb methods.
Step-II : Scientifically select employees and then train them to do the job as described in step-I.
Step-III : Supervise employees to make sure they follow the prescribed methods for performing their jobs.
Step-IV : **Continue to plan the work, but use workers to get the work done.**

Elements and Tools of Scientific Management

1. **Separation of Planning and Doing:** A worker will not plan how to do the work and with what instruments. Planning should be done by supervisor.
2. **Functional Foremanship:** Drastic reorganization of Supervision.
3. **Job Analysis:** Best way of doing the job based on time study, motion study and fatigue study.

4. **Standardization:** In respect of tools, period of work, amount of work, cost of production based on job analysis.
5. **Scientific Selection and Training of Workers:** Education, Experience, Aptitude, Physical strength.
6. **Financial Incentives:** Rate per piece, motivation behind incentive.
7. **Economy:** Profit, Cost estimated and controls to avoid wastage.
8. **Mental Revolution:** Cooperation between Management and Workers.
9. **Replacing Rule of Thumb:** Development of science for each part of men's job.
10. **Harmony in Group Action:**
    - Taylor has emphasized that attempts should be made in order to obtain harmony in group rather than discord.
    - There should be mutual give and take, cooperation in and along group members that they all contributes maximum.
11. **Cooperation:** Cooperation between management and workers can be developed through mutual understanding and a change in thinking.
12. **Maximum Output:** Scientific management involves continuous increase in production and productivity.
13. **Development of Workers:** All workers should be developed to the fullest possible extent for the prosperity of their and company. Development of workers requires scientific selection and adequate training. Training and development should be ongoing process so as to keep them fit according to the requirements of new methods of working.

Contributor of Scientific Management

1. Frederick Taylor

- Known as **"Father of scientific management."**
- Scientific Management is concerned with knowing exactly what you want men to do and then see in that they do it in the best and cheapest way.
- He put the emphasis on solving managerial problem in scientific way.
- He joined Midvale Company, USA as a worker and then promoted to supervisor.
- After completion of ME degree he joined Bethlehem Steel Company he carried experiments on how to increase efficiency in three companies: Midvale steel, Simond's Rolling Machines and Bethlehem Steel.
- He published many papers and books and all his contributions were compiled in his book **"Scientific Management".**
- Taylor believed that organizations should study tasks and develop precise procedures.
- He developed an incentive system that paid workers more money for meeting the new standard.

Important contributions:

1. Time and motion study
2. Differential payment
3. Drastic reorganization of Supervision.
   a. Separation of planning and doing
   b. Functional foremanship

4. Scientific recruitment and training
5. **Intimate Friendly Cooperation between the management and workers: "A complete mental revolution."**

2. Henry Gantt

- An associate of Taylor's developed the ***Gantt chart***, a bar graph that measures planned and completed work along each stage of production.
- Based on time instead of quantity, volume, or weight, this visual display chart has been a widely used planning and control tool since its development in 1910.

3. Frank and Lillian Gilbreth

- **A husband-and-wife team, studied job motions.**
- He was interested in standardization and method study.
- The first ***motion and fatigue study*** designed to isolate the best possible method of performing a given job.
- Frank and his wife Lillian studied job motions using a motion-picture camera and a split-second clock.
- Frank Gilberth classified all movements employed in industrial work into 17 basic types called ***"Therbligs"*** and provided shorthand symbols for each so that the analyst could easily and quickly jot down each motion as he observed the worker in action.
- ***Motion and fatigue studies raised workers morale.***

1.2.2. Administrative School (Administrative management)

- ***Henry Fayol: Father of Administrative management.***
- The classical administrative approach concentrates on the total organization.
- Focuses on the management process and principles of management.
- **The emphasis is on the development of managerial principles rather than work methods.**
- Contributors to this school of thought include ***Max Weber, Henry Fayol, Mary Parker Follett, Lyndal Urwick, and Chester I. Barnard***.
- These theorists studied the flow of information within an organization and emphasized the importance of understanding how an organization operated.
- *Henri Fayol* is the major contributor to this school of management thought.
- Three basic types of Administration considered in this school:

1. **Leader oriented:** There is no delegation of management function.
2. **Tradition oriented:** Managerial position is handed down from generation to generation.
3. **Bureaucratic:** Delegation of management responsibilities is based on the person's demonstrated ability to hold the position.

Contributor of Administrative Management

1. Henri Fayol: Administrative management

- ***Father of Modern Operational Management Theory Or Administrative Management.***
- Henri Fayol, French mining engineer was a management practitioner who brought his experience to bear on the subject of management functions and principles.
- These principles provide modern-day managers with general guidelines on how a supervisor should organize the department and manage their staff.
- He argued that management was a universal process consisting of functions, which he termed **planning, organizing, commanding, coordinating, and controlling (POCCC).**
- Wrote a monograph in French in 1916, entitled "General and Industrial Administration"
- His first published book ***"Administration Industrielle Generale."***
- Administration is common activity and universally applicable.
- Fayol believed that all managers performed these functions and that the functions distinguished management as a separate discipline of study apart from accounting, finance, and production.
- Administrative management criticized for rigid and inflexible.
- Gave emphasis on individual attitudes and behaviors and on group processes in organizations. Recognized the importance of behavioral processes in organizations.
- Fayol presented fourteen principles of management which are:

14 - Principles of management: Henry Fayol

1. **Division of work:** Division of work and specialization produces more and better work with the same effort.
2. **Authority and responsibility:** Authority is the right to give orders and the power to exact obedience. A manager has official authority because of her position, as well as personal authority based on individual personality, intelligence, and experience. Authority creates responsibility.
3. **Discipline:** Obedience and respect within an organization are absolutely essential. Good discipline requires managers to apply sanctions whenever violations become apparent.
4. **Unity of command:** An employee should receive orders from only one superior.
5. **Unity of direction:** Organizational activities must have one central authority and one plan of action.
6. **Subordination of individual interest to general interest:** The interests of one employee or group of employees are subordinate to the interests and goals of the organization.
7. **Remuneration of personnel:** The price of services rendered by employees in the form of salary should be fair and provide satisfaction both to the employee and employer.
8. **Centralization:** The objective of centralization is the best utilization of personnel. The degree of centralization varies according to the dynamics of each organization.
9. **Scalar chain: A chain of authority exists from the highest organizational authority to the lowest ranks for the purpose of communication.** Order of communications should pass through the proper channels of authority along the scalar chain. But in case there is need for swift action, the proper channels of authority may be short-circuited by making direct contact, called as **gang plank** with the concern authority.

10. **Order:** Organizational order for materials and personnel is essential. The right materials and the right employees are necessary for each organizational function and activity. *"The right place for everything and for every man."*
11. **Equity:** In organizations, equity is a combination of kindliness and justice. Both equity and equality of treatment should be considered when dealing with employees.
12. **Stability of tenure of personnel:** To attain the maximum productivity of personnel, a stable work force is needed.
13. **Initiative:** Thinking out a plan and ensuring its success is an extremely strong motivator. Zeal, energy, and initiative are desired at all levels of the organizational ladder.
14. **Esprit de corps: Teamwork is fundamentally important to an organization. Work teams and extensive face-to-face verbal communication encourages teamwork. "Union is strength".**

2. Max Weber: Father of Bureaucracy

- He believed that organizations should be managed impersonally and that a formal organizational structure, where specific rules were followed, was important.
- He thought authority should be something that was part of a person's job and passed from individual to individual as one person left and another took over.
- This non personal, objective form of organization was called a **bureaucracy.**
- **Bureaucratic management** focuses on the ideal form of organization.
- **Bureaucracy characterized by division of labor, hierarchy, formalized rules, impersonality, and the selection and promotion of employees based on ability, would lead to more efficient management.**
- Weber also contended that managers' authority in an organization should be based not on tradition or *charisma* but on the position held by managers in the organizational hierarchy.

Characteristics of bureaucracy

1. **A well-defined hierarchy:** All positions within a bureaucracy are structured in a way that permits the higher positions to supervise and control the lower positions. This clear chain of command facilitates control and order throughout the organization.
2. **Division of labor and specialization:** All responsibilities in an organization are specialized so that each employee has the necessary expertise to do a particular task.
3. **Rules and regulations:** Standard operating procedures govern all organizational activities to provide certainty and facilitate coordination.
4. **Impersonal relationships between managers and employees:** To avoid the impact of favoritism and personal prejudice on decision making managers should maintain an impersonal relationship with employees.
5. **Competence:** Competence, not "who you know," should be the basis for all decisions made in hiring, job assignments, and promotions in order to foster ability and merit as the primary characteristics of a bureaucratic organization.
6. **Records:** A bureaucracy needs to maintain complete files regarding all its activities.

Limitations of Bureaucracy

1. **Over conformity or Rigidity of the rules:**
   - "Stick to the rules"
   - Rules and regulations are very rigid and inflexible under bureaucracy.

- The initiative and creativity of employees are discouraged with rigid compliance of rules and regulations.
- There is a resistance to change on the part of employees also.

2. **Red Tapism :**
   - There is too much paper work and red tapism.
   - Every decision is taken after having detailed discussion with many persons. These discussions are recorded in a number of documents.
   - These documents cannot be cancelled after having been taken.
3. **Displacement of goal:**
   - An organization is divided into various units and sub units.
   - The objective of sub unit is also framed by the top management.
   - A person who is in charge of a sub unit may try to achieve its objective reelecting the overall objectives of the organization.
   - In such a case the management finds it very difficult to achieve the goals the organization.
   - Discovered by ***Robert Michels*** called *"Professional automation."*
4. **Impersonal nature of work:**
   - Service with devotion is not expected from the employees.
   - It does not faster in them a sense of belongingness.
   - The employees do not care about the well being of the organization.
   - This is because of impersonal nature of work.
5. **Failures of co-operation and co-ordination:**
   - Organizational rules and regulations are given priority over situation.
   - Jobs are performed according to norms and procedures.
   - It hampers the free flow of work.
   - So this restricts the management from getting the mutual co-operation and co-ordination.
6. **Mechanical treatment:**
   - Initiative and creative thinking of an employee are not recognized.
   - Employees are treated like machine and not like individuals.
7. **No Mutual understanding:**
   - Personal feelings views needs and opinions are not given any importance or consideration under bureaucracy.
   - Contractual obligations are given much importance over human relations. This results non existence of mutual understanding.
   - Inability to satisfy the needs of mature individuals: ***"The maturity-immaturity theory"*** propounded by ***Chris Argyris.***
8. **Empire Building:**
   - Every superior tries to increase the number of his subordinates.
   - The reason is that the maximum number of subordinates is considered a symbol of power and prestige.

3. Mary Parker Follett

- Emphasized on the importance of an organization establishing common goals for its employees.
- Encouraged managers to allow employees to participate in decision making.
- Stressed the importance of people rather than techniques.
- **Follett's Principles of Coordination:**

- **Principle of Early Stage:** Coordination must start at an early stage in the management process. It must start during the planning stage. This will result in making the best plans and implementing these plans with success. If coordination is started early only then all the management functions will be performed successfully. Thus by initiating proper coordination the organisation will achieve all its objectives easily and quickly.
- **Principle of Continuity:** Coordination must be a continuous process. It must not be a one-time activity. The process of coordination must begin when the organisation starts, and it must continue until the organisation exists. Coordination must be done continuously during the management process. It must be done during planning, organising, directing and controlling.
- **Principle of Direct Contact:** All managers must have a Direct Contact with their subordinates. This will result in good relations between the manager and their subordinates. This is because direct contact helps to avoid misunderstandings, misinterpretations and disputes between managers and subordinates. It enables the managers to coordinate all the different activities of their subordinates effectively and efficiently.
- **Principle of Reciprocal Relations:** The decisions and actions of all the managers, employees and departments of the organisation are inter-related. So, the decisions and actions of one person or department will affect all other persons and departments in the organisation. Therefore, before taking any decision or action all managers must first find out the effect of that decision or action on other persons and departments in the organisation.

4. Chester Barnard

- **Credited with developing** the ***acceptance theory of management*****, which emphasizes the willingness of employees to accept that managers have legitimate authority to act.**
- He was president of New Jersey Bell Telephone Company.
- **Cliques:** Introduced the idea of the *informal organization-**cliques*** (exclusive groups of people) that naturally form within a company.
- He felt that these informal organizations provided necessary and vital communication functions for the overall organization and that they could help the organization accomplish its goals.
- **Barnard felt that it was particularly important for managers to develop a sense of common purpose where a willingness to cooperate is strongly encouraged.**
- Barnard felt that four factors affected the willingness of employees to accept authority:
  1. The employees must understand the communication.
  2. The employees accept the communication as being consistent with the organization's purposes.
  3. The employees feel that their actions will be consistent with the needs and desires of the other employees.
  4. The employees feel that they are mentally and physically able to carry out the work.

1.3. NEO-CLASSICAL APPROACHES (BEHAVIORAL MANAGEMENT)

- **The behavioral management theory is often called the human relations movement because it addresses the human dimension of work.**
- The behavioral school focused on trying to understand the factors that affect human behavior at work.
- Behavioral theorists believed that a better understanding of human behavior at work, such as motivation, conflict, expectations, and group dynamics, improved productivity.

- The theorists who contributed to this school viewed employees as individuals, resources, and assets to be developed and worked with not as machines, as in the past.

1.3.1.Human Relations

- The ***Hawthorne Experiments began in 1924*** and continued through the early 1930s.
- The manager should possess skills for diagnosing the causes of human behavior at work, interpersonal communication, and motivating and leading workers.
- The focus became satisfying worker needs. If worker needs were satisfied, wisdom held, the workers would in turn be more productive.
- Focuses on issues of communication, leadership, motivation, and group behavior.
- The best-known contributors include ***Mary Parker Follett, Chester Barnard, Abraham Maslow, Kurt Lewin, Renais Likert , and Keith Davis.***
- The human relations school of thought still influences management theory and practice, as contemporary management focuses much attention on human resource management, organizational behavior, and applied psychology in the workplace.
- Researchers participated in the studies, including ***Clair Turner, Fritz J. Roethlisberger, and Elton Mayo.***

1.3.2 Behavioural Science

- The behavioral science school was a natural progression of the human relations movement.
- It focused on applying conceptual and analytical tools to the problem of understanding and predicting behavior in the workplace.
- The study of behavioral science in business schools was given increased credence by the **1959 Gordon and Howell report** on higher education, which emphasized the importance to management practitioners of understanding human behaviour.
- The behavioural science school has contributed to the study of management through its focus on personality, attitudes, values, motivation, group behaviour, leadership, communication, and conflict, among other issues.
- Major contributors to this school include ***Douglas McGregor, Chris Argyris, Frederick Herzberg, Rensis Likert, and Ralph Stogdill,*** etc.

Contributor of Behavioural Management

1. Elton Mayo :

- **Hawthorne Studies:** Human Relationship approach of Management (1927-1932)
- Carried out at Hawthorne Plant of GE at Chicago, 30000 Employees.
- **Elton Mayo (psychologist), Roethlisberger (Sociologist)** and **William Dickson** carried out this study.
- Despite material benefits to the workers such as pension, sickness benefits and other recreational facilities there was great deal of dissatisfaction among workers and productivity was not up to the mark.

1. Experiments to determine the effects of illumination on productivity (1924-27).
2. Experiments to determine the effects of changes in hours and other working conditions on productivity, Relay assembly test room experiments (1927-28).
3. Conducting plant wide interviews to determine workers attitude and sentiments, Mass interviewing program (1928-30).
4. Determination and Analysis of social organization at work, Bank wiring observation room experiments. (1931-32).

Implication of Hawthorne Studies

1. Social factors in output
2. Group Influence
3. Conflicts
4. Leadership
5. Supervision
6. Communication

Stages of Hawthorne experiments

1. Illumination Experiment
2. Relay Assembly Test Room
3. Mass Interviewing Programme
4. Bank Wiring Observation Test Room

Remember : IRMB

Conclusions of the Hawthorne studies

1. A second group of experiments began. Harvard researchers **Mayo and F. J. Roethlisberger** supervised a group of five women in a bank wiring room.
2. Mayo and Roethlisberger concluded that *the increase in productivity resulted from the supervisory arrangement rather than the changes in lighting or other associated worker benefits.*
3. The general conclusion from the Hawthorne studies was that *human relations and the social needs of workers are crucial aspects of business management.*
4. Workers attitudes are associated with productivity.
5. The workplace is a social system and informal group influence could exert a powerful effect on individual behavior.
6. The style of supervision is an important factor in increasing workers' job satisfaction.
7. Organizations should take steps to assist employees in adjusting to organizational life by fostering collaborative systems between labor and management.

1.4. MODERN APPROACHES OF MANAGEMENT : QUANTITATIVE SCHOOL OF MANAGEMENT

- The **quantitative approach** to management involves the use of quantitative techniques, such as statistics, information models, and computer simulations, to improve decision making.
- The quantitative approach facilitates disciplined thinking, while defining management problems and establishing relationship among the variables involved.
- This quantitative school of management consists of several branches as under:

1. Management science
2. Operations management

3. Management information systems
4. Systems management theory

1.4.1 Management Science

- The management science school emerged to treat the problems associated with global warfare. Encourages managers to use mathematics, statistics, and other quantitative techniques to make management decisions.
- Managers can use computer models to figure out the best way to do something as saving both money and time. Managers use several science applications.
- Mathematical forecasting helps make projections that are useful in the planning process.
- Inventory modeling helps control inventories by mathematically establishing how and when to order a product.
- **Queuing theory** helps allocate service personnel or workstations to minimize customer waiting and service cost.
- It developed during World War II as strategists tried to apply scientific knowledge and methods to the complex problems of war. Industry began to apply management science after the war.
- ***George Dantzig*** developed linear programming, an algebraic method to determine the optimal allocation of scarce resources.
- Other tools used in industry include inventory control theory, goal programming, queuing models, and simulation.
- Management science approach also known as mathematical or quantitative measurement approach, visualizes management as a logical entity, the action of which can be expressed in terms of mathematical symbol relationships and measurement data.

1.4.2 Operations management

- This school focuses on the operation and control of the production process that transforms resources into finished goods and services.
- Operations management emphasizes productivity and quality of both manufacturing and service organizations.
- **W. Edwards Deming exerted a tremendous influence in shaping modern ideas about improving productivity and quality.**
- Major areas of study within operations management include capacity planning, facilities location, facilities layout, materials requirement planning, scheduling, purchasing and inventory control, quality control, computer integrated manufacturing, just-in-time inventory systems, and flexible manufacturing systems.
- Focuses on managing the process of transforming materials, labor, and capital into useful goods and services.
- The product outputs can be either goods or services; effective operations management is a concern for both manufacturing and service organizations.
- The resource inputs, or factors of production, include the wide variety of raw materials, technologies, capital information, and people needed to create finished products.
- The transformation process, in turn, is the actual set of operations or activities through which various resources are utilized to produce finished goods or services of value to customers or clients.

- Pays close attention to the demands of quality, customer service, and competition.
- The process begins with attention to the needs of customers: What do they want? Where do they want it? When do they want it? Based on the answers to these questions, managers line up resources and take any action necessary to meet customer expectations.

1.4.3 Management information systems

- A management information system organizes past, present, and projected data from both internal and external sources and processes it into usable information, which it then makes available to managers at all organizational levels.
- The information systems are also able to organize data into usable and accessible formats.
- As a result, managers can identify alternatives quickly, evaluate alternatives by using a spreadsheet program, pose a series of "what-if" questions, and finally, select the best alternatives based on the answers to these questions.
- Focuses on providing needed information to managers in a useful format and at the proper time.
- Decision support systems (DSS) attempt to integrate decision models, data, and the decision maker into a system that supports better management decisions.

1.4.4 Systems management theory

- The systems school focuses on understanding the organization as an open system that transforms inputs into outputs.
- This school is based on the work of a biologist, ***Ludwig von Bertalanffy***, who believed that a general systems model could be used to unite science.
- Early contributors to this school included ***Kenneth Boulding, Richard Johnson, Fremont Kast, and James Rosenzweig.***
- The systems school focuses on the organization as a whole, its interaction with the environment, and its need to achieve equilibrium.
- Many of the ideas inherent in the systems school formed the basis for the contingency school of management
- The **systems management theory** has had a significant effect on management science.
- A system is an interrelated set of elements functioning as a whole.
- System approach of management lacks universality and its precepts cannot be applied to all organizations.
- An organization as a system is composed of four elements:

1. **Inputs**: Raw material, human resources and money.
2. **Transformation processes:** Technological and managerial processes.
3. **Outputs:** Products or services.
4. **Feedback:** Reactions from the environment

Important terminology used in systems approach:

- **Closed system:** An organization that interacts little with its external environment (outside environment) and therefore receives little feedback from it.
- **An open system:** In contrast, interacts continually with its environment. Therefore, it is well informed about changes within its surroundings and its position relative to these changes.
- A **subsystem:** It is a part of a larger system.

- **Entropy:** The tendency of systems to deteriorate or break down over time.
- **Synergy:** The ability of the whole system to equal more than the sum of its parts.

1.5. CONTINGENCY SCHOOL OF MANAGEMENT

- The contingency school originated in the 1960s.
- Major contributors to this school of management thought include ***Joan Woodward, Paul Lawrence, Jay Lorsch, and Fred Fiedler, etc.***
- Management action is contingent on certain outside system or subsystem.
- Organizational action should be based on the behavior of action outside the system so that organization should be integrated with the environment.
- Because of specific organization-environment relationship no action can be universal. It varies from situation to situation.
- Focuses on applying management principles and processes as dictated by the unique characteristics of each situation.
- It emphasizes that there is no one best way to manage and that it depends on various situational factors, such as the external environment, technology, organizational characteristics, characteristics of the manager, and characteristics of the subordinates.
- Contingency theorists often implicitly or explicitly criticize the classical school for its emphasis on the universality of management principles; however, most classical writers recognized the need to consider aspects of the situation when applying management principles.
- It has been applied primarily to management issues such as organizational design, job design, motivation, and leadership style.
- **Can be summarized as an *"it all depends"* approach.**
- The appropriate management actions and approaches depend on the situation.
- Managers with a contingency view use a flexible approach, draw on a variety of theories and experiences, and evaluate many options as they solve problems.
- In the contingency perspective, managers are faced with the task of determining which managerial approach is likely to be most effective in a given situation.
- **Contingency thinking avoids the classical *"one best way"* arguments and recognizes the need to understand situational differences and respond appropriately to them.**
- It does not apply certain management principles to any situation.
- Contingency theory is recognition of the extreme importance of individual manager performance in any given situation.
- The contingency approach is highly dependent on the experience and judgment of the manager in a given organizational environment.
- The basic idea of contingency approach is that there cannot be a particular management action which will be suitable for all situations. Rather, and appropriate action is one which is designed on the basis of external environment and internal states and needs.
- Contingency approach tries to fill this gap by suggesting what should be done in response to an event in the environment.
- Contingency approach, on the other hand suggests an active interrelationship between the variables in a situation and the managerial actions devised.

Limitations Contingency School of Management

- **Inadequate Literature:** Contingency approach suffers from inadequacy of literature.
- **Complex:** Determination of situation in which managerial action is to be taken involves analysis of a large number of variables with multifarious dimensions.
- **Reactive not Proactive: Contingency approach is basically reactive in nature. It merely suggests what managers can do in given situation.**

1.6. CONTEMPORARY SCHOOLS OF MANAGEMENT

1.6.1. Total quality management (TQM)

- Total quality management (TQM) is a philosophy or approach to management that focuses on managing the entire organization to deliver quality goods and services to customers.
- This approach to management was implemented in Japan after World War II and was a major factor in their economic renaissance.
- TQM has at least four major elements.

1. Employee involvement is essential in preventing quality problems before they occur.
2. A customer focus means that the organization must attempt to determine customer needs
3. Wants.
4. Deliver products and services that address them.

- **Benchmarking** means that the organization is always seeking out other organizations that perform a function or process more effectively and using them as a standard, or benchmark, to judge their own performance.
- The organization will also attempt to adapt or improve the processes used by other companies.
- A philosophy of continuous improvement means that the organization is committed to incremental changes and improvements over time in all areas of the organization.
- TQM has been implemented by many companies worldwide and appears to have fostered performance improvements in many organizations.
- **W. Edward Deming was the best-known proponent of this school of management.**

1.6.2. The Learning organization

- All employees are involved in identifying and solving problems, which allows the organization to continually increase its ability to grow, learn, and achieve its purpose.
- The organizing principle of the learning organization is not efficiency, but problem solving.
- Three key aspects of the learning organization are:
  1. A team-based structure
  2. Empowered employees
  3. Open information.
- **Peter Senge** is one of the best-known experts on learning organizations.
- The dimension that distinguishes learning from more traditional organizations is the mastery of certain basic disciplines or 'component technologies'.

- The five that Peter Senge identifies are said to be converging to innovate learning organizations. They are:

a) Systems thinking
b) Personal mastery
c) Mental models
d) Building shared vision
e) Team learning

1.7. QUALITY SCHOOLS OF MANAGEMENT

- Comprehensive concept for leading and operating an organization, aimed at continually improving performance by focusing on customers while addressing the needs of all stakeholders.
- This concept focuses on managing the total organization to deliver high quality to customers.
- Quality management involves employees in decision making as a way to prevent quality problems.
- The quality school of management considers the following in its theory:
  - ❖ **Organization makeup:** Organizations are made up of complex systems of customers and suppliers. Every individual, executive, manager, and worker functions as both a supplier and a customer.
  - ❖ **Quality of goods and services:** Meeting the customers' requirements is a priority goal and presumed to be a key to organizational survival and growth.
  - ❖ **Continuous improvement in goods and services: Recognizing the need to pinpoint internal and external requirements and continuously strive to improve. It is an idea that says, "the company is good, but it can always become better."**
  - ❖ **Employees working in teams:** These groups are primary vehicles for planning and problem solving.
  - ❖ **Developing openness and trust:** Confidence among members of the organization at all levels is an important condition for success.

1.7.1. Kaizen approach

- **Kai means *Change* and Zen means *Good* and Kaizen means *Continual improvement & Elimination of waste.***
- The Kaizen philosophy is drawn from the Japanese word kai which means "continuous" and zen meaning "improvement" or "wisdom".
- **The Kaizen management philosophy, therefore, is defined as making "continuous improvement :-slow, incremental but constant."**
- Kaizen Events are when work groups set aside a few day or up to a week to simplify a process or work area - eliminating waste, creating space.
- The **Kaizen** approach uses incremental, continuous improvement for people, products, and processes.
- The very notion of continuous improvement suggests that managers, teams, and individuals learn from both their accomplishments and their mistakes.
- Quality managers help their employees gain insights from personal work experiences, and they encourage everyone to share with others what they have learned.

- In this way, everyone reflects upon his or her own work experiences, including failures, and passes their newfound knowledge to others.
- Sharing experiences in this manner helps to create an organization that is continuously discovering new ways to improve.
- Kaizen is the commitment to work toward steady, continual improvement.
- The best support for continuous improvement is an organization of people who give a high priority to learning. In this process, everyone in the organization participates by identifying opportunities for improvement, testing new approaches, recording the results, and recommending changes.

Types of Kaizen Events

- Value Stream Mapping
- 5S – Simplify, Straighten, Scrub, Stabilize, Sustain.
- Standard Work – One Piece Flow

1.7.2. Reengineering approach

- The reengineering approach focuses on sensing the need to change, seeing change coming, and reacting effectively to it when it comes.
- The reengineering approach to management focuses on creating change, big change and fast.
- It centers on sensing the need to change, seeing change coming, and reacting effectively to change when it comes.

Reengineering :

- **Hammer & Champy:** Defined the process of reengineering as "the fundamental rethinking and radical redesign of business processes to achieve dramatic improvements in critical, contemporary measures of performance, such as cost, quality, service and speed."
- The radical redesign of business processes to achieve dramatic improvements in cost, quality, service, and speed requires that every employee and manager look at all aspects of the company's operation and find ways to rebuild the organizational systems to improve efficiency, identify redundancies, and eliminate waste in every possible way.
- Reengineering is neither easy nor cheap, but companies that adopt this plan have reaped remarkable results.
- Reengineering efforts look at how jobs are designed, and raise critical questions about how much work and work processes can be optimally configured.
- Although many people believe that reengineering is a euphemism for downsizing or outsourcing, this is not true. Yes, downsizing or outsourcing may be a byproduct of reengineering.
- The goal of reengineering is to bring about a tight fit between market opportunities and corporate abilities. After organizations are able to find this fit, new jobs should be created.

Business process re-engineering (BPR) :

- It is a business management strategy, originally pioneered in the early 1990s, focusing on the analysis and design of workflows and processes within an organization.
- BPR aimed to help organizations fundamentally rethink how they do their work in order to dramatically improve customer service, cut operational costs, and become world-class competitors.

- BPR seeks to help companies radically restructure their organizations by focusing on the ground-up design of their business processes.
- According to **Davenport** a business process is a set of logically related tasks performed to achieve a defined business outcome. Re-engineering emphasized a holistic focus on business objectives and how processes related to them, encouraging full-scale recreation of processes rather than iterative optimization of sub processes.
- Business process re-engineering is also known as business process redesign, business transformation, or business process change management.

- **Davenports Five-step approach to the Business Process Reengineering model:**

1. **Develop the business vision and process objectives:** The BPR method is driven by a business vision which implies specific business objectives such as cost reduction, time reduction, output quality improvement.
2. **Identify the business processes to be redesigned:** Most firms use the 'high-impact' approach which focuses on the most important processes or those that conflict most with the business vision. A lesser number of firms use the 'exhaustive approach' that attempts to identify all the processes within an organization and then prioritize them in order of redesign urgency.
3. **Understand and measure the existing processes:** to avoid the repeating of old mistakes and to provide a baseline for future improvements. Compare: Scientific Management
4. **Identify IT levers:** awareness of IT capabilities can and should influence BPR.
5. **Design and build a prototype of the new process:** the actual design should not be viewed as the end of the BPR process. Rather, it should be viewed as a prototype, with successive iterations. The metaphor of prototype aligns the Business Process Reengineering approach with quick delivery of results, and the involvement and satisfaction of customers.

1.8. OTHER APPROACHES TO THE STUDY OF MANAGEMENT

1.8.1. Empirical approach

- The empirical school of management bases its methods on a close study of past managerial experiences and management cases.
- According to this approach, management is considered a study of manager in practice.
- Offers the most conventional way of acquiring skills in management, that is, learning through the experience of others.
- This approach also helps in classroom, situations for developing diagnostic and analytical skills in management students.

Limitations

- This empirical approach, basing its generalizations on cases and past experiences has not contributed anything fundamental to the development of management as discipline because of obvious contradictions in various management experiences.

1.8.2. Social system approach

- Closely resembling the human behavior approach and often confused intermixed with it is the social system approach.

- The real pioneer of social system approach is ***Vilfred Pareto***, a sociologist. His ideas were later developed by ***Chest Bernard*** who has really developed the concept of social systems approach management.
- According to this approach, the organization is essentially a culture system composed of people who work in cooperation.
- As such, for achieves organization goals, a co-operative system of management can be developed only understanding the behavior of people in groups.
- The social system approach has real significance to the practicing managers in the sense that all managers operate n a social system and the organization is likely to succeed if the demands of the society in which it operates as fully recognized.
- The approach, however, spreads the boundary and application of management beyond the true concept of organizations.

1.8.3. Social technical systems approach

- This approach believes that to solve organizational problems, it is not enough to look at the cooperative social systems alone but technical systems (methods and machines) and how it affects and is affected by social systems and a technical system.
- The real pattern of behavior in the organization is determined by the interaction of the two.
- The major contribution of this approach is that while analyzing management problem of getting things done by people, adequate consideration should be given to technology as well as informal interactions of people.
- Thus any change in technology must be viewed in subsequent change in social interactions at the workplace.
- This approach is more suitable for managing the problems at the shop floor leave rather than dandling the total management problems.

1.8.4. Decision theory approach

- The major emphasis of this approach is that decision making is the job of every manager.
- The manager is a decision maker and organization is a decision-making unit. Therefore, the basic problem in managing is to make rational decision.
- The approach contributes to the sharpening of managerial tools specially for making suitable decisions in the organization.
- The approach demonstrates how managers can discharge their functions effectively.
- Decision-making is vital in every school of management. The vital aspect cannot be denied but management is more than mere decision making.

1.9. MANAGEMENT IN THE FUTURE

- Modern management approaches respect the classical, human resource, and quantitative approaches to management. However, successful managers recognize that although each theoretical school has limitations in its applications, each approach also offers valuable insights that can broaden a manager's options in solving problems and achieving organizational goals.
- Successful managers work to extend these approaches to meet the demands of a dynamic environment.
- Modern management approaches recognize that people are complex and variable.

- Employee needs change over time; people possess a range of talents and capabilities that can be developed. Organizations and managers, therefore, should respond to individuals with a wide variety of managerial strategies and job opportunities.
- Key themes to be considered, as the twenty-first century progresses, include the following:
  - ❖ The commitment to meet customer needs 100 percent of the time guides organizations toward quality management and continuous improvement of operations.
  - ❖ Today's global economy is a dramatic influence on organizations, and opportunities abound to learn new ways of managing from practices in other countries.
  - ❖ Organizations must reinvest in their most important asset, their people. If organizations cannot make the commitment to lifelong employment, they must commit to using attrition to reduce head count. They will not receive cooperation unless they make it clear that their people will not be working themselves out of a job.
  - ❖ Managers must excel in their leadership responsibilities to perform numerous different roles.

Table: 1 The Emergence of management thoughts and, their promoter and relative areas of emphasis:

Management Schools	Promoters	Emphasis
Scientific Management	**Frederick Taylor** *Shop Management(1903) *Principles of Scientific Management(1911) *Testimony before the Special house committee(1912)	*Father of Scientific Management. *Primary concern was to increase productivity through greater efficiency in production and increased pay for workers, through the application of the Scientific methods.
	Henry Gantt Gantt Chart(1901)	*Called for scientific selection of workers and "harmonious cooperation" between labour and management. *Developed the Gantt chart stressed the need for training.
	Frank and Lillian Gilbreth	*Frank is known primarily for his time and motion studies. *Lillian, an industrial psychologist, focused on the human aspects of work and the understanding of workers personalities and needs.
Modern operational management theory	**Henri Fayol** *Administration Industrielle et Generale(1916)	*Referred to as "The father of modern management theory." *Divided Industrial activities into six groups: technical, commercial, financial, security, accounting and managerial. *Recognized the need for teaching management. *Formulated 14 principles of management such as

		authority and responsibility, unity of command, scalar chain and espirit de corps.
Bureaucratic Management	**Max Weber**	Theory of Bureaucracy.
Behavioral sciences		Understanding human behavior in the organization.
	Hugo Munsterberg (1912)	* Application of Psychology to industry and management.
	Walter Dill Scott(1901, 1911)	* Application of Psychology to advertising, marketing and personnel.
	Vilfredo Pareto	* Father of the "social systems approach" to organization and management.
	Elton Mayo and F. J. Roethlisberger	Famous studies at the Hawthorne plant of Western Electric company. Influence of social attitudes and relationships of work groups on performance.
Systems theory	**Chester Bernard** The functions of the Executives(1938)	The task of managers is to maintain a system of cooperative effort in a formal organization. He suggested a comprehensive social systems approach to managing.

1.10 OBJECTIVE QUESTION – ANSWERS

1. Who is attributed with developing the scientific management perspective?
   (A) Elton Mayo (B) Robert Owens
   (C) Frank Gilbreth (D) Frederick Taylor

Answer: D

2. Match List – I with List – II and Select the correct answer from the codes given follow :

List – I (Definitions)	**List – II (Authors)**
(a) Henry Fayol	(i) An employee should receive orders from one superior only.
(b) Pfiffner and Presthus	(ii) A man cannot serve two leader masters.
(c) Dimock and Dimock	(iii) Every member of an organization should report to one and only one.
(d) Gullick and Urwick	(iv) Each employee should have only one boss.

Codes :

	a	b	c	d
(A)	(i)	(ii)	(iii)	(iv)
(B)	(i)	(iii)	(ii)	(iv)
(C)	(ii)	(iii)	(iv)	(i)
(D)	(iii)	(ii)	(iv)	(i)

Answer : A

3. The doctrine of Management By Objectives is introduced by :
   (A) Peter Drucker
   (B) Elton Mayo
   (C) Henri Fayol
   (D) McGregor

Answer: A

4. Taylor differential piece rate system is related to
   (A) Time wage system
   (B) Piece wage system
   (C) Incentive wage system
   (D) None of the above

Answer: B

5. The main drawback of the functional organization developed by F. W. Taylor is that it fails to recognize the__________
   (A) Scalar Principle
   (B) Principle of equity
   (C) Principle of Unity of Command
   (D) Principle of esprit-de-corps

Answer : D

Explanation: Principle of esprit-de-corps (Union is Strength)is given by Henry Fayol.

6. Match the following :

List-I

(a) F. J. Roethlisberger& Dickson
(b) Elton Mayo
(c) Douglas Mc Gregor
(d) Rensis Likert

List-II

(i) New Patterns of Management
(ii) The Human side of enterprise
(iii) The Management and Worker
(iv) The Human problems of industrial civilization

Codes :	(a)	(b)	(c)	(d)
(A)	(ii)	(iv)	(i)	(iii)
(B)	(iii)	(iv)	(ii)	(i)
(C)	(iv)	(iii)	(i)	(ii)
(D)	(ii)	(iii)	(iv)	(i)

Answer: B

7. Match the following :

List-I

(a) Fourteen Principles of management
(b) Time and motion study
(c) Hawthorne experiment
(d) Bureaucracy
(e)Systems Approach
(f)Universalist Approach

List-II

(i) Max Weber
(ii) Elton Mayo
(iii) F. W. Taylor
(iv) Henry Feyol

(v) Koontz and Donnell
(vi) Herbert Simon

Codes :	(a)	(b)	(c)	(d)	(e)	(f)
(A)	(ii)	(iv)	(i)	(iii)	(v)	(vi)
(B)	(iii)	(iv)	(ii)	(i)	(vi)	(v)
(C)	(iv)	(iii)	(ii)	(i)	(vi)	(v)
(D)	(ii)	(iii)	(iv)	(i)	(vi)	(v)

Answer: C

8. Who propagated the quality of work life as a descending participation mechanism?
(A) Frederick Herzberg
(B) Eric Tryst
(C) A. K. Rice
(D) John T. Dunlop

Answer: B

9. Match List I with List II and select the correct answers using the code given below :

List I	**List II**
(a) Henry Fayol	(i) Scientific Management
(b) Elton Mayo	(ii) Human Relations
(c) Peter Deucker	(iii) Espirits de corps
(d) F.W. Taylor	(iv) M.B.O.

Code :
(A) (a) –(iii),(b) – (ii), (c) – (iv),(d) –(i)
(B) (a) – (ii), (b) – (i),(c) – (iii), (d) – (iv)
(C) (a) – (i), (b) – (ii), (c) – (iv), (d) – (iii)
(D) (a) – (iv), (b) – (iii),(c) – (ii), (d) – (i)

Answer: A

10. Match the following :

Name of the Book
(a) Human side of Enterprise
(b) Management and Worker
(c) Social Problems of an Industrial Civilisation
(d) The Human Organization

Authors
(i) F.J. Roethlisberger
(ii) Elton Mayo
(iii) Rensis Likert
(iv) Douglas McGregor

	(a)	(b)	(c)	(d)
(A)	(iv)	(i)	(ii)	(iii)
(B)	(iv)	(iii)	(i)	(ii)
(C)	(iii)	(i)	(iii)	(iv)
(D)	(ii)	(iii)	(iv)	(i)

Answer: A

11. Match the following :

List - I (Name of the Contributor)	**List - II (Contribution)**
(a) Charles Babbage	(i) Systems approach
(b) F.J. Roethlisberger and Dickson	(ii) X, Y theory
(c) Douglas Murray McGregor	(iii) Hawthorne Experiments
(d) Talcot Parsons	(iv) Fair day's work

Code :	(a)	(b)	(c)	(d)
(A)	(ii)	(i)	(iv)	(iii)
(B)	(iii)	(iv)	(ii)	(i)
(C)	(iv)	(iii)	(ii)	(i)
(D)	(iv)	(ii)	(i)	(iii)

Answer: C

12. Match the following:

Group A	**Group B**
(a) Managerial Grid	(i) Peter F. Drucker
(b) Bureaucracy	(ii) Blake & Mouton
(c) M.B.O	(iii) George Elton Mayo
(d) Hawthorne Studies	(iv) Max Weber

	(a)	(b)	(c)	(d)
(A)	(ii)	(i)	(iv)	(iii)
(B)	(ii)	(iv)	(i)	(ii)
(C)	(iii)	(ii)	(iv)	(i)
(D)	(iv)	(iii)	(i)	(ii)

Answer: B

13. Match the following :

Proponents	**Management thought**
(a) F. W. Taylor	(i) Systems theory
(b) Elton Mayo	(ii) 'Z' theory
(c) William Ouchi	(iii) Scientific Management
(d) Rensis Likert	(iv) Human Relations

	(a)	(b)	(c)	(d)
(A)	(ii)	(iv)	(iii)	(i)
(B)	(iii)	(ii)	(iv)	(i)
(C)	(i)	(iii)	(ii)	(iv)
(D)	(iii)	(iv)	(i)	(ii)

Answer: D

14. Match the following :

Name of the Book	**Author**
(a) Management and Worker	(i) Rensis Likert
(b) The Human Side of Enterprise	(ii) Elton Mayo
(c) The New Patterns of Management	(iii) Roethlisberger and Dickson
(d) The Human Problems of Industrial Civilization.	(iv) Douglas McGregor

Codes :

	(a)	(b)	(c)	(d)
(A)	(ii)	(iv)	(iii)	(i)
(B)	(iii)	(ii)	(iv)	(i)
(C)	(i)	(iii)	(ii)	(iv)
(D)	(iii)	(iv)	(i)	(ii)

Answer: D

15. Match the following :

Contributor	**Organisation Theory**
(a) Chester I. Barnard	(i) Functional Foremanship
(b) Max Weber	(ii) Acceptance Theory of Authority
(c) F.W. Taylor	(iii) Open System Theory
(d) Katz and Kahn	(iv) Bureaucracy

Codes :

	(a)	(b)	(c)	(d)
(A)	(iv)	(i)	(ii)	(iii)
(B)	(iii)	(iv)	(i)	(ii)
(C)	(ii)	(iii)	(iv)	(i)
(D)	(ii)	(iv)	(i)	(iii)

Answer: D

16. Match the following :

Management Thinkers	**Contributions**
(a) F.W. Taylor	(i) Application of psychology to management
(b) Henri Fayol	(ii) Sociological concept of Group Behaviour
(c) Elton Mayo	(iii) Time and Motion Study
(d) Hugo Munsterberg	(iv) 14 Principles of Management

	(a)	(b)	(c)	(d)
(A)	(ii)	(iii)	(i)	(iv)
(B)	(iii)	(iv)	(ii)	(i)
(C)	(iv)	(ii)	(iii)	(i)
(D)	(iii)	(i)	(ii)	(iv)

Answer: B

17. Match the following :

Approach to Management	**Characteristics**
(a) Management science approach	(i) Focus on leadership and motivation
(b) Situational approach	(ii) Managerial practices depend on circumstances
(c) Interpersonal behaviour approach	(iii) Use of mathematical symbol and relationship
(d) System approach of management functions and sub- system	(iv) Recognising importance of inter- relatedness

	(a)	(b)	(c)	(d)
(A)	(i)	(ii)	(iii)	(iv)
(B)	(ii)	(iii)	(i)	(iv)
(C)	(iii)	(ii)	(i)	(iv)
(D)	(iii)	(ii)	(iv)	(i)

Answer: C

18. Match the following :

Name of Thinker	**Major Contribution**
(a) F.W. Taylor	(i) Application of psychology to industry and management
(b) Max Weber	(ii) Systems approach to management
(c) Chester Barnard	(iii) Emphasis on rules and regulations
(d) Hugo Munsterberg	(iv) Increased productivity through efficiency in production

	(a)	(b)	(c)	(d)
(A)	(iv)	(iii)	(ii)	(i)
(B)	(iii)	(ii)	(iv)	(i)
(C)	(ii)	(iii)	(iv)	(i)
(D)	(iv)	(iii)	(i)	(ii)

Answer: A

19. 'Case of Schimdt' which School of Management thought ?
(A) Human Relations School
(B) Behavioural School
(C) Systems Approach
(D) Scientific Management

Answer: D

Explanation: Taylor used the example of *Schmidt* at the Bethlehem Steel Company to test his theories.

20. Scalar chain means:
(A) Chain of services provided by management.
(B) Chain of relations between superior and subordinate.
(C) A line of authority from superior to subordinate used for proper communication.
(D) A process of communication in management.

Answer: C

21. During his days at Midvale Steel Company F.W. Taylor saw that employees soldiering – deliberately working at a pace slower than their capabilities. He identified that, worker indulge in soldiering primarily for the following reasons :
(A) Fear of losing jobs if they increase their output.
(B) Faulty wage systems.
(C) Out-dated methods of working
(D) All of the above

Answer: D

22. Espirit-de-corps means:
(A) Union is strength.
(B) A feeling of pride and loyalty, uniting members of a group.
(C) A and B both.
(D) None of the above.

Answer: C

23. Who has given time study technique of management?
(A) Charles Babbage
(B) Henry Fayol
(C) F. W. Taylor
(D) Joseph L. Massie

Answer: A

24. Which of the following are correct?
(i) Theory of Social and Economic Organisation : Max Weber
(ii) Models of Man : H.A. Simon
(iii) Organisation and Management : F.W. Taylor
(iv) Elements of Public Administration : F.M. Marx

Codes :
(A) (i), (ii) and (iv)
(B) (i), (ii) and (iii)
(C) (ii), (iii) and (iv)
(D) (iv), (i) and (iii)

Answer: A

25. Match List – I with List – II and select the correct answer from the codes given below :

List – I	List – II
a. Chester Barnard	i. Models ofMan
b. Herbert Simon	ii. The Human Side of Enterprise
c. M.P. Follett	iii. The Functions of the Executive
d. Douglas McGregor	iv. Creative Experience

Codes:

	a	b	c	d
(A)	ii	i	iii	iv
(B)	i	ii	iv	iii
(C)	iii	i	iv	ii
(D)	iii	ii	i	iv

Answer: C

26. Match List – I with List – II and select the correct answer from the codes given below :

List – I	List – II
a. Classical Theory	i. Interaction between Organisation and Environment
b. Behavioural Approach	ii. Shop floor activities of Organisation
c. Systems Approach	iii Formulation of Principles of Organisation
d. Scientific Management	iv. People in the Organisation

Codes :

	a	b	c	d
(A)	iv	iii	i	ii
(B)	ii	iv	iii	i
(C)	iii	iv	i	ii
(D)	i	ii	iv	iii

Answer: C

27. Match List – I with List – II and select the correct answer from the codes given below :

List – I	List – II
(a). M.P. Follett	i. The Ecology of Public Administration
(b). Hergberg	ii. Dynamic Administration
(c). F.W. Riggs	iii. Motivation and Personality
(d). A. Maslow	iv. TheMotivation to work

Codes :

	(a)	(b)	(c)	(d)
(A)	ii	iv	i	iii
(B)	i	iv	iii	ii
(C)	iii	ii	i	iv
(D)	iv	iii	ii	i

Answer: A

28. According to Peter Drucker, which of the following is the basic tool for an entrepreneur?

(A) Searching for change
(B) Innovation
(C) Providing something of value.
(D) Exploiting opportunities

Answer: B

Explanation: Explained by Peter Drucker's in his classic book on "innovation and entrepreneurship".

29. Who is author of the book "General and Industrial Administration"

(A) Henry Fayol
(B) Edwin B. Flippo
(C) Leonard Nadler
(D) Keith Davis

Answer: A

30. Who is called as Father of Bureaucracy?

(A) Henry Fayol.
(B) Edwin B. Flippo
(C) Leonard Nadler
(D) Max Weber

Answer: D

31. Henry Ford is noted for his contributions to

(A) Standardization of parts
(B) Statistical quality control
(C) Assembly line operations
(D) Scientific management
(E) Time and motion studies

Answer: C

32. The scientific management stressed upon:

(A) Rationality
(B) Specialization
(C) Technical competence
(D) Predictability
(E) All the above

Answer: E

33. Taylor and Deming would have both agreed that

(A) Whirlpool's global strategy is a good one
(B) Eli Whitney was an important contributor to statistical theory
(C) management must do more to improve the work environment and its processes so that quality can be improved
(D) productivity is more important than quality
(E) the era of Operations Management will be succeeded by the era of scientific management

Answer: C

34. The term 'Charisma' used by Max Weber in the ideal type is taken from which of the following languages ?

(A) German (B) Greek
(C) Italian (D) Roman

Answer: B

35. Match of the following statements are correct in relation to F.W. Taylor's 'Scientific Management'?

(i) Time and methods of study may be used to find out the best way of performing a job.
(ii) Specialists may be employed to perform the tasks.
(iii) Workers must perform the job in whichever way they like.
(iv) Work place and incentives are not linked to output.

Select the correct answer from the codes given below :

Codes :

(A) Only (i) (B) (i), (ii)
(C) (i), (iii) (D) (iii), (iv)

Answer: B

36. Identify the principle of F.W. Taylors Scientific Management :

(A) Scalar Chain
(B) M.B.O
(C) Functional Foremanship
(D) Unity of Command

Answer: C

37. With which school of management thought 'Case of Schimadt' is associated ?

(A) Scientific Management School
(B) Human Relations School
(C) Behaviour School
(D) Systems Approach

Answer: A

38. Which of the following principles of management was not given by Fayol?

(A) Unity of direction
(B) Subordination of individual interest to common interest
(C) Stability of tenure
(D) Standardization

Answer: D

39. The paper "Engineer as Economist", which influence F. W. Taylor to develop his Scientific Management Principles authored by

(A) Charles A. Babbage
(B) Henry Gnatt
(C) Henry R. Towne
(D) Louis D. Brandies

Answer: C

40. Who coined the term Scientific Management?

(A) Louis D. Brandies
(B) F. W. Taylor
(C) Douglas Mc Gregor
(D) None of the above

Answer: B

41. Who is called the Father of Scientific Management?
(A) Charles Babbage
(B) F. W. Taylor
(C) Douglas Mc Gregor
(D) Henry L. Gantt

Answer: B

42. Gang Plank theory given by Henry Fayol is associated with :
(A) Upward Communication
(B) Lateral Communication
(C) Downward Communication
(D) Informal Communication

Answer: B

Explanation: Henry Feyol explained in his principle of Scalar chain: In case there is need for swift action, the proper channels of authority may be short-circuited by making direct contact, called as *gang plank* with the concern authority.

43. Match the following :

Thinker	Management Principle
a. F.W. Taylor	i. Authority and Responsibility
b. Henri Fayol	ii. Hierarchy
c. Weber	iii. Separation of planning from doing
d. Elton Mayo	iv. Human Relations Approach

Codes :

	a	b	c	d
(A)	iii	i	iv	ii
(B)	iii	iv	i	ii
(C)	iii	i	ii	iv
(D)	iii	ii	i	iv

Answer: C

44. The classical theorists favoured organisation based on
(A) Civilian model
(B) Strategic model
(C) Military model
(D) None of the above

Answer: C

45. Which one of the following is not Taylor's mechanisms of Management?
(A) Using a routing system
(B) Employing a mnemonic system
(C) Employing a modern cost system
(D) Using a gang plank.

Answer: D

46. What does Unity of Command indicate?
(A) Person giving command must have authority
(B) An employee should receive order from one superior.
(C) Unified command and control
(D) None of the above

Answer: B

47. Assertion (A): The satisfying administrative man is different from the maximising man.

Reason (R): The administrative man does not search for the optimal decision but a satisfactory one

Codes :
(A) Both (A) and (R) are correct and(R) is the correct explanation of(A).
(B) Both (A) and (R) are correct, but (R) is not the correct explanation of (A).
(C) (A) is true, but (R) is false.
(D) (A) is false, but (R) is true.

Answer: A

48. Neo-Classical theory focuses attention on :
(A) Employees
(B) Management
(C) Welfare of employees
(D) Bargainable employees

Answer: A

Explanation: The neoclassical theory was an attempt at incorporating the behavioral sciences into management thought in order to solve the problems caused by classical theory practices. The premise of this inclusion was based on the idea that the role of management is to use **employees** to get things done in organizations. Rather than focus on production, structures, or technology, the neoclassical theory was concerned with the employee. Neoclassical theorists concentrated on answering questions related to the best way to motivate, structure, and support employees within the organization.

49. Mayo's studies at the Hawthorne plant made valuable contributions about :
(A) Formal Organisation
(B) Formal Work Group
(C) Informal Organisation
(D) Formal Communication

Answer: B

50. Who is associated with The 'illumination experiment' of The Hawthorne experiment
(A) Elton Mayo
(B) George A. Pennock
(C) F. J. Roethlisberger
(D) None of the above

Answer: B

51. Arrange different phases of Hawthorne experiments in their right sequence :
a. Relay assembly test room experiment
b. Bank wiring observation test
c. Illumination experiment
d. Personal counseling
e. Mass interviewing programme
(A) a, b, c, d, e
(B) c, a, e, b, d
(C) c, b, e, a, d
(D) e, d, c, b, a

Answer: B
Remember: IRMB

52. Elton Mayo's study concludes that employee productivity is more related to :
(A) Work itself
(B) Reward system
(C) Working conditions
(D) Social Relations at work place

Answer: C

53. Which approach emerged from the findings of Hawthorne experiments ?
(A) Systems Approach
(B) Human Behaviour Approach
(C) Human Relations Approach
(D) Process Approach

Answer: C

54. Who among the following undertook the famous Hawthorne experiments ?
(A) Elton Mayo and Blake
(B) Elton Mayo Roethlisberger
(C) Elton Mayo, Blake
(D) Elton Mayo, Blake and Juran

Answer: B

55. The field of operations management is shaped by advances in which of the following fields?
(A) chemistry and physics
(B) industrial engineering and management science
(C) biology and anatomy
(D) information sciences
(E) all of the above

Answer: E

56. Who among the following is associated with contributions to quality control in operations management?
(A) Charles Babbage
(B) Henry Ford
(C) Frank Gilbreth
(D) W. Edwards Deming

Answer: D

57. The field of operations management is shaped by advances in which of the following fields?
(A) chemistry and physics
(B) industrial engineering and management science

(C) biology and anatomy
(D) information sciences
(E) all of the above

Answer: E

58. The school of thought typified by Joan Woodward says that
(A) size is the most critical determinant of structure
(B) technology is the most critical determinant of structure
(C) structure follows strategy
(D) strategy follows structure

Answer: B

59. What are the management principles given by Henry Fayol:
(A) Division of work
(B) Discipline
(C) Authority and responsibility
(D) All of the above

Answer: D

60. Under mechanism of scientific management, scientific task setting includes :
(A) Time study
(B) Motion study
(C) Method study
(D) All of the above

Answer: D

61. Management is multidisciplinary, it includes knowledge from:
(A) Psychology
(B) Economics
(C) Math's
(D) All of the above

Answer: D

62. Fredrick Winslow Taylor's Mechanism of scientific management includes:
(A) Scientific task setting
(B) Planning task setting
(C) Standardization of tools
(D) All of the above

Answer: D

63. Peter Drucker is an expert on :
(A) Japanese art
(B) History of technology
(C) History of American statesman
(D) All of the above

Answer: D

64. The names of the experts who have given recent contribution to management are:
(A) William Ouchi
(B) W. Edward Deming
(C) Peter F. Drucker
(D) All of the above

Answer: D

65. The steps included in the process of MBO are:
(A) Preliminary setting of goals at the top
(B) Clarification of organizational goals
(C) Recycling of objectives
(D) All of the above

Answer: D

66. Modern developments in management theory are:
(A) Decentralization of decision making
(B) Increased recognition
(C) Development of the Personnel function
(D) All of the above

Answer: D

67. Who has designed the first *motion and fatigue study* to isolate the best possible method of performing a given job.
(A) Frank and Lillian Gilbreth
(B) Henri Fayol
(C) Peter Drucker
(D) Max Weber

Answer: A

68. Who is considered as Father of Administrative management?
(A) Frank and Lillian Gilbreth
(B) Henri Fayol
(C) Peter Drucker
(D) Max Weber

Answer: B

69. What are the characteristics of bureaucracy?
(A) A well-defined hierarchy
(B) Division of labor and specialization
(C) Rules and regulations
(D) All the above
Answer: D

70. Who is the author of book "Administration Industrielle Generale"?
(A) Frank and Lillian Gilbreth
(B) Henri Fayol
(C) Peter Drucker
(D) Max Weber
Answer: B

71. Who is credited with developing the "Acceptance theory of management"
(A) Frank and Lillian Gilbreth
(B) Henri Fayol
(C) Peter Drucker
(D) Chester Barnard
Answer: D

72. Who is the real pioneer of social system approach?
(A) Frank and Lillian Gilbreth
(B) Vilfred Pareto
(C) Peter Drucker
(D) Chester Barnard
Answer: B

73. Who among the following is associated with contributions to quality control in operations management?
(A) Charles Babbage
(B) Henry Ford
(C) Frank Gilbreth
(D) W. Edwards Deming
Answer: D

74. The experts who dealt in Behavioral Sciences are :
(A) Max Weber
(B) Vilfredo Pareto
(C) Elton Mayo
(D) All the above
Answer: D

75. The term 'span of control' is also referred to as:
(A) Span of management
(B) Span of supervision
(C) Span of authority
(D) All the above
Answer: D

76. The different kinds of relationships for selecting the span of control would be :
(A) One to one
(B) Cross relationship
(C) Direct group
(D) All the above
Answer: D

77. The tools and techniques used in the learning organizations are
(A) creativity
(B) Brainstorming
(C) Observing outcomes
(D) Reframing knowledge
(E) All the above
Answer: E

78. Collective learning requires skills for sharing information and knowledge, the key skills mentioned are:
(A) Listening and observing
(B) Holistic perspective
(C) Coping with challenge and uncertainty
(D) All the above
Answer: D

79. Advantages of learning organizations should be
(A) Free exchange and flow of information
(B) Commitment to learning, personal development
(C) Climate of openness and trust
(D) All the above
Answer: D

80. Henry Ford is noted for his contributions to
(A) Standardization of parts
(B) Statistical quality control
(C) Assembly line operations
(D) Scientific management
(E) Time and motion studies
Answer: C

81. Who called scientific management thought as a 'rabble hypothesis' ?
(A) Frederick Winslow Taylor
(B) Henry R. Towne
(C) Elton Mayo
(D) Louis D. Brandies
Answer: C
Explanation: Elton Mayo and Chester Barnard both were critical of F. W. Taylor's 'scientific management'-'one best way of designing jobs' and of what they called economists' 'rabble hypothesis' regarding workers' puta- tively individualistic and exclusive interests in wages.

82. Who has developed Functional Approach to management?
(A) F.W.Taylor (B) Henry Fayol
(C) Koontz (D) Elton Mayo
Answer: B

83. Who is the founder of Behavioural Science Approach to management?
(A) F.W.Taylor
(B) Henry Fayol
(C) Koontz
(D) Elton Mayo
Answer: D

84. Who is the author of Book "The making of scientific management".
(A) F.W.Taylor
(B) Henry Fayol
(C) Urwick and Breach
(D) Elton Mayo
Answer: C

85. Which of the following is the oldest type of the organization?
(A) Committee organization
(B) Line organization
(C) Functional organization
(D) Bureaucratic organization
Answer: B

86. Henry Fayol authored the book:
(A) The making of scientific management
(B) General and industrial management
(C) .The philosophy of management
(D) Innovation and Entrepreneurship
Answer: B

87. Who is the author of Book "The philosophy of management".
(A) F. W. Taylor (B) Henry Fayol
(C) Oliver Sheldon (D) Elton Mayo
Answer: C

88. Which principle denotes 'Union is Strength'?
(A) Equity (B) Imitative
(C) Espirit de corps (D) Division of work
Answer: C

89. The concept of management " getting things done by other people" is described by:
(A) Robinson
(B) Marry Parker Follett
(C) F. W. Taylor
(D) Henry Fayol
Answer: B

90. Elton Mayo emphasized the concept of :
(A) Complex Man
(B) Social Man
(C) Administrative Man
(D) Organizational Man
Answer: B

91. Max Weber's Ideals is based on:
(A) Taylorism
(B) Structure of the organization
(C) Time and motion study
(D) Scientific management
Answer: B

92. Functional organization is suitable for:
(A) Small undertaking
(B) Manufacturing undertakings
(C) Non-manufacturing undertakings
(D) Large undertakings

Answer: C

93. Unity of command is violated in the organization:
(A) Line organization
(B) Line and staff organization
(C) Functional organization
(D) All the above
Answer: D

94. "Employees selected for the work should be as perfectly matched to the demand of the job as possible." Which of the following theories says this :
(A) Scientific Management Theory
(B) Bureaucracy Theory
(C) Classical Theory
(D) Traditional Theories
Answer: A

Explanation: Taylor argued that individuals selected to do the work should be as perfectly matched (physically and mentally) to the demands of the job as possible and that overqualified individuals should be excluded. Employees should be trained carefully by supervisors.

95. Functional type of organization was first developed by :
(A) Pavlov
(B) Taylor
(C) Henry Fayol
(D) Elton Mayo
Answer: B

96. 'Gang-plank' means :
(A) Quick Communication
(B) Vertical Communication
(C) Horizontal Communication
(D) Lateral Communication
Answer: D

97. The Book "Human Behaviour at work" was written by :
(A) McGregor (B) Abraham Maslow
(C) Herzberg (D) Keith Davis
Answer: D

98. Who divided all activities organizations into six Technical, Commercial, Security, Accounting and Managerial?
(A) Peter Drucker (B) D. E. Mc Forland
(C) Henry Fayol (D) George R. Terry
Answer: C

99. Hawthorne Experiment is related to the
(A) Systems theory
(B) Classical theory
(C)Human relations theory
(D) Scientific management theory
Answer: C

100. The number of subordinates a superior can effectively handle is called
(A) Organizing people
(B) Span of control
(C) Direction
(D) Coordination
Answer: B

101. Match the following :

List – I	List – II
a. Functional Organisation	1. F.W. Taylor
b. Transactional Analysis	2. Mc Clelland
c. Managerial Grid	3. Eric Berne
d. Need Theory	4. Blake and Mouton

Codes :

	a	b	c	d
(A)	1	3	4	2
(B)	1	2	3	4
(C)	4	3	2	1
(D)	2	1	4	3

Answer: A

102. Who is father of Administrative Management Theory ?
(A) Max Weber
(B) Frank Gilbraith
(C) Henry Fayol
(D) Henry Gantt
Answer: C

103. Today's organizations are working on the principle of
(A) Production-orientation
(B) Product-orientation
(C) Selling-orientation
(D) consumer-orientation
Answer: D

104. F.W. Taylor has done the following studies for improving the production process :
(A) Time Study, Fatigue Study and Fatal Study.
(B) Time Study, Motion Study and Fatal Study.
(C) Time Study, Motion Study and Fatigue Study.
(D) Time Study, Motivation Study and Fatigue Study.
Answer: C

105. The principle of organization that no employee should report to more than one superior is called
(A) Scalar principle
(B) Span of control
(C) Unity of command
(D) Unity of direction
Answer: C

Explanation: The chain of command, sometimes called the scaler chain, is the formal line of authority, communication, and responsibility within an organization. By utilizing the chain of command, and its visible authority relationships, the principle of unity of command is maintained. Unity of command means that each subordinate reports to one and only one superior.

106. Which is the oldest and simplest form of organisation ?
(A) Functional organisation
(B) Committee organisation
(C) Line organization
(D) Line and staff organisation
Answer: C

Explanation: Line organization is the oldest and simplest method of administrative organization. According to this type of organization, the authority flows from top to bottom in a concern. The line of command is carried out from top to bottom. This is the reason for calling this organization as scalar organization which means scalar chain of command is a part and parcel of this type of administrative organization. In this type of organization, the line of command flows on an even basis without any gaps in communication and co-ordination taking place.

107. Management by Objective(MBO) was first proposed by:
(A) Henry Fayol
(B) Elton Mayo
(C) Peter Drucker
(D) J.T. Dunlop

Answer: C

108. The number of persons a manager can effectively manage refers to the:
(A) Coordination
(B) Span of control
(C) Unity of command
(D) Expertise
Answer: B

109. The key management processes in the learning organizations would be
(A) competitor analysis
(B) performance measurement
(C) capability planning
(D) All the above
Answer: D

110. Lean production aims at :
(A) Continuous improvement
(B) Aim at zero defects
(C) Just-in-time inventory system
(D) All of the above
Answer: D

111. ____________means gradual, unending improvement doing little things better, setting and achieving higher standards.
(A) Organisation development
(B) Six sigma
(C) Kaizen
(D) None of the above
Answer: C

112. Who had advanced the 'Business Process Reengineering' concept ?
(A) K. Pang and N. Oliver
(B) R. Stablein and W. Nord
(C) Micheal Hammer and James Champy
(D) M. Mandenhall and U.Oddon
Answer: C

113. Arrange the following aspects of 'system' in the sequence in which they occur :
(i) Throughput (ii) Output
(iii) Input (iv) Feedback
(A) (iii), (i), (iv), (ii)
(B) (iii), (ii), (i), (iv)
(C) (iv), (iii), (ii), (i)
(D) (iii), (i), (ii), (iv)
Answer: D

Explanation: Input is the operating substance and energizer of a system. Input consists of information, materials or forces that enter a system.

Throughput is the process by which a system converts input into output.

Output is the end result of the system throughput.

Feedback loops are essential mechanism used to monitor and evaluate performance of a system.

114. Which perspective is hailed as being responsible for launching research into such topics as leadership effectiveness and group dynamics?
(A) Human relations approach
(B) Scientific management
(C) Contingency approach
(D) Hawthorne effect
Answer: A

115. Which of these approaches argues that there is no single best way to manage behavior?
(A) Hawthorne
(B) Scientific Management
(C) The cornerstone skill
(D) Contingency
Answer: D

116. The different disciplines mentioned in the fifth discipline field book by Peter Senge are:
(A) Personal mastery
(B) Mental models
(C) Shared vision
(D) All the above
Answer: D

117. The features of Management as a art is as follows:
(A) Skill
(B) knowledge
(C) creativity
(D) All the above
Answer: D

118. Science as a discipline has the following features
(A) body of organized knowledge
(B) establishes cause
(C) effect relationship
(D) All the above
Answer: D

119. Management is the combination of
(A) Arts
(B) Science
(C) profession
(D) All the above
Answer: D

120. "Organizational learning" and "Learning organization" are
(A) Same
(B) Different
(C)Reverse to each other
(D) Complementary to each other
Answer: D

121. Which of the following statements is <u>not</u> true about the five disciplines identified by Peter Senge?
(A) Personal Mastery in the first discipline
(B)Mental models is not included in the five disciplines
(C)Building shared vision is a part of the five disciplines
(D) System thinking is the last discipline
Answer: B
Explanation: Five Disciplines by Peter Senge:
"**<u>Personal mastery</u>** is a discipline of continually clarifying and deepening our personal vision, of focusing our energies, of developing patience, and of seeing reality objectively."
"**<u>Mental models</u>** are deeply ingrained assumptions, generalizations, or even pictures of images that influence how we understand the world and how we take action."
"**<u>Building shared vision</u>** a practice of unearthing shared pictures of the future that foster genuine commitment and enrollment rather than compliance."
"**<u>Team learning</u>** starts with dialogue, the capacity of members of a team to suspend assumptions and enter into genuine thinking together."
<u>Systems thinking</u> - The Fifth Discipline that integrates the other four discipline.

122. A Learning Organization is most accurately described as which of the following?
(A) A company that facilitates the learning of all its members and consciously transforms itself and its context
(B) A company in which Human Resource Development is aligned to the business strategy
(C) A company where a lot of training takes place
(D) All the above
Answer: A

123. The study of management theory is important for which of the following reasons:
(A) It helps decision making
(B) It is scientific
(C) Management theories are interpretive and evolve with organisational changes
(D) All of the above
Answer: C

124. Which of the following is not a feature of a bureaucracy?
(A) Generalism
(B) Hierarchy of authority
(C) Impersonality
(D) Specialisation
(E) None of the above
Answer: A

125. Which of the following is an example of the Hawthorne experiments?
(A) The relay assembly test room
(B) The interview programme
(C) The bank wiring observation room
(D) The illumination experiments
(E) All of the above
Answer: E

126. The systems approach is:
(A) Emphasises the technical requirements of the organisation and its needs
(B) Encourages managers to view the organisation both as a whole and as part of a larger environment
(C) Emphasises the psychological and social aspects
(D) All of the above
(E) None of the above
Answer: B

127. Consider the following statements:
1. Through the Hawthorne Studies, Elton Mayo could support Mary Parker Follett's theory that the lack of attention to human relationships was a major flaw in other management theories.
2. The book – The Human Problems of an Industrialized Civilization was written by Mary Parker Follett.

Which of the statements given above is/are correct?
(A) Only 1
(B) Only 2
(C) Both 1 and 2
(D) Neither 1 nor 2
Answer: A

128. Which of the following are among the 14 principles of management in the classical management work of Henri Fayol?
1. Personnel tenure
2. Unity of command
3. Core competence
4. Scalar chain

Select the correct answer using the code given below:
(A) Only 1, 2 and 3
(B) Only 2 and 4
(C) Only l and 3
(D) 1, 2, 3 and 4
Answer: B

129. Which of the following pairs is/are correctly matched?

Scholar	**Viewpoint**
1. F. Riggs	In developing countries, bureaucracy also performs political roles
2. Harold Laski	Bureaucracy is a threat to democratic government
3. S. Eisenstadt	Bureaucracy is the most rational form of organization

Select the correct answer using the code given below:
(A) 1 and 2 (B) Only 1
(C) Only 2 (D) 1 and 3
Answer: A

130. Which of the following pairs is/are correctly matched?
1. Cybernetic Theory : Norbert Weiner
2. Task-Technology : Joan Woodward
3. Classical Approach to organizational design : Frederick Taylor

Select the correct answer using the code given below:
(A) Only 1 and 2 (B) Only 2 and 3
(C) Only 1 (D) 1, 2, and 3
Answer: A

131. Consider the following statements:
1. Defects in co-ordination inherent in large-scale organizations may apply to an organization whether the organization is bureaucratic or not.
2. Chester Barnard criticized Weber for failing to analyze the correspondence of behaviour in organizations with organizational blueprints.

Which of the statements given above is/are correct?
(A) Only 1
(B) Only 2
(C) Both 1 and 2
(D) Neither 1 nor 2
Answer: C

132. Consider the following statements:

1. Henri Fayol was the first to describe the fly functions of management.
2. Henri Fayol was a French management theorist whose theories concerning human relations were widely influential in the beginning of the 20th Century.

Which of the statements given above is/are correct?

(A) Only 1 (B) Only 2
(C) Both 1 and 2 (D) Neither 1 nor 2

Answer: A

133. Consider the following statements:

1. Much of current knowledge of selection techniques, employee training and work design is built on the work of Hugo Munsterberg.
2. Hugo Munsterberg combined scientific management and industrial psychology in his work.

Which of the statements given above is/are correct?

(A) Only 1 (B) Only2
(C) Both 1 and 2 (D) Neither 1 nor 2

Answer: C

134. Which one of the following is not i component of Max Weber's ideal bureaucracy?

(A) Job specialization
(B) Impersonality
(C) Career orientation
(D) Organization as a social system

Answer: D

135. Who among the following conducted one of the most widely cited pig iron experiment as an example of scientific management?

(A) Robert Owen
(B) Frederick W. Taylor
(C) Chester Barnard
(D) Mary Parker Follett

Answer: B

136. The systems approach is mainly based on the work of which one of the following?

(A) Chris Argyris
(B) Chester Barnard
(C) Ludwig Bertalanffy
(D) A. Etzioni

Answer: C

137. What is a 'Shadow Cabinet' in the British system?

(A) A group of young members of the ruling party
(B) A group of members from the opposition party who scrutinize some functions of the government and present alternative policy
(C) A team of intellectuals who advise the Cabinet
(D) A Cabinet Committee that functions under the guidance of the Cabinet

Answer: B

138. Consider the following statements about the features of the administrative system in France:

1. Ministers are more concerned with direct administration in the provinces.
2. Specialist personnel are found only in small numbers in the advisory and policy-making roles.
3. Freedom of executive action from the legislature's supervision increased under the Fifth Republic.

Which of the statements given above are correct?

(A) 1, 2 and 3 (B) Only 1 and 2
(C) Only 2 and 3 (D) Only 1 and 3

Answer: A

139. Which of the following Departments of the Government of India were put under the Cabinet Secretariat at the time of their creation?

1. Department of Electronics

2. Department of Scientific and Industrial Research
3. Department of Personnel

Select the correct answer using the code given below:

(A) Only 1 and 2 (B) Only 2 and 3
(C) Only 1 and 3 (D) 1, 2 and 3

Answer: D

140. Consider the following statements:

1. The Administrative Reforms Commission (ARC) had recommended that the Department of Personnel of a State should be put under the charge of the Chief Secretary of the State.
2. Chief Secretary of a State is not involved in any manner in the promotion of State Civil officers to the All-India Services.

Which of the statements given above is/are correct?

(A) Only 1 (B) Only 2
(C) Both 1 and 2 (D) Neither 1 nor 2

Answer: A

141. Consider the following statements:

1. The rationalist paradigm of public policy is dominated by scholars of public administration rather than by political scientists.
2. The increment list paradigm of public policy making and implementation is theoretical, effectual, prescriptive and nonnative.

Which of the staten1ts given above is/are correct?

(A) Only 1 (B) Only 2
(C) Both 1 and 2 (D) Neither 1 nor 2

Answer: A

142. Match List -I (**Person**) with List- II (**Major Area**) and select the correct answer using the code given below the lists:

List-I (Person)	**List- II (Major Area)**
A. Robert Owen	1. Motivation Theories
B. Henry L. Gantt	2. Personnel Management
C. W. Clay Hammer	3. Incentive Scheme for workers
D. Clayton Alderfer	4. Behaviour Modification Techniques

Code:

	A	B	C	D
(A)	2	4	3	1
(B)	1	3	4	2
(C)	2	3	4	1
(D)	1	4	3	2

Answer: C

143. The Wagner Act which proved to be the Magna Carta of labour was introduced in which country?

(A) United Stats1of America
(B) Great Britain
(C) France
(D) Japan

Answer: A

144. Assertion (A): Any legislative power of the Executive Independent of the Legislature is unimaginable in the United States of America.

Reason (R): The Doctrine of Separation of Powers underlies the American Constitution.

Answer: A

****

UNIT - II

FUNCTIONS OF MANAGEMENT

2.1. MANAGEMENT

- **Mary Parker Follett** defines management as the art of getting things done through people.
- **F. W. Taylor:** "Management is an art of knowing what you want to do and then seeing that is done in the best and cheapest way."
- **Henry Fayol:** "To manage is to forecast, to plan, to organize, to command, to co-ordinate and control.
- **George R. Terry:** "Management is a distinct process consisting of planning, organizing, actuating and controlling performance to determine and accomplish the objectives by the use of people and resources."
- **Koontz and O'Donnel:**"Management is the creation and maintenance of internal environment in an enterprise where individuals working in groups can perform efficiently and effectively toward the attainment of group goals. It is an art of getting the work done through and with people in formally organized groups."
- Management is a set of activities directed at an organization's resources with the aim of achieving organizational goals in an efficient and effective manner.
- Management for any organization is a function of organizing and channeling the people together to accomplish desired goals.
- In common understanding, management is also referred to the body or group of persons who perform the various functions of management.
- Management is a process to achieve desired goal.
- A series of activities and operations, such as planning, deciding, evaluating, assembling and using sets of resources by people with different functions intentionally structured and coordinated to achieve common purposes.
- Management is the process of designing and maintaining an environment in which individuals working together in groups to accomplish selected aims efficiently.
- The concept management may be used as: functions to be performed to attain the organizational objectives-planning, organizing direction, co-ordination and control.
- In a more important sense, management is a vital function concerned with all aspects of the working of an enterprise.
- The management is considered as a body of knowledge consisting of several concepts, principles, techniques and theories which can be adopted in any group endeavour.

2.1.1. Concept of Managèment

1. **Management as a discipline:** A field of study having well defined concepts and principles.

2. **Management as a group of people:** Includes all those personnel who perform managerial functions.
3. **Management as a Process:** A process can be defined as systematic method of handing activities.

2.1.2. Features of Management

- The important characteristics of management as a business function are:
  1. It is an art of getting things done through and with people.
  2. Art and science of decision making and leadership.
  3. It is universal process for achieving results.
  4. It is a profession which involves specialized training and is governed by an ethical code.
  5. It coordinates human factor and physical resources for the accomplishment of group objectives by balancing and integration (or) by innovation and adaptation.
- Organized activities.
- Existence of objective.
- Relationship among resources.
- Working with and through people.
- Decision making.

2.1.3. Nature of Management

1. **Multidisciplinary:** Emerging from Physiology, Psychology, Economics, etc.
2. **Dynamism:** Cause and effect, change with the environment. This body of knowledge is going on changing continuously with respect to changes that are taking place in the organizational environment.
3. **Relative not absolute Principles:** It embraces all business functions at different levels.
4. **Management Science or Art**: It is Science and Art both.
5. **Universality of Management**: Management is universal but principles of management are not universal. It has universal application in all kinds nature and size of business activities.
6. **Regularity of human nature:** It helps to shape the human behaviour in the work environment.

2.1.4. Hierarchical levels of Management

- **Top management**: The members of the board of directors of the company- responsible for strategic management.
- **Senior management or upper management:** The heads of various departments- responsible for operations management.
- **Middle management**: Responsible for operational management.
- **Junior or lower management**: Supervisors, team leaders, foreman etc. responsible for transaction control.

2.1.5. Administration and Management

- Although the two terms administration and management are being used interchangeably for all practical purposes but these two terms are different from each other.
- **Oliver Sheldon** summaries the distinction as follows:

- o "Administration is the function in the industry concerned in the determination of corporate policy, the co-ordination of finance production and distribution, the settlement of complaints of the organization and ultimate control of executive".
- o "Management is the function in the industry concerned in the execution of policy within the limits setup by the administration and the employment of the organization for the particular object set before it".

- **William Sprigeal** distinguishes "Administration as the determinate function and management as the executive function."
- Management is primarily concerned with carrying out of the broad policies laid down by the administration". Thus the administration is concerned with the thinking function and management with doing function.
- **Donald Clagh:** Describe management as the art and science of decision making and leadership. Art of getting things done through people and with people.
- Human factor in industry has endless capacity for work provided planning and resources are made available to it.
- The manager's goal of attainment of enterprise objectives is the more efficient manner can be accomplished only when the people in the enterprise work to the best of their ability in the spirit of cooperation and zeal.

Management as an Art :

- **George Terry:** Art is "Bringing about a desired result through the application of will in any activity is called as an art,' The emphasis is on applying skills with knowledge and accomplishing an end through deliberate effort.
- Thus the function of the art is accomplishing concrete ends efforts, results; predict situations that would not come about without the deliberate effort, to secure them.

Management as a Science:

- Science has been defined as "body of systemized knowledge accumulated and accepted with respect to the understanding of general tools concerning particular phenomenon subject or object of study."
- It is absolutely necessary that it should have codified principles and techniques that explain certain truth with respect to basic phenomenon.
- In this sense management is certainly regarded as science as it has also developed into a systemized knowledge regarding a particular phenomenon, namely, managerial function.

Management as a profession:

Profession is defined as an occupation based upon the specialized intellectual study and training, the purpose of which is to supply skilled service or advice to others for the definite fee or salary.

Characteristics of profession: McFarland

1. **Existence of an organized and systematic knowledge**
2. **Acquisition of knowledge:** Formalized Methods of acquiring training and experience.
3. **Professional association:** Existence of an association with professionalization as its goal.
4. **Ethical code:** Existence of an ethical code to regulate the behavior of the members of the profession.

5. **Service motive:** Charging of fees based on service, but with due regard for the priority of service over the desire for monetary reward.

2.1.6. The Business Environment

- **External environment**: A set of forces and conditions outside the organization that can influence its performance. It includes Customers, Competitors, Suppliers, Regulators, Strategic Partners and Labours, etc.
    - **Task environment**: Forces that have a high potential of affecting the organization on a immediate basis.
    - **General environment**: Forces that typically influence the organization's external task environment and through them, the organization itself.
- **Internal environment:** Key factors and forces inside the organization affecting its operation. It includes Owners, Board of Directors, Management, Employees, etc.

2.1.7. Approaches in Management Process

1. **Production or Efficiency Oriented :**

- **Fredric Taylor**: "Management is the art of knowing what you want to do and then seeing that it is done in the best and cheapest way."
- **John Mee:** "Management is the art of securing maximum results with minimum efforts so as to secure maximum prosperity and happiness for both employer and employee."

Decision Oriented Definitions :

- **Stanly Vance:** Management is the simply process of making decision making and control over the action of human beings from the expressed purpose of attaining pre-determined goals.

2. **People Oriented Definitions :**

- **Koontz**: "Management is the art of getting things done through and with people in formally organized groups."

3. **Function Oriented Definition :**

- **Henry Fayol:** To manage is to forecast and to plan, to organize , to coordinate and to control(**POCCC**).
- **Newman and Summer:** Recognize only four functions namely planning, organizing, leading and controlling (**POLC**).
- **Koontz and O'Donnell:** Management is the a process of involving planning, organizing, staffing, directing and controlling human efforts to achieve stated objective in an organization (**POSDC).**
- **Luther Gulick:** States seven such functions as planning, organizing, staffing, directing, coordinating, reporting and budgeting **(POSDCORB).**
- **George & Jerry:** "There are four fundamental functions of management i.e. planning, organizing, actuating and controlling (**POAC**)".

2.1.8. Role of Management Principles or Purpose

1. To increase efficiency

- The established principles of management provide managers guidelines as to how they should work in different situations.
- These principles increase managerial efficiency.
- Management Principles are modified according to situation in question.

2. To Crystallize the Nature of Management

- Lack of understanding of management principles makes it difficult to analyze the management job and to define the exact scope of managerial function.
- According to **Henry Fayol**, it is necessary to train and educate future managers with management principles, rules, methods and procedures.

3. To Carry on Research

- In any subject when certain fundamental principles are developed, the scope and limitations defined, this becomes the basis of future research.
- In the absence of these principles, researches become difficult and future horizons of knowledge cannot be expanded.
- In the Globalized world, it is necessary to come with the Universal principles.
- For a systematic theory to evolve it is necessary to carry out empirical research.
- Given the nature of interdisciplinary nature of management it is necessary that management field is well integrated with other disciplines.

4. To Attain social Objective

- Management itself is a part of society, it takes input from society and gives output to society thus the standards of society depends on the quality of management.

5. To Increase Efficiency: Process of management helps to enhance the efficiency.

2.1.9. Ten Roles of a Manager: *Henry Mintzberg*

A. Interpersonal contact

1. **Figurehead**: The Manager performs ceremonial and symbolic duties as head of the organization.
2. **Leader:** Fosters a proper work atmosphere and motivates and develops subordinates.
3. **Liaison**: Develops and maintains a network of external contacts to gather information.

B. Information processing

4. **Monitor**: Gathers internal and external information relevant to the organization.
5. **Disseminator**: Transmits factual and value based information to subordinates.
6. **Spokesperson**: Communicates to the outside world on performance and policies.

C. Decision making

7. **Entrepreneur**: Designs and initiates change in the organization.
8. **Disturbance handler**: Deals with unexpected events and operational breakdowns.

9. Resource allocator: Controls and authorises the use of organisational resources.
10. Negotiator: Participates in negotiation activities with other organisations and individuals.

2.1.10. Managerial skills: *Robert L. Katz*

- Social psychologist Robert L. Katz in 1974, in his article, ***"Skills of an Effective Administrator"*** in Harvard Business thought about the relationship of managerial skills (competences) and hierarchical management levels.

1. **Technical skills:** Competencies important, particularly for lower management
2. **Human skills:** Competencies needed for all levels of management
3. **Conceptual skills:** Competencies with a substantial importance, particularly for top management

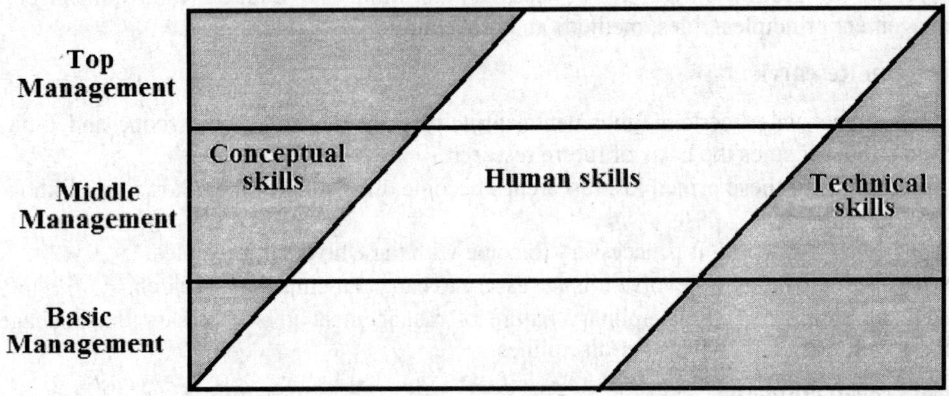

2.2. FUNCTIONS OF MANAGEMENT

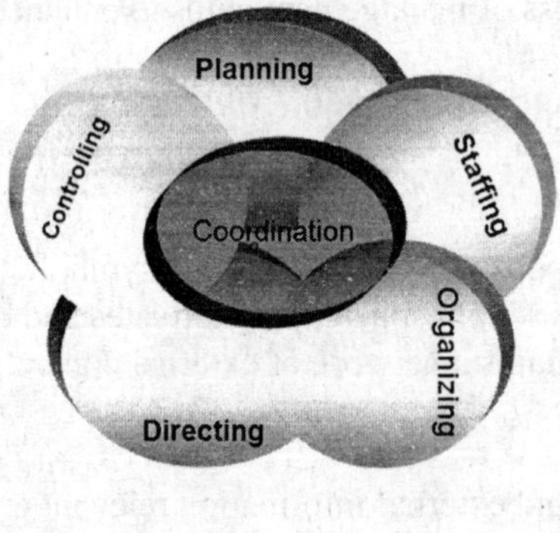

2.2.1. Planning

- Planning is an intellectual process of determining what is to be done, how, when and by whom it is to be done. *Decision making* thus an integral part of planning.
- A plan is a blue print for goal achievement and specifies the necessary resource allocations, schedules, tasks and other actions. Goals specify future ends, plans specify today's means.

- It lays down and object to pursuit and chalks out a specific course of action to achieve it.
- It is the first step in the management process concerned with establishment of objectives and goals to be attained in the future in the light of an analysis of present limitations for attaining such goals with a views to their removal or reduction, anticipation and designing the course of action and programmes for attaining such pre-determined goals.
- **Koontz & O'donnel:** "Planning is deciding in advance - what to do, when to do & how to do. It bridges the gap from where we are & where we want to be. It makes it possible for things to occur which would not otherwise happen."
- **George Terry:** "Planning is the selecting and relating of facts and the making and using of assumptions regarding the future in the visualization to achieve desire results."
- **Alford & Beatty:** "Planning is the thinking process, the organized, foresight, the vision based on facts and experience that is required for intelligent action."
- Generating plans of action for immediate, short term, medium term and long term periods.
- It is a conscious determination of future course of action.
- This evolves why an action, what action, how to take an action, and when to take an action.
- Planning involves taking decisions on vision, mission, values, objectives, strategies and policies of an organization.
- Planning is done for immediate, short term, medium term and long term periods.
- It is a guideline for execution or implementation.
- It is a measure to check the effectiveness and efficiency of an organization.
- It deals with chalking out a future course of action & deciding in advance the most appropriate course of actions for achievement of pre-determined goals.
- It is an exercise in problem solving & decision making.
- Planning is a systematic thinking about ways & means for accomplishment of pre-determined goals.
- Planning is necessary to ensure proper utilization of human & non-human resources.
- It is all pervasive, it is an intellectual activity and it also helps in avoiding confusion, uncertainties, risks, wastages etc.

Features of Planning

- It is thinking process.
- "Choosing" is at the root of planning.
- It is pervasive – prevailing in all activities
- Accomplishment of enterprise objectives.
- Primacy of planning – Prime
- It is all embracing.
- It leads to increase in efficiency.
- It is an integrated process consisting of objectives, policies, procedures

Importance of planning

- To tackle increasing complexity in modern business.
- To face increasing competition.
- To provide for complex technological changes.
- To insure against business failure.
- To meet the changing economic and political situations.
- To exercise effective control.
- To bring greater economy.

Merits of planning

- Selection of best objectives can be made with the help of planning, profits, prestige, favorable consumer reaction, High morale of workers, Man-power development, etc.
- Unity of action could be ensured.
- Aid to co-ordination and control
- Aid to growth and Expansion.
- Aid to employee co-operation.
- Aid to increase economy.
- Aid to foreseeing the future.
- Increases the effectiveness of manager.

Levels of planning

1. **Strategic planning:** Involves defining organizations long term goal and strategies. Top managers are responsible for the development and execution of strategic plans.
2. **Tactical planning:** Tactical planning translates broad strategic goals and plans into specific goals and plans for each activity of the organization. Tactical planning is done by mid-managers.
3. **Operational planning:** Identifies the specific procedures and processes required at lower levels of the organization. Front-line managers usually develop this type of plans for short. duration.

Process of planning

1. Situational Analysis
2. Alternative Goals and plans
3. Goal and Plan Evaluation
4. Goal and Plan Selection
5. Implementation
6. Monitor and Control

Limitations of planning

1. **Uncertainty:** Planning is based on forecasted results which will not hold good in uncertain situations.
2. **Rigidity:** Prior determination of policy, programme, etc. makes it rigid.
3. **Unsuitability:** Business is a dynamic activity and hence plan may not be suitable in all situations.
4. **Costly:** Planning is time consuming and costly affair.

Types of Planning

1. **Management by Objective (MBO):** Refers to a set of procedures that begins with goal setting and continuous through performance review.

Process in MBO :

a) The superior and subordinate managers jointly fix common objectives.
b) The superior and subordinate managers jointly make plans for achieving the objectives.
c) The subordinate manager implements the plans.

d) Then the actual performance of the subordinate manager is compared with the objectives and the deviations are found out.
e) Necessary corrective action is taken or the plans are modified.

2. **Contingency Plans:** It is also called as ***scenarios***. Scenario is the company responses to change in the environment includes socio-cultural, economic, technological, political, legal, etc.

3. **Crisis planning:** To response the events which are happening suddenly and devastating.

4. **Strategic management:** Strategic management is one specific type of planning.

5. **Single use and standing plans**
   - Developed to achieve a set of goals those are not likely to be repeated in the future.
   - Typically include programmes and projects.
   - **Standing plans are organizational policies, rules and procedures.**
   - They pertain to employee illness, absences, smoking, discipline, hiring and dismissals.

5.1. Standing or repeated use plans consist of:

1. Objectives
2. Policies
3. Procedures
4. Rules
5. Strategies

1. Objectives

- It may be defined as the specific goals or targets to be accomplished viz., profit making, cost reduction, increase in productivity goodwill, personnel development.
- Healthy employee relations, social responsibility.
- Fixing of objectives in an organizational planning function ensures the following advantages.
  - o It is vital to planning function.
  - o It helps to integrate planning.
  - o It ensure performance control.

Limitations of Objectives:

- Difficult to define the objectives.
- Difficult to devise suitable means.
- Difficult to avoid conflict.

Remedies:

1. Objectives should be specific.
2. Objective should be realistic.
3. Objective should be backed by suitable sub-goals.
4. Objectives should be flexible.

2. Policies

- ***A policy is general guideline for decision making***.
- It may be defined as a guide to thinking and action of those who have to make decisions in the course of accomplishment of the enterprise objectives.

- **George R. Terry:** "Policy is a verbal, written or implied overall guide, setting up boundaries that supply the general limits and direction in which managerial actions will take place."
- They are formulated in broad forms and provide a compressive and flexible course of action to be pursued to attain the given objectives.

Features:

- It is a broad outlines about the things to be done and the way in which they should done.
- It is consistent with that of the organizational plan.
- It is to be adequate in number to achieve organisationals goals.
- It should be a sound one.
- It must ensure flexibility.

Kinds of policies

1. Internal or originated polices.
2. External or imposed policies.
3. Addealed policies.
4. State or explicit policies.
5. Unstated or implied policies.

Factors to be considered while formulation policies are:

1. Values, Beliefs, Ambitions, and Foresight of the owners and members of the top management.
2. Prevalent Technology.
3. Finance availability.
4. Employee reaction.
5. Accomplishment and activities of competitors,
6. Governmental regulation and control.
7. General business environment.
8. Price levels.
9. Public attitudes and behaviour.

Merits:

1. Guide to think and act.
2. Ensures Consistency in all actions.
3. Broader applicability.
4. Confidence booster.

Demerits:

1. It won't help to solve all problems.
2. Instant solutions to problems may not be available.
3. It cannot substitute human judgment.
4. It may nor encourage initiative.

Instrument of management policy:

1. Time bound
2. Specific targets.
3. Synthesis of past, present and future.
4. Right motivation.

5. Basis of control.

Limitations

1. Cabined and confined.
2. Excessive reliance on past experience.
3. Danger of inaccuracy in estimates.
4. Hampers initiative: Rational and pragmatic initiative is stiffed.

3. Procedures or Methods

- "The process of establishing time sequences for work to be done."
- They may be described as plans prescribing the exact chronological sequence of specific tasks required to perform designated work.
- To determine the specific tasks to be performed.
- The time when those tasks will be performed.
- The person who will perform them.

Merits:

1. Basis of control
2. Standardization of activities can be done.
3. Ensure consistency in all operations.
4. Aid to communication and co-ordination.

Limitations:

1. Redundancy may takes place in course of time.
2. Updating becomes must.

4. Rules:

- Rules are detailed and recorded instructions that a specific action must or must not be performed in a given situation.
- It is decision made by the management regarding what is to be done and what is not to be done in a given situation.
- It applies to specific situations.
- Rules do not leave any scope for decision making nor do they permit any deviation.

5. Strategies:

- It means the art of projecting and planning the choice of means by which the enterprises forces may be employed most effectively in order to accomplish it's intended goal.
- It is said to be formulated only to meet the challenge posed by competitions policies and activity.
- The following factors may be considered for formulating strategies.
  - Correct assessment of reaction of the parties concerned.
  - Human and physical resources are available to draw up a strategy.
  - Temperamental make-up of the persons to check-mate whom the strategy is being would up.

Types of strategies

- Strike while the iron is hot-act prompt a while the action is likely to get results.
- Camel's head in the tent – creation of confidence regarding plan to some

- Unity is strength
- Time is greater heater.
- Offence if the best form of a defence.
- Divide and rule.

Successful implementation of strategies

1. Communicating strategies to all key decision-making managers.
2. Developing and communicating planning premises.
3. Ensuring that action plans contribute to and reflect major objectives and strategies.
4. Reviewing strategies regularly.
5. Developing contingency strategies and program.
6. Making the organization structure fit planning needs.
7. Continuing to emphasis planning implementing strategy.
8. Creating a company climate that forces planning.

5.2. Single use of plans:

1. Programme
2. Budgets

1. Programme

- It is single use plans.
- It lays down the operation to be carried out to accomplish a given work.
- It prescribes how enterprise resources should be used.

Merits

1. Action based – practical guide to managerial action.
2. Greater motivation.

Demerits

1. Greater risk of failure
2. Inadequate motivation.

2. Budget

- It is single use plans.
- It is a plan relating to a period of time expressed in numerical terms. "as a pre-determined statement of management policy, during a given period, which provide a standard for comparison with the results actual achieved.

Objectives of Budgeting

1. To ensure effective planning.
2. To facilitate Co-ordination function.
3. To exercise Controlling effective and achieving desire goals.
4. To motivate the workforce for achieving desired results.

Planning premises

- ***Managerial plans are based on certain assumptions which are called planning premises.***

- They constitute the ground on which plans will stand. Meaningful premises facilitate consistency and coordination of plans.
- The premises may be of non-controllable premises such as economic conditions, political situations, tastes, preferences of people etc.
- Semi-controllable premises such as firms market shares, union management relations etc.
- Controllable premises such as policies of the organization, procedures, rules etc.

Guideline for Effective Premising

- Selection of the premises that bear materially on program.
- Development of alternative premises for contingency planning.
- Verification of the consistency of premises
- Communication of the premises.

2.2.2. Decision making

- Decision refers to making a choice among available alternatives.
- Decision Making is the process of choosing the best alternative for reaching objectives.
- Decision making is the process of identifying problems and opportunities and then resolving them.
- **George Terry:** "It is the process selection an alternative from two or more alternatives to determine an opinion or a course of action."
- **Greshams Law of Planning and Decision Making:** This law states that there is a general tendency for programmed activities to overshadow non-programmed activities. Hence, if a series of decisions are to be made, those that are more routine and repetitive will tend to be made before the ones that are unique and require considerable thought.

Factors involved in decision making

1. Tangible factors: Profits, Quality of output and all other quantitative factors such as Man-hours, Machine hours, etc.

2. Intangible factors:

- o Employee morale.
- o The prestige of business concern.
- o Consumer behaviour.
- o Such other abstract factors.

3. Need: Weighing the consequences of each alternative course of action.

Steps in Decision-making process:

1. Defining and analyzing (Diagnose) the problem.
2. Goal setting.
3. Search for alternative solution.
4. Evaluate alternative solution and select the best.
5. Implementing solution.
6. Follow up and control.

Types of Decisions

1. **Programmed Decisions**
   - Programmed decisions are routine and repetitive, and the organization typically develops specific ways to handle them.
   - A programmed decision might involve determining how products will be arranged on the shelves of a supermarket.
   - For this kind of routine, repetitive problem, standard arrangement decisions are typically made according to established management guidelines.
2. **Non- programmed decisions**: Typically one shot decisions that are usually less structured than programmed decision.
   - **Strategic decisions:** Relating to the identification of long-term or overall aims and interests and the means of achieving them. Most groups seek a maximum of participation and agreement for strategic decisions, while letting operational decisions be made in small groups or work teams.
3. **Organizational decisions:** Relating to the way different aspects and parts of a group are arranged with the aim of being more orderly and efficient.
4. **Operational decisions:** Relating to the way a group or organization works on a daily basis.

Barriers to effective decision making

- Ethical issues
- Escalation of commitment
- Technology
- Psychological biases

Models of Decision Making

1. **The Rational Model:** Consists of a structured four-step sequence:
   a. Identifying the problem
   b. Generating alternative solutions
   c. Selecting a solution
   d. Implementing and evaluating the solution
2. **Simon's Normative Model:** Based on premise that decision making is not rational. Decision making is characterized by:
   a. Limited information processing
   b. Use of rules of thumb or shortcuts
   c. Satisfying

Group Decision Making

- Groups can accumulate more knowledge and facts
- Groups have a broader perspective and consider more alternative solutions
- Individuals who participate in decisions are more satisfied with the decision and are more likely to support it.
- Group decision making processes serve an important communication function as well as a useful political function.

Liabilities of Group Decision Making

- Groups often work more slowly than individuals.
- Groups decisions involve considerable compromise that may lead to less than optimal decisions.
- Groups are often dominated by one individual or a small clique, thereby negating many of the virtues of group processes.
- Overreliance on group decision making can inhibit management's ability to act quickly and decisively when necessary.

Individual vs. Group Decision Making

- In ***establishing objectives***, groups are probably superior to individuals because of the greater amount of knowledge available to groups.
- In ***identifying alternatives***, the individual efforts of group members encourage a broad search in various functional areas of the organization.
- In ***evaluating alternatives***, the collective judgment of the group, with its wider range of viewpoints, seems superior to that of the individual decision maker.
- In ***choosing an alternative***, group interaction and the achievement of consensus usually result in the acceptance of more risk than would be accepted by an individual decision maker.
- ***Implementing a decision***, whether or not it was made by a group, is usually accomplished by individual managers.

Strategies for improving group decisions

1. **Brainstorming:**
   - Developed by ***Alex Osborn***.
   - The idea in brainstorming is to create an atmosphere of enthusiasm and non- judgment in terms of the usefulness of ideas.
   - Four rules typically govern the brainstorming process:
   1. All criticism is ruled out.
   2. Freewheeling is welcome.
   3. Quantity is wanted.
   4. Combination and improvement are sought.
2. **Normal group technique (NGT):** It controls the amount of personal interaction and adds structure to the group process. It integrates the advantages of both group creativity and individual creativity.
3. **Delphi technique:** Developed by the ***Rand Corporation*** to allow for the benefits of group decision making without members having to meet face to face.

2.2.3. Business Forecasting

- Business forecasting is a process used to estimate or predict future patterns using business data.
- Forecasting provides an important benchmark for firms which have a long-term perspective of operations.
- **Henry Fayol:** "Forecasting includes both assessing the future and making provisions for it."
- Forecasting helps a businessmen in number of ways:
  - o Making planning possible.
  - o Ensures coordination.
  - o Facilitates control

- Business forecasting supports executives, analysts and end users in decision-making using decision support systems such as business intelligence.
- **Short-term forecasts**: Needed for scheduling of personnel, production and transportation.
- **Medium-term forecasts:** Needed to determine future resource requirements in order to purchase raw materials, hire personnel, or buy machinery and equipment.
- **Long-term forecasts:** Used in strategic planning. Such decisions must take account of market opportunities, environmental factors and internal resources.
- A planning tool that helps management in its attempts to cope with the uncertainty of the future, relying mainly on data from the past and present and analysis of trends.

Techniques of forecasting:

1. **Qualitative and Judgmental Methods**
   - Qualitative technique used in Economic forecasting are the jury of executive opinion, sales force composite and survey methods.
   - Qualitative techniques most commonly used in technological forecasting are the ***Delphi method, Brainstorming and scenario construction.***

2. Operation Research techniques

2.1. Queuing Theory

- Queueing theory is the mathematical study of waiting lines, or queues.
- In queueing theory a model is constructed so that queue lengths and waiting times can be predicted.
- Queueing theory is generally considered a branch of operations research because the results are often used when making business decisions about the resources needed to provide service.
- Queueing theory started with research by **Agner Krarup Erlang** when he created models to describe the Copenhagen telephone exchange.

2.2. Linear Programming

- Linear programming is a mathematical method for determining a way to achieve the best outcome such as maximum profit or lowest cost in a given mathematical model for some list of requirements represented as linear relationships.

2.3. Simulation method

- Simulation is the imitation of the operation of a real-world process or system over time.
- The act of simulating something first requires that a model be developed; this model represents the key characteristics or behaviors of the selected physical or abstract system or process. The model represents the system itself, whereas the simulation represents the operation of the system over time.

2.4. Game theory

- Developed by two US mathematicians, **Oskar Morgenstern** and **John von Neumann** in their 1944 book "*Theory of Games and Economic Behavior.*"
- Game theory is a study of strategic decision making. It is "the study of mathematical models of conflict and cooperation between intelligent rational decision-makers."
- An alternative term suggested "as a more descriptive name for the discipline." is *interactive decision theory.*

- Set of concepts aimed at decision making in situations of competition and conflict (as well as of cooperation and interdependence) under specified rules.
- In business schools, game theory is closely associated with decision-theory, and is used to study situations where management-psychology can play an important part.

2.2.4. Organizing

Introduction of an organization

- The term organization is derived from the word "organism" which means structure with parts so integrated that their relation to each other is governed by their relation to whole.
- **Amitai Etizoni:** "Organizations are social units deliberately constructed and reconstructed to seek specific goals. Corporations, armies, schools, hospitals, churches, and prisons are included; tribes, classes, ethnic groups, friendship groups and families are excluded."
- **Organizations are characterized by:**
    - o Divisions of labor, power, and communication responsibilities, divisions, which are not random or traditionally patterned, but deliberately planned to enhance the realization of specific goals.
    - o The presence of one or more power centers which control the concerted efforts of the organization and direct them toward its goals; these power centers also must review continuously the organization's performance and re – pattern its structure, where necessary, to increase its efficiency.
    - o Substitution of personnel i.e., unsatisfactory persons can be removed and others assigned their tasks. The organization can also recombine its personnel through transfer and promotion
- The term organization is used both structural and functional sense. As a structure it means a developed enterprise being operated to achieve the given goals. As a function it refers to establishing relationship between activities and authority pertaining to an enterprise.
- Organization is nothing but a process of integrating and co-ordinating the efforts of men and materials for the accomplishment of a set objective.
- Process of bringing together physical, financial and human resources and developing productive relationship amongst them for achievement of organizational goals.
- **Henry Fayol:** "To organize a business is to provide it with everything useful or its functioning i.e. raw material, tools, capital and personnel's".
- **Allen:** "Organization is the process of identifying and grouping work to be performed defining and delegating responsibility and authority and establishing relationship for the purpose of enabling people to work most effectively together in accomplishing objectives.
- **Sehein:** An Organization as the rational coordination of the activities of a number of people for the achievement of some common explicit purpose or goal, through division of labour and function, and through a hierarchy of authority and responsibility."
- **Pfiffner and Sherwood:** An Organization is the pattern of ways in which large number of people, too many have intimate face to face contact with all others, and engaged in a complexity of tasks, relate themselves to each other in the conscious, systematic establishment and accomplishment of mutually agreed purposes.

- To organize a business involves determining & providing human and non-human resources to the organizational structure, in the best possible manner.
- Organizing involves determination and grouping of the activities. Designing organization structures and departmentation based on this grouping.
- Defining the roles and responsibilities of the departments and of the job positions within these departments.
- Defining relationships between departments and job positions.
- Defining authorities for departments and job positions.
- Organizing as a process involves:
  - o Identification of activities.
  - o Classification of grouping of activities.
  - o Delegation of authority and creation of responsibility.
  - o Coordinating authority and responsibility relationships.

Types of Organization

1. Formal Organisation

- It is formed when two or more persons come together. They have a common objective or goal. They are willing to work together to achieve this similar objective.
- Formal Organisation has its own rules and regulation. These rules must be followed by the members (employees and managers).
- A formal organisation has a system of co-ordination.
- It also has a system of authority.
- It has a clear superior-subordinate relationship.
- All the members are given specific duties and responsibilities. Examples of formal organisation are a company, a school, a college, a bank, etc.
- A formal organisation is formed by the top level management.
- In a formal organisation, the duties, responsibilities, authority and accountability of each member is well-defined.
- In a formal organisation, the objectives or goals are specific and well-defined. The main objectives of a formal organisation are productivity, growth, and expansion.
- The members of the formal organisation get financial benefits and perks like wages or salaries, bonus, travelling allowances, health insurance, etc.
- A formal organisation is stable.
- A formal organisation uses formal channels of communication.
- In a formal organisation, there exists a superior-subordinate relationship.

2. Informal Organisation

- An informal organisation exists within the formal organisation.
- An informal organisation is a network of personal and social relationships.
- There are many groups of friends in a formal organisation.. These groups are called informal organisation.
- An informal organisation does not have its own rules and regulation.

- It has no system of co-ordination and authority. It doesn't have any superior-subordinate relationship or any specific and well-defined objectives.
- **In an informal organisation, communication is done through the *grapevine*.**
- An informal organisation is formed by social forces within the formal organisation.
- The members of an informal organisation do not have to follow any rules and regulations.
- In an informal organisation, there are no fixed duties, responsibilities, authority, accountability, etc. for the members.
- In an informal organisation, the objectives are not specific and well-defined. The main objectives of an informal organisation are friendship, security, common interest, individual and group satisfaction, etc.
- The members of informal organisation get social and personal benefits like friend circle, community, groups, etc.
- An informal organisation is not stable.
- An informal organisation uses informal channels of communication (i.e. grapevine)
- In an informal organisation, there is no such superior-subordinate relationship.

Factors included in the concept of organization

1. Assembly of business elements such as men, money and materials.
2. Creation of formal relationships between men employed at different levels through a hierarchy of authority.
3. Defining the functional role of the personnel and laying down the range of their responsibility for business performance.
4. Operating the organizational activities in conformity with the establishment objectives of the enterprise.

Elements of an organization

1. Division of work
2. Grouping of activities
3. Assignment of Duties
4. Delegation of Authority
5. Establishment of relationship

2.2.4.1. Organization Structure: Departmentation

1. **Mechanistic or Classical Organizational structure**

- It is usually Pyramid shaped structure.
- Mechanistic organizations is comparatively simpler and easy to organize, but find it difficult to cope with rapid change.

Hierarchical, bureaucratic, organizational-structure characterized by:

a) Centralization of authority,
b) Formalization of procedures and practices, and
c) Specialization of functions.

2. **An Organic or Behavioural structure**

- It has wider span of control.

- Organic organizations are comparatively more complex and harder to form, but are highly adaptable, flexible, and more suitable where external environment is rapidly changing and is unpredictable.
- Also called ***open organizations***, they are contrasted with mechanistic organizations.
- A term created by ***Tom Burns and G.M. Stalker*** in the late 1950s.
- An organic organization is a fluid and flexible network of multi-talented individuals who perform a variety of tasks.
- Organic Organizations Leads to Teamwork.

Organizational structure characterized by:

a) **Flatness:** Communications and interactions are horizontal,
b) **Low specialization:** Knowledge resides wherever it is most useful and
c) **Decentralization:** Great deal of formal and informal participation in decision making.

3. Collateral organization

- **Dale Zand:** A manager should develop a collateral mode of functioning which he should shift to be able to operate in tandem with the problem without displacing the existing formal structure.
- This is reserved for a collateral design, one that coexists with the formal, operational design but is structured as a flexible, open, loose, "organic-adaptive" system of problem-solving groups.
- A number of key steps are presented for designing such a collateral organization so that the operational design and the collateral design will combine to sense problems, define problems, derive solutions, and implement solutions.

4. Virtual organization

- Virtual organization is one that does not have a physical presence but exists electronically (virtually) on the internet.
- It is not constrained by the legal definition of a company, or is formed in an informal manner as an alliance of independent legal entities.
- A network of continually evolving independent organizations that share skills, costs, and access to one another's markets.

Departmentation

- First task in designing an organization structure is the identification of activities and to group them properly.
- The process of grouping activities is commonly known as departmentation.

Importance of departmentation

1. Advantages of specialization
2. Fixation of responsibility
3. To develop managers
4. Facility in Appraisal
5. Feeling of Autonomy

Types of Departmentation

1. **Functional departmentation:** The grouping of common or homogeneous activities to form an organization unit is known as functional departmentation.
2. **Productwise departmentation:** Product departmentation involves the grouping together of all activities necessary to manufacture a product or product line.
3. **Territorywise departmentation:** Territorial or geographical departmentation is specially useful to large-sized organizations having activities which are physically or geographically spread such as banking, insurance, transportation etc.
4. **Production processeswise departmentation:** Processes involved in production or various types of equipments used are taken as basis for departmentation.
5. **Customerwise departmentation :** Basically market – oriented in which departments are created around the markets served or around marketing channels.
6. **Choice of bases for departmentation:** The selection of bases for departemntation involves a consideration of the relative advantages of each base for the organization.

Characteristics of departmentation

a) **Specialization:** The basis of departmentation should reflect the specialization in performing the work.
b) **Coordination:** Coordination involves that all the related activities are performed in a way that their performance is synchronized so that each activity contributes to others.
c) **Economy:** A balance should be maintained between the cost of creating a department and its contribution. The existence of a department is desirable only when it contributes more than its cost.
d) **Focus on Result:** Those activities which contribute to the achievement to these results should be given proper attention.
e) **Local Conditions:** Local requirements of the organization should also the taken into account while creating departments.
f) **Human Considerations:** Departments should be created on the basis of availability of personnel, their aspirations and value systems, informal work groups and attitudes of people towards various forms of organization structure.

2.2.4.2. Organizational chart

- **George Terry**: "It is diagrammatic form which shows important aspects of an organization, including the major function and their respective relationship, the channels of supervision and the relative authority of each employee who is incharge of each respective function."
- It is important tool for portraying net work of an organization structure. It shows the main portion, nature of relationship between levels of management.

Types of Organizational charts

1. Vertical chart
2. Horizontal chart
3. Circular chart
4. Tree chart

Merits of Organizational Chart

1. Clarity in relationship
2. Easy to understand at a glance
3. Familiarizing new employees
4. Helps in formulating training programme
5. Helps to organizational change
6. It serves as a better method of visualizing the tone and character of an organisation.

Limitations of Organizational Chart

1. Likely to be outdated.
2. Rigidity.
3. It shows only relationships.
4. Shifting of responsibility to somebody else.
5. Does not show extents of authority or responsibility.
6. It may go against team spirit.
7. It ignores the informal aspects of an organization.

2.2.5. Authority, Responsibility and Accountability

1. Authority

- **Henri Fayol:** Authority is the right to give orders and the power to exact obedience.
- ***Superior can delegate to a subordinate the authority to perform and accomplish specific job.***
- Authority may be of formal authority, acceptance authority, authority of situation, position authority, and technical authority.
- Authority is the basis of organization in as much as organization is described as a system of authority relationships.
- In **line authority**, a superior exercises direct command over a subordinate. Line authority is represented by the standard chain of command that starts with the board of directors and extends down through the various levels of an organization.
- Staff authority is merely advisory in nature.
- Authority is the power to command others to act in a manner deemed by the possessor of the authority to further enterprise or departmental purpose.
- It is the power to make decisions which guide the actions of others.
- The person who makes the decisions is the superior and the person who accepts them and is guided by them is called one subordinate.
- Authority is different from power, which is the ability to influence or to cause a person to perform an act.
- **French and Raven:** Suggested five types of power as ***Reward, Coercion, Reference, Expertise and Legitimacy.***
- A subordinate accepts his superior's authority because he considers it to be legitimate.
- According to **Max Weber,** the three major bases of legitimacy are ***tradition, rationality and charisma.***
- **Herbert A. Simon:** Most subordinates are unwilling to accept the authority of the superiors outside certain limits, which refers to as ***"zones of acceptance"***.
- **Chester I. Bernard:** Four conditions must exist to make an order acceptable to a person:

1. He must understand the order.
2. He must believe that it is not inconsistent with the purpose of the organization.
3. He must believe that it is not incompatible which his personal interest.
4. He must be mentally and physically able to comply with it.

Difference between Authority and Power

	Authority	Power
1	It is the institutionalized right of a superior to command and compel his subordinates to perform a certain act.	It is the ability of a person to influence another person to perform an act.
2	It rests in the chair	It rests in the person
3	It is delegated	It is earned by own efforts
4	It is well defined	It is undefined
5	It is what exists in the eye	It exists in fact
6	It is a dejure concept	It is defacto concept
7	Basis for formal organization	Basis for informal organization

Use of Authority

- It enforces obedience to norms.
- It secures expertise in the making of decisions.
- It permits centralization of decision-making and coordination of activity.

1.1 Delegation of Authority

- **Louis A. Allen:** "If the managers require his subordinate to perform the work, he must entrust him with part of the rights and powers which he otherwise would have to exercise himself to get that work done."
- **Terry:** "It is something like imparting knowledge. You share with others who then process the knowledge, but you still remain the knowledge too."
- **F.C. Moore**, "Delegation means assigning work to the others and giving them authority to do so."
- **O. S. Miner**, "Delegation takes place when one person gives another the right to perform work on his behalf and in his name and the second person accepts a corresponding duty or obligation to do that is required of him."
- **Louis Allen**, "Delegation is the dynamics of management, it is the process a manager follows in dividing the work assigned to him so that he performs that part which only he, because of his unique organizational placement, can perform effectively, and so that he can get others to help him with what remains."

- Delegation means assigning of certain responsibilities along with the necessary authority by a superior to his subordinate managers.
- Delegation of authority is the base of superior-subordinate relationship.
- It involves following steps:
  a) Assignment of duties to subordinates.
  b) Granting of authority to enable the subordinates to perform the duties assigned.
  c) Creation of obligation on the part of subordinate to perform duties in an orderly manner.

Objectives of Delegation of Authority

1. To reduce the excessive burden on the superiors i.e., executives and managers functioning at different levels.
2. To provide opportunities of growth and self development to junior executives.
3. To create a team of experienced and matured managers for the organization. It acts as a technique of management and human resource development.
4. To improve individual as well as overall efficiency of the organization.

Process of Delegation of Authority

1. Assignment of duties to subordinates
2. Transfer of authority to perform the duty
3. Acceptance of the assignment
4. Creation of Obligation / Accountability / Responsibility

Advantages of Delegation of Authority

1. Relieves manager for more challenging jobs
2. Leads to motivation of subordinates
3. Facilitates efficiency and quick actions
4. Improves employee morale
5. Develops team spirit
6. Maintains cordial relationships
7. Facilitates management development

Barriers to Effective Delegation of Authority

1. Unwillingness of the manager to delegate authority: The attitude that 'I can do it better myself' on the part of superior acts as an obstacle to delegation.
2. Fear of competition
3. Lack of confidence in subordinates
4. Lack of ability to direct
5. Absence of controls that warn of coming troubles
6. Conservative and cautious temperament of the manager
7. Desire to dominate subordinates

Principles of Effective Delegation of Authority

1. Knowledge of Objectives
2. Parity of Authority and Responsibility
3. Unity of Command
4. The Scalar Principle

5. Clarity of Delegation
6. Absoluteness of Responsibility
7. Use of Exception Principle
8. Completeness of Delegation
9. Effective Communication Support System
10. Reward for Effective Delegation

1.2. Decentralization of Authority

- It is the situation which exists as a result of systematic delegation of authority throughout the organization.
- The term decentralization carries different meanings to different people.
- Decentralization is an extension of delegation.
- Decentralization implies a systematic delegation of authority throughout the whole organization.

Need of decentralization

- Large companies having independent product or service lines may adopt a form of decentralization.
- Under decentralization the whole organization is divided in to self-sufficient divisions.
- Having experienced many difficulties in the smooth running of such centralizes organizations, decentralizations of authority has been suggested and largely resorted to particularly to achieve the following purposes.
  - o Easing burden of chief executive
  - o Facilitating diversification
  - o Providing product of market emphasis
  - o Developing managers and
  - o Improving motivation

Advantages of decentralization

- o Decentralization leads to specialization.
- o Encourages decision making and assumption of authority and responsibility.
- o Decentralization makes the subordinates to work with involvement
- o Facilitates diversification in large scale.
- o Promote the development of general managers.
- o Aids in adoption of fast changing Environment.

Disadvantages of decentralization

- o Makes it more difficult to have a uniform policy.
- o Decentralization leads to problem in co – ordination.
- o May be limited to external forces.
- o Leads to increase in cost.
- o May some time leads to mis-use of power in high levels.
- o Leads to expenses in training a manager.
- o May be limited by the availability of qualified managers.

Delegation Vs decentralization

1. Delegation is the process while decentralization is the end result.

2. Superior is responsible for delegation where as in decentralization subordinates are responsible.
3. Delegation is vital and decentralization is optional.

2. Responsibility

- **Keith Davis:** "Responsibility is an obligation of the individual to perform assigned duties to the best of his ability under the direction of his executive leader."
- Responsibility refers to duty, activity or sometimes even authority.
- It really means that the obligation of a subordinate to perform the duty assigned to him. The essence of responsibility is, then obligation.
- In the normal functioning of an enterprise much of the responsibility in the nature of continuing obligation which means that the subordinate has an obligation to discharge his functions as required by the superior continually.
- Responsibility involves compliance, obedience and dependability.
- A failure to observe these elements may call forth a penalty, punishment or disciplinary action against the erring subordinate.
- ***Responsibility cannot be delegated or transferred:*** Superior can delegate to a subordinate the authority to perform and accomplish specific job.

Relationship between Authority and Responsibility

- Authority is the legal right of person or superior to command his subordinates while accountability is the obligation of individual to carry out his duties as per standards of performance.
- Authority flows from the superiors to subordinates, in which orders and instructions are given to subordinates to complete the task.
- It is only through authority, a manager exercises control. In a way through exercising the control the superior is demanding accountability from subordinates.

Differences between Authority and Responsibility

Authority	Responsibility
It is the legal right of a person or a superior to command his subordinates.	It is the obligation of subordinate to perform the work assigned to him.
Authority is attached to the position of a superior in concern.	Responsibility arises out of superior-subordinate relationship in which subordinate agrees to carry out duty given to him.
Authority can be delegated by a superior to a subordinate	Responsibility cannot be shifted and is absolute
It flows from top to bottom.	It flows from bottom to top.

3. Accountability

- The term accountability can also be used as a substitute for responsibility.
- Accountability refers to the liability of a subordinate for a proper discharge of his functions.
- It includes responsibility and arises from it. But accountability cannot be delegated.

- Thus to be accountable is to be answerable for the fulfillment or non-fulfillment of the authority or responsibility assigned.

2.2.6. Staffing

- The main purpose o staffing is to positioning right people to right jobs at right time. i.e. square pegs in square holes and round pegs in round holes.
- **Koontz & O'Donell:** "Managerial function of staffing involves manning the organization structure through proper and effective selection, appraisal & development of personnel to fill the roles designed on the structure".
- It includes manpower or human resource planning.
- It is the function of manning the organization structure and keeping it manned.
- Involves managing the various positions created by the organizing process.
- It involves conducting Gap analysis between existing and required manpower.
- It involves selection, training and development, retraining, mentoring, counseling, fixing remuneration, appraising them periodically and designing and administering the motivational packages.
- In nutshell Staffing involves:
  - Manpower Planning
  - Recruitment, selection & placement.
  - Training & development.
  - Remuneration.
  - Performance appraisal.
  - Promotions & transfer.

2.2.7. Directing

- Direction is instructing the subordinates to follow a certain process to attain given objectives.
- It is getting the work done through instructions and orders.
- It is the function of diversion in the management process to get the work from the subordinates by means of guiding, motivation, communication, supervising, leading and if need be commanding.
- It is sum of total of managerial efforts that is applied for guiding and inspiring the working teams to make better accomplishments in the organization.
- ***It is the heart and soul of management.***
- Ever manager in the organization gives direction to his subordinates as superior and receives direction subordinate from his superior.
- Direction may be defined as the function of management which is related with instructing, guiding and inspiring human factor in the organization to achieve organization objective.
- The direction is not merely issuing orders and instructions by a superior to his subordinates, but is includes the process of guiding and inspiring them.
- The analysis of definition reveals that direction function consist of three elements.
  a. Motivation
  b. Leadership
  c. Communication

Process of direction

1. Defining the objectives.
2. Organizing the efforts.
3. Measuring the work.
4. Developing the people.

Characteristics of direction

- Direction is an important managerial function. Through direction management can initiates actions in the organization.
- Direction function is performed at every level of management.
- Direction is a continuous process and it continuous throughout the life of the organization.
- Direction initiates at the top level in the organization follows and bottom through there hierarchy. It emphasizes that a subordinates is to be directed by his own superior only.

Importance of direction

- Direction initiates action.
- Direction integrates employees efforts.
- Direction attempts to get maximum out of individuals.
- Direction facilitates charges in the organization.
- Direction provides stability and balance in the organization

Principles of direction

- Direction is one of the most complex function of the management as it ideals with people whose nature itself is quite complex and unpredictable.

1. Principles of relating to the purpose of directing :

a. Principles of maximum individual contribution.
b. Principle of harmony of objectives.
c. Principle of efficiency of direction.

2. Principle relating to direction process :

a. Principle of unity of command.
b. Principle of appropriateness of direction technique.
c. Principle of managerial communication.
d. Principle of comprehension.
e. Principle of use of informal organization.
f. Principle of leadership.
g. Principle of follow through.

- Thus one of the basic functions of management is direction.
- Direction means the use of leadership and motivation to guide the performance of subordinates towards the achievement of the organization's goals.
- Important requirements for effective direction: Harmony of objectives, Unity of command, direct supervision, efficient communication and follow-up.
- Includes leading, motivating, communicating and coordinating. Communicate and coordinate with people to lead and enthuse them to work effectively together to achieve the plans of the organization.

- It is one of the most important functions of management to translate company's plans into execution.
- It includes providing leadership to people so that they work willingly and enthusiastically.
- Directing people involves motivating them all the time to enthuse them to give their best.
- Interacting effectively in group and team situations.
- Communicating in support of others efforts on behalf of achieving their work and organizational goals.
- Communicating companies plans throughout the organization is an important directing activity.
- It also means coordinating various people and their activities.
- Directing aims at achieving the best not just out of an individual but achieving the best through the groups or teams of people through team building efforts.
- Actuates the organizational methods to work efficiently for achievement of organizational purposes.
- Direction is that inert-personnel aspect of management which deals directly with influencing, guiding, supervising, motivating sub-ordinate for the achievement of organizational goals.

Direction has following elements:

- **Supervision:** Overseeing the work of subordinates by their superiors. It is the act of watching & directing work & workers.
- **Motivation:** Inspiring, stimulating or encouraging the sub-ordinates with zeal to work. Positive, negative, monetary, non-monetary incentives may be used for this purpose.
- **Leadership:** A process by which manager guides and influences the work of subordinates in desired direction.
- **Communications:** The process of passing information, experience, opinion etc from one person to another. It is a bridge of understanding.

2.2.8. Controlling

- **Theo Haimann:** "Controlling is the process of checking whether or not proper progress is being made towards the objectives and goals and acting if necessary, to correct any deviation".
- **Koontz & O' Donell :** "Controlling is the measurement & correction of performance activities of subordinates in order to make sure that the enterprise objectives and plans desired to obtain them as being accomplished".
- Control is any process that guide activity towards some predetermined goals.
- Thus control can be applied in any field such as price control, distribution control pollution control etc.
- Control process tries to find out deviations between planned performance and actual performance and to suggest corrective action wherever needed.
- **Terry:**"Controlling is determining what is being accomplish, that is evaluating the performance and, if necessary, applying corrected measures so that the performance takes place according to plan."
- Control is checking event performance against pre-determined standards contained in the plans, with a view to ensuring adequate progress and satisfactory performance.
- Controlling consists in verifying whether everything occurs inconformity with the plan adopted, the instructions issued and principles established.
- Its object is to point out weakness and errors in order to rectify them and prevent recurrence.

- Includes review and monitoring: evaluating the progress against the plans and making corrections either in plans or in execution.
- It includes verifying the actual execution against the plans to ensure that execution is being done in accordance with the plans.
- It measures actual performance against the plans.
- It sets standards or norms of performance.
- It measures the effective and efficiency of execution against these standards and the plans.
- It periodically reviews, evaluates and monitors the performance.
- If the gaps are found between execution levels and the plans, controlling function involves suitable corrective actions to expedite the execution to match up with the plans or in certain circumstances deciding to make modifications in the plans.
- An efficient system of control helps to predict deviations before they actually occur.
  1. Control is forward looking
  2. Control is both executive process and from the point of view of the organization of the system, a result
  3. Control is a continuous process.
  4. A control system is a coordinated – integrated system.
- Regulating the work of those for whom a manager is responsible which may include:
  - o Setting standards of performance in advance.
  - o Monitoring ongoing (real-time) performance.
  - o Assessing a completed performance.
  - o Results of the control process (evaluation) are fed back into the planning process.

Importance of control

1. **Adjustment in operations:** A control system acts as an adjustment in organizational operations. Every organization has certain objectives to achieve which become the basis for control.
2. **Policy verification:** Various policies in the organization generate the need for control. For organizational functioning, managers set certain policies and other planning elements which later become the basis and reason for control.
3. **Managerial responsibility:** In every organization, managerial responsibility is created through assignment of activities to various individuals. This process starts at the top level and goes to the lower levels.
4. **Psychological pressure:** Control process puts a psychological pressure on the individuals for the better performance. The performance of the individuals is evaluated in the light of targets set for them.
5. **Coordination in action:** Control system area designed in such a way that they focus not only on the operating responsibility of a manager but also on his ultimate responsibility. This forces a manager to co-ordinate the activities of his subordinate in such a way that each of them contributes positively towards the objectives of the superior.
6. **Organizational efficiency and effectiveness:** Proper control ensures organizational efficient and effectiveness various factors of control, namely, making managers responsible, motivating them for higher performance, and achieving coordination in their performance, control, ensures that their organization works efficiently.

Steps in controlling

1. Establishment of control standards: Every function in the organizations begins with plans which are goals, objectives or targets to be achieved. In the light of these standards are established which are criteria against which actual results are measured.

2. **Measurement of performance:** The second major step in control process is the measurement of performance. The step involves measuring the performance in respect of a work in terms of control standards.

3. Comparing actual and standard performance: The third major step in control process is the comparison of actual and standard performance. It involves two steps :

- o Finding out the extent of deviations and
- o Identifying the causes of such deviations.

4. Correction of deviations: This is the last step in the control process which requires that actions should be taken to maintain the desired degree of control in the system or operation.

Essentials of effective control system

- Control is necessary in every organization to ensure that everything is going properly. Therefore every manager should have an effective and adequate control system to assist him in making sure that events conform to plans.
- In this tailoring of control system, there are certain requirements which should be kept in mind.

1. **Reflecting organizational Needs:** All control systems and techniques should reflect the jobs they are to perform.
2. **Forward looking:** Control should be forward looking. Though many of the controls are instance, they must focus attention as to how future actions can be confirmed with plans.
3. **Promptness in reporting deviations:** The success of a thermostat lies in the fact that it points the deviation promptly and takes corrective actions immediately.
4. **Pointing out exceptions at critical points:** Control should point exception at critical points and suggest whether action is to be taken for deviations or not.
5. **Objectives:** The control should be objective, definite and determinable in a clear and positive way.
6. **Flexible:** Control system should be flexible so that it remains workable in the case of changed plans, unforeseen circumstances or failures.
7. **Economical:** Control should be economical and must be worth its costs. Economy is relative since the benefits vary with the importance of the activity, the size of the operation the expense that might be incurred in the absence of control and the contribution the control system can make.
8. **Simple:** Control system must be simple and understandable so that all managers can use it effectively.
9. **Motivating:** Control system should motivate both controller and controlled.
10. **Reflecting organizational pattern:** The control should reflect organizational pattern by focusing attention on positions in organization structure through which deviations are corrected.

Feedback loop of management control

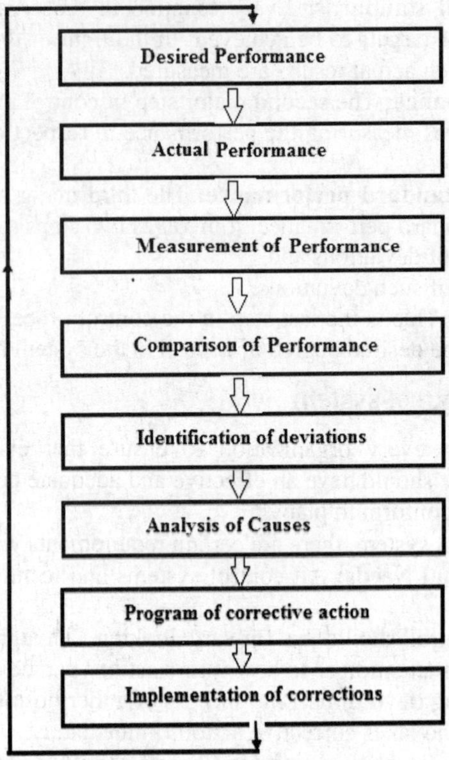

Techniques of control

To control the activities in the organization, managers can use variety of tools and techniques. They are broadly grouped under two heads.

1. Traditional techniques of conrol:

Traditional techniques are those which have long been used by the managers. Some of the important techniques under this heads are budgetary control, financial statement and ratio analysis, auditing, break-even analysis and report writing etc.

1.1. Budgeting

- **George R. Terry:** "Budgetary control is a process of comparing the actual results with the corresponding budgeting data in order to approve accomplishments or to remedy differences by either adjusting the budget estimates or correcting the cause of the difference."

- The different budgets such as production budget, sales budget, overhead budget, labour budget etc. clearly indicate the limits for expenses and also the results to be achieved in a given period. It ensures effective co-ordination of the work of the entire organization. It promotes co-operation and team spirit among the employees.

1.2. **Standard costing:** It is one of the techniques of cost control and it is being increasingly used by modern business concerns for the purpose of cost reduction and cost control. It involves a comparison of actual with the standards and the discrepancy is called variance.

1.3. **Break-even analysis:** It is useful in planning and control because it emphasize the marginal cost and benefit concept. It helps to make profit estimation at the different levels of activity, ascertaining turnover for desire profit and estimating the impact of the variations of fixed and variable costs. It magnifies a set of relationships of fixed costs, variable cost, price, level of output and sales mix to the profitability of the organization.

1.4. **Financial statement analysis:** Such as found flow analysis, cash flow analysis and ratio analysis help to know the financial performance and financial position of the business unit. The liquidity, profitability and solvency position of the business unit can be ascertained and efforts can be taken to maintain these factors in an optimum proportion.

1.5. **Auditing:** It is the process of investigating financial and other operation of a business establishment. It may be carried out by internal and external members. It helps to scrutinizes the applicability and relevance of policy, procedure and method which have a tendency to become obsolete. This helps in choosing a suitable working procedures and methods.

1.6. **Adoption of reporting system:** Helps to analyze a particular problem and to take necessary corrective action over it. Reports may be prepared regarding taxation, legislation and its effect on profit, make or buy decisions, replacement of capital equipment, social pricing analysis etc. A manager can also exercise effective control over his subordinates by observing them while they are engaging in work. Personal observation helps the managers not only in knowing the workers attitude towards work but also n correcting their work and method, if necessary.

2. Modern techniques of control

- These are of recent origin, which provide information not readily available with traditional methods. These techniques help to give sharper focus and promise increasingly to improve the quality of control.
- **Program Evaluation Review Technique (PERT) and Critical Path Method (CPM): PERT** has been, developed by an U.S. Office in 1958 in connection with the Polaris Weapon System and is credited with reduction the completion time of the program by two years. **CPM** has been jointly developed by DUPoint and Remington Rand USA in order to facilitate the control of large, complex industrial projects.
- These techniques are used to minimize total time, minimize to cost, minimize idle resources etc.
- It is helpful in solving problems of scheduling the activities of on-time projects. These tools are widely being used in construction industry, planning and launching a new projects, scheduling ship construction etc. It ensures improved management of resources by facilitating better decision making. It aims to have future oriented control mechanism for the organization.
- **Management Information System (MIS):** Provides needed information to each manager at the right time, in right form which aids his understanding and stimulate his action. MIS is a refined form of traditional information collection and supply to the organization points.

- **Management Audit:** It is an evaluation of management as a whole. It examine the total managerial process of planning, staffing, directing and controlling. To evaluate the management achievement, the organization plans, policies, procedures, organization structure, system of control personnel relation should be measure with its end results.

Human Resource Accounting (HRA)

- In 1891, first **William Patty** calculate the value of human resource in the form of money.
- Lev and Schwartz (1971) is the first person who discover above formula of value of employee.
- Most popular book of human resource accounting is Human Resource Accounting: Past, Present and Future which is written by **Caplan, Edwin H. and Landekich, Stephen**.
- Human Resource Accounting is the process of identifying and measuring data about Human Resources and communicating this information to the interested parties. It is an attempt to identify and report the Investments made in Human Resources of an organisation that are currently not accounted for in the Conventional Accounting Practices.
- Thus, Human Resource Accounting is a term applied by the Accountancy Profession to quantify the cost and value of employees of their employing organisation.
- Human Resource Accounting is the process of assigning, budgeting, and reporting the cost of human resources incurred in an organization, including wages and salaries and training expenses.
- Human Resource Accounting is the activity of knowing the cost invested for employees towards their recruitment, training them, payment of salaries & other benefits paid and in return knowing their contribution to organization towards its profitability.
- The American Accounting Association's Committee on Human Resource Accounting (1973) has defined Human Resource Accounting as "the process of identifying and measuring data about human resources and communicating this information to interested parties". HRA, thus, not only involves measurement of all the costs/ investments associated with the recruitment, placement, training and development of employees, but also the quantification of the economic value of the people in an organisation.
- **Flamholtz** has offered a similar definition for HRA. They define HRA as "the measurement and reporting of the cost and value of people in organizational resources".
- Human Resource Accounting (HRA) means to measure the cost and value of the people (i.e. of employees and managers) in the organisation. It measures the cost incurred to recruit, hire, train and develop employees and managers.
- **American Accounting Society Committee on HRA:** "Human Resource Accounting is the process of identifying and measuring data about human resources and communicating this information to interested parties."
- **Woodruff:**"Human Resource Accounting is an attempt to identify and report investments made in human resources of an organisation that are presently not accounted for in conventional accounting practice. Basically it is an information system that tells the management what changes over time are occurring to the human resource in the business."
- **Davidson and Roman L Weel:** "A term used to describe a variety of proposals that seek to report and emphasize the importance of human resources – knowledgeable, trained and loyal employees in a company earning process and total assets."
- **Eric Flamholtz of university of California, Los Angeles:** "Human resource accounting is the measurement of the cost and value of the people for the organisation."

- HRA also finds out the present economic value of its employees and managers. After measuring the cost and value of its employees and managers, the organisation prepares a report. This report is called **HRA Report**. It is shown to the top level management. It can also be shown to the employees, managers and outside investors.

Concept of human resource accounting

- Human Resource Accounting (HRA) is a new branch of accounting. It is based on the traditional concept that all expenditure of human capital formation is treated as a charge against the revenue of the period as it does not create any physical asset. But now a day this concept has changed and the cost incurred on any asset (as human resources) should be capitalized as it yields benefits measurable in monetary terms.
- Human Resource Accounting means accounting for people as the organisational resources. It is the measurement of the cost and value of people to organisations. It involves measuring costs incurred by private firms and public sectors to recruit, select, hire, train and develop employees and judge their economic value to the organisation.
- According to **Likert**, HRA serves the following purposes in an organisation:
  - ❖ It furnishes cost/value information for making management decisions about acquiring, allocating, developing, and maintaining human resources in order to attain cost-effectiveness;
  - ❖ It allows management personnel to monitor effectively the use of human resources;
  - ❖ It provides a sound and effective basis of human asset control, that is, whether the asset is appreciated, depleted or conserved;
  - ❖ It helps in the development of management principles by classifying the financial consequences of various practices.

Meaning of human resource accounting

- Human resource accounting is an attempt to identify and report investments made in the human resources of an organisation that are not presently accounted for under conventional accounting practice. Basically, it is an information system that tells the management what changes overtime are occurring to the human resources of the business, and of the cost and value of the human factor to the organisation. The system may serve both the internal and external users, providing management (internal users) with relevant data on which to base recruiting, training and other development decisions and supplying investors, lenders and other external users of financial statement with information concerning the investment in and utilisation of human resources in the organisation.
- Accounting is a man-made art and its principles and procedures have been evolved over a long period to aid business in reporting for the management and public. Of the four factors of production, viz., man, money, material and land, the last three of them are amenable to conventional accounting, but the first one, i.e., the human resource has not been subject to such accounting. Over the last two decades the idea of accounting for human resources is gaining active consideration.
- Much of the work on accounting for human resources focused primarily on development or validation of HRA concepts. The traditional practice of treating all expenditure on human capital formation as an immediate charge against income is not consistent with the

treatment accorded to comparable outlays in physical capital. The American Accounting Association strongly critised the practice of assigning a Zero value to an asset and stated that 'Costs should be capitalised when they are incurred in order to yield future benefits and when such benefits can be measured.'

- Management of any concern continuously strives hard for obtaining maximum efficiency. In order to measure the effectiveness of any firm the normal method is to examine financial statements. These statements include balance sheets in which physical assets such as cash accounts receivables, inventory and plant are recorded. These statements normally do not mention the productive capacity of the workers or goodwill of the company.
- HRA is the art of valuing, recording and presenting systematically the work of human resources in the books of accounts of an organisation. Thus, it is primarily an information system, which informs the management about the changes that are taking place in the human resource of an organisation.

Objectives of HR Accounting

- The objective of HRA is not merely the recognition of the value of all resources used by the organisation, but it also includes the management of human resource which will ultimately enhance the quantity and quality of goods and services. The main objectives of HR Accounting system are as follows:
- To furnish cost value information for making proper and effective management decisions about acquiring, allocating, developing and maintaining human resources in order to achieve cost effective organisational objectives.
- To monitor effectively the use of human resources by the management.
- To have an analysis of the human assets i.e. whether such assets are conserved, depleted or appreciated.
- To aid in the development of management principles. and proper decision making for the future by classifying financial consequences of various practices.
- In all, it facilitates valuation of human resources recording the valuation in the books of account and disclosure of the information in the financial statement.
- It helps the organisation in decision making in the following areas:
- Direct Recruitment vs. promotion, transfer vs. retention, retrenchment vs. retention, impact on budgetary controls of human relations and organisational behaviour, decision on reallocation of plants closing down existing units and developing overseas subsidiaries etc.
- The Aim of HR Accounting is to depict the Potential of the Employees in Monetary Terms. This concept can be examined from 2 directions i.e.
- Cost of Human Resources i.e. the expenditure incurred for recruiting, staffing and training the Quality of the Employees and
- Value of Human Resources i.e. the yield which the above investment can yield in the future.

Advantages of HR Accounting

1. **Information for manpower planning:** HRA provides useful information about the cost and value of human resources. It shows the strengths and weakness of the human resources. All this information helps the managers in planning and making the right decisions about human resources. Thus, it provides useful information for Manpower Planning and Decision Making. Human Resource Planning anticipates not only the required kind and number of employees but

also determines the action plan. It provides scope for advancement and development of employees by effective training and development.

2. **Information for making personnel policies:** HRA provides useful information for making suitable personnel policies about promotion, favorable working environment, job satisfaction of employees, etc. It checks the corporate plan of the organisation. The corporate plan aiming for expansion, diversification, changes in technological growth etc. has to be worked out with the availability of human resources for such placements or key positions. If such manpower is not likely to be available, HR accounting suggests modification of the entire corporate plan.

3. **Utilization of human resources:** HRA helps the organisation to make the best utilization of human resources.

4. **Proper placements:** HRA helps the organisation to place the right man in the right post depending on his skills and abilities. It offsets uncertainty and change, as it enables the organisation to have the right person for the right job at the right time and place. It aims to see that the human involvement in the organisation is not wasted and brings high returns to the organisation. It helps to take steps to improve employee contribution in the form of increased productivity.It provides different methods of testing to be used, interview techniques to be adopted in the selection process based on the level of skill, qualifications and experience of future human resources.

5. **Increases morale and motivation:** HRA shows that the organisation cares about the employees and their welfare. This increases their morale and it motivates them to work hard and achieve the objectives of the organisation. It helps individual employee to aspire for promotion and better benefits. It can foresee the change in value, aptitude and attitude of human resources and accordingly change the techniques of interpersonal management

6. **Attracts best human resources:** Only reputed organisations conduct HRA. So, competent and capable people want to join these organisations. Therefore, it attracts the best employees and managers to the organisation.

7. **Designing training and development programs:** HRA helps the organisation to design (make) a suitable training and development program for its employees and managers.

8. **Valuable information to investors:** HRA provides valuable information to present and future investors. They can use this information to select the best company for investing their money.

There are many benefits of HRA accounting which can be explained in following way.

- HRA provides the information of total cost of human assets which can use for calculating their benefits for business by comparing it with the benefits provided by employees.
- HRA is top work in the field of accounting because in accounting , we includes all physical assets and intangible assets but before making of HRA accounting we are ignoring a very important asset and its name is human being who works in any company or industry.
- Human resource accounting is very important where human element is more important than any other factor of production or services. For instance education sector is top sector who human resource accounting must be used for maintaining the accounts of education department.

Limitations of HRA

1. The valuation of human assets is based on the assumption that the employees are going to remain with the organisation for a specified period. However, this assumption is wrong because employee mobility is very high.
2. The human resource accounting may lead to the dehumanization in the organisation. If the valuation is not done correctly or the results of the valuation are not used properly.
3. In the case of financial accounting, there are certain specified accounting standards which every organisation must follow. However, there are no standards for HRA. Each organisation has its own standards for it. So, there are no uniform standards for it. Therefore, the HRA of two organisations cannot be compared.
4. There are no specific and clear cut guidelines for 'cost' and 'value' of human resources of an organisation. The present valuation systems have many limitations.
5. The life of a human being is uncertain. So its value is also uncertain.
6. Calculation the value of human resources is not so easy because it is most difficult to calculate the value of the quality of any person. What worth will be of honesty, morality, benevolence and generosity? But these moral values are so important for developing any company from bottom point.
7. Jealousy to see the high value of other employee can decrease the efficiency of any employee because he can think why my price is sow low and other employee's price is so high.
8. From human resource accounting, we cannot get short period benefits like general historical accounting system.
9. Indian company law 1956 , Indian Income tax law 1961 and other legal laws are no rule for showing human resource assets in the balance sheet .

Methods of Human Resource Accounting

- Quite a few Models have been suggested in the past for the Human Resource Accounting and these can be classified into 2 parts each having various Models. Some of the Important ones are:

A. COST BASED MODELS

1. Capitalisation of Historical Costs

- As per this Method of HR Accounting, the sum of all costs related to Human Resources (i.e. Recruitment, Acquisition, Formal Training, Informal Training, Informal familiarisation, experience and development) is taken together to represent the value of the human resources.
- The value is amortised annually over the expected length of the service of individual employees and the unamortised cost is shown as Investments in the Human Assets. If an employee leaves the firm (i.e. Human Assets expire) before the expected service life period, then the net value to that extent is charged to the Current Revenue.

Limitations

- This Model of HR Accounting is simple and easy to understand and satisfies the basic principles of matching the costs and revenues.
- As the historical costs are sunk costs and are irrelevant for decision making, this model was severely criticised as it failed to provide a reasonable value to the human resources.

- This method of HR Accounting capitalises only the Training and Development Costs incurred on the employees and ignores the future expected costs to be incurred for their maintenance.
- This Model of HR Accounting distorts the value of the highly skilled human resources as such employees require less training and therefore, according to this model, they will be valued at a lesser cost.

1. Replacement Costs

- The Historical Cost Method was highly criticised as it only takes into account the Sunk Costs which are irrelevant for Decision Making. Thus, a new model for Human Resource Accounting was conceptualised which took into the account, the costs that would be incurred to replace its existing human resources by an identical one.
- **Individual Replacement Costs**: Which refers to the cost that would have to be incurred to replace an individual by a substitute who can provide the same set of services as that of the individual being replaced.
- **Positional Replacement Costs**: Which refers to the cost of replacing the set of services referred by an incumbent in a defined position
- Thus, the Positional Replacement Cost takes into account the position in the organisation currently held by the employee and also the future positions expected to be held by him.

Limitations

- As per this method of HR Accounting, the determination of replacement cost of an employee is highly subjective and often impossible.
- Particularly at the management cadre, finding out an exact replacement is very difficult. The exit of a top management person may substantially change the human assets value.

2. Opportunity Cost Model

- This model was advocated by Hekimian and Jones in the year 1967 and is also known as the Market Value Method.
- This method of measuring Human Resources under this Model is based on the concept of opportunity cost i.e. the value of an employee in its alternative best use, as a basis of estimating the value of human resources.
- The opportunity cost value may be established by competitive bidding within the firm, so that in effect, managers bid for any scarce employee.
- A human asset therefore, will have a value only if it is a scarce resource, that is, when its employment in one division denies it to another division.

Limitations

- One of the serious limitations of this method for Human Resource Accounting is that it excludes employees of the type which can be hired readily from outside the firm.
- Thus, this approach seems to be concerned with only one section of a firm's human resources, having special skills within the firm or in the labour market.

B. ECONOMIC VALUE MODELS

1. Present Value of Future Earnings Model

- This Model of human resource accounting was developed by Lev and Schwartz in the year 1971 and involves determining the value of human resources as per the present value of estimated future earnings discounted by the rate of return on Investment (Cost of Capital).
- As per this valuation model of Human Resource Accounting, the following expression is used for calculating the expected value of a person's human capital

Limitations

- This Model of HR Accounting ignores the possibility and probability that an Individual may leave an organisation for reasons other than Death or Retirement.
- This Model of HR Accounting also ignores the probability that people may make role changes during their careers. For example, an Assistant Engineer will not remain in the same position throughout the expected service life in the Organisation.
- Despite the above limitations, this model is the most commonly used model across the Globe for the purpose of Human Resource Accounting.

2. Reward Valuation Model/ Flamholtz Model

- Flamholtz advocated that an Individual's Value to an organisation is determined by the services he is expected to render.
- This model of Human Resource Accounting is an improvement to the "Present Value of Future Earnings Model" as it takes into account the probability that an individual is expected to move through a set of mutually exclusive organisational roles or service states during a time interval. Such movement can be estimated probabilistically by using the following model

Limitations:

- The major drawback of this model of Human Resource Accounting is that it is difficult to estimate the probabilities of likely service states of each employee.
- Determining the monetary equivalent of service states is also very difficult and costly affair.
- Since the analysis is restricted to Individuals, it ignores the value added element of Individuals working as groups.

3. Valuation on Group Basis

- While applying the above models, the Accountants realised that proper Valuation as per Human Resources Accounting is not possible unless the contributions of the Individuals as a Group are taken into consideration.
- An Individual's expected service tenure in the organisation is difficult to predict but on a group basis it is relatively easier to estimate the percentage of people in a group likely to leave the organisation in the future.
- This model of Human Resource Accounting attempted to calculate the present value of all existing employees in such in each rank. Such Present Value is ascertained with the help of the following steps:
- Ascertain the number of employees in each rank: Estimate the probability that an employee will be in his rank within the organisation or will be terminated in the next period. This probability will be estimated for a specified time period.

- Ascertain the economic value of an employee in a specified rank during each time period.
- The present value of existing employees in each rank is obtained by multiplying the above three factors and applying an appropriate discount rate.

Limitations

- Although this process simplifies the process valuation of Human Resource Accounting by considering a group of employees as a valuation base, but this method ignores the exceptional qualities of certain skilled employees.
- Thus, the performance of a group may be seriously affected in the event of exit of a single individual.

Position of HRA in India

In India, very few companies use HRA. It is not compulsory in India. **Infosys** Technologies and **BPL** are the leading companies in India, which uses HRA. HRA reports give useful information to the company management, employees and investors.

In nutshell various techniques of control leads to as follows:

1. Budgetary control: Financial performance.
2. Cost control: Cost performance.
3. Production control: PERT, CPM , Production, performance, quality.
4. Inventory control: Stores function performance.
5. Profit & Loss Control ROL control: Overall organizational objective performance.
6. External audit control: Statutory performance.
7. Management self audit.

2.2.9. Co-ordination

- It is the integration, synchronization or orderly pattern of group efforts in the enterprise towards the accomplishment of objectives.
- Coordination is the management of interdependence in work situations.
- It may be defined as balancing and keeping the teams together by ensuring a suitable allocation of working activities to the various members and seeing that they are performed with due harmony among the members themselves.

Need for coordination

- Systematic sequence of operation
- Fulfillment of activities as per planned schedules
- Avoidance of interruptions in the operations
- Eliminating inconsistencies in objectives and policies
- Removal of conflicts among individuals
- Developing the team spirit and cooperation.

Advantages of coordination

1. Increases the efficiency, Increases in the productivity, economizing the activities etc.
2. Improve the morale of the employees.
3. Develop and retain good personnel.

Types of co-ordination

1. **Internal co-ordination:** It is the establishment of relationship with a view to coordinate the employees of all the departments. It may be vertical or horizontal.

2. **External Co-ordination:** It refers to establishment or relationship with a view to coordinate the activity of those who are not part of the organization.

Principles of coordination

1. Early beginning
2. Direct contact
3. Reciprocity
4. Continuity

Techniques of coordination

"A manager in managing must coordinate the work for which he is accountable by balancing, timing and integrating.

- o Balancing-Support,
- o Timing -Time schedule
- o Integrating-Unification.

Problems of coordination

- Complex organizational structure
- Improper communication
- Higher labour turnover
- Lack of motivation and morale
- Favoritism
- Red-tapism
- Improper leadership
- Weak public relations.

Follett's Four Principles of Coordination

Mary Parker Follett gave **four** main Principles of Coordination. These four principles of co-ordination are called are Follett's **Principles of Coordination**. These four principles must be followed to make co-ordination effective. Mary P. Follett's four main principles of coordination are discussed below:

1. **Principle of Early Stage:** According to this principle, coordination must start at an early stage in the management process. It must start during the planning stage. This will result in making the best plans and implementing these plans with success. If coordination is started early only then all the management functions will be performed successfully. Thus by initiating proper coordination the organisation will achieve all its objectives easily and quickly.

2. **Principle of Continuity:** According to this principle, coordination must be a continuous process. It must not be a one-time activity. The process of coordination must begin when the organisation starts, and it must continue until the organisation exists. Coordination must

be done continuously during the management process. It must be done during planning, organising, directing and controlling.

3. **Principle of Direct Contact:** According to this principle, all managers must have a Direct Contact with their subordinates. This will result in good relations between the manager and their subordinates. This is because direct contact helps to avoid misunderstandings, misinterpretations and disputes between managers and subordinates. It enables the managers to coordinate all the different activities of their subordinates effectively and efficiently.

4. **Principle of Reciprocal Relations:** The decisions and actions of all the people (i.e of all managers and employees) and departments of the organisation are inter-related. So, the decisions and actions of one person or department will affect all other persons and departments in the organisation. Therefore, before taking any decision or action all managers must first find out the effect of that decision or action on other persons and departments in the organisation. This is called the Principle of Reciprocal Relations. Co-ordination will be successful only if this principle is followed properly.

Additional Principles of Coordination

After Mary Parker Follett, modern management experts have extended her list by adding four additional principles of coordination. These additional or supplementary principles of coordination are explained as follows:

1. **Principle of Effective Communication:** Co-ordination will be successful only in the presence of an effective communication. Good communication must be present between all departments, within employees themselves and even between managers and their subordinates. All communication barriers and gaps must be avoided and fixed. Good communication helps to avoid misunderstandings in the organization. This overall helps in coordination.

2. **Principle of Mutual Respect:** Coordination will be successful only if there exist a mutual respect throughout the organization. All managers working at different levels (top, middle or lower) must respect each other. Similarly, all employees must show a friendly attitude and should respect each other during interactions. There must also exist a feeling of brotherly hood among managers and employees. The managers must respect the feelings and emotions of the employees. On the other hand, employees too must understand and acknowledge their bosses. Without mutual respect, coordination may not survive, and it will eventually fail.

3. **Principle of Clarity of Objectives:** Co-ordination will be successful only if the organisation has set its clear objectives. Everyone in the organisation must know the objectives very clearly. No one must have any doubts about the objectives of the organisation. Clear objectives can be achieved easily and quickly.

4. **Principle of Scalar Chain:** Scalar Chain is a line of authority. This line joins all the members (managers and employees) from top to bottom. Every member must know who is his superior. He must also know who is his subordinate. Scalar Chain is necessary for good communication. Scalar Chain must not be broken in norm circumstances. However, if quick action is necessary, then this chain can be broken. This is done using "**Gang Plank**" / "**Bridge**" / "**Direct Contact**".

Scalar Chain is shown in diagram below with Gang plank as dotted line BK.

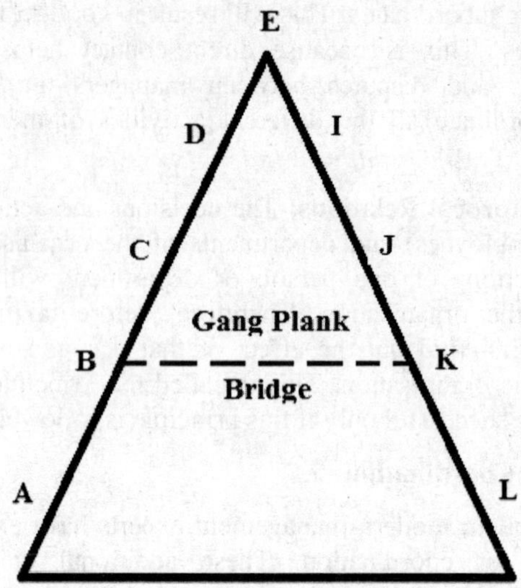

- The Scalar Chain is shown by a double ladder E to A and E to L. E is the head of the organisation. D and I are the next level, and so on. If quick action is necessary, then a "Gang Plank" "BK" is made. Now B and K can contact each other directly but they should inform C and J about their decisions.

2.3. OBJECTIVE QUESTION-ANSWER

1. Match the thinkers with the management functions advocated by them.

Thinker	Function
(a) Newman and Summer	(i) Organising, planning, leading and controlling
(b) Henry Fayol	(ii) Planning, Organising, Commanding, Coordinating and Controlling
(c) Luther Gullick	(iii) Planning, organising, staffing, directing and controlling
(d) Koontz and O'Donnell	(iv) POSDCORB"

	(a)	(b)	(c)	(d)
(A)	(i)	(ii)	(iv)	(iii)
(B)	(ii)	(i)	(iii)	(iv)
(C)	(i)	(ii)	(iii)	(iv)
(D)	(ii)	(i)	(iv)	(iii)

Answer: A

2. Who has called the POSDCORB a folklore'?
(A) Michael Armstrong (B) Michael Poole
(C) Rosemary Stewart (D) Henry Mirzberg
Answer: D

3. Every person has different ways and means of performing art, similarly, every individual has different styles of management and these are categorized as:
(A) Democratic (B)Autocratic
(B) Bureaucratic (D) All the above

Answer: D

4. Features of Management are as follows
(A) Goal oriented (B) Universal
(C) Continuous process (D)All the above
Answer: D

5. Management is multidisciplinary, it includes knowledge/ information from
(A)Economics (B)Maths
(C) Psychology (D)All the above
Answer: D

6. Match the following :

List - I	List - II
(a) Top Management	(i) Human Skill
(b) Middle Management	(ii) Conceptual Skill
(c) Junior Management	(iii) Technical Skill

Code :	(a)	(b)	(c)
(A)	(iii)	(i)	(ii)
(B)	(ii)	(i)	(iii)
(C)	(i)	(ii)	(iii)
(D)	None of the above		

Answer : B

7. Match the following managerial activities with the managerial functions :

(a) Forecasting	(i) Controlling
(b) Communication	(ii) Planning
(c) Selection of Managers	(iii) Leading
(d) Established performance standards	(iv) Staffing

Code:

	(a)	(b)	(c)	(d)
(A)	(ii)	(iii)	(iv)	(i)
(B)	(i)	(ii)	(iv)	(iii)
(C)	(ii)	(iv)	(i)	(ii)
(D)	(i)	(iii)	(iv)	(ii)

Answer: A

8. Match the following :

(a) Staff Executives	(i) Advisory Function
(b) Directing	(ii)Manpower Development
(c) Line Executive	(iii) Guiding Function
(d) Staffing	(iv) Managerial Authority

Code:

	(a)	(b)	(c)	(d)
(A)	(i)	(iv)	(iii)	(ii)
(B)	(i)	(iii)	(iv)	(ii)
(C)	(ii)	(iii)	(iv)	(i)
(D)	(ii)	(i)	(iii)	(iv)

Answer: A

9. Match the following:

Group A	Group B
(a) Grapewine	(i) Tool of control
(b) Units of Direction	(ii) Scientific Management
(c) Time and Motion Study	(iii) Form of Communication
(d) Budget	(iv) Management Principle

	(a)	(b)	(c)	(d)
(A)	(iii)	(ii)	(iv)	(i)
(B)	(ii)	(iii)	(i)	(iv)
(C)	(iii)	(iv)	(ii)	(i)
(D)	(iv)	(iii)	(i)	(ii)

Answer: C

10. The five elements in the management process are
(A) Plan, direct, update, lead, and supervise
(B) Accounting/finance, marketing, operations, and management
(C) Organize, plan, control, staff, and manage
(D) Plan, organize, staff, lead, and control
(E) Plan, lead, organize, manage, and control
Answer : E

11. The responsibilities of the operations manager include
(A) Planning, organizing, staffing, procuring, and reviewing
(B) Forecasting, designing, planning, organizing, and controlling
(C) Forecasting, designing, operating, procuring, and reviewing
(D) Planning, organizing, staffing, leading, and controlling designing and operating
Answer: D

12. Which of the following is not an element of the management process?
(A) Pricing (B) Staffing
(B) Planning (D) Controlling
Answer: A

13. An operations manager is not likely to be involved in :
(A) The design of products and services to satisfy customers' wants and needs
(B) The quality of products and services to satisfy customers' wants and needs
(C) The identification of customers' wants and needs
(D) Work scheduling to meet the due dates promised to customers
(E) Forecasting sales
Answer: C

14. All of the following decisions fall within the scope of operations management except for
(A) Financial analysis
(B) Design of products and processes
(C) Location of facilities
(D) Quality management
(E) All of the above fall within the scope of operations management
Answer: A

15. Which of the following are the primary functions of all organizations?
(A) Operations, marketing, and human resources
(B) Marketing, human resources, and finance/accounting
(C) Sales, quality control, and operations
(D) Marketing, operations, and finance/accounting
(E) Research and development, finance / accounting, and purchasing
Answer: D

16. A major problem with a task force type of management is
(A) There is no logical basis for task force information
(B) Its status is too inflexible
(C) Accountability
(D) Lack of planning
Answer: C

17. Match the following :

List I	List II
(a) Innovation and representation as	(i) Mary Parker Follet two additional managerial functions
(b) Characteristics of profession	(ii) Henry Mintzberg
(c) Management is the art of getting	(iii) E. F. L. Brech
(d) Roles of manager	(iv) McFarland
(e) Management is a comprehensive generic term.	(v) Ernest Dale things done through people.

Codes :

	(a)	(b)	(c)	(d)	(e)
(A)	(i)	(iii)	(iv)	(ii)	(v)
(B)	(v)	(iv)	(i)	(ii)	(iii)
(C)	(ii)	(iii)	(iv)	(i)	(v)
(D)	(ii)	(i)	(iii)	(iv)	(v)

Answer: B

18. Some of the management functions mentioned by Henry Fayol are:
(A) Planning
(B) Control
(C) Co-ordination
(D) All the above
Answer: D

19. What type of skills does management require?
(A) Conceptual
(B) Human relations
(C) Technical
(D) All the above
Answer: D

20. Characteristics of formal organization are :
(A) Arbitrary structure
(B) Predetermined objectives and policies
(C) Well defined rules and regulations
(D) All the above
Answer: D

21. A vision statement should have the following components :
(A) Ability to inspire people
(B) Achievable
(C) Precise and objective
(D) All the above
Answer: D

22. Key ethical principles include the following:
(A) Fulfilling commitments
(B) Caring and compassion
(C) Being accountable for decision
(D) All the above
Answer: D

23. The three major functions of business organizations
(A) Are mutually exclusive
(B) Exist independently of each other
(C) Overlap
(D) Function independently of each other
(E) Do not interface with each other
Answer: C

24. Which of the following are the primary functions of all organizations?
(A) Operations, marketing, and human resources
(B) Marketing, human resources, and finance/accounting
(C) Sales, quality control, and operations
(D) Marketing, operations, and finance/accounting
(E) Research and development, finance/accounting, and purchasing
Answer: D

25. The products that are grouped under strategic business units share common factors, like
(A) Underlying technology (B) The market
(C) The skill (D) All the above
Answer: D

26. What type of skills does management require?
(A) Conceptual (B) Human relations
(C) Technical (D) All of the above
Answer: D

27. According to Robert L. Katz, the right sequence of relative importance of various managerial skills from top to bottom is
(a) Technical (b) Human (c) Conceptual
(A) c, b, a (B) a, b, c
(C) c, a, b (D) b, c, a
Answer: A

28. Which one of the following is not an interpersonal role identified by Henry Mintzberg ?
(A) The Figure head role
(B) The Leader role
(C) The Liason role
(D) The Resource – allocator role
Answer: D

29. Components of planning would include:
(A) Objectives (B)Budgets
(B) procedures (D)All the above
Answer: D
Explanation: Planning is the process of determining the organization's objectives and deciding how to accomplish them.

30. Essentials of a good plan are
(A) Must be continuous
(B) Should be time bound
(C) Must motivate people
(D) All the above
Answer: D

31. Objectives can be classified as:
(A) On the basis of time
(B) On the basis of functions
(C) On the basis of levels
(D) All the above
Answer: D

32. Some of the limitations of business planning are
(A) Time Consuming
(B) Expensive device
(C) Heavy cost of planning
(D) All the above
Answer: D

33. A Programme is a :
(A) Multi-use plan
(B) Single-use plan
(C) Fixed plan
(D) Flexible plan
Answer: C

34. Planning involves the following:
(A) Assigning tasks
(B) Defining goals
(C) Making corrections
(D) Using influence
(E) Determining appropriate tasks and resources
Answer: B

35. Arrange the following steps in Policy Analysis in the correct sequence and select the correct answer from the codes given below :
(i) Problem identification
(ii) Forecasting and evaluating the alternatives.
(iii) Determining alternative courses of action.
(iv) Policy choice
Codes :
(A) (i), (ii), (iii), (iv)
(B) (i), (iii), (ii), (iv)
(C) (ii), (iv), (i), (iii)
(D) (ii), (iii), (iv), (i)
Answer: B

36. Arrange the following steps of planning in a proper sequence
(i) Developing premises
(ii) Evaluating alternative courses
(iii) Being aware of opportunities
(iv) Selecting a course
(v) Establishing objectives
(A) (i) (iii) (iv) (ii) (v)
(B) (i) (iii) (ii) (v) (iv)
(C) (iii) (v) (i) (ii) (iv)
(D) (iii) (v) (i) (iv) (ii)
Answer: C

37. Which of the following is the major element of planning process ?
(A) Developing leadership abilities
(B) Selecting right people
(C) Perception of opportunities
(D) Motivating people
Answer: C

38. Which one of the following identifies the basic function or task of an organization?
(A) Policy (B) Objective
(C) Mission (D) Programme
Answer: D

39. Which of the following is a single use plan?
(A) Budget (B) Rule
(C) Procedure (D) Policy
Answer: A

40. The basic role of policy is
(A) To provide guidelines for action
(B) To set procedures
(C) To give direction for motivation
(D) To prescribe methods
Answer: A

41. Process of planning begins with :
(A) Forecasting
(B) Setting objectives
(C) Setting policies
(D) Setting procedures
Answer : A

42. Planning does not include :
(A) Deciding in advance what to do
(B) Identifying Priorities
(C) Implementation
(D) Focus on target groups
Answer: C

43. A special kind of plan formulated in order to meet the challenge of competitors is called:
(A) Single use plan (B) Programme
(C) Strategy (D) Project
Answer: C

44. Arrange the following steps in the planning process in which they occur :
(i) Establishing objectives
(ii) Determining planning premises
(iii) Analyzing opportunities
(iv)Evaluation
(v) Identifying alternatives
(vi)Selection
(vii) Review
(viii) Implementation
(A) (iii) (i) (ii) (v) (iv) (vi) (viii) (vii)
(B) (i) (iii) (ii) (iv) (vi) (v) (vii) (viii)
(C) (ii) (i) (iii) (v) (vi) (viii) (iv) (vii)
(D) (iii) (ii) (v) (i) (iv) (vi) (vii) (viii)
Answer: B

45. Planning does not include :
(A) Deciding in advance what to do
(B) Identifying Priorities
(C) Implementation
(D) Focus on target groups
Answer: C

46. What are the advantages of a procedure?
(A) Ensures uniformity of action
(B) Increases co-ordination
(C) Provides good standard for the manage
(D) All the above
Answer: D

47. Policies are sometimes defined as a(n)
(A) Shortcut for thinking
(B) Action plan
(C) Substitute for strategy
(D) Substitute for management authority
Answer: A

48. 'No Smoking in the factory' is an example of________.
(A) Policy (B) Procedure
(C) Rule (D) Strategy
Answer: C

49. What does strategy indicate?
(A) A method for a particular plan
(B) An indication of correct action
(C) Programme of actions to achieve objectives
(D) Specific indication to an action
Answer: C

50. Strategic planning as a broad concept consists of
(A) Corporate strategy and business strategy
(B) Strategy formulation and strategy implementation
(C) Inputs and outputs
(D) Environmental analysis and internal analysis
Answer: B

51. Early theories about how individuals make decisions were based on the concept of a(n)
(A) Utilitarian philosophy (B) Action man
(C) Economic man (D) Attentive man
Answer: C

52. Some policies are imposed by external forces, such as
(A) Governmental regulatory agencies
(B) Employee demands
(C) Management decisions
(D) Lack of funding
Answer: A

53. Rules offer a definite direction to the planning process, they are also names as
(A) Specific (B) Rigid
(C) non-flexible (D) All the above
Answer: D

54. According to Urwick, features of good plan is that which is
(A) Sample
(B) Balanced
(C) Flexible
(D) All the above
Answer: D

55. Determining an organization's objectives and deciding how to accomplish them are part of the management function known as:
(A) Planning (B) organizing
(C) Staffing (D) controlling
(E) directing
Answer: A

56. The type of planning conducted on a short-term basis to implement activities and objectives is called
(A) Strategic
(B) Static
(C) Tactical
(D) Comprehensive
(E) timely
Answer: C

57. The type of planning conducted on a long-range basis by top managers is usually called
(A) Incremental
(B) Tactical
(C) Strategic
(D) Crisis
(E) Static
Answer: C

58. Crisis management plans generally cover maintaining business operations during a crisis and

(A) Firing those responsible for the crisis.
(B) Avoiding responsibility for the crisis.
(C) Communicating with others about the situation and the company's response to it.
(D) Preventing the situations from occurring.
(E) All of the above.
Answer: C

59. Top managers spend most of their time performing which of the following management functions?
(A) Directing (B) Controlling
(C) Organizing (D) Staffing
(E) Planning
Answer: E

60. Which of the following refers to conscious choice among alternative course of action?
(A) Decision making (B) Control
(C) Coordination (D) Direction
Answer: A

61. Decision making is an important aspect of:
(A) Planning (B) Control
(C) Organizing (D) All the above
Answer: D

62. Which of the following provides a guideline to decision making ?
(A) Strategy (B) Policy
(C) Procedure (D) Programme
Answer: A

63. Who defined decision– making is a conscious choice among alternative course of action.
(A) Phillip Kotler (B) F.W.Tayler
(C) Henry Fayol (D) Max Weber
Answer: A

64. The defination of decision involves following characteristics
(A) Involves Rationality
(B) Involves Commitment
(C) Involves Mental Process
(D) All the above
Answer: D

65. Specific procedures developed for repetitive and routine problems are
(A) Autocratic decisions
(B) Programmed decisions
(C) Easy decisions
(D) Non-programmed decisions
Answer: B

66. Match List – I with List – II and select correct answer from the codes given below :

List – I
a. Autocratic decision making
b. Democratic decision making
c. Rational decision making
d. Consultative decision making

List – II
i. Making decision with participation
ii. Making decision with little consultation
iii. Making decisions on the basis of calculation and choosing thebest option
iv. Making decision by inviting opinions

Codes :

	A	b	c	d
(A)	i	ii	iii	iv
(B)	ii	I	iii	iv
(C)	iv	iii	ii	i
(D)	iii	ii	iv	i

Answer: B

67. Which one of the following is not a decision role identified by Henry Mintzberg
(A)The spokesperson role
(B)The Entrepreneurial role
(C) The Disturbance handler role
(D)The Resource allocator role
Answer: A

68. What are the important guidelines for effective decision making?
(A) Adopt a diagnostic approach to decision making
(B) Involve subordinates in decision making process
(C) Evaluate the results
(D) All the above
Answer: D

69. All of the following steps are a part of the decision-making process *except*
(A) defining the situation
(B) developing options
(C) analyzing options
(D) delegating the decision
(E) implementing the decision.
Answer: D

70. The process of forecasting is based on:
(A) Future trends (B) Current analysis
(C) Past performance (D) All the above
Answer: D

71. Some of the popular forecasts are
(A) Demand forecast
(B) Sales forecast
(C) Specific industry forecast
(D) All the above
Answer: D

72. The three major types of forecasts used by business organizations are
(A) Strategic, tactical, and operational
(B) Economic, technological, and demand
(C) Exponential smoothing, delphi, and regression
(D) Causal, time-series, and seasonal
(E) Departmental, organizational, and territorial
Answer: B

73. Which of the following is **not** a step in the forecasting process?
(A) Determine the use of the forecast
(B) Eliminate any assumptions
(c) Determine the time horizon
(d) Select a forecasting model(s)
(e) Validate and implement the results
Answer: B

74. The two general approaches to forecasting are
(A) Qualitative and quantitative
(B) Mathematical and statistical
(c) Judgmental and qualitative
(d) Historical and associative
(e) Judgmental and associative
Answer: A

75. Which of the following uses three types of participants: decision makers, staff personnel, and respondents?
(A) Executive opinions
(B) Sales force composites
(C) The delphi method
(D) Consumer surveys
(E) Time series analysis
Answer: C

76. Which of the following is **not** a type of qualitative forecasting?
(A) Executive opinions
(B) Sales force composites
(C) Consumer surveys
(D) The Delphi method
(E) Moving average
Answer: E

77. The forecasting model that pools the opinions of a group of experts or managers is known as the
(A) Sales force composition model
(B) Multiple regression
(C) Jury of executive opinion model
(D) Consumer market survey model
(E) Management coefficients model
Answer: C

78. Which of the following techniques uses variables such as price and promotional expenditures, which are related to product demand, to predict demand?
(A) Associative models
(B) Exponential smoothing
(C) Weighted moving average
(D) Simple moving average time series
Answer: A

79. Forecasting is most closely associated with
(A) Organizing (B) Directing
(C) Staffing (D) Planning
(E) Controlling.
Answer: D

80. Effective implementation of a major decision requires
(A) Perseverance (B)Luck
(C)Directing (D) Planning
(E)Controlling
Answer: D

81. The managerial function of organising is to :
(A) Review and adjust plans as circumstances alter.
(b) Establish a programme for accomplishment of objectives.
(c) Get things done through others.
(d) Create a structure of functions and duties for a group of people.
Answer: D

82. Sequence the following steps of organising process :
(A) Forming supportive objectives
(B) Delegating the authority require to perform activities.
(C) Establising enterprise objectives
(D) Identifying and classifying activities

(A)	(c)	(a)	(d)	(b)
(B)	(c)	(d)	(a)	(b)
(C)	(d)	(c)	(b)	(a)
(D)	(b)	(c)	(a)	(d)

Answer: A

83. Dividing work into small units and assigning it to individuals are tasks related
(A) Planning (B) Organizing
(C) Staffing (D) Controlling
(E) Directing.
Answer: B

84. Name the following topics that give an idea about the concept of organizing.
(A)Decentralization
(B)Staffing process
(C)Span of management
(D)All the above
Answer: D

85. Characteristics of informal organization
(A) Spontaneous development
(B) Informal authority
(C) Both
(D) None of the above
Answer: C

86. The liberalization and globalization has lead to restructuring of industry through
(A) Merger
(B) Outsourcing
(C) Downsizing
(D) (D)All the above
Answer: D

87. A manager may delegate any of the following except
(A) Authority (B) Work load
(C) Responsibility (D) None of the above
Answer: C

88. Decentralization means:
(A) Creating an account
(B) Determination of results expected
(C) Transfer of authority from one individual to another
(D) Doing things in a central place.
Answer: C

89. Decentralization in an organization is achieved by :
(A) Functional Departmentation
(B) Delegation of Powers
(C) Both (A) and (B)
(D) None of the above
Answer: C

90. Authority means:
(A) Getting work done
(B) Right to get work done
(C) Sports authority of India
(D) Being in a managerial position
Answer: B

91. Factors determining decentralization of authority
(A) Uniformity of policy
(B) Desire for independence
(C) Control techniques
(D) All the above
Answer: D

92. Generally delegation moves from:
(A) Downward
(B) Upward
(C) Vertical
(D) Horizontal
Answer: A

93. Name the factors determining decentralization of authority:
(A) Size of the organization
(B) Uniformity of policy
(C) History of the enterprise
(D) All the above
Answer: D

94. Principles of effective delegation are:
(A) Train the subordinates
(B) Reward delegation
(C) Appropriate reporting system
(D) All the above
Answer: D

95. Barriers to delegation of authority would be :
(A) Lack of trust in subordinates
(B) Fear of loosing status by managers
(C) Over-confidence among managers
(D) All the above
Answer: D

96. Who of the following has described authority as the supreme co-ordinating power ?
(A) Karl Marx (B) F.W. Riggs
(C) Max Weber (D) Mooney and Reiley
Answer: D

97. The concept of power refers to
(A) Defined authority and responsibility
(B) A relative hierarchical position in an organization
(C) The ability to influence the behavior of others
(D) The specialized knowledge possessed by an individual
Answer: C

98. Individuals such as Albert Einstein, Edwin Land and Steven Jobs lead through which type of power?
(A) Legitimate (B)Reward
(C) Expert (D)Charismatic
Answer: C

99. Types of degree of delegations are:
(A) Low degree (B)Moderate degree
(C) High degree (D)All the above
Answer: D

100. Functional authority works only when,
(A) Assignment is clarified
(B) The subordinates are allowed to participate
(C) Feedback control is established
(D) All the above
Answer: D

101. Advantages of delegation of authority would be:
(A) Prompt decision making
(B) Opportunity to subordinates to grow and develop
(C) Satisfaction to subordinates in terms of recognition
(D) All the above

Answer: D

102. Delegation becomes a necessity due to the following reasons:
(A) Structure of authority
(B) Accountability
(C) Superiors need to address important issues
(D) All the above

Answer: D

103. Name the following topics that gives an idea about the concept of organizing.
(A) Decentralization (B) Staffing process
(C) Span of management (D)All the above

Answer: D

104. Delegation becomes a necessity due to the following reasons:-
(A) Structure of authority
(B) Accountability
(C) Superiors need to address important issues
(D) All the above

Answer: D

105. Accountability :
(A) Is the requirement of answerability for one's performance
(B) Is right to give orders and the power to exact obedience
(C) One's obligation to perform the functions
(D) None of the above

Answer: C

106. In 'delegation'
(A) Only authority is delegated not responsibility
(B) Both authority and responsibility are delegated
(C) Only responsibility is delegated, not authority
(D) Neither responsibility, nor authority is delegated

Answer: A

107. Major barriers to entry for a newcomer into the industry are
(A) Access to distribution channels
(B) Govt. policies
(C) Economies of scale
(D) All the above

Answer: D

108. Nilesh and Prachi have just finished interviewing four candidates who want to work for PCE, Inc. They are involved in which of the following management functions?
(A) Planning (B)Analyzing
(C) Staffing (D)Controlling
(E) Directing

Answer: C

Explanation: Staffing is the hiring of people to carry out the work of the organization.

109. Downsizing is an aspect most closely associated with
(A) Staffing (B) planning.
(C) organizing (D) controlling.
(E) directing.

Answer: A

110. Staffing includes the following :
(i) Selection (ii) Appraisal
(iii) Placement (iv) Recruitment
Which of the above is/are correct ?
(A) (i) only (B) (i) and (ii)
(C) (i), (ii) and (iv) (D) (iv), (i) and (iii)

Answer: D

111. Few of the benefits of direction are
(A) Ensures stability and balance
(B) Secures employees co-operation
(C) Facilitates change in organisation
(D) All the above
Answer: D

112. Elements of direction are :
(A) Maintaining discipline
(B) Motivation of subordinates
(C) Rewarding good performance
(D) All the above
Answer: D

113. Directing function of management includes :
(A) Issuing orders to subordinates
(B) Supervising subordinates
(C) Guiding and teaching subordinates
(D) All the above
Answer: D
Explanation: Directing refers to motivating and leading employees to achieve organizational objectives.

114. The important characteristics of direction are :
(A) Helps utilize capabilities
(B) Initiates action
(C) Irreplaceable task
(D) All the above
Answer: D

115. Features of direction would be:
(A) Pervasive function
(B) Communication
(C) Continuous process
(D) All the above
Answer: D

116. Giving people incentives to achieve objectives relates to the management function of
(A) Planning
(B) Organizing.
(C) Staffing
(D) Controlling.
(E) Directing.
Answer: E

117. Identify the correct sequence of control cycle:
(A) Feedback - Evaluation -Adjustment - Action.
(B) Action -Evaluation -Feedback - Adjustment.
(C) Action - Feedback -Evaluation - Adjustment.
(D) Adjustment -Action -Feedback - Evaluation.
Answer: C

118. Which of the following is a reason for supporting a wider span of control?
(A) To reduce opportunities for delegations
(B) To have tighter control within the organisation
(C) To increase contact between managers and employees
(D) To reduce a process of delaying
Answer: C

119. Narrow span of control results into
(A) Tall structure
(B) Flat structure
(C) Mechanistic structure
(D) All the above
Answer: A

120. The meaning and purpose of control is:
(A) Knowing exactly what work is to be done
(B) Knowing that the work has been done or being done

(C) Knowing immediately of any delays, hold ups
(D) All the above
(E) **Answer: D**

Explanation: Controlling is the process of evaluating and correcting activities to keep the organization on course.

121. The external factors that limit control are:
(A) Govt. policies (B)Market changes
(C)Economic changes (D)All the above
Answer: D

122. Control function cannot be performed without :
(A) Planning (B) Organising
(C) Staffing (D) All the above
Answer: D

123. Limitation of control are :
(A) External factors
(B) Fixing of responsibility
(C) Variation and its causes
(D) All the above
Answer: D

124. What are the elements of control?
(A) Authority and knowledge
(B) Guidance and direction
(C) Constraint and restraint
(D) All the above
Answer: D

125. It is agreed that control is vital to an organization due to the following reasons
(A) Positive impact
(B) Detection of weaknesses
(C) Proper implementation of plans
(D) All the above
Answer: D

126. The old control techniques which were used through years are
(A) Unity of policies
(B) Break-even analysis
(C) Budgetary control
(D) All the above
Answer: D

127. Budgetary control involves budgets such as:
(A) Sales (B) Production
(B) Cash (D) All the above
Answer: D

128. Elements of effective control are
(A) Understandable (B) Corrective
(C) Flexible (D)All the above
Answer: D

129. Budgeting, paying the bills, and collection of funds are activities associated with the
(A) Management function
(B) Control function
(C) Finance/accounting function
(D) Production/operations function
(E) Staffing function
Answer: C

130. Which of the following involves careful analysis of inputs and corrective actions before operation is completed?
(A) Feed forward control
(B) Concurrent control
(C) Feedback control
(D) All the above
Answer: A

131. When Prachi pointed out to the supervisor that the number of nails used by the table assemblers had increased by 20 percent from the preceding month, she was involved in
(A) Planning (B) Organizing
(C) Staffing (D) Controlling
(E) Directing
Answer: D

132. The first step in the control process is to
(A) Ask your employees to fix any problems.
(B) take corrective actions when necessary.
(C) investigate the causes of any deviations.
(D) measure the actual performance.
(E) identify deviations from the standard.
Answer: D

133. Determining whether an organization has fulfilled a certain objective is most closely associated with which of the following management functions?
(A) Planning (B) Staffing
(C) Controlling (D) Organizing
(E) Directing
Answer: C

134. Internal coordination will be coordination between:
(A) Branch offices
(B) Workers and managers
(C) Coordination with employees of same dept.
(D) All the above
Answer: D

135. The coordination functions of management aims at:
(A) Providing manpower resources
(B) Bringing harmony in various activities
(C) Prompt decision making
(D) Achieve targets
Answer: B

136. Which is important element of coordination?
(A) Resistance
(B) Integration
(C) Semantic
(D) Emotional attitude
Answer: B

137. Some of the important techniques of coordination are:
(A) Hierarchy
(B) effective communication
(C) indoctrination
(D) All the above
Answer: D

138. If coordination takes place between the two parties within the organization is called:
(A) Internal coordination
(B) External coordination
(C) Horizontal coordination
(D) Vertical coordination
Answer: A

139. Name the factors governing the span of management.
(A) Ability of the manager
(B) Ability of the employees
(C) Geographic location
(D) All the above
Answer: D

140. The components of competitive analysis are :
(A) Future goals (B) Current strategy
(C) Capabilities (D) All the above
Answer: D

141. Most Indian business houses go for restructuring exercise, through,
(A) Demerger (B) Merger
(C) Takeover (D) All the above
Answer: D

142. The functions of the board of directors are
(A) Succession planning
(B) Establishing performance standards
(C) Determination of board policies
(D) All the above
Answer: D

143. Key ethical principles include the following:
(A) Caring and compassion
(B) Being fair and open minded
(C) Fulfilling commitments
(D) All the above
Answer: D

144. What are important Generic Competitive Strategies?
(A) Overall cost leadership
(B) Differential
(C) Focus
(D) All the above
Answer: D

145. The qualities that matter for International teamwork are:
(A) Mutual respect (B) Sense of time
(C)Team spirit (D)All the above
Answer: D

146. Services are defined as the art and science of managing:
(A) The expectations of others
(B) The experiences of people
(C) The demands of the customer
(D) All the above
Answer: D

147. Name the tactics used in the intensity of rivalry amongst existing competitors.
(A) Price competition
(B) Advertising battles
(C) Product introduction
(D) All the above
Answer: D

148. The main strategies adopted by business families for growth are:
(A) Raising their capital
(B) Appoint professional manager
(C) Technology upgradation
(D) All the above
Answer: D

149. Due to liberalization the changes that has taken place can be summarized as:
(A) Competition (B) pressure on prices
(C) market revolution (D) All the above
Answer: D

150. Steps that a whistle blower should take into consideration
(A) Stick to facts
(B) Consult lawyer
(C) Determine the type of wrong
(D) All the above
Answer: D

151. The channels through which corporate governance may bear on performance are:
(A) Managerial incentives
(B) Disciplining
(c) Corporate restructuring
(D) All the above
Answer: D

152. The functional management challenges in service sector are:
(A) Human resource
(B) Marketing and advertising
(c) Finance and taxation
(D) All the above
Answer: D

153. The aspects of corporate governance are:
(A) Attracting public attention
(B) Indispensable
(C) Trust
(D) All the above
Answer: D

154. The external environmental factors that influence management are
(A) Economic
(B) Political
(C) Technological
(D) All the above
Answer: D

155. Under the role of management consultant, consultant acts as a
(A) Motivator (B) Leader
(C) Counselor (D)All the above
Answer: D

156. The various tools employed by the companies to improve and sustain employee morale
(A) Building of responsibility
(B) Rotation of jobs
(C) Job enrichment
(D) All the above
Answer: D

157. The non-financial type of motivators would be
(A) Encouragement
(B) Freedom
(C) Recognition
(D) All the above
Answer: D

158. The different A's of the service sector are
(A) Acceptability (B) Awareness
(B) Availability (D) All the above
Answer: D

159. The objective in corporate governance are :
(A) Shareholders value maximization
(B) Growth
(c) Stability
(D) All the above
Answer: D

160. In the complex new liberalized economy, business families face common problems such as
(A) Unproductive labor
(B) Falling share values
(C) Transnational attack
(D) All the above
Answer: D

161. The characteristics of professional managers are
(A) Focus (B) Objectivity
(C) Creativity (D) All the above
Answer: D

162. The objectives in corporate governance are
(A) Growth
(B) Stability
(C) Shareholders value maximization
(D) All the above
Answer: D

163. The various tools for corporate governance are :
(A) Audit
(B) Professionalism
(C) Proper functioning of the board
(D) All the above
Answer: D

168. In general, if a policy is not thought out and established:
(A) A situation requiring action will arise
(B) Social issues will cause change in the organization
(C) Managers will be hired from the outside
(D) There will be significant staff turnover
Answer: A

169. The problem-solving process begins with
(A) Clarification of the situation
(B) Establishment of alternatives
(C) Identification of the difficulty
(D) Isolation of the cause
Answer: C

170. Which one of the following statements is not correct'? In the matrix structure of organization, there is:
(A) dual chain of command
(B) better communication
(C) more flexibility
(D) less conflict
Answer: D

171. Consider the following statements:
1. Model synthesis of organization is based on the fact that all organizations must deal with uncertainty
2. Sources of uncertainty are external as well as internal
3. If the sources of organizational uncertainty are internal, then the organization will try to reduce uncertainty by decentralizing

Which of the statements given above are correct?

(A) Only 1 and 2 (B) Only 2 and 3
(C) Only I and 3 (D) 1, 2 and 3

Answer: A

172. Consider the following statements:
1. Activities classified for line authority differ in each organization.
2. For small organizations, all positions may be line positions.
3. Staff authority is based on expert power.

Which of the statements given above are correct'?

(A) 1, 2 and 3 (B) Only 1 and 2
(C) Only 2 and 3 (D) Only 1 and 3

Answer: C

173. Consider the following statements:
1. Decentralization has the same advantages as delegation.
2. Decentralization leads to more flexibility in an organization.
3. Decentralization leads to slower decision making in raidly changing environment

Which of the statements given above are correct'?

(A) 1, 2 and 3 (B) Only l and 2
(C) Only 2 and 3 (D) Only I and 3

Answer: B

174. Consider the following statements:
1. Control helps to monitor environment changes and their effects on the organization's progress.
2. Delegation of authority in participative management does not change the nature of the control process.

Which of the statements given above is/are correct?

(A) Only 1 (B) Only 2
(C) Both 1 and 2 (D) Neither 1 nor 2

Answer: A

175. Which of the following techniques used by organizations engaged in public administration are based on network analysis?
1. Organization and Methods (O. and M.)
2. PERT
3. Critical Path Method
4. Work Study

Select the correct answer using the code given below:

(A) 1, 2, 3 and 4 (B) Only 1 and 2
(C) Only 2 and 3 (D) Only 1 and 4

Answer: C

176. Which one of the following is not a defense public sector undertaking?

(A) Bharat Dynamics Ltd.
(B) Mishra Dhatu Nigam Ltd.
(C) Bharat Earth Movers Ltd.
(D) Bharat Heavy Electrical Ltd.

Answer: D

177. Which of the following is/are essential to delegate authority in an organization?
1. Establish feedback channels
2. Others must not know that delegation has occurred
3. Delegate's range of discretion should not be specified

Select the correct answer using the code given below:

(A) Only 1 (B) Only 2 and 3
(C) Only 1 and 3 (D) 1, 2 and 3

Answer: A

178. Which one of the following statements is not correct?
Wider span of control is consistent with efforts of the organizations to
(A) get closer to customers
(B) speed up decision making
(C) reduce cost
(D) improve supervision
Answer: D

179. Consider the following statements:
Computer technology has made the concept of:
1. authority more relevant
2. authority less relevant
3. chain of command more relevant
4. unity of command less relevant
Which of the statements given above is/are correct?
(A) l and 3 (B) Only 3
(C) 2 and 4 (D) 1 and 4
Answer: C

180. Consider the following statements:
1. Defects in co-ordination inherent in large-scale organizations may apply to an organization whether the organization is bureaucratic or not.
2. Chester Barnard criticized Weber for failing to analyze the correspondence of behaviour in organizations with organizational blueprints.
Which of the statements given above is/are correct?
(A) Only 1 (B) Only 2
(C) Both 1 and 2 (D) Neither 1 nor 2
Answer: C

181. Who among the following expressed the view that virtually all the decisions in an organization are such that they do not maximize, but only suffice?
(A) George Miller
(B) Herbert A. Simon
(C) Kurt Lewin
(D) Abraham Maslow
Answer: B

182. Consider the following statements about open model of organization:
1. Means (or the proper way to do a job) are emphasized in the open model.
2. Non-routine tasks occur in unstable conditions in the open model.
3. The beginning of the open model can be traced to Saint-Simon and Auguste Comte.
Which of the statements given above is/are correct?
(A) Only 2
(B) 1 and3
(C) 2 and 3
(D) 1 and 2
Answer: C

183. Which one of the following statements is not correct in respect of the rational comprehensive approach of decision-making in an organization?
(A) It cannot be simulated under laboratory conditions.
(B) Values to be realized are usually not set out distinctly.
(C) Individual decision-maker cannot take a comprehensive view of the whole problem.
(D) The need for speed compels decisions to be taken on the basis of incomplete data.
Answer: D

184. Which one of the following statements is not correct?
Decision making in the public sector, in comparison to the private sector, involves
(A) higher levels of constraint
(B) more complexity
(C) less consultation
(D) more conflict
Answer: C

185. Consider the following statements:

1. The Management Information System (MIS) provides decision making assistance for unstructured problems.
2. Decision Support System (DDS) is structured around analytic decision models on a specialized management database.

Which of the statements given above is/are correct?

(A) Only 1 (B) Only 2
(C) Both 1 and 2 (D) Neither 1 nor 2

Answer: B

****

UNIT-III

HUMAN RESOURCE MANAGEMENT (HRM)

3.1. INTRODUCTION : OBJECTIVES - SCOPE - FUNCTIONS – IMPORTANCE – SIGNIFICANCE - ROLE

- Human resource management means employing people, developing their resources, utilizing, maintaining and compensating their services in tune with the job and organizational requirements with a view to contribute to the goals of the organizations, individual and the society.
- **Leon C. Megginson :** "Human resources are the total knowledge, skills, creative abilities, talents and aptitudes of an organizations workforce, as well as the value, attitude and beliefs of the individuals involved."
- **Ivancevich and Gluck :** "Human resource management is the function performed in organizations that facilitates the most effective use of employees to achieve organizational and individual goals."
- The policies and practices involved in carrying out the 'people' or human resource aspects of a management position, including recruiting, screening, training, rewarding, and appraising.
- **Michael J. Jucius :** Personnel Management as "the field of management which has to do with planning, organizing, directing and controlling the functions of procuring, developing, maintaining and utilizing a labour force ,such that the:
  (a) Objectives for which company is established are attained economically and effectively.
  (b) Objectives of all levels of personnel are served to the highest possible degree and
  (C) Objectives of society are duly considered and served."
- Personnel means persons employed. Hence *Personnel Management views the man as **economic man** who works for money or salary.*
- Human resource management treats the people as human beings having economic, social and psychological needs.
- "HRM is a series of integrated decisions that form the employment relationships; their quality contributes to the ability of the organizations and the employees to achieve their objectives."
- "HRM is concerned with the people dimensions in management. Since every organization is made up of people, acquiring their services, developing their skills, motivating them to higher levels of performance and ensuring that they continue to maintain their commitment to the organization are essential to achieving organizational objectives. This is true, regardless of the type of the organization – government, business, education, health, recreational, or social action."

Objectives of HRM

1. **Societal Objectives:** To be ethically and socially responsible to the needs and challenges of the society while minimizing the negative impact of such demands upon the organization.

2. **Organizational Objectives :** To recognize the role of HRM in bringing about organizational effectiveness. HRM is only means to achieve to assist the organization with its primary objectives.
3. **Functional Objectives:** To maintain department's contribution and level of services at a level appropriate to the organization's needs.
4. **Personal Objectives:** To assist employees in achieving their personal goals, at least in so far as these goals enhance the individual's contribution to the organization. This is necessary to maintain employee performance and satisfaction for the purpose of maintaining, retaining and motivating the employees in the organization.

Scope of HRM

- Human Resource Management embraces a very wide field of activities.
- The HR manager plays multiple roles like a researcher, a counselor, a bargainer, a mediator, a peacemaker and a problem solver, etc.
- Employee selection, employee remuneration, employee motivation, employee health and safety, industrial relations, employee education, etc.

Functions of HRM

1. Managerial Functions of HRM

1. **Planning:** Plan and research about wage trends, labor market conditions, union demands and other personnel benefits. Forecasting manpower needs etc.
2. **Organizing:** Organizing manpower and material resources by creating authorities and responsibilities for the achievement of organizational goals and objectives.
3. **Staffing:** Recruitment & Selection of an employee.
4. **Directing:** Issuance of orders and instructions, providing guidance and motivation of employees to follow the path laid-down.
5. **Controlling:** Regulating personnel activities and policies according to plans. Observations and comparisons of deviations.

2. Operational Functions of HRM

1. **Procurement:** Planning, Recruitment and Selection, Induction and Placement.
2. **Development:** Training, Development, Career planning and counseling.
3. **Compensation:** Wage and Salary determination and administration
4. **Integration:** Integration of human resources with organization.
5. **Maintenance:** Sustaining and improving working conditions, retentions, employee communication.
6. **Separations:** Managing separations caused by resignations, terminations, lay-offs, death, medical sickness etc.

All activities connected with employees of an organization and all decisions related to human relations come within the *functional areas of personnel management.*

According to **Dale Yoder and Robert Nelson**, these functions can be categorized into seven types:

- **Department administration** which looks after the planning, policy decision and general administration.

- **Employment** which includes recruitment, selection and placement of workers, job analysis, job description and performance appraisal.
- **Training and induction** which include induction training and in-service training.
- **Wage and salary administration** which include wage payments, job evaluation, job analysis surveys, etc.
- **Benefits and services** which include administration of various benefit schemes for employees like insurance, medical facilities, retirement benefits, etc.
- **Collective bargaining** which includes labour bargains with management to obtain its due share.
- **Personnel research** which includes preparation of plans and their implementation.

Importance of HRM

- Human resources, along with financial and material resources contribute to the production of goods and services in an organization.
- It is through the combined and concerted efforts of people that monetary and material resources are harnessed to achieve organizational goals.
- **Personnel management policies:** ***A policy is a statement or general guidelines for employees to make decisions in respect of to any course of action.***
- Personnel policies provide guidelines for a variety of employment relationships and identify the organization's intentions in recruitment, selection, development, promotion, compensation, motivation etc.

The significance of HRM

1. **Corporate:** Good human resource practices help in attracting and retaining the best people in the organization.
2. **Professional :** Effective management of human resource helps to improve the quality of work life.
3. **Social:**
   - Sound human resource management has a great significance for society.
   - Employment opportunities multiply.
   - Scarce talents are put to best use.
4. **National:**
   - Human resources and their management play a vital role in the development of a nation.
   - Development of a country depends primarily on the skills, attitudes and values of its human resources.
   - Employment opportunities.

Role of HRM

1. **Advisory Role:** HRM advises management on the solutions to any problems affecting people, personnel policies and procedures.
   - **Personnel Policies:** Organization Structure, Social Responsibility, Employment Terms & Conditions, Compensation, Career & Promotion, Training & Development and Industrial Relations.

- **Personnel Procedures:** Relating to manpower planning procedures, recruitment and selection procedures, and employment procedures, training procedures, management development procedures, performance appraisal procedures, compensation procedures, industrial relations procedures and health and safety procedures.

2. **Functional Role:** The personnel function interprets and helps to communicate personnel policies. It provides guidance to managers, which will ensure that agreed policies are implemented.

3. **Service Role:** Personnel function provides services that need to be carried out by full time specialists. These services constitute the main activities carried out by personnel departments and involve the implementation of the policies and procedures.

Changing role of HRM

- The challenge of HR managers today is to recognize talent and nurture the same carefully and achieve significant productivity gains over a period of time.
- The role of HR manager is shifting from one of a protector and screener to that of a planner and change agent.
- HR professionals can help an organization to select and train employees for emerging roles.
- HRM function can transform its outlook from an internally focused, reactive, activity-driven, and control-oriented to being business-oriented, customer-focused, proactive, effectiveness-driven, and empowerment-oriented.

3.2. ROLE OF HR MANAGER

Role of HR Managers

1. **Humanitarian Role:** Reminding moral and ethical obligations to employees.
2. **Counselor:** Consultations to employees about marital, health, mental, physical and career problems.
3. **Mediator:** Playing the role of a peacemaker during disputes, conflicts between individuals and groups and management.
4. **Spokesman:** To represent of the company because he has better overall picture of his company's operations.
5. **Problem Solver:** Solving problems of overall human resource management and long-term organizational planning.
6. **Change Agent:** Introducing and implementing institutional changes and installing organizational development programs
7. **Management of Manpower Resources:** Broadly concerned with leadership both in the group and individual relationships and labor-management relations.

Changing Role of the HR Manager

1. **Flatter organizations:** The reducing levels of hierarchy mean that more people report to one manager.
2. **Employee empowerment:** Knowledge workers need to be provided with greater autonomy though information sharing and provision of control over factors that affect performance.

3. **Team work:** modern workers do not remain confined to a single function but can do more than one function. Employees contribute to organization are as members of the team.
4. **Ethical management:** Ethical issues pose fundamental questions about fairness, justice, truthfulness and social responsibility.

3.3. STRUCTURE OF HR DEPARTMENT

- The internal organization structure of HR department varies depending upon the nature and size of the enterprise, its management philosophy and its external environment.
- According to **Agyris:** "Organizations are usually formed to satisfy objectives that can be met collectively"
- It is said that *HRM is a line manager's responsibility but a staff function.*
- The HR department provides specialized advice assistance and information to line executives so that they may concentrate on their respective functions.
- An organizational structure consists of activities such as task allocation, coordination and supervision, which are directed towards the achievement of organizational aims.
- An organization can be structured in many different ways, depending on their objectives.
- The structure of an organization will determine the modes in which it operates and performs.
- Organizational structure affects organizational action in two big ways. First, it provides the foundation on which standard operating procedures and routines rest. Second, it determines which individuals get to participate in which decision-making processes, and thus to what extent their views shape the organization's actions.
- The structure of one industrial organization differs from that of another organization and it depends upon
  1. Size of the organization
  2. Nature of the product being manufactured
  3. Complexity of the problems being faced

General Structure of HR Department

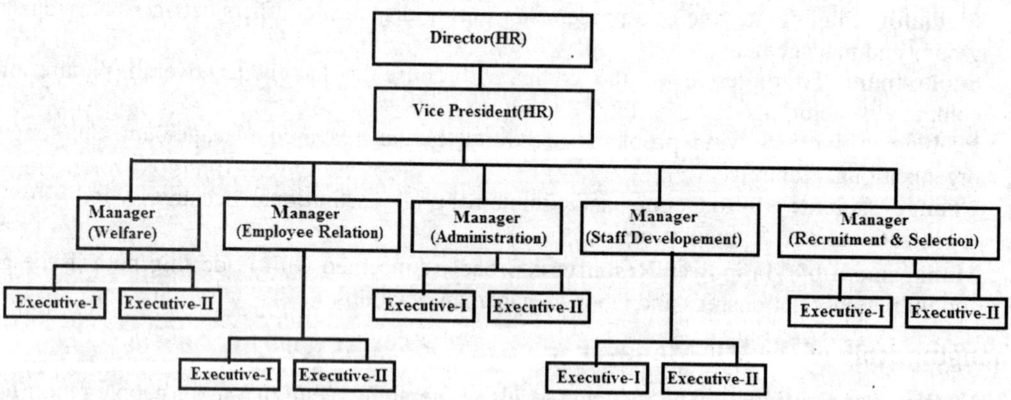

Description of line and staff functions

- All managers are HR managers as they all get involved in activities like selecting, training, compensating employees.
- Line managers have the final responsibility for achieving the organization's goals.
- They also have the authority to direct the work of subordinates.
- Staff managers usually help and advice line managers in achieving organizational goals.
- HR managers are staff experts. They assist line managers in areas like recruiting, selecting, training and compensating. Managing people, in a broader context, is every manager's business and successful organizations generally combine the experience of line managers with the experience of HR specialists while utilizing the talents of employees to their greatest potential.
- HR managers have to win the hearts of employees working alongside line mangers and deliver results in a cost-effective manner.
- HR managers as indicated earlier are assuming a greater role in top management planning and decision making-a trend that indicates the growing realization among executives that HRM can make significant contributions to the success of an organization.

3.4. FACTORS FACILITATING ACCELERATION OF HRM IN INDIA

1. Slow growth of HRM in India due to:

a. Late arrival of the Factory System.

b. Low Status of the Industrial Worker.

2. Professionalization of Human Resource Management.
3. Social Responsibilities of Business: Fair wages; adequate benefits; good working conditions; opportunity for growth; recognition of worker's rights etc.
4. Change of Government attitude.
5. Abundance of cheap labour.
6. Weak labour movement.
7. Highly authoritarian culture.
8. Technological backwardness.
9. Instability in Employment.
10. Unhealthy growth of Trade Unions.
11. Migratory character of Indian Labour.

Evolving Role of HR Professional in India

- The origin of Personnel Management in India can be traced to the recommendations of the Royal Commission on Labour in India (1921-31).

- The Royal Commission emphasized recruitment and dismissal as the primary responsibilities of the labour officer.
- The Government passed ***The Bombay disputes conciliation act, 1934***, which provided for the ***appointment of a government labour officer*** to deal with labour grievances.
- **Role as a Police Man:** The labour officer, at this stage was also visualized as having to perform police functions as the position between the employers and workers was often viewed as a law and order problem.
- **The Welfare Man:** After the enactment of the ***Factories Act 1948***, the labour officer's function changed from mere employment function to welfare activities. The Factories Act created the institution of ***labour welfare officers*** making it compulsory for factories with ***500 or more*** workers to employ the prescribed number of welfare officers.
- **The Law Man:** With the acceptance of the idea of welfare state, laws and regulations were enacted to define the rights of employees and to limit the employer's prerogatives. Legal knowledge thus became a preferential attribute of the personnel man.
- **The Liaison Man:** Someone was required to deal and negotiate with the union on behalf of the management. Industrial relations become important with the advent of the trade union. The personnel man became a shock absorber.
- **The HR Professional:** A gradual shift of emphasis from that of a liaison man to personnel administration has taken place.
- The function of a personnel manager includes labour, welfare, industrial relation and personnel administration.
- To provide training facilities, motivate employees to put their best effort, and do manpower planning and development.

3.5. HRM MODEL

In recent years there has been relative agreement among HRM. The model developed by the American Society for Training and Development (ASTD) identifies nine human resource areas:

1. Training and Development
2. Organization Development
3. Organization or Job Design
4. Planning
5. Selection and Staffing
6. Personnel Research and Information systems
7. Compensation or Benefits
8. Employee Assistance
9. Union or Labour Relations

3.6. ENVIRONMENTAL INFLUENCE ON HRM

The external environment consists of factors that affect an organization's human resources from outside it.

- Technological innovation
- Economic factors
- Employee's organizations
- Labour markets
- Changing demand of employers
- Legal factors
- Human resource in the country

3.7. RECENT CHALLENGES IN HRM

3.7.1. Work force diversity

- The Indian work force is characterized by diversity such as more women entering the work force, minority group members, older workers, etc.
- The diverse work force has become a challenge for the HR manager. One is that organizations claim they seek to maximize diversity in the workplace.
- The second is that the traditional human resource system will not allow diversity, only similarity.
- Economic and technological change: Technology has become the hall mark of modern organizations. The explosive growth of information technology linked to the internet has ushered in many changes throughout the organization.
- The **'fall of hierarchy'** has given birth to the **'virtual organization.'**
- Globalization: New Economic Policy, 1991, has globalized the Indian economy and Globalization has given rise to MNCs.
- The MNCs are characterized by their cultural diversity, intensified competition and variations in business practices.

3.7.2. Organizational Restructuring

- Organizational restructuring is used to make the organization competitive.
- As a part of organizational changes, many organizations have **'right sized'** themselves in various ways such as eliminating layers of managers, closing facilities, merging with other organizations, or out placing workers.
- **Downsizing:** Downsizing occurs when a company permanently reduces its workforce. Corporate downsizing is often the result of poor economic conditions and/or the company's need to cut jobs in order to lower costs or maintain profitability.
- Downsizing may occur when one company merges with another, a product or service is cut, or the economy falters.

- Downsizing also occurs when employers want to "streamline" a company – this refers to corporate restructuring in order to increase profit and maximize efficiency.
- Downsizing results in layoffs that are often followed by other restructuring changes, such as branch closings, departmental consolidation, and other forms of cutting pay expenses. In some cases, employers are not fired, but instead become part-time or temporary workers (to trim costs).

3.7.3. Changing nature of work

- With change in technology, the nature of jobs and work has also changed.
- One of the significant changes in the nature of work is from manual to knowledge work.
- The challenge posed by the changed environment is fostering HRM practices to respond to the need and requirement of knowledge workers.
- Every organization depends increasingly on knowledge –patents, processes, management skills, technologies and intellectual capital.
- As a result of these changes, organizations are giving growing emphasis to their human capital, i.e. knowledge, education, training skills and expertise of their employees.

3.7.4. Golden Handshake

- A stipulation in an employment agreement which states that the employer will provide a significant severance package if the employee loses their job.
- A golden handshake is usually provided to top executives for loss of employment through layoffs, firing or even retirement.
- Payment can be made several ways, such as cash, or stock options.
- A golden handshake is a hefty severance package which is offered to senior executives and other high ranking employees. Often, the terms of a golden handshake are included in a hiring contract, and they are viewed as insurance against sudden or involuntary job termination.
- A golden handshake may also be offered to an employee to encourage him or her to retire; this is common in systems like schools, where long-term employees make more money, and it can be more cost efficient to hire entry level teachers.
- The specifics of a golden handshake vary, depending on the position. Typically it includes a lump sum of money, and it may also include stock options or securities, continued insurance coverage, or payment into retirement accounts.
- A golden handshake also typically includes a few weeks of full pay, especially if the employment termination was sudden, allowing the former employee a chance to recover.
- Golden handshakes can also be sweeteners for mandatory retirement. In industries where retiring long-term employees is a cost effective business decision, a golden handshake is almost used like a punishment. If the employee declines to retire, the offer will be retracted, and the employee may take a loss. Employees may also be asked to retire due to declining job performance or age, in which case a company may wish to provide recognition of the employee's years of loyal service.

- In an instance where a golden handshake is part of an employment contract, it pays to read the terms carefully, and to clarify questionable terms.
- Employees may want to ask whether golden handshakes will still be offered if companies liquidate or go into bankruptcy.
- It is also important to ask about conditions in which the severance package will not be offered.

3.7.5. Total Quality Management (TQM)

- TQM describes a management approach to long–term success through customer satisfaction. In a TQM effort, all members of an organization participate in improving processes, products, services, and the culture in which they work.
- In a TQM effort, all members of an organization participate in improving processes, products, services and the culture in which they work.
- The methods for implementing this approach come from the leaders as **Philip B. Crosby**, **W. Edwards Deming**, **Armand V. Feigenbaum**, **Kaoru Ishikawa**, and **Joseph M. Juran**.
- Total quality management is a management system for a customer-focused organization that involves all employees in continual improvement. It uses strategy, data, and effective communications to integrate the quality discipline into the culture and activities of the organization.
- Total quality management is an integrative philosophy of management for continuously improving the quality of products and processes.
- TQM is based on the premise that the quality of products and processes is the responsibility of everyone involved with the creation or consumption of the products or services offered by an organization, requiring the involvement of management, workforce, suppliers, and customers, to meet or exceed customer expectations.

Common TQM practices: Cua, McKone, and Schroeder identified nine common TQM practices:

1. Cross-functional product design
2. Process management
3. Supplier quality management
4. Customer involvement
5. Information and feedback
6. Committed leadership
7. Strategic planning
8. Cross-functional training
9. Employee involvement.

Elements of TQM

1. Customer-focused
2. Total employee involvement
3. Process-centered
4. Integrated system
5. Strategic and systematic approach

6. Continual improvement
7. Fact-based decision making
8. Communications

TQM Model

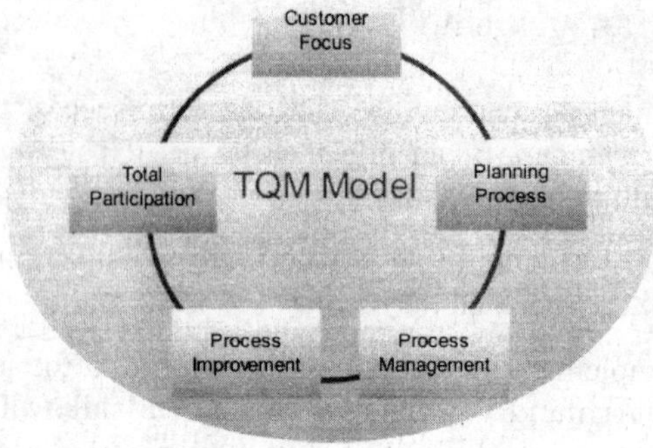

3.7.6. Six Sigma

- **Six Sigma** is a set of tools and strategies for process improvement originally developed by Motorola in 1985.
- Six Sigma became well known after ***Jack Welch*** made it a central focus of his business strategy at General Electric in 1995.
- Six Sigma seeks to improve the quality of process outputs by identifying and removing the causes of defects or errors and minimizing variability in manufacturing and business processes.
- It uses a set of quality management methods, including statistical methods, and creates a special infrastructure of people within the organization ("Champions", "Black Belts", "Green Belts", "Orange Belts", etc.) who are experts in these very complex methods.
- Each Six Sigma project carried out within an organization follows a defined sequence of steps and has quantified financial targets (cost reduction and/or profit increase).
- The term *Six Sigma* originated from terminology associated with manufacturing, specifically terms associated with statistical modeling of manufacturing processes. The maturity of a manufacturing process can be described by a *sigma* rating indicating its yield or the percentage of defect-free products it creates.

3.8. FUNCTIONS OF HRM

3.8.1. Manpower planning or Human Resource Planning (HRP)

- The ongoing process of systematic planning to achieve optimum use of an organization's most valuable asset - its human resources.
- The objective of human resource (HR) planning is to ensure the best fit between employees and jobs, while avoiding manpower shortages or surpluses.

- The three key elements of the HR planning process are forecasting labor demand, analyzing present labor supply and balancing projected labor demand and supply.
- Human resources planning is a process that identifies current and future human resources needs for an organization to achieve its goals.
- **E.W. Vetter** has visualized resources planning as "a process by which an organization should move from its current manpower position to its desired manpower position. Through planning, management strive to have the right number and right kind of people at the right places, at the right time, doing things which result in both the organization and the individuals receiving maximum long-run benefit."
- **Bulla and Scott**: Human resource planning is 'the process for ensuring that the human resource requirements of an organization are identified and plans are made for satisfying those requirements'.
- **Reilly:** 'Workforce planning as a process in which an organization attempts to estimate the demand for labour and evaluate the size, nature and sources of supply which will be required to meet the demand.'
- Human resource planning includes creating an employer brand, retention strategy, absence management strategy, flexibility strategy, talent management strategy, recruitment and selection strategy.
- **Leon C Megginson:** "Human resources planning is an integrated approach to performing the planning aspects of the personnel function in order to have a sufficient supply of adequately developed and motivated people to perform the duties and tasks required to meet organizational objectives and satisfy the individual needs and goals of organizational members."

Objectives of Human Resources Planning

1. To recruit and retain the human resources of required quantity and quality.
2. To foresee the employee turnover and make the arrangements for minimizing turnover and filling up of consequent vacancies.
3. To meet the needs of the program of expansion, diversification etc.
4. To foresee the impact of technology on work, existing employees and future human resources requirements.
5. To improve the standards, skill ,.knowledge,, ability, discipline etc.
6. To assess the surplus or shortage of human resources and take measures accordingly.
7. To maintain congenial industrial relations by maintaining optimum level and structure of human resources.
8. To minimize imbalances caused due to non-availability of human resources of right kind, right number in right time and right place.
9. To make the best use of its human resources and
10. To estimate the cost of human resources.

Characteristics of human resource planning

1. Human resources plan must incorporate the human resources needs in the light of organizational goals.
2. Human resource plan must be directed towards well-defined objectives.
3. Human resource plan must ensure that it has the right number of people and the right kind of people at the right time doing work for which they are economically most useful.
4. Human resource planning should pave the way for an effective motivational process.

5. A human resource plan should take into account the principle of periodical reconsideration of new developments and extending the plan to cover the changes during the given period.
6. Adequate flexibility must be maintained in human resources planning to suit the changing needs of organization.

Factors affecting human resource planning

1. External factors

- Government legislation
- Job mobility factors
- Population shifts
- Economic cycles and condition
- Geographical concerns
- Educational levels of workers
- Technological changes
- Changes in social views
- Political changes
- International events

2. Internal factors

- Strategies of the company
- HR policies of the company
- Formal and informal groups
- Job Analysis
- Time Horizons
- Type and quality of information
- Company's Production Operations policy
- Trade Unions

Process of Human Resource Planning

1. **Analyzing the Corporate Level Strategies:** Human Resource Planning should start with analyzing corporate level strategies which include expansion, diversification, mergers, acquisitions, reduction in operations, technology to be used, method of production etc. Therefore Human Resource Planning should begin with analyzing the corporate plans of the organization before setting out on fulfilling its tasks.
2. **Demand forecasting:** There are two types of HR demand forecasting :
   - A. **Quantitative Approach:** This approach involves the use of statistical or mathematical technique.
   - B. **Qualitative Approach:** This relies on the opinions of supervisors, departmental managers and experts.
   - In forecasting the supply of employees, an organization has to forecast its future requirements of employees.
   - It must determine if there are sufficient numbers and types of employees available to staff the anticipated openings.

- Forecasting the overall human resource requirement in accordance with the organizational plans is one of the key aspects of demand forecasting.
- Forecasting of quality of human resources like skills, knowledge, values and capabilities needed in addition to quantity of human resources is done through the following methods:

I. **Executive or Managerial Judgment:** Here the managers decide the number of employees in the future. They adopt one of the three approaches mentioned below.

a. **Bottom-Up approach:** Here the concerned supervisors send their proposals to the top officials who compare these with the organisational plans, make necessary adjustments and finalise them.

b. **Top-Down approach:** Here the management prepares the requirements and sends the information downwards to the supervisory –level who finalises the draft and approves it.

c. **Participative Approach:** Here the supervisors and the management sit together and projections are made after joint consultations.

Drawbacks : The chief drawback of these methods is that estimation of manpower is made using guesswork.

II. **Statistical Techniques:** These methods use statistical methods and mathematical techniques to forecast and predict the supply and demand of Human Resources in the future.

- **Ratio-Trend analysis:** In this method depending on the past data regarding number of employees in each department, like production department, sales department, marketing department and workload level, etc ratios for manpower are estimated. Past values are plotted and extrapolated to get fairly accurate future projections.

III. **Work Study method:** This technique is suitable to study the correlation between volume of work and labour i.e. demand for human resources is estimated based on the workload. Work study method is more appropriate for repetitive and manual jobs when it is possible to measure work and set standards.

IV. **Delphi Technique:** *'Delphi'* Technique is named after the Greek Oracle at the city of Delphi. In this method, the views of different experts related to the industry are taken into consideration and then a consensus about the Human Resource requirement is arrived at. Delphi technique is used primarily to assess long-term needs of human resource.

3. **Analyzing Human Resource Supply** : Every organisation has two sources of supply of Human Resources: Internal & External. Internally, human resources can be obtained for certain posts through promotions and transfers. In order to judge the internal supply of human resources in future human resource inventory or human resource audit is necessary. Human resource inventory helps in determining and evaluating the quantity of internal human resources available. Once the future internal supply is estimated, supply of external human resources is analysed.

Techniques of HR supply forecasting

1. **Staffing Table:** A staffing table is a graphic representation of all jobs in the organization along with the number of employees currently occupying those jobs and future employment requirements.

2. **Markov Analysis:** Invented by the Russian mathematician and a probability theory pioneer, **Andrei Andreevich Markov** (1856-1922).

- Marko analysis is a method for tracking the pattern of employee movements through various approaches.
- Statistical technique used in forecasting the future behavior of a variable or system whose current state or behavior does not depend on its state or behavior at any time in the past in other words, it is random.
- For example, in the flipping of a coin, the probability of a flip coming up heads is the same regardless of whether the previous result was heads or tails.
- In accounting, Markov analysis is used in estimating bad debt or uncollectible accounts receivable.
- In marketing, it is used in modeling future brand loyalty of consumers based on their current rate of purchases and repurchases.
- In quality control, Markov analysis is applicable to common-cause problems and other sequence dependent events, and can handle system degradation.

3. **Talent Inventories:** Skill inventories can be prepared to include the employee's education, past work experience, vocational interests, specific abilities and skills, job tenure, etc.
4. **Replacement Chart:** Replacement chart provides information on the current job performance and promotability of possible replacements.
5. **Succession Planning:** Succession planning is the process of identifying, developing, and tracking key individuals for executive positions.
6. **Estimating manpower gaps**: Manpower gaps can be identified by comparing demand and supply forecasts. Such comparison will reveal either deficit or surplus of Human Resources in the future. Deficit suggests the number of persons to be recruited from outside, whereas surplus implies redundant employees to be re-deployed or terminated. Employees estimated to be deficient can be trained while employees with higher, better skills may be given more enriched jobs.
7. **Action Planning**: Once the manpower gaps are identified, plans are prepared to bridge these gaps. Plans to meet the surplus manpower may be redeployment in other departments and retrenchment. People may be persuaded to quit voluntarily through a golden handshake. Deficit can be met through recruitment, selection, transfer and promotion. In view of shortage of certain skilled employees, the organization has to take care not only of recruitment but also retention of existing employees. Hence, the organization has to plan for retaining of existing employees.
8. **Modify the Organizational plans**: If future supply of human resources form all the external sources is estimated to be inadequate or less than the requirement, the manpower planner has to suggest to the management regarding the alterations or modifications in the organizational plans.
9. **Controlling and Review**: After the action plans are implemented, human resource structure and the processes should be controlled and reviewed with a view to keep them in accordance with action plans.

Problems in Human Resource Planning

1. Resistance by Employers and Employees.

2. Uncertainties.

3. Inadequacies of Information System.

3.8.2. Recruitment

- Recruitment is the process of searching for prospective employees and stimulating and encouraging them to apply for jobs in an organization.
- The process of finding and hiring the best-qualified candidate from within or outside of an organization for a job opening, in a timely and cost effective manner.
- The recruitment process includes analyzing the requirements of a job, attracting employees to that job, screening and selecting applicants, hiring, and integrating the new employee to the organization.
- **Edwin Flippo**: "Recruitment is the process of searching for prospective employees and stimulating them to apply for jobs in the Organization."

Objectives of recruitment

- Support the organization ability to acquire, retain and develop the best talent and skills.
- Determine present and future manpower requirements of the organization in coordination with planning and job analysis activities.
- Obtain the number and quality of employees that can be selected in order to help the organization to achieve its goals and objectives.
- Create a pool of candidates so that the management can select the right candidate for the right job from this pool.
- Attract and encourage more and more candidates to apply in the organization
- Increase the pool of candidates at minimum cost.
- Acts as a link between the employers and the job seekers
- Infuse fresh blood at all levels of the organization
- Meet the organization's legal and social obligations regarding the composition of its workforce.
- Increase the effectiveness of various recruiting techniques

Sources of recruitment:

1. **Internal sources**
2. **External sources**

1. Internal sources

1. Promotions
2. Transfers, and
3. Response of employees to notified vacancy and
4. Re-employment of ex-employees: It is one of the internal sources of recruitment in which employees can be invited and appointed to fill vacancies in the concern. There are situations when ex-employees provide unsolicited applications also.

Merits of internal sources of recruitment

1. The internal sources of recruitment have the advantage of absorbing people already acquainted with the company culture.
2. Our employees are tried and tested people and we can depend on them.

3. It is a useful signal to employees and assures them that their services are recognized and this helps in maintaining their motivation and morale.
4. It reduces labour turnover as it gives employees a sense of job security and opportunity for advancement.
5. Our employees are fully acquainted with the organization. Hence, job training can be reduced.
6. Internal sources of recruitment are less costly than the other sources of recruitment.
7. It is a return of investment in human capital.

Disadvantages of internal sources of recruitment

1. It limits the choice to a few employees only.
2. The likes and dislikes of the superiors play an important role in the selection of an employee.
3. It creates frustration among those employees who are not selected.
4. Creates inbreeding of ideas.

2. External sources

1. **Advertising in newspapers, trade journals and magazines:** The advantage of advertisement is that it covers a vide area of market and scattered applicants can get information from advertisement.
2. **Employment exchanges:** There are certain employment exchange which are run by Government. Most of the government undertakings and concern employ people through such exchanges. Now-a-days recruitment in government agencies has become compulsory through employment exchange.
3. **Campus recruitment:** There are certain professional Institutions which serve as an external source for recruitment fresh graduates from these institutes. This kind of recruitment done through such educational institutions is called as Campus Recruitment. They have special recruitment cells which help in providing to fresh candidates.
4. **Unsolicited applicants**
5. **Labour contractors:** These are the specialist people who supply manpower to the Factory or Manufacturing plants. Through these contractors, workers are appointed on contract basis, i.e. for a particular time period. Under conditions when these contractors leave the organization, such people who are appointed have to also leave the concern.
6. **Employee referrals**
7. **Private Employment agencies/Consultants:** There are certain professional organizations which look towards recruitment and employment of people. i.e. these private agencies run by private individuals supply required manpower to needy concerns.
8. Professional Associations
9. Data Banks
10. Casual Applicants
11. Similar Organizations/Competitors
12. Trade Unions
13. Walk-in
14. Consult in
15. Head Hunting
16. Body Shopping
17. Mergers and Acquisitions
18. Tele recruitment
19. Outsourcing

Merits of external sources of recruitment

1. Fresh talent and skill comes into the organization.
2. New employees may try to change old habits.
3. New employees may be selected at the terms and conditions of the organization.
4. Highly qualified and experienced employees may help the organization to come up with better performance.
5. Since persons are recruited from a large market, the best selection can be made.
6. External sources provide the requisite type of personnel for an organization, having the required skill and standard.
7. External sources of recruitment are economical because potential employees do not need extra training for their skills.

Demerits of external sources of recruitment

1. External sources of recruitment reduce the morale of employees.
2. External sources of recruitment deny career advancement for employees.
3. Proper evaluation of outside candidates may not be possible because of time availability, this may result in faulty selection of employees.
4. Outsiders are not fully acquainted with the policies and procedures of the organization. Therefore, may need expensive training.
5. According to **Yoder**, 'the hiring process is of one or many 'go-no-go' gauges. Candidates are screened by the employer and the short-listed applicants go on to the next hurdle, while unqualified ones are eliminated.'

Recruitment Techniques

1. Traditional Techniques

- Promotions
- Transfers
- Advertising

2. Modern Techniques of Recruitment

Modern recruiting Model is a new-age solution designed to overcome problems in traditional recruitment approaches like demand prediction, and critical skill-set supply.

I. Knowledge Based Recruitment Method

II. E-Recruitment / Online Recruitment Method

I. The Knowledge-Based Recruiting Method

- The way that this method of recruiting works is that together, both the client and the recruiting company define the anticipated skill-set requirements over a period of time; say a twelve-month period.

- Once this has been established, a minimum rate of ongoing recruiting activity can be agreed upon. From this activity, candidates who become available immediately will be hired on an ongoing basis.
- Candidates who are potentially interested in making a move, but are not available immediately, can be tracked until they are available.
- In addition, all information pertaining to recruiting sites is captured and entered into the knowledge database. The process requires continuous monitoring of both the long-term and short-term needs of the client and, whenever necessary, redirecting both the amount and focus of the recruiting effort in line with the client's changing needs.
- In other words, knowledge-based recruiting is an ongoing, flexible retained search that allows for a rapid response to the needs of the organization.
- Knowledge-based recruiting is targeted search, taken to a new level of client relationship. It is a client-directed, continuous, yet flexible recruiting initiative designed to overcome the problems of critical skill shortage or sustained growth.
- It means that we do not have to "re-invent the wheel" every time a new opening occurs. It delivers a better quality of candidate, better value-for-money, and better time-to hire periods.
- It is based on a mutual agreement between client and recruiting firm to invest in a long-term strategic relationship.
- The philosophy behind knowledge-based recruiting is that all information gleaned from a recruiting activity should be stored for use at a later date.
- In other words, Recruiting is viewed as not only a short-term process – to fill today's position now – but as an opportunity to build a database of knowledge which will result in rapid future hires.
- Knowledge-based recruiting is based on the concept of sharing Information and updating information on an ongoing basis, in order to continuously build a pool of talent.
- The database which is generated contains information pertaining not just to target candidates, but also to target sites identified by location, product, or technology.

II. E-Recruitment / Online Recruitment Method:

- The buzzword and the latest trends in recruitment is the "E-Recruitment". Also known as "Online recruitment", it is the use of technology or the web based tools to assist the recruitment processes.
- The tool can be either a job website like naukri.com, the organization's corporate web site or its own intranet. Many big and small organizations are using Internet as a source of recruitment.
- They advertise job vacancies through worldwide web. The job seekers send their applications or curriculum vitae (CV) through an e-mail using the Internet.
- Alternatively job seekers place their CV□s in worldwide web, which can be drawn by prospective employees depending upon their requirements

Flow of E- Recruitment

1. **Resume Bank portals**: i.e. posting the position with the job description and the job specification on the job portal and also searching for the suitable resumes posted on the site corresponding to the opening in the organization.
2. **Creating a complete online recruitment/application section in the company's own website:** Companies have added an application system to its website, where the passive job

seekers can submit their resumes into the database of the organization for consideration in future, as and when the roles become available.

3. **Resume Scanners:** Resume scanner is one major benefit provided by the job portals to the organizations. It enables the employees to screen and filter the resumes through pre-defined criterias and requirements.
4. **Job sites**: Provide a 24x7 access to the database of the resumes to the employees facilitating the just-in-time hiring by the organizations. Also, the jobs can be posted on the site almost immediately and is also cheaper than advertising in the employment newspapers. Sometimes companies can get valuable references through the "passers-by" applicants.
5. **Online recruitment:** Helps the organizations to automate the recruitment process, save their time and costs on recruitments. Online recruitment giving a detailed job description and job specifications in the job postings to attract candidates with the right skill sets and qualifications at the first stage. E-recruitment should be incorporated into the overall recruitment strategy of the organization. A well defined and structured applicant tracking system should be integrated and the system should have a back-end support. Along with the back-office support a comprehensive website to receive and process job applications (through direct or online advertising) should be developed. Therefore, to conclude, it can be said that e-recruitment is the "Evolving face of recruitment."

Concepts in Modern Recruitment Methods

1. **Scouting:** Scouting means sending the representation of the organizations to various sources of recruitment with a view to persuading or stimulating the candidates to apply for jobs. The representatives provide information about the company and exchange information and ideas and clarify the doubts of the candidates.
2. **Networking:** This is a very good job finding technique and is usually carried out by most HR professionals. Relevant and sustained relationships over a period of time can help the HR professionals in networking with their colleagues to acquire resources from different fields.
3. **ESOP's:** Companies recently started stimulating the employees by offering stock ownership to the employees through their Employees Stock Ownership Programmed (ESOPs)
4. **Body shopping**: It is also known as employee leasing activity.
5. **Event Recruiting:** Sponsoring events where the candidates you are seeking attend to. By giving a presentation and advertising your company in a way which will attract the candidates and letting them know that your company knows what the participants are looking for, you can bring in the most suitable candidates which you might consider hiring.
6. **Re-Recruiting:** When you are most qualified or experienced staff leave the company let them know that they are welcome back. The reasons they leave maybe for a change of location, a new challenge or higher pay which you can't afford at the moment. But if they are not satisfied at the new place, they all always appreciate the old one. This can also reduce on training cost and time which you might have to spend for a newly hired employee. This of course cannot be applied to all employees.
7. **Make Every Employee a Recruiter:** This does not mean asking employees to refer their friends and family to the company. This also can be a way of advertising. Equip every employee with a company card stating the company contact details and an attractive "we are always looking out for dynamic individuals....." This can be very useful when employees know how to effectively hand out these cards to the most eligible individuals.
8. **Cast A Wider Net:** Expand your recruiting to include some people who do not have all the skills you would like, but who have potential to contribute if they are trained.

Innovative Modern Recruitment Practices

1. **Sending of SMS:** Converges provide individuals an easy option to send their application by simply texting the word "APPLY" to a specific number and in turn receives a reply from the organization to proceed with the application process.
2. **Video / Visual Networks:** Nowadays, Companies also using Online Video channels like You tube, Google Video portal.
3. **Blogging on Social Networking Sites:** e.g.: Twitter, Face book, Multiply, HRLink, CiteHR, LinkedIn, Orkut etc.
4. Job Fairs, Job Application Banners, Pamphlets, Hoardings, Advertisement in Public transport by using visual and audio aids.
5. **Advertisement through public address system:** Radio, Television etc. Even though advertising in the media still remains a powerful source in attracting candidates, pioneers in the field say that "the most suitable, qualified and talented candidates aren't even looking". So approaching this set of candidates should be done after careful observations and by being attractive and making the candidates want to join your organization for his or her career growth.

Advantages from Modern Recruitment Procedures:

- Structure and systematically organize the entire recruitment processes.
- Facilitates faster, unbiased, accurate and reliable processing of applications from various applications.
- Helps to reduce the time-per-hire and cost-per-hire.
- Helps to incorporate and integrate the various links like the application system on the official website of the company, the unsolicited applications, outsourcing recruitment, the final decision making to the main recruitment process.
- Maintains an automated active database of the applicants facilitating the talent management and increasing the efficiency of the recruitment processes.
- Provides and a flexible, automated and interactive interface between the online application system, the recruitment department of the company and the job seeker.
- Offers tolls and support to enhance productivity, solutions and optimizing the recruitment processes to ensure improved ROI.
- Helps to communicate and create healthy relationships with the candidates through the entire recruitment process.

Factors affecting Recruitment

1. External Factors

- Supply and Demand
- Labour Market
- Image/Goodwill
- Political-Social-Legal Environment
- Unemployment rate
- Competitors

2. Internal Factors

- Recruitment policy

- Human resource planning
- Size of the firm
- Cost of recruitment
- Growth and expansion

3.8.3. Selection

- Selection is next step after recruitment.
- It is the process of choosing the most suitable candidates (Properly qualified and competent) out of many interested candidates.
- It is a process of selecting the best and rejecting the rest.
- In this selection process, interested applicants are differentiated in order to identify those with a greater likelihood of success in a job. Such candidates are selected and appointed.
- Selection is a negative function as it relates to elimination of unsuitable candidates.
- 'Right man for the right job' is the basic principle in selection.

Order of the Employee selection Process

1. Preliminary Interviews
2. Application blanks
3. Written Tests
4. Employment Interviews
5. Medical examination
6. Appointment Letter

Steps in Scientific Selection process :

1. **Job Analysis:** Job analysis is the formal process of identifying the content of a job in terms activities involved and attributes needed to perform the work and identifies major job requirements. Job analysis was conceptualized by two of the founders of industrial or organizational psychology, **Frederick Taylor and Lillian Moller Gilbreth** in the early 20th century.Job analyses provide information to organizations which helps to determine which employees are best fit for specific jobs.

2. **Recruitment:** Recruitment refers to the process of attracting, screening, selecting, and on boarding a qualified person for a job. At the strategic level it may involve the development of an employer brand which includes an 'employee offering'. The stages of the recruitment process include: job analysis and developing a person specification; the sourcing of candidates by networking, advertising, or other search methods; matching candidates to job requirements and screening individuals using testing (skills or personality assessment); assessment of candidates' motivations and their fit with organisational requirements by interviewing and other assessment techniques. The recruitment process also includes the making and finalising of job offers and the induction and on boarding of new employees.

3. **Preliminary Interviews**: It is used to eliminate those candidates who do not meet the minimum eligibility criteria laid down by the organization. The skills, academic and family background, competencies and interests of the candidate are examined during preliminary interview. Preliminary interviews are less formalized and planned than the final interviews.

The candidates are given a brief up about the company and the job profile; and it is also examined how much the candidate knows about the company. Preliminary interviews are also called screening interviews.

4. **Application blank:** The candidates who clear the preliminary interview are required to fill application blank. It contains data record of the candidates such as details about age, qualifications, reason for leaving previous job, experience, etc.

5. **Written Examination:** Various written tests conducted during selection procedure are aptitude test, intelligence test, reasoning test, personality test, etc. These tests are used to objectively assess the potential candidate. They should not be biased.

6. **Initial interview of the candidate:** It is a one to one interaction between the interviewer and the potential candidate. It is used to find whether the candidate is best suited for the required job or not. But such interviews consume time and money both. Moreover the competencies of the candidate cannot be judged. Such interviews may be biased at times. Such interviews should be conducted properly. No distractions should be there in room. There should be an honest communication between candidate and interviewer.

7. **Business Games:** Business Games and their Utility in selection process as follows:

   a) **Case Study:** Analytical, Judgmental and decision making skills.
   b) **Role play:** Human relation skills
   c) **In-basket method:** Situational judgment, social relations, decision-making skills, problem solving skills.
   d) **Sensitivity:** Degree of openness, concern for others, tolerance for individual differences.
   e) **Simulations:** Encountering skills

8. **Employment tests :**

   a) **Aptitude tests:**
      i. Intelligence test(IQ)
      ii. Emotional Quotient
      iii. Skill tests
      iv. Mechanical aptitude
      v. Psychomotor Tests
      vi. Clerical Aptitude tests

   b) **Performance or achievement test**
      i. Job knowledge test
      ii. Work sample test

   c) **Situational tests**
      i. Group discussion
      ii. In Basket

   d) **Interest test**
   e) **Personality test**
      i. Thematic Apperception Test (TAT)
      ii. Ink-Blot Test

f) **Other tests**
   i. Cognitive Ability Tests
   ii. Wechsler Adult Intelligence Scale
   iii. Wonderlic Personal Tests
   iv. Polygraph Tests
   v. Honesty Test

9. **Formal Interviews**

10. **Physical or medical examination:** Medical tests are conducted to ensure physical fitness of the potential employee. It will decrease chances of employee absenteeism.

11. Checking references
    a) Educational.
    b) Social and
    c) Employment.

12. Line Managers Decisions

13. **Job offer or Appointment Letter:** A reference check is made about the candidate selected and then finally he is appointed by giving a formal appointment letter.

14. Employment

3.8.4. Placement

- After selecting a candidate, they should be placed on a suitable job. It involves assigning a specific rank and responsibility to an employment.
- Placement of individuals in job matching their abilities. Personnel offices interview and test applicants for the purpose of achieving suitable job placements where there is a good match between management needs and employee qualifications.
- Placement basically refers to the system of assessment and selection by which vacancies are filled by staff serving in an organization.
- Placement can also be defined as the internal filling of vacancies as distinguished from external recruitment.
- Placement is a process of assigning a specific job to each of the selected candidates. It involves assigning a specific rank and responsibility to an individual.
- It implies matching the requirements of a job with the qualifications of the candidate.

Significance of placement

- It improves employee morale.
- It helps in reducing employee turnover.
- It helps in reducing absenteeism.
- It helps in reducing accident rates.
- It avoids misfit between the candidate and the job.
- It helps the candidate to work as per the predetermined objectives of the organization.

Employee placement process

- Collect details about the employee
- Construct the employees profile
- Match between sub-group profile and individual's profile
- Compare sub-group profile to job family profile
- Match between job family profiles and sub-group profiles
- Assign the individuals to the job family
- Assign the individual to specific job after further counseling and assessment

Problems in placement

- Employee expectations from the job.
- Expectation from the employers is more than the employee's ability or skills.
- Technological changes might result in mismatch between the job and the employee.
- Changes in organizational structure.
- Social and Psychological factors.

Factors responsible for Effective Placement

- Job rotation
- Team work
- Training & Development
- Job enrichment
- Empowerment

3.8.5. Induction and Orientation

- Induction program is a technique by which a new employee is rehabilitated into the changed surroundings and introduced to the practices, policies and purposes of the organization.
- "Induction is the process of receiving and welcoming an employee when the first joins a company and giving him the basic information he needs to settle down quickly and happily and start work"
- Proper employee orientation/socialization helps to accommodate the new employee with existing employees.

  - ❖ Handbook, Lecture, Film, group seminar, etc used to impart the information to new employees about the environment of the job and the organization includes:
  - ❖ About the company
  - ❖ About the Department
  - ❖ About the Superiors, Subordinates, etc.

Types of induction programs

- General induction program
- Specific orientation program
- Follow-up induction program.

Objectives of induction

- To help the new comer to overcome his shyness and overcome his shyness nervousness in meeting new people in a new environment.

- To give new comer necessary information such as location of a café, rest period etc.
- To build new employee confidence in the organization.
- It helps in reducing labor turnover and absenteeism.
- It reduces confusion and develops healthy relations in the organization.
- To ensure that the new comer do not form false impression and negative attitude towards the organization.
- To develop among the new comer a sense of belonging and loyalty to the organization.

Advantages of formal Induction

- Induction helps to build up a two-way channel of communication between management and workers.
- Proper induction facilitates informal relation and team work among employee.
- Effective induction helps to integrate the new employee into the organization and to develop a sense of belonging.
- Induction helps to develop good relation.
- A formal induction programme proves that the company is taking interest in getting him off to good start.
- Proper induction reduces employee grievances, absenteeism and labor turnover.
- Induction is helpful in supplying information concerning the organization, the job and employee welfare facilities.

Contents of induction programme

- Brief history and operations of the company.
- The company's organization structure.
- Policies and procedure of the company.
- Products and services of the company.
- Location of department and employee facilities.
- Safety measures.
- Grievances procedures.
- Benefits and services of employee.
- Standing orders and disciplinary procedures.
- Opportunities for training, promotions transfer etc.
- Suggestion schemes.
- Rules and regulations.

3.9. CHALLENGES OF HRM

1. **Globalization:** Growing internationalization of business has its impact on HRM in terms of problems of unfamiliar laws, languages, practices, competitions, attitudes, management styles, work ethics and more. HR managers have a challenge to deal with more functions, more heterogeneous functions and more involvement in employee's personal life.
2. **Corporate Re-organizations:** Reorganization relates to mergers and acquisitions, joint ventures, take over, internal restructuring of organizations. In these situations, it is difficult to imagine circumstances that pose a greater challenge for HRM than reorganizations itself. It is a

challenge to manage employees' anxiety, uncertainties, insecurities and fears during these dynamic trends.

3. **New Organizational forms:** The basic challenge to HRM comes from the changing character of competitions. The competition is not between individual firms but between constellations of firm. Major companies are operating through a complex web of strategic alliances, forgings with local suppliers, etc. These relationships give birth to completely new forms of organizational structure, which highly depend upon a regular exchange of people and information. The challenge for HRM is to cope with the implications of these newly networked relations more and more, in place of more comfortable hierarchical relationships that existed within the organizations for ages in the past.

4. **Changing Demographics of Workforce:** Changes in workforce are largely reflected by dual career couples, large chunk of young blood between old age superannuating employees, working mothers, more educated and aware workers etc. These dynamic workforces have their own implications for HR managers and from HRM point of view is a true challenge to handle.

5. **Employee expectations:** With the changes in workforce demographics, employee expectations and attitudes have also transformed. Traditional allurements like job security, house, and remunerations are not much attractive today; rather employees are demanding empowerment and equality with management. Hence it is a challenge for HRM to redesign the profile of workers, and discover new methods of hiring, training, remunerating and motivating employees.

6. **New Industrial Relations Approach:** In today's dynamic world, even unions have understood that strikes and militancy have lost their relevance and unions are greatly affected by it. The trade union membership has fallen drastically worldwide and the future of labor movement is in danger. The challenge before HRM is to adopt a proactive industrial relations approach which should enable HR specialist to look into challenges unfolding in the future and to be prepared to convert them into opportunities.

7. **Renewed People Focus:** The need of today's world and business is the people's approach. The structure, strategy, systems approach which worked in post war era is no more relevant in today's economic environment which is characterized by over capacities and intense competition. The challenge of HR manager is to focus on people and make them justifiable and sustainable.

8. **Managing the Managers:** Managers are unique tribe in any society, they believe they are class apart. They demand decision-making, bossism, and operational freedom. However in the post liberalization era, freedom given to managers is grossly misused to get rid of talented and hard working juniors. The challenge of HRM is how to manage this tribe? How to make them realize that the freedom given to them is to enable them make quick decisions in the interest of the organization and not to resort to witch-hunting.

9. **Work force diversity:** Another challenge for HRM is to protect the interest of weaker sections of society. The dramatic increase of women workers, minorities and other backward communities in the workforce has resulted in the need for organizations to reexamine their policies, practices and values. In the name of global competition, productivity and quality the interests of the society around should not be sacrificed. It is a challenge of today's HR managers to see that these weaker sections are neither denied their rightful jobs nor are discriminated against while in service.

10. **Contribution to the success of organizations:** The biggest challenge to an HR manager is to make all employees contribute to the success of the organization in an ethical and socially responsible way. Because society's well being to a large extent depends on its organizations.

3.10. SOCIAL RESPONSIBILITIES OF BUSINESS

- The obligation of any business to protect and serve public interest is known as social responsibility of business.
- Social responsibility is an ethical or theory that an entity, be it an organization or individual, has an obligation to act to benefit society at large.
- Social responsibility is a duty of every individual or organization has to perform so as to maintain a balance between the economy and the ecosystem.
- Social responsibility means sustaining the equilibrium between the two. It pertains not only to business organizations but also to everyone whose any action impacts the environment.
- This responsibility can be passive, by avoiding engaging in socially harmful acts, or active, by performing activities that directly advance social goals.
- In 1960, **Keith Davis** suggested that social responsibility refers to businesses' "decisions and actions taken for reasons at least partially beyond the firm's direct economic or technical interest."
- **Eells and Walton:** "CSR refers to the problems that arise when corporate enterprise casts its shadow on the social scene, and the ethical principles that ought to govern the relationship between the corporation and society."
- Social responsibility entails developing businesses with a positive relationship to the society which they operate in.

Benefits of social responsibility

- Social responsibility is a voluntary effort on the part of business to take various steps to satisfy the expectation of the different interest groups. As you have already learnt, the interest groups may be owners, investors, employees, consumers, government and society or community.

1. **Public Image:** The activities of business towards the welfare of the society earn goodwill and reputation for the business. The earnings of business also depend upon the public image of its activities. People prefer to buy products of a company that engages itself in various social welfare programmes. Again, good public image also attracts honest and competent employees to work with such employers.
2. **Government Regulation:** To avoid government regulations businessmen should discharge their duties voluntarily. For example, if any business firm pollutes the environment it will naturally come under strict government regulation, which may ultimately force the firm to close down its business. Instead, the business firm should engage itself in maintaining a pollution free environment.
3. **Survival and Growth**: Every business is a part of the society. So for its survival and growth, support from the society is very much essential. Business utilizes the available resources like

power, water, land, roads, etc. of the society. So it should be the responsibility of every business to spend a part of its profit for the welfare of the society.

4. **Employee satisfaction**: Besides getting good salary and working in a healthy atmosphere, employees also expect other facilities like proper accommodation, transportation, education and training. The employers should try to fulfill all the expectation of the employees because employee satisfaction is directly related to productivity and it is also required for the long-term prosperity of the organization. For example, if business spends money on training of the employees, it will have more efficient people to work and thus, earn more profit.

5. **Consumer Awareness:** Now-a-days consumers have become very conscious about their rights. They protest against the supply of inferior and harmful products by forming different groups. This has made it obligatory for the business to protect the interest of the consumers by providing quality products at the most competitive price.

3.11. OBJECTIVES QUESTION - ANSWER

1. The following concept is developed on unitarism , individualism, commitment and strategic alignment.
(A) Personnel Management
(B) Human Resource
(C) Management
(D) Industrial Relations

Answer: B

2. Which of the following is not a function of human resource management?
(A) Planning
(B) Organizing
(C) Directing
(D) Accounting

Answer: D

3. People should be regarded as assets rather than variable costs was emphasized in:
(A) Personnel Management
(B) Human Resource Management
(C) Personnel Administration
(D) Public Administration

Answer: B

4. Human Resource Management is improving quality of employees as well as:
(A) Performance (B) Effectiveness
(C) Efficiency (D) Outputs

Answer: C

5. Which of the following is not an operative function of Personnel/Human Resource Management ?
(A)Procuring (B) Planning
(C)Developing (D) Maintaining

Answer: D

6. Human Resource Management is primarily concerned with :
(A) Sales
(B) Dimension of People
(C) External Environment
(D) Internal Environment

Answer: B

7. Reducing the number of employees at operational level and reorganizing the work system in order to attain greater productivity.
(A)Downsizing
(B)Manpower inventory
(C)Manpower forecasting
(D)All the above

Answer: A

8. Dramatic reduction of manpower is called
(A)Termination (B) Retrenchment
(C) Downsizing (D) Right sizing

Answer: B

9. What are the operative functions of HRM ?
(A) Organising (B) Directing
(C) Controlling (D)All of the above

Answer: D

10. Which of the following is/are new challenge/s in the field of human resource management ?
(A)Rightsizing
(B)Outsourcing
(C)Diversity Management
(D)All the above

Answer: D

11. Selection of persons in an organization is the responsibility of :
(A) Security Department
(B) Personnel Department
(C) Trade Unions
(D) Canteen Department

Answer: B

12. Human Resource Management is the management of :
(A) Man
(B) Machine
(C) Material
(D) All the above

Answer: A

13. Which of the following objective of human resource management?
(A) Productivity
(B) Quality of work life
(C) Organizational change
(D) All the above

Answer: D

14. The book "HR Champions" is authored by :
(A) Mintzberg
(B)J. Pfeffer
(C)M. Porter
(D)Dave Ulrich

Answer: D

15. Reduction of Labour Force is called
(A)Termination
(B)Retrenchment
(C)Lay-off
(D)Right sizing

Answer: D

16. Dramatic reduction of manpower is called
(A) Termination
(B) Retrenchment
(C) Downsizing
(D)Rightsizing

Answer: B

17. Which of the following is not a fringe benefit?
(A) Transport
(B) Subsidized canteen facilities
(C) Free education to the children
(D) Dearness Allowance

Answer: D

18. The policy of introducing "New Blood" is
(A) Steriotypic
(B) Bureacratic as well as redtapic
(C) Innovative and challenging, making the corporate dynamic
(D) Innovative, challenging, but often resisted

Answer: C

19. Human Resource Management (HRM) is a part of the broad Human Resource Development (HRD) System, as this focus to
(A) Selection, Induction, Training and Development
(B) Operational and Organisational Options
(C) (A) and (B) above
(D) None of the above

Answer: C

20. Exit Policy primarily emphasises in the broad sense, for policy makers as
(A) Removing employees
(B) Down sizing
(C) Retiring people and Rehabilitating them
(D) Bringing new blood to the Corporate

Answer: C

21. The development of a performance-appraisal system is primarily the concern of
(A) Financial management
(B) Human resources management.
(C) Production and operations management.
(D) Marketing management.
(E) Administrative management.

Answer: B

22. Having good human relations skills means that a manager is able to
(A) Use a computer
(B)Train employees and solve problems.
(C) Think creatively
(D) Work with others.
(E) All of the above.

Answer: D

23. In which company 'Six Sigma' was first experimented?
(A)Toyota (B) Motorola
(C) Sony (D) Ford

Answer: B

24. The word 'Kaizen', which refers to improvement in performance and productivity has been borrowed from :
(A)Japan (B) Germany
(C)Korea (D) Sweden

Answer: A

25. Kanban is associated with all of the following except:
(A)signaling when it is time for the next batch
(B) reducing setup time
(C)reducing batch size
(D) increasing material handling

Answer: D

26. The word "kanban" means
(A) low inventory
(B) employee empowerment
(C) card
(D) continuous improvement

Answer: C

27. The word "Kanban" refers to :
(A) A means of effective dialogue
(B) A meaning of effective communication and visual control
(C) A means of potential appraisal
(D) All the above

Answer: A

28. Which one is not a general concept of T.Q.M. ?
(A) Continuous Improvement
(B) Team Work
(C) Strategy
(D) Quality Education

Answer: C

29. The total dedication of continuous improvement so that customers' needs are met is known as :
(A)Theory X
(B)Theory Y
(C)Total Quality Management
(D) Change Management

Answer: C

30. Match the following contributions to TQM with the contributors :

List – I (Contributors)	**List – II (Contributions)**
a. Walter A.	i. Concept of Shewart Internal Customer
b. Joseph M. Juran	ii. Product Design Quality
c. Kaoru Ishikawa	iii. Statistical control charts
d. Genichi Taguchi	iv. Quality as 'fitness for use'

Codes:

	a	b	c	d
(A)	ii	i	iii	iv
(B)	iv	iii	i	ii
(C)	ii	iii	i	iv
(D)	iii	iv	i	ii

Answer: D

31. The philosophy of 'never-ending improvement' in total quality management is called :
(A)Kanaban
(B)Business Process Re-engineering
(C)Benchmarking
(D)Kaizan

Answer: D

32. Which one of the following is not a step in planning ?
(A) Establishing objectives
(B) Developing premises
(C) Determining alternative courses
(D) Identifying needs of employees

Answer: D

33. Which one of the following refers to plan of action:
(A) Objectives
(B) Policy
(C) Principle
(D) Strategy

Answer: B

34. Planning is looking ahead and control is:
(A) Scanning environment
(B) Looking back
(C) Setting targets
(D) Defining objectives

Answer: B

35. The ultimate mission or purpose is to relate human resources to future enterprise needs, so as to maximize the future return on investment in human. resources. It is referred as
(A) Demand and Supply
(B) Forecasting
(C) Human Resource Planning
(D) Human Resource Development

Answer: C

36. Human Resource Planning include:
(A)Scenario planning
(B)Action planning
(C)Demand and Supply forecasts
(D)All the above

Answer: D

37. Human Resource Planning is the _______step in the management function.
(A)Primary (B) Middle
(C)Final (D) None of the above

Answer: A

38. Arrange the steps in Manpower Planning in the order in which they occur.
(a) Identifying sources of manpower supply.
(b) Manpower forecasting.
(c) Determining manpower requirements.
(d) Manpower Inventory
(e) Selection
(f) Recruitment
(g) Placement
(A) (c) (b) (d) (a) (f) (e) (g)
(B) (a) (c) (b) (d) (e) (f) (g)
(C) (d) (a) (b) (c) (f) (e) (g)
(D) (c) (d) (a) (b) (f) (e) (g)

Answer: A

39. Which of the following is the meaning of Human Resource Planning?
(A) Evaluation of job
(B) Satisfaction of the employees on the job
(C) Appraising the performance of employees
(D) It is the process by which an organisation ensures that it has the right number and kind of people at the right place, at the right time.

Answer: D

40. In which order the following aspects of Manpower planning operate in established organisations ?
(i) Recruitment
(ii) Job analysis
(iii) Manpower Inventory
(iv) Manpower Forecasting
(A) (iii), (ii), (iv), (i)
(B) (ii), (iv), (iii), (i)
(C) (iv), (iii), (ii), (i)
(D) (iii), (ii), (i), (iv)

Answer: C

41. Which of the following is the techniques of the Human Resource Demand Forecasting?
(A)Ratio-Trend Analysis
(B)Work-Study method
(C) Managerial Judgement
(D)All of the above

Answer: A

42. Human Resource Planning is the process of :
(A)Managing people at work
(B)Stimulating people to work effectively
(C)Getting maximum out of employee
(D)Demand and supply forecasting of manpower

Answer: D

43. Which of the following is not true in case of manpower planning ?
(A) It is a process by which an organisation should move from its current manpower position to its desired manpower position.
(B) It is an integrated approach to performing the personnel function required to meet organisational and individual objectives.
(C) It involves forecasting human resource requirements.
(D) It is a process to discover the sources of manpower.

Answer: B

44. The main advantage of the Delphi technique over other judgemental forecasting technique is :
(A)The opinion of others are not allowed to influence individual experts
(B)It requires that a consensus be reached
(C)It is based on the majority decision
(D)For this less information is required

Answer: B

45. Decision theory helps management in:
(A)Analysing a problem
(B)Deciding sequence of activities
(C)Selecting the most cost effective alternative
(D)Postpone administrative action

Answer: C

46. Which is the most inaccurate method of forecasting?
(A) Delphi method
(B) Market research
(C) Exponential smoothing
(D) Time series

Answer: C

47. Delphi technique is used in
(A) Organizing (B) Operating
(C) Staffing (D) Forecasting

Answer: D

48. In demand forecasting important method used in trend projection is:
(A)Scientific Method
(B) Box-Jenkins Method
(C)Delphi Method
(D) Logistics Method

Answer: B

49. Decision on plant layout and location are concerned with :
(A) System design
(B) System operations
(C) System control
(D) None of the above

Answer: C

50. One of the following is training provided to enhance decision making skills:
(A)On the job training
(B) Behavioural modeling
(C)Management games
(D) Action learning

Answer: C

51. Which one of the following is the functions of personnel management ?
(A) Planning, Organising, Staffing, Directing and Controlling
(B) Planning, Organising, Coordinating, Budgeting and Controlling
(C) Procurement, Development, Compensation, Integration and Maintenance
(D) Perception, Development, Learning, Organisation and Behaviour

Answer: C

52. Recruitment is concerned with
(A) Selecting the right candidate
(B) Developing a pool of job candidates
(C) Getting applications
(D) None of the above

Answer: B

53. Which of the following is the internal sources of recruitment?
(A) Advertisement
(B) Selection
(C) Both (A) and (B)
(D) None of the above

Answer : D

54. Which of the following is the process of searching for perspective employees and stimulating them to apply for the jobs in the organizations:
(A) Recruitment (B) Selection
(C) Promotion (D) Retrenchment

Answer : A

55. When an organization outsources the responsibilities for the end-to-end delivery of the recruitment/selection process covering all vacancies is
(A) Recruitment process and screening
(B) Business process and screening
(C) Knowledge process and screening
(D) All the above

Answer : D

56. Which one is not a part of recruitment process?
(A) Determining requirements
(B) Planning recruitment campaign
(C) Attracting candidates
(D) Selecting candidates

Answer: D

57. Which one is the appropriate sequence in recruitment and selection process?
(A) Recruitment, Job analysis, Manpower planning
(B) Manpower planning, Job analysis, Recruitment
(C) Manpower planning, Recruitment, Job analysis
(D) Job analysis, Manpower planning, Recruitment

Answer: B

58. An organisation secretly tries to lure the employee of another organisation. It is called:
(A) Consulting
(B) Poaching
(C) Negotiating
(D) Persuading

Answer : B

59. Recruitment Refers to :
(A) Process of searching for prospective employee
(B) Basis for selecting the right candidate
(C) Solicit necessary information from prospective applicant
(D) Know the suitability of candidates

Answer : A

60. Which of the following is not a method of recruitment ?
(A) Scouting
(B) Employment exchanges
(C) Advertisement
(D) Application Blank

Answer: D

61. Which of the following method of recruiting is from external sources?
(A) Personnel Consultants
(B) Employment exchanges
(C) Advertisement
(D) All the above

Answer: D

62. Which of the following source is the most relevant for recruitment of managerial personnel ?
(A) Employment Exchange
(B) Advertisement
(C) Gate Hiring
(D) Trade Unions

Answer: B

63. What are benefits of external recruitment?
(A) Easy and heap method
(B) Acquiring new skills and talent
(C) To save training cost
(D) To increase production
Answer: B

64. (1)Recruitment is influenced by the internal labour market conditions
(2) Recruitment is influenced by the external labour market conditions
Which option is correct?
(A)Statement (1)
(B)Statement (2)
(C)Both of the above
(D)None of the above
Answer: B

65. Which of the following is not a method of selection ?
(A) Advertisement
(B)Interview
(C)Tests
(D)Reference checking
Answer: A

66. Match the following :

(a) Interest Tests	(i) Recruitment
(b) Voluntary Retirement	(ii) Interview rating
(c) Disposition	(iii) Separation
(d) Deputation	(iv) Selection

	(a)	(b)	(c)	(d)
(A)	(i)	(ii)	(iii)	(iv)
(B)	(ii)	(i)	(iii)	(iv)
(C)	(iv)	(iii)	(ii)	(i)
(D)	(iv)	(ii)	(i)	(iii)

Answer : C

67. Which of the following is not a model of selection ?
(A)Multiple Choice Model
(B)Multiple Cut-off Model
(C)Multiple Hurdles Model
(D)Predictor Criterion Model
Answer : D

68. Tests devised to assess a person's ability to undertake a particular type of work or to learn a particular skill are called
(A)Aptitude Test
(B) Knowledge Test
(C)Intelligence Test
(D)Attitude Test
Answer : A

69. Which of the following is **not** a type of test pertaining to selection procedure?
(A) Aptitude Test
(B) Achievement Test
(C) Situational Test
(D) Statistical Test
Answer: D

70. Achievement Test is also known as:
(A) Proficiency Test
(B)Interest Test
(C) Aptitude Test
(D)Personality Test
Answer: A

71. Which of the following is Psychological Test ?
(A) Aptitude Test
(B) Physical Test
(C) Ability Test
(D)Knowledge Test
Answer: B

72. Which of the following test is used to measure the mental ability or mental alertness of the applicant:
(A) Performance Test
(B) Intelligence Test
(C) Aptitude Test
(D)Personality Test
Answer: B

73. Arrange the following in a proper sequence to show selection procedure :
(a) Medical Test
(b) Screening of applications

(c) Interview
(d) Application of Psychological Test
(e) Written Test
(f) Checking of references
(g) Issuance of Appointment letter
(A) b, e, d, c, f, a, g
(B) e, d, b, c, a, g, f
(C) d, b, e, c, a, g, f
(D) f, a, g, b, c, d, e

Answer: A

74. Technique of drawing conclusions from a candidate's hand writing about future performance in a role is
(A)Graphology (B) Physiognomy
(C)Phrenology (D) Astronomy

Answer: A

75. What is not an advantage of seniority principle of promotion ?
(A) It is more objective and easier in application.
(B) It eliminates internal strife for advancement.
(C) It promotes general morale of the personnel.
(D) It affects the self-improvement efforts of personnel.

Answer: D

76. The art of judging, character of a person from appearance specially the face, based on the assumption that face is an index of mind, is known as :
(A)Graphology (B) Physiognomy
(C)Phrenology (D) None of the above

Answer: B

Explanation: Physiognomy is the assessment of a person's character or personality from his outer appearance, especially the face. The term *physiognomy* can also refer to the general appearance of a person, object or terrain, without reference to its implied characteristics, as in the physiognomy of a plant community.

77. An interview process must be:
(A)Direct questions
(B) Open Ended
(C) FAQ
(D) Personal Questions

Answer: B

78. Excess & Deficiency of employees is generally observed in which of following
(A) Recruitment
(B) Selection
(C) H.R.P
(D) Wages and admin

Answer: B

79. The use of predesigned set of questions used in an interview process leads to:
(A) Behavioural interview
(B) Situational interview
(C) Non-directional interview
(D) Structured interview

Answer: D

80. Interviews conducted for knowing why an employee is leaving the organisation is called :
(A)Exit Interview
(B)Separation interview
(C)Termination interview
(D)Retrenchment interview

Answer: A

81. Selection is the process in which candidates for employment are divided into two classes – those who are to be offered employment and those who are not." This is stated by-
(A) Dale Yoder
(B) Milton M. Mandell
(C) R.D. Agarwal
(D) Edwin Flippo

Answer: A

82. The use of predesigned set of questions used in an interview process leads to :
(A)Behavioural interview
(B)Situational interview
(C)Non-directional interview
(D)Structured interview
Answer: D

83. One of the following is training provided to enhance decision making skills:
(A)On the job train
(B) Behavioural modeling
(C)Action learning
(D) Management games
Answer: D

84. An "Assessment Centre" is
(A)A place
(B)A technique
(C)Both (A) and (B)
(D)None of the above
Answer: A

Explanation: An assessment centre is a place at which a person, such as a member of staff, is assessed to determine their suitability for particular roles, especially management or military command. The candidates' personality and aptitudes are determined by a variety of techniques including interviews, examinations and psychometric testing.

85. The following are the three components of creativity:
(A) Expertise, creativity skills and task motivation
(B) Expertise, innovation and rationality
(C) Expertise, rationality and relevance
(D) Expertise, novelty and performance
Answer: B

86. While considering promotion of an employee, the following is the most important consideration :
(A) Seniority
(B) Competence
(C) Loyalty
(D) Only (A) and (B)
Answer: D

87. Which type of promotion described by W. R. Spriegel ?
(i) Departmental Promotion
(ii) Inter-departmental Promotion
(iii) Inter-plant Promotion
(iv) Inter-company Promotion
(A) (i), (ii), (iii) (B) (ii), (iii), (iv)
(C) (i), (ii), (iv) (D) (i), (iii), (iv)
Answer: A

88. Induction means :
(A) The determination of the job to which an accepted candidate is to be assigned
(B) Introducing the new employee who is designated as a probationer to the job
(C) Measuring the efficiency of labour
(D) Absorbing human resources as organs of the company
Answer: B

89. Introducing the new employee to the job, location, surroundings is called
(A) Placement (B) Job design
(C) Recruitment (D) Induction
Answer: D

90. What is the term used to describe the process of helping a new employee to settle quickly into their job so they become efficient and productive workers?
(A)Action learning
(B)Discovery learning
(C)Sitting by Nellie
(D) Induction
Answer: D

91. Induction training is also called as:
(A) Orientation (B) Refresher
(C) Indoctrination (D) Both A and C
Answer: D

92. Giving general information's regarding organization to the newly appointed personnel is called :
(A) Training (B) Development
(C)Induction (D) Promotion

Answer: C

93. Induction refers to
(A) Giving training to the employees.
(B) Giving incentive to the employees.
(C) Introducing employees to the organization culture and situation.
(D) Increasing the morale of the employees.

Answer: C

94. Ethical values are derived from:
(A)Corporate objectives
(B)Organizational culture
(C)The Bible, the Kuran and the Geeta
(D)Corporative philosophy

Answer: D

95. Which one of the following is not the social responsibility of business?
(A)Adopting villages for development
(B)Setting up educational institutes
(C)Opening research and development department
(D)Construction of temples

Answer: D

96. Social responsibility is a responsibility towards :
(A)Employees (B) Government
(C)Society (D) All of these

Answer: D

97. The most appropriate goal of corporate social responsibility is centered around :
(A)Philanthropic activities
(B)Voluntary activities
(C)Ethical based activities
(D)Legalistic activities

Answer: B

98. Social responsibility is not :
(A)Legal behaviour
(B)Legal compliances
(C)Ethical compulsion
(D)All of the above

Answer: B

99. Which one of the following is not the Social Responsibility of business?
(A) Adopting villages for development
(B) Setting up educational institutes
(C) Opening research and development department
(D) Construction of temples

Answer: D

100. Social responsibility means that a business
(A) Functions efficiently without harming the society
(B) Abjures the profit motive
(C) Keeps pollution under check
(D) Pays its Taxes to Government

Answer: A

101. Which o of the following is not related to Business Ethics?
(A)Environmental ethics
(B) Social responsibility of business
(C) Profiteering
(D) Ecological consciousness

Answer: C

102. PERT stands for:
(A)Production Estimation & Research Technique
(B)Project Evaluation and Review Technique
(C)Project Estimation & Research Technique
(D)None of the above

Answer: B

103. TQM's major emphasis is on:
(A) Product quality
(B) Company profitability
(C)Customer delight
(D) Employee training
Answer: A

104. External environment of business is:
(A) Physical
(B) Demographic
(C)Economic
(D)All of these
Answer: D

105. Which of the following is not an essential feature of social environment?
(A) Competitiveness
(B) Respect for the individual
(C)Better quality of life
(D) Bailment
Answer: D

106. Consider the following:
1. Measurement
2. Projection
3. Selection
4. Observation
5. Comparison
6. Decision making
The correct sequence of the above ingredients of management by exception is:
(A) 12 3 45 6
(B) 12 3 54 6
(C) 12 3 64 5
(D) 12 3 65 4
Answer: A

107. The Social Responsibility of a Business is important to
(A) Owners and Investors
(B) Employees
(C) Government
(D) All the above
Answer: D

108. Find the 'odd' in the 'Benefits of Strategic HR Planning'
(A) Encouragement of proactive in place of reactive behaviour
(B) Explicit communication of organization goals
(C) Identification of gaps in current situation and future vision
(D) Coping with the environment
Answer: D

109. Promotion means:
1. Elevation to higher position.
2. Elevation to higher position with financial benefits.
3. Elevation to higher position with more power.
(A) 1 and 2 only (B) 1 and 3 only
(C) 2 and 3 only (D) All the above
Answer: D

110. Which of the following constitute manpower planning ?
1. Determine human resource requirements both qualitatively and quantitatively.
2. Find the source of talented individuals.
3. Planning for the human resource needs of an organization.
4. Processing the right people.
(A) 1, 2 and 4 (B) 2 and 3
(C) 1 and 3 (D) 1, 2, 3 and 4
Answer: D

111. Who among the following are administratively linked with the Department of Personnel and Training?
1. Central Bureau of Investigation
2. Union Public Service Commission
3. Central Vigilance Commission
Select the correct answer using the code given below:
(A) Only 1 and 2 (B) Only 2 and 3
(C) Only 1 and 3 (D) 1, 2 and 3
Answer: D

112. The use of predesigned set of questions used in an interview process leads to :
(A) Behavioural interview
(B) Situational interview
(C) Non-directional interview
(D) Structured interview
Answer: D

113. Human Resource Management (HRM) is a part of the broad Human Resource Development (HRD) System, as this focus to
(A) Selection, Induction, Training and Development
(B) Operational and Organisational Options
(C) (A) and (B) above
(D) None of the above
Answer: C

114. Exit Policy primarily emphasises in the broad sense, for policy makers as
(A) Removing employees
(B) Down sizing
(C) Retiring people and Rehabilitating them
(D) Bringing new blood to the Corporate
Answer: C

115. Selection is the process in which candidates for employment are divided into two classes – those who are to be offered employment and those who are not." This is stated by
(A) Dale Yoder (B) Milton M. Mandell
(C) R.D. Agarwal (D) Edwin Flippo
Answer: A

116. The ultimate mission or purpose is to relate human resources to future enterprise needs, so as to maximize the future return on investment in human resources. It is referred as
(A) Demand and Supply
(B) Forecasting
(C) Human Resource Planning
(D) Human Resource Development
Answer: C

117. Recruitment is concerned with
(A) Selecting the right candidate
(B) Developing a pool of job candidates
(C) Getting applications
(D) None of the above
Answer: B

118. Which of the following is the internal sources of recruitment ?
(A) Advertisement
(B) Selection
(C) Both (A) and (B)
(D) None of the above
Answer: D

119. Changes in the population characteristics such as age, gender, marital status, income and education are the examples of
(A) Demographic characteristics
(B) Cultural characteristics
(C) Geographic characteristics
(D) None of the above
Answer: A

****

UNIT-IV
HUMAN RESOURCE DEVELOPMENT (HRD)

4.1. INTRODUCTION: FEATURES – NEED – OBJECTIVES – FUNCTIONS – OUTCOMES

- HRD is mainly concerned with overall development of human resources in order to contribute to the well-being of the employees, organization and the society at large. It includes development of skills, knowledge and competencies of people.
- It is people oriented concept.HRD consider People are the real assets of an organization and organizations depend on people for their survival and growth.
- HRD is a positive concept in human resource management. It is based on the belief that an investment in human beings is necessary and will invariably bring in substantial benefits to the organization in the long run.
- HRD aims at helping people to acquire competencies required to perform their functions effectively thereby making organizations do well.
- The concept of HRD was formally introduced by ***Leonard Nadler*** in 1969 in conference organized by ASTD.
- **Leonard Nadler: "**HRD as those learning experiences which are organized for a specific time and designed to bring about the possibility of behavioral changes."
- **T.V. Rao:** "HRD is a process by which the employees of an organisation are helped in a continuous and planned way to:
  (i) acquire or sharpen capabilities required to perform various functions associated with their present or expected future roles.
  (ii) develop their journal capabilities as individual and discover and exploit their own inner potential for their own and /or organisational development purposes.
  (iii) develop an organisational culture in which superior-subordinate relationship, team work and collaboration among sub-units are strong and contribute to the professional well being, motivation and pride of employees."
- **T. V. Rao** is considered as a **Father of Indian HRD.**
- **M.M. Khan:** "Human resource development is across of increasing knowledge, capabilities and positive work attitudes of all people working at all levels in a business undertaking."
- According to **Udai Pareek and T. V. Rao ; the attributes of HRD Manager are:**
  a) Technical
  b) Managerial and
  c) Personality

Salient Features of HRD

- Human resource development is a process in which employees of the organizations are recognized as its human resource. It believes that human resource is most valuable asset of the organization

- It stresses on development of human resources of an organization. It helps the employees of the organization to develop their general capabilities in relation to their present jobs and expected future role.
- It emphasize on the development and best utilization of the capabilities of individuals in the interest of the employees and organization.
- It helps in establishing better inter-personal relations. It stresses on developing relationship based on help, trust and confidence.
- It promotes team spirit among employees.
- It tries to develop competencies at the organisation level. It stresses on providing healthy climate for development in organisation.
- HRD is a system. It has several sub-systems. All these sub-systems are inter-related . It stresses on collaboration among all the sub-systems.
- It aims to develop an organisational culture in which there is good senior-subordinate relations, motivation, quality and sense of belonging.
- It tries to develop competence at individual, inter-personal, group and organisational level to meet organisational goal.
- It is an inter-disciplinary concept. It is based on the concepts, ideas and principles of sociology, psychology, economics etc.
- It form on employee welfare and quality of work life. It tries to identify employee needs and meeting them to the best possible extent.
- It is a continuous and systematic learning process. Development is a lifelong process, which never ends.

Need for HRD

1. Changes in Economic Policies in 1991(LPG)
2. Changing Job Requirements
3. Need for Multi-skilled Human Resources
4. Organizational Complexity
5. Human Relations
6. Organizational Viability and Transformation Process
7. Technological Advances

Objectives of HRD

- **Work Opportunity**: HRD provides an opportunity and a systematic framework for the development resource in the organisation for full expression of their talents.
- **Development of Traits**: HRD is associated with the development of total personality so that these can show and use their talent for the benefit of the organisation.
- **Ability development**: HRD makes capable employees. Thus they can develop their capability by which they can do their present job easily.
- **Creative Motivation:** HRD manager motivates employees and improve their level of performance.
- **Good Relation**: HRD manager stresses the need of coordination which is used for the benefits of himself and for the benefits of those who come in their contact.
- **Develop team spirit**: HRD manager develops the spirit of teamwork; team work for it is used for the effective cooperation and coordination of each employee which ultimately checks industrial unrest.

- **Organisational Growth**: HRM manager is responsible for developing health, culture and effective work plan which always result in more profitability.
- **Human Resource Information**: HRM manager in general keeps all records to employees working in his organisation; these can be used at any time when these are needed.

Functions of HRD

1. Performance appraisal
2. Employee Training
3. Employee Development
4. Organizational Change
5. Organizational Development
6. Career planning and development
7. Involvement in social and religious Organizations
8. Involvement in Quality Circles
9. Involvement in Workers Participation in Management
10. Job rotation
11. Rewards
12. Feedback and Counseling

Outcomes of HRD

- People in organizations become more competent because: they become better aware of the skills required for job performance; there is greater clarity of norms and standards.
- People understand their roles better because of increased communication.
- People become more committed to their jobs because there is greater objectivity.
- People develop greater trust and respect for each other.
- There is greater collaboration and team work which produces synergy effect.
- People find themselves better equipped with problem – solving capabilities.
- Useful and objective data on employees is generated which facilitates better human resource planning.
- The top management becomes more sensitive to employees' problems and human processes due to increased openness in communication.

4.2. COMPARISON BETWEEN HRM AND HRD FUNCTION

HRM Function

- The HRM function is a routine, maintenance oriented administrative function.
- HRM function is seen as an independent function with independent sub-functions.
- HRM function is regarded as mainly a reactive function responding to the demands of the organization as and when they arise.
- HRM is supposed to be an exclusive responsibility of the personnel department.
- HRM takes a very narrow view of its scope and aims only at developing and administering people.
- HRM function considers salary, economic rewards, job simplification and job specialization as important motivators.
- HRM function considers improved satisfaction and morale as the cause of improved performance.

HRD Function

- HRD is a continuous development function. The major attention of HRD is on improving the human process.
- HRD is viewed as a sub-system of a larger system. This means that the design of HRD cannot be considered in isolation.
- ***HRD is regarded as a proactive function:*** The function of HRD is not merely to cope with the needs of the organization but to anticipate them and to act on them in advance in a continuous and planned way.
- HRD aims at developing the capabilities on all line managers to carry out various personnel functions themselves.
- HRD takes a much wider view of its scope and aims at developing the total organization.
- HRD emphasizes the importance of higher needs in motivating individuals. It considers informal organization, autonomous work groups, job enrichment, job challenge and creativity as the main motivating forces.
- HRD considers improved performance as the cause and improved satisfaction and morale of as its results.

4.3. MAJOR FUNCTIONS OF HRD

- Major functions of HRD include Employee, Training, Management Development, Performance Management, Career Planning etc.

4.3.1. Employee Training

- Training of employees take place after orientation.
- Training is the process of enhancing the skills, capabilities and knowledge of employees for doing a particular job.
- Training process moulds the thinking of employees and leads to quality performance of employees. It is continuous and never ending in nature.
- Training is crucial for organizational development and success.
- It is fruitful to both employers and employees of an organization. An employee will become more efficient and productive if he is trained well.
- Training is given on four basic grounds:
  1. New candidates who join an organization are given training. This training familiarize them with the organizational mission, vision, rules and regulations and the working conditions.
  2. The existing employees are trained to refresh and enhance their knowledge.
  3. If any updations and amendments take place in technology, training is given to cope up with those changes. For instance, purchasing a new equipment, changes in technique of production, computer implantment. The employees are trained about use of new equipments and work methods.
  4. When promotion and career growth becomes important. Training is given so that employees are prepared to share the responsibilities of the higher level job.
- In order to achieve its objective, any training program should try to bring positive changes in :
  1. **Knowledge:** It helps a trainee to know facts, policies, procedures and rules pertaining to his job.
  2. **Skills**: It helps him to increase his technical and manual efficiency necessary to do the job.

3. **Attitude:** It moulds his behaviour towards his co-workers and supervisors and creates a sense of responsibility in the trainee.

Need for training

- To match the Employee specifications with the job Requirements and Organizational needs.
- Organizational viability and the transformation process.
- Technological Advances.
- Organizational Complexity.
- Human Relations.
- Change in the job assignments
- To increase productivity
- To improve quality of the products and services
- To improve organizational climate
- To improve health and safety
- To prevent obsolescence
- Effect personal growth
- Minimize the resistance to change
- To act as a mentor

Assessment of training methods

1. Organizational requirements or weakness
2. Departmental requirements or weaknesses
3. Job specifications and employee specifications
4. Identifying specific problems
5. Anticipating future problems
6. Managements requests
7. Observation
8. Interviews
9. Group conferences
10. Questionnaire surveys
11. Test of examinations
12. Check lists
13. Performance Appraisal

Importance of training

- Training enables the management to face the pressure of changing environments.
- Training usually results in the increase of quantity and quality of output.
- Training leads to job satisfaction and higher morale of the employees.
- Trained workers need lesser supervision.
- Trained workers enable the enterprise to face competition from rival organization.
- Training enables employees to develop and rise within the organization and increase their earning capacity.
- It moulds the employee's attitudes and helps them to achieve better co-operation with the organization.

- Trained employees make better economic use of materials and equipment resulting in reduction of wastage and spoilage.
- Training instructs the workers toward better job adjustment and reduces the rate of labour turnover and absenteeism.

Benefits of training programs

- Personal growth.
- Development of new skills.
- Higher earning capacity.
- Helps to adjust with changing technology.
- Increased safety.
- Confidence building.
- Improves morale of employees.
- Less supervision.
- Chances of promotion.
- Increased productivity.

Important steps in training

1. Discovering or identifying training needs.
2. Preparing the instruction or getting ready for the job.
3. Preparing the trainee.
4. Presenting the operation.
5. Try out the trainee's performance.
6. Follow-up or rewards and feedback.

Methods of Training

1. On the job training

- On the job training methods are those which are given to the employees within the everyday working of a concern.
- It is a simple and cost-effective training method.
- Inproficient as well as semi- proficient employees can be well trained by using such training method. Employees are trained in actual working scenario.
- The motto of such training is "learning by doing."
- ***Instances of such on-job training methods are job-rotation, coaching, temporary promotions, etc.***

On-The-Job Training Methods

(a) Job Rotation: This type of training involves the movement of the trainee from one job to another.

The trainee receives job knowledge and gains experience from his supervisor or trainer in each of the different job assignments. Though this method of training is common in training managers for general management positions, trainees can also be rotated from job to job in workshop jobs. This method gives an opportunity to the trainee to understand the problems of employees on other jobs and respect them.

(b) Coaching: The trainee is placed under a particular supervisor who functions as a coach in training the individual. The supervisor provides feedback to the trainee on his performance and offers him some suggestions for improvement. Often the trainee shares some of the duties and responsibilities of the coach and relieves him of his burden.

A limitation of this method of training is that the trainee may not have the freedom or opportunity to express his own ideas.

(c) Job Instruction: This method is also known as training through step by step. Under this method, trainer explains the trainee the way of doing the jobs, job knowledge and skills and allows him to do the job. The trainer appraises the performance of the trainee, provides feedback information and corrects the trainee.

(d) Committee Assignments: Under the committee assignment, group of trainees are given and asked to solve an actual organisational problem. The trainees solve the problem jointly. It develops team work.

(e) Apprenticeship: Apprenticeship is a formalized method of training curriculum program that combines classroom education with on-the-job work under close supervision. The training curriculum is planned in advance and conducted in careful steps from day to day. Most trade apprenticeship programs have duration of three to four years before an apprentice is considered completely accomplished in that trade or profession. This method is appropriate for training in crafts, trades and technical areas, especially when proficiency in a job is the result of a relatively long training or apprenticeship period, e.g., job of a craftsman, a machinist, a printer, a tool maker, a pattern designer, a mechanic, etc.

(f) Internship: Internship is one of the on-the-job training methods. Individuals entering industry in skilled trades like machinist, electrician and laboratory technician are provided with thorough instruction though theoretical and practical aspects.

Apprenticeship training programmes are jointly sponsored by colleges, universities and industrial organisations to provide the opportunity to the students to gain real-life experience as well as employment. Most of the Universities and Colleges encourage students for internship as part of the curriculum as it is beneficial to all concerned.

Advantages of On-the-Job Training:

- It is directly in the context of job
- It is often informal
- It is most effective because it is learning by experience
- It is least expensive
- Trainees are highly motivated
- It is free from artificial classroom situations

Disadvantages of On-the-Job Training:

- Trainer may not be experienced enough to train or he may not be so inclined.
- It is not systematically organized
- Poorly conducted programs may create safety hazards.

2. Off the job training

- Off the job training methods are those in which training is provided away from the actual working condition.
- It is generally used in case of new employees.
- ***Instances of off the job training methods are workshops, seminars, conferences, etc.***

- Such method is costly and is effective if and only if large number of employees have to be trained within a short time period.
- Off the job training is also called as ***vestibule training***, i.e., the employees are trained in a separate area (may be a hall, entrance, reception area, etc. known as a vestibule) where the actual working conditions are duplicated.

Methods of Off the Job Training

Off the job training refers to method of training given outside the company. The different methods adopted in off the job training are the following:

(a) Classroom method/Lecture method:

- The classroom method is used when a group of managers have to be trained in theoretical aspects.
- The training involves using lectures, audio visuals, case study, role play method, group discussions etc. The method is interactive and provides very good results.
- In lecture method trainers used to communicate with spoken words which they want the trainees to learn, it is primarily one way communication of learned capabilities from trainer to audience.
- Lecture method is a popular training methods despite of advanced new technologies such as interactive video and computer assisted instruction, it is least expensive and least time consuming way to present large amount of information efficiently in organized manner.
- It can be employed with large groups of trainees, it also supports other training methods like behavior modeling and technology based techniques.

Advantage :

- It can be used for large groups.
- Cost per trainee is low.
- It reinforces trainers credibility and authority.
- Information is concentrated and organised as desired.
- Efficient and simple and lots of material can be presented within given time.
- Can be personalozed easily.

Disadvantages:

- Low interest of employees.
- It is not learning by practice.
- No authentic feedback mechanism.
- Likely to lead to boredom for employees.
- One way communication with relatively less participation or passive participation.
- The attention span of listener is normally 15-20 minutes.
- Depends completely on trainers effectiveness and information.
- A clear and rigorous verbal presentation requires a great deal of preparation and hence time consuming preparation.

(b) Audio-Visual:

- Audio visual instruction includes overheads, slides and video.
- Video can be used for improving communication skills and customer service skills, it can also illustrate how procedures can be followed.

- Video is rarely used alone, it is normally used along with lectures to show trainees real life experiences and examples.

Merits of Audio visual techniques

- Trainers can review, slow down or speed up the lesson according to expertise of trainees.
- It can be watched multiple times.
- It gives exposure of equipment, problems and events that cannot be easily demonstrated, I.e equipment malfunctions, angry customers or emergencies.
- Training content is not affected by interests and goals of a particular trainer.
- It requires minimum technical knowledge.
- Wide range of realistic examples, quality control possible.

Demerits of Audio visual techniques

- To much content for trainee to learn.
- Poor dialogue between actors.
- Overuse of humor or music.
- Important learning points of training can be confused by drama in the video.
- One-way communication, No feedback mechanism.
- No flexibility for different audience.

(c) Simulation:

- Simulation involves creating atmosphere which is very similar to the original work environment.
- The method helps to train manager handling stress, taking immediate decisions, handling pressure on the jobs etc.
- An actual feel of the real job environment is given here.
- It represents real life situations regarding trainees decisions resulting in outcomes that reflects what would happen if they were on the job.
- Simulations allow trainees to see impact of their decisions in an artificial, risk free environment.
- It is used to teach production and process skills as well as management and interpersonal skills. Simulation closely mimics work environment.
- Simulators replicate the physical equipment that employees use on the job.

Merits of Simulation

- Trainee can concentrate on learning without involving much risk.
- Interest and motivation are high as real job conditions are duplicated.
- This method is helpful in cases where on the job training might result in a serious injury and destruction of valuable equipment and material.
- **Example:** Aeronautical industry

Demerits of Simulation

- It is an expensive method.
- Need constant updating as new informaiton about work environment is obtained

(d) Vestibule Training:

- Mostly this method of training will be used to train technical staff, office staff and employees who deal with tools and machines.

- Employees learn their jobs on the equipment they will be using, but the training is conducted away from the actual work floor by bringing equipments or tools to certain place where training is provided, but not work place.
- Vestibule training allows employees to get a full feel for doing task without real world pressures. Additionally, it minimizes the problem of transferring learning to the job.
- Vestibule training is provided to employees when new or advanced equipment or tools introduced in to the organisation to do a particular job by using them.
- For this purpose such equipment is brought to a separate place to give demonstration and train how to use and that handle it by employees safely.

(e) Case Studies:

- This method involves studying cases from all perspectives, analyzing the various options available to the company for solving problems or address issues and arriving at most suitable answers.
- Trainers develop a habit of looking at problems from various perspectives and hence their decisions as managers will be more realistic and based on sound study and analysis.

Merits of Case Studies

- It promotes analytical thinking.
- It encourages open mindedness.
- It is acceptable to everyone as it deals with detailed description of real life situations.

Demerits of Case Studies

- It may suppress the voice of average trainees as only those having analytical and vocal skills will dominate the sessions
- Preparation of cases involve expenditure and time and the outcome is not quite certain.

(f) Role Playing :

- The trainees act out a given role as they would in a stage play.
- Role players are informed of a situation about the respective roles that they have to play.
- Role playing basically covers topics such as employee-employer relationships, hiring, firing, conducting a post-appraisal interview.

Merits of Role Play

- The outcome and feedback is known immediately.
- Trainees participate in entire proceedings and so they take interest and are involved.
- It develops skill in applying knowledge in areas of human relations.
- It brings about desired changes in behavior and attitudes as the trainees are motivated to think.

Demerits of Role Play

- Role playing may sometimes not adhere to the objectives of training program. The trainees may deviate from the subject being discussed and start giving unrelated examples and explanations.
- Re-enforcement of the desired behavior may be lacking unless follow-up discussion are organized to asses the impact of the session.

(g) Programmed Instructions:

- This involves two essential elements:
- (a) a step-by-step series of bits of knowledge, each building upon what has gone before, and

- (b) a mechanism for presenting the series and checking on the trainee's knowledge.
- Questions are asked in proper sequence and indication given promptly whether the answers are correct.
- This programme may be carried out with a book, a manual or a teaching machine.
- It is primarily used for teaching factual knowledge such as Mathematics, Physics, etc.

(h) Management/Business Games:

- This method involves providing a market situation to the trainee manager and asking him to provide solutions.
- If there are many people to be trained they can be divided into groups and each group becomes a separate team and play against each other.
- This method requires trainees to gather information, analyze it and make decisions.
- Business games are primarily used for management skill development.
- Games stimulate learning because participants are actively involved and because games mimic the competitive nature of business.
- The type of decisions that participants make in games may include all aspects of management practice i.e labour relations, ethics, marketing and finance.

Merits of Business games

- The game helps dealer to develop skills needed for business success.
- Participant must work as team.
- Cohesive groups are developed.

Demerits of Business games: Factual information cannot be taught through this training.

(i) Committee:

- A committee refers to a group of people who are officially appointed to look into a problem and provide solution.
- Trainee managers are put in the committee to identify how they study a problem and what they learn from it.

(j) Readings:

- This method involves encouraging the trainee manager to increase his reading related to his subject and then ask him to make a presentation on what he has learned.
- Information can be collected by trainee manager from books, magazines and internet etc.

Advantages of Off-the-Job Training

- Trainers are usually experienced enough to train
- It is systematically organized
- Efficiently created programs may add lot of value

Disadvantages of Off-the-Job Training:

- It is not directly in the context of job
- It is often formal
- It may not be based on experience.
- It is expensive.
- Trainees may not be much motivated
- It is artificial in nature.

Evaluation of Training Programme

- "Any attempt to obtain information on the effect of training performance and to asses the value of training in the light of that information"
- Evaluation leads to controlling and correcting the training programme.
- **Hamblin** suggested five levels at which evaluation of training can takes place:
  - ❖ Reactions
  - ❖ Learning
  - ❖ Job behavior
  - ❖ Organization
  - ❖ Ultimate value

Criteria to evaluate the effectiveness of training

1. Reaction of participants.
2. Performance of trainees.
3. Performance of the training itself.
4. Behavioral changes in the trainees.
5. Organizational effectiveness.

Kirkpatrick model of training evaluation

- He laid out four levels for evaluation of any training.
- This model is arguably the most widespread for evaluation in use. It is simple, very flexible and complete.
- The four levels as described by Kirkpatrick are as follows:
  1. **Reaction of the Trainee:** Thoughts and feelings of the participants about the training.
  2. **Learning:** The increase in knowledge or understanding as a result of the training.
  3. **Behaviour:** Extent of change in behaviour, attitude or capability
  4. **Results**: The effect on the bottom line of the company as a result of the training.
     - o The fifth level which is the Return on Investment (ROI) has been recently added which is not but a part of the original model.

Systems Model of Training

- Phase 1 : Conducting the needs assessment
- Phase 2 : Designing the training program
- Phase 3 : Implementing the training program
- Phase 4 : Evaluating the training program.

4.3.2. Management development

- Management development providing managerial skills and knowledge to employees.
- Management development is the overall concept that describes the many ways that organizations help employees develop their personal and organizational skills, either as managers in a management job or with an eventual management job in mind.
- Executive or management development is a long – term educational process utilising a systematic and organized procedure by which managerial personnel learn conceptual and theoretical knowledge.

- Management development should produce change in behaviour which is more in keeping with the organization goals than the previous behaviour.
- Management development is a systematic process of growth and development by which the managers develop their abilities to manage.

Objectives of management development

- To provide adequate leaders.
- To increase the efficiency of performance of existing executives.
- To serve as a means of control in operations.
- To train managers for higher assignment who show potential for growth greater than those of their colleagues.
- To prepare them for adaptation to changes, environmental, ideological and technological.
- To develop unity of purpose and improve morale.

Need for executive development

- If there is a shortage of trained managers then organization has to develop the talented employees and maintain an inventory of executive skills to meet the future demands.
- The performance of a company depends upon the quality of its managers. Executive development, therefore, is of paramount importance to have effective and desired managerial talents to meet the organization's demand.
- Obsolescence of managerial skills is another factor, which calls for continuous executive development. A manager must continuously update himself to successfully meet new challenges as they occur.
- To ensure a steady source of competent people at all levels to meet organizational needs at all times.
- To prevent managerial obsolescence by exposing the managers to new concepts and techniques in their respective fields of specialization.
- To prepare the present employees for higher assignments so that they may be promoted from within.
- To develop a second line of competent managers for future replacements.
- To promote a high morale and good organizational climate.

Methods of management development

1. On the Job technique Development carried out during job.

a) **Coaching:** In coaching the trainee is placed under a particular supervisor who acts as an instructor and teaches job knowledge and skills to the trainee.

b) **Job rotation:** This is particularly useful in the development of diversified skills and to give executive a broader outlook, which are very important to the upper management levels.

c) **Understudy:** An understudy is normally chosen with forethought of making available to the organization a subordinate who is equal to his superior in the event of retirement, illness or death of the superior. The subordinate will be able to take over his position and manage as effectively as his boss could.

d) **Multiple management:** This technique is mainly useful in bringing the managers out of their narrow shells and helps them gain a broader outlook and knowledge in different functional areas.

e) **Special projects:** The trainees' may ask to work on special projects related with departmental objectives. By this, the trainees will acquire the knowledge of the assigned work and also learn how to work with others.

f) **Experience:** It refers to learning by doing. This is one of the oldest methods of on-the-job training. Although this is very effective method but it also very time-consuming and wasteful. Thus it should be followed by other training methods.

g) **Committee assignment:** In this, the trainees become members of a committee. The committee is assigned a problem to discuss and make recommendations.

2. Off-the-Job Methods

- These methods require trainees to leave their workplace and concentrate their entire time towards the training objectives.
- These days off-the-job training methods have become popular due to limitations of the on-the-job training methods such as facilities and environment, lack of group discussion and full participation among the trainees from different disciplines, etc.
- In the off-the job methods, the development of trainees is the primary task rest everything is secondary. Following are the main off-the-job training methods:

(a) **Special courses and lectures:** These are the most traditional and even famous today, method of developing personnel. Special courses and lectures are either designed by the company itself or by the management/professional schools. Companies then sponsor their trainees to attend these courses or lectures. These are the quick and most simple ways to provide knowledge to a large group of trainees.

(b) **Conferences and seminars:** In this, the participants are required to pool their thoughts, ideas, viewpoints, suggestions and recommendations. By attending conferences and seminars, trainees try to look at a problem from different angles as the participants are normally from different fields and sectors.

(c) **Selected reading:** This is the self-improvement training technique. The persons acquire knowledge and awareness by reading various trade journals and magazines. Most of the companies have their own libraries. The employees become the members of the professional associations to keep abreast of latest developments in their respective fields.

(d) **Case study method:** This technique was developed by Harvard Business School, U.S.A. It is used as a supplement to lecture method. A case is a written record of a real business situation/problem faced by a company. The case is provided to the trainees for discussion and analysis. Identification and diagnose of the problem is the aim in case study method. Alternate courses of action are suggested from participants.

(e) **Programmed instruction/learning:** This is step-by-step self-learning method where the medium may be a textbook, computer or the internet. This is a systematic method for teaching job skills involving presenting questions or facts, allowing the person to respond and giving the learner immediate feedback on the accuracy of his or her answers."

(f) **Brainstorming:** This is creativity-training technique, it helps people to solve problems in a new and different way. In this technique, the trainees are given the opportunity to generate ideas openly and without any fear of judgement. Criticism of any idea is not allowed so as to reduce inhibiting forces. Once a lot of ideas are generated then they are evaluated for their cost and feasibility.

(g) **Role-playing:** In this method, the trainees are assigned a role, which they have to play in an artificially created situation. For example, a trainee is asked to play the role of a trade union leader and another trainee is required to perform the role of a HR manager. This technique results in better understanding of each other's situation by putting foot in other's shoes.

(h) **Vestibule schools:** Large organisations frequently provide what are described as vestibule schools a preliminary to actual shop experience. As far as possible, shop conditions are duplicated, but instruction, not output is major objective." A vestibule school is operated as a specialised endeavor by the personnel department. This training is required when the amount of training that has to be done exceeds the capacity of the line supervisor; a portion of training is evolved from the line and assigned to staff through a vestibule school." The advantage of a vestibule school is specialisation.

(i) **Apprenticeship training:** This training approach began in the Middle Ages when those who wanted to learn trade skill bound themselves to a master craftsman and worked under his guidance. Apprenticeship training is a structured process by which people become skilled workers through a combination of classroom instruction and on-the-job training.

(j) **In-basket exercise:** In this technique, the trainees are provided background information on a simulated firm and its products, and key personnel. After this, the trainees are provided with in-basket of memos, letters, reports, requests and other documents related with the firm. The trainee must make sense out of this mass of paperwork and prepare memos, make notes and delegate tasks within a limited time period."

(k) **Business games**: Business games involve teams of trainees. The teams discuss and analyse the problem and arrive at decisions. Generally, issues related with inventories, sales, R&D, production process, etc. are taken up for consideration.

(l) **Behaviour modeling**: This is structured approach to teach specific supervisory skill. This is based on the social learning theory in which the trainee is provided with a specific model of behaviour and is informed in advance of the consequences of engaging in that type of behaviour.

(m) **Sensitivity (T-group) training**: In this type of training, a small group of trainees consisting of 10 to 12 persons is formed which meets in an unstructured situation. There is no set agenda or schedule or plan. The main objectives are more openness with each other, increased listening skills, trust, support, tolerance and concern for others. The trainers serve a catalytic role. The group meets in isolation without any formal agenda. There is great focus on inter-personal behaviour. And, the trainer provides honest but supportive feedback to members on how they interacted with one another.

(n) **Multiple management:** This technique of training was first introduced by McCormick, President of McCormick & co. of Baltimore in 1932. He gave the idea of establishing a junior board of directors. Authority is given to the junior board members to discuss any problem that could be discuss in senior board and give recommendations to the senior board. Innovative and productive ideas became available for senior board.

4.3.3. Career Planning

- Career planning aims at matching individual potential for promotion and individual aspirations with organizational needs and opportunities.
- It opens avenues for growth to higher levels of responsibilities for each and every employee of the organization through hierarchy of position and training and development activities to equip the individuals with the requisites for succession.
- The process of establishing career objectives and determining appropriate educational and developmental programs to further develop the skills required to achieve short term or long-term career objectives.

- Career planning is an ongoing process through which an individual sets career goals and identifies the means to achieve them. The process by which individuals plan their life's work is referred to as career planning.
- **Schermerhorn:** "Career planning is a process of systematically matching career goals and individual capabilities with opportunities for their fulfillment."
- **McMahon and Merman:** "Career Planning is a deliberate process of becoming aware of self, opportunities, constraints, choices and consequences; identifying career-related goals; and "career pathing" or programming work, education and related developmental experiences to provide the direction, timing and sequence of steps to attain a specific career goal."
- The tern career denotes all the jobs that are held during one's working life. It is viewed as a sequence of positions held by an individual during the course of his lifetime.
- **Edwin B. Flippo**: "Career as a sequence of separate but related work activities that provide continuity, order and meaning in a person's life."
- **Douglas T. Hall:** "Career as an individually perceived sequence of attitudes and behaviors associated with work related experiences and activities over the span of the person's life."
- **John Lees :**"Effective career planning is about finding a job that works for you, matching who are to the life you are going to lead"
- **James M. Barrie:**"It is not in doing what you like, but liking what you do that is the secret of happiness."

Importance of Career Planning

- To attract competent persons and retain them in the organization.
- To provide suitable promotional opportunities,
- Map out careers of employees suitable to their ability, and their willingness to be trained and developed for higher positions.
- To ensure better utilisation of managerial reserves within an organization.
- To reduce employee dissatisfaction and turnover.
- To correct employee placement.
- To improve employee morale and motivation by matching their skills to job requirements.
- To achieve higher productivity and organization developments.
- To provide guidance and encourage employees needs to fulfill their potentials.

Objectives of Career Planning

- To provide and maintain appropriate manpower resources in the organisation by offering careers, not jobs.
- To provide environment for the effectiveness, efficiency and growth of its employees and motivating them to contribute effectively towards achieving the objectives of the organisation.
- To map out careers of various categories of employees suitable to their ability, and their willingness to be 'trained and developed for higher positions.
- To have a stable workforce by reducing absenteeism and employee turnover.
- To cater to the immediate and future human resourcesss need of the organisation on a timely basis.
- To increase the utilisation of managerial reserves within organisation.

Nature of Career Planning

- **A Process:** Career planning is a process of developing human resources rather than an event.

- **Upward movement:** It involve upward movement in the organizational hierarchy, or special assignments, project work which require abilities to handle recurring problems, human relations issues and so on.
- **Mutuality of Interest:** The individual's interest is served as his needs and aspirations are met to a great extent and the organization's interest is served as each of its human resources is provided an opportunity to develop and contribute to the organizational goals and objectives to the optimum of its ability and confidence.
- **Dynamic:** Career planning is dynamic in nature due to an ever changing environment.

Career Anchors

- **Career anchors** are distinct patterns of self – perceived talents, attitudes, motives and values that guide and stabilize a person's career after several years of real world experiences and feedback.
- Career anchors denote the basic drives that create the urge to take up a certain type of a career. These drives are as follows:
  - **a. Managerial Competence:** Person having this drive seek managerial positions that provide opportunities for higher responsibility, decision making, control and influence over others.
  - **b. Technical Competence:** People having this anchor seek to make career choices based on the technical or functional content of the work. It provide continuous learning and updating one's expertise in a technical or specialised area such as quality control, engineering, accounting, advertising, public relations etc.
  - **c. Security:** If one's career anchor is security than he is willing to do what is required to maintain job security (through compliance with organisational prescriptions), a decent income and a stable future.
  - **d. Creativity:** This drive provides entrepreneurial and innovative opportunities to the people. People are driven by an overwhelming desire to do something new that is totally of their own making.
  - **e. Autonomy:** These people seek a career that provides freedom of action and independence.

Steps in Career Planning Process

1. **Self-Assessment:** The first and foremost step in career planning is self assessment. For this one must need to collect information about them while deciding about a particular career option. Also person must analyze their interests, abilities, aptitudes, desired lifestyle, and personal traits and then study the relationship between the career opted for and self.
2. **Goal Setting:** Set the goals according to academic qualification, work experience, priorities and expectations in life. Once the goal is identified, then determine the feasible ways and objectives how to realize it.
3. **Academic or Career Options:** Analyze the career option by keeping in mind present educational qualification and what more academic degrees one must need to acquire for it. Narrow the general occupational direction to a particular one by an informatory decision making process.
4. **Plan of Action:** Recognize those industries and particular companies where a person wants to get into. Make the detailed plan about length of service in a selected company in order to achieve maximum success, and then switch to another. Decide the position after five years and accordingly work on it.
5. **Catch Hold of Opportunities:** Opportunity comes but once.

Different phases in the career of an employee :

1. **Exploration Stage:** This is the stage where an individual builds expectations about his career. Some of them are realistic and some are not. But the fact is that these could be a result of the individual's ambitions.
2. **Establishment Stage:** This could be at the stage where the individual gets his first job, gets accepted by his peers, learns in this job, and also gains the first tangible evidence of success or failure. The establishment/advancement stage tends to occur between ages 25 and 44. In this stage, the individual has made his or her career choice and is concerned with achievement, performance, and advancement. This stage is marked by high employee productivity and career growth, as the individual is motivated to succeed in the organization and in his or her chosen occupation. Opportunities for job challenge and use of special competencies are desired in this stage. The employee strives for creativity and innovation through new job assignments. Employees also need a certain degree of autonomy in this stage so that they can experience feelings of individual achievement and personal success.
3. **Mid-Career Stage:** The individual's performance levels either continue to improve, or levels, or even deteriorates.
4. **Late Career:** This is regarded as a pleasant phase, where one is allowed to relax and play the role of an elderly statesman in the organization.
5. **Decline:** The stage, where the individual is heading towards retirement.

Remember: E^2MLD

Career Development

- A career is a sequence of work-related positions occupied by a person during a lifetime.
- Career development involves making decisions about an occupation and engaging in activities to attain career goals.
- A career plan is an individual's choice of occupation, organization, and career path.

Five Aspects of a Career

1. Career success or failure is best determined by the individual, in terms of his/her personal goal achievement.
2. No absolute career evaluation standards exist.
3. Examine a career subjectively e.g., values and personality fit and objectively e.g., job choices, competencies needed.
4. Make decisions about occupation and pursue activities to attain career goals lifetime.
5. Consider cultural factors as they impact performance and career opportunities.

Career Resilience

- **Collard:** "The ability to adapt to changing circumstances, even when the circumstances are discouraging or disruptive"
- "The result or outcome of being career self-reliant"
- No longer are individuals advised to think in terms of spending their entire careers in one organization. Rather, they are being led to recognize the temporary nature of all jobs and the need to prepare themselves for redefined career paths that require resilience and an ability to be self-reliant.

- Change in the workplace continues at a rapid pace, affecting careers and career development. Mergers, acquisitions, reengineering, and downsizing are influencing employment patterns and altering the career directions of many. These leads to the concept of Career Resilience.

4.3.4. Performance Appraisal

- **Edwin Flippo:** "Performance Appraisal is the systematic, periodic and impartial rating of an employee's excellence, in matters pertaining to his present job and his potential for a better job,"
- **Dale Beach:** "Performance Appraisal is the systematic evaluation of the individual with regards to his or her performance on the job and his potential for development."
- Organizations use performance appraisals for three purposes:
  1. Administrative
  2. Employee development
  3. Program assessment
- Appraising the performance of individual groups is a common practice of all societies. Appraisal process is formal or informal and is integral part of daily activities.
- Performance appraisal is a method of evaluating the behavior of employees in the work spot, normally including both the qualitative & quantitative aspect of job performance.
- Performance refers to the degree of accomplishment of the task that makes up an individual job. It indicates how well an individual is fulfilling the job demands. Performance is always measured in terms of result and not in efforts.
- Effective performance management systems enable an organization to objectively and systematically rate employee performance, while providing the tools necessary to take that performance level and equate it to compensation actions.

Elements of a good appraisal system

- Reliability and validity
- Standardization
- Training to Appraisers
- Employee access to results
- Post Appraisal Interview
- Not vindictive in nature
- Job relatedness
- Practical viability
- Clear Objectives
- Periodic Review.

Goals of Performance appraisal

- Recognize the efforts and contributions of current staff.
- Reward staff with compensation directly linked to performance.
- Motivate staff to improve performance.
- Orient staff towards goal achievement
- Retain key employees through the use of competitive compensation programs
- Attract quality employees with an effective performance management system
- The key elements of a Performance Management System include the following:
  - ❖ A formal Compensation Philosophy Statement
  - ❖ Salary Administration Program

- A Formal Audit/Success Rating overview on an annual or periodic basis with disclosure of results to management.

Need of Performance appraisal

1. To create and maintain satisfactory level of performance.
2. To contribute to the employees growth & development through training and self & management development program.
3. To help the superior to have a proper understanding about their subordinate.
4. To grid, the job changes with the help of continuous ranking.
5. To facilitate fair and equitable compensation based on performance.
6. To facilitate for resting & validating selection test, interview techniques through comparing their scores with performance appraisal.
7. To providing information for making decision regarding lay off, retrenchment, retirement.
8. To suggest changes in employees behavior.

Purpose of Performance appraisal

1. Identify employees who are eligible for salary increase.
2. Generate data to take personnel decisions such as promotion, transfer and lay-off or termination decision.
3. Determine the training and development needs of the employees.
4. Validate the selection process.
5. To measure whether standards laid down has been achieved by the employees or not.
6. Estimate the future requirement of work force.
7. Helps to recognize potential of promising employees.
8. Helps in motivating employees by providing feedback about their level of performance.

Process of performance appraisal

1. Job analysis, job description and job specification.
2. Establish performance standards.
3. Communicate standards/ expectation to employees.
4. Measure the actual performance.
5. Adjust the actual performance due to environmental influence.
6. Compare performance with that of other and previous.
7. Compare actual performance with standards and find out deviation if any.
8. Communicate actual performance to concerned employees.
9. Suggest changes in job analysis and standards if necessary.
10. Follow up performance appraisal report.

Advantages of Performance Appraisal

1. **SWOT Analysis:** Performance Appraisal gives a complete idea of the employee's strength, weaknesses and based on that their opportunities and threats.
2. **Career Planning:** On the basis of one's own SWOT analysis, an employee can have his career plans.
3. **Suitable Placement:** Performance appraisal enables a company to give suitable placement to an employee based on their talents and skills.
4. **Self-Development:** Performance Appraisal is very much a positive activity which enables an employee to know his own weaknesses and also enables him to remove their weaknesses and lead to self-development.

5. **Effective Training Program:** Training programmes can be drawn out on the basis of the needs of employees to remove their weaknesses.
6. **Sound Personnel Policies:** Personnel policies for promotions, transfer must be sound and objective. Performance Appraisal provides valuable information and reliable data for such decisions.
7. **Employee-Employer Relations:** Will be healthy if performance Appraisal information will be used for personnel management. This will minimize grievances and improve confidence in the management.
8. **Higher Employee Productivity:** Employer morale will be high because there can be a system of rewards for employees with higher performance. This will improve organization productivity.
9. **Human resource planning:** Performance Appraisal will help in potential human resource planning.

Limitations of Performance Appraisal

1. **Personal Bias:** The biggest limitation of performance Appraisal is subjectivity. Due to human element in Appraisal, there is always a fear of one's own opinion coming in the way of Appraisal.
2. **Halo Effect:** The tendency of an individual to rate an employee consistently high due to some earlier good performance rather than his existing performance is called as carrying a halo around oneself.
3. **Horn Effect:** The tendency of a superior to rate a subordinate lower than his performance justifies due to some recent or earlier failures.
4. **Lack of Uniform Standards:** The standards used by different departments in the organisation may not be the same, hence, rating becomes unscientific and employees suffer. Some raters are too liberal while others are too strict causing lack of uniformity.
5. **Appropriate Appraisal Technique:** Selection of appropriate appraisal technique is important to give the correct result. Some of the techniques are time-consuming and costly and so avoided. If wrong techniques are applied performance appraisal results may prove defective.
6. **Wrong Appraisal by Superior :** Superiors have continuous and daily relations with the subordinates, giving accurate ratings may lead to spoiling relations with them which the superiors may want to avoid, hence higher rating to the subordinates.
7. **Stress on Individual and not on Performance:** Performance Appraisal must lay stress on the performance of the individual and not on his individual and not on his personal characteristics. Many a times this is overlooked and the personnel characteristics come in the way of his performance appraisal.
8. **Central Tendency:** Many a times to be on the safer side the rater would put the ratee on average scores. This happens because of two reasons: first of all if the rater does not want low scores to the ratee. Secondly, if he himself is not competent and would not like to show his incompetency.
9. **Lack of Importance to Self-Development:** Performance Appraisal is not for witch hunting but for finding out strengths as well as weaknesses. The strengths can be consolidated upon and the weaknesses too be removed through appropriate training. However, this aspect is not given importance and so the main objective of performance appraisal is neglected.
10. **Lack of Communication and Participation with Employees:** Performance appraisal is not complete without communicating to the employee the results of the appraisal and also gives him a

chance to give his opinion; otherwise it is a one-sided affair without participation of employee and will not lead to their development.

11. **Time-Consuming and Huge Paperwork:** Performance appraisal is a continuous job for the superiors. There is need to continuously observe the subordinates, keep records, fill documents, write reports, hence time-consuming and costly.

Methods of Performance Appraisal

1. **Traditional Methods:** These methods lay more emphasis on rating of individuals' personality traits, such as initiative, dependability, drive, creativity, integrity, intelligence, leadership potential, etc.
   1. Graphic Rating Scale
   2. Ranking Method
   3. Paired Comparison Method
   4. Forced Distribution method
   5. Forced Choice Method
   6. Essay Method
   7. Group Appraisal
   8. Confidential Report
   9. Field Review Method
   10. Check List Method
       a. Simple Check List
       b. Weighted Check List
       c. Critical Incident Method

1.1 Graphic Rating scale or Linear Rating Scale:

- This method lists a set of performance factors such as job knowledge, work quality, cooperation that the supervisor uses to rate employee performance using an incremental scale.
- This is the most commonly used method of evaluating an employee's performance. In this method questionnaire is used to collect the data.
- The questionnaire consists of set of questions covering aspects such as:
  a. Employee characteristics include factors such as initiative, leadership, dependability, attitude, loyalty, creative ability, analytical ability etc.
  b. Employee contribution includes factors such as quantity and quality of work, specific goals achieved regularity, attitude and approach towards supervisors and colleagues, etc.

1.2. Ranking Method: It is the oldest and simplest method of performance appraisal. In this method the employee is ranked from the highest to the lowest or from best to the worst. Thus, if there are five employees the best employee is given the first rank and the worst employee in the group is given the fifth rank.

1.3. Paired Comparison Method: In this method, each employee is compared with the other on one-to-one basis. This method makes judgment easier as compared to ranking method. The number of times the employee is rated as better in comparisons with others determines his or her final ranking.

1.4. Forced Distribution Method: This technique was contributed by ***Joseph Tiffin.*** The method operates under the assumption that an employee's performance can be plotted in a bell-shaped curve. According to a forced distribution performance appraisal, an employee is judged on his own accomplishments. This is rewarding for an employee who values individual achievements over teamwork and team-based goals.

1.5. Forced Choice Method: This method was contributed by ***J.P. Guilford.*** Here, an evaluator rates an employee on the basis of a group of statements. These statements are a combination of positive and negative statements and are arranged in blocks of two or more. The rater is required to identify the most or least descriptive statement pertaining to an employee.

1.6. Essay Method: In this method, the rater writes a narrative description of an employee's strengths, weaknesses, past performance, potential and suggestions for improvement. As the essays are descriptive in nature, it only provides qualitative information about the employee.

1.7. Group Appraisal : In **group rank ordering** the supervisor places employees into a particular classification such as "top one-fifth" and "second one-fifth". If a supervisor has ten employees, only two could be in the top fifth, and two must be assigned to the bottom fifth.

- In **individual ranking** the supervisor lists employees from highest to lowest. The difference between the top two employees is assumed equivalent to the difference between the bottom two employees.
- In **paired comparison** the supervisor compares each employee with every other employee in the group and rates each as either superior or weaker of the pair. After all cômparisons are made, each employee is assigned a summary or ranking based on the number of superior scores received.

1.8. Confidential Report : This is a traditional method of evaluating an employee's performance. It is normally used in Government departments and small business units. Here, the evaluation is done by the immediate boss or supervisor. The main limitation of this method is the ratings are generally not discussed with the ratee (only in case of adverse remark).

1.9. Field Review Method: If during the appraisal process there are reasons to believe that the employee is given a higher rating because of rater bias, a review process is initiated. The review process is generally conducted by the personnel officer of the HR department. This method is also used for making promotional decisions at the managerial level and when information is required from employees of different units and location.

1.10. Check List Method: The main purpose of this method is to reduce the evaluator's burden of rating the employee. In this method a dichotomous questionnaire (A question with two answer choices namely `Yes' or `No') is used. A rater is required to put a tick mark against the respective column. This questionnaire is prepared and scored by the HR department. The main disadvantage of this method is the rater is not given the flexibility to add or delete the statements.

a) Simple Check List: A checklist represents, in its simplest form, a set of objectives or descriptive statements about the employee and his behavior. If the rater believes strongly that the employee possesses a particular listed trait, he checks the item; otherwise, he leaves the item blank.

b) Weighted Check List: A more recent variation of the checklist method is the weighted list. Under this, the value of each question may be weighted equally or certain questions may be weighted more heavily than others. A rating score from the checklist helps the manager in evaluation of the performance of the employee.

Limitation of the checklist method:

- The rater may be biased in distinguishing the positive and negative questions. He may assign biased weights to the questions.
- Another limitation could be that this method is expensive and time consuming.
- Finally, it becomes difficult for the manager to assemble, analyze and weigh a number of statements about the employee's characteristics, contributions and behaviors.
- In spite of these limitations, the checklist method is most frequently used in the employee's performance evaluation.

c) Critical Incident Method

- The supervisor's attention is focused on specific or critical behaviors that separate effective from ineffective performance.
- This method evaluates an employee on the basis of certain `events' or `episodes' known as critical incident. The underlying principle of this method is "there are certain significant acts in each employee's behaviour and performance, which can make all the difference between success and failure on the job."
- Thus, in this method the rater focusses his attention on all those factors, that can make a difference between performing a job in a noteworthy manner

2. Modern Methods :

1. 360^0 Performance Appraisal
2. Behaviourally Anchord Rating Scales(BARS)
3. Assessment Centres
4. Human Resource Accounting
5. Management by Objectives(MBO)
6. Behaviour Observation scales
7. Psychological Appraisal
8. Result Method
9. Productivity Measures
10. Balance Scorecard

2.1. 360^0 performance appraisal

- 360 Degree appraisal is a method of appraisal in which people receive performance feedback from those on all sides of them in the organization their boss, their colleagues and peers and their subordinates.
- Multiple raters are involved in evaluating performance; the technique is called 360-degree appraisal viz.: Supervisors, Peers, Subordinates, Self Appraisal, Customers and Consultants etc.
- The 360-degree technique is understood as systematic collection of performance data on an individual or a group derived from a number of stakeholders: the stakeholders being the immediate team members, customers, peers and self.
- The 360-degree appraisal provides a broader perspective about an employee's performance. In addition, the technique facilitates greater self-development of the employee. It enables an employee to compare his evaluation about self with perceptions of others. Though this method was developed to bring about a degree of objectivity, it still suffers from subjectivity.
- This multi-source feedback method provides a comprehensive perspective of employee performance by utilizing feedback from the full circle of people with whom the employee

interacts: supervisors, subordinates and co-workers. It is effective for career coaching and identifying strengths and weaknesses.

2.2 Behaviorally Anchored Rating Scales (BARS)

- In order to overcome the problem of judgmental evaluation, this method was conceived by some organizations. This method combines the benefits of Essay Method, Critical Incident and Rating scales.
- In this method the employee's behaviour and performance dimensions are analyzed and used for evaluating the performance of the employee. The HR department is involved in the process of preparing the BARS.
- Based on the Employee's performance and behaviour, employees are anchored in different slots of good, average and poor. The rater is required to give corresponding ratings to the employee.
- BARS combine elements from critical incident and graphic rating scale approaches. The supervisor rates employees according to items on a numerical scale.

Construction of BARS

a. Collect critical incident
b. Identify performance dimension.
c. Reclassification of incidents
d. Assessing scale values to the incidents.
e. Producing final instruments.

2.3 Assessment Centres

- This method was used to appraise army officers in Germany way back in 1930s. The concept was adapted from army to business arena in 1960s.
- In India, the concept has been adopted by organisations such as Crompton Greaves, Eicher, Hindustan Lever and Modi Xerox recently.
- This method is mainly used to evaluate executive and supervisory potential. Here employees are taken to a place away from work and a series of tests and exercises are administered. For example, assesses are asked to participate in; in-basket exercise, simulations, group exercise and role plays.
- Performance of the employee is evaluated in each of these tests and feedback is provided to the ratee, in terms of strengths and weaknesses.
- In this approach, individuals from various departments are brought together, to spend two or three days working, as an individual or group assignment similar to the ones they would be handling when promoted.
- Observers rank the performance of each and every participant in order of merit. This appraisal is mainly used for promotion purpose.

2.4 Human Resource Accounting (HRA)

- This method evaluates an employee's performance in relation to the contribution of an employee in monetary terms.
- Human Resource Accounting measures the cost and contribution of human resources in the organisation. The cost includes the cost of recruitment, selection, induction, training, salaries and other facilities, etc. Contribution is the money value of the service of the employees. This service is measured by labour productivity. If the contribution is more than the cost, then the employee performance is positive and vice-versa.

- Here the rater evaluates the employee in terms of cost of retaining the employee and the benefits the organisation derives from him or her.
- The following factors are taken into account in this method :
    - o Cost of training the employee.
    - o Quality of product or service rendered.
    - o Accidents, damages, errors, spoilage, wastages etc.
    - o The time spent in appraising the employee.

2.5 Management by objectives (MBO)

- This method was propounded by ***Alfred Sloans and Donaldson Brown*** in 1920s. However, it was further popularised by ***Peter Drucker*** in his book ***"The Practice of Management"*** in 1954.
- **George S. Odiorne:** MBO can be described as "a process whereby the superior and the immediate subordinate of an organisation jointly identify the common goals, define each individual's major areas of responsibility in terms of results expected of him and use these measures as guides for operating the unit and assessing the contribution of each of its members."
- In this method emphasis is laid on stating objectives for *Key Result Areas (KRAs) in Quantifiable terms.*
- MBO is used as a performance appraisal technique, as it is easy to measure whether the stated objectives have been achieved or not.
- MBO evaluates how well an employee has accomplished objectives determined to be critical in job performance.
- This method aligns objectives with quantitative measures such as sales, profits, zero-defect units produced.
    - ❖ Joint goal setting
    - ❖ Action planning
    - ❖ Self-control
    - ❖ Periodic progress review

2.6 Behaviour Observation Scales

- Rating system used in identifying how often employees or trainees display the preferred behavior.
- Behavioral observation is a method used to measure the behavior and value of employees whose job performance cannot be evaluated on the basis of productivity alone. Such measurements are usually made based on a behavioral observation scale that is used to evaluate everyone in a comparable manner.
- Such scales are generally used to record whether or not an employee engages in a certain type of behavior or action and, if so, how often.
- Each employee's result from the behavioral observation scale can be compared to other employees' results or to some objective baseline for expected behavior.
- Evaluation of this sort can be used to ensure that an employee is meeting expectation or to determine if disciplinary action is necessary.

2.7 Psychological Appraisal

- Psychological appraisal is done to find out the conceptual skills, human skills, technical skills, etc. of the employee. It is done by different methods, such as in-depth interviews, psychological tests, consultations and discussions with the employees, superiors, subordinates and others, who are working with the employee.
- Large organizations employ full time industrial psychologist.

- Here psychologists are used for evaluations they assess an individual's future potential and not past performance.

2.8 Result Method

Organizations of the contemporary periods evaluate employee performance based on accomplishments they achieved rather than on the behavioural traits. An employee accomplishment includes sales turnover, number of units produced, number of customers served, number of complaints settled etc.

2.9 Productivity Measures

In this method employees are appraised based on the ratio of output they turned out to the input they used. example, sales to employee salary and benefits, number of clients served per day etc. These measures are not free from limitations as measurement of all kinds of output as well as all kinds of input would be difficult.

2.10 Balance Scorecard

- The balanced scorecard is a strategic planning and management system that is used extensively in business and industry, government, and nonprofit organizations worldwide to align business activities to the vision and strategy of the organization, improve internal and external communications, and monitor organization performance against strategic goals.
- It was originated by ***Dr. Robert Kaplan*** and ***David Norton*** as a performance measurement framework that added strategic non-financial performance measures to traditional financial metrics to give managers and executives a more 'balanced' view of organizational performance.
- Robert S. Kaplan and David P. Norton published the book, *"The Balanced Scorecard : Translating Strategy into Action"*
- 'A strategic planning and management system used to align business activities to the vision statement of an organization'.
- The Balanced Scorecard goes beyond standard financial measures to include the following additional perspectives: the customer perspective, the internal process perspective, and the learning and growth perspective.
    - **Financial perspective** - Includes measures such as operating income, return on capital employed, and economic value added.
    - **Customer perspective** - Includes measures such as customer satisfaction, customer retention, and market share in target segments.
    - **Business process perspective** - Includes measures such as cost, throughput, and quality. These are for business processes such as procurement, production, and order fulfillment.
    - **Learning & growth perspective** - Includes measures such as employee satisfaction, employee retention, skill sets, etc.
- Each perspective of the Balanced Scorecard includes objectives, measures of those objectives, target values of those measures, and initiatives, defined as follows:
    - **Objectives** - major objectives to be achieved, for example, profitable growth.
    - **Measures** - the observable parameters that will be used to measure progress toward reaching the objective. For example, the objective of profitable growth might be measured by growth in net margin.

- **Targets** - the specific target values for the measures, for example, +2% growth in net margin.
- **Initiatives** - action programs to be initiated in order to meet the objective.

Balanced Scorecard as a Strategic Management System

- The Balanced Scorecard originally was conceived as an improved performance measurement system. However, it soon became evident that it could be used as a management system to implement strategy at all levels of the organization by facilitating the following functions. These functions have made the Balanced Scorecard an effective management system for the implementation of strategy.

1. **Clarifying strategy** - The translation of strategic objectives into quantifiable measures clarifies the management team's understanding of the strategy and helps to develop a coherent consensus.
2. **Communicating strategic objectives** - The Balanced Scorecard can serve to translate high level objectives into operational objectives and communicate the strategy effectively throughout the organization.
3. **Planning, setting targets, and aligning strategic initiatives** - Ambitious but achievable targets are set for each perspective and initiatives are developed to align efforts to reach the targets.
4. **Strategic feedback and learning** - Executives receive feedback on whether the strategy implementation is proceeding according to plan and on whether the strategy itself is successful ("double-loop learning").

A Performance Evaluation Tool (PET)

- The performance evaluation is conducted between the employee and their immediate supervisor, in which the supervisor evaluates the performance of the employee.
- The supervisor provides feedback to the employee regarding their performance and areas of concern.
- The evaluated performance level during the evaluation will be used for justifying personnel actions relative to promotion, transfer, and salary adjustments.
- It is the intent of the Company to make salary increases and related personnel actions based on an employee's evaluated performance in their assigned position, and the individual's overall contribution.
- Performance evaluations are to be conducted at the completion of the introductory period, on an as-needed basis during the year, and no less than two times every twelve months.
- It is intended that this should provide adequate feedback, allows for corrective action, and substantiate salary increases and related personnel actions.
- The prime consideration in the performance appraisal system is enhancement in overall performance.
- The process is expected to enhance the development of meaningful communication between the employee and their supervisor, which in turn should lead to such improvement in the employee's overall performance.

1. **Outstanding:** Performance substantially and consistently above required standards for the position.

2. **Competent:** Consistently meets objectives and produces the desired results that are expected for a qualified employee in this position. Performance meets required standards for the position.
3. **Needs Improvement:** Areas of improvement are noted. Performance is less than expected, and below required standards for the position. Consideration must be given to probationary status pending improvement of performance.
4. **Unsatisfactory:** Does not meet objectives. Performance substantially and consistently below required standards for the position. If significant improvement is not made, termination will follow.

4.3.5. Promotions

- **Paul Pigors and C.A. Myers** defined "Promotion is advancement of an employee to a better job: better in terms of greater responsibility, more prestige or status, greater skill and especially increased rate of pay or salary."
- **Prof. Mamoria:** 'Promotion is a term which covers a change and calls for greater responsibilities, and usually involves higher pay and better terms and conditions of service and, therefore, a higher status or rank.'
- **Arun Monappa and Mirza S.Saiyadain:** "The upward reassignment of an individual in an organization's hierarchy, accompanied by increased responsibilities, enhanced status and usually with increased income though not always so."
- Employees expect to be informed about ladders of promotion, how they can prepare themselves for advancement and what will be expected of them from the higher rated jobs.

Types of Promotion

1. **Limited Promotion**: also known as upgrading, means an increase of pay on the same job or moving to a higher scale without changing the job.
2. **Dry Promotion**: is a promotion as a result of which there is no increase in the employee's pay.
3. **Multiple Chain Promotion:** provides for a systematic linking of each position to several other positions.
4. **Up and Out Promotion:** means that a person must either earn a promotion or seek employment elsewhere.
5. **Vertical Promotion:** Employee is move to the next higher level, in the organizational hierarchy with greater responsibility, authority, pay and status.

Basis of Promotion

1. **Promotion based on Seniority:** The employees are promoted to higher positions purely based on their length of service irrespective of their qualifications, experience, performance and track record. Trade unions prefer seniority as a basis of promotion.
2. **Promotion based on Merit:** Employees are promoted to higher positions purely on their performance and work record. The management will look into the qualifications, experience, previous work record, performance capability, etc.
3. **Merit –cum-Seniority Promotion:** Both the service seniority and work efficiency will be taken into account in promoting an employee. This is considered as the best method of promotion as it gives due weightage to the skill, efficiency, and better service record of the employee.
4. **Promotion by Selection:** A process through which employees are promoted after undergoing rigorous test and screening.

5. **Time Bound Promotion:** Employees would be promoted according to standards of time set for promotions to higher cadre subject to the condition that they possess the minimum qualifications required.
6. **Temporary Promotion:** Also known as officiating promotion scheme, officials are promoted temporarily to higher positions in case there are vacancies.

Promotion Policy

- There should be a definite promotion policy which should be effective and protect the interests of the employees due for promotion.
- Leads to more job satisfaction and retention.
- Promotion policy should be evolved considering the following points :
  - ❖ Promotion Policy Statement.
  - ❖ Ratio of Internal Promotion vs External Recruitment.
  - ❖ Decide the Basis for Promotion.
  - ❖ Decide the Routes for Promotion.
  - ❖ Communicate the Promotion Policy.
  - ❖ Lack of Promotional Avenues.
  - ❖ Determination of Seniority.
  - ❖ Relationship of Disciplinary Action to Promotion.

4.3.6. Demotions

- Demotion is a process by which the employee is downgraded and sent to a lower position from the one he is holding at present, with less responsibility, status or compensation.

Causes of Demotion

- Demotion may be used as a disciplinary weapon.
- Demotion may be resorted to when employees, because of ill health or personal reasons, cannot do their job properly.
- If a company curtails some of its activities, employees are often required to accept lower-level position until normalcy is restored.
- If an employee finds it difficult to meet job requirements standards, following his promotion he may be reverted to his old position.

4.3.7. Transfer

- Transfers may be either organization-initiated or employee-initiated.
- **Yoder** : "A lateral shift causing movement of individuals from one position to another usually without involving any marked change in duties, responsibilities, skills needed or compensation."
- A transfer may be either temporary or permanent, depending upon the need, and may occur within a department, between departments and divisions, or between plants within a company.

Types of Transfers

1. **General:** Such transfers are normally affected during a particular period of the year wherein all employees having completed a given period of service in a post or at a place are involved, especially government departments.
2. **Production:** transfers are normally made from one department to another where the need for the employee is more, especially to avoid lay-off.
3. **Replacement:** transfers are affected to replace persons leaving the organization, due to resignations, retirements, dismissal or death.
4. **Shift:** This type of transfers is transfers of workers from one shift to another on the same type of work.
5. **Remedial:** Transfers are made to remedy some situation primarily concerned with the employee on the job.
6. **Versatility:** A transfer increases the versatility of the employee by shifting him from one job to another.
7. **Punishment or Penal:** Transfer is made as punishments to erring employees.
8. **Request Transfers:** Normally done on humanitarian grounds.
9. **Mutual Transfers:** Mutual transfer between two employees.

Transfer Policy

- Every organization should have a just and impartial transfer policy which should be known to each employee.
- The absence of a well-formulated transfer policy will breed a state of uncertainty amongst the employees.

4.3.7. Separation

- Separation means cessation of service of agreement with the organization which can be a result of:

1. **Resignation:** A resignation is a voluntary separation. A study of exit interviews over a period of time is needed.
2. **Discharge:** This involves permanent separation of an employee from the organization because of poor performance , violation of rules or poor code of conduct. Discharges are generally made in accordance with the standing orders.
3. **Dismissal**: The termination of the services of an employee by way of punishment for some misconduct, or for prolonged absence from duty. It must be supported with a just and sufficient cause.
4. **Retrenchment**: It is termination of service due to redundancy. The principle in the procedure of retrenchment is that the last person employed in each category must be the first person to be retrenched.
5. **Golden Handshake**: It is a method of retrenchment wherein the employees with a certain minimum service can opt for voluntary retirement and get a fat lumpsum in return .
6. **Lay off:** A layoff refers to an indefinite separation of the employee from the pay roll due to factors beyond the control of the employer. The employee is expected to be called back in the forseeable future. Layoff is resorted to by the employer for factors beyond his control such as :
   a. Fluctuations in the market resulting in loss of sales.

b. Shortage of raw materials or power.
c. Accumulation of stock.
d. Breakdown of machinery.
e. Production delays.

7. **Retirement:** In India, the retirement age is 58 or 60 years. Workers may need preparation through counseling.

4.4. QUALITY OF WORK LIFE (QWL)

- Quality of Work Life comprises systematic efforts made by organizations to give workers a greater opportunity to affect the way they do their jobs and the contributions they make to the organization's overall effectiveness.
- Quality of work environment shapes the personality of the employees of an organization and leads to their commitment to the organization.
- **Richard and Loy:** "QWL is the degree to which members of a work organization are able to satisfy important personal needs through their experience in the organization".
- High morale, job satisfaction, a sense of security, healthy and safe environment at the work place, concern for labour welfare go a long way in enhancing production, improving quality and overall growth of the employee and employer alike.
- Quality of work means incorporating socio–physiological needs of employees into the requirements of particular technology and structures or processes of an organization.
- It also involves economic rewards and benefits for the employees.
- Quality of work ensures the satisfaction of workers towards their job, which in turn ensures higher productivity.
- There are many factors that can contribute to QWL. They are:
  - ❖ Adequate compensation to meet the needs of the socially determined standard of living.
  - ❖ Healthy and safe working conditions.
  - ❖ Respect for individual's personal rights and the principles of natural justice and equity.
  - ❖ Balance between work and family life.
  - ❖ Security and growth opportunity.

Effects of Quality of Work Life

- **Job involvement**: Job involved people spend more time on job and turn out better performance.
- QWL gives employee job satisfaction. High job satisfaction leads to high work performance, less employee turnover and less absenteeism.
- As employees engage themselves more and more in work activities, they acquire a great sense of competence and experience and higher level of job involvement.
- The general perception is that an improvement in QWL costs much to the organization.
- But it may not be so as the financial costs incurred on improving the QWL may be offset by the increase in productivity.

4.5. QUALITY CIRCLES (QCs)

- Started in Japan in the early 1960s, QCs have spread all over the world.
- Quality Circles became extremely popular in the 1980s, particularly in the aerospace, automobile, steel and consumer goods industries.

- The primary topics of discussion in most QCs are related to quality, but they also consider others such as cost, safety and efficiency.
- QC members identify a problem, study it and present their recommendations for change and improvement to a committee.
- A quality circle (QC) is a group of employees that meet regularly to solve problems affecting its work area. The ideal size of the group is six to eight members.
- A quality circle generally recommends solutions for quality which may be implemented by management.
- The main features of a quality circle are as follows:
  - A quality circle is a voluntary group.
  - Members meet at periodic intervals to discuss quality-related activities.
  - A quality circle has its own terms of reference and offers recommendations to management for implementation.
  - Members of a quality circle vary between six to eight members and generally they come from a particular work area.
  - The ultimate purpose of a quality circle is to improve organizational functioning.

Advantage of Quality Circles

- Generation of Creative Ideas.
- Improvement in Productivity.
- Better Teamwork.
- Higher Motivation.
- Development of Problem Solving Skills.

Necessary Conditions for making Quality Circles effective

- Top management support.
- Education and training of managers and workers.
- Timely implementation of ideas generated by quality circles.
- Sharing gains in productivity with workers.
- Facilities for meetings and discussions.
- Regular monitoring of working of quality circles.

4.6. HR AUDIT

- HR records provide information regarding the utilization of human resources in an objective way.
- Human resource audit implies a critical examination and evaluation of policies, programs and procedures in the area of HR management.
- It is a periodic review to measure the effectiveness of HR management and also to determine further steps for a more effective use of human resources.

Significance of HR Audit

1. The management now feels that employee participation in organizational activities is essential for the success of the organization.
2. It provides the required feedback.
3. Rising labor costs and increasing opportunities for competitive advantage in human resource management.
4. It can be used to avoid the intervention of Government to protect employee interests.

4.7. THE McKINSEY 7S FRAMEWORK

- Ensuring That All Parts of Your Organization Work in Harmony.
- The McKinsey 7S framework developed in the early 1980s by ***Tom Peters and Robert Waterman***, two consultants working at the McKinsey & Company.
- The basic premise of the model is that there are seven internal aspects of an organization that need to be aligned if it is to be successful.
- The 7S model can be used in a wide variety of situations where an alignment perspective is useful in following manner:
    - ❖ Improve the performance of a company.
    - ❖ Examine the likely effects of future changes within a company.
    - ❖ Align departments and processes during a merger or acquisition.
    - ❖ Determine how best to implement a proposed strategy.

The Seven 'S' Elements :

A. **Hard Elements**: "Hard" elements are easier to define or identify and management can directly influence them.

1. **Strategy:** The plan devised to maintain and build competitive advantage over the competition.
2. **Structure:** The way the organization is structured and who reports to whom.
3. **Systems:** The daily activities and procedures that staff members engage in to get the job done.

B. **Soft Elements:** "Soft" elements, on the other hand, can be more difficult to describe, and are less tangible and more influenced by culture.

4. **Shared Values:** called "super ordinate goals" when the model was first developed, these are the core values of the company that are evidenced in the corporate culture and the general work ethic.
5. **Style:** The style of leadership adopted.
6. **Staff:** The employees and their general capabilities.
7. **Skills:** the actual skills and competencies of the employees working for the company.

Interdependency of the elements:

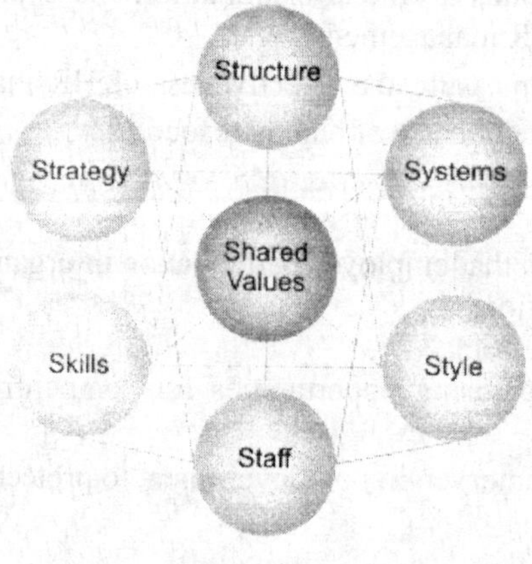

4.8. OCTAPACE CULTURE

- **OCTAPACE:** Openness, Confrontation, Trust, Authenticity, Proactively, Autonomy, Collaboration, and Experimenting.
- Organizational Culture can be defined as cumulative, crystallized and quasi-stable shared life style of people as reflected in the presence of some states of life over others, in the response predispositions towards several significant issues and phenomena (attitudes), in the organized ways of filling time in relation to certain affairs (rituals), and in the ways of promoting desired and preventing undesirable behavior (sanctions) The most important aspect of organizational culture are the values it practices.
- Eight values may be examined to develop the profile of an organizational culture that is called OCTAPACE.

1. **Openness**: The comparative openness in the system should influence the design of HRS. The degree of openness of the organizations will be an important factor in determining the nature of the various dimensions of HRD being designed, as well as the way in which these dimensions should be introduced. Organizations which are fairly open may start with several confronting designs of HRS.
2. **Confrontation**: Confrontation is used in relation to problem putting the front rather than the back to escaping the problems. A better term would be confrontation exploration that implies facing a problem and working jointly with other concerned to find its solution. If an organization encourages people to recognize a problem, bring it to people concerned, explore with them to under it and search possible ways of dealing with it.
3. **Trust:** Trust introducing the HRD in an organization trust in another factor which should be considered along with openness. If the level of trust is low, the various dimensions of HRS are likely to be seen with suspicion and therefore the credibility of the system may go down.
4. **Authenticity:** Authenticity is the value underlying trust. It is the willingness of a person to acknowledge the feelings he has, and accept himself as well as other who relate to him as persons. Authenticity is reflected in the narrowest gap between the stated vales and the actual behavior. This value is important for the development of a culture of mutuality.
5. **Proactive**: Proactive can be contrasted with the term react. It in the later action is in response to an act from some source, while in the former the action is taken independently of act form the other source. Pro-action means anticipating issues in advancing to take advantage of this undertaking conflict or responding to needs of the future in fact creating the future.
6. **Autonomy**: Autonomy is the willingness to use power without fear and helping other to do same. It multiplies power in system and the basis is collaboration.
7. **Collaboration:** Collaboration involves working together during one another strengths for a common cause. Individuals instead of solving their problems by themselves share their concerns with one another and prepare strategies working out plan of actions and implement them together.
8. **Experimenting**: Experimenting as a value emphasizes the importance given to innovating and trying out new ways of dealing with problems in the organization.
A profile of an organization on these aspects may help to decide what elements of HRS should be introduced in what sequences in the organization.

4.9 HRD MATRIX

- **T.V. Rao** has evolved the HRD matrix linking HRD subsystems with different development dimensions.
- HRD Matrix identifies the interrelationships between HRD instruments, processes, outcomes and organizational effectiveness.
- HRD instruments include performance appraisal, counseling, role analysis, potential development, training, reward system, job enrichment, etc.
- These mechanisms may vary depending upon the size of the organization, the commitment of the top management, the environment, the culture and climate, the perception of the people, technology used, methods employed by the competitors, etc.
- These instruments lead to generation of HRD processes like role clarity, development planning, development climate, risk-taking and dynamism in employees. Such HRD processes should result in more competent, satisfied and dynamic people is likely to do better than which does not believe in HRD concept and committed people who, by their contributions, would make the organisation grow.
- Such HRD outcomes influence organisational effectiveness in the long-run. It may be noted that organisational effectiveness also depends on a number of other variable like environment, technology, competitors, etc. However, other things being the same, an organisation that has competence.

4.10. HR SCORECARD

- HR scorecard measures the HR function's effectiveness and efficiency in producing employee behaviors needed to achieve the company's strategic goals.
- HR scorecards are developed based on the work of ***Robert Kaplan and David Norton.***
- There are seven steps required to develop HR score card ,so that the result are statistically measure :
  1. Define business strategy
  2. Outline company value chain
  3. Identify business required organizational outcomes strategy
  4. Identify required workforce
  5. Identify relevant HR system
  6. Design of HR score card for measurement purpose
  7. A periodic revaluation based on measurement system from score card.
- The goal of an HR scorecard is to help businesses determine the value of their human resources departments. The challenge often is daunting because unlike most departments or divisions within a company, measurement tools traditionally have been lacking for HR purposes.

HRD Score Card :

1. Aims at evaluating and improving HRD competencies in any organization
2. Applicable to all types of organizations.

3. Based on integrated HRD systems models and HRD Audit methods developed by ***T.V. Rao and Udai Pareek*** in India.
4. Focuses on People and HR practices
5. Based on HRD: HRD strategies, structure, competencies, styles, and culture and takes into consideration Quality concerns and OD
6. Does not believe that organization could be classified into any one stage or level, assumes that any organization could be assessed on a 10-point maturity scale on any given dimension.
7. Useful to improve HRD competencies (strategies, structure, systems, people competencies) of any organization.
8. Provides insights into strengthening HRD and making it more business driven.

4.11. HUMAN DEVELOPMENT INDEX (HDI)

- The **Human Development Index (HDI)** is a composite statistic of life expectancy, education, and income indices to rank countries into four tiers of human development.
- It was created by economist **Mahbub ul Haq**, followed by economist Amartya Sen in 1990, and published by the United Nations Development Programme.
- To produce the Human Development Reports, Mahbub ul Haq brought together a group of well-known development economists including: Paul Streeten, Frances Stewart, Gustav Ranis, Keith Griffin, Sudhir Anand and Meghnad Desai. But it was Nobel laureate Amartya Sen's work on capabilities and functionings that provided the underlying conceptual framework.

4.12.5S- HOUSEKEEPING PRACTICES

- The elements of 5S are all valuable in their own right but they simply form part of the bigger picture of establishing good practice.
- They sit alongside the other elements of Lean , or Just in Time, or World Class and some of the elements in, for example, Seiton (standardisation) are in fact straight lifts from textbooks on other forms of improvement activity.
- 5S is the beginning of a healthy, comfortable and productive life for every at work. This is fundamental to productivity improvement.
- When implemented successfully in a company, 5S brings about amazing changes.
- The driving force for a 5S program comes from people.
- 5S is an acronym for five Japanese words, i.e. ***Seiri, Seiton, Seiso, Seiketsu and Shitsuke.***

1	Seiri	Sorting	Sisih
2	Seiton	Simplify, Set in order	Susun
3	Seiso	Sweep, shine	Sapu
4	Seiketsu	Standardize	Seragam
5	Shitsuke.	Sustain, Self-disciplined	Sentiasa Amal

Definition of 5S

1. **Seiri :** To sort and systematically discard items that are not needed in the workplace.
2. **Seiton:** To arrange necessary items in a neat and systematic manner so that they can be easily retrieved for use and to return after use.
3. **Seiso:** To clean and inspect the workplace thoroughly so that there is no dirt on the floor, machines and equipments.
4. **Seiketsu :** To maintain a high standard of workplace organization by keeping everything clean and orderly at all times.
5. **Shitsuke:** To train people to practise the 5S system continuously so that it becomes habitual and ingrained in the culture of organization.

4.13. OBJECTIVE QUESTION - ANSWER

1. The sequence of human resource development activities according to Leonard Nadler are
(A)Education, training and development
(B)Development, training and education
(C)Training, education and development
(D)Training, development and education

Answer: C

2. Which of the following is the focus of the Human Resource Development System?
(A) Individuals and Dyads
(B)Collectives and Organization
(C) Both (A) and (B)
(D)None of the above

Answer : C

3. Which of the following are the sub systems of HRD?
(A) Training
(B) Performance appraisal
(C)Career development and counseling
(D)All the above

Answer : D

4. Match the following :

(a)	Fish-Bone Analysis	(i) Paul Branthal et. al
(b)	Balance Score Card	(ii) Frederick Herzberg
(c)	Learning and Performance Cycle	(iii) Ishikawa
(c)	Job Enrichment	(iv) Kaplan and Norton

Codes :

	(a)	(b)	(c)	(d)
(A)	(ii)	(iv)	(iii)	(i)
(B)	(iii)	(i)	(iv)	(ii)
(C)	(iv)	(ii)	(i)	(iii)
(D)	(iii)	(iv)	(i)	(ii)

Answer: D

5. Who is associated with 'The Human Capital Approach' of HRD ?
(A)Dalton E. McFarland
(B)T.W. Schultz
(C)T.V. Rao
(D)Rensis Likert

Answer: B

6. The goal of HRD system is to develop the capabilities of each employee:
(A) as an individual and in relation to his or her present role
(B) in relation to his or her expected future role and dyadic relationship between employee and his/her supervisor.
(C) Both (A) and (B)
(D) None of the above

Answer: C

7. Which of the following is not a sub-system of HRD?
(A)Training and Development
(B) Career Planning
(C) Performance Appraisal
(D) None of the above

Answer: D

8. The HRD matrix linking HRD sub-systems with development dimensions has been evolved by
(A)Dharani P. Sinha
(B) D.M. Pestonjee
(C)T.V. Rao
(D) Udai Pareek

Answer: C

9. Who is not associated with development of human development index?
(A)Mahabub-ul-Haq
(B)Manmohan Singh
(C)Meghnad Desai
(D)Sudhir Anand

Answer: B

10. Which of the following factors are included in the calculation of human development index?
(A) Life expectancy
(B) Adult literacy
(C) Decent standard of living
(D) All the above

Answer: D

11. The concept of HRD scorecard was introduced in India by
(A) Udai Pareek
(B) Rao and Pareek
(C) T.V. Rao
(D) Arun Honappa

Answer: C

12. Which of the following is most important for HRD?
(A) to be clearly related to the organization's objectives
(B) to be clearly related to the expertise in the department
(C) to be flexible to be able to respond to sudden crisis
(D) to operate as an extension of the HRM department

Answer: A

13. Who has given the concept of OCTAPACE culture
(A) Dharni P. Sinha
(B)T. V. Rao
(C) D. M. Pestonjee
(D) Udai Pareek

Answer: D

14. In OCTAPACE instrument of HRD culture , the words O, T, and P stand for :
(A)Openness, Team, and Performance
(B)Organisation, Training, and Potential
(C)Opinion, T-Group, and Probability
(D)Openness, Trust, and Pro-action

Answer: D

15. OCTAPACE culture means
(A) Openness-cooperation-Truth-Authenticity-Proaction-Autonomy-Collaboration-Experimentation
(B) Openness-Confrontation-Trust-Autonomy-Proaction-Authority-Collaboration-Experimentation
(C) Openness-Confrontation-Trust-Authority-Proaction-Autonomy-cooperation-Experimentation
(D) Openness-Confrontation-Trust-Authenticity-Proaction-Autonomy-Collaboration-Experimentation

Answer: D

16. Empowerment means authority to make decisions in ones area of operation
(A) by taking approval from the senior
(B) without having to get approval from anyone else
(C) without caring for the consequences
(D) All the above

Answer: B

17. Who has advanced the Bottom of the Pyramid concept ?
(A) Garry Dessler (B) Peter Drucker
(C) C.K. Prahlad (D) Michael Porter

Answer: C

18. Which one is part of Michael Porter's generic strategies ?
(A) Cost leadership strategy
(B) Focus strategy
(C) Differentiation strategy
(D) All the above

Answer: D

19. Which one is not a part of M.C. Kinsy's 7's frame work ?
(A) Standards (B) Structure
(C) Skills (D) Strategy

Answer: A

20. Under McKinsey's 7 S model, the soft S's are:
(A) Style (B) Staff
(C) Skills (D)All the above

Answer: D

21. Which of the following is not one of the 5s of housekeeping ?
(A) Sort (B) Systemize
(C) Specialize (D) Shine

Answer: C

22. "A place for everything, everything in its place" is
(A)American Management
(B) 5S Practice
(C) Peter Principle
(D)A Chinese Practice

Answer: B

23. Robert Kaplan is associated with
(A)A Benchmark Practice
(B)Balanced Score Card
(C)Kaizen
(D) Quality of Life

Answer: B

24. During whose prime ministership the New Economic Policy was introduced in India ?
(A) Indira Gandhi (B) Rajiv Gandhi
(C) P.V.Narasimha Rao (D)A.B.Vajpayee

Answer: C

25. Who has advance the PDCA cycle of Quality Management ?
(A)Joseph M. Juran
(B) W. Edwards Deming
(C)Kaoru Ishikawa
(D)Phillip Crosby

Answer: B

26. Who has given the 'Balance Score Card' as a measurement based performance management strategy ?
(A) Robert S. Kaplan and David P.Norton
(B) Hammel and Prahallad
(C) Stablein and Nord
(D) Pascale and Athos

Answer: A

27. The components of Marvin Weisbord's six box model are:
(A) Purposes, structure, rewards, mechanisms, relationships and leadership
(B) Processes, structure, resources, mechanisms, relationships and leadership
(C) Performance, structure, rewards, machines,relationships and leadership
(D) Purposes, structure, resources, machines, relationships and Leadership

Answer: A

28. The process of comparing work and service methods against the best practices and outcomes in industry is known as
(A) Benchmarking (B) Kaizens
(C) Quality Circles (D) None of the above

Answer: A

29. Which one is not a part of Mc Kinsy's 7's' framework?
(A)Systems (B) Strategy
(C)Standards (D) Style

Answer: C

30. HRD Matrix was conceptualized by :
(A) Leonard Nadler
(B) Leon C. Megginson
(C) T. V. Rao
(D) Udai Pareekh
Answer: C

31. Which of the following explain the HRD concept ?
(A) It is competence building exercise.
(B) It is a subprocess of OD.
(C) It brings about attitudinal changes in people.
(D) All of the above.
Answer: D

32. Which of the following is (are) the goal(s) of HRD ?
(A) Attracting people to organisation and retaining them
(B) Maximising performance in assigned roles
(C) Maximising performance in future roles
(D) All the above
Answer: D

33. HRD develops competencies at which level (s) ?
(A)Individual level
(B)Group level
(C)Organisation level
(D)All the above
Answer: D

34. Moonlighting means
(A) Working simultaneously in two organisations.
(B) Working under moonlight.
(C) Working in the night.
(D) Encouraging employee to improve productivity.
Answer: A

35. Which of the following is the correct sequence of training evaluation?
(A) Reaction, learning, behaviour and results
(B) Learning, reaction, behaviour and results
(C) Learning, behaviour, reaction and results
(D) Reaction, learning, results and behaviour
Answer: A

36. The following is the right process of training :
(A) Instructional design, validation, need analysis, implementation and evaluation
(B) Need analysis, instructional design, validation, implementation and evaluation
(C) Need analysis, validation, instructional design, implementation and evaluation
(D) Instructional design, need analysis, implementation, validation and evaluation
Answer: B

37. Sensitivity Training is known as_______.
(A) T - group training
(B) Operative training
(C) In - basket exercise
(D) Problem solving Training
Answer: A

38. Identify the factors which do not help organization in dealing with knowledge management:
(A) Improve the returns
(B) Improve competency
(C) Do not exploit opportunity
(D) Great value for core business
Answer: C

39. Training refers to:
(A) An act of increasing the knowledge and skill of an employee for doing a particular job
(B) A short term educational process and utilizing systematic and organized procedure by which employees learn technical knowledge and skills for a definite purpose.
(C) It bridges the differences between job requirements and employee's present specifications
(D) All of the above

Answer: D

40. Which of the following is not an objectives of sensitivity training?
(A) Awareness of behavioural pattern of oneself and others
(B) Increased openness and greater concern for others
(C) Increased tolerance and less ethnic prejudice
(D) Potentialities for the next level job

Answer: D

41. Off the job training does not include :
(A) Role playing
(B) Lecture method
(C)Coaching
(D) Conference or discussion

Answer: C

42. Arrange the following steps of training procedure in proper sequence
a. Preparing the trainee
b. Preparing the instructor
c. Presenting the operation
d. Getting ready to teach
e. Tryout the trainee's performance
f. Follow up
(A) a, b, c, d, e, f
(B) b, a, d, c, e, f
(C) f, e, d, c, a, b
(D) a, d, c, e, b, f

Answer: B

43. Which of the following is not a method of operative training ?
(A) Grid Training
(B) Vestibule Training
(C) Apprenticeship Training
(D) Demonstration

Answer: B

44. Match the following :

(Training Programmes)	**(Skills Imparted)**
(a) Inbasket Exercize	(i) Problem solving
(b) Role Playing	(ii) Skills required for promotion
(c) Sensiticity Training	(iii)Time Management
(d) Understudy	(iv) Group Skills

Code:

	(a)	(b)	(c)	(d)
(A)	(iii)	(i)	(iv)	(ii)
(B)	(ii)	(iii)	(i)	(iv)
(C)	(iii)	(ii)	(iv)	(i)
(D)	(iv)	(iii)	(ii)	(i)

Answer: B

45. Which of the following is not on the job training programme :
(A)Vestibule Training (B) Role Playing
(C)Simulation (D) All the above

Answer: D

46. Arrange the following in the sequence in which they occur in a training and development programe.
(a) training programmes
(b) training evaluation
(c) determining training needs
(d) feedback
(A) (a) (d) (b) (c)
(B) (b) (a) (c) (d)
(C) (c) (a) (b) (d)
(D) (c) (b) (a) (d)

Answer: C

47. Which of the following labs are in use in the sensitivity training ?
(A)Stranger lab (B) Cousin lab
(C)Family lab (D) All of the above

Answer: D

48. What is the correct order of the following phases of training?
(i) Development Phase
(ii) Design Phase
(iii) Need Analysis Phase
(iv) Implementation Phase
(v) Evaluation Phase

(A) (iii)	(ii)	(i)	(iv)	(v)
(B) (ii)	(i)	(iii)	(v)	(iv)
(C) (iii)	(iv)	(i)	(ii)	(v)
(D) (iv)	(ii)	(i)	(iii)	(v)

Answer: A

49. Training Evaluation at Reaction, Learning, Job behaviour and results levels is the model advanced by:
(A) Donald Kirkpatrick
(B) Goldstein
(C) Brinkerhoff
(D) Phillips

Answer: A

50. On–the–job training does not include :
(A) Coaching
(B) Job rotation
(C) Under study
(D) The case study

Answer: D

51. When situation is duplicated in such a way that it carries a closer resemblance to the actual job setting, it is called:
(A) Sensitivity Training
(B) Simulation
(C) Managerial Grid
(D) In Basket Method

Answer: B

52. What may be particularly necessary as part of the training process where people are working in another country?
(A) e-learning
(B) discovery learning
(C) cross-cultural training
(D) activist learning

Answer: A

53. Which of the following is *not* a stage in the systematic training cycle?
(A) evaluation
(B) assessing training needs
(C) planning the training
(D) job instruction on a one to one basis

Answer: D

54. Sensitivity Training is
(A) Sensitization of employee for organization.
(B) Kind of group for discussing the interpersonal behavior
(C) Related with organization change
(D) Induction training

Answer: A

Explanation: Sensitivity Training is a form of training that claims to make people more aware of their own prejudices, and more sensitive to others. Sensitivity training involves such groupings as T groups (T for training), encounter groups, laboratory training groups, and human awareness groups are all names usually associated with what is known as sensitivity training.

55. One of the following is a Training provided to enhance decision making skills :
(A)On the job training
(B)Behavioural modeling
(C)Management games
(D)Action learning

Answer: C

56. Group-building training techniques are most effective for:
(A) Developing specific skills or dealing with interpersonal issues on the job.
(B) Teaching new facts or alternative problem-solving solutions.
(C) Continuously attempting to learn new things to apply for quality improvements.

(D) Sharing ideas and experiences and getting to know one's strengths and weaknesses.

Answer: D

57. One of the acceptable methods for obtaining feedback of training is called
(A) Structured Interview
(B) Performance after Training
(C) Improvement after Training
(D) Employee Turnover Rate

Answer: A

58. Match the following :

(i) Sensitivity training	(a) Leadership
(ii) Hygiene factors	(b) Organisational Development
(iii) Number of subordinates	(c) Motivation
(iv) Likert's management system	(d) Span of management

Codes :

	(i)	(ii)	(iii)	(iv)
(A)	(b)	(c)	(d)	(a)
(B)	(a)	(c)	(d)	(b)
(C)	(d)	(c)	(a)	(b)
(D)	(a)	(b)	(c)	(d)

Answer: A

59. Sensitivity training method is a part of:
(A) On-the-job training method
(B) Off-the-job training method
(C) Vestibule training method
(D) None of the above

Answer: C

60. Which of the following techniques may be used for management development?
(A)Planned progression
(B)Creation of 'Assistants to' position
(C)Sensitivity training
(D)All the above

Answer: C

61. Human values in regard to Management Development do not include
(A)Dignity and forgiveness
(B)Arrogance and anger
(C)Gratitude and gentleness
(D)Humility and Honesty

Answer: B

62. Management development is concerned with learning of
(A)Mechanical skills
(B)Specific job skills
(C)Conceptual and creative skills
(D)All the above

Answer: D

63. Management Development Programmes are required :
(A) To increase production
(B) To increase effectiveness and personality of a manager
(C) To increase morale
(D) To increase team work

Answer: C

64. The following definition "development of awareness and sensitivity to behavioural patterns of oneself and others" refers to which of the following methods of training?
(A)In-Basket
(B)Case study
(C)Management games
(D)T-Group

Answer: D

65. In organizing an Executive Development Programme, how would you arrange the following steps?
I. Actual conduct of the programme.
II. Evaluation of the programme.
III. Inventory of Management Talent.
IV. Analysis of Developmental Needs

(A)	I	III	II	IV
(B)	IV	III	I	II
(C)	I	IV	III	II
(D)	II	I	III	IV

Answer: B

66. Which of the following is the correct sequence of management development process?
(i)Designing Development Programmes
(ii)Conducting Development Programmes
(iii)Evaluating Development Programmes
(iv) Defining Parameters to Development
(v) Identifying Development needs
(A) (ii), (iii), (i), (iv), (v)
(B) (iii), (ii), (iv), (i), (v)
(C) (iv), (iii), (ii), (v), (i)
(D) (v), (iv), (i), (ii), (iii)

Answer: D

67. Which of the following is not a simulation technique of development ?
(A)In - Basket
(B)Case study
(C)T - group
(D)Management games

Answer: C

68. The term human resource development reflects the fact that it is no longer appropriate in modern organizations to focus on just the development of which group?
(A) Workers
(B) employees
(C) Consultants
(D) part timers

Answer: B

69. The method of management development which purports to develop awareness and sentiments to one's own and others' behavioural patterns, is known as :
(A)Structured Insight
(B)The syndicate system
(C)Business games
(D) Sensitivity training

Answer: D

70. When the career progression stagnates at a point, it is called
(A)Career Resilience
(B)Career Anchor
(C)Career Insight
(D)Career Plateau

Answer: D

71. Which of the following is the correct sequence of career development stages ?
(i) Mid career
(ii) Late career
(iii) Exploration
(iv) Decline
(v) Establishment

(A)	(i)	(ii)	(iii)	(iv)	(v)
(B)	(ii)	(iii)	(i)	(v)	(iv)
(C)	(i)	(iv)	(v)	(ii)	(iii)
(D)	(iii)	(v)	(i)	(ii)	(iv)

Answer: D

72. Career planning linked with multiskilling results into :
(A) linear career planning
(B) protean career planning
(C) Vertical career planning
(D) none of the above

Answer: B

73. Which of the following factors may be levelled as career anchor?
(A) Managerial competence
(B) Creativity
(C) Functional competence
(D) All the above

Answer: D

74. Self perceived talents, motives and values that influence career of an individual are known as
(A) career anchors (B) career plans
(C) career aims (D)none of the above

Answer: A

75. Arrange the following steps involved in establishing a career development system in proper sequence:
(a) Vision (b) Needs
(c) Action plan (d) Results
(A) d, c, b, a (B) b, a, c, d
(C) b, d, a, c (D) c, a, b, d

Answer: B

76. Which of the following is ***not*** one of the career anchors :
(A) Managerial competence
(B) Technical - functional competence
(C) Personal competence
(D) Security
Answer: C

77. Career resilience means
(A) Ability to switch careers
(B) Ability to remain with same competencies refining suitably for organizations
(C) Lack of capacity to remain in career
(D) None of the above
Answer: B

78. The process of retaining suitable successors is called :
(A) Alternative staffing
(B) Succession planning
(C) Position replacement
(D) Promotion
Answer: B

79. Monitoring employees through a preplanned series of position is called:
(A) Promotion
(B) Succession planning
(C) Job reporting
(D) Job rotation
Answer: B

80. All of the following are phases of career development except:
(A) Performance Phase
(B)Direction Phase
(C)Assessment Phase
(D)Development Phase
Answers: A

81. Which of the following provides direction, serves as standards for evaluating performance and motivates members of the organization?
(A) Mission (B) Values
(C) Objectives (D) Goals
Answer: C

82. Performance Appraisal is a double edged tool to
(A) Create space for the employee to organisationally survive.
(B) Offering challenges for promotion.
(C) Accompanying the course of Demotion.
(D) All of the above.
Answer: D

83. The process of evaluating an employee's current and/or past performance relative to his or her performance standards is called ______.
(A) Recruitment
(B) employee selection
(C) performance appraisal
(D) organizational development
(E) training
Answer: C

84. Which one is a part of performance measurement?
(A)Trait (B) Behaviour
(C) Outcome (D) All the above

Answer: D

85. Which one is not a performance appraisal error arising from rater?
(A) Halo error (B) Content error
(C) Contrast error (D) Recency error
Answer: A

86. Performance appraisal helps in :
(A)Training (B) Career planning
(C)Promotion (D) All the above
Answer: D

87. Which of the following is not a method of Performance Appraisal ?
(A)Paired comparison method
(B)360^0 Appraisal
(C)Assessment centres
(D)None of the above
Answer: C

88. BARS stand for :

(A) Behaviourally Anchored Ranking Scales

(B) Behaviour Aptitude Reaction Syndrome

(C) Behaviourally Anchored Rating Scales

(D) Behavioural Alternative Reaction Syndrome

Answer: C

89. 360^0 Appraisal refers to the appraisal to be done by :

(A) Superiors and Subordinates

(B) Superiors Subordinates and Customers

(C) Superiors Subordinates, Customers and Peers

(D) None of the above

Answer: C

90. Assertion: Management of performance is a better substitute to the performance appraisal.

Reason: Appraisal of performance is affected by many errors as in human processes biases are bound to occur.

(A) Both asseration and reason are wrong

(B) Assertion is wrong but reason is right

(C) Assertion is right and it will control reason

(D) None of the above

Answer: C

91. Arrange the following aspects of performance appraisal objectives in the proper sequence:

(i) to identify potential for promotion

(ii) to help develop individuals

(iii) to assess training needs

(iv) to review past performance

(v) to set targets for future performance

(vi) to audit the skills within an organisation

(A) (i) (iii) (iv) (vi) (v) (ii)

(B) (i) (ii) (iii) (v) (vi) (iv)

(C) (iv) (v) (vi) (iii) (ii) (i)

(D) (iv) (iii) (ii) (vi) (v) (i)

Answer: C

92. Which of the following would be the correct sequence of various phases in performance coaching ?

(i) Report building

(ii) Exploration

(iii) Action Planning

(A) (iii) (ii) (i)

(B) (i) (iii) (ii)

(C) (i) (ii) (iii)

(D) (ii) (iii) (i)

Answer: D

93. Consider following steps in performance appraisal process and arrange them in proper sequence :

(i) Comparison of actual performance with performance standards

(ii) Communicate performance expectations

(iii) Initiate corrective action, if any

(iv) Establish performance standards

(v) Measurement of actual performance

(A) (iv), (ii), (v), (iii), (i)

(B) (i), (ii), (iii), (iv), (v)

(C) (iv), (ii), (v), (i), (iii)

(D) (i), (iv), (iii), (ii), (v)

Answer: C

94. Every evaluator has his/her own value system that acts as a standard against which appraisals are made. Relative to the true or actual performance an individual exhibits, some evaluators mark high and others low. Such errors are known as:

(A) Similarity errors

(B) Central tendency

(C) Strictness/Leniency error

(D) Recency Vs Primacy effect

Answer: C

95. The influence of rater's general impression on ratings of specific rate qualities is called :
(A)Halo effect
(B)Central tendency
(C) Leniency
(D) Howthorne Effect

Answer: A

96. Match the following :

List - I
(a) Forced Distribution method
(b) Critical Incident method
(c) Alternation Ranking method
(d) Management by objectives

List - II
(i) Keeping record of uncommonly examples of work related behaviour
(ii) Predetermined percentages of employees placed in various performance categories
(iii) Ranking employees from best to worst on a particular trait until all are ranked
(iv) Setting goals and periodically measuring performance

Codes:

	(a)	(b)	(c)	(d)
(A)	(ii)	(i)	(iii)	(iv)
(B)	(i)	(ii)	(iii)	(iv)
(C)	(iii)	(i)	(ii)	(iv)
(D)	(iii)	(ii)	(i)	(iv)

Answer: A

97. Which of the following is the correct sequence of Performance Appraisal Process?
I. Setting standards for performance.
II. Measuring the performance.
III. Comparing the actual performance with the standard set.
IV. Communicating the standards set to the employees.

(A)	I	II	III	IV
(B)	I	II	IV	III
(C)	I	IV	II	III
(D)	II	III	IV	I

Answer: A

98. Which of the following is not a method of Performance Appraisal?
(A)Behaviourally Anchored Rating Scales
(B)Critical Incidence Method
(C)Grading Method
(D)Weighted Check List Method

Answer: B

99. Which of the following statements is not true about Performance Appraisal?
(A) Key performance areas are developed for role clarity.
(B) Key result areas are developed for accountability.
(C) KSA stands for knowledge, skill and attitude.
(D) Attributes and traits are of no importance in Performance Appraisal.

Answer: D

100. Behaviourally Anchored Rating Scale is associated with
(A) Training and Development
(B) Performance Appraisal
(C) Career Planning
(D) Workers' Participation in Management

Answer: B

101. Performance Appraisal is a primary human resource management process that links employees and organizations and provides input for other processes through these means :
(A) Identification, measurement, management
(B) Assessment, direction, development.
(C) Recruitment, Selection, onboarding
(D) Skill, effort, responsibility

Answer: A

102. Who has advanced the Goal setting theory of Performance Management?
(A) E.A. Locke & Gary Lutham
(B) F. Trompenaavs and Charles Hamp
(C) R. Tung and Arthur Anderson

(D) J.C. Usunier and P.N. Gharvi

Answer: A

103. Performance appraisal by all the following parties is called 360^0performance appraisal :

(A) Supervisors and Peers
(B) Subordinates and Employees themselves
(C) Users of Service and Consultants
(D) All the above

Answer: D

104. The term BARS stands for :

(A) Behavioural Abnormality Rating Scales
(B) Behavioural Abnormality Response Scales
(C) Behaviourally Anchored Response Scales
(D) Behaviourally Anchored Rating Scales

Answer: D

105. When goal setting, performance appraisal, and development are consolidated into a single, common system designed to ensure that employee performance supports a company's strategy, it is called _____.

(A) strategic organizational development
(B) performance management
(C) performance appraisal
(D) human resource management
(E) strategic management

Answer: B

106. Performance management combines performance appraisal with _____ to ensure that employee performance is supportive of corporate goals.

(A) goal setting
(B) training
(C) incentive systems
(D) all of the above
(E) none of the above

Answer: D

107. Managers following a performance management approach to appraisals will usually meet with employees on a _____ basis.

(A) Weekly (B) monthly
(C) bi-annual (D) yearly
(E) bi-monthly

Answer: A

108. Managers following a traditional performance appraisal system will typically meet with employees on a _____ basis.

(A) Daily (B) weekly
(C) Monthly (D) bi-monthly
(E) yearly

Answer: E

109. The component of an effective performance management process that communicates the organization's higher level goals throughout the organization and then translates these goals into departmental goals is called _____.

(A) role clarification
(B) goal alignment
(C) developmental goal setting
(D) direction sharing
(E) coaching and support

Answer: D

110. The component of an effective performance management process that explains each employee's role in terms of his or her day-to-day work is called _____.

(A) role clarification
(B) goal alignment
(C) developmental goal setting
(D) direction sharing
(E) coaching and support

Answer: A

111. Which of the following is <u>not</u> one of the guidelines for effective goal setting?

(A) assign specific goals
(B) assign measurable goals

(C) assign challenging but doable goals
(D) assign consequences for performance
(E) encourage participation

Answer: D

112. The S in the acronym for SMART goals stands for _____.
(A) specific
(B) straightforward
(C) strategic
(D) source
(E) support

Answer: A

113. The M in the acronym for SMART goals stands for _____.
(A) Moderate
(B) measurable
(C) Meaningful
(D) mid-range
(E) merit

Answer: B

114. The A in the acronym for SMART goals stands for _____.
(A) Actionable
(B) appropriate
(C) Attainable
(D) attitude
(E) asset

Answer: C

115. Participatively set goals result in higher performance than assigned goals when _____.
(A) participatively set goals are more difficult
(B) assigned goals are more difficult
(C) the rewards are also higher
(D) participatively set goals are used consistently
(E) the goals are doable

Answer: A

116. When using goal setting in performance management, the goals should be _____.
(A) Difficult
(B) challenging
(C) Doable
(D) specific
(E) all of the above

Answer: E

117. Who is the primary person responsible for doing the actual appraising of an employee's performance?
(A) the employee's direct supervisor
(B) the company appraiser
(C) the human resource manager
(D) the EEO contact person
(E) none of the above

Answer: A

118. Which of the following is not a role played by the HR department regarding performance appraisals?
(A) Training of supervisors
(B) Monitoring the appraisal system
(C) Appraising of employees
(D) Ensuring compliance with EEO laws
(E) Advising regarding appraisal tools and procedures

Answer: C

119. When designing an actual appraisal method, the two basic considerations are _____.
(A) who should measure and when to measure
(B) when to measure and what to measure
(C) what to measure and who should measure
(D) what to measure and how to measure
(E) when to measure and how to measure

Answer: D

120. The most popular technique for appraising performance is the _____ method.
(A) alternation ranking
(B) graphic rating scale
(C) Likert
(D) MBO
(E) constant sum rating scale

Answer: B

121. Which performance appraisal technique lists traits and a range of performance?
(A) alternation ranking
(B) graphic rating scale
(C) Likert
(D) MBO
(E) constant sum rating scale

Answer: B

122. What do performance appraisals measure?
(A) generic dimensions of performance
(B) performance of actual duties
(C) employee competency
(D)achievement of objectives
(E) all of the above

Answer: E

123. If a performance appraisal focuses on an employee's quality and quantity of wok, then the performance appraisal is focused on measuring _____.
(A) generic dimensions of performance
(B) performance of actual duties
(C) employee competency
(D) achievement of objectives

Answer: A

124. The _____ method of performance appraisal involves listing all the subordinates to be rated, crossing out the names of any not known well enough to rank, indicating the employee who is the highest on each characteristic being measured and who is the lowest, and then alternating between the next highest and lowest until all employees have been ranked.
(A) alternation ranking
(B) graphic rating scale
(C) Likert
(D) MBO
(E) constant sum rating scale

Answer: A

125. Alternation ranking refers to an appraisal method, which _____.
(A) is based on progress made toward the accomplishment of measurable goals
(B) combines the benefits of narratives, critical incidents, and quantified scales by assigning scale points with specific examples of good or poor performance
(C) requires that the supervisor keep a log of positive and negative examples of a subordinate's work-related behavior
(D) requires a supervisor to evaluate performance by assigning predetermined percentages of those being rated into performance categories
(E) involves listing all the subordinates to be rated, crossing out the names of any not known well enough to rank, indicating the employee who is the highest on each characteristic being measured and who is the lowest, and then alternating between the next highest and lowest until all employees have been ranked

Answer: E

126. The most popular method for ranking employees is the _____ method.
(A)graphic ranking scale
(B)constant sum ranking scale
(C)alternation ranking
(D)paired comparison
(E)forced distribution

Answer: C

127. Suppose you have five employees to rate. You make a chart of all possible pairs of employees for each trait being evaluated. Then, you indicate the better employee of the pair for each pair. Finally, you add up the number of positives for each employee. In this case, you have used the _____ method of performance appraisal.
(A) graphic ranking scale
(B) constant sum ranking scale
(C) alternation ranking
(D) paired comparison
(E) forced distribution

Answer: D

128. Forced distribution refers to an appraisal method, which _____.
(A) is based on progress made toward the accomplishment of measurable goals
(B) combines the benefits of narratives, critical incidents, and quantified scales by assigning scale points with specific examples of good or poor performance
(C) requires that the supervisor keep a log of positive and negative examples of a subordinate's work-related behavior
(D) requires a supervisor to evaluate performance by assigning predetermined percentages of those being rated into performance categories
(E) involves listing all the subordinates to be rated, crossing out the names of any not known well enough to rank, indicating the employee who is the highest on each characteristic being measured and who is the lowest, and then alternating between the next highest and lowest until all employees have been ranked

Answer: E

129. When a supervisor evaluates performance by assigning predetermined percentages of ratees into performance categories, he or she has used the _____ method of performance appraisal.
(A)graphic ranking scale
(B)constant sum ranking scale
(C)alternation ranking
(D)paired comparison
(E)forced distribution

Answer: E

130. John, the supervisor of the manufacturing department, is in the process of evaluating his staff's performance. He has determined that 15% of the group will be identified as high performers, 20% as above average performers, 30% as average performers, 20% as below average performers, and 15% as poor performers. John is using a _____ method.
(A)graphic rating scale
(B)constant sum ranking scale
(C) forced distribution
(D) alternation ranking
(D) paired comparison

Answer: C

131. Which of the following measurement methods rates employee performance relative to other employees?
(A)graphic rating scale
(B)forced distribution
(C) likert scale
(D)constant sums rating
(E) critical incident method

Answer: B

132. With the _____ method, the supervisor keeps a log of positive and negative examples of a subordinate's work-related behavior.
(A) alternation ranking
(B)constant sums rating
(C) forced distribution
(D) narrative forms
(E) critical incident

Answer: E

133. The critical incident technique refers to an appraisal method, which _____.
(A) is based on progress made toward the accomplishment of measurable goals
(B) combines the benefits of narratives, critical incidents, and quantified scales by assigning scale points with specific examples of good or poor performance
(C) requires that the supervisor keep a log of positive and negative examples of a subordinate's work-related behavior
(D) requires a supervisor to evaluate performance by assigning predetermined percentages of those being rated into performance categories
(E) involves listing all the subordinates to be rated, crossing out the names of any not known well enough to rank, indicating the employee who is the highest on each

characteristic being measured and who is the lowest, and then alternating between the next highest and lowest until all employees have been ranked

Answer: C

134. All of the following are advantages of using the critical incident method for appraising performance <u>except</u> that _____.

(A) it provides examples of good performance
(B) it does not include a numerical rating
(C) it provides examples of poor performance
(D) it reflects performance from throughout the appraisal period
(E) incidents can be tied to performance goals

Answer: B

135. Which appraisal method combines the benefits of narratives, critical incidents, and quantified scales by assigning scale points with specific examples of good or poor performance?

(A)behaviorally anchored rating scale
(B)graphic rating scale
(C)constant sums rating scale
(D)alternation ranking
(E)none of the above

Answer: A

136. Behaviorally anchored rating scale (BARS) refers to an appraisal method, which _____.

(A) is based on progress made toward the accomplishment of measurable goals
(B) combines the benefits of narratives, critical incidents, and quantified scales by assigning scale points with specific examples of good or poor performance
(C) requires that the supervisor keep a log of positive and negative examples of a subordinate's work-related behavior
(D) requires a supervisor to evaluate performance by assigning predetermined percentages of those being rated into performance categories
(E) involves listing all the subordinates to be rated, crossing out the names of any not known well enough to rank, indicating the employee who is the highest on each characteristic being measured and who is the lowest, and then alternating between the next highest and lowest until all employees have been ranked

Answer: B

137. The first step in developing a behaviorally anchored rating scale is to _____.

(A)develop performance dimensions
(B)generate critical incidents
(C) reallocate incidents
(D) scale incidents
(E) develop a final instrument

Answer: B

138. Which step in developing a behaviorally anchored rating scale involves clustering critical incidents into a smaller set of performance dimensions?

(A) First
(B) second
(C) Third
(D) fourth
(E) fifth

Answer: B

139. Which step in developing a behaviorally anchored rating scale involves clustering definitions and critical incidents, reassigning each incident to the cluster where it fits best and then determining the level of agreement among the group as to the allocation of incidents?

(A) First
(B) Second
(C) Third
(D) Fourth
(E) Fifth

Answer: C

140. All of the following are advantages of behaviorally anchored rating scales (BARS) except that they _____.
(A)are more accurate
(B)provide clearer standards
(C) are time consuming
(D)are reliable

Answer: C

141. Management by objectives (MBO) refers to an appraisal method, which _____.
(A) is based on progress made toward the accomplishment of measurable goals
(B) combines the benefits of narratives, critical incidents, and quantified scales by assigning scale points with specific examples of good or poor performance
(C) requires that the supervisor keep a log of positive and negative examples of a subordinate's work-related behavior
(D) requires a supervisor to evaluate performance by assigning predetermined percentages of those being rated into performance categories
(E) involves listing all the subordinates to be rated, crossing out the names of any not known well enough to rank, indicating the employee who is the highest on each characteristic being measured and who is the lowest, and then alternating between the next highest and lowest until all employees have been ranked

Answer: A

142. Which of the following is a problem with using MBO?
(A) a tendency to set unclear objectives
(B) a tendency to set unmeasurable objectives
(C) it is time consuming
(D) tug of war between subordinate and manager regarding goals
(E) all of the above

Answer: E

143. Graphic rating scales are subject to all of the following problems except _____.
(A) unclear standards
(B) halo effects
(C) complexity
(D) central tendency
(E) leniency

Answer: C

144. When different supervisors define levels of performance (good, fair, poor) differently, unfair appraisals could result due to a problem with _____.
(A) unclear standards
(B) halo effects
(C) complexity
(D) central tendency
(E) leniency

Answer: A

145. _____ is defined as the influence of a rater's general impression on ratings of specific ratee qualities.
(A) Impression management
(B) Halo effect
(C) Central tendency
(D) Stereotyping
(E) Bias

Answer: B

146. Prashant is generally considered unfriendly at work. His supervisor rates him low on the trait "gets along well with others" but also rates him lower on other traits unrelated to socialization at work. Prashant's performance appraisal may be unfair due to _____.
(A) impression management
(B) bias
(C) stereotyping
(D) halo effects
(E) strictness

Answer: D

147. Some supervisors, when filling in rating scales, tend to avoid the highs and lows on the scale and rate most people in the middle. This _____ means that all employees may be rated average.
(A) halo effect
(B) stereotyping
(C) central tendency
(D) strictness
(E) leniency

Answer: C

148. The best way of reducing the problem of central tendency in performance appraisals is to _____.
(A) rank employees
(B) be aware of the problem
(C) train supervisors to avoid it
(D) impose a distribution for performance
(E) consider the purpose of the appraisal

Answer: A

149. The _____ problem occurs when supervisors tend to rate all their subordinates consistently high.
(A) central tendency
(B) leniency
(C) strictness
(D) bias
(E) halo effect

Answer: B

150. The _____ problem occurs when supervisors tend to rate all their subordinates consistently low.
(A) central tendency
(B)leniency
(C) strictness
(D)bias
(E)halo effect

Answer: C

151. Which big five personality trait is associated with performance appraisal ratings that are too strict?
(A) Agreeableness
(B) extraversion
(C) conscientiousness
(D) openness
(E) neuroticism

Answer: C

152. Which big five personality trait is associated with performance appraisal ratings that are too lenient?
(A) Agreeableness
(B) extraversion
(C) Conscientiousness
(D) openness
(E) neuroticism

Answer: A

153. The best way of reducing the problems of leniency or strictness in performance appraisals is to _____.
(A) rank employees
(B) be aware of the problem
(C) train supervisors to avoid it
(D) impose a distribution for performance
(E) consider the purpose of the appraisal

Answer: D

154. When an employee's personal characteristics such as age, race, and gender influence a supervisor's evaluation of his or her performance, the problem of _____ has occurred.
(A) Bias
(B) stereotyping
(C) central tendency
(D) halo affect
(E) strictness

Answer: A

155. Which of the following could result in a legally questionable appraisal process?
(A) conduct a job analysis to establish criteria and standards for successful performance
(B) base appraisals on subjective supervisory observations
(C) administer and score appraisals in a standardized fashion
(D) use clearly defined job performance dimensions

(E) avoid abstract trait names when using graphic rating scales
Answer: B

156. Who is in the best position to observe and evaluate an employee's performance for the purposes of a performance appraisal?
(A) Peers
(B) customers
(C) rating committees
(D) top management
(E) immediate supervisor
Answer: E

157. Performance appraisals may be conducted by _____.
(A) the immediate supervisor
(B) peers
(C) rating committees
(D) subordinates
(E) all of the above
Answer: E

158. Rating committees, made up of an employee's immediate supervisor along with other supervisors, usually have _____ members.
(A) 2-3
(B) 4-5
(C) 6-7
(D) 8-9
(E) 10 or more
Answer: B

159. While peer appraisals have many benefits, one problem is _____, when several peers collaborate to rate each other highly.
(A) social loafing
(B) group think
(C) logrolling
(D) alliance forging
(E) impression management
Answer: C

160. Peer appraisals have been shown to result in a(n) _____.
(A) reduction of social loafing in the team
(B) reduction of group cohesion
(C) decrease in satisfaction with the group
(D) lower task motivation
(E) tendency to inaccurately predict who would be promoted
Answer: A

161. What usually occurs when employees rate themselves in a performance appraisal?
(A) interrater reliability is higher
(B) appraisals are subject to halo effects
(C) logrolling could occur
(D) ratings are higher than when rated by supervisors or peers
(E) ratings are about the same as when determined by peers
Answer: D

162. Firms that use _____ let subordinates anonymously rate their supervisor's performance.
(A) downward feedback
(B) upward feedback
(C) MBO
(D) narratives
(E) critical incidents
Answer: B

163. What process allows top management to diagnose the management styles of supervisors, identify potential "people" problems, and take corrective action with individual supervisors as necessary?
(A) strategic performance appraisal
(B) organizational development
(C) upward feedback
(D) MBO
(E) critical incidents
Answer: C

164. When subordinates provide feedback for supervisors, the comments should be anonymous because identifiable responses tend to result in _____.
(A) more critical ratings
(B)increased comfort with the process

on the part of the subordinate more negative attitudes from managers receiving the feedback
(C) more inflated ratings
(D) all of the above

Answer: D

165. What is another term for 360-degree feedback?
(A) feedback loop
(B) multi-source assessment
(C) upward feedback
(D) circle feedback
(E) wheel feedback

Answer: B

166. You are conducting an appraisal interview with an employee who is satisfactory, but not promotable. Which incentive listed below would likely be the least effective for maintaining satisfactory performance in this situation?
(A) time off
(B) small bonus
(C) compliments
(D) additional professional development
(E) additional authority

Answer: D

167. Which is the easiest type of appraisal interview to conduct?
(A) satisfactory-not promotable
(B) satisfactory-promotable
(C) unsatisfactory-correctable
(D) unsatisfactory-uncorrectable
(E) final warning

Answer: B

168. When conducting an appraisal interview, supervisors should do all of the following <u>except</u>
(A) talk in terms of objective work data
(B) compare the person's performance to a standard
(C) encourage the employee to talk
(D) give specific examples of poor performance
(E) compare the person's performance to that of other employees

Answer: E

169. Which of the following responses is <u>not</u> typical during a negative appraisal interview?
(A) Denial (B) Anger
(C) Relief (D) Aggression
(E) Retreat

Answer: C

170. When a supervisor must criticize a subordinate in an appraisal interview, it is best to _____.
(A) hold the meeting with other people who can diffuse the negative situation
(B) provide examples of critical incidents
(C) acknowledge the supervisor's personal biases in the situation
(D) provide feedback once per year
(E) surprise the employee so they cannot develop excuses for poor performance

Answer: B

171. Subordinates may feel dissatisfied with their appraisal interview when they _____.
(A) feel threatened during the interview
(B) have an opportunity to express their ideas
(C) have an opportunity to influence the course of the interview
(D) have a constructive interviewer conduct the interview
(E) are shown specific examples of their poor performance

Answer: A

172. When an employee's performance is so poor that a written warning is required, the warning should _____.
(A) identify the standards by which the employee is judged

(B) provide examples of employees who met the standards
(C) provide examples of times when the employee did meet the standards
(D) be sent to the employee in question, to the manager's superior, and to the EEO office
(E) all of the above
Answer: A

173. If a performance appraisal focuses on an employee's ability to "identify and analyze problems" or to "maintain harmonious and effective working relationships," then the performance appraisal is focused on measuring _____.
(A)generic dimensions of performance
(B)performance of actual duties
(C) employee competency
(D)achievement of objectives
(E) all of the above
Answer: C

174. Self-assessment is a part of :
(A)Interview followed by written test
(B)Competency mapping
(C)Induction
(D)Performance Appraisal System
Answer: D

175. Which of the following is called a negative process?
(A) Recruitment
(B) Selection
(C) Induction
(D) Performance Appraisal
Answer: D

176. Which of the following provides directions, serves as standard for evaluating performance and motivates members of the organization?
(A) Mission
(B) Values
(C) Objectives
(D) Goals
Answer: C

177. The systematic collection and feedback of performance data on an individual or group derived from a number of stake holders in their performance is called :
(A)180^0Appraisal
(B)360^0 Appraisal
(C)Confidential reports
(D)None of these
Answer: C

178. When the water allows one aspect of a person's character or performance to influence the enitre evaluation, the error will be :
(A)Constant error (B) Halo effect
(C)Central tendency (D) Similar to me
Answer: B

179. The main objective of 360^0Appraisal is to bring :
(A)Subjectivity
(B)Objectivity
(C)Uniformity of standards
(D)None of these
Answer: C

180. Who introduced the concept of MBO?
(A) Mary Parker Foilet (B) Keith Davice
(C)Peter Drucker (D) F. W. Taylor
Answer: C

181. The concept of management by objectives was given by
(A) Peter F. Drucker
(B) Luther Gulick
(C) Rensis Likert
(D) Blake and Mouton
Answer: A

182. MBO was popularised as an approach to planning by :
(A) P.F. Drucker
(B) Henry Fayol
(C) F. W. Taylor
(D) None of the above
Answer: A

183. MBO cannot be implemented effectively in an organisation which is prone to rapid changes, either internal or environmental, because :
(A) It becomes difficult to set objectives in a changing environment
(B) It becomes difficult to assign responsibilities in a changing situation
(C) Unforeseen changes may refer most objectives unachievable
(D) None of the above

Answer: B

184. Which one is not a performance appraisal method ?
(A) 360^0 performance appraisal
(B) Balanced score card
(C) Rank method
(D) Interview method

Answer: D

185. Who had given the 'Work linked democracy' explanation of Quality of Work Life.
(A) Evic Tryst
(B) Evic Frank
(C) Fred Luthans
(D) None of the above

Answer: A

186. Fish-bone Analysis is used in which of the following :
(A) Collective bargaining
(B) Quality circles
(C) Quality of work life
(D) Training and Development

Answer: B

187. The doctrine of Quality Circle got popularity in which of the following countries :
(A) U.S.A (B) India
(C) Japan (D) U.K

Answer: C

188. Which of the following aims control through setting productivity measures based on best-industry practices?
(A) Pareto diagram
(B) Quality circles
(C) Kaizens
(D) Benchmarking

Answer: B

189. Fish bone analysis as a tool of quality circle was advanced by
(A) Edward Deming
(B) Joseph Juran
(C) Kouru Ishi Kawa
(D) Phillip Crosby

Answer: C

190. Who introduced the concept of quality circles in India ?
(A) P. V. Rao (B) Udai Pareek
(C) Dharani P. Sinha (D) S. R. Udpa

Answer: D

191. In which industry, Quality circles in India were first introduced ?
(A) Bharat Electronics Ltd.
(B) Bharat Heavy Electricals Ltd.
(C) Bharat Heavy Plates and Vessels
(D) Bharat Earth Movers Ltd.

Answer: B

192. In which public sector organization quality circles was first introduced in India.
(A) Hindustan Aeronautics Ltd.
(B) Bharath Earth Movers Ltd.
(C) Bharath Heavy ElectricalsLtd.
(D) Hindustan Machine Tools Ltd.

Answer: C

193. A voluntary group of workers, to examine work-related problems that affect quality of output, is called :
(A) Quality of work life
(B) Quality team
(C) Quality circle
(D) All the above

Answer: C

194. The concept of quality circle is a brain child of :

(A) Ishikawa Japanese engineer
(B) Munchu, H.R.M. Expert
(C) Peter Drucker
(D) Japanese union for scientists and engineers

Answer: A

195. Who is the father of Quality Circles?

(A) Lewin (B) Ishikawa
(C) Udpa (D) Robert Owen

Answer: B

196. Arrange the following processes of quality circle in the order in which they occur.

(i) Pareto Analysis
(ii) Fish Bone Analysis
(iii) Pie Chart
(iv) Brain Storming Exercise

Code:

(A)	(i)	(iv)	(ii)	(iii)
(B)	(iv)	(ii)	(i)	(iii)
(C)	(iii)	(i)	(iv)	(ii)
(D)	(iv)	(i)	(ii)	(iii)

Answer: B

197. Match the following development dimensions of HRD function :

(a) Job enrichment	(i) Analyzing the job
(b) Career development	(ii) Matching the role and the person
(c) Key performance areas	(iii) Developing the person in the role
(d) Succession Planning	(iv) Developing the role for the person

	(a)	(b)	(c)	(d)
(A)	(iv)	(iii)	(ii)	(i)
(B)	(i)	(iv)	(iii)	(ii)
(C)	(iv)	(iii)	(i)	(ii)
(D)	(i)	(iii)	(ii)	(iv)

Answer: D

198. Who coined the term 'informal sector'?

(A) Keith Davis (B) Amartya Sen
(C) Mahabub Ul Haq (D) Keith Hart

Answer: D

199. Power distance, uncertainty avoidance, individualism and masculinity as dimensions of cross–cultural comparative model is given by

(A) Kluckhohn & Strodthbeck
(B) Geert Hofstede
(C) Andres Lauvent
(D) Hall and Trompenaar

Answer: B

200. The training analysis is required to :

(A) Find out the training needs
(B) Find out additional requirement of manpower
(C) Find out working problems
(D) Maintain industrial democracy at work

Answer: A

201. 'Cousin Lab', 'Stranger lab' and 'Family lab' are terms associated with which OD technique?

(A) Survey Feedback
(B) Managerial Grid
(C) Sensitivity Training
(D) Process Consultation

Answer: C

202. The method of management development which purports to develop awareness and sentiments to one's own and others' behavioural patterns, is known as :

(A) Structured Insight
(B) The syndicate system
(C) Business games
(D) Sensitivity training

Answer: D

203. Which of the following is not a method of Performance Appraisal ?

(A) 360^0 Performance Appraisal
(B) Ranking Method
(C) Graphic Rating Scales Method
(D) Man Power Planning

Answer: D

204. The process of providing employees with specific skills or helping them correct deficiencies in their performance is called
(A) Counselling
(B) Motivation
(C) Recruitment and selection
(D) Training
Answer: D

205. Vestible training is provided
(A) in the class room
(B) off the job
(C) on the job
(D) in the training dept.
Answer: B

206. Group Training means
(A) Sensitivity training
(B) Class room training
(C) Role playing
(D) Training conference
Answer: A

207. Simuflite expected to combat competition with
(A) Curriculum Based Training
(B) Competition Based Training
(C) Combat Based Training
(D) Computer Based Training
Answer: D

****

UNIT-V
JOB ANALYSIS AND SALARY MANAGEMENT

5.1. JOB ANALYSIS

- **Job:** "Job is a 'group of tasks to be performed every day."
- **Job analysis is** primary tool in personnel management. In this method, a personnel manager tries to gather, synthesize and implement the information available regarding the workforce in the concern.
- Job analysis is the process by means of which a description is developed of the present methods and procedures of doing a job, physical conditions in which the job is done, relation of the job to other jobs and other conditions of employment.
- Job analysis is useful in:
  - o Recruitment and selection : A personnel manager has to undertake job analysis so as to put right man on right job.
  - o Establishing a base for compensation of employees
  - o Can be used for employee development, performance appraisal and training.
- **U. S. Department of Labour:** "The process of determining, by observation and study and reporting pertinent information relating to the nature of a specific job. It is the determination of the tasks which comprise the job and of the skills, knowledge, abilities and responsibilities required of the worker of a successful performance and which differentiate one job from all others."
- **Process of Collecting Information:** "Job Analysis is a process of studying and collecting information relating to operations and responsibilities of a specific job. The immediate products of this analysis are 'Job Description' and 'Job Specifications'."
- **Systematic Exploration of Activities:** "Job Analysis is a systematic exploration of activities within a job. It is a basic technical procedure that is used to define duties and responsibilities and accountabilities of the job."
- **Identifying Job Requirement:** "Job is a collection of tasks that can be performed by a single employee to contribute to the production of some product or service, provided by the organization. Each job has certain ability requirements as well as certain rewards associated with it. Job Analysis is a process used to identify these requirements."
- **Functional Job Analysis:** It is a worker oriented job analytical approach which attempts to describe the whole person on the job.

Advantages of Job Analysis

1. **Provides First Hand Job-Related Information:** The job analysis process provides with valuable job-related data that helps managers and job analyst the duties and responsibilities of a particular job, risks and hazards involved in it, skills and abilities required to perform the job and other related information.
2. **Helps in Creating Right Job-Employee Fit:** This is one of the most crucial management activities. Filling the right person in a right job vacancy is a test of skills, understanding and

competencies of HR managers. Job Analysis helps them understand what type of employee will be suitable to deliver a specific job successfully.

3. **Helps in Establishing Effective Hiring Practices:** Who is to be filled where and when? Who to target and how for a specific job opening? Job analysis process gives answers to all these questions and helps managers in creating, establishing and maintaining effective hiring practices.
4. **Guides through Performance Evaluation and Appraisal Processes:** Job Analysis helps managers evaluating the performance of employees by comparing the standard or desired output with delivered or actual output. On these basis, they appraise their performances. The process helps in deciding whom to promote and when. It also guides managers in understanding the skill gaps so that right person can be fit at that particular place in order to get desired output.
5. **Helps in Analyzing Training & Development Needs:** The process of job analysis help to select the person and need of training required to accomplish the specific task.
6. **Helps in Deciding Compensation Package for a Specific Job:** A genuine and unbiased process of job analysis helps managers in determining the appropriate compensation package and benefits and allowances for a particular job. This is done on the basis of responsibilities and hazards involved in a job.

Disadvantages of Job Analysis

1. **Time Consuming:** It is very time consuming. It is a major limitation especially when jobs change frequently.
2. **Involves Personal Biasess:** If the observer or job analyst is an employee of the same organization, the process may involve his or her personal likes and dislikes. This is a major hindrance in collecting genuine and accurate data.
3. **Source of Data is Extremely Small:** Because of small sample size, the source of collecting data is extremely small. Therefore, information collected from few individuals needs to be standardized.
4. **Involves Lots of Human Efforts:** The process involves lots of human efforts. As every job carries different information and there is no set pattern, customized information is to be collected for different jobs. The process needs to be conducted separately for collecting and recording job-related data.
5. **Job Analyst May Not Possess Appropriate Skills:** If job analyst is not aware of the objective of job analysis process or does not possess appropriate skills to conduct the process, it is a sheer wastage of company's resources. He or she needs to be trained in order to get authentic data.
6. **Mental Abilities cannot be directly observed:** Mental abilities such as intellect, emotional characteristics, knowledge, aptitude, psychic and endurance are intangible things that cannot be observed or measured directly. People act differently in different situations. Therefore, general standards cannot be set for mental abilities.

Steps in Job Analysis

1. Collecting and recording job information.
2. Checking the job information for accuracy.
3. Writing job description based on information collected to determine the skills, knowledge, abilities and activities required.
4. Updating and upgrading this information.

7 Basic Steps of Job Analyais / Process of Job Analysis

1. **Strategies**
   William P. Antony: Four strategic choices

a) The extent of employee involvement in job analysis
b) The level of details of job analysis
c) Timing and frequency of analysis
d) Past-oriented Vs future-oriented job analysis

2. Collection of background information
3. Selection of representative position to be analyzed
4. Collection of job analysis data
5. Developing a job description
6. Developing a job specification
7. Developing employee specification

Techniques of Data Collection for Job Analysis

1. Interviews
2. Direct observation
3. Maintenance of long records
4. Questionnaires
5. Critical incident method

Barriers of job analysis

- Less Support from top management
- Single means and source, reliance on single method rather than combination
- No Training or Motivation to Jobholders
- Activities and data may be distorted

Methods of Job Analysis

5.1.1. Job description

5.1.2. Job specification

5.1.1. Job description

- Job description is an organized factual statement of job contents in the form of duties and responsibilities of a specific job.
- The preparation of job description is very important before a vacancy is advertised.
- It tells in brief the nature and type of job.
- ***"Job Description implies objective listing of the job title, tasks, and responsibilities involved in a job."***
- Job description is a word picture in writing of the duties, responsibilities and organizational relationships that constitutes a given job or position.
- It defines continuing work assignment and a scope of responsibility that are sufficiently different from those of the other jobs to warrant a specific title.
- Job description is a broad statement of purpose, scope, duties and responsibilities of a particular job.

Contents of Job Description

1. Job Identification
2. Job Summary
3. Job Duties and Responsibilities
4. Supervision specification

5. Machines, tools and materials
6. Work conditions
7. Work hazards
8. Definition of unusual terms

Format of Job Description

- Job Title
- Region/Location
- Department
- Reporting to (Operational and Managerial)
- Objective
- Principal duties and responsibilities

Features of Good Job Description

1. Up to date
2. Proper Job Title
3. Comprehensive Job Summary
4. Clear duties and responsibilities
5. Easily understandable
6. State job requirements
7. Specify reporting relationships
8. Showcase degrees of difficulties
9. Indicates opportunities for career development
10. Offer bird's-eye-view of primary responsibilities

Advantages of Job Description

1. It helps the supervisors in assigning work to the subordinates so that he can guide and monitor their performances.
2. It helps in recruitment and selection procedures.
3. It assists in manpower planning.
4. It is also helpful in performance appraisal.
5. It is helpful in job evaluation in order to decide about rate of remuneration for a specific job.
6. It also helps in chalking out training and development programmes.

5.1.2. Job specifications

- Job specification is a statement which tells us minimum acceptable human qualities which helps to perform a job.
- Job specification translates the job description into human qualifications so that a job can be performed in a better manner.
- "Job Specification involves listing of employee qualifications, skills and abilities required to meet the job description. These specifications are needed to do job satisfactorily."
- It is a statement of minimum and acceptable human qualities necessary to perform job properly.
- Job specifications seeks to indicate what kind of persons may be expected to most closely approximate the role requirements and thus it is basically concerned with matters of selection, screening and placement and is intended to serve as a guide in hiring.
- Job specifications can be divided into three broad categories:

  - o Essential Attributes
  - o Desirable Attributes
  - o Contra-Indicators – Indicators hampering the success of job.
- Job specification helps in hiring an appropriate person for an appropriate position.

Contents of Job Specifications

a. Job title and designation
b. Educational qualifications for that title
c. Physical and other related attributes
d. Physique and mental health
e. Special attributes and abilities
f. Maturity and dependability
g. Relationship of that job with other jobs in a concern.

Advantages of Job Specification

1. It is helpful in preliminary screening in the selection procedure.
2. It helps in giving due justification to each job.
3. It also helps in designing training and development programmes.
4. It helps the supervisors for counseling and monitoring performance of employees.
5. It helps in job evaluation.
6. It helps the management to take decisions regarding promotion, transfers and giving extra benefits to the employees.

5.2. JOB DESIGN

- The first operative function of HRM is job design and job analysis.
- ***Job design follows job analysis i.e. it is the next step after job analysis.***
- Job design means to decide the contents of a job. It fixes the duties and responsibilities of the job, the methods of doing the job and the relationships between the job holder (manager) and his superiors, subordinates and colleagues.
- It aims at outlining and organizing tasks, duties and responsibilities into a single unit of work for the achievement of certain objectives.
- It also outlines the methods and relationships that are essential for the success of a certain job. In simpler terms it refers to the what, how much, how many and the order of the tasks for a job/s.
- Job design essentially involves integrating job responsibilities or content and certain qualifications that are required to perform the same. It outlines the job responsibilities very clearly and also helps in attracting the right candidates to the right job. Further it also makes the job look interesting and specialized.
- Job design is a continuous and ever evolving process that is aimed at helping employees make adjustments with the changes in the workplace. The end goal is reducing dissatisfaction, enhancing motivation and employee engagement at the workplace.
- **Integration of work, rewards and qualification:** "Job Design integrates work content (tasks, functions, relationships), the rewards and qualifications required including skills, knowledge and abilities for each job in a way that meets the needs of employees and the organization."
- The whole process of job design is aimed to address various problems within the organizational setup, those that pertain to ones description of a job and the associated relationships. More specifically the following areas are fine tuned:

- Checking the work overload.
- Checking upon the work under load.
- Ensuring tasks are not repetitive in nature.
- Ensuring that employees don not remain isolated.
- Defining working hours clearly.
- Defining the work processes clearly.

Steps in Job Design

1. Specification of Individual Tasks
2. Specification of Methods of Tasks Performance
3. Combination of Tasks into Specific Jobs to be assigned to individuals

Benefits of Job Design

1. **Employee input:** A good job design enables a good job feedback. Employees have the option to vary tasks as per their personal and social needs, habits and circumstances in the workplace.
2. **Employee training:** Training is an integral part of job design. Contrary to the philosophy of "leave them alone' job design lays due emphasis on training people so that are well aware of what their job demands and how it is to be done.
3. **Work / Rest Schedules:** Job design offers good work and rest schedule by clearly defining the number of hours an individual has to spend in his/her job.
4. **Adjustments:** A good job designs allows for adjustments for physically demanding jobs by minimizing the energy spent doing the job and by aligning the manpower requirements for the same.

Factors Affecting Job Design

1. Environmental Factor
2. Organizational Factor
3. Behavioral Factor
4. Proper scope of job
5. Full-time challenge of the job
6. Managerial skills
7. Organization's requirements
8. Individual likes and dislikes
9. Organizational structure
10. Technology

Approaches to Job design

Job design is the next step after job analysis that aims at outlining, and organizing tasks and responsibilities associated with a certain job. It integrates job responsibilities and qualifications or skills that are required to perform the same. There are three important approaches to job design namely:

1. Engineering approach
2. Human approach
3. The job characteristics approach

1. Human Approach

- The human approach of job design laid emphasis on designing a job around the people or employees and not around the organizational processes. In other words it recognizes the need of designing jobs that are rewarding (financially and otherwise) and interesting at the same time.

- According to this approach jobs should gratify an individual's need for recognition, respect, growth and responsibility. Job enrichment as popularized by Herzberg's research is one the ways in human approach of job design. Herzberg classified these factors into two categories - the hygiene factors and the motivators.
- Motivators include factors like achievement, work nature, responsibility, learning and growth etc that can motivate an individual to perform better at the work place.
- Hygiene factor on the other hand include things like working conditions, organizational policies, salary etc that may not motivate directly but the absence of which can lead to dissatisfaction at the work place.

2. Engineering Approach

- The engineering approach was devised by ***FW Taylors et al.*** They introduced the idea of the task that gained prominence in due course of time.
- According to this approach the work or task of each employee is planned by the management a day in advance. The instructions for the same are sent to each employee describing the tasks to e undertaken in detail. The details include things like what, how and when of the task along with the time deadlines.
- The approach is based on the application of scientific principles to job design. Work, according to this approach should be scientifically analyzed and fragmented into logical tasks.
- Due emphasis is then laid on organizing the tasks so that a certain logical sequence is followed for efficient execution of the same.
- The approach also lays due emphasis on compensating employees appropriately and training them continuously for work efficiency.

3. The Job Characteristics Approach

- The job characteristics approach was popularized by ***Hackman and Oldham.***
- According to this approach there is a direct relationship between job satisfaction and rewards. They said that employees will be their productive best and committed when they are rewarded appropriately for their work.
- They laid down five core dimensions that can be used to describe any job - skill variety, task identity, task significance, autonomy and feedback.
  1. **Skill variety:** The employees must be able to utilize all their skills and develop new skills while dealing with a job.
  2. **Task Identity:** The extent to which an identifiable task or piece or work is required to be done for completion of the job.
  3. **Task Significance:** How important is the job to the other people, what impact does it create on their lives?
  4. **Autonomy:** Does the job offer freedom and independence to the individual performing the same.
  5. **Feedback:** Is feedback necessary for improving performance.

- These are different approaches but all of them point to more or less the same factors that need to be taken into consideration like interest, efficiency, productivity, motivation etc. All these are crucial to effective job design.

Techniques of Job Design or Job design alternatives

1. Job Simplification: *Taylor*
2. Job Enrichment: *Herzberg*
3. Job Enlargement & Rotation
4. Automation
5. Self-Managing Teams

5.2.1. Job Rotation

- Job Rotation Refers to the movement of an employee from one job to another. This measure relieves the employee from boredom and monotony, improves employees skills regarding various jobs, prepare the competent employees and provide competent advantage to company.
- Here jobs remain unchanged, but the incumbents shift from one job to another.
- On the positive side, it increases the intrinsic reward potential of a job because of different skills and abilities needed to perform it.
- Periodic job changes can improve interdepartmental cooperation.

Disadvantages of Job Rotation

- On the negative side, it may not be much enthusiastic or efficiency may not be more.
- Besides jobs may not improve the relationships between task, while activities and objectives remain unchanged.
- Further training costs also rise and it can also de-motivate intelligent and ambitious trainees who seek specific responsibilities in their chosen specialties.

5.2.2. Job Enlargement

- Job Enlargement adding more and different tasks to a specialized job to provide greater variety.
- This process is called ***Horizontal job loading*** or ***Horizontal Job Enlargement.*** It is with same skills taking additional responsibilities like extending working hours etc. Job enlargement may involve breaking up of the existing work system and redesigning a new work system.
- For this employees also need to be trained to adjust to the new system. Job enlargement is said to contribute to employee motivation but the claim is not validated in practice.
- It means expanding the number of tasks, or duties assigned to a given job. Job enlargement is naturally opposite to work simplification. Adding more tasks or duties to a job does not mean that new skills and abilities are needed.

Benefits of Job Enlargement

1. Task Variety
2. Meaningful Work Modules
3. Full Ability Utilization
4. Worker Paced Control
5. Meaningful Performance Feedback

Disadvantages of Job Enlargement

1. High Training Costs
2. Redesigning existing work system required
3. Productivity may not increase necessarily

4. Workload increases
5. Unions demand pay–hike
6. Jobs may still remain boring and routine

5.2.3. Job Enrichment

- Job Enrichment loads the job ***vertically***.
- Job Enrichment means adding duties and responsibilities that will provide for skill variety, task identity, task significance, autonomy and feedback on job performance.
- The employee does more planning and controlling with less supervision but more self-evaluation.
- In other words, transferring some of the supervisor's tasks to the employee and making his job enriched.

Benefits of Job enrichment

1. It benefits employee and organization in terms of increased motivation, performance, satisfaction, job involvement and reduced absenteeism.
2. Additional features in job meet certain psychological needs of jobholders due to skill variety, identity, significance of job etc.
3. It also adds to employee self-esteem and self-control.
4. Job enrichment gives status to jobholder and acts as a strong satisfier in one's life.
5. Job enrichment stimulates improvements in other areas of organization.
6. Empowerment is a by-product of job enrichment. It means passing on more authority and responsibility.

Demerits of Job Enrichment

1. Lazy employees may not be able to take additional responsibilities and power. It won't fetch the desired results for an employee who is not attentive towards his job.
2. Union's resistance, increased cost of design and implementation and limited research on long term effect of job enrichment are some of the other demerits.
3. Job enrichment itself might not be a great motivator since it is job-intrinsic factor. As per the two-factor motivation theory, job enrichment is not enough. It should be preceded by hygienic factors etc.
4. Job enrichment assumes that workers want more responsibilities and those workers who are motivated by less responsibility, job enrichment surely de-motivates them
5. Workers participation may affect the enrichment process itself.
6. Change is difficult to implement and is always resisted as job enrichment brings in a changes the responsibility.

5.2.4. Work Simplification

- In work Simplification Job is simplified or specialized.
- The job is broken down into small parts and each part is assigned to an individual.
- To be more specific, work simplification is mechanical pacing of work, repetitive work processes, working only on one part of a product, predetermining tools and techniques, restricting interaction amongst employees, few skills requirement.
- Work simplification is used when jobs are not specialized.

1. **Autonomous of Self-Directed Teams:** Empowerment results in self-directed work teams. A self –directed team is an intact group of employees responsible for whole work segment, they work together, handle day-to-day problems, plan and control, and are highly effective teams.
2. **High Performance Work Design:** Improving performance in an environment where positive and demanding goals are set leads to high performance work design. It starts from the principle of autonomous groups working and developing an approach, which enables group to work effectively together in situations where the rate of innovation is very high. Operational flexibility is important and there is the need for employees to gain and apply new skills quickly with minimum supervision. However due to bureaucracy high performance work design does not work.

5.3. JOB EVALUATION

- **Kimball and Kimball**: " Job evaluation represents an effort to determine the relative value of every job in a plant and to determine what the fair basic wage for such a job should be."
- Helps in removing inequalities.
- **Wendell French:** "Job Evaluation is a process of determining the relative worth of the various jobs within the organization so that differential wages may be paid to jobs of different worth. "
- It is a process which is helpful even for framing compensation plans by the personnel manager.
- Job evaluation is the process of analyzing and assessing the various jobs systematically to ascertain their relative worth in an organization.
- To be objective, job evaluation should "rate the job not the man." Should be clear, easily understood, and sold to employees. Should not result in salary decrease/demotions for existing employees.
- Job evaluation is the process that establishes every position's internal relative worth to a company by measuring a position's potential fulfillment of duties against the amount of value being given by the present employee.
- Job evaluation measures job worth in an internal sense, as well as in an economic one.

Advantageous of Job evaluation

1. **Reduction in inequalities in salary structure:** It is found that people and their motivation is dependent upon how well they are being paid. Therefore the main objective of job evaluation is to have external and internal consistency in salary structure so that inequalities in salaries are reduced.
2. **Specialization:** Because of division of labour and thereby specialization, a large number of enterprises have got hundred jobs and many employees to perform them. Therefore, an attempt should be made to define a job and thereby fix salaries for it. This is possible only through job evaluation.
3. **Helps in selection of employees:** The job evaluation information can be helpful at the time of selection of candidates. The factors that are determined for job evaluation can be taken into account while selecting the employees.
4. **Harmonious relationship between employees and manager:** Through job evaluation, harmonious and congenial relations can be maintained between employees and management, so that all kinds of salaries controversies can be minimized.
5. **Standardization:** The process of determining the salary differentials for different jobs become standardized through job evaluation. This helps in bringing uniformity into salary structure.
6. **Relevance of new jobs:** Through job evaluation, one can understand the relative value of new jobs in a concern.

Procedure of Job evaluation: IIPM

1. Analyse and Prepare Job Description
2. Select and prepare a Job Evaluation Plan
3. Classify Jobs
4. Install the Programme
5. Maintain the Programme

Methods of Job Evaluation

1. Non-Analytical Methods

1. **Job Ranking:** Ranking system is a very simple method of job evaluation. Under this system the job raters simply rank one job against various others without assigning point value.
2. **Job Classification and Grading Method:** Numbers of predetermined grades or classifications are first established and then various jobs are assigned within each grade or class.

2. Analytical Methods

3. **Point Rating System:** Assumes it is possible to assign points to the different job factors as well as to each degree of each factor involved in jobs and the sum total of these points gives an index of relative value of jobs.
4. **Factor Comparison System:** A mixture of point & simple ranking .After locating major common factors, each job is ranked for each compensable factor and then ratings are combined for each job in an overall numerical rating for the job. It is easy now to assign money value to jobs in direct proportion to points assigned.

Pitfalls of Job Evaluation

- Encourages employees on how to advance in position when there may be limited opportunities for enhancement as a result of downsizing.
- It promotes internal focus instead of customer orientation
- Not suitable for forward looking organizations, which has trimmed multiple job titles into two or three broad jobs.

5.4. MERIT RATING

- Main aim of merit rating is the evaluation of the performance of employees.
- Employer can give reward on the basis of merit of employees.
- It is also helpful to compare the quality of different employees.
- **James Lundy**: "The process of evaluating an employee's performance on the job."
- **Kimball and Kimball:** "The evaluation of any given worker as to his fitness for a given job in terms of assigned factors by which he may be intelligently appraised."

Personal abilities evaluate in merit rating

1. Knowledge and work experience
2. Interest in the work
3. Quality which he produced
4. Punctuality
5. Trust and Faith
6. Confidence

7. Leadership quality
8. Discipline and co-operation
9. Flexibility according to situation and time
10. Hardworking

Importance of Merit Rating

1. It is helpful to measure the performance of employees. On the basis of performance, we can utilize him in better works.
2. After telling the weak points of employees, we can increase the performance of employees.
3. It is the helpful to promote of employees.
4. Merit rating tells the strength and weakness of employee with proper record. So, it is helpful to give more training to employee. With training, we can convert his work points into strength points.

5.5. WAGES AND SALARY ADMINISTRATION

- Wage and Salary Administration is the administrative procedure of establishing and supervising wage levels and operations in an organization.
- Job evaluation is the basis to determine wage or salary.
- Wage and salary administration affect levels of employee commitment to the organization.
- A large part of the compensation that people receive from work is monetary.
- Administration of employee compensation is called ***wage and salary administration.***
- **D.S. Beach**: "Wage and Salary Administration refers to the establishment and implementation of sound policies and practices of employee compensation. It includes such areas as job evaluation, surveys of wage and salaries, analysis of relevant organizational problems, development and maintenance of wage structure, establishing rules for administrating wages, wage payment incentives, profit sharing, wage changes and adjustments, supplementary payments, control of compensation costs and other related items."
- The **wage and salary administration** aims to establish and maintain an equitable wage and salary structure and an equitable labor cost structure. Generally both the terms are taken as similar and same but there is some difference.
- **Wage:** "ILO defined wage as the remuneration paid by the employer for the services of hourly, daily, weekly and fortnightly employees."
- The remuneration paid to blue collar employees for production and maintenance.
- Wages are compensation of wage earners. The numerous employees who use the tools and equipments for their employers to produce goods and services that are sold by their employers.
- **Wages for Salary:** Wage is compensation to the employees for services rendered to the organization. In case the quantum of services rendered is difficult to measure, then the payment is called salary. Normally the wage period is shorter than the salary period.
- **Salary:** The remuneration paid to the clerical and managerial personnel employed on monthly or annual basis for production and maintenance.
- All remuneration capable of being expressed in terms of money, which would, if the terms of employment expressed or implied were fulfilled, be payable to a worker in respect of his/her employment, or of work done in such employment.
- Wage represent hourly rates of pay, and Salary refers to the monthly rate of pay, irrespective of the number of hours put in by an employee. They differ from employee to employee, and depend upon the nature of job, seniority and merit.
- **Nominal wage:** Wage paid or received in monetary terms. It is also known as money wage.

- **Real Wage:** The amount of wage arrived after discounting nominal wage by the living cost. ***It represents the purchasing power of money wage.***

Importance of wages

- Wages are most important component of labour costs, which also include non-wage costs such as employer's social contributions and taxes.
- Wages represent an important variable taken into account by employers in their attempt to improve their competitive position in national and international markets.
- Importance of wages within labour costs, collecting information on the different components of labour costs while identifying how far they influence employers decision with regard to employment, investment and capital relocations.
- It may be direct use of governments, trade unions and employers to better understand the role played by wage and labour costs in a highly competitive and globalized environment.

Objectives of Wage and Salary Administration

- To establish a fair and equitable compensation offering similar pay for similar work.
- To attract competent and qualified personnel.
- To retain the present employees by keeping wage levels in tune with competitive units.
- To keep labor and administrative costs in line with the ability of the organization to pay.
- To improve motivation and morale of employees and to improve union management relations.
- To project a good image of the company and to comply with legal needs relating to wages and salaries.
- To establish job sequences and lines of promotion wherever applicable.
- To minimize the chances of favoritism while assigning the wage rates.

Factors Affecting Wage or Salary level

1. Remuneration in comparable industries
2. Firms ability to pay
3. Relating to price index
4. Productivity
5. Union pressure and strategies
6. Government Legislations

Type of wages

1. **Subsistence Wage:** The wage that can meet only bare physical needs of a worker and his family is called subsistence wage.
2. **Minimum Wage:** Minimum wage is the wage that is able to provide not only for bare physical needs but also for preservation of efficiency of worker plus some measure of education, health and other things. The National Commission on Labour stated : Among the competing clauses on value added in industry, the first claim is of the worker for a basic minimum wage irrespective of the worker for a basic minimum wage irrespective of any other consideration. Beyond this however, in the determination of wages differentials the capacity to pay becomes relevant.:
3. **Fair Wage:**
    - Fair wages is an adjustable step that moves up according to the capacity of the industry to pay, and the prevailing rates of wages in the area of industry.
    - The wages must be fair, i.e. sufficiently high to provide standard family with food, shelter, clothing, medical care and education of children appropriate to the workmen.

- A fair wage lies between the minimum wage and the living wage which is the goal.
- Wages must be paid on an industry wise and region basis having due regard to the financial capacity of the unit.

4. **Living Wage:** Living wage is that which workers can maintain the health and decency, a measure of comfort and some insurance against the more important misfortune of lie.
Remember: SMILE

- It is wage which can offer an employee, incentive to work and produce enough in quantity, without sacrificing quality, so that the payment of such wage is justifiable by the industry. A literate and intelligent worker will use living wage for steady size in his standard of living i.e. healthy living, with a few comforts and provision for contingencies.
- **Incentive wage**: The amount of remuneration paid to worker over and above the normal wage as an incentive for employee's contribution to the increased production or saving in time or material.
- It is the wage equal to that received by employees performing equal work demanding equal skills, equal difficulty and equal unpleasantness. It is reflected in the slogan 'equal pay for equal work'.
- It is the wage equal to that received by employees performing equal work demanding equal skills, equal difficulty and equal unpleasantness. It is reflected in the slogan 'equal pay for equal work'.

Theories of Wages

1. Subsistence theory of wages

- This theory advanced by ***David Ricardo*** and other classical economist, was based on the population theory of Thomas Malthus.
- The market price of labour would always tend towards the minimum required for subsistence.
- According to this theory, the wage in the long run tends to be equal to the level of subsistence. By minimum level of subsistence means the amount which is just sufficient to meet the basic necessities of life of the workers and their family.
- It is argued that if wages exceed the subsistence level the labour will marry and will produce children. The supply of labour will increase then the demand and money wages will fall to the level of subsistence.
- If wages remain below the subsistence level, the labour will not be able to maintain their families. The death rate will increase due to hunger and supply of labour will fall than its demand. Again wages will rise to the subsistence level.

Criticism

- **Relation between marriages and wages:** It is incorrect to say that when the money income of a person increases about the subsistence level, he marriages and increases the birth rate. While infect when income increases, people improve their standard of living instead of having the marriage.
- **Demand side ignored:** This theory gives more importance to the supply side and ignores the demand side labour, for the determination of wages.
- **Difference in wages:** This theory falls to explain that why wages differ from occupation to occupation and from person to person.
- **Trade unions ignored:** This theory ignores the role of trade unions. But in the present age these are playing very important role in the determination of wages.

2. The wages fund theory

- This theory is associated with ***Adam Smith and J.S.Mill***.

- Wage fund is that amount of floating capital which is set a part by employer for paying wages to the labour. The average wage rate is determined by dividing the wages fund by the total number of workers employed.
- Wage rate = Wage Fund / Total no. of workers.
- If we want to increase the rate of wages, there are two methods. We should increase the fund or we should decrease the supply of labour. We cannot increase the fund quickly, because the savings increase slowly. Further if any group of labour succeeds in getting higher wages, the result will be that other workers would get less.

Criticism

- **Difference in wages:** According to this theory, all the workers receive the equal wages while infect wages differ from worker to worker.
- **Demand factor ignored:** In this theory supply of labour has given much importance while the demand factor has been ignored.
- **Existence of fund:** According to this theory there is a separate fund for the payment of wages, while in reality there is no special fund which is particularly meant for the payment of wages to the workers.
- **Objection on homogeneous labour:** This theory assumes that labour is homogeneous and they should be paid equally but all the units of labour cannot be homogeneous.

3. Residual claimant theory

- This theory is offered by American economist ***Francis A. Walker***. He says, "Wages equal the whole product minus rent interest and profit."
- *According to this theory labour receives what remains after the payment of rent, profits, taxes and interest out of the national income.*
- **Jevon** says, "The wages of working man are ultimately coincident with what he produces, after the deduction of rent, taxes and the interest on capital."

Criticism:

- **Supply influence ignored:** This theory ignores the influence or supply side in the determination of wages.
- **Role trade unions:** It fails to explain as to how the trade unions raise their wages.
- **Entrepreneur right:** Residual claimant is the right of entrepreneur and not the labour. The labour receives its share during the process of production.
- **Case of loss:** If the firms suffers a loss, in that case how labour will bear the loss.

4. Marginal productivity theory

- This theory proposed by ***J .B. Clark.***
- "Marginal productivity means the net addition or net subtraction caused in the total production by employing or withdrawing one unit of production."
- A producer always compares the marginal product value with the price of a marginal input unit. This theory states that price of each factor of production tends to be equal to its marginal productivity.

Assumptions :

1. **Homogeneous units:** It has been assumed that all the input units are exactly same. While it is not possible that all units should be same.

2. **Perfect competition:** It is assumed in this theory that the law of diminishing return also applies to the business organization.

5. Demand and supply theory

- This theory Propounded by ***Alfred Marshal.***
- Just as the price of commodity is determined by the interaction of the forces of demand and supply, the rate of wages can also be determined in the same way with help of demand and supply forces.
- **Supply of labour:** Supply of labour depends upon the following factors.
  a. **Size of population:** If the size of population is greater than the supply of labour will also be greater.
  b. **Mobility of labour:** The supply of labour also depends upon the mobility of labour. Because if any occupation or country supply of labour decreases it can be increased.
  c. **Social structure:** Supply of labour also depends upon the social set up of a country. If any society allows the women to work, then the supply of labour will be greater.
- The wages will be determined at the point where demand and supply both are equal to each other.

Criticism: In this theory it is assumed that there is perfect competition in the market while perfect competition is absent in the market of labour and goods.

6. The Bargaining theory of wages

- The bargaining theory of wages holds that wages, hours, and working conditions are determined by the relative bargaining strength of the parties to the agreement.
- This idea of bargaining was developed to a considerable extent by ***John Davidson***, who proposed in *The Bargain Theory of Wages* (1898) that the determination of wages is an extremely complicated process involving numerous influences that interact to establish the relative bargaining strength of the parties.
- In the **bargaining theory of wages**, there is no single economic principle or force governing wages. Instead, wages and other working conditions are determined by workers, employers, and unions, who determine these conditions by negotiation.

Limitations

- Collective bargaining can be seen as the reduction of two risks to which the worker is exposed through individual bargaining.
- There is first the risk that the worker will be merely one of a number of applicants for a single vacancy and that competition between them will force the pay down.

6. Surplus value theory

- Surplus value is a specific expression of the capitalist form of exploitation, in which the surplus product takes the form of surplus value.
- The production and appropriation of surplus value constitute the essence of the fundamental economic law of capitalism. ***Karl Marx*** pointed out that "production of surplus value is the absolute law" of the capitalist mode of production.

7. Equity theory

- Equity theory is a theory that attempts to explain relational satisfaction in terms of perceptions of fair or unfair distributions of resources within interpersonal relationships.
- Equity theory was first developed in 1963 by ***John Stacey Adams***, who asserted that employees seek to maintain equity between the inputs that they bring to a job and the outcomes that they receive from it against the perceived inputs and outcomes of others.
- The belief is that people value fair treatment which causes them to be motivated to keep the fairness maintained within the relationships of their co-workers and the organization.
- The structure of equity in the workplace is based on the ratio of inputs to outcomes. Inputs are the contributions made by the employee for the organization.

5.6 WAGE BOARDS AND PAY COMMISSIONS

Wage Policy in India

- Recent wage practices in India in the organized sector are such that dearness allowances are paid to neutralize at least partially, price increases, bonus paid as per the bonus act and fringes benefits given under the employees state insurance act and the employees provident fund act.
- Wage boards have attempted to settle wage disputes taking into account the principle of fair wages first set forth by the report of committee on fair wages.
  (a) Productivity of labour.
  (b) Prevailing rates of wages in the same and similar occupations in the same neighbouring localities.
  (c) Level of the national income and its distribution.
  (d) Place of the industry connected in the economy of the country. The committees' recommendations are similar to the requirement laid down above.

Constituents of a National Wage Policy

Three reports on National Wage Policy were presented after independence.

1. National Commission on Labour (1969) – Concern with the evolution of wage policy and the conditions of labour.

2. A committee under the chairmanship of Prof. S. Chakravorty was appointed by the planning commission, they have submitted report in 1973.

3. The Janata Gpvernment appointed a study group on Wages, Incomes and Prices under the chairmanship of Mr. S. Bhootlingam which submitted its report in May 1978.

Objectives National Wage Policy

- To eliminate malpractices in the payment of wages.
- To minimum wages for workers.
- To rationalize inter-occupational, inter-industrial and inter-regional wage differentials.
- To compensate workers for the rise in the cost of living.
- To obtain for the worker's a just share in the fruits of economic development.
- To permit bilateral collective bargaining within the national framework so that high wage islands are not created.
- The regulations adopted by the State to achieve the objectives of the national wage policy are:
- Prescribing minimum rates of wages.

- Compulsory conciliation and arbitration.
- Wage boards.

Second National Commission on Labour

- On 15th Oct. 1999, Govt of India decided to set up the 2nd National Commission with Mr. Ravindra Varma as a chairperson indicating the following terms of reference.

  A. To suggest rationalization of existing laws relating to labour in the organized sector and

  B. To suggest an 'umbrella' legislation for ensuring a minimum level of protection to the works in the unorganized sector.

Formulation of Wage policies in India

- A tripartite Committee Viz., "The Committee on Fair Wage" was set up in 1948 to provide guidelines for wage structures in the country. The report of this Committee was a major landmark in the history of formulation of wage policy in India. Its recommendations set out the key concepts of the 'living wage', "minimum wages" and "fair wage" besides setting out guidelines for wage fixation.
- Article 39 states that the State shall, in particular, direct its policy towards securing (a) that the citizen, men and women equally shall have the right to an adequate livelihood and (b) that there is equal pay for equal work for both men and women.
- Article 43 states that the State shall endeavour, by suitable legislation or economic organization or in any other way, to give all workers, agricultural, industrial or otherwise, work, a living wage, conditions of work ensuring a decent standard of life and full enjoyment of leisure, and social and cultural opportunities.

Collective Bargaining and Adjudication

- In organized , collective bargaining is the method whereby workers organize together (usually in unions) to meet, converse, and negotiate upon the work conditions with their employers normally resulting in a written contract setting forth the wages, hours, and other conditions to be observed for a stipulated period.
- It is the practice in which union and company representatives meet to negotiate a new labor contract. It is the coming together of workers to negotiate their employment.
- A collective agreement is a labor contract between an employer and one or more unions. Collective bargaining consists of the process of negotiation between representatives of a union and employers in respect of the terms and conditions of employment of employees, such as wages, hours of work, working conditions and grievance-procedures, and about the rights and responsibilities of trade unions.
- The parties often refer to the result of the negotiation as a Collective Bargaining Agreement or as a Collective Employment Agreement .
- Collective bargaining includes not only negotiations between the employers and unions but also includes the process of resolving labor-management conflicts. Thus, collective bargaining is, essentially, a recognized way of creating a system of industrial jurisprudence.
- It acts as a method of introducing civil rights in the industry, that is, the management should be conducted by rules rather than arbitrary decision making.
- It establishes rules which define and restrict the traditional authority exercised by the management.

- **Mechanics of Wage Fixation in India**: Collective bargaining can be used for negotiating wages and hours of work. Unfortunately the trade unions lack solidarity. The multiplicity of unions often makes workers bargaining power rather weak. The state therefore, has provided conciliation and adjudication machinery. The industrial tribunals usually attempt to find a reasonable rate to wage. Very often however a tribunal's award was not found satisfactory either by the employer or the workers.

Wage boards

- A wage board is a ***tripartite body*** with representatives of management and workman presided over by an independent person nominated by the government.
- The board is required to fix wages in accordance with a principles of wage fixation and discussed earlier.
- The wage board helps to resolve the disputes in a democratic manner by bringing the parties together, without compulsion on either side.
- It may however be pointed out that a wage board can only make recommendations as there is no legal sanction behind it but for all practical purposes, a board's recommendations are regarded as awards, and if unanimous, are made binding on the parties.

Pay Commissions

- The Pay Commission is an administrative system or mechanism that the government of India set up in 1956 to determine the salaries of government employees.
- The First Pay Commission was established in 1956, and since then, every decade has seen the birth of a commission that decides the wages of government employees for a particular time-frame.
- The second Pay Commission was set up in August 1957 and gave its report in two years.
- The third Pay Commission, set up in April 1970, submitted its report in March 1973.
- The recommendations of the Fourth Pay Commission covered the period between 1986 and 1996.
- The Fifth Pay Commission covered the period between 1996 and this year. The Union Cabinet, under the stewardship of Prime Minister Manmohan Singh , approved the setting up of the 6th Pay Commission to revise the payscales of central government employees in July 2006.
- The 6th Pay Commission is headed by ***its Chairman Justice B N Srikrishna, and has Ravindra Dholakia, J S Mathur and Sushama Nath as its other members.***

5.7. OTHER IMPORTANT ASPECTS OF WAGES AND SALARY

5.7.1. Profit Sharing

- An arrangement in which an employer shares some of its profits with its employees.
- The compensation can be stocks, bonds, or cash, and can be immediate or deferred until retirement.
- Profit-sharing allows for changing contributions each year. Contributions are determined by a formula to allocate the overall contribution and distribution of accumulated funds after the retirement age.
- Unless the plans are defined as an elective deferral plan, the contributions are not tax deductible. Contributions and earnings can grow tax-deferred until withdrawal.

- **Profit-Sharing Plan**: A plan that gives employees a share in the profits of the company. Each employee receives a percentage of those profits based on the company's earnings. Also known as "deferred profit-sharing plan" or "DPSP."
- This is a great way to give employees a sense of ownership in the company. The company decides what portion of the profit will be shared. And there are typically restrictions as to when and how you can withdraw these funds without penalties.
- One of the aspects of organization wide incentive system is profit sharing under which an employee receives a share of the profit fixed in advance under an agreement freely entered into. The major objective of the profit sharing system is to strengthen the unity of interest and the spirit of cooperation. Some of the advantages of such a scheme are:
- (i) it inculcates in employees' a sense of economic discipline as regards wage costs and productivity;
- (ii) it engenders improved communication and increased sense of participation;
- (iii) it is relatively simple and its cost of administration is low; and
- (iv) it is non-inflationary, if properly devised.
- One of the essentials of a sound profit sharing system is that it should not be treated as a substitute for adequate wages but provides something extra to the participants. Full support and cooperation of the union is to be obtained in implementing such a scheme.

5.7.2. Bonus

- Bonus pay is compensation over and above the amount of pay specified as a base salary or hourly rate of pay. The base amount of compensation is specified in the employee offer letter, in the employee personnel file, or in a contract. Bonus pay can be distributed randomly as the company can afford to pay a bonus, or the amount of the bonus pay can be specified by contract.
- Bonus pay that is specified by contract is used most frequently to reward executives. While employees might wish that executive bonus payments were tied to performance results, this is not always the case. A structure of bonus payments is frequently found in sales organizations to reward sales performance at specified levels over and above commission. Some sales organizations reward employees with bonus pay without commission.
- Bonus pay is used by many organizations as a thank you to employees or a team that achieves significant goals. Bonus pay is also used to improve employee morale, motivation, and productivity. As long as bonus pay is discretionary by the employer, it is not considered to be a contract. If the employer promises a bonus, however, the employer may be legally liable to pay the bonus.

Performance bonus

- Compensation for work performed above and beyond normal or expected duties. Performance bonuses are often used as incentives for increased productivity of an individual or team in a corporate environment.
- A predetermined performance bonus for meeting a specific goal or target is common in the sales industry and for C-suite executive's at large companies. Occasionally, performance bonuses are awarded in recognition of exceptional work even when the employer has no contractual obligation to do pay a bonus.

Recommendation of Bonus Commission (1961)

- Chairman: **M. R. Mehar**

- Bonus Commission suggested that the Bonus payment should be done when 'profits exceed a certain base, laborers should legitimately have a share in them'.
- Bonus is a right of the worker.
- Bonus should be paid unit-wise, with a view to creating a sense of belongingness among the workers.
- Bonus should be paid from the available surplus.
- ***Available surplus=Gross profit-(depreciation according to Income tax act+ Actual return Preferences Capital+7% return on equity capital+4% Reserves and surplus).***
- Allocation of surplus for the payment of bonus should be 60% of the available surplus. Minimum bonus payable to worker is 4% of the basic + DA or Rs.400 whichever is higher. If the minimum bonus is more than 60% of the surplus, the industry has to pay minimum bonus. Maximum bonus is 20% of the basic.
- The Bonus should be paid to employees whose salary is upto Rs.1600.In case of employees whose salary is beyond Rs.700, this salary would be taken as Rs.700 for the purpose of calculations of bonus.
- Employees in public sector competing with the private sector to the tune of 20% are eligible to get the bonus.

5.7.3. The Minimum Wages Act: 1948

- The act empowers the central and state governments.
- To fix minimum rates of wages and to revise such wages from time to time in respect of schedule employments The state governments are required to appoint advisory board for fixing minimum wages and there is to be a central advisory board to advise on the wage fixation matters in general and for the co-ordination of the work of the state advisory boards

5.8. WAGE STRUCTURE IN INDIA

Designing a Wage Structure

- Ascertain and establish the market rate survey and the studies on the existing salary structure from the senior to the junior grade.
- Draw up a salary grade structure ranging from the lowest limit to the highest limit along with the salary gaps between jobs.
- Make a job evaluation and rank the jobs into a hierarchy.
- Procure market data to establish external equity in the pay scale.
- Based on the result of the job evaluation and market rate survey or studies arrange all jobs in the grades in a hierarchical order.

Determining Wage Structure

- While constructing a salary structure two points have to be borne in mind:
- Salary progression: sequence of increase in salary to merit/seniority.
- **Broad Banding:** collapsing salary grades into a few broad and wide levels or "bands" each consisting of a relatively wide range of jobs and salary levels.

Prerequisites of Wage Structure

There are three pre requisites of a sound primary compensation structure; they are:

1. Internal Equity.

2. External Competitiveness
3. Performance – based payment.

- The employee benefit package normally contains apart from basic wage, a dearness allowance, overtime payment, annual bonus, incentive systems, and a host of fringe benefits.

1. Basic Wage

- The concept of basic wage is contained in the report of the Fair Wages Committee.
- According to this Committee, the floor of the basic pay is the "minimum wage" which provides "not merely for the bare sustenance of life but for the preservation of the efficiency of the workers by providing some measure of education, medical requirements and amenities."
- The basic wage has been the most stable and fixed as compared to dearness allowance and annual bonus which usually change with movements in the cost of living indices and the performance of the industry.

2. Dearness Allowance

- The fixation of wage structure also includes within its compass a fixation of rates of dearness allowance.
- In the context of a changing pattern of prices and consumption, real wages of the workmen are likely to fluctuate greatly.
- Ultimately, it is the goods and services that a worker buys with the help of wages that are an important consideration for him.
- The real wages of the workmen thus require to be protected when there is a rise in prices and a consequent increase in the cost of living by suitable adjustments in these wages. In foreign countries, these adjustments in wages are effected automatically with the rise or fall in the cost of living.
- In India, the system of dearness allowance is a special feature of the wage system for adjustment of the wages when there are frequent fluctuations in the cost of living.
- In our country, at present, there are several systems of paying dearness allowance to the employees to meet the changes in the cost of living.
- In practice, they differ from place to place and industry to industry.
- One of the methods of paying dearness allowance is by a flat rate, under which a fixed amount is paid to all categories of workers, irrespective of their wage scales.
- The second method is its linkage with consumer price index numbers published periodically by the government.
- It indicates the changes in the prices of a fixed basket of goods and services customarily bought by the families of workers.
- In other words, the index shows the rise or falls in the cost of living due a rise or fall in consumer prices.
- The Consumer Price Index (CPI) is a monthly index published by the Bureau of Labor Statistics.
- The CPI is compiled by price data collected throughout the country for a fixed set of goods, such as food, clothing, shelter, fuels, prescriptions, transportation fares, and medical fees. The CPI is important as a predictor of wage increases and of employees' need for greater income.
- The third method of paying dearness allowance is on a graduated scale according to slabs. Under this method, workers are divided into groups according to the slabs of wage scales to whom fixed amounts of dearness allowance are paid on a graduated scale. After a limit, there will not be any increase in the amount of dearness allowance at all, however high the wage rate may be. This method is popular because it is convenient and also considered to be equitable.

3. Overtime Payment

- Working overtime in industry is possibly as old as the industrial revolution.
- The necessity of the managements' seeking overtime working from employees becomes inevitable mainly to overcome inappropriate allocation of manpower and improper scheduling, absenteeism, unforeseen situations created due to genuine difficulties like breakdown of machines.
- In many companies, overtime is necessary to meet urgent delivery dates, sudden upswings in production schedules, or to give management a degree of flexibility in matching labour capacity to production demands.
- The payment of overtime allowance to the factory and workshop employees is guaranteed by law.
- All employees who are deemed to be workers under the Factories Act or under the Minimum Wages Act are entitled to it at twice the ordinary rate of their wages for the work done in excess of 9 hours on any day or for more than 48 hours in any week.
- The major benefit of overtime working to workers is that it offers an increase in income from work.

4. Annual Bonus

- The bonus component of the industrial compensation system, though a quite old one, had assumed a statutory status only with the enactment of the Payment of Bonus Act, 1965. The Act is applicable to factories and other establishments employing 20 or more employees.
- **Eligibility:** Every employee not drawing salary/wages beyond Rs. 10,000 per month who has worked for not less than 30 days in an accounting year, shall be eligible for bonus for minimum of 8.33% of the salary/wages even if there is loss in the establishment whereas a maximum of 20% of the employee's salary/wages is payable as bonus in an accounting year.
- However, in case of the employees whose salary/wages range between Rs. 3500 to Rs. 10,000 per month for the purpose of payment of bonus, their salaries/wages would be deemed to be Rs. 3500.

5. Incentive Systems

- The term "incentive" has been used both in the restricted sense of participation and in the widest sense of financial motivation.
- It is used to signify inducements offered to employees to put forth their best in order to maximize production results.
- Incentives are classified as financial and non-financial. Important financial incentives are attractive wages, bonus, dearness allowance, traveling allowance, housing allowance, gratuity, pension, and provident fund contributions.
- Some of the non-financial incentives are designation, nature of the job, working conditions, status, privileges, job security, opportunity for advancement and participation in decision making.

Essentials of a Sound Wage Incentive Plan

- Measurement of the amount of work done.
- Establishment of standard output on the basis of which the incentive has to be worked out.
- Setting up a suitable rate of incentive.

6. Fringe Benefits

- Certain supplementary benefits and services other than salary and wages are known as **"fringe benefits"** are also available to them.

- **Fringe Benefits:** In almost all industrial organizations the employees receives several employee benefits, commonly known as fringe benefits.
- In India fringe benefits for the labour personnel in common use may be categorized as Dearness Allowance, City Compensatory Allowance and Special Housing Assistance Allowance To these may be added cleaning charges for uniforms, travelling allowance, canteen subsidy, food subsidy, special financial assistance to workers educational schemes, leave with wages for attending basic education school etc.
- The characteristics of fringe benefits are:
  - ❖ These benefits are distinctly additional to the regular wages paid to the workers. As such, they are not provided as a substitute for wages or salaries of the employees.
  - ❖ These benefits are meant primarily to be of advantage to the employees.
  - ❖ The advantages accrued to the employees through the provision of fringe benefits are as such they cannot be secured through their own individual efforts.
  - ❖ Only those benefits fall within the purview of fringe benefits which are or can be expressed in cash terms.
  - ❖ The scope of fringe benefits is different from that of welfare services. Fringe benefits are provided by the employers alone whereas welfare services may be provided by other agencies as well. Benefits that have no relation to employment should not be regarded as fringe benefits.
- Fringe benefits have been classified in several ways. In terms of their objectives, ***Meggison*** classifies them into two groups: those providing for employees' security and those purporting to increase employees' job satisfaction causing reduction in labour turnover and improvement in productivity. The former group includes retirement programmes, workmen's compensation, unemployment compensation, social insurance, and other provisions. The later group incorporates vacations, holidays, sick leave, discounts on company goods and services, and allied tangible and intangible benefits.
- Fringe benefits are also categorised as statutory, contractual, and voluntary. Statutory benefits include social security and medical care, unemployment compensation, workmen's compensation, provident fund, and gratuity. The benefits provided by the employers in pursuance of agreements with workers may include dearness allowance, house rent allowance, city compensatory allowance, medical allowance, night-shift allowance, heat allowance, transport, housing and educational allowances. Voluntary fringe benefits which are provided unilaterally by the company include group insurance, death benevolent fund, washing allowance, leave encashment, leave travel concession, conveyance allowance, incentive for family planning, service awards, and suggestion awards.
- Currently fringe benefits are a significant part of employee compensation system and the employees tend to take them for granted and do not link these items with wages or income as they do not have any direct bearing on payments. They are no more on the fringe of compensation but form an integral component of individual's earnings involving spiraling costs for the company.

  However, the fringe benefit system can become effective if attempts are made to gear them to the needs of human resource in organisational settings.

- **Fringe benefits help in**:
  - Lesser fatigue.
  - Oppose labour unrest.
  - Satisfy employee objectives.
  - Promote recruitment.
  - Minimize turnover.
  - Reduce overtime costs.

Methods of Compensation

1. **Time Rate System**: It is one of the simplest and oldest methods of wage payment. Under it, remuneration is based upon the amount of time spent on the work. The wage rate increases with an increase in hours of work done and vice-versa. Here wages are calculated on hourly, daily, weekly, monthly or yearly basis and are usually prescribed in advance. It is more widely used as it is very simple to compute the earnings quite easily.It provides guaranteed and secured income, thereby removing the fear of irregularity of income.It facilitates payroll function.
2. **Piece Rate System**: This method takes into consideration the efficiency of the workers. Under it, wages are based upon the amount of work done by the workers. The wage rate rises or falls with increase or decrease in the output of the worker. Here wage rates are prescribed per piece.It can offer direct connection between effort and reward. Hence, it is the best method to ensure higher productivity.Wage-cost determination is easy.
3. **Incentive Wage Plan**: It is the co-ordinated form of both the above mentioned methods for wage payment. Under it, the workers get additional wages based upon their efficiency in addition to the minimum guaranteed wages. Incentive wage rate rises or falls with increase or decrease in the quantity of production.

Incentive schemes: ***Dunn and Rache*** categories incentive schemes in three broad types:

a) Simple incentive plan.
b) Sharing incentive wage.
c) Group incentive plan.

5.9 SALARY ADMINISTRATION PROGRAM

5.9.1. Pay-for-Performance Salary Programs

- A program which provides small increases to most employees based on changes in the labor market, but with large, meaningful increases granted to a limited number of exceptional employees.
- Increases are based on realistic performance evaluations with some employees not receiving any increase.

Design Features :

- Performance standards are established for activities that employees can impact or control.
- Traditional Cost of Living and Seniority increases are eliminated.
- Increases are withheld from poor performers until their evaluated performance improves.

- Increases may take the form of additional salary and/or cash bonuses.
- Salary Administration Program
- Pay-for-Performance Salary Programs.

Advantages :

- Increases are tied to productivity and results, rather than length of service, etc.
- Improves employee communication and teamwork.
- Provides greater job satisfaction.
- Additional compensation dollars result in attainment of desired results.

Disadvantages:

- Requires considerable effort to install and monitor.
- Is based on a foundation of trust and credibility between management and employees.
- Requires an accurate and well-accepted Performance Evaluation System.
- Eliminates length of service as a significant pay determinant. This initially negatively impacts the concept of "loyalty“ because it diminishes the impact of the ever-present “Good Ol’ Boy” system.

5.9.2 Wage incentives

- Incentive pay, also known as "pay for performance" is generally given for specific performance results rather than simply for time worked. While incentives are *not* the answer to all personnel challenges, they can do much to increase worker performance.
- In order to remove the defects of time wage system and piece wage system, management authorities of wage payments which blended the two systems in such a manner that the interests of both - the workers and the employees might be protected under these systems, time and speed form the basis of wage payment.
- Technically, these methods are called "incentive plans". These plans provide an incentive to workers to produce more and are paid bonus or premium for additional work.
- **Hummel and Nickerson:** "It refers to all the plans that provide extra pay for extra performance in addition to regular wages for a job."
- **The National Commission on Labour:** "Wage incentives are extra financial motivation. They are designed to stimulate human effort by rewarding the person, over and above the time rated remuneration, for improvements in the present or targeted results."
- **Florence:** “It refers to increased willingness as distinguished from capacity.Incentives do not create but only aim to increase the national momentum towards productivity.”
- **Scott: “**It is any formal and announced programme under which the income of an individual, a small group, a plant work force or all the employees of a firm are partially or wholly related to some measure of productivity output.”

Types of Wage Incentive Plans

1. Individual Incentive Programs
2. Group Incentive Plans
3. Reward Programs
4. Compensation Communications

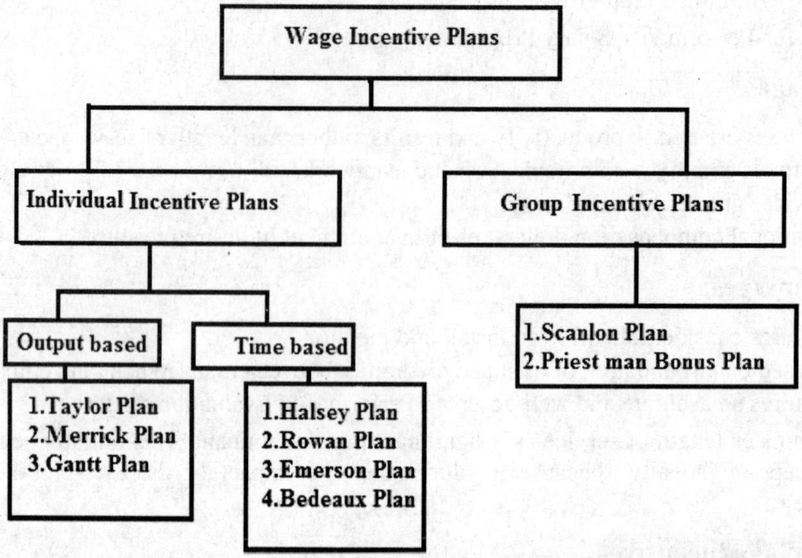

1. Individual Incentive Plans

- Under individual incentive plans, earnings are related directly to the performance of the individual worker.
- In case of group incentive schemes, earnings of a group are related to the performance of the group as a whole.
- Individual incentives may be based on time or output. Under time based plans, a standard time is determined and bonus is given if a worker completes the job in less than standard time.
- Under output based plans, a standard of output is determined and workers producing more than the standard output are given bonus.

1.11 Time Based Individual Incentive

1.1.1. Halsey or Weir Plan

- This plan was developed by **F.A. Halsey** and was first introduced in the Weir Engineering Works, England.
- Under this plan, a standard time is fixed on the basis of past performance records.
- A worker who completes his job within or more than the standard time is paid a guaranteed time wage.
- A bonus (usually 50 per cent) of the time saved is paid to a worker who completes his job in less than the standard time. The bonus is calculated o the basis of time rate.
- The Halsey plan is useful during the transitionary period when a well-conceived plan based on scientific standards is being introduced. In some textile mills this plan is used while an employee is learning the job.

Merits of Halsey or Weir Plan

- The plan is simple to understand. A worker can easily calculate his earnings.
- Both the employee: and the workers get equal benefit of time saved.
- A guaranteed minimum wage to every worker provides a sense of security.
- The plan encourages the workers to be efficient because bonus is based on time saved.

Demerits Halsey or Weir Plan

- Standards based on past performance may not be scientific and fair.
- Workers get only half of the benefit of their efficiency.
- If the workers rush through the job to save more time, the quality of production may suffer. Wastage and spoilage may also increase.
- Much clerical work is involved because records of time saved and bonus earned have to be kept for each worker.

1.1.2. Rowan Plan

- This is a modified form of Halsey Plan.
- It was developed by **James Rowan** of England.
- Under it, a minimum time wage is guaranteed to every worker. A standard time is determined in advance. The bonus is that proportion of the wages which the time saved bears to the standard time.

Merits of Rowan Plan

- The guarantee of minimum wage gives a feeling of security.
- Both the employer and the workers share the benefits of time saved.
- The efficient workers get bonus at a diminishing rate if they save more than 50% of the standard time. This provides a check against over-speeding and deterioration in quality.

Demerits of Rowan Plan

- The plan is difficult to understand for an average worker.
- Efficient workers are discouraged to save more than half of the standard time.

1.1.3. Emerson Efficiency Plan

- This plan was developed by **Harrington Emerson.**
- Under this plan, standard time for the job is determined scientifically and a minimum time wage is guaranteed to all workers.
- Bonus is given at an increasing percentage beyond the prescribed level of efficiency (usually 66.67 per cent). Efficiency is measured by comparing the actual time taken with the standard time.

Merits of Emerson Efficiency Plan

- Guaranteed time wage provides a sense of security to all workers.
- It encourages healthy competition among workers.
- Bonus begins at 66.67 per cent efficiency which is within the reach of many workers.

Demerits of Emerson Efficiency Plan

- There is little incentive after 100 per cent efficiency level.

- Employer may fix the standard time at a low level making it impossible for most of the worker s to earn bonus.
- The plan is not very flexible or selective.

1.1.4. Bedeaux Point Plan

- This plan was developed by Charles E. Bedeaux in 1911.
- Under it, standard time for the job is set scientifically and it is expressed in terms of B. For instance, a standard time of 240 B means the job should be completed within 240 minutes.
- In determining the Bs, the time of operation and the rest time both are taken into account, minimum time wage is guaranteed to all workers.
- The workers who complete the job within or more than the standard time are paid at the normal time rate. Those who complete the job in less than the standard time are paid bonus for the time saved.
- Generally, 75% of the wages for the time saved are paid as bonus to the worker and 25% of the foreman.
- Total Wages = S × R + 75% of R (S – T)

Merits of Bedeaux Point Plan

- Minimum wages are guaranteed to all workers.
- The foreman is motivated to increase productivity as one fourth of the value of time saved is paid to him.
- This plan is suitable in factories wherein a worker is expected to perform different types of jobs. All the jobs can be reduced to standard units called Bs.
- Efficiency of different section/workers in the factory can be compared.

Demerits of Bedeaux Point Plan

- Workers may resent sharing the bonus with foreman.
- Calculations involved are complicated and workers may not be able to understand them.
- Much clerical work is involved.

1. 2. Output Based individual incentive plan

1. 2.1. Taylor's Differential Piece Rate Plan

- F.W. Taylor, the Father of Scientific Management devised this plan.
- Under this system, standard task is established through time and motion study.
- Two piece rates are laid down. The lower rate for those workers who fail to complete the standard task within the allotted time and the hither rate for those who completer the task within or less than the allotted time.
- The objective is to provide sufficient incentive to workers to work hard and achieve the standard.

Merits of Taylor's Differential Piece Rate Plan

- it provides sufficient incentives to efficient workers to put forth their best efforts.
- Inefficient workers are penalized but encouraged to reach the standard.
- Use of time and motion study help to improve and standardize work methods.
- Workers have not to share the reward with the foreman.

Demerits of Taylor's Differential Piece Rate Plan

- There is no guarantee of minimum wage to workers.
- The plan is harsh to workers who are just below the standard.
- It treats the workers as machines rather than as human beings.
- The employer may fix a very high standard which workers may find difficult to achieve.

1.2.2. Merrick's Multiple Piece Rate Plan

- This plan was developed to overcome a drawback in Taylor's plan.
- This drawback relates to an abrupt change I piece rate. Under it, three graded piece rates are prescribed. Workers' producing less than 83% of the standard output are paid at a basic piece rate.
- Those producing from 83% to 100% of the standard output are paid 110% of the basic piece rate. Workers producing more than the standard output are paid at 120% of the basic piece rate.

Merits of Merrick's Multiple Piece Rate Plan

- This plan reduces the severity of the Taylor's plan.
- It is less harsh to beginners or learners.
- It is more flexible.
- It is useful where the performance level is to be increased to 100 per cent.

Demerits of Merrick's Multiple Piece Rate Plan

1. Minimum wage is not guaranteed to workers.
2. It is liberal for the efficient workers. But all workers producing from 1% to 82.9% of the standard output are classified as sub-standard and are paid at the same piece rate.

1.2.3. Gantt's Task and Bonus Plan

- This plan was developed by Henry L. Gantt, a close associate of F.W. Taylor.
- Under it, standard time for every task is fixed through time and motion study.
- Minimum time wage is guaranteed to all workers.
- A worker who fails to complete the task within the standard time receives wage for actual time spent at the specified rate.
- Workers who achieve or exceed the standard get extra bonus varying between 20% to 50% of the hourly rate for the time allowed for the task.

Merits of Gantt's Task and Bonus Plan

1. Minimum wage is assured to all workers.
2. Wage increase progressively with increase in efficiency. Therefore, there is sufficient incentive for efficient workers.
3. Inefficient workers are not penalized severally.

2. Group Incentive Plans

- Individual members of the group who occupy jobs requiring special care and attention have not to bear the whole loss of slow speed.
- Charges of favoritism in the assignment of 'though' and 'easy' jobs are not likely to occur.
- The skilled and experienced workers are motivated to help and train inexperienced and new members.

- All these factors create teamwork and cooperative spirit in the group.
- Need for supervision and control is reduced.

Disadvantages:

- An efficient worker may be penalized for the inefficiency of some inefficient members of the group.
- The incentive for an individual worker may not be strong enough to motivate.
- Rivalry among the members of the group may defeat the very purpose of team work and cooperation.

2.1. Priestman Bonus Plan

- This system of wage payment was first used by Priestman's of Hull in 1917.
- It is applied to workers who work in groups.
- It provides for payment of group bonus in addition to the ordinary time rate to the individual workers.
- Thus if during a year, an enterprise is able to reach the predetermined standard output or exceed the previous year's output, workers are paid increased wages in the same ratio in which output has increased.
- If the group as a whole works well, this is bound to add to overall output of the enterprise and in that case all the workers would stand to benefit.
- A minimum wage is guaranteed to each worker.
- The group gets bonus when actual output exceeds the standard.
- The group supervisor also gets a share in the group bonus.
- The plan is easy and promotes team spirit among employees.

Disadvantage:

- It makes no distinction between efficient and inefficient workers.
- It may be insufficient to motivate individual workers, particularly these who possess greater skills and experience.
- Under this plan, a committee of workers and management sets the standards of performance.

2.2. Towne's gain-sharing plan

- Under this plan half of the savings in labour cost as a result of output in excess of the standard is distributed among workers and the foreman.
- The foreman gets a certain percentages as fixed in advance.
- The bonus is paid half yearly.

2.3. Scanlon Plan :

- Named after ***Mr. Joseph Scanlon*** of United States, this plan is the most popular for shaving the gains from increase in productivity.
- It provides for payment of 10% participating bonus for every 10% increase in productivity.
- The benefit is extended to all employees except the members of top management. Under the plan, workers are not paid the entire amount of bonus earned by them in any month. One half of the first 15% of such bonus is set apart for the creation of a reserve fund.

- This fund is used to neutralize the effects of any fluctuations in labour costs.
- In case a part of such fund remains unused, it too is distributed among the workers in the last month of the year and then a new fund is a created for the New Year.
- It is a plant-wide scheme designed to involve workers in making suggestions for reducing the cost of operations and improving work methods by showing the gains of increased productivity.

Other Group Incentive Plan

1. Productive Bargaining

- Management and workers of an enterprise may reach an agreement under which workers agree to give up unproductive wasteful practices such as go-slow and work to rule and in return, the management agrees to link the wages and concessions of increase in productivity.
- For this, it is necessary that there should be a strong trade union to force the workers to honour the agreement. In case there are too many unions not cooperating with one another such agreement has little chance of succeeding.

2. Co-partnership

- Under this certain employees are given the option of buying the shares of the enterprise at reduced price in installments.
- The employees are choosen on the basis of seniority or wage levels.
- Its assumption is that as a shareholder of the company. An employee is likely to show greater understanding of the company's viewpoint and behave more responsibly.
- As for management, it can cite such schemes as proof of its enlightened outlook and thus brighten the public image of the enterprise.

3. Profit sharing

- It is formal or informal agreement freely entered into, by which an employee receives a share fixed in advance of the profits.

• Reward Programs

- The success of any Individual Reward Program (IRP) requires that a number of different areas to be addressed:
  - Open communication
  - Capacity to administer
  - Commitment to success
  - Patience and perseverance
  - Management commitment
  - Clear-cut objectives and strategy
  - Good management and employee relations
  - Recognition of resources: time, expense, manpower.

3.1. Individual Employee Oriented Reward Programs

Design Features :

- Performance standards are established for activities that employees can impact or control.
- Traditional Cost of Living and Seniority increases are eliminated.
- Increases are withheld from poor performers until their evaluated performance improves.
- Increases may take the form of additional salary and/or cash bonuses.

Advantages:

- Increases are tied to productivity and results, rather than length of service, etc.
- Improves employee communication and teamwork.
- Provides greater job satisfaction.
- Additional compensation dollars result in attainment of desired results.

Disadvantages:

- Requires considerable effort to install and monitor.
- Is based on a foundation of trust and credibility between management and employees.
- Requires an accurate and well-accepted Performance Evaluation System.
- Eliminates length of service as a significant pay determinant. This negatively impacts the concept of "loyalty".

3.2. Skill Based Reward Programs :

- A program that rewards employees for attainment of additional skills and knowledge on a formalized basis.

Design Features:

- Establishes an environment in which attainment of skill and knowledge is considered to be highly desirable.
- Provides increased compensation and/or rewards for skill attainment.
- Clarifies career path for each position and the associated educational support.

Advantages :

- Encourages skill acquisition and commitment by individual employees.
- Permits flexibility in worker assignments which may result in reduced staffing requirements.
- Typically results in increased job satisfaction and lower turnover of skilled employees.

Disadvantages :

- Very complicated program to install and maintain, requiring considerable time, resources, and money.
- Training is very expensive and can easily be underestimated.
- Emphasis is on attainment of skills and knowledge, and is not necessarily results oriented.
- Unless carefully monitored, may end up with too many high skilled, high priced employees.
- Does not enhance teamwork.

3.3 Alternative Reward Programs

- Initial analysis and problem definition
- Review of alternatives
- Selection of plan elements
- Test and finalize
- Review and approval
- Implementation
- Monitoring and refinement

The success of any Individual Reward Program (IRP) requires that a number of different areas be addressed:

Limitations of Alternative Reward Programs

- Imagination
- Fear of new and untested
- Ability to accurately forecast or budget
- Administrative ability of organization

State of employee/management relations.

3.4 Reward Programs – Broad-banding

- Broadbanding is a job grading structure that falls between using spot salaries vs. many job grades to determine what to pay particular positions and incumbents within those positions.
- While broadbanding gives the organization using it some broad job classifications, it does not have as many distinct job grades as traditional salary structures do.
- Broadbanding reduces the emphasis on 'status' or hierarchy and places more of an emphasis on lateral job movement within the company.
- In a broadbanding structure an employee can be more easily rewarded for lateral movement or skills development, whereas in traditional multiple grade salary structures pay progression happens primarily via job promotion.
- Broadbanding is a more flexible pay system. This flexibility, however, can lead to internal pay relativity problems as there isn't as much control over salary progression as there would be within a traditional multi-level grading structure.
- Broadbanding eliminates the present hierarchical grading structure and narrow salary ranges.
- In broadbanding, jobs with similar responsibilities and skill requirements are grouped in "bands" or job families.
- Employees can receive salary increases when they improve job knowledge, skills and abilities without having to be reclassified.
- Enhances organizational effectiveness by producing flatter organizational structures and reduces the perceived need to create additional levels of classification and/or supervision to justify higher pay.
- Broad Banding is a type of salary program that replaces multiple grades and ranges with a limited number of wide ranges. Employees move through salary ranges without traditional promotions or job delineation, based on individual skill attainment, and expansion of duties, rather than on any prescribed time pattern.

Design Features :

- Substantially fewer grade levels and titles.
- Multiple job levels are combined into a single range.
- Large range spreads, e.g., 75%, 100% or more vs. 40% to 50%.
- Provides a method to recognize dual career tracks (management and professional).

Advantages :

- Better accommodates a flat organizational hierarchy.
- Emphasizes skill development rather than vertical promotions.
- Eliminates need to establish artificial job titles and hierarchy.
- Provides greater organizational flexibility since the organization is not encumbered by narrowly focused job titles.
- Simplifies salary administration by eliminating promotions that are not bona fide changes in duties and responsibilities.

Disadvantages:

- May not be compatible with the organization's culture and is less successful in highly structured organizations.
- Loss of control points for salary planning and may result in overpaid employees, requiring greater emphasis on monitoring.
- Difficult to use as management tool for determining relationship between jobs.
- Limits promotional opportunities.

4. Compensation Communications

- It is a company's responsibility to commit to effective communication of salary administration plans and their modifications.
- At the minimum, a company is responsible for: providing each employee with applicable salary information regarding his/her own total compensation level, salary range, position in range (PIR), the method for determining salary increases, and other pertinent aspects of the total compensation package.
- communicating changes to policies and procedures to the appropriate personnel in a timely manner, and for ensuring that the staff understands and can effectively implement the changes
- ***The goal is to design a customized alternative reward and recognition program.***
- Recognize extraordinary employee contributions in the areas of effectiveness, quality of work, cost savings, and productivity.
- Strengthen communications between employees and management.
- Provide a systematic method of identifying outstanding individual contributions.
- Provide financial rewards to employees who have demonstrated performance or contribution in excess of their assigned duties and responsibilities.
- Enhance the Company's ability to meet or exceed its target goals.

5.10. ABSENTEEISM

- Absenteeism means unauthorized absence of the worker from his job or the absence of worker when work is available.

- **Rate of Absenteeism:** It is important to reduce the rate of absenteeism for increasing industrial production. Hence, the success of an industry will depend on to the extent to which absenteeism is reduced.
- **Labour Bureau Simla:** "The failure of worker to report for work when he is scheduled to work."
- It is the manifestation of a decision by employees not to present themselves at their place of work, at a time when it is planned by the management that they should be in attendance.
- **Websters Dictionary:** "Absenteeism is the practice or habit of being an 'absence' and an absentee is one who habitually stays away"

Causes of Absenteeism

1. Maladjustment with Factory Conditions.
2. Social and Religious Functions.
3. Stress.
4. Alcoholism and Drug Abuse.
5. Unsatisfactory Housing Conditions.
6. Sickness.
7. Unhealthy Working Conditions.
8. Rural Exodus.
9. Absence of Adequate Welfare Facilities.
10. Managerial Attitude.
11. Over-identification with Family Affairs.
12. Desire for Money, Status and Power.

Types of Absenteeism

1. Authorized Absenteeism
2. Unauthorized Absenteeism
3. Willful Absenteeism
4. Absenteeism caused by circumstances beyond one's control.

Measures to Control Absenteeism

- Provision of suitable housing facilities in industrial towns will definitely improve attendance.
- A sense of responsibility should be created among workers through proper education and training.
- Introduction of an incentive bonus scheme and linking it with attendance should be encouraged.
- No single measure can be effective in controlling absenteeism; rather a skilful combination of various measures.

Calculation of Absenteeism

$$\text{Absenteeism Rate} = \frac{\text{Number of Mandays lost}}{\text{Number of Mandays scheduled to work}} X\,100$$

Five Categories of Absenteeism: K. N. Vaid

1. Entrepreneurs
2. Status seekers

3. **Epicureans:** This class of absentee does not like to take up the jobs which demand initiative, responsibility, discipline and discomfort. They wish to have money, power, status but are unwilling to work for their achievement.
4. Family Oriented
5. The sick and old

5.12. LABOUR TURNOVER

- Labour turnover is the rate of change in the number of employees of a concern during period.
- It is a measure of the extent to which old employees leave and new employees enter the service of the concern.
- **Pigors and Myers:** "Labour turnover involves costs not only in human values but also in money." These include:
  - o Costs incurred in hiring and training each new employee.
  - o Costs of overtime work required from regular workers in order to maintain the required levels of production until the new employee can do his share.
  - o Loss of production in the interval between separation of the former employee and the time when his replacement is fully broken in.
  - o Expense in equipment or facilities not being fully utilised during the training period.

Types of Labour Turnover

1. **Accessions:** Addition of new candidates to the existing employees.
2. **Seperation:** Termination of employment. They are also called employee turnover.They incudes:
   a. Resignation
   b. Lay off or Lack of work
   c. Disciplinary Lay off or Discharge
   d. Retirement and Deaths

Formulae

- Labour turnover is defined as the **proportion of a firm's workforce that leaves during the course of a year.**
- The formula for calculating labour turnover is :

$$\text{Labour turnover} = \frac{\text{Number of Employees leaving during period}}{\text{Average Number of Employees employed during period}} X\ 100$$

Measures to Reduce Labour Turnover

- Increase pay levels to meet competition.
- Introduce procedures for relating rewards to performance.
- Provide better career opportunities.
- Workers organizations should be encouraged to maintain contact with the workers and redress their grievances.
- Reorganize work and arrangement of offices or workshops to increase group cohesiveness.
- Improve working conditions; adopt policy of welfare, sickness insurance and pension.
- Improve recruitment and selection procedures to ensure that job requirements are specified accurately and the selected employees fit the specifications.
- Provide adequate training or adjustment periods when working conditions change.

5.12. OBJECTIVE QUESTION - ANSWER

1. Job - analysis includes :
   (A) Job description
   (B) Job specification
   (C) Both (A) and (B)
   (D) Job evaluation

Answer: C

2. Which of the following is not a method of Job Analysis?
   (A) Critical Incident Approach
   (B) Job Elements Approach
   (C) Position Analysis Questionnaire
   (D)Application Blank

Answer: D

3. Which of the following case of methods of Job analysis information?
   (A)The interview
   (B)Questionnaire
   (C)Observation and Diary
   (D)All the above

Answer: D

4. By-product of Job Analysis are :
   (A) Job Enrichment and Job Evaluation
   (B) Job Description and Job Specification
   (C) Job Rotation and Job Transfer
   (D)Job Satisfaction and Job Specification

Answer: B

5. Job analysis includes :
   (A) Job description and job enlargement
   (B) Job enlargement and job enrichment
   (C) Job description and job specification
   (D) All of the above

Answer: C

6. Monitoring employees through a preplanned series of position is called :
   (A) Promotion
   (B) Succession planning
   (C) Job reporting
   (D) Job rotation

Answer: B

7. Approaches to job design includes :
   (A) Engineering approach
   (B) Human approach
   (C)The job characteristic approach
   (D) All the above

Answer : D

8. Restructuring of job content and division of responsibility between jobs to increase the amount of responsibility is called :
   (A) Job Enlargement
   (B) Job Enrichment
   (C) Job Analysis
   (D) Job evaluation

Answer: B

9. The provision of training and practice in increased range of skills is known as____ :
   (A)Job enlargement
   (B)Job enrichment
   (C)Job Analysis
   (D)Job Evaluation

Answer: B

10. The internal wage differentials and relative worth of the job for the organization are determined by
    (A)Job Analysis
    (B)Job Design
    (C)Job Enrichment
    (D)Job Evaluation

Answer: D

11. Which of the following is a strategy of job design that increases job depth by meeting employee's needs for psychological growth?
    (A) Job rotation
    (B) Job enrichment
    (C) Job enlargement
    (D) Job enrichment and job enlargement

Answer: B

12. Job design does not involve which one of the following considerations :
(A) How much autonomy should be given to individual employees?
(B) What tasks should be allocated?
(C) Who should be involved / consulted?
(D) Ignoring where the job is located

Answer: A

13. When a worker has a say in the work methods that he/she wishes to utilise in his/her job is characterised by :
(A)Skill variety
(B)Job identity
(C)Job significance
(D)Autonomy

Answer: A

14. The job design would be LEAST formal in a
(A) matrix structure
(B) professional bureaucracy
(C) divisionalized structure
(D) machine bureaucracy

Answer: B

15. While formulating a wage structure, a Wage Board should consider:-
a. Requirements of social justice
b. Capacity of the industry to pay
c. Possibility of reduction in work force
d. Periodicity for review of wage structure
(A) D (B) b & d
(C) C (D) a & b

Answer: D

16. The purpose of job enrichment is to
(A) expand the number of tasks an individual can do
(B) increase job efficiency
(C) increase job effectiveness
(D) increase job satisfaction of middle management

Answer: C

17. Which one is not a non-quantitative job evaluation method?
(A)Ranking method
(B)Grading method
(C)Point rating method
(D)Job-classification method

Answer: C

18. The systematic process of making job evaluation determinations about a job based upon its content and the way is which it actually functions within the organization is called:
(A) Job Determination
(B)Job Analysis
(C)Job Evaluation
(D) Job Grading

Answer: C

19. Match the following with List-A to List-B

List-A
(a) Job Rotation
(b) Job Instruction
(c) Vestible training
(d)Programmed Instruction

List-B
(i) The trainer appraises the performance of the trainee, provides feedback information and corrects the trainee
(ii) The movement of the trainee from one job to another
(iii) Simulation of actual work conditions in a class room
(iv) The subject matter to be learned is presented in a services of carefully planned sequential units.

	(a)	(b)	(c)	(d)
(A)	(iv)	(iii)	(ii)	(i)
(B)	(ii)	(i)	(iii)	(iv)
(C)	(iii)	(iv)	(ii)	(i)
(D)	(i)	(ii)	(iii)	(iv)

Answer: B

20. The method by which relative worth of Jobs in an organization is determined is called as :
(A)Job Specification
(B)Job Description
(C)Job Analysis
(D)Job Evaluation

Answer: D

21. Which of the following is the most analytical method of evaluation?
(A)Ranking Method
(B)Grading Method
(C)Factor-Comparision Method
(D)Point Method

Answer: C

22. Under job Evaluation techniques ranking method includes :
(A)Simple ranking
(B)Ranking the key jobs
(C) Paired comparison
(D)All the above

Answer: D

23. An organized factual statement of the duties and responsibilities of a specific job is known as :
(A)Job description
(B)Job specification
(C)Job evaluation
(D) Job enrichment

Answer: A

24. Match the following :

Personal management Function	**Deals with**
(a) Job enrichment	(i) determining relative worth of various jobs
(b) Job description	(ii) restructuring job content to include more responsibility
(c) Job specification	(iii) qualification of job performers
(d) Job evaluation	(iv) functions required to be performed on the job

	(a)	(b)	(c)	(d)
(A)	(i)	(iii)	(iv)	(ii)
(B)	(ii)	(iv)	(iii)	(i)
(C)	(i)	(iv)	(iii)	(ii)
(D)	(i)	(iii)	(iv)	(ii)

Answer: B

25. Match the following :

Group A	**Group B**
(a) Point ranking method	(i) Non-Analytical method of job-evaluation
(b) Paid holidays	(ii) Fringe benefits
(c) Provident fund	(iii) Analytical method of job-evaluation
(d) Job grading method	(iv) Perquisites

	(a)	(b)	(c)	(d)
(A)	(iii)	(iv)	(ii)	(i)
(B)	(iii)	(ii)	(i)	(iv)
(C)	(ii)	(i)	(iii)	(iv)
(D)	(i)	(iv)	(ii)	(iii)

Answer: D

26. Arrange the following steps of job evaluation process in the correct sequence :
(i) Job description / Specification
(ii) Employee Classification
(iii) Job Evaluation Programme
(iv) Job Analysis

(A)	(i)	(ii)	(iii)	(iv)
(B)	(iv)	(i)	(iii)	(ii)
(C)	(iv)	(iii)	(ii)	(i)
(D)	(ii)	(i)	(iii)	(iv)

Answer: B

27. Organize the following steps in job evaluation in the sequence of their occurrence :
(a) Preparing key or benchmarking job
(b) Selecting comparable and compensable factors

(c) Job analysis data
(d) Administration of Position Analysis Questionnaire
(A) (c), (a), (b), (d)
(B) (a), (c), (d), (b)
(C) (a), (c), (b), (d)
(D) (b), (c), (a), (d)

Answer: A

28. Match the following :

List I	List II
(a) Job specification	(i) Procedure for determining duties and skills for a job and the kind of person required to perform
(b) Career	(ii) List of Job's duties, responsibilities, reporting, relations, working conditions
(c) Job analysis	(iii) List of job's human requirements in terms of education, skills, personality etc.
(d) Job description	(iv) The occupational positions a person has had over many years

Codes :

	(a)	(b)	(c)	(d)
(A)	(i)	(ii)	(iii)	(iv)
(B)	(i)	(iii)	(ii)	(iv)
(C)	(iii)	(iv)	(i)	(ii)
(D)	(iv)	(iii)	(ii)	(i)

Answer: C

29. A broad statement of the purpose, duties and responsibilities of a job or position, may be referred to as :
(A)Job Analysis
(B)Task Analysis
(C)Job Description
(D)Job Specification

Answer: C

Job Description: A broad, general, and written statement of a specific job, based on the findings of a job analysis. It generally includes duties, purpose, responsibilities, scope, and working conditions of a job along with the job's title, and the name or designation of the person to whom the employee reports. Job description usually forms the basis of job specification.

30. Match List – I with List – II. Select the correct answer from the codes given below :

List – I	List – II
a. Theory – X	i. Integration of behaviour is the key process in Management.
b. Theory – Y	ii. Calls for vertical job loading.
c. Job Enrichment	iii. Based on the traditional conception of control and command.
d. Job Enlargement	iv. To provide more control over one's activities and greater participation in decisions.

Codes:

	a	b	c	d
(A)	i	ii	iii	iv
(B)	iii	i	ii	iv
(C)	iii	i	iv	ii
(D)	i	iv	ii	iii

Answer : B

31. What is broad-banding ?
(A)Clubbing manpower structure
(B)Integrating information system
(C)Flexible pay-banding allowing grade mobility performance
(D)None of the above

Answer: C

32. Job description provides information about characteristics required to perform activities.
(A)Forming supportive objectives

(B) Delegating the authority
(C)Establishing enterprise objectives
(D) Identifying and classifying activities.

Answer: A

33. Monitoring employees through a preplanned series of position is called:
(A)Promotion
(B)Succession planning
(C)Job reporting
(D)Job rotation

Answer: B

34. The provision of training and practice in an increased range of skills is known as :
(A)Job enrichment
(B)Job enlargement
(C)Job evaluation
(D)Job analysis

Answer: A

35. The process of establishing the value of jobs in a Job hierarchy, is known as :
(A)Job Analysis
(B)Job Evaluation
(C)Job Requirement
(D)Performance Evaluation

Answer: B

Explanation: Kimball and Kimball: " Job evaluation represents an effort to determine the relative value of every job in a plant and to determine what the fair basic wage for such a job should be."

36. A list of Jobs duties, Responsibilities, reporting relationships and working conditions is called :
(A) Job enhancement
(B) Job specification
(C) Job description
(D) Job enlargement

Answer: C

Explanation: Job description is a broad statement of purpose, scope, duties and responsibilities of a particular job.

37. The process of studying and collecting information relating to a specific job is known as :
(A) Job Analysis
(B) Job Specification
(C) Job Description
(D) Motion Study

Answer: A

Explanation: Job analysis is primary tool in personnel management. In this method, a personnel manager tries to gather, synthesize and implement the information available regarding the workforce in the concern.

38. The horizontal expansion of jobs is termed as :
(A)Job enrichment
(B)Job enlargement
(C)Job sharing
(D)Job involvement

Answer: B

39. Job analysis involves
(A)Job description and job specification
(B)Job order and job description
(C)Job specification and job order
(D)Job satisfaction and job description

Answer: A

40. A written statement of the human qualification, education and experience needed to perform a job is referred to as:
(A) Job enrichment
(B) Job specification
(C) Job design
(D) Job description

Answer: C

41. Job evaluation is the evaluation of ______
(A) Work
(B) Worker
(C)Working Conditions
(D)All the above
Answer: D

Explanation: Job evaluation is the process of analyzing and assessing the various jobs systematically to ascertain their relative worth in an organization.

42. A systematic comparison done in order to determine the value of Job is called :
(A) Job upgradation
(B) Job enrichment
(C) Job Evaluation
(D) Job analysis
Answer: C

43. When monotony in work is reduced by giving a wider variety of duties to employees, this is known as :
(A)Job rotation
(B)Job redesign
(C)Job enlargement
(D)Job enrichment
Answer: A

44. Modifying methods of performing a job to reduce the levels of skill or skills demanded is known as :
(A) Multi - tasking
(B) De - skilling
(C) Multi - skilling
(D) None of these
Answer: B

45. The process of establishing the value of jobs in a job hierarchy is known as
(I) Job analysis
(II) Job requirement
(III) Job evaluation
(IV) Performance evaluation

Find the correct combination according to the **Code.**
(A) I & II
(B) II & III
(C) III & IV
(D) I & IV
Answer: C

46. The distinction between 'job enrichment' and 'job enlargement' is
(A) semantics
(B) 'job enrichment' is vertical loading while 'job enlargement' is horizontal loading
(C) 'job enrichment' is the outgrowth of Hertzberg's theory while 'job enlargement' is of Maslow's orientation.
(D) 'job enrichment' is more for the individual and the other is more of organisation making
Answer: B

47. Minimum wages are fixed by :
(A) Trade unions
(B) Employees
(C) State Governments
(D) Court of law
Answer: C

48. Which of the following is not a determinant of wages?
(A) Prevailing wages
(B) Bargaining strength of Unions
(C) Job Evaluation
(D) Performance Appraisal
Answer: D

49. Wage Boards set right
(A) Inter-regional differentials
(B) Inter-sectoral differentials
(C) Intra-industry differentials
(D) Inter-industry differentials
Answer: C

50. Wage Boards evolve wage structure for :
(A) Single Firm
(B) Different Industries
(C) One Industry
(D) Nation as a whole

Answer: D

51. Wage survey method is used for getting information regarding :
(A) Prevailing Wages
(B) Variable Pay
(C) Dearness Allowance
(D) All the above

Answer: D

52. Who among the following are not included as members of Wage Board?
(A) Employers' Representatives
(B) Workers' Representatives
(C) Consumers' Representatives
(D) Economists, Wage Experts and Members of Parliament

Answer: C

53. Which of the following is a method of state regulation of wages ?
(A) Wage Boards
(B) Enactment of Minimum Wage Legislation
(C) Labour Courts and Tribunals
(D) All of the above

Answer: D

54. Which of the following is not a method of State Regulation of Wages?
(A) Minimum Wage Legislation
(B) Ordinances
(C) Wage Boards
(D) Industrial Tribunals

Answer: D

55. Which of the following is not a method for fixation of minimum wages in India under the Minimum Wage Act, 1948?
(A) Notification Method
(B) Committee Method
(C) Wage Boards
(D) None of the above

Answer: C

56. Who among the following was the chairman of the Second National Commission on Labour :
(A) Dr. P.B. Gajendragadkar
(B) Dr. Ravindra Verma
(C) Dr. Satya Narayan Jatia
(D) Justice P.N. Bhagwati

Answer: B

57. Which of the following is not a wage incentive plan ?
(A) Halsey Plan
(B) Rowan Plan
(C) Barth System
(D) Beveridge Plan

Answer: C

58. Which of the following is not a type of wage differential?
(A) Occupational wage differential
(B) Geographical wage differential
(C) Wage - Differentials on the basis of sex
(D) Personal wage differential

Answer: D

59. Which of the following statements about characteristics of labour is not true?
(A) Labour is a perishable commodity.
(B) Labour cannot be separated from the person.
(C) Workers have no reserve price.
(D) Labour is as flexible and mobile as capital.

Answer: D

60. Which of the following statements about labour market is not true ?

(A) Labour market like commodity market is analyzed by supply, demand and price equilibrium.

(B) Labour Market is relatively more local than commodity market.

(C) Unlike a commodity market, the relationship between a buyer and seller in a labour market is not temporary.

(D) Monopoly in the labour market is high.

Answer: D

61. Money Wage is otherwise called as

(A) Real wage (B) Living wage

(C) Nominal wage (D) Fair wage

Answer: C

62. Which of the following requirements of a Perfect Market are not found in the Labour Market :

(A) Large number of buyers and sellers

(B) Same price

(C) Same quality

(D) None of the above

Answer: C

63. If money wages are fixed or constant, which of the following situation will be applicable :

(A) Real wages may also be constant

(B) Real wages may fall

(C) Real wages may rise

(D) All the above

Answer: B

64. Voluntary Retirement Scheme (VRS) is introduced to get rid off :

(A) Inefficient employees

(B) Surplus employees

(C) Problematic employees

(D) None of the above

Answer: A

65. Labour Market is :

(A) Perfect Market

(B) Imperfect Market

(C) Monopolistic Market

(D) None of the above

Answer: B

66. Who among the following are not included in the labour force of a country?

(A) Employees (B) Employers

(C) Domestic Servants (D) Housewives

Answer: D

67. Which of the following is not a characteristics of Indian Labour Market ?

(A) Migratory character

(B) Low level of literacy

(C) High Degree of Unionization

(D) High rates of Absenteeism and Labour Turnover

Answer: C

68. Who among the following propounded the marginal productivity theory of wages ?

(A) Davidson (B) Webbs

(C) Maurice Dobb (D) J.B. Clark

Answer: D

69. Under which of the following theories of wages, trade unions play a vital role in wage determination :

(A) Marginal Productivity theory of Wages

(B) Wage Fund Theory

(C) Residual Claimant Theory

(D) Collective Bargaining Theory

Answer: D

70. After all other factors of production are paid, wages are paid to labour from the left-out fund: is the theme of :

(A) Subsistence theory

(B) Marginal Productivity theory

(C) Wage fund theory

(D) Residual claimant theory

Answer: D

71. Match the following :

Theory of Wages	Propounders
(a) Exploitation theory	(i) J.S. Mill
(b) Subsistence theory	(ii) J.B. Clark
(c) Marginal Productivity theory	(iii) Karl Marx
(d) Wage fund theory	(iv) David Ricardo

	(a)	(b)	(c)	(d)
(A)	(iii)	(iv)	(ii)	(i)
(B)	(iii)	(ii)	(iv)	(i)
(C)	(ii)	(iii)	(iv)	(i)
(D)	(iii)	(i)	(ii)	(iv)

Answer: A

72. Match the following :

Theory of wage	Contributor
(a) Bargaining theory	(i) J.Stacy Adams
(b) Demand and Supply theory	(ii)A.C.Pigou
(c) Purchasing Power theory	(iii) John Davidson
(d) Equity theory	(iv) Alfred Marshall

	(a)	(b)	(c)	(d)
(A)	(iii)	(iv)	(ii)	(i)
(B)	(iv)	(ii)	(i)	(iii)
(C)	(ii)	(i)	(iii)	(iv)
(D)	(iii)	(ii)	(iv)	(i)

Answer: A

73. The Residual Claimant Theory of Wages was propounded by :

(A) Karl Marx
(B) David Ricardo
(C) David John
(D) Francis A. Walker

Answer: D

74. Karl Marx is said to be the proponent of which of the following theories of wages?

(A) Subsistence Theory of Wage
(B) Wage Fund Theory
(C) Surplus Value Theory of Wage
(D) Marginal Value Theory of Wage

Answer: C

75. Match the following :

Contributors	Wage Theories
(a) David Ricardo	(i) Marginal Productivity Theory
(b) James Stuart Mill	(ii) Residual Claimant Theory
(c) F.W. Walker	(iii) Wage Fund Theory
(d) J.B. Clark	(iv) Subsistence Theory

Codes :

	(a)	(b)	(c)	(d)
(A)	(iv)	(ii)	(i)	(iii)
(B)	(iii)	(ii)	(iv)	(i)
(C)	(iv)	(iii)	(ii)	(i)
(D)	(ii)	(iv)	(iii)	(i)

Answer: C

76. Match the following :

Theories of Wages	Propounders
(a) Subsistence Theory	(i) Karl Marx
(b) Wage FundTheory	(ii) Francis Walker
(c) Residual Claimant Theory	(iii) J.S. Mill
(d) Surplus Value Theory	(iv) David Ricardo

	(a)	(b)	(c)	(d)
(A)	(iii)	(iv)	(i)	(ii)
(B)	(iv)	(iii)	(ii)	(i)
(C)	(ii)	(i)	(iii)	(iv)
(D)	(i)	(iii)	(iv)	(ii)

Answer: B

77. Out of the following theories of wages which one is also called as Iron Law of Wages?

(A) Wage Fund Theory
(B) Subsistence Theory
(C) Marginal Productivity Theory
(D) Collective Bargaining Theory

Answer: B

78. Match the following :

Theory of wages	Propagators
a. Wage Fund Theory	i. John Bates Clark
b. Marginal Productivity Theory	ii. John Davidson

c. Bargaining Theory iii. John Stuart Mill
d. Investment Theory iv. Gilelman

Codes :

	a	b	c	d
(A)	ii	iv	i	iii
(B)	iii	I	ii	iv
(C)	iv	ii	iii	i
(D)	i	iii	ii	iv

Answer: B

79. The "Marginal Discounted Product of Labour" as a modified version of Marginal Productivity Theory was advanced by
(A) Taussig (B) Kalecki
(C) Ricardo (D) Adam Smith

Answer: A

80. Wages paid on the basis of units produced are called :
(A)Time Rated
(B) Money Wages
(C) Piece Rated
(D)Real Wages

Answer: C

81. Give the correct sequence of the following :
(i) LivingWage (ii) Minimum Wage
(iii) Fair Wage (iv) Subsistence Wage

Codes :

(A)	(iv)	(i)	(iii)	(ii)
(B)	(iv)	(ii)	(iii)	(i)
(C)	(ii)	(iv)	(iii)	(i)
(D)	(ii)	(iv)	(i)	(iii)

Answer: B

82. Which of the following is not a component of wages?
(A) Basic Wage
(B) Dearness Allowance
(C) Fringe Benefits
(D) Incentives

Answer: C

83. Which of the following theory of migration explains the pressures of the places of origin and attraction of the places of destination?
(A)Affluence driven skill scarcity theory
(B)Population ecology theory
(C)Push and pull theory
(D) None of the above

Answer: C

84. Which of the following is concerned with intra-industry wage differentials?
(A)Wage Survey
(B)Job Evaluation
(C)Wage Board
(D) None of the above

Answer: B

85. Formula for Labour Turnover rate is :

(A)Labour Turnover = $\frac{\text{Temporary total loss}}{\text{Temporary partial loss}} \times 100$

(B)Labour Turnover = $\frac{\text{Permanent total loss}}{\text{Permanent partial loss}} \times 100$

(C)Labour Turnover = $\frac{\text{Number of Employees left during specified period}}{\text{Average Number of Employees during the same period}} \times 100$

(D)Labour Turnover = $\frac{\text{Number of Employees present}}{\text{Number of Employees left}} \times 100$

Answer: C

86. Wages expressed in terms of money are called :
(A) Nominal wages
(B) Real wages
(C) Wage scales
(D) Fringe Benefits

Answer: B

87. If a wage rate is determined by job evaluation, it is called :
(A) Real wage
(B) Standard wage rate
(C) Piece - rate
(D) Time - rate

Answer: B

88. The committee on Fair Wages was appointed in India in the year ________

(A) 1946 (B) 1947
(C) 1948 (D) 1949

Answer: C

89. Minimum wage is :

(A) The wage paid or received in monetary terms
(B) The total amount of remuneration received by an employee during a given period
(C) The amount of wage arrived after discounting nominal wage from the living cost
(D) The amount of remuneration which could meet the nominal needs of the average employee

Answer: A

90. In an inflationary economy like ours to–day, which of the following components of wages becomes more important :

(A) Overtime (B) Incentive
(C)Bonus (D) Dearness Allowance

Answer: D

91. Which of the following is not an incentive plan that relates wages with productivity ?

(A)Taylor's differential piece-rate system
(B)The Beveridge Plan
(C)The Scanlon Plan
(D)The Halsey Premium Plan

Answer: D

92. Which of the following is not an objective of wage incentive programmes?

(A) Developing ownership interest
(B) Improving employee retention
(C) Reducing labour cost
(D) Facilitating the separation of employees

Answer: D

93. When the same rate of incentives is paid to the employees for each unit of goods produced by them, it is called

(A) Straight piece rate
(B) Differential piece rate
(C) Task and time bonuses
(D) None of the above

Answer: A

94. When more than one piece rate is offered to the individuals for goods produced by them, it is called :

(A) Straight piece rate
(B) Differential piece rate
(C) Priestman bonus plan
(D) None of the above

Answer: B

95. Which of the following methods discourages too much speed in the production by the employees?

(A) Straight piece rate
(B) Differential piece rate
(C) Task and time bonuses
(D) None of the above

Answer: C

96. Evaluating the relative worth of the employees in the organization and then deciding the awards for them is called :

(A) Merit rating
(B) Differential piece rate
(C) Task and time bonuses
(D) Straight piece rate

Answer: A

97. Which of following incentive systems recommends a two-piece rate for wage determination?

(A) Merrick multiple piece rate plan
(B) Taylor's differential piece rate plan
(C) Emerson efficiency plan
(D) Gnatt task and bonus system

Answer: B

98. In which of the following methods is the standard time stated as minutes and points?
(A) Bedeaux system
(B) Barth variable incentive plan
(C) Task and time bonus
(D) None of the above

Answer: A

99. Which of the following incentive plans has the following equation for computing the earnings of employees? (Actual hours worked × Time rate) + (Actual time worked / Standard time) × Time saved × Time rate
(A) Emerson efficiency plan
(B) Rowan incentive plan
(C) Halsey incentive plan
(D) Barth variable incentive plan

Answer: B

100. Which of the following is not usually a group incentive plan?
(A) Halsey incentive plan
(B) Priestman bonus plan
(C) Rucker incentive plan
(D) Towne's incentive plan

Answer: A

101. Achieving cost saving not only on labour cost but also on overheads is the crux of
(A) Towne's incentive plan
(B) Priestman bonus plan
(C) Rucker incentive plan
(D) Halsey incentive plan

Answer: C

102. In which method is the standard time expressed in terms of man-minutes called "MANT"?
(A) Hayne's incentive plan
(B) Rowan incentive plan
(C) Barth variable incentive plaN
(D) Bedeaux system

Answer: A

103. Which of the following is an example of fringe benefits?
(A) Health and accident insurance
(B) Contribution to superannuation funds
(C) Leave facilities
(D) All of the above

Answer: D

104. The machinery of wage board in India is primarily used in connection with
(A) Settlement of Industrial Disputes
(B) State Regulation of Wages.
(C) Determination of Wages
(D) Promoting Equal Wages For Equal Work.

Answer: D

105. After the report of the Royal Commission on Labour, which of the following legislations was first enacted ?
(A) Minimum Wages Act
(B) Equal Remuneration Act
(C) Payment of Wages Act
(D) Payment of Gratuity Act

Answer: C

106. Most of the social security benefits to workers in India are calculated on the basis of
(A) Basic wage
(B) Basic wage and Dearness Allowance
(C) Basic wage, D.A. and Medical allowance
(D) Basic wage, D.A., Medical and House rent allowance

Answer: A

107. Which of the following is true of Indian Labour Market ?
(A) It is a Perfect Market

(B) Monopolistic Market
(C) Imperfect Market
(D) None of the above

Answer: C

108. Which of the following statements is false ?
(A)Good wage structure shall address to internal equity and external parity.
(B)Pay related decisions need not base on employer's capacity to pay.
(C)Wage survey is the method for knowing the 'prevailing wages'.
(D)Low wages and high productivity is exploitation.

Answer: A

109. Which of the following is given to workers in the unorganised sector or sweated industries ?
(A) Living Wages
(B) Fair Wages
(C) Statutory Minimum Wages
(D) None of the above

Answer: C

110. Arrange the following according to their comparative position from lowest to the highest:
(a) Statutory Minimum Wage
(b) Subsistence Wage
(c) Living Wage
(d) Fair Wage

(A)	(a)	(c)	(b)	(d)
(B)	(b)	(d)	(a)	(c)
(C)	(b)	(a)	(d)	(c)
(D)	(a)	(c)	(d)	(b)

Answer: C

111. Which of the following statements appear to be correct?
(A)Wage differential is desirable for the growth and development of the society.
(B)There should be no wage differential in the country.
(C)The state through regulation of wages can eliminate wage differentials.
(D) None of the above

Answer: C

112. Which of the following is not a characteristic of labour market ?
(A) Same wage rate
(B) More sellers than buyers
(C) Heterogeneity in labour services
(D) Limited mobility of labour

Answer: A

113. Which of the following factors affect supply of labour ?
(A) Population and Labour Force Participation Rate
(B) Skill, Experience and Job Qualification
(C) Mobility of Labour and Organization of Buyers and Sellers
(D) All the above

Answer: D

114. Which of the following cannot be said to be a type of wage differential ?
(A) Occupational Wage Differential
(B) Geographical Wage Differential
(C) Inter-industry Wage Differential
(D) National Wage Differential

Answer: D

115. Fixing lower retirement age for workers will result in
(A) increased supply of labour
(B) reduced supply of labour
(C) will have no effect on supply of labour
(D) None of the above

Answer: C

116. Which of the following industries lead to seasonal unemployment?
(A) Sugar industry
(B) Construction industry
(C) Ice-cream industry
(D) All the above
Answer: C

117. Who among the following is not included in the labour force?
(A) Workers / employees
(B) Self-employed people
(C) Domestic servants
(D) House-wives
Answer: D

118. Which of the following types of unemployment is also known as Disguised Unemployment ?
(A)Frictional unemployment
(B)Technological unemployment
(C)Seasonal unemployment
(D)Under employment
Answer: D

119. Outsourcing, when it is done internationally, affects which of the following in the country which out–sources :
(A) Supply of labour
(B) Demand for labour
(C) Both supply and demand
(D) None of the above
Answer: C

120. Which of the following can be said to be a correct concept of wages?
(A) Wage is a reward
(B) Wage is a compensation
(C) Wage is the price of labour
(D) Wage is an incentive to work more
Answer: C

121. Tripartite Wage Boards in India followed which of the following principles while making their recommendations?
(A) Minimum Wage Principle
(B) Fair Wage Principle
(C) Living Wage Principle
(D) None of the above
Answer: A

122. The amount sufficient to enable a worker to live in reasonable comfort, having regard to all obligations to which an average worker would ordinarily be subject to
(A) Minimum Wage
(B) Fair Wage
(C) Living Wage
(D) Nominal Wage
Answer: A

Explanation: Minimum Wage: Minimum wage is the wage that is able to provide not only for bare physical needs but also for preservation of efficiency of worker plus some measure of education, health and other things.

123. A test which measures, what it is intended to measure is
(A) Reliable test
(B) Standardised test
(C) Objective test
(D) Valid test
Answer: D

124. The wage which has to be paid by an employer to his workers, irrespective of his ability, is known as :
(A) Living wage
(B) Fair wage
(C) Minimum wage
(D) None of the above
Answer: A

Explanation: Living Wage: Living wage is that which workers can maintain the health and decency, a measure of comfort and some insurance against the more important misfortune of lie.

125. Fair wage is defined as :
(A) Monthly wage paid with Dearness Allowance
(B) Wage that is lower than living wage but more than minimum wage
(C) Wages paid with incentive
(D) Fair wage includes all allowances

Answer: B

Explanation: A fair wage lies between the minimum wage and the living wage which is the goal.
Wages must be paid on an industry wise and region basis having due regard to the financial capacity of the unit.

126. Labour Turnover is :
(A)The rate of change in the working staff of a concern during a definite period
(B)Number of Employees joining the organization
(C)Number of Employees promoted during a year
(D)Number of Employees transferred to other departments

Answer: A

127. The Gregory Committee recommended that _____.
a. The payment of dearness allowance should be limited to an income level below Rs.100/- per month
b. The amount of dearness allowance should be fixed in terms of rupees and not as a percentage of actual income
c. Either to equate the absolute amount of dearness allowance to full compensation for the weighted average of the earnings of all wage groups below the ceiling wage of Rs.200/-
d. To equate the same to full compensation for the weighted average earnings of all wage groups below the weighted average as calculated
(A) d
(B) b, c & d
(C) a & b
(D) All of the above

Answer: B

128. During the second World War, a Board of Conciliation under the chairmanship of Sir S. S. Ranganekar was setup. He was a retired _____ judge.
(A) High Court
(B) Supreme Court
(C) Industrial Court
(D) None of the above

Answer: A

129. The minimum remuneration for a class four employee on entry as recommended by the Third pay commission was:
(A) Rs.285/- per month
(B) Rs.165/- per month
(C) Rs.185/- per month
(D) Rs.175/- per month

Answer: C

130. The NCL has attempted to assess the General Wage Policy of the Government since independence. For this purpose, it chose the following indicators. They are:
a. The state of industrial harmony
b. Changes in workers level of living
c. Changes in productivity
d. Impact of wages on prices
(A) b, c & d (B) a, b, c & d
(B)a & c (D) None of the above

Answer: B

131. The plans having skill-based structures in which employees are paid for the jobs they perform are grouped into two types. These are as follows:-

a. Knowledge plans which link pay differentials to the depth of knowledge related to one occupation
b. Multi-skill plans which link pay differentials to the number of different sets of tasks an employee is supposed to perform
c. Semi-skill plans
d. Skilled plans
(A) D (B) b, c & d
(C) a & b (D) None of the above

Answer: C

132. The following are the major component of compensation system:
a. Salary
b. Basic salary
c. Advanced salary
d. Consolidated salary
(A) a, b, d (B) a, b, c & d
(C) b, c & d (D) b

Answer: C

133. Flexible benefits plan will help:-
a. Control costs
b. Enhance employee satisfaction
c. Increase efficiency
d. Imply rigidity
(A) a & b (B) c & d
(C) a, b, c & d (D) a, c & d

Answer: A

134. Which are the administrative problems caused due to individual incentives
(A)The difficulty in setting production standards that are accepted by both management and workers
(B)The cost of tracking output in the multiple jobs and calculating payments
(C)The cost of time study to set and keep current production standards for multiple jobs
(D)All of the above

Answer: D

135. One of the salient features of The Payment of Wages (Amendment) Bill, 2002 is to substitute the expressions a 'Central Government' or a 'State Government' by the expression '_____', in conformity with the other labour laws.
(A) Union Government
(B) Appropriate Government
(C) Home ministry
(D) Finance Ministry

Answer: B

136. A corporate wide pay plan that uses a structured formula to allocate a portion of annual company profits to employees is known as :
(A) Gain sharing
(B) Profit sharing
(C) ESOPS sharing
(D) All of the above

Answer: B

137. Standing Labour Conference (SLC) was constituted in line with the recommendations of Royal Commission on Labour in the year :
(A) 1942
(B) 1944
(C) 1946
(D) 1948

Answer: A

138. An incentive plan, where improvements in group productivity determines the total amount of money that is allocated, is described as :
(A) Profit sharing
(B) Gain sharing
(C) Bonus sharing
(D) None of these

Answer: B

139. The Employee Stock Ownership Plan (ESOP) was developed by :
(A) Michael Porter
(B) Kaplan
(C) P. F. Drucker
(D) Louis Kelso

Answer: D

Explanation: An **employee stock ownership plan (ESOP)** is an employee-owner scheme that provides a company's workforce with an ownership interest in the company. In an ESOP, companies provide their employees with stock ownership, often at no cost to the employees. Shares are given to employees and may be held in an ESOP trust until the employee retires or leaves the company. The shares are then sold. In 1956, Louis Kelso, invented the first ESOP, which allowed the employees of Peninsula Newspapers to buy out the company founders.[13] Chairman of the Senate Finance Committee, Senator Russell Long, a Democrat from Louisiana, helped develop tax policy for ESOPs within the Employee Retirement Income Security Act of 1974 (ERISA), calling it one of his most important accomplishments in his career.[14] ESOPs also attracted interest of Republican leaders including Barry Goldwater, Richard Nixon, and Gerald Ford, and ESOPs won praise from Ronald Reagan.

In 2001, the United States Congress enacted Internal Revenue Code section 409(p), which effectively requires that S ESOP benefits be shared equitably by investors and workers. This ensures that the ESOP includes everyone from the receptionist to the CFO.

140. Wage determination is mostly done through tools which are
(A) Objective
(B) Subjective
(C) Both of (A) & (B)
(D) None of these

Answer: C

141. Job Evaluation criterion comes from:
(A) Job manual
(B) Job description
(C) Job specification
(D) Job duration

Answer: C

142. The process of determining the tasks that make-up a job and the skills, abilities and responsibilities needed to perform the job is called
(A) Job Analysis
(B) Job Description
(C) Job Enrichment
(D) All of the above

Answer: A

143. One of the following is not included in job descriptions :
(A) Job title (B) Location
(C) Penal actions (D) Duties

Answer: C

144. Match the following :

List – A	List – B
(i) Job Analysis	(a) Grading jobs according to scale of pay
(ii) Job Description	(b) A statement of human qualities to fill the job
(iii) Job Specification	(c) A process of obtaining job facts
(iv) Job Classification	(d) A statement of duties and responsibilities of a job

Codes :

	(i)	(ii)	(iii)	(iv)
(A)	(c)	(d)	(b)	(a)
(B)	(c)	(d)	(a)	(b)
(C)	(a)	(b)	(c)	(d)
(D)	(b)	(c)	(d)	(a)

Answer: A

145. _____ is the procedures through which one determines the duties associated with positions and the characteristics of people to hire for those positions.
(A) Job description
(B) Job specification
(C) Job analysis
(D) Job context
(E) None of the above

Answer: C

146. The information resulting from job analysis is used for writing:
(A) job descriptions
(B) work activities
(C) work aids
(D) job context
(E) performance standards

Answer: A

Explanation: Job analysis produces information used for writing job descriptions and job specifications.

147. Which of the following types of information can be collected via a job analysis?
(A) work activities
(B) human behaviors
(C) performance standards
(D) job context
(E) all of the above

Answer: E

Explanation: The information gathered during a job analysis is primarily used for listing what jobs entail and what kind of people to hire for the job.

148. Information regarding job-related knowledge or skills and required personal attributes is included in the information about _____ an HR specialist may collect during a job analysis.
(A) work activities
(B) human behaviors
(C) human requirements
(D) performance standards
(E) job context

Answer: C

148. What describes the tasks, duties and responsibilities of a Job?
(A) Job Analysis
(B) Job Enrichment
(C) Job Description
(D) Job Empowerment

Answer: C

150. Information regarding job demands such as lifting weights or walking long distances is included in the information about _____ an HR specialist may collect during a job analysis.
(A) work activities
(B) human behaviors
(C) machines, tools, equipment, and work aids
(D) performance standards
(E) job context

Answer: B

151. Information regarding how, why, and when a worker performs each activity is included in the information about _____ an HR specialist may collect during a job analysis.
(A) work activities
(B) human behaviors
(C) machines, tools, equipment, and work aids
(D) performance standards
(E) job context

Answer: A

152. Information regarding the quantity or quality levels for each job duty is included in the information about _____ an HR specialist may collect during a job analysis.
(A) work activities
(B) human behaviors

(C) machines, tools, equipment, and work aids
(D) performance standards
(E) job context

Answer: D

153. Information regarding matters such as physical working conditions and work schedule is included in the information about _____ an HR specialist may collect during a job analysis.
(A) work activities
(B) human behaviors
(C) machines, tools, equipment, and work aids
(D) performance standards
(E) job context

Answer: E

154. How many steps are included in job analysis?
(A) three (B) four
(C) five (D) six

Answer: D

155. The first step in conducting a job analysis is:
(A) deciding how to use the information
(B) reviewing relevant background information
(C) selecting representative positions
(D) collecting data on job activities
(E) developing a job description and job specification

Answer: A

Explanation: Step-1: To decide how one will use the information.
Step-2: To review relevant background information such as organization charts, process charts, and job descriptions.
Step-3: To select representative positions.
Step-4: To analyze the job by collecting data on job activities, required employee behaviors, working conditions, and human traits and abilities needed to perform the job.
Step-5: To verify the job analysis information with the worker performing the job and with his or her immediate supervisor.
Step-6: To develop a job description and job specification.

156. Which is the final step in conducting a job analysis?
(A) deciding how to use the information
(B) reviewing relevant background information
(C) selecting representative positions
(D) collecting data on job activities
(E) developing a job description and job specification

Answer: E

157. Who is interviewed by managers collecting job analysis data?
(A) individual employees
(B) groups of employees with the same job
(C) supervisors who know the job
(D) all of the above
(E) none of the above

Answer: D

158. Which of the following is ***not*** an advantage of using interviews to collect job analysis data?
(A) it is simple to use
(B) some information may be exaggerated or minimized
(C) it is quick to collect information
(D) it can identify uncommon, but important activities
(E) it can be used to explain need for job analysis

Answer: B

159. Interviews often include questions about:
(A) supervisory responsibilities
(B) job duties
(C) education
(D) experience
(E) all of the above
Answer: E

160. What shows the flow of inputs to and outputs from the job being analyzed?.
(A) organization chart
(B) process chart
(C) value chain
(D) job preview
(E) job description
Answer: B

161. Which term refers to a written statement that describes the activities and responsibilities of the job?
(A) job specification
(B) job analysis
(C) job report
(D) job description
(E) job context
Answer: D

162. A _____ summarizes the personal qualities, traits, skills, and background required for getting the job done.
(A) job specification
(B) job analysis
(C) job report
(D) job description
(E) job context
Answer: A

163. Which of the following is included in the job specifications?
(A) personal qualities
(B) traits
(C) skills
(D) required background
(E) all of the above
Answer: E

164. Which of the following methods is used to gather job analysis data?
(A) interviews
(B) questionnaires
(C) observation
(D) all of the above
(E) none of the above
Answer: D
Explanation: The interview is the most widely used method for identifying job duties and responsibilities.

165. In addition to identifying the specific duties associated with a job, a job analysis should also seek to identify the:
(A) length of time an employee has held the position
(B) order of importance
(C) frequency of occurrence
(D) all of the above
(E) b and c only
Answer: E

166. For which of the following jobs is direct observation ***not*** recommended to collect data used in a job analysis?
(A) assembly-line worker
(B) accounting clerk
(C) engineer
(D) receptionist
(E) salesperson
Answer: C

167. A _____ is the time it takes to complete a job.
(A) job specification
(B) work cycle
(C) work week
(D) shift
(E) none of the above
Answer: B

168. The average cycle time is a(n) _____.
(A) minute
(B) hour
(C) day
(D) week
(E) it depends on the specific job

Answer: E

169. When a worker changes what he or she would normally do because they are being watched, _____ has occurred.
(A) proactivity
(B) reactivity
(C) cycling
(D) diverting
(E) none of the above

Answer: B

170. Which two data collection methods are frequently used together?
(A) direct observation and interviewing
(B) questionnaires and direct observation
(C) interviewing and questionnaires
(D) diaries and interviewing
(E) most are used individually

Answer: A

171. Prachi records every activity she participates in at work along with time in a log. This approach to data collection for job analysis is based on:
(A) diaries
(B) interviews
(C) direct observation
(D) questionnaires
(E) supervisor verification

Answer: A

172. Which of the following is considered a qualitative approach to job analysis?
(A) position analysis questionnaire
(B) interviews
(C) Department of Labor approach
(D) functional job analysis
(E) all are qualitative approaches

Answer: B

173. Which of the following is considered a quantitative approach to job analysis?
(A) Interviews
(B) diaries
(C) Department of Labor Procedure
(D) direct observation
(E) questionnaires

Answer: C

174. Which of the following is included in a functional job analysis?
(A) the extent to which specific instructions are necessary to perform the task
(B) the extent to which reasoning and judgment are required to perform the task
(C) the mathematical ability required to perform the task
(D) the verbal and language facilities required to perform the task
(E) all of the above

Answer: E

Explanation: Functional job analysis rates the job not just on data, people, and things, but also on four more dimensions: the extent to which specific instructions are necessary to perform the task; the extent to which reasoning and judgment are required to perform the task; the mathematical ability required to perform the task; and the verbal and language facilities required to perform the task. Second, functional job analysis also identifies performance standards and training requirements.

175. Most job descriptions contain sections that cover:
(A) job summary
(B) standards of performance
(C) working conditions
(D) all of the above
(E) none of the above
Answer: D

176. One uses information from the _____ to write a job specification.
(A) job summary
(B) job identification
(C) job description
(D) standards for performance
(E) job advertisement
Answer: C

177. What type of information is contained in the job identification section of a job description?
(A) job title
(B) job summary
(C) relationships statement
(D) major functions or activities
(E) all of the above
Answer: A

178. What form of data collection involves recording work activities in a log?
(A) interviews
(B) diaries
(C) direct observation
(D) questionnaires
(E) none of the above
Answer: B

179. Which of the following is ***not*** one of the basic activities included in a position analysis questionnaire?
(A) performing skilled activities
(B) being physically active
(C) operating equipment
(D) processing information
(E) all are included in a position analysis questionnaire
Answer: E

180. The _____ assigns a quantitative score to each job based on its decision-making, skilled activity, physical activity, equipment operation, and information-processing characteristics.
(A) Department of Labor Procedure
(B) position analysis questionnaire
(C) functional job analysis
(D) log approach
(E) all of the above
Answer: B

181. Which quantitative job analysis technique can be conducted online?
(A) position analysis questionnaire
(B) Department of Labor Procedure
(C) functional job analysis
(D) all of the above
(E) none of the above
Answer: A

182. FLSA status is located in the _____ section of a job description.
(A) job summary
(B) job identification
(C) relationships
(D) responsibilities and duties
(E) none of the above
Answer: B
Explanation: The FLSA status section of a job description permits quick identification of a job as exempt or nonexempt from overtime and minimum wage provisions.

183. The _____ classifies all workers into one of 23 major groups of jobs.
(A) Department of Labor Procedure
(B) Job analysis
(C) Standard Occupational Classification
(D) Federal Professions Classification System
(E) None of the above
Answer: C

184. Under the _____, the individual must have the requisite skills, educational background, and experience to perform the job's essential functions.
(A) SOC (B) DOL
(C) ADA (D) FCC
(E) SIC
Answer: C

185. Which section of a job description should define the limits of the jobholder's authority, direct supervision of other personnel, and budgetary limitations?
(A) job identification
(B) job summary
(C) relationships
(D) responsibilities and duties
(E) pay levels
Answer: D

186. Job duties that employees must be able to perform, with or without reasonable accommodation, are called:
(A) essential job functions
(B) job requirements
(C) primary job activities
(D) work activities
(E) all of the above
Answer: A

187. The job specification takes the job description and answers the question, _____?
(A) What human traits and experience are required to do this job well
(B) When will the supervisor be completely satisfied with a worker's work
(C) What are the four main activities making up this job
(D) How many other employees are available to perform job functions
(E) What are the performance standards for the job
Answer: A

188. When filling jobs with untrained people, the job specifications may include:
(A) quality of training
(B) length of previous service
(C) previous job performance
(D) physical traits
(E) all of the above
Answer: D

189. Which of the following work behaviors is considered "generic" or important to all jobs?
(A) industriousness
(B) intelligence
(C) experience
(D) morality
(E) motivation
Answer: A

190. All of the following work behaviors are considered "generic" or important to all jobs ***except:***
(A) thoroughness
(B) attendance
(C) experience
(D) schedule flexibility
(E) industriousness
Answer: C

191. _____ means assigning workers additional same-level activities, thus increasing the number of activities they perform.
(A) Job rotation
(B) Job enrichment
(C) Job assignment
(D) Job enlargement
(E) Job adjustment
Answer: D
Explanation: Job enlargement means assigning workers additional same-level activities to increase the number of activities they perform.

192. Systematically moving workers from one job to another is called:
(A) Job rotation
(B) Job enrichment
(C) Job assignment
(D) Job enlargement
(E) Job adjustment

Answer: A

193. Redesigning jobs in a way that increases the opportunities for the worker to experience feelings of responsibility, achievement, growth, and recognition means:
(A) Job rotation
(B) Job enrichment
(C) Job assignment
(D) Job enlargement
(E) Job adjustment

Answer: B

Explanation: Job enrichment means redesigning jobs in a way that increases the opportunities for the worker to experience feelings of responsibility, achievement, growth, and recognition

194. Who argued that the best way to motivate workers is to build opportunities for challenge and achievement into their jobs via job enrichment?
(A) Adam Smith
(B) Frederick Taylor
(C) Frederick Herzberg
(D) Abraham Maslow
(E) Milton Friedman

Answer: C

195. _____ refers to broadening the responsibilities of the company's jobs, and encouraging employees not to limit themselves to what's on their job descriptions.
(A) Job rotation
(B) Job enrichment
(C) Job assignment
(D) Job enlargement
(E) Dejobbing

Answer: E

196. Dejobbing can be described as:
(A) assigning workers additional work at the same level
(B) redesigning jobs to increase opportunities for responsibility
(C) moving workers from one job to another
(D) encouraging employees not to limit themselves to what's on their job descriptions
(E) focusing workers on highly specialized jobs

Answer: D

197. Job enrichment can be described as:
(A) assigning workers additional work at the same level
(B) redesigning jobs to increase opportunities for responsibility
(C) moving workers from one job to another
(D) encouraging employees not to limit themselves to what's on their job descriptions
(E) focusing workers on highly specialized jobs

Answer: B

198. Jack works at a Hilton hotel. Some weeks he works in catering but he also works in housekeeping, and in reservations periodically. This is an example of:
(A) job enlargement
(B) job rotation
(C) job enrichment
(D) dejobbing
(E) job specialization

Answer: B

199. The fundamental rethinking and radical redesign of business processes to achieve dramatic improvements in performance is called:
(A) job redesign
(B) reengineering
(C) process engineering
(D) job enlargement

(E) outsourcing

Answer: B

200. Describing the job in terms of the measurable, observable, and behavioral competencies necessary for good job performance is called a:
(A) competency-based job analysis
(B) Department of Labor Procedure
(C) functional job analysis
(D) SOC classification system
(E) none of the above

Answer: A

201. Competency analysis mainly focuses on:
(A) what is accomplished
(B) how work is accomplished
(C) when work is accomplished
(D) who accomplishes the work
(E) where the work is accomplished

Answer: B

Explanation: Competency analysis focuses on how the worker meets the job's objectives or actually accomplishes the work.

202. The major focuses of Traditional job analysis is:
(A) what is accomplished
(B) how work is accomplished
(C) when work is accomplished
(D) who accomplishes the work
(E) where the work is accomplished

Answer: A

203. Job competencies are always:
(A) measurable
(B) observable
(C) based on goals
(D) both a and b
(E) all of the above

Answer: D

204. When a supervisor bases an employee's training, appraisals, and rewards on the skills and competences he or she needs to achieve his or her goals, the supervisor is using:
(A) competency analysis
(B) traditional analysis
(C) performance management
(D) functional systems management
(E) none of the above

Answer: C

Explanation: Job analysis provides information for recruitment and selection by laying out what the job entails and what human characteristics are required to perform these activities. This information helps management decide what sort of people to recruit and hire. Job analysis information is also crucial for estimating the value of each job and its appropriate compensation. A performance appraisal compares each employee's actual performance with his or her performance standards. Managers use job analysis to determine the job's specific activities and performance standards.

205. Job Analysis involves

1. Developing training skills
2. Identifying Machine tools
3. Identification of the task to be performed by an individual
4. Determination of the materials and products.

Write the correct sequence of steps in Job Analysis

(A) 3, 2, 4, 1
(B) 3, 2, 1, 4
(C) 2, 3, 4, 1
(D) 2, 3, 1, 4

Answer: A

206. A wage period shall not exceed :
(A)Forty days
(B) One week
(C)One month
(D) Thirty - five days
Answer: C

207. "Employees selected for the work should be as perfectly matched to the demand of the job as possible." Which of the following theories says this :
(A)Scientific Management Theory
(B)Bureaucracy Theory
(C)Classical Theory
(D)Traditional Theories
Answer: A

******

UNIT-VI
ORGANIZATION BEHAVIOR

6.1. ORGANIZATION

- Organization is a consciously coordinated social unit composed of a group of people functioning on a relatively continuous basis to achieve a common goal or set of goals.
- Organizations are sets of people who work together to achieve shared goals.
- Groups of people who work interdependently toward some purpose:
  - o Structured patterns of interaction
  - o Coordinated tasks
  - o Work toward some purpose.

6.2. ORGANIZATIONAL BEHAVIOR (OB)

- **Robbins:** "Organisation Behaviour is concerned with the study of what people do in an organisation and how that behaviour affects the performance of the organisation."
- OB is field of study that investigates the impact of individuals, groups, and structure on behavior within organizations for the purpose of applying such knowledge toward improving organizational effectiveness.
- OB refers to the behavior of individuals and groups within organization and the interaction between organizational members and their external environments.
- The study of individual behavior and group dynamics in organizations.
- The study and application of how employees behave within organizations.

Interrelated dimensions influencing behaviour

1. **The Individual:** Working environment should satisfy individual needs as well as attainment of organisational goals.
2. **The Group:** Groups are formal and informal. Understanding of groups complements knowledge of individual behaviour.
3. **The Organisation:** Impact of organisation structure and design, and patterns of management, on behaviour.
4. **The Environment:** Technological and scientific development, economic activity, governmental actions etc. Comes under the term environment of an organization.

Evolution of Organizational Behavior (OB)

1. **<u>Industrial Revolution:</u>**

- Industrial Revolution brought about materialism, discipline, monotony, boredom, impersonally and work interdependence.
- **1800: Robert Owen**, a Welsh factory owner and ***"Father of Personnel management"*** emphasizes the human needs of employees. He could demonstrate ***'vital machines'*** as to ***'inanimate machines.'***

- **1835: Andrew Ure** publishes his ***"The Philosophy of Manufactures"*** based on human factor as one of the factor of production.
- **1886: J. N. Tata** instituted a pension fund and in 1895began to pay accident compensation.

2. **Scientific Management**
   - **Fredrick Taylor** is called the ***'Father of scientific management'***
   - In 1911 Taylor published his work in ***'Principles of scientific management'***
   - Taylors ideas were criticized- particularly, his belief in rationalizing everything and holding the assumptions that human behavior is based on ***'rabble hypothesis.'***
   - **Frank and Lillian Gilberth** pioneered ***time and motion study,*** a type of applied research designed to classify and streamline the individual movements needed to perform jobs with the intent of finding ***"the one best way"*** to perform them.

3. **The Human relation movement**
   - Human relation movement is characterized by heavy emphasis on employee cooperation and morale.
   - There are varied complex reasons for this human relation position. The most contributing factors would be the great depression, the labour movement, the results of the new *Hawthorne studies.*

4. **Hawthorne studies**
   - Carried out at the Western Electric Company's Hawthorne works in Cicero, a suburb of Chicago by **Father of Human relation movement: Elton Mayo.**
   - Studies were conducted by the National Research council. The research involves three sets of studies.
   - **Illumination studies (1924-1927):** Referring originally to the fact that peoples knowledge that they are being studied leads them to modify their behavior.
   - **The Relay Assembly Room study (1927-1933):** A Harward university research group finally concluded that the change in supervisory arrangement was the major reason for the increase in the productivity in this study and in two related studies involving different work groups. The researcher felt that the physical changes such as rest pauses, free lunches, and incentive payments were of lesser importance.
   - **The Bank wiring Room Study (1931-1932):** The behavioral norms set by the work group had a powerful influence over the productivity of the group. The higher the norms, the greater the productivity. The power of the peer group and the importance of group influence on individual behavior and productivity were confirmed in the bank wiring room.
   - Hawthorne studies laid foundation for understanding people's social and psychological behavior in the workplace.
   - Hawthorne researchers concluded that the behavioral norms set by the work group had a powerful influence over group's productivity.

Challenges in OB

1. **Challenges at the Individual Level**
   - Individual Differences
   - Job Satisfaction
   - Motivation
   - Empowerment
   - Behaving ethically

2. **Challenges at the Group Level**
   - Working With Others
   - Workforce Diversity
3. **Challenges at the Organizational Level**
   - Productivity
   - Developing effective employees
   - Putting people first
   - Global competition
   - Managing and working in a multicultural world.
4. **Challenges at the Organizational Level**
   - Productivity.
   - A performance measure including effectiveness and efficiency.
   - Effectiveness.
   - The achievement of goals.
   - Efficiency.
   - The ratio of effective work output to the input required to produce the work.
   - Developing Effective Employees.
   - Organizational Citizenship Behaviour (OCB).
   - Discretionary behaviour that is not part of an employee's formal job requirements, but that nevertheless promotes the effective functioning of the organization.
   - Putting people first generates a committed workforce and positively affects the bottom line.
   - People will work harder when they feel they have "more control and say in their work."

6.3. GROUP DYNAMICS

- Group dynamics means the action of a group engaged in a common endeavor. The word dynamics comes from the Greek word meaning force.
- The phrase Group Dynamics thus means a study of cohesive and disruptive force operating within a group.
- The group dynamics will be structured around the three key elements such as basic element of group behaviour, group cohesiveness and the group structure.
- These three basic elements generally of use in understanding the behavior of a group are activities, interactions and sentiments.
- **Group cohesiveness** refers to the degree to which its members are attracted to the group, are motivated to remain in the group, and mutually influence on another. Highly cohesive groups are more likely to confirm to group pressures than are members of low-cohesive groups.
- **Group structure:** Means that the nature and characteristics of the interrelationships among the members of a group and the roles they play in it.
- **Reason behind joining groups:** People join groups because of needs for security, esteem, affiliation, power, identity, huddling and task functions.
- Ideal group size is 5 to 7 members. Group size has impact on productivity. Bigger the size, lesser the productivity.

Nature of Groups

1. Interaction among members
2. Shared goals

3. People see themselves as a group member.
4. Two or more individuals needed to form group.

Types of Groups

1. **Formal groups:** Deliberately created to perform a specific task.
2. **Informal groups:** Also called a **clique,** is a neither formally structured, nor organizationally determined. This may be a group of friends, like-minded people, etc. created by themselves.
3. **A standing task group or Command group:** Permanently specified in the organizational structure and consists of a supervisor who exercises formal authority over subordinates.
4. **A task group:** Temporarily formal group that is created to solve specific problems.
5. **An interest group:** It is made up of individuals who affiliate to achieve an objective of mutual interest that may have nothing to do with their formal task group memberships.
6. **A friendship group:** It develops on common characteristics such as marital status, political views, college affiliation, sports, etc. This type of group satisfies affiliation needs of their members.
7. **A reference group:** Group with which an individual identifies for the purpose of forming opinions or making decisions. It may exist outside the organization. It is based on factors such as race, gender, politics, religion; social class, education level, profession, etc.
8. **Open and Closed group:** Open group is constant in a state of change whereas close group is quite stable. Open groups differ from closed groups in four aspects as changing membership, frame of reference, time perspective and equilibrium.
9. **In-groups and Out-groups:** The groups to which we belong are in-groups and groups to which we do not belong are out-groups.

Stages of Group development: Bruce W. Tuckman

1. **Forming:** Group members learn about each other, and the task at hand. Indicators of this stage might include: unclear objectives, confusion, and low morale.
2. **Storming:** As group members continue to work, they will engage each other in arguments about the structure of the group which often are significantly emotional and illustrate a struggle for status in the group. Lack of cohesion marks this phase.
3. **Norming:** Group members establish implicit or explicit rules about how they will achieve their goal. They address the types of communication that will or will not help with the task. Indicators include: Questioning performance, Reviewing/clarify objective, Changing/ confirming roles, Opening risky issues, Assertiveness, Listening, Testing new ground, Identifying strengths and weaknesses.
4. **Performing:** Groups reach a conclusion and implement the conclusion. Indicators include: Creativity, Initiative, Flexibility, and Open relationships.
5. **Adjourning:** This is the final stage of team development. It is also called ***'mourning'***. The process of "unforming" the group, that is, letting go of the group structure and moving on.

In nutshell five stages includes:

1. **Forming:** Awareness: Commitment, Acceptance.
2. **Storming:** Conflict: Clarification, Belonging.
3. **Norming:** Cooperation: Development, Support.
4. **Performing:** Productivity: Achievement, Pride
5. **Adjourning:** Separation: Recognizing, Satisfaction.

Remember: FSNPA

Roles or Processes required for group formation: McGrath

Mode I: Inception and acceptance of a project (goal choice).
Mode II: Technical problem solving: Solution of technical issues (means choice).
Mode III: Conflict resolution: Resolution of political issues conflict (policy choice).
Mode IV: Execution: The performance requirements of the project (goal attainment).

Pitfalls of Groups

- Status differential.
- Group norms.
- Risky and cautious shifts.
- **Polarization:** Magnifying a dominant viewpoint.
- **Groupthink:** It leads to conformity. It involves the involuntary suppression of members.

Characteristics of Group

- Shared values and Norms
- Interdependence
- Interaction
- Activities
- Conformity

Theories of group formation

1. **Propinquity theory:** The propinquity theory explains a basic factor, i.e., proximity of people at the workplace, which leads to formation of groups.
2. **Homans' theory:** According to George C. Homans, "the more activities persons share, the more numerous will be their interactions and the stronger will be their shared activities and sentiments; and the more sentiments persons have for one another, the more will be their shared activities and interactions". The members of a group share activities and interact with one member of a group share activities and interact with one another not just because of physical proximity, but also to accomplish group goals. They key element is interaction because of which they develop common sentiments for one another.
3. **Balance theory:** This theory is proposed by ***Theodore Newcomb*** states that "persons are attracted to one another on the basis of similar attitudes towards commonly relevant objects and goals. Once a relationship is formed, it strives to maintain a symmetrical balance between the attraction and the common attitudes. If an imbalance occurs, attempts are made to restore the balance. If the balance cannot be restored, the relationship dissolves". Both propinquity and interaction play a role in the balance theory. Thus, the balance theory is additive in nature in the sense that it introduces the factor of 'balance' to the propinquity and interaction factors. There must be a balance in the relationship between the group members for the group to be formed and for its survival.
4. **Exchange theory:** This theory is based on reward -cost outcomes of interaction between people. To be attracted towards a group, a person thinks in terms of what he will get in exchange of interaction with the group members. Thus, there is an exchange relationship in terms of rewards and costs of associating with the group.

6.4. TEAM DYNAMICS

- A team is a small number of people having shared goals and has an approach for which they hold themselves mutually accountable.
- **Team differs from groups:** Group member possesses diverse skills but teams possess complementary skills.
- When individuals with a common interest, goal, attitude, need and perception come together, a team is formed. Individuals need to come and work together to form a team for the accomplishment of complicated tasks.
- In a team, all team members contribute equally and strive hard to achieve the team's objective which should be predefined.
- In any organization, no one works alone. Every employee is a part of a team and works in close coordination with the team members to perform his level best and in turn benefit the organization. The team members should complement each other and come to each other's need whenever required.
- Teams can be formed anywhere, anytime whenever the task is little difficult and complicated.

Types of teams

1. **Permanent teams:** These teams perform on a permanent basis and are not dissolved once the task is accomplished. Organization never asked them to leave or ever dissolved their team. Such teams are called permanent teams. Work or no work, the human resources team, operation team, administration team always function effectively throughout the year and hence are permanent teams.
2. **Temporary teams:** Unlike permanent teams, temporary teams loose their importance, once the task is accomplished. Such teams are usually formed for a shorter duration either to assist the permanent team or work when the members of the permanent team are busy in some other project. When organizations have excess of work, they generally form temporary teams which work in association with the members of the permanent team for the accomplishment of the task within the stipulated time.
3. **Task Force:** Such teams are formed for a special purpose of working on any specific project or finding a solution to a very critical problem. The government generally appoints special teams to investigate critical issues like bomb blasts, terrorist attacks and so on. The task force explores all the possible reasons which led to a severe problem and tries to resolve it within a given deadline.
4. **Committee:** Committees are generally formed to work on a particular assignment either permanently or on a temporary basis. Individuals with common interests, more or less from the same background, attitude comes together on a common platform to form a committee and work on any matter. To organize any cultural event, organizations generally make committees to raise funds, invite celebrities and all the major tasks involved to successfully organize any event. The committee members work together, design strategies to successfully accomplish the task.
5. **Organization/Work Force:** Such groups are formed in organizations where team members work together under the expert guidance of leader. A leader or a supervisor is generally appointed among the members itself and he along with his team works hard to achieve a common goal. The leader all through must stand by his team and extract the best out of each team member. He must not underestimate any of his team members and take his team along to avoid conflicts.

6. **Self Managed Teams:** Self Managed Teams consist of individuals who work together again for a common purpose but without the supervision of any leader. Here as the name suggests every individual is accountable for his individual performance. The team members of self managed teams must respect each other and should never loose focus on their target. No leader is appointed and the team members have to take their own responsibility. Individuals take the initiative on their own and are their own guides and mentors.
7. **Cross Functional Team:** Ideally the employees should be more or less on the same level to avoid ego hassles. Individuals from different areas come and work together for a common objective to form a cross functional team. In such teams, people from different areas, interests and likings join hands to come out with a unique idea to successfully complete a task.
8. **Virtual Teams:** Virtual teams consist of individuals who are separated by distances and connected through computer. Here individuals communicate with each other online through internet. Such teams are helpful when employees need to connect with each other and are located at different places. Individuals supporting any community in social networking sites such as facebook or orkut also form a virtual team as all the members are from different locations but support a common community. They all have a common objective -to support and promote their community.

6.4.1 Quality Circles (QCs)

- Quality Circle is a small group of 6 to 12 employees doing similar work who voluntarily meet together on a regular basis to identify improvements in their respective work areas using proven techniques for analyzing and solving work related problems coming in the way of achieving and sustaining excellence leading to mutual upliftment of employees as well as the organization.
- Started in 1962 in Japan.
- ***Kaoru Ishikawa*** is the creator of Quality Circles
- Movement in Japan is coordinated by Japanese Union of Scientists and Engineers (JUSE).
- In India Quality Circles is promoted by QCFI (Quality Circle Forum of India).
- A method of continuous quality improvement in an organization by direct involvement of employees in quality.
- They operate on the basic principle that employee participation in decision making and problem solving improves the quality of work. They are:
  - ❖ Voluntary group of persons
  - ❖ Meet on regular basis
  - ❖ Work on similar tasks
  - ❖ Share area of responsibility
  - ❖ Solve problems related to work
- In India first time quality circle implemented in :

Characteristics of Quality Circles

- Volunteers – Activity carried out voluntarily.
- Set Rules and Priorities
- Decision made by consensus
- Organized approach to problem solving
- Members of a circle need to receive training
- Support of senior management required
- Members need to be empowered

Basics of Quality Circle

- Adopt prevention procedures rather than corrective measures
- Minimize scrap and downtime
- Improving quality, increase productivity.
- QC relies on visual representations:
  - ❖ scatter diagrams
  - ❖ flow charts,
  - ❖ Cause & effect diagram etc.

Quality Assurance

- Covers all activities from design, development, production, installation, servicing and documentation
- Includes regulation of quality for:
  - ❖ Raw Material
  - ❖ Assemblies
  - ❖ Product
  - ❖ Components & other services related to production

Three major attributes of QC

1. Quality Circle is a form of participation management.
2. Quality Circle is a human resource development technique.
3. Quality Circle is a problem solving technique.

Structure of quality circle

- **A steering committee:** This is at the top of the structure. It is headed by a senior executive and includes representatives from the top management personnel and human resources development people. It establishes policy, plans and directs the program and meets usually once in a month.
- **Coordinator:** He may be a Personnel or Administrative officer who co-ordinates and supervises the work of the facilitators
- **Facilitator:** He may be a senior supervisory officer. He co-ordiates the works of several quality circles through the Circle leaders.
- **Circle leader:** Leaders may be from lowest level workers or Supervisors. A Circle leader organizes and conducts Circle activities.
- **Circle members:** They may be staff workers. Without circle members the porgramme cannot exist. They are the lifeblood of quality circles.

Basic problem solving techniques or tools of QC

1. **Brain storming:** Brainstorming is a group or individual creativity technique by which efforts are made to find a conclusion for a specific problem by gathering a list of ideas spontaneously contributed by its members. The term was popularized by ***Alex Faickney Osborn*** in the 1953 in book *"Applied Imagination."*
2. **Pareto diagrams:** A Pareto chart, named after ***Vilfredo Pareto***, is a type of chart that contains both bars and a line graph, where individual values are represented in descending order by bars, and the cumulative total is represented by the line. Analyses different causes by frequency to illustrate the vital cause.

3. **Cause and effect analysis:** Also called fishbone diagrams, Ishikawa diagrams (Shows hierarchies of causes contributing to a problem), herringbone diagrams, cause-and-effect diagrams, or Fishikawa are causal diagrams created by ***Kaoru Ishikawa*** (1968) that show the causes of a specific event. Common uses of the Ishikawa diagram are product design and quality defect prevention, to identify potential factors causing an overall effect. Each cause or reason for imperfection is a source of variation. Causes are usually grouped into major categories to identify these sources of variation. The categories typically include :
   - **People:** Anyone involved with the process.
   - **Methods:** How the process is performed and the specific requirements for doing it, such as policies, procedures, rules, regulations and laws.
   - **Machines:** Any equipment, computers, tools, etc. required to accomplish the job.
   - **Materials:** Raw materials, parts, pens, paper, etc. used to produce the final product.
   - **Measurements:** Data generated from the process that are used to evaluate its quality.
   - **Environment:** The conditions, such as location, time, temperature, and culture in which the process operates.
4. **Data collection**
5. **Data analysis**
6. **PDCA (Plan, Do, Check, Act):** Deming wheel, as described by ***W. Edwards Deming.***

The operation of quality circle

- Problem selection
- Problem analysis
- Generate alternative solutions
- Select the most appropriate solution
- Problem identification
- Prepare plan of action
- Present solution to management for approval
- Implementation of solution

Benefits of QC's

- Increased productivity
- Improved quality of work life
- Boost employee morale
- Enhances creativity
- Improved teamwork
- Employee involvement

Teams Competency

1. **Managing Teams Competency:** Involves the ability to develop, support, facilitate, and lead groups to achieve organizational goals.
2. **Core Abilities of the Managing Teams Competency**
   - Determine when and how to use teams.
   - Set clear performance goals directly or participatively

- Define responsibilities and tasks directly or participatively
- Show accountability for goal achievement.
- Use appropriate decision-making methods.
- Effectively manage conflicts.
- Assess performance and take corrective action as needed.

6.5. ORGANIZATIONAL CHANGE

- Change is understood as doing things differently.
- Organizational change is the process by which Organizations move from their present state to some desired future state to increase their effectiveness.
- **Managing Change Competency:** Involves the ability to recognize and implement needed adaptations or entirely new transformations in the people, tasks, strategies, structures, or technologies in a person's area of responsibility.
- **Transition Management:** Ensures that business continues while the change is occurring.

The change process

1. Becoming aware of the pressure for change
2. Recognizing the need for change
3. Diagnosing the problem
4. Planning the change
5. Implementing the change
6. Following up on the change

Levels of Change

1. **Individual-level change:** Change is reflected in such developments as changes in job assignment, physical move to different location or the change in maturity of a person which occurs overtime.
2. **Group-level change:** Changes at the group level can affect work flows, job design, social organization, influence and status systems and communication patterns.
3. **Organization-level change:** It includes reorganization of the organizational structure and responsibilities, revamping of employee remuneration system or major shifts in an organizational objective.

Organization change targets :

1. **Strategy:** Clarify or create strategic and operational plans.
2. **Objectives:** Set or modify specific performance targets.
3. **Purpose:** Clarify and create mission and objectives
4. **Technology:** Improve equipment, facilities and work flows.
5. **Structure:** Update organizational design and coordination mechanisms.
6. **Tasks:** Update job designs for individuals and groups.
7. **People:** Update recruiting and selection practices; improve training and development.
8. **Culture:** Clarity or create core beliefs and values.

6.5.1 Total Quality Management (TQM)

Evolutionary change: It is gradual, incremental and specially focused.

- Technique developed by ***Edward Demming*** to improve the efficiency of flexible work teams.

- TQM firms value their employees both as individuals as well as for their contribution to the growth of the organization.
- The broad goal of TQM is continuous improvement.
- TQM is rational technique which is driven by hard statistical data on the need for change.
- TQM seeks to introduce change through four components:
  - o System
  - o Process
  - o People
  - o Management

6.5.2. Business process Re-engineering (BPR)

- **Revolutionary change:** It is sudden, drastic and organization-wide.
- It involves rethinking and redesign of business processes to increase organizational effectiveness.

Components of Re-engineering

- Business Processes
- Values and beliefs
- Jobs and structure
- Management and measurement.

The Reengineering Process

- Prepare the organization
- Specify the organization's strategy and objectives
- Fundamentally rethink the way work gets done
  - ❖ Identify and analyze core business processes
  - ❖ Define performance objectives
  - ❖ Design new processes
- Restructure the organization around the new business processes.

Characteristics of Reengineered Organizations

- Work units change from functional departments to process teams
- Jobs change from simple tasks to multidimensional work
- People's roles change from controlled to empowered
- The focus of performance measures and compensation shifts from activities to results.
- Organization structures change from hierarchical to flat
- Managers change from supervisors to coaches; executives change from scorekeepers to leaders

Characteristics of Transformational Change

- Triggered by Environmental and Internal Disruptions
- Aimed at Competitive Advantage
- Systemic and Revolutionary Change
- Demands a New Organizing Paradigm
- Driven by Senior Executives and Line Management
- Involves Significant Learning

6.5.3. Forces for Change in organizations

1. External Forces

- Globalization
- Workforce diversity
- Technological change
- Managing ethical behaviour
- Economic shocks
- Competition
- Social Needs
- World Politics

2. Internal forces

- Falling effectiveness
- Crisis
- Differing employee expectations
- Change in work climate

6.5.4. Change Agents

- Persons in organization responsible for managing change activities or acts as a catalyst for change.
- Can be managers or non managers, current employees, newly hired employees or outside consultants.

Characterization of Change Agent :

1. Clear vision.
2. Patient yet persistent.
3. Asks though questions.
4. Knowledgeable and leads by example.
5. Strong relationships built on trust.

6.5.5. Forces of Resistance to Change

1.1. Organizational level forces:

- Organization Structure
- Organization Culture
- Organization Strategy
- Over-determination

1.2. Group-level forces:

- **Group norms:** Unspoken and often unwritten set of informal rules that govern individual behaviors in a group. Group norms vary based on the group and issues important to the group. Without group norms, individuals would have no understanding of how to act in social situations.
- **Group cohesiveness:** "The resultant of all the forces acting on members to remain in the group." Group cohesiveness is the 'stick togetherness' of the group, its peanut butter. Group

cohesiveness provides the bonds that hold a group together. It is a stumbling block to change.

- **Groupthink:** Groupthink is a psychological phenomenon that occurs within a group of people, in which the desire for harmony or conformity in the group results in an incorrect or deviant decision-making outcome. Group members try to minimize conflict and reach a consensus decision without critical evaluation of alternative ideas or viewpoints, and by isolating themselves from outside influences.

1.3. Sub-unit-level forces:

- Differences in orientation
- Power and conflict

1.4. Individual-level forces:

- Cognitive Biases
- Uncertainty
- Fear of loss
- Selective perception
- Habit
- Logical reasons

Overcoming Resistance to Change

1. Education and Communication
2. Participation
3. Building Support and Commitment
4. Selecting People who Accept Change
5. **Coercion:** Coercion is the practice of forcing another party to act in an involuntary manner (whether through action or inaction) by use of threats or intimidation or some other form of pressure or force, and describes a set of various different similar types of forceful actions that violate the free will of an individual to induce a desired response. These actions can include, but are not limited to, extortion, blackmail, torture, and threats to induce favors.

6.5.6.Force field theory of change

- Force field theory of change demonstrates how forces for and against change balance and how the organization is balanced at anytime.
- Force field theory of change is developed by Kurt Lewin .
- Demonstrates how forces for and against change balance and how the organization is balanced at anytime, between these two opposing forces.

5.6.7. Kurt Lewin's change model:

1. **Unfreezing:** Process by which people become aware of the need for change. Unfreezing can be achieved by Increasing driving forces that direct behavior away from the status quo and decrease restraining forces that hinder movement from the existing equilibrium.
2. **Moving or Changing:** Developing new attitudes, values and behaviors. Movement from the old way of doing things to a new way.
3. **Refreezing:** Reinforcing new values, attitudes and behaviors. Process of making new behaviors relatively permanent and resistant to further change.

6.5.8. Mergers and Acquisitions

- **Merger:** The integration of two previously independent organizations into a completely new organization
- **Acquisition:** The purchase of one organization by another for integration into the acquiring organization.
- Distinct from trans-organizational systems, such as alliances and networks, because at least one of the organizations ceases to exist.

Merger and Acquisition Rationale

- Diversification
- Vertical integration
- Gaining access to global markets, technology, or other resources
- Achieving operational efficiencies, improved innovation, or resource sharing.

Merger and Acquisition Application Stages

1. **Pre-combination Phase:** The organization must identify a candidate organization; work with it to gather information about each other, and plan the implementation and integration activities.
2. **Legal Combination Phase:** The two organizations settle on the terms of the deal, gain approval from regulatory agencies and shareholders, and file appropriate legal documents.
3. **Operational Combination Phase:** Implementing the operational, technical and cultural integration activities.

6.5.9.The Downsizing

- Downsizing is reducing the number of employees on the operating payroll.
- Downsizing distinguish from a layoff, with downsizing intended to be a permanent downscaling and a layoff intended to be a temporary downscaling in which employees may later be rehired.
- Businesses use several techniques in downsizing, including providing incentives to take early retirement and transfer to subsidiary companies, but the most common technique is to simply terminate the employment of a certain number of people.
- **Rightsizing** is downsizing in the belief that an enterprise really should operate with fewer people.
- **Dumbsizing** is downsizing that, in retrospect, failed to achieve the desired effect.

The Downsizing Process

- Clarify the organization's strategy
- Assess downsizing options and make relevant choices
- Implement the changes
- Address the needs of survivors and those who leave
- Follow through with growth plans

Downsizing Tactics

Tactic	Characteristics	Examples
Workforce Reduction	• Reduces headcount • Short-term focus • Fosters transition	• Attrition • Retirement/buyout • Layoffs
Organization Redesign	• Changes organization • Medium-term focus • Fosters transition & transformation	• Eliminate functions, layers, products • Merge units • Redesign tasks
Systemic	• Changes culture • Long-term focus • Fosters transformation	• Change responsibilities • Foster continuous improvement • Downsizing is normal

6.6. ORGANIZATIONAL DEVELOPMENT (OD)

- Organization Development (OD) is a planned process of change in an organization's culture through the utilization of behavioral science technology, research, and theory.
- OD refers to a long-range effort to improve an organization's problem-solving capabilities and its ability to cope with changes in its external environment with the help of external or internal behavioral-scientist consultants.
- OD is an effort: Planned, organization-wide, and managed from the top, to increase organization effectiveness and health through planned interventions in the organization's "processes," using behavioral science knowledge.
- Organization Development is a system wise application and transfer of behavioral science knowledge to the planned development, improvement, and reinforcement of the strategies, structures, and processes that lead to organization effectiveness.
- The basic characteristics of OD are the following:
  1. Planned change or change intervention
  2. Comprehensive Change
  3. Emphasis upon work groups
  4. Long-range change
  5. Participation of a change agent
  6. Emphasis on intervention
  7. Collaborative management
  8. Organizational culture
  9. Action Research

Organization Development Interventions

- Organization Development (OD) interventions techniques are the methods created by OD professionals and others.
- Single organization or consultant cannot use all the interventions. They use these interventions depending upon the need or requirement.
- The most important interventions are:

1. **Survey feedback:** The intervention provides data and information to the managers. Information on Attitudes of employees about wage level, and structure, hours of work, working conditions and relations are collected and the results are supplied to the top executive teams. They analyze the data, find out the problem, evaluate the results and develop the means to correct the problems identified. The teams are formed with the employees at all levels in the organization hierarchy i.e. from the rank and file to the top level.
2. **Process Consultation:** The process consultant meets the members of the department and work teams observes their interaction, problem identification skills, solving procedures etc. He feeds back the team either the information collected through observations, coaches and counsels individuals & groups in molding their behavior.
3. **Goal setting and planning:** Each division in an organization sets the goals or formulates the plans for profitability. These goals are sent to the top management which in turn sends them back to the divisions after modification. A set of organization goals thus emerge thereafter.
4. **Managerial grid:** This identifies a range of management behavior based on the different ways that how production/service oriented and employee oriented states interact with each other. Managerial grid is also called as instrumental laboratory training as it is a structured version of laboratory training. It consists of individual and group exercises with a view to developing awareness of individual managerial style interpersonal competence and group effeciveness. Thus grid training is related to the leadership styles. The managerial grid focuses on the observations of behaviour in exercises specifically related to work. Participants in this training are encouraged and helped to appraise their own managerial style.

Six phases in grid OD:

- First phase is concerned with studying the grid as a theoretical knowledge to understand the human behavior in the Organization.
- Second phase is concerned with team work development. A seminar helps the members in developing each member's perception and the insight into the problems faced by various members on the job.
- Third phase is inter group development. This phase aims at developing the relationships between different departments
- Fourth phase is concerned with the creation of a strategic model for the organization where Chief Executives and their immediate subordinates participate in this activity.
- Fifth phase is concerned with implementation of strategic model.. Planning teams are formed for each department to know the available resources, required resources, procuring them if required and implementing the model Sixth Phase is concerned with the critical evaluation of the model and making necessary adjustment for successful implementation.

5. **Management by Objectives (MBO)**: MBO is a successful philosophy of management. It replaces the traditional philosophy of "Management by Domination". MBO led to a systematic ***Goal setting and Planning***. Peter Drucker the eminent management Guru in 1959 has first propagated the philosophy since then it has become a movement.MBO is a process by which managers at different levels and their subordinates work together in identifying goals and establishing objectives consistent with Organizational goals and attaining them.

6. **Team building**: It is an application of various techniques of Sensitivity training to the actual work groups in various departments. These work groups consist of peers and a supervisor.

7. **Sensitivity training**: It is called a laboratory as it is conducted by creating an experimental laboratory situation in which employees are brought together. The Team building technique and training is designed to improve the ability of the employees to work together as teams.

8. **Job enrichment**: It is currently practiced all over the world. It is based on the assumption in order to motivate workers; job itself must provide opportunities for achievement, recognition, responsibility, advancement and growth. The basic idea is to restore to jobs the elements of interest that were taken away. In a job enrichment program the worker decides how the job is performed, planned and controlled and makes more decisions concerning the entire process.

OD Intervention Categories

1. **Human Process Interventions:**

The following interventions deal with interpersonal relationships and group dynamics.

- **T Groups:** The basic T Group brings ten to fifteen strangers together with a professional trainer to examine the social dynamics that emerge from their interactions.
- **Process Consultation:** This intervention focuses on interpersonal relations and social dynamics occurring in work groups.
- **Third Party Interventions:** This change method is a form of process consultation aimed at dysfunctional interpersonal relations in organizations.
- **Team Building:** This intervention helps work groups become more effective in accomplishing tasks.

The following Interventions deal with human processes that are more system wide than individualistic or small-group oriented.

- **Organization Confrontation Meeting:** This change method mobilize organization members to identify problems, set action targets, and begin working on problems.
- **Intergroup Relations:** These interventions are designed to improve interactions among different groups or departments in organizations.
- **Large-group Interventions:** These interventions involve getting abroad variety of stakeholders into a large meeting to clarify important values, to develop new ways of working, to articulate a new vision for the organization, or to solve pressing organizational problems.
- **Grid Organization Development:** This normative intervention specifies a particular way to manage an organization.

2. **Techno-structural Interventions:**

These interventions deal with an organization's technology (for examples its task methods and job design) and structure (for example, division of labor and hierarchy). These interventions are rooted in the disciplines of engineering, sociology, and psychology and in the applied fields of socio-technical systems and organization design. Practitioners place emphasis both on productivity and human fulfillment.

- **Structural Design:** This change process concerns the organization's division of labour – how to specialize task performances. Diagnostic guidelines exist to determine which structure is appropriate for particular organizational environments, technologies, and conditions.
- **Downsizing:** This intervention reduces costs and bureaucracy by decreasing the size of the organization through personnel layoffs, organization redesign, and outsourcing.
- **Re-engineering:** This recent intervention radically redesigns the organization's core work processes to create tighter linkage and coordination among the different tasks
- **Parallel Structures**
- **High-involvement Organizations (HIO's)**
- **Total Quality Management**
- **Work design:** This refers to OD interventions aimed at creating jobs, and work groups that generate high levels of employee fulfilment and productivity.

3. Human Resource management Interventions

- **Goal Setting:** This change program involves setting clear and challenging goals. It attempts to improve organization effectiveness by establishing a better fit between personal and organizational objectives.
- **Performance Appraisal:** This intervention is a systematic process of jointly assessing work-related achievements, strengths and weaknesses,
- **Reward Systems:** This intervention involves the design of organizational rewards to improve employee satisfaction and performance.
- **Career Planning and development:** It generally focuses on managers and professional staff and is seen as a way of improving the quality of their work life.
- **Managing workforce diversity:** Important trends, such as the increasing number of women, ethnic minorities, and physically and mentally challenged people in the workforce, require a more flexible set of policies and practices.
- **Employee Wellness:** These interventions include employee assistance programs (EAPs) and stress management.

4. Strategic Interventions:

These interventions link the internal functioning of the organization to the larger environment and transform the organization to keep pace with changing conditions.

- **Integrated Strategic Change:** It argues that business strategies and organizational systems must be changed together in response to external and internal disruptions. A strategic change plan helps members manage the transition between a current strategy and organization design and the desired future strategic orientation.
- **Trans organization development:** This intervention helps organizations to enter into alliances, partnerships and joint ventures to perform tasks or solve problems that are too complex for single organizations to resolve
- **Merger and Acquisition Integration:** This intervention describes how OD practitioners can assist two or more organizations to form a new entity.
- **Culture Change:** This intervention helps organizations to develop cultures (behaviours, values, beliefs and norms) appropriate to their strategies and environments.
- **Self-designing organizations:** This change program helps organizations gain the capacity to alter themselves fundamentally. It is a highly participative process, involving multiple stakeholders in setting strategic directions and designing and implementing appropriate structures and processes.
- **Organization learning and knowledge management.**

5. Action research

- Action research is a research initiated to solve an immediate problem or a reflective process of progressive problem solving led by individuals working with others in teams or as part of a "community of practice" to improve the way they address issues and solve problems. It sometimes called participatory action research.
- Action research involves the process of actively participating in an organization change situation whilst conducting research.
- Action research can also be undertaken by larger organizations or institutions, assisted or guided by professional researchers, with the aim of improving their strategies, practices and knowledge of the environments within which they practice. As designers and stakeholders, researchers work with others to propose a new course of action to help their community improve its work practices.

- **Kurt Lewin,** first coined the term "action research" in 1944. In his 1946 paper "Action Research and Minority Problems" he described action research as "a comparative research on the conditions and effects of various forms of social action and research leading to social action" that uses "a spiral of steps, each of which is composed of a circle of planning, action and fact-finding about the result of the action".

Action Research Model

It is a data based problem-solving process of organizational change and development.

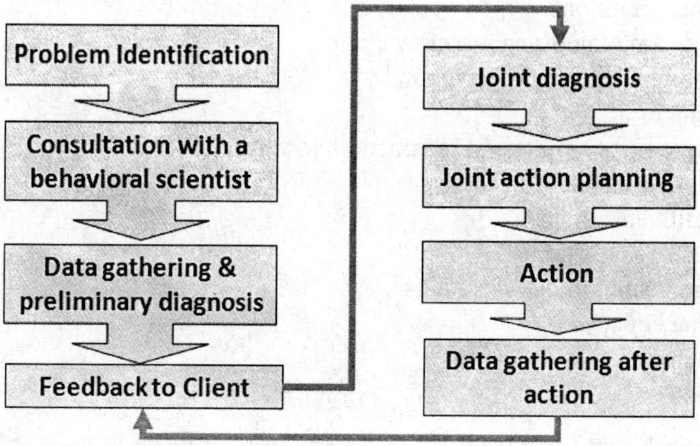

6.7. ORGANIZATIONAL EFFECTIVENESS

- Efficiency focuses on ***activities***, Effectiveness focuses on ***results.***

Effective organization:

- An effective organization, one that excels, is one that continually strives to identify and focus on factors critical to its customers and improves its processes in order to provide the highest-quality product or service possible.
- Organizations try different strategies in order to achieve their goals.
  - o Disjointed efforts
  - o Flavor of the month
  - o Most efforts are successful in the short run
- Generating success requires an organization-wide approach that improves and enhances the whole process of providing a product or service, enabling the organization to exceed customer expectations, each time and every time.
- People need a sense of how to pull a variety of knowledge and skills together to make improvements in a complex environment.

Approaches to measuring organizational effectiveness

1. **Goal Approach:** Effectiveness is the ability to excel at one or more output goals.
2. **Internal Process Approach:** Effectiveness is the ability to excel at internal efficiency, coordination, motivation, and employee satisfaction.

3. **System Resource Approach:** Effectiveness is the ability to acquire scarce and valued resources from the environment.
4. **Constituency Approach:** Effectiveness is the ability to satisfy multiple strategic constituencies both within and outside the organization.
5. **Domain Approach:** Effectiveness is the ability to excel in one or more among several domains as selected by senior managers.

Benefits from an effective organization

- Improved profitability
- Increased customer retention
- Reduced customer complaints and warranty claims
- Reduced costs through less waste, rework
- Greater market share
- Increased employee involvement and satisfaction, lower turnover
- Increased ability to attract new customers
- Improved competitiveness
- Improved customer satisfaction
- Improved management-employee relations
- Improved focus on key goals
- Improved communication
- Improved teamwork

6.8. ORGANIZATIONAL DESIGN

- Organization design can be defined narrowly, as the process of reshaping organization structure and roles, or it can more effectively be defined as the alignment of structure, process, rewards, metrics and talent with the strategy of the business.
- The words "lean" and "flat" are used to describe organization design as well as it's structure.
- In fact, organizational design encompasses much more than simply the structure: Organization design is the process of aligning an organization's structure with its mission. This means looking at the complex relationship between tasks, workflow, responsibility and authority, and making sure these all support the objectives of the business.
- Good organizational design helps communications, productivity, and innovation. It creates an environment where people can work effectively.

Organization Design Components

- **Strategy:** The way an organization uses its resources (human, economic, or technical) to gain and sustain a competitive advantage.
- **Technology:** The way an organization converts inputs into products and services.
- **Structure:** how attention and resources are focused on task accomplishment.
- **Human Resource Systems:** The mechanisms for selecting, developing, appraising, and rewarding organization members.
- **Measurement Systems:** Methods of gathering, assessing, and disseminating information on the activities of groups and individuals in organizations.
- **Organization Culture:** The basic assumptions, values, and norms shared by organization members. Represents both an "outcome" of organization design and a "foundation" or "constraint" to change.

Outputs of Organization Design

- **Organization Performance:** Profits, profitability, stock price.
- **Productivity:** Cost/employee, cost/unit, error rates, quality.
- **Stakeholder Satisfaction:** Market share, employee satisfaction, regulation compliance.

Making Organization Design Decisions

- **Strategy:** The organization design must support the strategy.
- **Size:** The design must take into account the size of organization. A small organization could be paralyzed by too much specialization. In larger organizations, on the other hand, there may be economies of scale that can be gained by maintaining functionally specialist departments and teams. A large organization has more complex decision making needs and some decision making responsibilities are likely to be devolved or decentralized.
- **Environment:** If the market environment where me work in (customers, suppliers, regulators, etc.) is unpredictable or volatile, then the organization needs to be flexible enough to react to this.
- **Controls:** Some activities need special controls (such as patient services in hospitals, money handling in banks and maintenance in air transport) whilst others are more efficient when there is a high degree of flexibility.
- **Incentives:** Incentives and rewards must be aligned with the business's strategy and purpose. When these are misaligned, there is a danger that units within the organization become self-serving. Using the earlier example of a company that wants to grow by acquiring new customers, the sale team is incentivized on customer retention, and therefore is self-serving rather than aligned with the business purpose.

6.9. CLASSICAL, NEO-CLASSICAL AND MODERN THEORIES OF ORGANIZATIONAL STRUCTURE

6.9.1. Organizational structure

- Organizational structure is defined as the relatively enduring allocation of work roles and administrative mechanisms that creates a pattern of interrelated work activities and allows the organization to conduct, co-ordinate and control its work activities.
- Organizational structure refers to the levels of management and division of responsibilities within an organization.
- In an organization of any size or complexity, employees' responsibilities typically are defined by what they do, who they report to, and for managers, who reports to them. Over time these definitions are assigned to positions in the organization rather than to specific individuals. The relationships among these positions are illustrated graphically in an organizational chart.
- The typically hierarchical arrangement of lines of authority, communications, rights and duties of an organization.
- Organizational structure determines how the roles, power and responsibilities are assigned, controlled, and coordinated, and how information flows between the different levels of management.
- A structure depends on the organization's objectives and strategy. In a centralized structure, the top layer of management has most of the decision making power and has tight control over departments and divisions.
- In a decentralized structure, the decision making power is distributed and the departments and divisions may have different degrees of independence.
- An organizational chart illustrates the organizational structure.

6.9.2 Theories of organizational structure

1. Classical Organization Theory

- Classical organization theory was developed in the first half of the 20th century as a way of bringing together scientific management, bureaucratic theory and administrative theory.
- Scientific management focused on getting the best people and equipment, and scrutinizing each production task. Bureaucratic theory involved establishing a hierarchy to describe the division of labor in a company and recognizing the importance of specialization.
- Administrative theory worked to establish a set of management principles that applied to all organizations. Classical organization theory didn't work because it described motivation only as a function of economic rewards.
- **Classical approach** Emphasis on purpose, formal structure, hierarchy of management, technical requirements and common principles of organisation.
- This perspective was concerned with structuring organisations effectively.
- Two major sub-groupings of this approach are: ***Bureaucracy and Scientific Management.***

2. Neo-Classical Organization Theory

- Improvements in organization theory led to consideration of the work environment.
- Productivity improves in an environment with coherence of values and purpose.
- Organizations can succeed with a cohesive environment where subordinates are accepting of managerial authority.
- The key to this theory is maintaining equilibrium. Of course, there can be unpredictable responses to managerial authority.

3. Contingency Theory

- Contingency theory deals primarily with conflict, which previous theories considered something to be avoided at all costs.
- Conflict is unavoidable, but according to contingency theory it is manageable.
- Organizations evolve to meet their own strategic needs in rational, sequential and linear ways.
- Adapting to changes in the environment is important to managerial and organizational success. Managers must be able to make decisions contingent on current circumstances.

4. Systems Theory

- Systems theory describes the interrelatedness of all parts of an organization and how one change in one area can affect multiple other parts.
- Systems may not always interact in a lineal manner. Small changes in one part may cause big changes in another part, while large changes in one area may only result in small changes in another.
- Organizations act as systems interacting with their environment. Any equilibrium is constantly changing as the organization adapts to its changing environment.

6.9.1. Types of organization Structure

1. Line organization
2. Staff Organisation
3. Functional Organisation

4. Line and Staff Organisation
5. Matrix Organisation
6. Projectised Organisation

1. Line organization

- This is the oldest form of organization.
- This is known by different names, i.e. military, vertical, scalar, departmental, organization.
- All other types of organization structure have mostly been either modifications of this organization.
- The concept of line organization holds that in any organization derived from a scalar process, there must be a single head who commands it.
- Although an executive can delegate authority, he has ultimate responsibility for results. According to ***McFarland,*** "Line structure consists of the direct vertical relationship which connects the positions and tasks of each level with those above and below it.
- "According to ***Allen,*** "Organizationally, the line is the chain of command that extends from the board of directors through the various delegations and redelegation of authority and responsibility to the point where the primary activities of the enterprise are performed."

Features of line organization :

- There are many levels of management depending upon the scale of business and decision-making ability of managers. Each level of management has equal rights.
- There is vertical flow of authority and responsibility. The lower positions derive authority from the positions above them.
- There is unity of command. Every person is accountable to only one person i.e. immediate boss. A person receives orders only from his immediate boss.
- There is ***scalar chain*** in line organization. The flow of orders, communication of suggestions and complaints etc. are made as it is in the case of a ladder. One cannot defy the claim.
- There is limit on subordinates under one manager. A manager has control only over the subordinates of his department.
- It is the oldest type of organization in use in which authority flows from the men at the top to the lowest man vertically. i.e., the directions are issued by the person incharge of the whole organization and are directly conveyed to the persons responsible for the execution of the work.
- There is a hierarchical arrangement of authority.
- Each department is self contained and works independently of other departments.
- Lines of authority are vertical i.e. from top to bottom.
- There are no staff specialists.

Typical Structure of Line organization

- Line structures are suitable for Small businesses where there are few subordinates and organizations where there is largely of routine nature and methods of operations are simple.

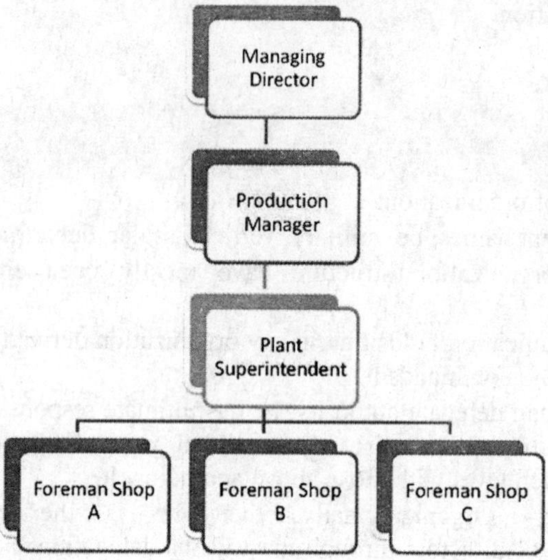

Advantages:

1. **Simplicity:** Simple to understand and develop. It is the simplest of all types of organizations. It can be easily established and easily understood by the workers.
2. **Clear-cut division of authority and responsibility**: The authority and responsibility of every person is clearly defined. Everyone knows as to whom he can issue orders and to whom he is accountable. Further it is easier to fix up the responsibility if there is any lapse anywhere in the performance of activities.
3. **Strong Discipline**: Because of direct authority-responsibility relationships, discipline can be maintained more effectively. Direct supervision and control also helps in maintaining strong discipline among the workers.
4. **Unified control**: Since the orders are given by one superior, there is no confusion among the subordinates. This ensures better understanding and quick action.
5. **Prompt Decisions**: As the superiors enjoy full authority, quick decisions are taken by them. Such decisions are executed promptly also.
6. **Flexibility**: Since each departmental head has sole responsibility for his department, he can easily adjust the organization to changes in business situation.
7. **Communication:** Communication is fast and easy as there is only vertical flow of communication.

Limitations

1. **Heavy Burden of work**: Since the departmental head has to look after all the activities of his department, he is over burdened with work. He may neglect some of the duties and there may be inefficiency in management.
2. **Concentration of Authority**: It is dictatorial in nature as all important powers are concentrated in the hands of a few top executives. If they are not able the enterprise will not be successful.
3. **Lack of specialization**: Line organisation suffers from lack of specialised skill of experts. It is extremely difficult for one person to handle activities of diverse nature. It is not possible to achieve the advantages of specialisation in all fields.
4. **Lack of communication:** There is failure to get correct information and to act upon it due to lack of communication. Although there is communication from top to bottom there is usually no communication from the lower ranks to higher ranks and executives. They are not provided with

an opportunity to put forward their view point or problems or suggestions to persons at the top level. Thus, they lose their capacity for independence thinking.

5. **Scope for favouritism**: Since the departmental head is almost all-in-all for the activities of his department. There is scope for favouritism. There may be a good deal of nepotism and jobbery and personal prejudices. The executive may appoint and promote his own men in various positions ignoring the claim of efficient persons.

2. Line and staff organization

- A manager today cannot hope to think of all possible factors in a given situation. Therefore, he has a set of expert advisers.
- Those functions which have direct responsibility for accomplishing the major objectives of the firm are called line functions.
- The staff functions are supposed to help and assist the line in discharging their responsibility.
- The staff position established as a measure of support for the line organization may be of personal staff, specialized staff and general staff.

Advantages

- It is based planned specialization
- It brings expert knowledge to bear upon management
- It provides more opportunity for advancement for able workers.

Limitations

- Relationship between line and staff member may creates confusion.
- Lack of authority may affect the interest of the staff member.
- Prestige and influence of line member may suffer in front of specialist.

3. Functional Organization

- Whole task of management and direction of subordinates should be divided according to the type of the work involved.
- The functional management carries this idea to its logical limit and divides up management into a number of functions such as production, sales, finance and personae, and research and development etc.
- Each of these departments would serve its best for the organization.

Advantages:

- It ensures a greater division of labour
- It improves the efficiency of the organization.
- It brings specialization and innovations.
- It facilitates mass production.

Limitations:

- Strict enforcement of discipline is questionable.
- Creates complexity in structuring activities.
- Responsibility cannot be fixed effectively.

A model of line staff and functional organization structure:

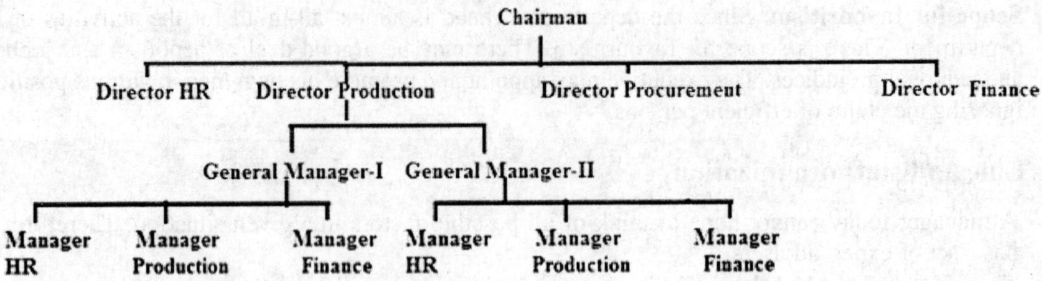

4. Formal organization and Informal Organization

- "A Network of personal and social relation not established or required by the formal organization but arising spontaneously as people associate with one another."

Types of informal groups

1. Social overlays
2. Functional overlays
3. Decision overlays
4. Power overlays
5. Communication overlays

Advantages

1. Sense of belonging
2. Safety value for emotional problem
3. Aid to the job
4. Breeding ground for innovation and originality
5. Important channel of communication
6. Social control
7. Check of authority
8. Self – policing
9. Fills gaps in a managers abilities
10. Gives the managers feedback about employees and their work experience

Limitations

1. Resistance to change
2. Suboptimization
3. Rumor
4. Group think philosophy

Mintzberg's five basic elements of structure

- Mintzberg's five basic elements of structure which Serve as co-ordinating mechanisms for the work of the organisation.
  1. Mutual adjustment
  2. Direct supervision
  3. Standardisation of work processes

4. Standardisation of work output
5. Standardisation of worker skills

Advantages of centralisation

- Easier implementation of a common policy for the organisation as a whole.
- Prevents sub-units becoming too dependent.
- Easier co-ordination and management control.
- Improved economies of scale and a reduction in overhead costs.
- Greater use of specialisation, including better facilities and equipment.
- Improved decision-making which might otherwise be slower.

Limitations:

- More mechanistic structure.
- Lengthens scalar chain (number of different levels in the structure of an organisation).

Advantages of decentralisation

- Enables decisions to be made closer to the operational level of work.
- Support services will be more effective if they are closer to the activities they are intended to serve.
- Opportunities for training in management.
- Tends to be easier to implement in private sector organisations rather than the public sector - accountability, regularity, uniformity.

Key elements of Structure designing:

1. Work Specialisation
2. Departmentalisation
3. Chain of Command (Scalar Chain)
4. Span of Control (Number of subordinates reporting directly to a manager or supervisor.)
5. Centralisation and Decentralisation
6. Formalisation

Types of Organization Structure

- Most organizations are designed, or evolve, to have elements of both hierarchy and more flexible, organic structures within.
- Organic structures are more informal, less complex and more "ad-hoc" than hierarchical structures.
- They rely on people within the organization using their initiative to change the way they work as circumstances change.

Characteristic	Hierarchical structure	Organic structure
Complexity	**High:** with lots of horizontal separation into functions, departments and divisions.	**Usually lower:** Less differentiation or functional separation.
Formality	**High**: Lots of well defined lines of control and responsibility.	**Lower:** No real hierarchy and less formal division of responsibilities.
Participation	**Low:** Employees lower down the organization have little involvement with	**Higher participation**: lower level employees have more

	decision making.	influence on decision makers.
Communication	**Downward**: Information starts at the top and trickles down to employees.	**Lateral, upward, & downward communication**: Information flows through the organization with fewer barriers.

1. **Functional structure:** In a functional structure, functions viz. accounting, marketing, Human Resource etc. are quite separate; each led by a senior executive who reports to the CEO. The advantage can be efficiency and economies of scale where functional skills are paramount. The main disadvantage is that functional goals can end up overshadowing the overall goals of the organization.
2. **Divisional structure**: In a divisional structure, the company is organized by office or customer location. Each division is autonomous and has a divisional manager who reports to the company CEO. Each business unit is typically structured along functional lines. The advantage here relates to local results, as each division is free to concentrate on its own performance. The disadvantage is that functions and effort may be duplicated. For example, each division may have a separate marketing function, and so risk being inefficient in its marketing efforts.
3. **Organic structures**: It includes simple, flat structures, matrix organizations and network structures.
4. **Simple Structure:** Often found in small businesses, the simple organization is structure is flat. It may have only two or three levels; employees tend to work as a large team with everyone reporting to one person. The advantages are efficiency and flexibility, and responsibilities are usually clear. The main disadvantage is that this structure can hold back growth when the company gets to a size where the founder or CEO cannot continue to make all the decisions.
5. **Matrix Structure:** In a matrix structure, people typically have two or more lines of report. ***For example, a matrix organization may combine both functional and divisional lines of responsibility.*** The advantage is that the organization focuses on divisional performance whilst also sharing functional specialist skills and resources.
6. **Network Structure:** Often known as a ***lean structure***, this type of organization has central, core functions that operate the strategic business. It outsources or subcontracts non-core functions which, depending on the type of business, could include manufacturing, distribution, information technology marketing and other functions. This structure is very flexible and often can adapt to the market almost immediately. The disadvantage is inevitable loss of control; dependence on third parties and the complexity of managing outsource and sub-contract suppliers.

6.10. UNDERSTANDING AND MANAGING INDIVIDUAL BEHAVIOR

- Individual differences in hereditary and diversity factors, personality, ability and skills, perception, attitude,'etc. will affect work behavior like productivity, creativity and performance.
- These all aspects viz. Personality, Perception, Values, Attitudes, Learning, Motivation, Communication, Leadership, Managing change, Managing conflicts, Job satisfaction, Morale, Fatigue and monotony are discussed below in detailed.

6.10.1.Personality

- The overall profile or combination of characteristics that capture the unique nature of a person as that person reacts and interacts with others.

- Combines a set of physical and mental characteristics that reflect how a person looks, thinks, acts, and feels.
- Personality refers to a set of unique characteristics that make an individual different from others.
- **Personality dynamics:** The ways in which an individual integrates and organizes social traits, values and motives, personal conceptions, and emotional adjustments.
- **Self-concept:** The view individuals have of themselves as physical, social, and spiritual or moral beings. It includes ***Self-esteem*** and ***Self-efficacy***.
- **Oedipus complex** states that a child loves and hates his parents, with these feelings being strongest towards the parents of the same sex as the child.

Theories of personality

1. Type theory

- In type theories, individuals are categorized depending upon their physical characteristics.
- ***Kretschmer and Sheldon*** classified personalities on the basis of structure of body.
- ***Carl Jung*** divided all personalities into introverts and extroverts.

2. Trait theory

- Trait theories classify individuals on the basis of traits.
- A personality trait is understood as being an enduring attribute of a person that appears consistently in a variety of situations.

3. Psychoanalytic theory

- Developed by ***Sigmund Freud.***
- According to Freud, personality comprises Id, ego and super-ego.
- Id is the innate component of personality.
- Superego judges whether an action is right or wrong according to the standards of society.

4. Social learning theory: Social learning theory stresses on the change of behavior through learning from several sources.

5. Humanistic theory

- Emphasis on mans potential for self direction and freedom of choice.
- ***Carl Rogers*** *and* ***Abraham Maslow*** is credited with the humanistic theory of personality.

The Shaping of Personality: Stages

1. Freudian Stages

- Oral Stage
- Anal stage
- Phallic stage
- Genital stage

2. Eriksons stage

- Infancy
- Early childhood
- Play age
- School age
- Puberty and adolescence

- Young adulthood
- Middle adulthood
- Late adulthood

3. **John Piagets stages**
   - Sensorimotor
   - Preoperational
   - Concrete operational
   - Formal operational

4. **Chris Argyris' stages**
   - Immaturity to maturity.

Factors affecting on personality

1. **Heredity**
   - Physical characteristics
   - Gender
2. **Environment**
   - Cultural
   - Social
   - Situational factors

"Big Five" personality dimensions

1. **Extraversion:** Being outgoing, sociable, assertive.
2. **Agreeableness:** Being good-natured, trusting and cooperative.
3. **Conscientiousness:** Being responsible, dependable and persistent.
4. **Emotional stability:** Being unworried, secure, relaxed.
5. **Openness to experience:** Being imaginative, curious, and broad-minded.

Personal conception traits

1. **Locus of control:** The extent to which a person feels able to control his or her own life.
   - **Externals:** More extraverted in their interpersonal relationships and more oriented toward the world around them.
   - **Internals:** More introverted and more oriented towards their own feelings and ideas.
   - **Information processing:** Internals make more attempt to acquire information, are less satisfied with the amount of information they possess and are better at utilizing information.
   - **Job Satisfaction:** Internals are generally more satisfied, less alienated and there is strong job satisfaction relationship for them
   - **Performance:** Internals perform better on learning and problem solving tasks, when performance leads to valued rewards.
   - **Self control, risk & anxiety:** Internals exhibit better self control, are more cautious, engage in less risky behavior and are less anxious.
   - **Motivation, expectancies and results:** Internals display greater work motivation, see a stronger relationship between what they do and what happens to them, expect that working hard leads to good performance, feel more control over their time.
   - **Response to others:** Internals are more independent, more reliant on their own judgment and less susceptible to the influence of others; they are more likely to accept information on its merit.

2. **Authoritarianism/dogmatism**
    - **Authoritarianism:** Tendency to adhere rigidly to conventional values and to obey recognized authority.
    - **Dogmatism:** Tendency to view the world as a threatening place.
3. **High-Machiavellian personality:**Approach situations logically and thoughtfully:
    - Are capable of lying to achieve personal goals.
    - Are rarely swayed by loyalty, friendships, past promises, or others opinions.
    - Are skilled at influencing others.
    - Try to exploit loosely structured situations.
    - Perform in a perfunctory or detached manner in highly structured situations.
4. **Low-Machiavellian personality**
    - Accept direction imposed by others in loosely structured situations.
    - Work hard to do well in highly structured situations.
    - Are strongly guided by ethical considerations.
    - Are unlikely to lie or cheat.
5. **Self-monitoring:** A person's ability to adjust his/her behavior to external situational factors.

    High self-monitors

    ❖ Sensitive to external cues.
    ❖ Behave differently in different situations.

    Low self-monitors.

    ❖ Not sensitive to external cues.
    ❖ Not able to disguise their behaviors.

Personality Test

- A personality test is a questionnaire or other standardized instrument designed to reveal aspects of an individual's character or psychological makeup.
- The first personality tests were developed in 1920s and were intended to ease the process of personnel selection, particularly in the armed forces.
- Since these early efforts of these test, a wide variety of personality tests have been developed, notably the ***Myers Briggs Type Indicator (MBTI), the MMPI,*** and a number of tests based on the Five Factor Model of personality.
- Personality test used in a range of contexts, including individual and relationship counseling, career planning, and employee selection and development.

Myers-Briggs Indicator

- The **Myers-Briggs Type Indicator** (**MBTI**) assessment is a psychometric questionnaire designed to measure psychological preferences in how people perceive the world and make decisions.
- These preferences were extrapolated from the typological theories proposed by ***Carl Gustav Jung*** and first published in his 1921 book ***'Psychological Types'.***
- Jung theorized that there are four principal psychological functions by which we experience the world: ***sensation, intuition, feeling, and thinking***. One of these four functions is dominant most of the time.

6.10.2. Perception

- "The study of perception is concerned with identifying the process through which we interpret and organize sensory information to produce our conscious experience of objects and object relationship."
- "Perception is the process of receiving information about and making sense of the world around us. It involves deciding which information to notice, how to categorize this information and how to interpret it within the framework of existing knowledge.
- "A process by which individuals organize and interpret their sensory impressions in order to give meaning to their environment.
- Perception is the act of seeing what is there to be seen.

Factors influencing Perception

1. Factors in the perceiver

- Attitudes
- Motives
- Interests
- Experience
- Expectations

2. Factors in the Target

- Size
- Background
- Proximity
- Similarity

3. Factors in the situation

- Time
- Work Setting
- Social Setting

Perceptual Process

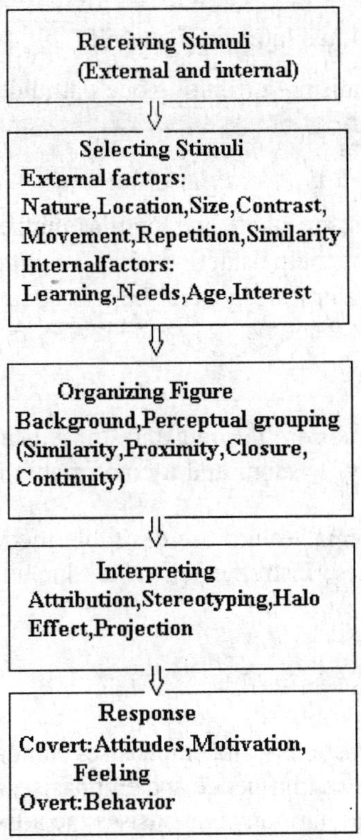

The process of interpreting

- Perceptual set, attribution, stereotyping, halo effect, context, defense and projection influence perceptual interpretation.
- Halo effect refers to the tendency of perceiving people in terms of good or bad and assigning all good qualities to one who is good and bad qualities to one who is bad.
- According to the principles of defense, an individual is likely to put up a defense when faced with conflicting stimuli.

Attribution Theory :

- Attribution Theory seeks to explain why people behave as they do.
- ***Fritz Heider*** and ***H.H. Kelly*** are contributors to the Attribution Theory.

Biases affecting perception

1. **Stereotypes:** It is the process of generalizing behavior of all members of a group.
2. **Frame of Reference:** Our frame of reference is our tendency to see things from a narrow focus that directly affects us.
3. **Expectations:** We perceive, select, organize, and interpret information as we expect it to appear.

4. **Selective Exposure:** People sometimes selectively pick information they want to hear and ignore information they don't want to hear.

5. **Interest**: Common or individual interest of oneself.

6. **Projection:** Defense mechanism - attributing one's attitudes or shortcomings to others.

6.10.3. Values

- Values are evaluative statements, are stable and long-lasting beliefs about what is important.
- "They are evaluative standard that help us define what is right or wrong, good or bad, in the world"
- Values differ from attitudes. Values are general beliefs about life, whereas attitudes are directed towards specific objects, events or people.

Types of Value

1. **Terminal values:** Terminal values are desired states of existence that we think are worth striving for. A world of beauty, equality, wisdom and a comfortable life are some of the terminal values that people might hold.
2. **Instrumental Values:** Instrumental values are desirable modes of behavior that help us to reach the objectives of terminal values. Instrumental values include being polite, courageous, logical, self- controlled and ambitious.

Gordon Allport : Six value types

1. **Economic:** Values utility and practically and emphasises standard of living.
2. **Political:** Values power,position and influence and emphasises competition and winning.
3. **Aesthetic:** Values from grace and harmony emphasises the artistic aspects of life.
4. **Social:** Values love of people and altruism emphasises concern for others.
5. **Religious:** Values unity and peoples relationship to the universe and emphasises high deals and the search for the purpose of being on earth.
6. **Theoretical:** Values the discovery of truth and emphasises critical and rational approach to the problems.

Louis Rath's Value Criteria

- **Choosing Freely:** No one can force you into a value.
- **Choosing from alternatives:** Choosing after consideration of the consequences.
- **Choosing after the thoughtful consideration:** Being committed to the choice.
- **Prizing and cherishing:** Being happy with your choice.
- **Affirming:** Letting others know where you stand.
- **Acted upon:** Your actions speak louder than words.
- **Repeated:** Consistent in your pattern of life.

The value theory (Schwartz-1992):

Adopts a conception of values that specifies six main features that are implicit in the writings of many theorists:

(1) **Values are beliefs** linked inextricably to affect. When values are activated, they become infused with feeling. People for whom independence is an important value become aroused if their independence is threatened, despair when they are helpless to protect it, and are happy when they can enjoy it.

(2) **Values refer to desirable goals** that motivate action. People for whom social order, justice, and helpfulness are important values are motivated to pursue these goals.

(3) **Values transcend specific actions and situations**. Obedience and honesty, for example, are values that may be relevant at work or in school, in sports, business, and politics, with family, friends, or strangers. This feature distinguishes values from narrower concepts like norms and attitudes that usually refer to specific actions, objects, or situations.

(4) **Values serve as standards or criteria:** Values guide the selection or evaluation of actions, policies, people, and events. People decide what is good or bad, justified or illegitimate, worth doing or avoiding, based on possible consequences for their cherished values. But the impact of values in everyday decisions is rarely conscious. Values enter awareness when the actions or judgments one is considering have conflicting implications for different values one cherishes.

(5) **Values are ordered by importance relative to one another:** People's values form an ordered system of value priorities that characterize them as individuals. Do they attribute more importance to achievement or justice, to novelty or tradition? This hierarchical feature also distinguishes values from norms and attitudes.

(6) **The *relative* importance of multiple values guides action:** Any attitude or behavior typically has implications for more than one value. Values contribute to action to the extent that they are relevant in the context (hence likely to be activated) and important to the actor.

Individualism as a Work-Related Value

- Individualism is the tendency of people to look after themselves and their immediate family, which implies a loosely integrated society
- In cultures that emphasize individualism, people view themselves as independent, unique, and special; value individual goals over group goals; value personal identity, personal achievement, pleasure, and competition; accept interpersonal confrontation; and are less likely to conform to other's expectations
- Such cultures include the United States, Australia, New Zealand and the United Kingdom
- **Example:** "Stand on your own two feet!"

Collectivism as a Work-Related Value

- Collectivism is the tendency of people to emphasize their belonging to groups and to look after each other in exchange for loyalty
- Cultures that emphasize collectivism are characterized by a tight social framework, concern for the common welfare, emotional dependence of individuals on larger social units, a sense of belonging, a desire for harmony, with group goals being viewed as more important than individual goals, and a concern for face-saving
- Such cultures include Japan, China, Venezuela, and Indonesia
- **Example:** "The nail that sticks up gets hammered down!"

6.10.4. Attitude

- Attitude is state of mind or feeling with regard to some matter.
- Attitudes represent beliefs, feelings and action tendencies towards objects, ideas or people.
- "An attitude is a mental state of readiness, learned and organized through experience, exerting a specific influence on person's response to people, object and situations with which it is related."
- Attitudes are learned predispositions towards aspects of our environment. They may be positively or negatively directed towards certain people, service or institutions."

- An attitude is "a relatively enduring organization of beliefs, feelings, and behavioral tendencies towards socially significant objects, groups, events or symbols."

Characteristics of Attitude

- **Difficult to measure:** Indicated by behavior, reactions to individual situations, social values
- **May create inflexibility and stereotypes:** Based on inconsistencies, incorrect assumptions or other false data
- **Demonstrated by behavior:** Formed largely from the continuous process of socialization. May be Positive or negative
- **Once formed not easily changed:** Takes a new conditions, new experience, and new information. Attitudes may be affected by age, position, and education.

ABC Model of attitude

1. **An Affective Component:** The feelings, sentiments, moods and emotions about some idea, person, event or object. For example: "I am scared of spiders".
2. **A behavioral component:** The predispositions to get on a favorable or unfavourable evaluation of something. the way the attitude we have influences how we act or behave. For example: "I will avoid spiders and scream if I see one".
3. **A cognitive element:** The beliefs, opinion, knowledge or information held by the individual. For example: "I believe spiders are dangerous".
   - This model is known as the ***ABC model of attitudes.***
   - The three components are usually linked. However, there is evidence that the cognitive and affective components of behavior do not always match with behavior.
   - This is shown in a study by LaPiere (1934).

The Function of Attitudes

- Attitudes can serve functions for the individual.
- *Daniel Katz* outlines four functional areas:

1. **Knowledge:** Attitudes provide meaning (knowledge) for life. The knowledge function refers to our need for a world which is consistent and relatively stable. This allows us to predict what is likely to happen, and so gives us a sense of control. Attitudes can help us organize and structure our experience. Knowing a person's attitude helps us predict their behavior. For example, knowing that a person is religious we can predict they will go to Church.
2. **Self / Ego-expressive:** The attitudes we express help communicate who we are and may make us feel good because we have asserted our identity. Self-expression of attitudes can be non-verbal too: think bumper sticker, cap, or T-shirt slogan. Therefore, our attitudes are part of our identify, and help us to be aware through expression of our feelings, beliefs and values.
3. **Adaptive:** If a person holds and/or expresses socially acceptable attitudes, other people will reward them with approval and social acceptance. For example, when people flatter their bosses or instructors (and believe it) or keep silent if they think an attitude is unpopular. Again, expression can be nonverbal [think politician kissing baby]. Attitudes then, are to do with being apart of a social group and the adaptive functions helps us fit in with a social group. People seek out others who share their attitudes, and develop similar attitudes to those they like.
4. **The ego-defensive**: Function refers to holding attitudes that protect our self-esteem or that justify actions that make us feel guilty. For example, one way children might defend themselves against the feelings of humiliation they have experienced in P.E. lessons is to adopt a strongly negative attitude to all sport. People whose pride has suffered following a defeat in sport might similarly adopt a defensive attitude: "I'm not bothered, I'm sick of rugby anyway…". This function has

psychiatric overtones. Positive attitudes towards ourselves, for example, have a protective function (i.e. an ego-defensive role) in helping us reserve our self-image.

Formation of attitude

- Direct experience with the object
- Classical conditioning and attitude
- Operant conditioning and attitude acquisition
- Vicarious learning
- Family and Peer groups
- Neighborhood
- Economic status and occupations
- Mass Communications

Benefits of Positive attitude

- Increases productivity
- Fosters teamwork
- Solves problems
- Improves quality
- Makes for congenial atmosphere
- Breeds loyalty
- Increase profits
- Fosters better relationship with employees, employers and customers.
- Reduces stress
- Makes for a pleasing personality.

6.10.5. Job Satisfaction

- Job satisfaction is the work related attitudes.
- **Job satisfaction:** Job satisfaction is positive attitude toward one's job.
- **Hoppock:** "Job satisfaction is ***the combination of psychological, physiological and environmental circumstances that cause a person to truthfully say 'I am satisfied with my job"***.
- Job satisfaction is different from morale. Satisfaction implies a positive emotional state whereas; morale implies a general attitude towards work and work environment.

Determinants of job satisfaction

1. Environmental factors

- Job Content
- Pay and Promotion
- Work Group
- Supervision

2. Personal characteristics

- Age
- Sex
- Educational Level
- Marital Status
- Experience

The Effect of Job Satisfaction on Performance

- Job Satisfaction and Productivity
- Job Satisfaction and Absenteeism
- Job Satisfaction and Turnover
- Job Satisfaction and Customer Satisfaction

Theories of Job satisfaction

1) **Herzberg's two factor theory:** Herzberg's distinction between motivators and hygiene factors is referred to as the two-factor theory of job satisfaction.
2) **Locke's value theory:** Job satisfaction is the relationship between job outcomes realized as compared to those desired. Locke's approach focuses on any outcomes that people value , regardless of what they are and not necessarily lower order needs. Key to satisfaction is the discrepancy between those aspects of the job one has and those one wants; the greater the discrepancy, lesser the satisfaction.

Causes of job satisfactions

1. **Organizational factors:** Pay, opportunities for promotion, nature of work, policies of the organization and working conditions.
2. **Group factors:** Includes group size and supervision.
3. **Individual factors:** Personality variables,Status, Job congruent with their interests, general life satisfaction.

Consequences of job satisfactions

- High job satisfaction tends to lead to improved productivity, reduced absenteeism, reduced accidents, less stress and lower unionization.

A. Measuring job satisfactions

1. **Rating scales:** These scales fall into two general categories.
   1) **Tailor-made scales:** which are constructed for a particular setting or a project .
   2) **Standardized scales:** which before their use have been developed to establish group norms on the scales and to ensure reliability and validity of the measuring instrument.Job descriptive index(JDI) is one of the Standardized scale developed by ***Smith, Kendall and Hulin***. The JDI has separate scales for satisfaction with pay, promotion, supervision, work and coworkers.
2. **Critical incidents:** Developed by Herzberg's to measure job satisfactions.
3. **Interviews**
4. **Action tendencies**
5. **Likert scale:** This method of standardized survey was developed by Likert in 1932.
6. **Use of existing information**
7. **Satisfaction and managerial implications**
8. **Responses to job dissatisfaction**

B. Organizational commitment :

It refers to the strength of an employee's involvement in the organization. There are three kinds of organizational commitment.

1. Affective commitment
2. Continuous commitment
3. Normative commitment

6.10.6. Learning

- Learning is change in behaviour acquired through practice, training or experience.
- Learning is defined by the outward expression of new behavior.
- **Driscoll:** "A persisting *change* in human performance or performance potential(brought) about as a result of the learner's interaction with the environment."
- **Mayer:** "The relatively permanent *change* in a person's knowledge or behavior due to experience"
- **Shuell :** **"**An enduring *change* in behavior, or in the capacity to behave in a given fashion, which results from practice or other forms of experience"
- The process of gaining knowledge.
- A process, by which behavior is changed, shaped or controlled.
- The individual process of constructing understanding based on experience from a wide range of sources.

Theories of Learning

1. **Classical Conditioning: Ivan Pavlov**
   - Classical Conditioning states that an event, repeated several times, evokes desired responses.
   - Pavlov conducted an experiment on a dog and tried to relate the dog's salivation and the ringing of bell.
   - Reflexes (Pavlov's Dogs).
   - A stimulus is presented in order to get a response.

2. **Operant conditioning: Skinner**
   - Operant Conditioning or *instrumental conditioning* refers to the process that our behaviour produces certain consequences and how we behave in the future will depend on what these consequences are.
   - Feedback/Reinforcement (Skinner's Pigeon Box)
   - The response is made first, then reinforcement follows.

3. **Cognitive learning**
   - Cognitive process is contemporary perspectives about learning.
   - Knowledge is stored cognitively as symbols
   - Learning is the process of connecting symbols in a meaningful & memorable way
   - Studies focused on the mental processes that facilitate symbol connection
   - ***Discovery Learning - Jerome Bruner***
   - ***Meaningful Verbal Learning - David Ausubel.***

4. **Social Learning**
   - Social learning theory emphasizes the ability of an individual to learn by observing others.
   - Popularly known as ***vicarious learning.***
   - Learning takes place through observation and sensorial experiences
   - Learning From Models -**Albert Bandura (1973)**

Critiques of Social Learning Theory

- Does not take into account individuality, context, and experience as mediating factors.

- Suggests students learn best as passive receivers of sensory stimuli, as opposed to being active learners.
- Emotions and motivation not considered important or connected to learning.

Principles of Learning

1. **Reinforcement**
   i. **Positive Reinforcement:** Strengthen and enhances behaviour by the presentation of positive reinforce.
   ii. **Negative Reinforcement:** An unpleasant event that precedes behaviour is removed when the desired behaviour occurs.
2. **Punishment:** It is an attempt to eliminate or weaken an undesirable behaviour.
3. **Extinction:** Extinction is the weakening of behaviour by ignoring it or making sure it is not reinforced. It is an alternate to punishing undesirable behaviour.

Learning Curves

- Graphical representation of the common sense principle that more one does something the better one gets at it. Learning curve shows the rate of improvement in performing a task as a function of time, or the rate of change in average cost (in hours or dollars) as a function of cumulative output.
- Used in resource requirements planning, learning curves are also employed in setting incentive rate schemes based on the statistical findings that as the cumulative output are doubled, the average unit cost declines by a constant percentage.
- A Learning Curve is a graphical representation of the increase of Learning (Y- axis) with Experience (x-axis).
- The term *Learning Curve* is used in two main ways : where the same task is repeated in a series of trials, or where a body of knowledge is learned over time.
- The first person to describe the learning curve was ***Hermann Ebbinghaus*** in 1885, in the field of the psychology of learning.
- In 1936, ***Theodore Paul Wright*** described the effect of learning on production costs in the aircraft industry. This form, in which *Unit Cost* is plotted against *Total Production*, is sometimes called an ***Experience Curve.***
- The familiar derogatory expression "***but it has a steep learning curve***" is intended to mean that the activity is difficult to learn. In fact, it means the exact opposite: if the curve is steep then one makes rapid progress.

6.10.7. Motivation

- Motivation is the level and direction of an effort expended at work.
- Derived from Latin word "movere" means to move.
- Motivation refers to the set of forces that causes people to behave in certain ways.
- Motivation is an art of stimulating someone or oneself or oneself to get designed course of action, to push the right button to get desire action. Motivation is an act of inducement.
- The basic principle of motivation is based upon the following policy i.e., **carrot or stick policy.** "Put a carrot in front of donkey to make it move or Job his with a stick being."
- "Motivation is the result of processes, internal or external to the individual that arouses enthusiasm and persistence to pursue a certain course of action."
- Motivated employees are quality driven.
- ***Dwight D. Eisenhower:*** "Motivation is getting people to do what you want them to do because they want to do it."

Nature of motivation

- It is a psychological concept.
- It is total not piecemeal.
- Determined by human needs.
- May be financial or non financial.
- It is constant process.

Need for motivation

- Maximum utilization of factors of production.
- Reduce labour turnover.
- Easy availability of right personnel.
- Increased the efficiency and output.
- Create sense of belonging.

Kinds of motivation

1. Positive motivation
2. Negative motivation
3. Financial motivation
4. Non-financial motivation

Theories of motivation

1. **Content theories:** Focus on profiling the needs that people seek to fulfill.
   1) Maslow's Hierarchy of needs theory.
   2) Herzberg's Two factor theory
   3) Alderfer's ERG theory
   4) Mc Clelland Achievement theory
2. **Process theories:** Focus on people's thought or cognitive processes. Emphasize controlling behavior by manipulating its consequences.
   1) Goal Setting theory
   2) Vroom's Expectancy theory
   3) Porters Performance satisfaction model
   4) Adams Equity theory

1. Content theories

- Focus on profiling the needs that people seek to fulfill.
- Focus on the individual needs that activate tensions which influence satisfaction and behaviour.

1.1. Maslow's Hierarchy of needs theory

- Abraham Maslow's book on motivation and personality emphasizes multiplicity of human needs are arranged in an order.
- Maslow's theory consisted of two parts:
  (1) The classification of human needs, and
  (2) Workers are not just motivated by money but also by having their human/social needs met.

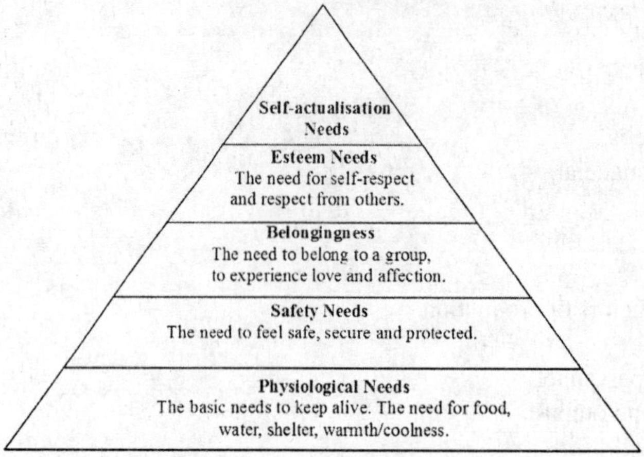

Fig: Maslow's Need hierarchy

Maslow's hierarchy of human needs	General Examples	Organisational Examples
1. Physiological needs	Sustenance Food and Shelter	Base Salary
2. Safety needs/Security	Stability, Union, Health insurance, protection against unemployment, loss of income through sickness etc.	Pension Plan Employee assistance plans
3. Social needs/Belongingness	Friendship, need for love and belonging.	Friends in the Work Group Teamwork Communication
4. Esteem needs	Status symbols	Job Title Promotion Banding
5. Self actualization.	Achievement Personal growth Realization of potential	Challenging Job

- The first two sets of needs are called ***Lower order needs*** (1,2)
- The other sets of needs are called ***Higher order needs*** (3,4)
- According to him when one need fulfils another need will emerge automatically.
- While going for achieving the particular need, people like to give priority to the pressing needs first and the rest in next.

Shortcoming of Maslow's theory :

- Order cannot be regarded as rigid.
- No indication regarding satisfaction of needs.
- It may not have universal applicatibility.

- Motivation is piecemeal exercise by means of splitting of human needs.

Critics of Maslow's theory

- Levels of needs are difficult to measure. It is difficult for businesses to measure the quantitative level of security, ego, esteem, and love or belonging in the workplace.
- Maslow assumed that everyone is motivated in the prescribed order of the model.
- There is no explanation of what motivates people once they have achieved self-actualization.

1.2. Herzberg's Two factor theory

- Herzberg's Two Factor Theory is a "content theory" of motivation"
- Needs priority, to a great extent, characterizes the types of behavior.
- A research study was conducted by Frederick. Herzbergls of Case-Western reserve University and associates.
- This study consisted of an intensive analysis of the experiences and feeling of 200 Engineers and accountants in 9 different companies in Pittsbrug area, U.S.A.
- Herzberg concluded that there were two categories of needs essentially independent of each other affecting behavior indifferent ways.
- His findings are that there are some job conditions which operate primarily to dis-satisfy employees when the conditions are absent, their presence does not motivate them in a strong way.
- Another set of job conditions operates primarily to build strong motivation and high job satisfaction, but their absence carely proves strongly dissatisfying.
- According to Herzberg, factors that give real satisfaction to an individual are motivators.
- Classified the factors into two factors:

1. Hygien or Maintenance factors:

1. Fair co-policy and administration
2. Supervisor knows the work
3. Supervisors relationship
4. Peers relationship
5. Fair salary
6. Job security
7. Subordinates relationship
8. Personal life
9. Status
10. Good working condition
    - Concerned basically with job environment.
    - Extrinsic to the work itself.
    - Leads to High Job dissatisfaction
    - **The maintenance seekers** tend to be more concerned with factors surrounding the job such as supervision; working conditions, pay etc.

2. Motivators :

Factors that give satisfaction (feeling of achievement, significance of growth)

1. Opportunity to accomplish something significant.
2. Recognition.
3. Chance for development
4. Opportunity to grow
5. Chance for increased responsibility

6. The job/work itself
   - **Motivators or Growth Factors** - concerned with job content. Intrinsic to the work itself.
   - Leads to High Job satisfaction
   - **The motivation seekers** generally are individuals who are primarily motivated by the satisfier's such as advancement, achievement and other factors associated with work itself.

The shortcomings of Herzberg's theory:

1. Infact job satisfaction and dis-satisfaction are two opposite points on a single continuum Individuals on the job are affected by any change either in the job environment or in the job content.
2. Herzberg model is method bound and a number of other methods used for similar study have shown different results not supporting his contentions other the theory has limitation is general acceptability.
3. This theory does not attach much importance to pay, status, or inter-personal relationships which are help generally as important contents of satisfaction.

Conclusion: According to Herzberg, management should focus on rearranging work so that motivator factors can take effect. He suggested three ways in which this could be done:

- o Job enlargement
- o Job rotation
- o Job enrichment

1.3. Alderfer's ERG theory

- To bring Maslow's need hierarchy theory of motivation in synchronization with empirical research, ***Clayton Alderfer*** redefined it in his own terms.
- His rework is called as ERG theory of motivation.
- He re-categorized Maslow's hierarchy of needs into three simpler and broader classes of needs:
  1. **Existence needs:** Desire for physiological and material well-being. These include need for basic material necessities. In short, it includes an individual's physiological and physical safety needs.
  2. **Relatedness needs:** Desire for satisfying interpersonal relationships. These include the aspiration individual's have for maintaining significant interpersonal relationships (be it with family, peers or superiors), getting public fame and recognition. Maslow's social needs and external component of esteem needs fall under this class of need.
  3. **Growth needs:** Desire for continued personal growth and development. These include need for self-development and personal growth and advancement. Maslow's self-actualization needs and intrinsic component of esteem needs fall under this category of need.

1.4. McClelland Achievement theory

- Employees with a high need for achievement derive satisfaction from achieving goals.
- The employees exhibiting the need for power derive satisfaction from the ability to control others.
- Individuals exhibiting need for affiliation derive satisfaction from social and interpersonal activities.
- The essence of McClelland's model is that individual needs along with congential work environment can create motivation and satisfaction.

1. **Need for achievement:** The desire to do something better or more efficiently, to solve problems, or to master complex tasks. Need for achievement must be given challenging tasks.
2. **Need for affiliation:** The desire to establish and maintain friendly and warm relations with others. Need for affiliation should be given opportunities to manage and lead a team of people. It should be provided with a cooperative working environment in order to gain their:
   Work Preferences: Prefers moderately challenging goals, Prefers performance feedback, Prefers individual responsibility
3. **Need for power:** The desire to control others, to influence their behavior, or to be responsible for others.

Conclusion: McClelland's main contribution is that people with different kinds of needs are motivated differently.

2. Process theories

- Focus on people's thought or cognitive processes. Emphasize controlling behavior by manipulating its consequences.
- Process theories of motivation look at the decision-making processes and behaviour of people to determine motivation.

2.1. Goal setting theory

- In 1960's, ***Edwin Locke*** put forward the Goal-setting theory of motivation.
- This theory states that goal setting is essentially linked to task performance. It states that specific and challenging goals along with appropriate feedback contribute to higher and better task performance.
- In simple words, goals indicate and give direction to an employee about what needs to be done and how much efforts are required to be put in.
- Goal setting theory proposes that a goal serves as a motivator because it causes people to focus their inputs and their jobs.
- Set realistic, attainable and time bound goals-performance takes place.
- SMART goals should be set by an employee to achieve desired level of production.
- Goal setting process consists of Goal; desire to meet the goal, self-efficacy belief, goal commitment, task performance and meeting the goal.

Features of goal-setting theory:

- The willingness to work towards attainment of goal is main source of job motivation. Clear, particular and difficult goals are greater motivating factors than easy, general and vague goals.
- Specific and clear goals lead to greater output and better performance. Unambiguous, measurable and clear goals accompanied by a deadline for completion avoids misunderstanding.
- Goals should be realistic and challenging. This gives an individual a feeling of pride and triumph when he attains them, and sets him up for attainment of next goal. The more challenging the goal, the greater is the reward generally and the more is the passion for achieving it.
- Better and appropriate feedback of results directs the employee behaviour and contributes to higher performance than absence of feedback. Feedback is a means of gaining reputation, making clarifications and regulating goal difficulties. It helps employees to work with more involvement and leads to greater job satisfaction.
- Employees' participation in goal is not always desirable.
- Participation of setting goal, however, makes goal more acceptable and leads to more involvement.

Eventualities of Goal setting theory:

- **Self-efficiency:** Self-efficiency is the individual's self-confidence and faith that he has potential of performing the task. Higher the level of self-efficiency, greater will be the efforts put in by the individual when they face challenging tasks. While, lower the level of self-efficiency, less will be the efforts put in by the individual or he might even quit while meeting challenges.
- **Goal commitment**: Goal setting theory assumes that the individual is committed to the goal and will not leave the goal. The goal commitment is dependent on the following factors:
  - o Goals are made open, known and broadcasted.
  - o Goals should be set-self by individual rather than designated.
  - o Individual's set goals should be consistent with the organizational goals and vision.

Advantages of Goal Setting Theory

- Goal setting theory is a technique used to raise incentives for employees to complete work quickly and effectively.
- Goal setting leads to better performance by increasing motivation and efforts, but also through increasing and improving the feedback quality.

Limitations of Goal Setting Theory

- At times, the organizational goals are in conflict with the managerial goals. Goal conflict has a detrimental effect on the performance if it motivates incompatible action drift.
- Very difficult and complex goals stimulate riskier behaviour.
- If the employee lacks skills and competencies to perform actions essential for goal, then the goal-setting can fail and lead to undermining of performance.
- There is no evidence to prove that goal-setting improves job satisfaction.

2.2. Vroom's Expectancy theory

- The expectancy theory of motivation given by ***Victor H. Vroom.***
- People will be motivated to do things to reach a goal if they believe in the worth of that goal and if they can see that what they do will help them in achieve it.
- Vroom makes the point that motivate is a product of the anticipated worth that an individual places on a goal and the chances of achieving that goal.
- This theory states that workers will only act when they have a reasonable expectation that their work will lead to the desired outcome.
- They need to believe that they possess the necessary ability and skill to achieve the given goal.
- Expectancy theory predicts that employees in an organization will be motivated when they believe that: putting in more effort will yield better job performance
- better job performance will lead to organizational rewards, such as an increase in salary or benefits these predicted organizational rewards are valued by the employee in question
- ***FORCE=VALENCE*** *X* ***EXPECTANCY***

Force: Strength of the person motivation.
Valence: Strength of an individual preference for an outcome.
Expectancy: Probability that a particular action will lead to a desired outcomes.

Basic concepts of the theory:

1. First and second level outcomes.
2. Instrumentality
3. Expectancy

4. **Motivation:** Motivation is the multiplicative function of the valence for each first level outcome (Vi) and the believed expectancy (E) that a given effort will be followed by a particular first level outcome.

Merits of Vroom's Theory

1. It recognizes the importance of various individual needs and motivations.
2. It fits the concept of harmony of objectives
3. It is completely consistent with the system of management by objectives.

Demerits of Vroom's Theory

1. Perception of value varies among individuals at different times and in various places.
2. Difficulty to apply the practice.

Conclusion

- The relationship between people's behavior at work and their goals was not as simple as was first imagined by other scientists.
- Vroom realized that an employee's performance is based on individuals factors such as personality, skills, knowledge, experience and abilities.
- In order to enhance performance managers should use reward systems that tie rewards very closely to performance.

2.3. Porters Performance satisfaction model

- Porters and Lawler seek to identify valence and expectancies and link effort with performance and satisfaction.
- This model attempted to:
    1. Identify the source of peoples valences and expectancies, and
    2. Link effort with performance and job satisfaction.

2.4. Adams Equity theory

- Equity theory proposes that motivation to act developes after the employee compares inputs/outcomes with the identical ratio of the relevant other.
- Adam's theory suggests that workers will naturally compare their efforts or rewards to those of others in the workplace (subordinates, peers and superiors).
- Each worker should receive a remuneration package that reflects his or her efforts.
- Adam's argued that workers will only be motivated if their remuneration package is seen to be fair in relation to others in the workplace.

6.10.8. Leadership

- Leadership is the ability to influence the behaviour of others.
- Leadership is an abstract quality in a human being to induce his followers to do whatever he is directed to do with the zeal and confidence.
- **Koontz & O' Donnel:** "Leadership is generally defined simply as the art of influencing people so that they will strive willingly towards the achievement of group goals."
- Leadership may be defined as the ability to influence and direct the task-related activities of the members of group.
- A leader is a goal-setter, planner, executive, expert, group representative, administrator of rewards and punishments and a symbol of the group.

- Leadership is "the process of encouraging and helping others to work enthusiastically towards objectives."
- Leadership is "the behaviour of an individual when he is directing the activities of a group towards a shared goal."
- Leadership is "interpersonal influence, exercised in a situation and directed, through the communication process, towards the attainment of a specified goal."
- Leadership is "an interaction between persons in which one presents information of a sort and in such a manner that the other becomes convinced that his outcomes will improve if he behaves in the manner suggested or desired."
- Leadership is "the relationship in which the leader influences others to work together willingly on related tasks to attain goals desired by the leader and or group."

Leadership and Management

- Managership and Leadership are management tools with which managers can influence the bahaviour of employees.
- **John Kotter:** "Management involves coping with complexity; while leadership is about coping with change."
- The ultimate aim of leadership is to lift the level of human conduct and ethical aspirations.
- Leaders have follower but manager do not have follower.
- Leaders have emotional appeal.
- Leaders fulfill follower's needs.
- **Peter Drucker and Warren Bennis:** "Management is doing things right, leadership is doing right things. Management lies in climbing the ladder of success; leadership determines whether the ladder is leaning against the right wall. "
- Leadership is a mutual influence process.
- **Leaders influence on followers:** A leader is able to change the behaviour of his followers because he enjoyes power which comes to him from at least five sources.
- One of the most notable studies on power was conducted by social psychologists ***John French and Bertram Raven*** in 1959. They identified five bases of power:
  1. **Legitimate:** This comes from the belief that a person has the right to make demands, and expect compliance and obedience from others.
  2. **Reward:** This results from one person's ability to compensate another for compliance.
  3. **Expert:** This is based on a person's superior skill and knowledge.
  4. **Referent:** This is the result of a person's perceived attractiveness, worthiness, and right to respect from others.
  5. **Coercive:** This comes from the belief that a person can punish others for noncompliance.

Importance of leadership

1. Initiates action
2. Motivation
3. Providing guidance
4. Creating confidence
5. Building morale
6. Builds work environment
7. Co-ordination

Ingredients of leadership

- Ability to use power effectively and in a responsible manner.
- Ability to comprehend the temperaments of human beings.
- Ability to inspire.
- Ability to act in a manner that will develop a climate conducive to and arousing motivations.

Leadership qualities

1. **Physical qualities:** Sound health to fulfill his obligation. Vitality and endurance to face al hardships.

2. **Psychological qualities.**
   a) Personal magnetism
   b) Enthusiasm.
   c) Co-operation.
   d) Exerting
   e) Resourcefulness.
   f) Ability to inspire and integrate.
   g) Tact and skillful handling.

3. **Intellectual traits**
   a) High degree of intelligence.
   b) Sound judgment.
   c) Capacity to deal with every situation.
   d) Scientific approach.
   e) Open mind.
   f) Best teacher.

4. **Qualities of character**
   a) Integrity
   b) Self discipline
   c) Good natured
   d) Willingness to work hard.
   e) Willingness to accept and share responsibilities.

Leadership theories

1. Trait Theory

- Trait theory focuses on the individual characteristics of successful leaders.
- This approach says that all of us possess certain abilities and share responsibilities. Such qualities are considered as god given and hence leaders are born.
- **Keith Davis** has summarized four of the major traits which might have an impact on successful organizational leadership. They are:
  (a) Intelligence
  (b) Social maturity and breath
  (c) Inner motivation and achievement drives

(d) Human relations attitude

2. Behavioural theory

- Behavioural theory focuses on leader behaviour while interacting with subordinates and not on his or her traits.
- In the 1930s, Kurt Lewin developed a framework based on a leader's behavior. He argued that there are three types of leaders:
  1. **Autocratic leaders**: Make decisions without consulting their teams. This style of leadership is considered appropriate when decisions need to be made quickly, when there's no need for input, and when team agreement isn't necessary for a successful outcome.
  2. **Democratic leaders**: Allow the team to provide input before making a decision, although the degree of input can vary from leader to leader. This style is important when team agreement matters, but it can be difficult to manage when there are lots of different perspectives and ideas.
  3. **Laissez-faire leaders**: Don't interfere; they allow people within the team to make many of the decisions. This works well when the team is highly capable, is motivated, and doesn't need close supervision. However, this behavior can arise because the leader is lazy or distracted.

3. Leader-Member Exchange (LMX) Theory

- It is also called as vertical dyad model.
- This approach more focuses on leader's behaviour.
- LMX theory focuses on two or three people who are close to each other.
- Informal observation of leadership behavior suggests that leader's action is not the same towards all subordinates. The importance of potential differences in this respect is brought into sharp focus by ***Graen's*** leader-member exchange model, also known as the ***vertical dyad linkage theory***.
- The theory views leadership as consisting of a number of dyadic relationships linking the leader with a follower.
- The quality of the relationship is reflected by the degree of mutual trust, loyalty, support, respect, and obligation.
- According to the theory, leaders formed different kinds of relationships with various groups of subordinates. One group, referred to as the ***in-group***, is favored by the leader. Members of in-group receive considerably more attention from the leader and have more access to the organizational resources. By contrast, other subordinates fall into the ***out-group***. These individuals are disfavored by the leader. As such, they receive fewer valued resources from their leaders.
- Leaders distinguish between the in-group and out-group members on the basis of the perceived similarity with respect to personal characteristics, such as age, gender, or personality.
- A follower may also be granted an in-group status if the leader believes that person to be especially competent at performing his or her job.
- The relationship between leaders and followers follows the stages:
  - ❖ **Role taking:** When a new member joins the organization, the leader assesses the talent and abilities of the member and offers them opportunities to demonstrate their capabilities.
  - ❖ **Role making:** An informal and unstructured negotiation on work-related factors takes place between the leader and the member. A member who is similar to the leader is more likely to succeed. A betrayal by the member at this stage may result in him being relegated to the out-group.
- The LMX 7 scale assesses the degree to which leaders and followers have mutual respect for each other's capabilities, feel a deepening sense of mutual trust, and have a sense of strong obligation to one another.

- Taken together, these dimensions determine the extent to which followers will be part of the leader's in-group or out-group.
- In-group followers tend to function as assistants or advisers and to have higher quality personalized exchanges with the leader than do out-group followers.
- These exchanges typically involve a leader's emphasis on assignments to interesting tasks, delegation of important responsibilities, information sharing, and participation in the leader's decisions, as well as special benefits, such as personal support and support and favorable work schedules.

Strengths of LMX Theory

- LMX theory is an exceptional theory of leadership as unlike the other theories, it concentrates and talks about specific relationships between the leader and each subordinate.
- LMX Theory is a robust explanatory theory.
- LMX Theory focuses our attention to the significance of communication in leadership. Communication is a medium through which leaders and subordinates develop, grow and maintain beneficial exchanges.
- When this communication is accompanied by features such as mutual trust, respect and devotion, it leads to effective leadership.
- LMX Theory is very much valid and practical in it's approach.

Criticisms of LMX Theory

- LMX Theory fails to explain the particulars of how high-quality exchanges are created.
- LMX Theory is objected on grounds of fairness and justice as some followers receive special attention of leaders at workplace and other followers do not.

6.10.8.1 Managerial grid

- It is forms of continuum which emphasize that leadership style consist of factors of both the task-oriented and people relations oriented behavior in varying degrees.
- It explains that whatever may be the type of leadership styles it ultimately relates with tasks to be performed and people with whom it is to be performed.
- Some styles emphasize on concern for production which means that the attitudes of superiors towards a variety of things, such as, quality of policy decisions, procedures and processes, creativeness of research, quality of staff service, work efficiency and volume of output.
- On the other hand there are certain leadership styles which emphasize on concern for people which means that degree of personal commitment towards goal achievement, maintaining the self-esteem of workers, responsibility based on trust, and satisfying inter-personal relations, Based on these two factors leadership styles can be identified n to 5 types as given in the diagram.

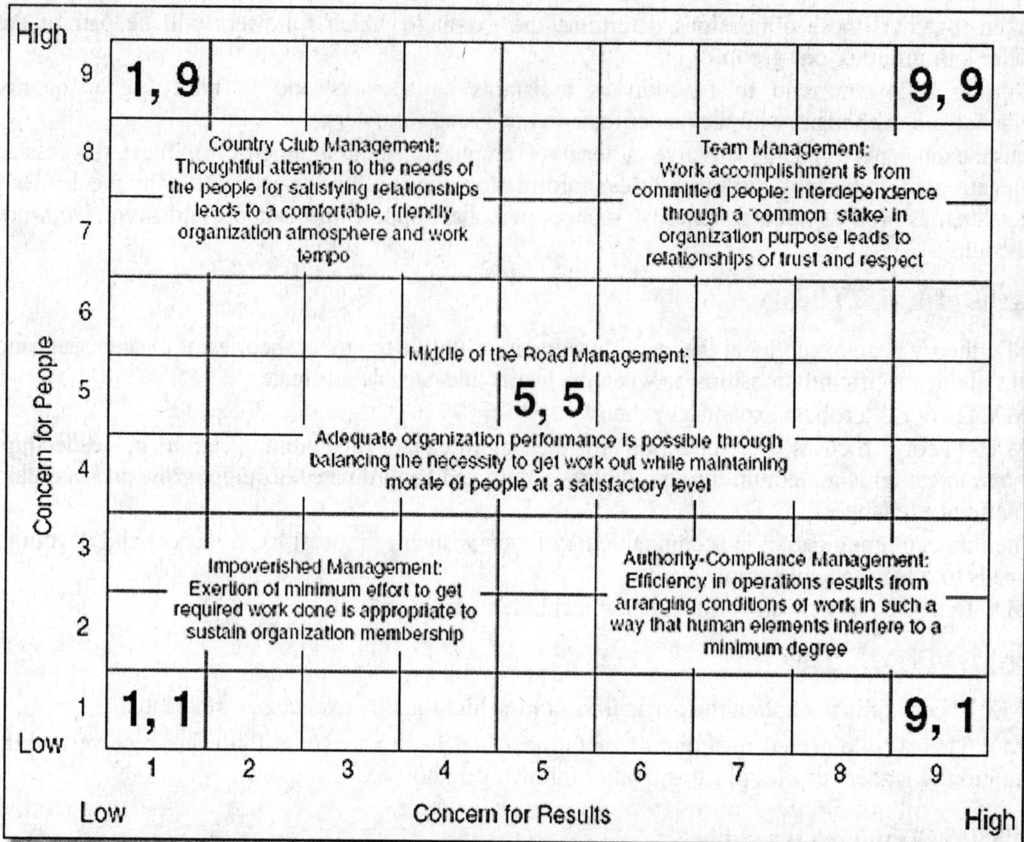

- This managerial grid concept has been developed by ***Blame and Mour.***
- The 5 styles depicted by the diagram are:
  - ❖ **Impoverished style** where exertion of minimum effort is require get work done and sustain organization morale.
  - ❖ **Country club style** where thoughtful attention to needs of people leads to friendly and comfortable organization atmosphere and work tempo.
  - ❖ **Task oriented style** which says that efficiency results from arranging work in such a way that human elements have little effect.
  - ❖ **Team model style** which highlights that work accomplished is from committed people with interdependence through a common stake in organization purpose and with trust and respect.
  - ❖ **Middle Road style** rightly pointed out that adequate performance through balance of work requirements and maintaining satisfactory morale.
- Among the five different styles, the most desirable leader behaviour is 9.9. So efforts have to be taken by developing suitable training programs that attempts to change managers towards 9.9 leadership style.
- Managerial gird helps the managers to identify and classify managerial styles and it helps to understand why he gets the reaction that he does from his subordinates. However, the midpoint of the grid i.e. 5.5 is highly emphasized in the pure form of working conditions.

4. Situational / Contingency approach

Paul Harsey and Kenneth Blanchard have developed a situational model of leadership that adds 'maturity' of the followers as a contingency variable which deserves due consideration.

Fielder's model: Fielder's theory emphasizes two variables:

1. Motivational styles
2. Favourableness of situations

- This is viewing that leadership qualities are determined by the situation in which he/she operates. It is not individual's characteristics.

5. Path goal theory

- According to the goal setting theory, leader's job is to create a favorable environment that helps employees reach the organizations goal.
- It suggests that the main functions of the leader are to clarify and set goals with subordinates them find the best path for achieving the goals and remove obstacles.
- **Group approach**: A leader is one who comes attuned to the feelings and actins of people whom he is supposed to lead. Thus, the leader is one who comes closest to living up to the norms and standards of his group.
- Path-goal theory identifies four kinds of leader behavior.
  1. **Directive leader behavior:** Letting subordinates know what is expected of them, giving guidance and direction, and scheduling work.
  2. **Supportive leader behavior:** Being friendly and approachable, showing concern for subordinate welfare, and treating members as equals.
  3. **Participative leader behavior:** Consulting subordinates, soliciting suggestions, and allowing participation in decision making.
  4. **Achievement-oriented behavior:** Setting challenging goals, expecting subordinates to perform at high levels, encouraging subordinates and showing confidence in subordinates' abilities.

6. Theory "Z": Team leader

a. Balances production and people issues
b. Builds a working team of employees
c. Team approach: *involves* subordinates
d. Organization is a *vehicle* for carrying out plans
e. Results of leadership styles
f. **"good manager"**
   i. High productivity, cooperation, low turnover, employee commitment
   ii. Origins of leadership
   iii. Evidence that both inherent personality and environment are factors

7. Theory L: Missing Management

Related to very low productivity.

8. McGregor's theory

- **McGregor** argued that the style of Management adopted is a function of the manager's attitudes towards human nature and behaviour at work.
- He put forward two suppositions called Theory X and Theory Y which are based on popular assumptions about work and people.
- Douglas Mc. Gregore has classified the prevalent theories into two groups:
  1. Traditional or theory X
  2. Modern or theory y .

Traditional or Theory .X

- It completely excludes workers from the process of managerial decision making the theory stress that would here only when forced to do so through ruthless exercise of managerial authority over them through constant rebuking scolding reprimanding.
- Decisions whether right or wrong have to be made by managers only, the only rule assigned to workers being to mainly incline the decision.

Assumptions of theory-X

1. **Lack of inclination to work:** People do not like work and try to avoid it.
2. **Fears can alone force action:** People do not like work, so managers have to control, direct, coerce, and threaten employees to get them to work toward organisational goals.
3. **Inbuilt dislike for responsibility:** People prefer to be directed, to avoid responsibility, to want security, and have little ambition.
4. **Living – off others :** Mc Gregor used the term "Theory X" to explain the negative management attitude about the workforce. Such management see their workforce as lazy people who avoid work if possible also they lack ambition and do not enjoy work.
5. **Obession with security :**
6. **Money alone can make the people to work :**
7. **Labour is only a factor of production :**
8. **Authority is synonymous with control:** Theory X managers follow an authoritarian management style where emphasis is on output and productivity rather than on the people in the organization.

In Nutshell Theory "X": Autocratic leader shows following characteristic:

- ❖ Lacks flexibility
- ❖ Controlling and demanding
- ❖ "carrot and stick" approach
- ❖ Focused solely on productivity
- ❖ "my way or the highway"
- ❖ Job stress; low satisfaction; unions form

Modern theory or Theory Y

- It is the exact opposite of theory X, it gives workers a pride of place in the process of management.
- It emphasis fuel and active cooperation, between workers and management to accomplish the enterprise objectives as per theory if workers are properly maturated, they would willingly accept responsibility and show the sense of creativity and imagination in their work performance.
- It can be said to be positive and optimistic outlook.

- Managers take a more positive approach and assume that employees are able to achieve organizational objectives out of their own accord and initiative.
- They believe that workers can gain satisfaction from work and that they are able to take on responsibility.

Assumptions of Theory - Y

1. Work is reward in itself
2. Inherent sense of responsibility
3. Recognition.
4. Sense of security.
5. Financial reward is not the only inspiration.
6. Decision – making ability is not the monopoly
7. Democratically inclined.
8. People do not naturally dislike work; work is a natural part of their lives.
9. People are internally motivated to reach goals to which they are committed.
10. People are committed to goals to the degree that they receive personal rewards when they reach their objectives.
11. People will seek and accept responsibility under favourable conditions.
12. People have the capacity to be innovative in solving organisational problems.
13. People are bright, but generally their potentials are under-utilised.

In Nutshell Theory "Y": Benevolent leader shows following characteristics:

- ❖ Very people oriented; encouraging.
- ❖ Organizes around people.
- ❖ Can be paternalistic.
- ❖ "country club" atmosphere: non-competitive.
- ❖ Low achievement; good people leave.

Conclusion: McGregor concluded that managers ought to adopt a Theory Y approach in order to get positive results for the whole organization.

Leadership styles:

- Leadership style is the behaviour exhibited by the leader while influencing the behaviour of followers.
- From the point of view of authority, leadership can be autocratic and democratic or free rein.

1. Authoritarian Style (An Autocratic leader):

- An Autocratic leader will not entertain any suggestions originate from subordinates.
- Under this type of leadership, one person decides for the whole group.
- An autocratic leader does not trust anybody.
- The leader alone determines policies and makes plans. He demands strict obedience and relies on power.

Merits of Authoritarian Style :

- It can increases the efficiency, save time and get good result.
- It works well employees who have a low tolerance for ambiguity feel insecure with freedom.
- Chain of command and division of work are clear and full understood by all.

Demerits of Authoritarian Style:

- One – way communication may create costly errors.
- Individual decision making may be dangerous in the changing environment.
- Resentment in form of massive resistance, low morale and low productivity.

2. Participative Style: (Democratic, Consultative and Consensual)

2.1. A democratic leader

- A democratic leader can win the cooperation of his group and can motivate them
- effectively and positively.
- The entire group is involved in and accepts responsibility for goal setting and achievement. Subordinates have considerable freedom of action.

Merits of Participative Style:

- The leader has the built-in personal motivation working for him.
- The leader consistently receives the benefit of the best information, ideas, suggestions and talents of his people.
- This style permits and encourages people to develop grow and rise in the organization.

Demerits of Participative Style:

- Time consuming.
- Leaders may avoid responsibility.

2.2. Consultative :

Consultative leaders solicit opinions from group before making a decision, yet they do not feel obliged to accept the group thinking; these leaders make it clear that they alone have final authority to make final decesions.

2.3. Consensual :

Consensual leaders encourage group discussion on an issue and then make a decision that reflects the general agreement of group members. Delegate more authority to group.

3. A paternalistic leader

A paternalistic leader takes care of his followers in the way the head of the family takes care of the family members.

4. Free rein leadership or Laissez faire

- Leader exercises absolutely no control.
- He provides only information, materials and facilities to hi men to enable them to accomplish group objectives.
- This type does not hold good when the leader does not know well the competence and integrity of his people and their ability to handle this kind of freedom.
- A free rein leader will leave the group entirely to itself such as a leader allows maximum freedom to subordinates.

5. System based on Task versus people emphasis: Likert's Four styles

- Rensis Likert identified four main styles of leadership, in particular around decision-making and the degree to which people are involved in the decision.

1. **Exploitative authoritative:** In this style, the leader has a low concern for people and uses such methods as threats and other fear-based methods to achieve conformance. Communication is almost entirely downwards and the psychologically distant concerns of people are ignored.
2. **Benevolent authoritative:** When the leader adds concern for people to an authoritative position, a 'benevolent dictatorship' is formed. The leader now uses rewards to encourage appropriate performance and listens more to concerns lower down the organization, although what they hear is often rose-tinted, being limited to what their subordinates think that the boss wants to hear. Although there may be some delegation of decisions, almost all major decisions are still made centrally.
3. **Consultative:** The upward flow of information here is still cautious and rose-tinted to some degree, although the leader is making genuine efforts to listen carefully to ideas. Nevertheless, major decisions are still largely centrally made.
4. **Participative:** At this level, the leader makes maximum use of participative methods, engaging people lower down the organization in decision-making. People across the organization are psychologically closer together and work well together at all levels.

Advantages

- With the help of the profile developed by Rensis Likert, it became possible to quantify the results of the work done in the field of group dynamics.
- Likert theory also facilitated the measurement of the "soft" areas of management, such as trust and communication.

Conclusion

- According to Rensis Likert, Participative style will lead to long-term improvement in staff turnover and high productivity, low scrap, low costs, and high earnings. If an organization wants to achieve optimum effectiveness, then the Participative style is the ideal system.

6.10.9. Conflict Management

- Conflicts occur when disagreements occur in a social situation.
- Conflict is a process that begins when one party perceives that another party has negatively affected, or is about to negatively affect, something that the first party cares about.
- It could also be defined as the appearance of difference i.e. difference of opinion, difference of interest.
- It can be viewed as a breakdown in the standard mechanism of decision making.
- Contemporary view advocates that certain conflict is inevitable and even desirable.
- Conflicts can be constructive or destructive.
- Excessive conflict can hamper the effectiveness of a group or an organization, reduce satisfaction of group members, increases absence and turnover rates, and lowers productivity.

Constructive conflict:

- Improves the quality of decisions.

- Encourages creativity and innovation.
- Develops interest and curiosity.
- Provides medium through which tensions can be released.
- Promotes an environment of self-evaluation and change.
- Constructive conflict prevents stagnation, encourages creativity, allows tension to be released.

Stages of Conflict

There are five stages in a conflict. These are latent conflict, perceived conflict, felt conflict, manifest conflict, and conflict aftermath.

1. **Latent Conflict:** The first stage of conflict is latent conflict in which the factors that could become a cause of potential conflict exist. These are the dry for autonomy, divergence of goals, role conflict and the competition for scarce resources.
2. **Perceived conflict:** Sometimes a conflict arises even if no latent conflict is present. In this stage one party perceived the others to be likely to thwart or frustrate his or her goals. The case, in which conflict is perceived when no latent conflict arises, is used to result from the parties misunderstanding each other's true position. Such conflict can be resolved by improving communication between the groups.
3. **Felt Conflict:** Felt conflict is the stage when the conflict is not only perceived but actually felt and cognized. The personalization of conflict is the mechanism which causes many people to be concerned with dysfunctions of conflict. In other words, it makes them feel the conflict.
   There are two reasons for the personalization of the conflict:
   (i) the inconsistent demands on efficient organization and individual growth which is caused within the individual. Anxieties may also result from crisis or from extra-organizational pressures. Individuals need to vent these anxieties in order to maintain equilibrium.
   (ii) Conflict becomes personalized when the whole personality of the individual is involved in the relationship. Hostile feelings are most common in the intimate relations that characterize various institutions and residential colleges.
4. **Manifest Conflict:** Manifest conflict is the stage when the two parties engage in behavior which evokes response from each other. The most obvious of these responses are open aggression, apathy, sabotage, withdrawal and perfect obedience to rules. Except for prison riots, political revolutions and extreme labor unrest, violence as a form of manifest conflict is rare. The motives towards violence may remain they tend to be expressed in less violent forms.
5. **Conflict Aftermath:** The aftermath of a conflict may have positive or negative repercussion for the organization depending upon the how conflict is resolved. If the conflict is genuinely resolved to the satisfaction of all participants, the basis for more cooperative relationship may be laid or the participants in their drive for a more ordered relationship may focus on latent conflicts not previously perceived and dealt with. On the other hand, if the conflict is merely suppressed but not resolved, the latent conditions of conflict may be aggravated and explode in a more serious from until they are rectified. This conflict episode is called conflict aftermath.

Levels of Conflict

1. **Intrapersonal level (conflict within the individual)**
   - Conflict from frustration
   - Goal conflict
   - Role conflict

Types of Intrapersonal conflict

a) Approach –approach conflict

b) Avoidance –avoidance conflict
c) Approach –avoidance conflict

2. **Interpersonal level (individual to individual conflict)**
   - Transactional Analysis(TA): Eric Berne
   - Johari window
   - Stroking
   - Life positions
3. **Inter-group level**
   - Task interdependence
   - Task ambiguity
   - Goal incompatibility
   - Limited resources
   - Reward system
4. **Inter-organizational level (Intra-group)**
   - Dispute between family members

Views about Conflict

1. **The Traditional View**
   - This approach assumes that all conflicts hamper performance.
   - Conflicts occur due to poor communication, lack of openness and trust between people, and the failure of managers to be open to their employees.
2. **The Human Relations View**
   - This approach assumes that conflicts occur naturally in all groups and organizations.
   - It is natural and cannot be avoided hence it should be accepted.
   - It cannot be removed and it may play a role in group performance.
3. **Functional Vs Dysfunctional Conflict**
   - Functional or constructive conflict supports the goals of the group and improves its performance.
   - Conflicts that hamper group performance are dysfunctional or destructive conflicts.
   - Task conflicts are related to the content and goals of the work.
   - Low to medium levels of task conflict is good because it improves group performance.
   - **Functional Conflict:** It refers to confrontation between two ideas , goals and parties that improve employees and the organizations performance .Well managed conflict helps workers anticipate and solve problems , feel confident ,strengthen their relationship and be committed to the organization.
   - **Dysfunctional Conflict:** Hinders and prevents organizational goals from being achieved.

Reasons for conflict

- Diversity of Goals
- Competition for scarce resources
- Organizational ambiguities
- Introduction to change

- Nature of Communication
- Difference in work orientation

Strategies for Conflict Resolution

1. Intrapersonal conflict

- Remove barriers
- Cognitive dissonance
- Refuse to select either approach
- Minimize and priorities roles
- Develop compatibility between personal and organizational goal
- Realizing that divided they stand, united they fall.

2. Interpersonal conflict

- Lose-Lose
- Lose-win
- Developing complementary transactions
- Altering behavioral inputs

3. Intergroup conflict

- Problem solving
- Organization redesign
- Super ordinate goals
- Expansion of resources
- Avoidance
- Smoothen

Conflict Management Approaches

1. Avoidance: In avoidance, every one shows that the conflict does not really exist and hopes that it will finish.

2. Accommodation: It involves hiding the differences between the conflicting parties and showing areas of agreement.

3. Compromise: It occurs when each party gives up something for the sake of the other. No party is fully satisfied.

4. Competition: It is a victory achieved due to force, superior skill, or domination of one party. It is a win-lose situation.

5. Collaboration: It involves appreciation by all conflicting parties that something is wrong and needs attention.

6.10.9.1. Transactional Analysis: Eric Berne

- Transactional analysis is an integrative approach to the theory of psychology and psychotherapy.
- It is described as integrative because it has elements of psychoanalytic, humanist and cognitive approaches.
- Transactional Analysis was founded by ***Eric Berne***, and the famous 'parent adult child' theory is still being developed today.

- Transactional Analysis has wide applications in clinical, therapeutic, organizational and personal development, encompassing communications, management, personality, relationships and behavior.
- In the 1950's Eric Berne began to develop his theories of Transactional Analysis. According to him verbal communication, particularly face to face, is at the centre of human social relationships and psychoanalysis.
- His starting-point was that when two people encounter each other, one of them will speak to the other. This he called the ***Transaction Stimulus***. The reaction from the other person he called the ***Transaction Response***.
- The person sending the Stimulus is called the Agent. The person who responds is called the ***Respondent***.
- Transactional Analysis became the method of examining the transaction wherein: ***'I do something to you, and you do something back'.***
- Berne also said that each person is made up of three alter ego states: Parent, Child and Adult.

1. Parent ego :

- This is our ingrained voice of authority, absorbed conditioning, learning and attitudes from when we were young.
- We were conditioned by our real parents, teachers, older people, next door neighbors, aunts and uncles, Father Christmas and Jack Frost.
- Our Parent is made up of a huge number of hidden and overt recorded playbacks. Typically embodied by phrases and attitudes starting with 'how to', 'under no circumstances', 'always' and 'never forget', 'don't lie, cheat, steal', etc.
- Our parent is formed by external events and influences upon us as we grow through early childhood. We can change it, but this is easier said than done.
- Parent is our 'Taught' concept of life.

2. Child ego :

- Our internal reaction and feelings to external events form the 'Child'.
- This is the seeing, hearing, feeling, and emotional body of data within each of us.
- When anger or despair dominates reason, the Child is in control. Like our Parent we can change it, but it is no easier.
- Child is our 'Felt' concept of life.

3. Adult ego :

- Our 'Adult' is our ability to think and determine action for ourselves, based on received data.
- The adult in us begins to form at around ten months old, and is the means by which we keep our Parent and Child under control.
- If we are to change our Parent or Child we must do so through our adult.
- Adult is our 'Thought' concept of life

6.10.9.2. Zohari window

- Developed by ***Joseph Luft and Harry Ingham*** (the word “Johari” comes from Joseph Luftand Harry Ingham).
- The Johari Window is a communication model that can be used to improve understanding between individuals.

- Individuals can build trust between themselves by disclosing information about themselves.
- They can learn about themselves and come to terms with personal issues with the help of feedback from others.
- Ingham and Luft's Johari Window model diagrams and examples - for self-awareness, personal development, group development and understanding relationships.
- The Johari Window model is a simple and useful tool for illustrating and improving self-awareness, and mutual understanding between individuals within a group.
- The Johari Window model can also be used to assess and improve a group's relationship with other groups.
- The Johari Window model was devised by American psychologists Joseph Luft and Harry Ingham in 1955, while researching group dynamics at the University of California Los Angeles.
- Today the Johari Window model is especially relevant due to modern emphasis on, and influence of, 'soft' skills, behaviour, empathy, cooperation, inter-group development and interpersonal development.

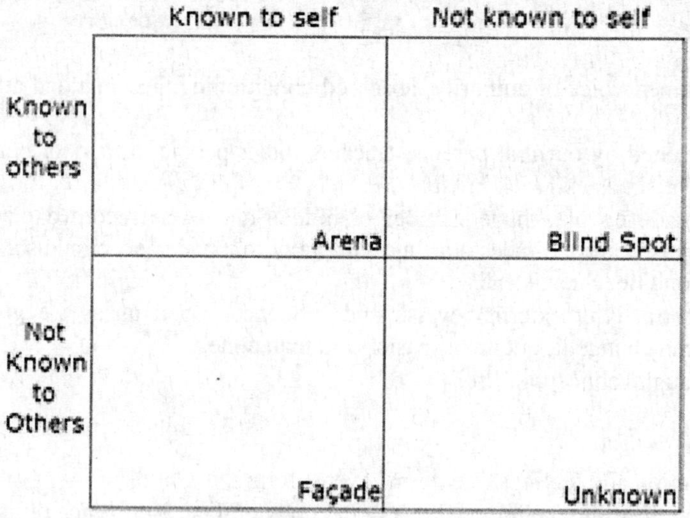

Fig. Zohari window

Four regions of Johari window

1. **Open area, open self, free area, free self, or 'the arena':** What is known by the person about him/herself and is also known by others.
2. **Blind area, blind self, or 'blind spot':** What is unknown by the person about him/herself but which others know.
3. **Hidden area, hidden self, avoided area, avoided self or 'facade':** What the person knows about him/ herself that others do not know.
4. **Unknown area or unknown self:** What is unknown by the person about him/herself and is also unknown by others.

6.10.10.Morale

- **Flippo:** *"morale is a mental condition or attitude of individuals or groups which determines their willingness to cooperate."*

- Morale is high when there is improved employee contribution, lower labour turnover and absenteeism.

Factors affecting morale

Morale building in the organization is a continuous process and a responsibility of every manager.

1. **The Organization:** If the goals set by management are worthwhile and acceptable the workers will develop a positive feeling towards the job and the organization.
2. **Job Enrichment:** It provides an opportunity to overcome monotony, fatigue, disinterestedness and creates an environment to satisfy needs leading to higher morale.
3. **Leadership:** The morale of employees would be high if their good work was recognized by their leader.
4. **Work Environment:** When employees are provided with clean, safe, comfortable and pleasant work conditions their morale will be high.
5. **Nature of Work:** If the nature of the work is interesting and challenging the morale will be high.
6. **Attitude of Co-Workers:** The attitude of co-workers can influence the morale.
7. **Conflict Handling:** Morale building effort includes conflict resolution.

Significant effects of low morale:

1. High rate of Absenteeism
2. Tardiness
3. High labour turnover
4. Strikes and Sabotage
5. Lack of Pride in Work
6. Wastage and Spoilage
7. Conflict

Measures to build high employee morale

1. **Unity of interests:** Integration of worker's goals with organization objectives.
2. **Leadership confidence:** Managers who are sincere, sympathetic and democratic in their attitudes towards employees.
3. **Sound wage structure:** Complete wage plan incorporates guaranteed base wages, incentive for productivity and other fringe benefits.
4. **Favorable work environment:** Good working conditions create job satisfaction.
5. **Higher-order need satisfaction:** Workers should be given ample opportunities to satisfy their social and personal wants.
6. **Other measures:** Employee counseling, sound promotion policy grievance procedure, proper selection techniques, induction training, and collective bargaining are some of the other measures to enhance employee morale.

6.10.11. Fatigue and Monotony

- Fatigue is the body's response to continued physical or mental activity or sleep loss, characterized by:
  - diminished ability to do work, loss of attention, slower reactions, poor response, deterioration of vigilance and alertness, impaired judgment, and other problems;
  - subjective feelings of tiredness, loss of motivation, desire for rest
- Fatigue is a complex state characterized by a lack of alertness and reduced mental and physical performance, often accompanied by drowsiness.
- The concepts of "fatigue", "sleepiness" and "drowsiness" are often used interchangeably.

- Sleepiness can be defined as the neurobiological need to sleep, resulting from physiological wake and sleep drives.
- Fatigue has from the beginning been associated with task performance.
- In addition, fatigue also has a psychological meaning: not having the energy to do anything, and a subjectively experienced reluctance to continue with a task.
- Thus, sleepiness is the drive for sleep while fatigue can be seen as a signal from the body that we should end the ongoing activity, whether it is physical activity, mental activity or just being awake.
- Although the causes of fatigue and sleepiness may be different, the effects of sleepiness and fatigue are very much the same, namely a decrease in mental and physical performance capacity.

Causes of fatigue

- Inadequate rest
- Sleep loss and/or disrupted sleep
- Displaced biological rhythms
- Excessive physical activity
- Excessive mental or cognitive work

Fatigue can occur in different parts of the body:

1) General body fatigue (cardiovascular system, Physiological).
2) Muscular fatigue (muscles, physiological),
3) Mental fatigue (brain, psychological).

Mental fatigue

- Feeling of tiredness after extended or repeated performance, particularly of tasks that are not predominantly physical.
- Feeling of monotony or boredom created by lack of novel stimulation.
- Mental fatigue is more pronounced and our alertness level decreases if we are tired and drowsy due to loss of anticipated sleep.

Factors affecting fatigue

- Quality and quantity of prior rest
- Individual physical fitness
- Endurance, exposure to level of task demand
- Environmental conditions
- Number of sustained work episodes
- Time of day
- Type of task
- Workload (mental or physical)
- Motivation and other individual differences

Effect of rest breaks

- The purpose of rest is to minimize the health effects of fatigue including musculoskeletal discomfort and mood disturbances associated with continuous work at computer workstation.
- *Rest* is a break or even a simple change of activity from a fatiguing task; we remain awake.
- Rest can restore energy, but it *cannot* substitute for sleep, nor can lack of sleep be corrected simply by resting.

Types of rest pauses :

1) **Spontaneous pauses:** Spontaneous pauses are the obvious pauses for the rest that the workers take on their own initiative. These are usually not very long. Nevertheless, may be frequent if the job is strenuous.
2) **Disguised pauses:** Disguised pauses are times when worker occupies himself or herself with some easier, routine task in order to relax from concentrating on the main job. Example: cleaning some part of the machine.
3) **Work-conditioned pauses:** Pauses arising from the nature of work are all those interruptions that arise either from the operation of the machine, or organization of the work; for example, waiting for the machine to complete a phase of its operation, for a tool to cool down.
4) **Prescribed pause:** Breaks in the work that are laid down by the management, for example, the midday break, and other pauses for snacks, e.g. coffee break.

Fatigue Signs and Symptoms

- Forgetfulness
- Poor communication
- Impaired decision making skills
- Lack of alertness
- Slow reaction time
- Micro sleep.
- Withdrawn behavior
- Depressed
- Moody
- Quick to anger
- No sense of humor
- Lack of interest
- Always tired.

6.10.12. Communication

- The word communication originates from the Latin word "***communis***" denoting common.
- Communication is the process of exchanging information and understanding between people.
- It involves imparting a common idea or understanding and covers any type of behavior resulting in an exchange of facts, ideas, opinions, or emotions by two or more persons.
- Management tasks of planning, directing, coordinating and motivation can be carried out by the process of receiving issuing recording and interpreting.
- **Louise Allen:** The information of facts and figures related to the varied aspects of business activities necessarily implies transmission of information intended to convey the idea of what is desired or required to be done. This would necessitate determination of information to link all the leavels and enable the concerned officers and operative to act upon such information. This process of transmitting information as between different levels of authority and among the officers at the same level is called communication.
- **Communication** can be defined as the process by which people share ideas, experience, knowledge and feelings through the transmission of symbolic messages.
- The means of communication are usually spoken or written words, pictures or symbols. But we also give information through body language, gestures, and looks, facial expressions can show how we feel and what we think about an issue or another person.

- **Murphy's Law:** "Communication usually fails, except by chance."
- **Grapevine:** Informal channel of communication.
- **Gang Plank:** Advanced by Henry Feyol. It is an lateral or Horizontal Communication.

Importance of communications

- Communication is described as one of the crucial fouls of management. It helps in handling the major managerial tasks of planning direction coordination motivating and controlling. It enables the top management.
- To formulate the comprehensive plans and policies on scientific basis.
- To put the policies and decisions into action results in accurate and efficient performance.
- Helps the management to remain informed to the problems difficulties, grievances of personnel. They arise mainly due to communication gap.
- It is essential for coordination which is the essence of management. It brings about mutual understanding between the officers and personnels at all levels and fosters the sprit of cooperation.
- It helps in securing largest possible participation or consumption indecision making, planning and general administration. This will give democratic character to managerial process and strengthen the moral of the staff.

Principles of good communication

1. Principle of clarity: It must give clear message n simple words and easily understandable form.
2. Principle of attention
3. Principle of adequacy: It should be consistent with plans, policies program and objective of the enterprise. It must be a complete one.
4. Principle of time: It should be give at proper time.
5. Principle of integration: It should ensure cooperation at all levels.
6. Principle of informality
7. Principle of feedback: Communication is two way traffic.

Interpersonal Communication (IPC)

- Interpersonal communication is a person to person, two-way, verbal and non verbal interaction that includes the sharing of information and feelings between individuals or in small groups that establish trusting relationships.
- **Elements of inter-personal Communication**
  - ❖ Message
  - ❖ Source (sender)
  - ❖ Channel
  - ❖ Receiver
  - ❖ Filter
  - ❖ Feedback
  - ❖ Encoding
  - ❖ decoding

Characteristics of communication

- Effective communication requires the ***message*** to be:
  - ❖ Clear and concise
  - ❖ Accurate
  - ❖ Relevant to the needs of the receiver

- ❖ Timely
- ❖ Meaningful
- ❖ Applicable to the situation

- Effective communication requires the ***sender*** to:
  - ❖ Know the subject well
  - ❖ Be interested in the subject
  - ❖ Know the audience members and establish a rapport with them
  - ❖ Speak at the level of the receiver
  - ❖ Choose an appropriate communication channel

- The ***channel*** should be:
  - ❖ Appropriate
  - ❖ Affordable
  - ❖ Appealing

- The ***receiver*** should:
  - ❖ Be aware, interested, and willing to accept the message
  - ❖ Listen attentively
  - ❖ Understand the value of the message
  - ❖ Provide feedback

An effective verbal communicator : CLEAR

- ❖ **C**larifies
- ❖ **L**istens
- ❖ **E**ncourages empathically
- ❖ **A**cknowledges
- ❖ **R**estates/repeats

An effective nonverbal communicator: ROLES

- ❖ **R**elaxes
- ❖ **O**pens up
- ❖ **L**eans toward the other person
- ❖ **E**stablishes eye contact
- ❖ **S**hows appropriate facial expressions

1. Giving information on matters regarding things done or to be done.
2. Receiving information on matters of actins expedited or yet to be expedited
3. Creating understanding in others about their responsibility and position and prospects of a situation concerning then.
4. Making others listen attentively to the facts, figures, views, opinions under transmissions.
5. Identifying the common intentions and interest by interaction of views through channels of commutations.

Effective Communication

- Functions of Communication
  - ❖ Control
  - ❖ Motivation
  - ❖ Emotional Expression
  - ❖ Information

Communication Fundamentals

Direction:

- ❖ Downward
- ❖ Upward
- ❖ Crosswise

Networks:

- ❖ Formal vs. Informal
- ❖ Communication Networks

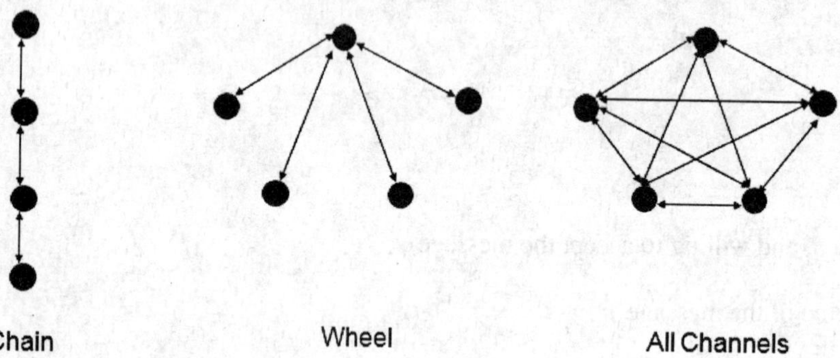

Key Communication Skills

- o Listening Skills
- o Feedback Skills
- o Presentation skills

Types of communication

1. On the basis of nature of passing information :

1.1. Formal communication

- Formal communication flows along prescribed channel which all members desires of communicating with one another are obliged to follow.
- Formal communication may more vertically or horizontally.
- **Vertical communication** can flow downward or upward.
- **Horizontal communication** flows between employees of equal or comparable status.
- **Downward communication:** Communication flows from a superior to a subordinate.

1.2. Informal communication:

Informal channel, often called a **grape vine**, that does not arise out of the organizational needs but that is never the less, an integral part of his communication system.

Grapevine

- In every organization an informal channel of communication exist called as the ***grapevine***.
- It follows no set lines, nor any definite rules, but spreads like the grapevine, in any direction anywhere and spared fast.
- **Keith davis** rightly pointed out that the grapevine is more a product of the situation then it is of the person.

- The grapevine is basically a channel of horizontal communication, for it is only people working at the same level of hierarchy who can informally communicate with one another with prefect case.
- Thus the workers may have one grapevine and the first line supervisors another. But the fact is that the grapevine does not follow any set pattern and it can be effective horizontal, vertically, and even diagonally.
- Professor Keith davis who has done some research in the nature of grapevine or the informal channel of communication classifies in the four basic types: Single strand, Gossi, Probability and Cluster.
  - **The single strand chain** involves the passing of information through a long line of persons to the ultimate recipient. A tells B who tells C who tells D and son on, till the information has reached most of the persons concerned.
  - **In the gossip chain**, A actively seeks and tells everyone. This chain is just like the wheel where A is at the centre and the information passes along the spokes of the wheel to others stationed on the rim.
  - **The probability chain** is a random process in which a transmits the information to others in accordance with the law of probability and them these others tell still others in a ultra manner. This chain may also be called random.
  - In **the cluster chain,** A feels selected persons who may in turn relay the information communication follows this chain.
  - A model if different forms of grapevines are depicted in the chart.

Importance of the grapevine

1. **Safety value:**
2. **Organizational solidarity and cohesion:** Properly used grapevine may even raise the morale of the workers.
3. Supplement to other channels
4. **Twice Transmission:** The speed with which information is transmitted through the grapevine is just remarkable.
5. **Feed Back:** The grapevine provide feedback to the management. It enable them to know what the subordinates think about the organization and its various activates

Demerits of grapevine

1. **Distortion:** One of the major drawbacks of the grapevine is that it may speed baseless or distorted news which may sometimes prove harmful even to the employees.
2. **Incomplete information:** The grapevine information is usually incomplete. So here is lively likelihood of its being misunderstood or misinterpreted.
3. **Damaging swiftness:** The swiftness with which the grapevine transmits information may even be damaging.

2. On the basis of direction i.e. flow of message:

2.1. Downwards Communication:

Message polices, programs, direction, opinions Highly Directive, from Senior to subordinates, to assign duties, give instructions, to inform to offer feedback, approval to highlight problems etc.

Objectives of downward communication

1. To give specific direction about the job being entrusted to a subordinate. The decision fallen at managerial levels are transmitted to states in the form of directives so an action may be initiated.

2. To explain the policies and organizational procedures. A clear understanding of policies given the lower state. A wider perspective so that they can grasp and relay their role more meaningfully.
3. To appraise the subordinates of their performance:
4. To give information about the rational of the job.

Media for downward communication

- Downward communication may be both oral and written.
- Important directives to initiate action may be communicated through letters policies and procedures may be announced house organs, manuals, bulletins etc, But the downward follow of communication is dominated by oral means.

Limitation of downward communication

1. Under – Communication and Over- Communication
2. Delay :
3. Loss of information
4. Distortion
5. Built – in resistance

Essentials of effective downwards communication

1. Managers should keep themselves well informed of the objectives and achievements of their organization. It they are themselves in possession of adequate information, they will be also to transmit information to their re-subordinated in an effective manner.
2. Managers must work according to communication plan. They must decide before how much information is to be communicated and at what time.
3. There should not be over communication of authority at the highest level. If an organization is so structured that orders and instructions can originate at various levels, the lines of communication will be shortened.
4. The information must be passed on to correct persons inherently.

2.2. Upwards Communications:

Grievances, complaints and suggestions etc. It is non directive in nature from down below, to give feedback, to inform about progress/problems, seeking approvals.

Upward communication: Bottom to Top (Subordinate to superior)

Importance of upward communication

1. Providing feed back
2. Out let for the sent-up emotions
3. Constructive suggestions
4. Easier introduction of new schemes
5. Greater harmony and cohesion

Methods of upward communication

1. Open door policy
2. Complaints and suggestions boxes
3. Social gatherings
4. Direct correspondence
5. Reports

6. Counseling

Limitations of upward communication

1. Employees are usually reluctant to initiative upward communication. The managers might keep their doors open, but they cannot force the employees to walk in to their problem.
2. Employees often feel that if they communicate their problems to their superiors, it may adversely reflect on their own efficiency.
3. Upward communication is more prone to distortion them downward communication. In downward communicate distortion is often unconscious. But upward communication is deliberately distorted.
4. Sometimes in the process of upward communication, workers become to bold, ignore their immediate superiors and directly approaches the top most authorities with their suggestions or complaints.

Essentials of effective upward communication

1. In order to enable the workers to over come the awe of authority, the managers should keep on encouraging them to come out of their shell and communicate freely.
2. Distortion by editing can be avoided if the lines of communication are kept as shortest possible.
3. All communicate should be properly analyzed genuine grievances deserve to be immediately resolved.

2.3. Lateral or Horizontal Communication

Among colleagues, peers at same level for information level for information sharing for coordination, to save time.

Horizontal communication

- Communication between departments or people on the same level in the managerial hierarchy of an organization may be termed as horizontal or lateral communication.
- Horizontal communication is extremely important for promoting understanding and coordinating among various departments.

Methods of horizontal communication

- Horizontal communication is most effectively carried on through oral means.
- Face to face exchanges of views or a brief conversation over the telephone in very convenient for horizontal communication.
- Formal channels tend to move managers status conscious so that they express their view in extremely measured items.
- This includes the free flow of communication takes place allow freedom of expression there is immediate feedback and all doubts and misunderstanding are sorted out.

3. On the basis of mode of operation

1) Oral communication
2) Written communication
3) Gesture communication

Barriers in communication

- Their might be a number of such barriers impeding the flow of communication in the organization. It includes Filtering, Selective Perception, Emotions, Language, etc.

- This may be classified as
  (i) External
  (ii) Organizational,
  (iii) Personal factors.

External barriers

1. **Semantic barriers:** Semantic barriers are obstruction caused in the process of receiving or understanding of the message during the process of encoding and decoding ideas and words.
   - ❖ Badly expressed message.
   - ❖ Faulty translations
   - ❖ Un-clarified Assumption.
   - ❖ Specialist's language.
2. **Emotional or psychological barriers:** Emotional or psychological factors are the prime barriers in inter-personal communication. The meaning ascribed to a message depends upon the emotional or psychological status of both the parties involved.
   - ❖ Premature evaluation.
   - ❖ Inattention
   - ❖ Loss by transmission and poor retention.
   - ❖ Undue reliance on the return word.
   - ❖ Distrust of communicator.
   - ❖ Failure to communicate.
3. **Organizational barriers:** An organization being a deliberate creations for the attainment of certain specified objectives, day-to-day happening within it require being regulated in such a manner that they contribute to attain these objectives in the most efficient manner.
   - ❖ Organizational policy
   - ❖ Organizational rules and regulations.
   - ❖ Status relationships.
   - ❖ Complexity in organization structure
   - ❖ Organizational facilities.
4. **Personal barriers :** While the organizational factors discussed above are, no doubt important influences operating on communication, a host of factors internal to the two parties-sender and receiver-to this process also exert important influences on its operation, s communication is basically an inter – personal processes.

Methods of overcoming the barriers

1. It is imperative that organizational policy must be clear explicit and encouraging the communication flow so that people at all levels realize the full significance of communication.
2. This policy should also specify the subject matter to be communicated.
3. Though the communication through proper channel is essential for orderly flow of information.
4. Even person in the organization shares the responsibility of good communication.
5. Organization should have adequate facilities for promoting communication.
6. Communication being an inter-personal process, the development of inter-personal relationship based on mutual respects, trust and confidence is essential for its promotion.
7. There should be continuous programme of evaluating the flow of communication in different directions.

6.11. OBJECTIVE QUESTION - ANSWER

1. Organization Behavior offers:
(A)Technical skills
(B) People skills
(C)Communication skills
(D) Wide knowledge

Answer: B

2. Organizational behaviour was popularized by :
(A) F.W. Taylor (B) Keith Davis
(C) Elton Mayo (D) David Cock

Answer: A

"**Frederic Winslow Taylor** (1856-1915): Taylor was one of the first to attempt to systematically analyze human behavior at work. His model was the machine with its cheap, interchangeable parts, each of which does one specific function. Taylor attempted to do to complex organizations what engineers had done to machines and this involved making individuals into the equivalent of machine parts. Just as machine parts were easily interchangeable, cheap, and passive, so too should the human parts be the same in the Machine model of organizations. "

3. According to the integrative model of organizational behavior, which of the following is an individual outcome?
(A) Job satisfaction
(B) Ability
(C) Personality
(D) Organizational commitment

Answer: D

Explanation: According to the integrative model of organizational behavior, the two individual outcomes are Job performance and Organizational commitment.

4. According to the integrative model of organizational behavior, trust, justice, and ethics are:
(A) Individual mechanisms
(B) Organizational mechanisms.
(C) Group mechanisms.
(D) Individual outcomes.

Answer: A

Explanation: According to the integrative model of organizational behavior, trust, justice, and ethics are part of the Individual mechanism.

5. According to the integrative model of organizational behavior, the two organizational-level variables that impact individual-level attitudes and behaviors are:
(A) Job performance and organizational commitment
(B) Culture and structure
(C) Team processes and team characteristics
(D) Personality and ability
(E) Stress and motivation

Answer: B

Explanation: Organizational culture and organizational structure are the two variables at the Organizational level that impact individual-level attitudes and behaviors.

6. While guiding organization members in appropriate directions, a manager exhibits:
(A) consideration behavior
(B) authoritarian behavior
(C) Theory Y behavior
(D) leadership behavior

Answer: D

7. The change in specialization and integration in organization context is called :
(A)Co-ordination
(B)Co-operation
(C)Organizational restructuring
(D) Feedback

Answer: C

8. ________ means willingness to exert high levels of effort on behalf of the organization.

(A) Organizational commitment
(B) Organization Effectiveness
(C) Organizational Control
(D) None of the above

Answer: A

9. Organizational Effectiveness is :
(A)Input - Output ratio
(B)Target achievement
(C)Doing right things
(D)Doing things right

Answer: A

Explanation: Organizational effectiveness is the concept of how effective an organization is in achieving the outcomes the organization intends to produce.

10. Organizational commitment is an example of :
(A) Job satisfaction
(B) Work attitude
(C) Personality
(D) Perception

Answer: A

11. OB can be contrasted with two other courses commonly offered in management departments_____ and strategic management.
(A)project management
(B)business management
(C)human resource management
(D)operations management

Answer: B

Explanation: Organizational behavior (OB) is a field of study devoted to understanding, explaining, and ultimately improving the attitudes and behaviors of individuals and groups in organizations. OB can be contrasted with two other courses: human resource management and strategic management.

12. An OB study might explore the relationship between pay and motivation, whereas a _______ study might examine the best way to structure compensation programs.
(A) Strategic management
(B) Anthropology
(C) Organizational development
(D) Economics
(E) Human resource management

Answer: E

Explanation: Human resource management takes the theories, principles studied in OB and explores the practical applications of those principles in organizations.

13. Factors contributing to unethical behaviour are :
(A)Poor leadership
(B)Poor internal communication
(C)Lack of management support
(D)All of the above

Answer: D

14. The Neo - classical theory of organizational structure was propounded by :
(A) Henry Fayol
(B) Elton Mayo
(C)Peter Drucker
(D) J.T. Dunlop

Answer: B

15. OB research on job performance and individual characteristics draws primarily from studies in:
(A) Industrial and organizational psychology
(B) Social psychology.
(C) Sociology.
(D) Sales management.

Answer: A

Explanation: The theories and concepts found in OB are actually drawn from a wide variety of disciplines. Research on job performance and individual characteristics draws primarily from studies in industrial and organizational psychology.

16. Research on satisfaction, emotions, and team processes found in OB draws heavily from studies in:
(A) Sociology.
(B) Organizational psychology.
(C) Industrial psychology.
(D) Social psychology.

Answer: D

Explanation: The theories and concepts found in OB are actually drawn from a wide variety of disciplines. Research on satisfaction, emotions, and team processes draws heavily from social psychology.

17. _____ is vital to research on team characteristics and organizational structure.
(A) Social psychology
(B) Industrial and organizational psychology
(C) Anthropology
(D) Economics
(E) Sociology

Answer: E

Explanation: The theories and concepts found in OB are actually drawn from a wide variety of disciplines. Sociology research is vital to research on team characteristics and organizational structure.

18. _____ research helps inform the study of organizational culture.
(A) Social psychology
(B) Industrial and organizational psychology
(C) Anthropology
(D) Sociology
(E) Economics

Answer: C

Explanation: The theories and concepts found in OB are actually drawn from a wide variety of disciplines. Anthropology research helps inform the study of organizational culture.

19. Study of organization culture is called:
(A)Organization Behaviour
(B)Organization Development
(C) Social Psychology
(D) Anthropology

Answer: A

20. Organization culture mostly effected by:
(A)Technology
(B)Market place
(C)Employees
(D)Top management

Answer: C

21. Which of the practice will *not* create an ethical culture in an organization?
(A) Visible role models from an organization
(B) Clearly communicating ethical expectations
(C) Provide ethical training
(D) Punishing whistle blowers

Answer: D

22. Models from ________ are used to understand motivation, learning, and decision making in OB.
(A) Marketing
(B) Economics
(C) Sociology
(D) Strategic management
(E) Anthropology

Answer: B

Explanation: The theories and concepts found in OB are actually drawn from a wide variety of disciplines. Models from economics are used to understand motivation, learning, and decision making.

23. The primary outcomes of interest to organizational behavior researchers are
(A) Job performance and organizational commitment.
(B) Organizational culture and organizational structure.
(C) Team processes and team characteristics.
(D) Personality and ability.
(E) Stress and motivation.

Answer: A

Explanation: The two primary outcomes of interest to organizational behavior researchers (and employees and managers in organizations) are job performance and organizational commitment.

24. Organisational Behaviour is a:
(A) Function of its consequences
(B) Study of character of people
(C) Study of team behavior
(D) Study of management behavior

Answer: A

25. Cross-functional groups that operate across space, time and organizational boundaries with members who communicate mainly through information technologies are
(A) Telecomputers (B) Virtual teams
(C) Teleworkers (D) Telemarketers

Answer: A

26. Which of these mechanisms dictate how the units within the firm link to other units?
(A) Organizational culture
(B) Organizational ability
(C) Organization size
(D) Organizational structure

Answer: D

Explanation: Organizational structure dictates how the units within the firm link to other units.

27. Which of the following mechanism captures "the way things are" in an organization?
(A) Organizational structure
(B) Organizational ability
(C) Organizational leadership
(D) Organizational performance
(E) Organizational culture

Answer: E

Explanation: Organizational culture captures "the way things are" in an organization.

28. Which of these mechanisms capture shared knowledge about the rules, norms, and values that shape employee attitudes and behaviors?
(A) Organizational structure
(B) Organizational ability
(C) Organizational culture
(D) Job performance
(E) Organizational leadership

Answer: C

Explanation: Organizational culture captures shared knowledge about the rules, norms, and values that shape employee attitudes and behaviors.

29. Which of the fóllowing statements about the resource-based view of organizations is false?

(A) It describes what exactly makes resources valuable.
(B) It describes what makes resources capable of creating long-term profits for the firm.
(C) A firm's resources include financial and physical resources.
(D) A firm's resources include resources related to organizational behavior.
(E) It suggests that the value of resources depends on a single factor.

Answer: E

Explanation: The resource-based view suggests that the value of resources depends on several factors. It describes what exactly makes resources valuable and capable of creating long-term profits for the firm.

30. According to resource-based view, a resource is more valuable when it is rare and
(A) Complex.
(B) Simple.
(C) Inimitable.
(D) Transparent.

Answer: C

Explanation: The resource-based view suggests that a resource is more valuable when it is inimitable.

31. An organizational memory includes the following except
(A) Information that employees possess
(B) Knowledge embedded in the organisation's systems and structures
(C) Documents
(D) Knowledge that is not documented

Answer: A

Explanation: Organizational memory is the accumulated body of data, information, and knowledge created in the course of an individual organization's existence. It has two repositories: an organization's archives, including its electronic data bases; and individuals' memories.

32. Nominal group technique is
(A) a consensus planning tool, generally used by groups to discuss, debate and decide on issues of strength-identification, problems and solutions.
(B) a consensus planning tool to arrive at decisions on issues, for instance man-power requirement, by involving group of experts through blind rounds of communication
(C) a majority based decision making tool
(D) None of the above

Answer: A

Explanation: Nominal group technique (NGT) is a structured method for group brainstorming that encourages contributions from everyone.

33. Which pattern reflects a pure executive form of management?
(A) Functional
(B) Line
(C) Line and Staff
(D) Committee

Answer: A

34. 'Appreciative Enquiry' is :
(A) Psychological Theory
(B) Training Method
(C) Business etiquette
(D) Problem Solving Method

Answer: D

Explanation: Appreciative Inquiry is a method of problem solving that was pioneered by ***David Cooperrider*** of Case Western Reserve University in the mid 1980s. It is primarily an organizational development method which focuses on increasing what an organization does well rather than on eliminating what it does badly.

35. OB is concerned with study of :
(A) Individuals, groups and organization system
(B) Individuals, groups and their institutions
(C) Organization, its roles and performance, and behaviour

(D)Organization, its environment, its strategies and performance

Answer: A

36. Graphical representation of Manpower in the organization is known as :

(A)Replacement chart
(B)Placement chart
(C)Organization structure
(D)Manpower inventory

Answer: C

37. Which of the following is a method of indicating the feeling of acceptance or rejection among members of a group?

(A) Mutuality
(B) Simulation
(C) T - group
(D) Sociometry

Answer: C

Explanation:

- **A T-group** or training group also referred to as **sensitivity-training group, human relations training group** or **encounter group** is a form of group psychotherapy where participants themselves learn about themselves through their interaction with each other. They use feedback, problem solving, and role play to gain insights into themselves, others, and groups.
- **Mutuality:** Having the same relationship each to the other.
- **Sociometry** is a quantitative method for measuring social relationships. It was developed by psychotherapist ***Jacob L. Moreno.***
- **Simulation** is the imitation of the operation of a real-world process or system over time.

38. What are the elements that a Mission Statement of an Organization should include?

(A) Self guidelines for Business Operations
(B) Identifies the reasons for existence of a company and its responsibilities to the stake-holders.
(C) Identifies the firms' customers and their needs and matches them to the products and services.
(D) All of the above

Answer: D

Explanation: The mission statement should guide the actions of the organization, spell out its overall goal, provide a path, and guide decision-making. It provides "the framework or context within which the company's strategies are formulated."

39. Group dynamics is the systematic study of :

(A) the forces operating outside the organization
(B) the forces operating within the group
(C) the forces operating between management and union
(D) the forces operating inside the organization

Answer: B

40. The group to which a person would like to belong is known as

(A)Primary Group
(B)Membership Group
(C)Reference Group
(D)None of the above

Answer: D

Explanation: When discussing ***social groups***, a group is said to be in a state of cohesion when its members possess bonds linking them to one another and to the group as a whole. Members of strongly cohesive groups are more inclined to participate readily and to stay with the group.

41. Sequence the following stages of group development :

(A)Forming, Norming, Storming, Performing
(B) Forming, Storming, Norming, Performing
(C) Norming, Forming, Storming, Performing
(D) Storming, Norming, Performing, Forming

Answer: B

Remember: FSNPA

42. Sensitivity training evolved from the group dynamics concept of
(A)French and Bell
(B) Eric Bernie
(C)Moreno
(D) Kurt Lewin
Answer: D

43. The theory which explains affiliation in Group formation and dynamics is called :
(A) Proximity theory
(B) Balance theory
(C) Exchange theory
(D) Propinquity theory
Answer: B

44. Group norms are strongly enforced by groups if they
(A) Aid in group survival
(B) Simplify expected behaviour of members
(C) Express central values of the group
(D) All the above
Answer: D

45. Which of the following is not a correct statement?
(A) Informal groups always hamper the performance of formal groups.
(B) Informal groups do not have prescribed goals and relationships.
(C) Informal and formal groups co-exist in organizations.
(D) Informal groups provide safety valve for employee emotions.
Answer: D

46. The process of grouping activities into units for the purpose of administration may be referred to as__________.
(A)Departmentation
(B)Decentralisation
(C)Coordination
(D)Specialisation
Answer: B
Explanation: Decentralization is the process of redistributing or dispersing functions, powers, people or things away from a central location or authority.

47. One method of bringing a group to agreement is called:
(A) proportional values
(B) consensus
(C) accordance
(D) conformance
Answer: B

48. Groups created by managerial decision in order to accomplish stated goals of the organization are called
(A) formal groups
(B) informal groups
(C) task groups
(D) interest groups
Answer: A

49. Continued membership in a group will usually require:
(A) supporting the group leader
(B) conforming to group norms
(C) encouraging cohesiveness in the group
(D) developing a status system
Answer: B

50. Which of the following decreases group cohesiveness?
(A) Agreement on group goals
(B) Frequency of interaction
(C) Large group size
(D) All the above
Answer: C

51. The way teams are formed, staffed, and composed, and the way members depend on one another is summarized by:
(A)Team processes.
(B)Team innovation.
(C)Team characteristics.
(D)Team policies.
(E) Team interaction.
Answer: C

Explanation : Team characteristics summarize the qualities that teams possess, such as their norms, their roles, and the way members depend on one another.

52. The basketball team at a local school has attributed their poor performance to the following: the team's coordination; inability to resolve conflict and cohesion. Which of the following is represented by the above scenario?
(A) Team responsibilities
(B) Team innovation
(C) Team characteristics
(D) Team processes
(E) Team problem solving

Answer: D

Explanation: Team processes summarize how teams behave, including their coordination, conflict, and cohesion.

53. Organization structures
(A) Affect group behavior more than individual behavior
(B) Change rapidly to meet environmental and market changes
(C) Contribute positively to organizational performance
(D) Can be defined simply as activities that occur regularly

Answer: D

Explanation: An organizational structure consists of activities such as task allocation, coordination and supervision, which are directed towards the achievement of organizational aims. It can also be considered as the viewing glass or perspective through which individuals see their organization and its environment.

54. Organization structure primarily refers to:
(A) How activities are coordinated and controlled
(B) How resources are allocated
(C) The location of departments and office space
(D) The policy statements developed by the firm

Answer: A

55. What is the key word in understanding organization structure?
(A) Control
(B) Change
(C) Process
(D) Delegation

Answer: A

56. 'Unity of Command' is violated under :
(A) Line and staff organization
(B) Line Organisation
(C) Matrix organisation
(D) Staff organization

Answer: C

57. In a line organization, authority flows from :
(A) Top to bottom
(B) Bottom to top
(C) Side by side
(D) None of these

Answer : A

58. Which of the following organizations is generally a combination of functionaland project patterns of departmentation ?
(A) Line and staff organization
(B) Matrix organisation
(C) Functional organization
(D) All the above

Answer: B

59. Functional managers are responsible
(A) for a single area of activity
(B) to the upper level of management and staff
(C) for complex organizational sub-units
(D) for obtaining copyrights and patents for newly developed processes and equipment

Answer: A

60. The line organisation structure is also called as:
(A) Matrix Organisation

(B)Scalar Organisation
(C)Functional Organisation
(D)Horizontal Organisation

Answer :B

61. The main advantage of functional organisation is :
(A)Simplicity (B) Hierarchical level
(C)Experience (D) Specialization

Answer: D

62. When the chain of command is longer than the span of control, the resultant organisation structure is :
(A)Balanced (B) Flat
(C)Tall (D)None of the above

Answer: C

63. Role of staff in 'line and staff' organization is
(A)Authoritative (B) Managerial
(C)Superior (D)Advisory

Answer: D

64. The principle of 'Unity of Command' is violated in
(A)Functional Organization
(B)Informal Organization
(C)Matrix Organization
(D)All the above

Answer: D

65. Which principle of management is violated by matrix organisation structure ?
(A) Division of Labour
(B) Unity of Direction
(C) Unity of Command
(D) None of the above

Answer: C

66. Feeling arising out of inadequate definition of roles is known as
(A)Role ambiguity
(B)Role conflict
(C)Role perception
(D)Role expectation

Answer: B

67. A type of group discussion process in which members of the group are encouraged to generate as many imaginative and creative ideas in a relatively short period of time is known as:
(A)Brain storming
(B)Group working
(C)Simulation
(D)Group effect

Answer: A

Explanation: Brainstorming is a group or individual creativity technique by which efforts are made to find a conclusion for a specific problem by gathering a list of ideas spontaneously contributed by its members. The term was popularized by ***Alex Faickney Osborn*** in the 1953 book Applied Imagination.

68. __________ is the third person acting as a catalyst, who assists in the achievement of the smooth introduction and implementation of change.
(A)Change manager
(B)Change supervisor
(C)Change player
(D)Change agent

Answer: D

69. The right sequence of steps in Kurt Lewin's change procedure is
(A) Unfreezing – Moving – Freezing
(B) Moving – Unfreezing – Freezing
(C) Unfreezing – Freezing – Moving
(D) Freezing – Moving – Unfreezing

Answer: A

70. Where do the following activities fall in Kurt Lewin's model of change process ? 'Reinforcing the newly learned behaviour, finding 'fits' between organizational components, and maintaining 'fits' between organizational components'
(A)Unfreezing (B) Moving
(C)Refreezing (D) None of the above

Answer: C

71. The change procedure of unfreezing, moving and refreezing was given by
(A) Kurt Lewin (B) P.F. Drucker
(C) French and Bell (D) Katz and Kahn

Answer: A

72. Lewin's theory is consistent with which view of organizational change?
(A) Continuous (B) contemporary
(C) Mayo's (D) "calm waters"

Answer: D

73. According to Kurt Lewin, which of the following is not a stage in the change process?
(A) unfreezing (B) changing
(C) refreezing (D) restraining

Answer: D

74. According to Kurt Lewin, increasing the driving forces, which direct behavior away from the status quo, is a means of doing which of the following?
(A) unfreezing (B) changing
(C) restraining forces (D) refreezing

Answer: A

75. The unfreezing step of the change process can be thought of as ______________.
(A) thawing the organization loose from the current status to the new status
(B) making the move to the new organizational condition
(C) loosening the organization from the old condition and moving it to the new codition
(D) preparing for the needed change

Answer: D

76. According to Lewin, which of the following is the objective of refreezing?
(A) directs behavior away from the status quo
(B) hinders movement away from existing equilibrium
(C) eliminates the need for future change
(D) stabilizes the new situation

Answer: D

77. The ______________ is consistent with uncertain and dynamic environments.
(A) calm waters metaphor
(B) white-water rapids metaphor
(C) contemporary metaphor
(D) continuous metaphor

Answer: B

78. In the white-water rapids metaphor, change is a natural state, and managing change is ____________.
(A) an accepted practice
(B) an expected practice
(C) a continual process
(D) a maintenance process

Answer: C

79. Changes in population characteristics such as age, gender, race, marital status, income and education are examples of change :
(A) Demographic (B) Cultural
(C) Geographic (D) Diversity

Answer: A

Explanation: Demographic change as a statistic characterizing human populations (or segments of human populations broken down by age or sex or income etc.)

80. Managing change is an integral part of ____________.
(A) Top management's job
(B) Middle-level management's job
(C) The first-line manager's job
(D) Every manager's job

Answer: D

81. Changing human resource management activities to attract and retain health care specialists due to increased needs for those workers is an example of what kind of environmental change factor?
(A) marketplace
(B) technology
(C) labor markets
(D) economic

Answer: C

82. Which of the following is not an internal force of change?
(A) technology
(B) strategy
(C) workforce
(D) employee attitudes
Answer: A

83. Which of the following is not an external force of change?
(A) marketplace
(B) government laws and regulations
(C) economic changes
(D) workforce
Answer: D

84. Internal forces that stimulate the need for change tend to originate primarily from the impact of external forces or from ________.
(A)the forces of competition
(B)change in technology
(C)customer demand for the products the company produces
(D)the internal operations of the organization
Answer: D

85. What change factor did Steve Bennett address in his turnaround of Intuit, Inc?
(A) technology
(B) workforce
(C) equipment
(D) strategy
Answer: D

86. Increasing the numbers of employed women and minorities forces managers to pay attention to what change factor?
(A) strategy
(B) workforce
(C) equipment
(D) technology
Answer: B

87. Labor strikes are an example of what change factor that may encourage a change in management thinking and practices?
(A) workforce
(B) equipment
(C) employee attitudes
(D) strategy
Answer: C

88. One of the primary views of the change process is ____________, while the other view is ____________.
(A) problematic; encouraged
(B) occasional; continuous
(C) costly; conservative
(D) optimistic; pessimistic
Answer: B

89. In organizations, people who act as catalysts and assume the responsibility for managing the change process are called ____________.
(A) change masters
(B) change agents
(C) operations managers
(D) charismatic leaders
Answer: B

90. In spurring organizational change, outside consultants are usually more ____, whereas internal managers may be more ________.
(A) drastic; thoughtful
(B) highly paid; risky
(C) resistant; bold
(D) cautious; friendly
Answer: A

91. As change agents, managers should be motivated to initiate change because they are committed to __________.
(A) promoting the welfare of their employees
(B) managing and want to do the best they can for everyone
(C) improving their organization's performance

(D) meeting the competition head-on in the market

Answer: C

92. Initiating change involves identifying what organizational areas might need to be changed and ____________.
(A) discussing it with the board of directors
(B) hiring a consultant to confirm that the change is needed
(C) forming a committee to determine that the need for change is real
(D) putting the change process in motion

Answer: D

93. Managers' options for change essentially fall into what three categories?
(A) environment, technology, and mission
(B) structure, technology, and people
(C) mission, structure, and people
(D) mission, environment, and process

Answer: B

94. What category of change involves work processes, methods, and equipment?
(A) technology
(B) people
(C) competitors
(D) structure

Answer: A

95. A company that decides to decentralize its sales procedures is managing what change category?
(A) technology (B) people
(C) competitors (D) structure

Answer: D

96. What type of change might include a shift from a functional to a product structure?
(A) a structural design change
(B) a structural component change
(C) automation
(D) computerization

Answer: A

97. Competitive factors or new innovations within an industry often require managers to introduce all of the following <u>except</u> new ____________.
(A) equipment
(B) tools
(C) operating methods
(D) employees

Answer: D

98. When grocery stores installed scanners to read the product price, this was an example of managing what change category?
(A) technology
(B) people
(C) competitors
(D) structure

Answer: A

99. If Kraft Foods hired a consultant to decrease group friction and enhance cooperative work relationships, this would be an example of managing what change category?
(A) technology (B) people
(C) competitors (D) structure

Answer: B

100. An individual is likely to resist change because of all of the following reasons <u>except</u> ____________.
(A) uncertainty
(B) increased productivity
(C) concern over personal loss
(D) belief that the change is not in the organization's best interest

Answer: B

101. To cope with the complexity of life, individuals rely on habits or ____________.
(A) programmed responses
(B) the status quo
(C) beliefs
(D) certainties

Answer: A

102. Which of the reasons for resistance to change expressed by an employee may be beneficial to the organization?
(A) uncertainty
(B) freezing
(C) change is incompatible with the interests of the organization
(D) refreezing

Answer: C

103. All of the following are mentioned as actions that managers can use to deal with resistance to change except ______________.
(A) education and communication
(B) diversification
(C) participation
(D) facilitation and support

Answer: B

104. For ________ to be effective, there must be mutual trust and credibility between managers and employees.
(A) education
(B) coercion
(C) negotiation
(D) participation

Answer: A

105. __________ may be necessary when resistance comes from a powerful source.
(A) Education and communication
(B) Coercion
(C) Facilitation and support
(D) Negotiation

Answer: D

106. ____________ is using direct threats or force on those who resist change.
(A) Negotiation
(B) Coercion
(C) Cooptation
(D) Education and communication

Answer: B

107. Which of the following represents the relationship between organizational culture and change?
(A) Culture and change are naturally compatible.
(B) Culture tends to be very resistant to change.
(C) Culture can change in months but not weeks.
(D) Culture can never be purposely changed.

Answer: B

108. Which of the following is not a favorable situational condition that may facilitate change in an organizational culture?
(A) a dramatic crisis occurs
(B) the culture is weak
(C) stock prices remain constant
(D) the organization is young and small

Answer: C

109. Cultural change is most likely to take place when ______________.
(A) the organization is old
(B) the organization is large
(C) the culture is strong
(D) there is a leadership change

Answer: D

110. What is a strategy for managing cultural change?
(A) Support employees who remain devoted to the old values.
(B) Redesign socialization processes to align with the new values.
(C) Keep the reward system the same.
(D) Terminate top managers who are positive role models.

Answer: B

111. A dynamic and uncertain organizational environment has created a large number of employees who are ____________.
(A) old enough to retire, but can't afford to retire
(B) young and energetic about the "next

day's work"
(C) overworked and stressed out
(D) overworked, but paid very well

Answer: C

112. An important potential environmental source of change is
(A) a new competitive product
(B) dissatisfied employee attitudes
(C) employee grievances
(D) a wildcat strike

Answer: A

113. USX (formerly U.S. Steel) has become mostly an energy company. This is an example of a change in
(A) executive
(B) policy
(C) strategy
(D) mission

Answer: D

114. Organizational change should be managed by:
(A) Top management
(B) Employees
(C) All mangers
(D) Consultants

Answer : C

115. The categories of human process, techno structural, human resources management and strategic applications are related to :
(A) Change management
(B) O. D. application
(C) Training
(D) Action research

Answer: A

116. Which of the following is not among the actions for change?
(A) Changing
(B) Forcing
(C) Unfreezing
(D) Refreezing

Answer: B

117. If the change is plotted on two axis of 'Time and difficulty involved in change ' then which of the following would be the correct sequence of change taking place in shortest time and difficulty to maximum period and difficulty ?
(i) Group Behaviour
(ii) Individual Behaviour
(iii) Organizational Behaviour
(iv) Knowledge
(v) Attitude

(A)	(iv)	(v)	(iii)	(ii)	(i)
(B)	(i)	(ii)	(iv)	(iii)	(v)
(C)	(ii)	(iii)	(i)	(v)	(iv)
(D)	(iv)	(v)	(ii)	(i)	(iii)

Answer: D

118. A person who will initiate change in the organization is called :
(A) Consultant
(B) Trainer
(C) Change Agent
(D) Counsellor

Answer: C

119. An organisation that has developed capacity to adapt and change is described as :
(A) Virtual organisation
(B) Learning organisation
(C) Developing organisation
(D) Changing organization

Answer: B

Explanation: A learning organization is the term given to a company that facilitates the learning of its members and continuously transforms itself. Learning organizations develop as a result of the pressures facing modern organizations and enables them to remain competitive in the business environment

120. Global economic pressures force organizations to become more ____________.
(A) price competitive
(B) quality conscious
(C) cost efficient
(D) conservative with raw materials

Answer: C

121. How can managers increase the likelihood of making change happen successfully?
(A) focus on how they want to change the organization
(B) understand the difficult task at hand
(C) increase the role of individual employees
(D) observe how competitors are changing

Answer: C

122. What is a characteristic of a change-capable organization?
(A) separates the present and the future
(B) makes controlling a way of life
(C) discourages mavericks
(D) shelters breakthroughs

Answer: D

123. A study of organizational change found that __________ percent of changes at the work-group level were reactions to a specific, current problem or to a suggestion from someone outside the work group; and __________ percent of those changes occurred in the course of employees' day-to-day work.
(A) 77; 68
(B) 35; 90
(C) 90; 35
(D) 68; 77

Answer: A

124. What organizational development (OD) technique is a technique for assessing attitudes and perceptions, identifying discrepancies in these, and resolving the differences by using survey information in feedback groups?
(A) team building
(B) intergroup development
(C) survey feedback
(D) sensitivity training

Answer: C

125. Which of the following is not a traditional method of organizational development?
(A) Survey feedback
(B) Sensitivity training
(C) Process consultation
(D) Managerial grid

Answer: C

126. What OD technique involves changing the attitudes, stereotypes, and perceptions that work groups have about each other?
(A) team building
(B) intergroup development
(C) survey feedback
(D) sensitivity training

Answer: B

127. Before using the same OD techniques to implement behavioral changes, especially across different countries, managers need to be sure that they've taken into account __________.
(A) cultural characteristics
(B) organizational differences
(C) employee attitudes
(D) societal differences

Answer: A

128. Techniques to change people and the quality of interpersonal work relationships are termed __________.
(A) operations
(B) organizational development
(C) downsizing
(D) robotics

Answer: B

129. Which of the following is correct about Organizational Development ?
(A) It is a planned change
(B) It aims at problem solving
(C) It is focused primarily on human and social relationships
(D) All the above

Answer: A

130. Among the following which is not OD technique
(A) Sensitivity training

(B) MBO
(C) Delphi technique
(D) Grid training and development

Answer: B

131. Which of the following is not correct about Organization Development?
(A) It is not a top management led and supported process.
(B) It is a process of planned change.
(C) It is an ongoing collaborative management of organization culture.
(D) It is a problem solving process.

Answer: A

132. Action research,as a methodology for behavioural science was proposed by :
(A) Wendell L. French
(B) P. F. Drucker
(C) Kurt Lewin
(D) Reddin

Answer: C

133. Which of the following is not an OD intervention?
(A) Grid Training
(B) Transactional Analysis
(C) Process Consultation
(D) None of the above

Answer: B

134. Arrange the following phases of Grid training in OD in the sequence in which they are held.
(a) Team development
(b) Organizational goal setting and attainment
(c) Inter-group development
(d) Laboratory-Seminar Training

(A) (d) (a) (c) (b)
(B) (a) (d) (b) (c)
(C) (c) (d) (b) (a)
(D) (d) (c) (b) (a)

Answer: A

135. Systematic collection of data on a problem, analysis, feedback and helping organization to take action to address the problem is called :
(A) Process Research
(B) Field Research
(C) Action Research
(D) Business Research

Answer: C

136. Who propounded Self Theory of Personality?
(A) Kretschmer
(B) Allport
(C) Eysenck
(D) Roger

Answer: D

137. Individual psychology of personality was given by:
(A) A. Adler
(B) Jung
(C) Eysenck
(D) None of these

Answer: A

138. Among the best known trait approaches to personality measurement – column A gives Traits and column B states the name of authority defining them. Match the correct combination

Traits	**Author**
(A)20 + needs	Murray
(B)16 traits	Eysenck
(C)3 traits	Cattell
(D)5 traits	Costa & Merree

Answer: A

Explanation: 3 traits given by Eysenck and 16 traits given by Cattel and 20 traits by Murray.

139. People's behavior at work, the kinds of tasks they are interested in, and how they react to events that happen on the job are associated with their _____
(A) Ability.
(B) Trust, justice, and ethics.
(C) Learning and decision making.
(D) Team characteristics.
(E) Personality and cultural values.

Answer: E

Explanation: Personality and cultural values affect the way people behave at work, the kinds of tasks they're interested in, and how they react to events that happen on the job.

140. Which of the following describes the cognitive abilities, emotional skills, and physical abilities that employees bring to a job?
(A) Ability
(B) Personality and cultural values
(C) Trust, justice, and ethics
(D) Individual's characteristics
(E) Intelligence

Answer: A

Explanation: Ability describes the cognitive abilities, emotional skills, and physical abilities that employees bring to a job.

141. Which of the following influences the kinds of tasks an employee is good at and those with which an employee may struggle?
(A) Personality
(B) Ability
(C) Trust, justice, and ethics
(D) Learning and decision making
(E) Cultural values

Answer: B

Explanation: Ability influences the kinds of tasks an employee is good at and those with which an employee may struggle.

142. The personality theory that emphasises the unconscious determinants of behaviour is known as :
(A) Cognitive theory
(B) Psychodynamic theory
(C) Perpetual theory
(D) Refreezing

Answer: B

143. The assumptions about human nature
(i) work is inherently distasteful to most people
(ii) most people would like to be directed, and
(iii) most people have little or no creativity are propounded by :
(A) Hygiene Theory
(B) Maslow's Theory
(C) Theory X
(D) Theory Y

Answer: C

144. In the theory of Mc Gregor following assumptions have been made about human nature, under theory X those are
(A) Self-centered
(B) Lacks ambitions
(C) Gullible
(D) All the above

Answer: D

145. The usual tendency with negative feedback is to find the reason to explain one's own behaviour. This tendency is termed as :
(A) Mutuality
(B) Displacement
(C) Rationalisation
(D) Projection

Answer: C

146. In which of the following inter - personal styles, people are critical of other's behaviour, develop rules and regulations and impose them on others :
(A)Rescuing style
(B)Prescriptive style
(C)Normative style
(D)Supportive style

Answer: B

147. A personality characteristic indicating one's willingness to do whatever it takes to get one's own way is known as
(A)Locus of control
(B)Machiavellism
(C)Job characteristic model
(D)Personality legitimacy
Answer: B

148. Emotional Intelligence includes :
(A) Self awareness, self management and self motivation
(B) Self awareness, self knowledge and self understanding
(C) Knowledge, belief, culture and perception
(D) All the above
Answer: A

149. Transactional Analysis (TA) is related to
(A) Learning
(B) Attitudes
(C) Perception
(D) Personality
Answer: D

150. In ______, a person is perceived on the basis of a single trait.
(A) Halo Effect
(B) Hawthorne Effect
(C) Stereotyping
(D) None of the above
Answer: A

151. Figure – Ground Theory explains the process of
(A)Cognition
(B) Sensation
(C) Perception
(D) Motivation
Answer: C

152. The process selecting, organizing and interpreting or attaining meaning to events happening in the environment is called:
(A) Perception
(B) Attitude
(C) Personality
(D) Learning
Answer: A

153. Organization value refers to :
(A) Individual belief
(B) Group belief
(C) Corporate believes and ethos
(D) None of the above
Answer: B

154. Dependability, predictability and faith are the three elements that constitute :
(A) Values
(B) Moral principles
(C) Trust
(D) Justice
Answer: C

155. ______ reflect the various traits and tendencies that describe how people act, with commonly studied traits including extraversion, conscientiousness, and collectivism.
(A) Leadership
(B) Motivation
(C) Social values
(D) Personality and cultural values
(E) Learning
Answer: D
Explanation: Personality and cultural values reflect the various traits and tendencies that describe how people act, with commonly studied traits including extraversion, conscientiousness, and collectivism.

156. Shared organizational values are
(A)unconscious, affective desires or wants that guide society's behavior
(B)influenced by international values
(C)different for the various components of a diverse work force
(D)a myth
Answer: C

157. Instrumental values are :
(A) Hardworking, sincerity, rationality and self-discipline
(B) Free of conflict, quality, happiness and self-esteem
(C) Social recognition, contentment and harmony
(D) All the above

Answer: A

Explanation: Instrumental Values are core values, permanent in nature, comprise personal characteristics and character traits. Instrumental Values refer to preferable modes of behaviour and include values like honesty, sincerity, ambition, independence, obedience, imaginativeness, courageousness, competitiveness, and also some negative traits too.

158. According to the integrative model of organizational behavior, two of the individual characteristics that impact individual attitudes and behaviors include:
(A) job performance and organizational commitment.
(B) organizational culture and organizational structure.
(C) team processes and team characteristics.
(D) personality and ability.
(E) stress and motivation.

Answer: D

Explanation: Two of the individual mechanisms that directly affect job performance and organizational commitment include personality and ability.

159. According to the integrative model of organizational behavior, the two types of group-level variables that impact individual-level attitudes and behaviors are:
(A) job performance and organizational commitment
(B) learning and decision making
(C) leadership and teams
(D) personality and ability
(E) stress and motivation

Answer: C

Explanation: Leadership and Teams are the two types of group level variables that impact individual-level attitudes and behaviors.

160. The conditioned - learning theory was propounded by :
(A)Thoradike
(B)Pavlov
(C)Maslow
(D)Luther Gullick

Answer: B

161. Classical conditioning is associated with:
(A) Repetition
(B) Generalization
(C) Discrimination
(D) All the above

Answer: A

162. Match the following expressions with the ego states mentioned against them :

Expressions	**Ego states**
(a) Rationality	(i) Parent
(b) Fantasising	(ii) Child
(c) Demonstrating	(iii) Adult

	(a)	(b)	(c)
(A)	(i)	(ii)	(iii)
(B)	(ii)	(i)	(iii)
(C)	(iii)	(ii)	(i)

(D) None of the above

Answer: C

163. The tools and techniques used in learning organizations are
(A) Creativity
(B) Brainstorming

(C) Observing outcomes
(D) Reframing knowledge
(E) All the above

Answer: E

164. According to Freud, Super Ego is properly developed during
(A) latency period
(B) anal period
(C) phallic period
(D) none of these

Answer: A

165. Which of the following theories is most quantitatively measurable?
(A) Pavlov's
(B) Skinner's
(C) Hull's
(D) None of these

Answer: C

166. Match the following List – I with List – II in correct order :

List – I	List – II
a. Classical conditioning	i. Kohler
b. Drive reduction	ii. Hull
c. Sign Gestalt learning	iii. Pavlov
d. Learning by insight	iv. Skinner
	v. Tolman

Codes:

	a	b	c	d
(A	iv	ii	v	i
(B)	iii	ii	v	i
(C)	iv	ii	I	v
(D)	iii	ii	i	v

Answer: B

167. "Assistant Manager, after observing the style of conducting a meeting of Senior Manager on number of occasions started conducting the meeting in similar manner" is an example of :
(A) Classical conditioning
(B) Social learning
(C) Insight learning
(D) Operant conditioning

Answer: A

168. In a learning organisation
(A) Vision is provided by top management
(B) Conflicts are resolved through power and hierarchical influence
(C) Formulation and implementation of ideas takes place at all levels of organization
(D) All the above

Answer: C

169. Who has advanced the single loop and double loop learning models?
(A) Albert Bandura
(B) Robert Blake
(C) Robert Katz
(D) Chris Argyris

Answer: D

170. Match the following :

Contributor	**Behavioural Models**
(a) Ivan Pavlor	(i) social learning model
(b) B.F. Skinner	(ii) cognitive framework
(c) Albert Bandura	(iii) classical conditioning
(d) Edward Tolman	(iv) operant conditioning

	(a)	(b)	(c)	(d)
(A)	(iii)	(iv)	(ii)	(i)
(B)	(ii)	(iii)	(i)	(iv)
(C)	(iii)	(iv)	(i)	(ii)
(D)	(iii)	(ii)	(iv)	(i)

Answer: C

171. Reinforcement given by removing a noxious or undesirable stimulus from the environment is known as :
(A) Positive Reinforcement
(B) Negative Reinforcement
(C) Punishment
(D) None of the above

Answer: B

Escape Learning (Negative reinforcement) Escape conditioning (Negative reinforcement). Stimulus → desired response → Removal of Noxious Consequence. Increase likelihood of desired behavior by taking away neg. consequences of that behavior. (pressing lever while noise is going on & it stops).

172. As employees gain experience, they obtain job knowledge and use this knowledge to make accurate judgments on the job. Which of the following is represented by this statement?
(A) Team processes
(B) Trust, justice, and ethics
(C) Learning and decision making
(D) Personality and ability
(E) Motivation

Answer: C

Explanation: Learning and decision making deals with how employees gain job knowledge and how they use that knowledge to make accurate judgments on the job.

173. Match the following :

List – I (Propagators)	List – II (Contributions)
a. Ivan Pavlov	i. Social Learning Thoery
b. B.F. Skinner	ii. S-O-B-C.Model
c. Albert Bandura	iii. Classical Conditioning
d. Freud Luthans	iv. Operant Conditioning

Codes:

	(a)	(b)	(c)	(d)
(A)	(iii)	(iv)	(ii)	(i)
(B)	(ii)	(iii)	(i)	(iv)
(C)	(iii)	(iv)	(i)	(ii)
(D)	(iii)	(ii)	(iv)	(i)

Answer: C

174. Which of the following statements correctly describe 'extinction'? When a previously reinforced behaviour :
(A) is reinforced immediately
(B) is reinforced for a short period
(C) is not reinforced for a long time
(D) both (B) and (C) above

Answer: C

Explanation: Extinction is observed in both operantly conditioned and classically conditioned behavior. When operant behavior that has been previously reinforced no longer produces reinforcing consequences the behavior gradually stops occurring.

175. In which of the following transactions, stimulus and response are parallel?
(A) Cross Transactions
(B) Complementary Transactions
(C) Ulterior Transactions
(D) All the above

Answer: B

176. Need-Hierarchy Theory was propounded by
(A) Peter F. Drucker
(B) Abraham Maslow
(C) Mc – Fraland
(D) Elton Mayo

Answer: B

177. Arrange Maslow's Hierarchy of Needs in descending order :
(i) Social Needs
(ii) Self-actualisation Needs
(iii) Physiological Needs
(iv) Ego Needs
(v) Security Needs

Codes :
(A) (iii), (v), (i), (iv) and (ii)
(B) (iii), (v), (i), (ii) and (iv)
(C) (ii), (iv), (i), (iii) and (v)
(D) (ii), (iv), (i), (v) and (iii)

Answer: D

178. Which is the correct sequence in Maslow's need hierarchy theory ?
(A) Security, Affiliation, Esteem
(B) Affiliation, Security, Esteem
(C) Security, Esteem, Affiliation
(D) None of the above are correct

Answer: A

179. In order from lowest to highest, what are Maslow's five classes of needs?
(A) Social.esteem.physiological.safety. self-actualization
(B) Physiological.safety.social.self-actualization.esteem

(C) Physiological.safety.social.esteem. self-actualization
(D) Self-actualization. esteem. safety. social. physiological

Answer: C

180. In Maslow's need hierarchy theory, which of the following are not high order needs?
(A) Safety
(B) Social
(C) Esteem
(D) Self-Actualisation

Answer: B

181. Who propounded the Two - Factor Theory ?
(A) Frederick Herberg
(B) Mc Gregor
(C) J. S. Mill
(D) Adam Smith

Answer: A

182. 'X' and 'Y' theory was prepared by
(A) Herzbeg
(B) Maslow
(C) Porter and Lawler
(D) McGregor

Answer: D

183. According to Herzberg, which of the following is a maintenance factor?
(A) Salary (B) Work itself
(C) Responsibility (D) Recognition

Answer: A

184. Which of the following is Herzberg's hygiene factor?
(A) Recognition at work place
(B) Reasonable salary
(C) Responsibility for work
(D) Sense of achievement

Answer: B

185. Which one of the following is a motivating factor according to Herzberg?
(A) Job itself
(B) Salary
(C) Working conditions
(D) Size of the organization

Answer: C

186. Among of following which is a hygiene factor
(A) Salary
(B) Reorganization
(C) Growth
(D) Self actualization

Answer: A

187. Which of the following is hygiene factor?

(A) Advancement (B) Growth
(C) Job Security (D) Achievement

Answer: C

188. **Assertion** : "All hygiene factors put together do not motivate a person on the job". **Reason** : "A satisfied need is not a motivator of behaviour."
(A) The Assertion is right but Reason is wrong
(B) The Assertion is wrong but Reason is right
(C) The Assertion distinguishes hyegiene factors from motivational factors thereby justifying the Reason.
(D) Neither the Assertion nor the Reason is right.

Answer: C

189. Under Alderfer's ERG theory, the three core needs are
(A) Emotional, Relational, and Growth
(B) Emotional, Rational and Growth
(C) Existence, Reliability and Gain
(D) Existence, Relatedness and Growth

Answer: D

190. Clayton Alderfer attempted to rework Maslow's need hierarchy to align it more closely with empirical research. His revised need hierarchy is labelled as
(A) Theory of Needs
(B) Self efficiency theory

(C) ERG theory
(D) Equity theory

Answer: C

191. Which of the following theories was propounded by McChelland ?
(A) Achievement motivation
(B) Need hierarchy
(C) Two factor theory
(D) ERG theory

Answer: A

192. What are the motives identified by David C Mc Celland ?
(A) Affiliation
(B) Power
(C) Achievement
(D) All the above

Answer: D

193. Need for achievement goes with
(A) F.W. Taylor
(B) Hertzberg
(C) McGregor
(D) McClelland

Answer: D

194. Which of the following is not a content theory of motivation?
(A) Maslow's Need Hierarchy Theory
(B) Alderfer's ERG Theory
(C) Vroom's Expectancy Theory
(D) Herzberg's Two Factor Theory

Answer: C

Explanation: Content theories focus on profiling the needs that people seek to fulfill.
Process theories: Focus on people's thought or cognitive processes. Emphasize controlling behavior by manipulating its consequences.

195. Which of the following is one of the process Theories of motivation?
(A) Alderfer's E R G Theory
(B) Achievement motivation Theory
(C) Manifest need Theory
(D) None of the above

Answer: D

196. Expectancy Theory of Motivation was propounded by
(A) Porter and Lawler
(B) McGregor
(C) Vroom
(D) J. Stacy Adams

Answer: C

197. In Vroom's theory, motivation is expressed as
(A) Valence + Expectancy
(B) Valence – Expectancy
(C) Valence × Expectancy
(D) Valence /Expectancy

Answer: C

198. Who has given the 'expectancy theory' of Motivation ?
(A) Abraham Maslow
(B) Victor Vroom
(C) Frederick Herzberg
(D) Clayton Adler

Answer: B

199. Which of the following is not the process theories of motivation?
(A) Vroom's expectancy model
(B) Adam's equity theory
(C) Porter's performance satisfaction theory
(D) Alderfer's ERG theory

Answer: C

200. Prachita is a new employee at a company. She feels very energetic and this drives her to perform well. Which of these individual mechanisms captures the energetic forces that drive employees' work efforts?

(A) Motivation
(B) Ability
(C) Job performance
(D) Personality
(E) Stress

Answer: A

Explanation: Motivation captures the energetic forces that drive employees' work effort.

201. The integrative model of organizational behavior includes a number of individual mechanisms that directly impact job performance and organizational commitment. Those mechanisms include:
(A) leader styles and behavior.
(B) team diversity and communication.
(C) team processes and team characteristics.
(D) personality and ability.
(E) stress and motivation.

Answer: E

Explanation: Stress and motivation are two of the individual mechanisms that directly impact job performance and organizational commitment.

202. 'Hot-Stove' rule was given by :
(A) Douglas Mc Gregor
(B) Mc Clleland
(C) Dale S. Beach
(D) Dale Yoder

Answer: A

203. The 'Cognitive Dissonance' theory of motivation was advanced by :
(A)Parter and Lawler
(B)Kelly and Rolter
(C)Lewin and Tolman
(D)Festinger and Homans

Answer: D

204. Match the following :

List-I	List-II
(a) Frederick Herzberg	(i)Scientific Management
(b) F.W. Taylor	(ii) Two Factor Theory
(c) Blake and Monton	(iii) Need Hierarchy Theory
(d) Abraham Maslow	(iv) Managerial Grid

	(a)	(b)	(c)	(d)
(A)	(ii)	(i)	(iv)	(iii)
(B)	(i)	(iii)	(ii)	(iv)
(C)	(i)	(ii)	(iii)	(iv)
(D)	(iv)	(iii)	(ii)	(i)

Answer: A

205. The subjective probability of efforts resulting in the outcome (the first level outcomes), is known as :
(A) Expectancy
(B) Instrumentality
(C) Incentive
(D) None of the above

Answer: A

206. Competency theory is given by
(A)Maslow
(B)McClendon
(C)Mc duologues
(D)Frederick Herzberg

Answer:A

207. Motivation is important to managers because
(A) it is a significant contributor to high performance
(B) it does not explain the differences in intensity of behavior
(C) it explains the differences in attitude and personality
(D) not all employees know how to use it effectively

Answer: A

208. Considering extrinsic rewards:
(A) money modifies behavior irrespective of the perceptions and preferences of the person being rewarded
(B) recognition is a powerful motivating reward for everyone

(C) upper management compensation is a strong incentive for lower-level employees to work harder
(D) benefits are usually based on longevity, not performance

Answer: D

209. Employees with relatively weak higher-order needs are _______ concerned with variety and autonomy.
(A) less
(B) more
(C) very
(D) extremely

Answer: A

210. Five forces model was developed by :
(A) Alderfer (B) Maslow
(C) Porter (D) Elton Mayo

Answer: C

211. What are the negative types of motivators?
(A) Fear
(B) Force
(C) Reprimands
(D) All the above

Answer: D

212. Some of the general motivators are:
(A) job security
(B) freedom at workplace
(C) interesting work
(D) All the above

Answer: D

213. Certain important motivational techniques are
(A) Monetary incentives
(B) Job-based techniques
(C) MBO techniques
(D) All the above

Answer: D

214. Which theory of motivation places a premium on the effort - reward relationship?
(A) Vroom's
(B) McClelland's
(C) Equity
(D) Hersberg

Answer: A

215. The assumption that employees like work, are creative and can exercise self direction is known as :
(A) Theory X
(B) Theory Y
(C) Theory Z
(D) None of these

Answer: B

216. The amount of satisfaction an individual anticipates from a particular outcome is known as
(A) Theory Y
(B) Theory Z
(C) Valence
(D) Stress

Answer: C

Explanation: Valence – a measure of attraction a given outcome holds for an individual or the satisfaction the person anticipates receiving from a particular outcome. Valence can be positive, negative or zero.

217. Employees with high self-esteem set
(A) Higher goals for others
(B) Higher goals for themselves and lower goals for others
(C) Higher goals for themselves
(D) None of the above

Answer: C

Explanation: Self-esteem is the degree to which a person has overall positive feelings about himself or herself. People with high self-esteem view themselves in a positive light, are confident, and respect themselves. In contrast, people with low self-esteem experience high levels of self-doubt and question their self-worth. High self-esteem is related to higher levels of satisfaction with one's job and higher levels of performance on the job.People with low self-esteem are attracted to situations where they will be relatively invisible, such as large companies.

218._____________ is a predisposition to behave in a certain way and to take particular point of view.
(A) Motivation
(B) Behaviour
(C) Perception
(D) Attitude
Answer: D

219. Theory " Z " has been propounded by :
(A) Mc Gregor
(B) Ouchi
(C) Maslow
(D) Skinner
Answer: B

220. Match the following :

List-I	**List-II**
(a) Z – Theory	(i) Hergberg
(b) Y – Theory	(ii) Maslow
(c) Hierarchy Needs Theory	(iii) Mc Gregor
(d) Hygiene Theory	(iv) Urwick

Codes :

	(a)	(b)	(c)	(d)
(A)	(iv)	(i)	(iii)	(ii)
(B)	(iii)	(ii)	(iv)	(i)
(C)	(iv)	(iii)	(ii)	(i)
(D)	(iii)	(iv)	(i)	(ii)

Answer: C

221. Porter and Lawler model is related to
(A) Perception
(B) Attitudes
(C) Motivation
(D) Leadership
Answer: C

222. Emotional intelligence is said to be the ability to sense, understand and effectively apply the power and acumen of emotions as a source of
(A) Information
(B) Trust
(C) Human energy
(D) All the above
Answer: D

223. Who among the following has advanced the Power, Affiliation and Achievement motivation concepts?
(A) J. Stacey Adams
(B) BR Skinner
(C) Victor Vroom
(D) David C. McClelland
Answer: D

224. Who among the following has advanced Transactional Analysis as an explanation of interpersonal communication strategy?
(A) Thomas A Harris
(B) Eric Frank
(C) Muriel James
(D) Eric Beme
Answer: D

225. Match List-I with List- II and select the correct answer using the code given below the Lists:

List -I (Theory of Motivation)	**List-II (Contributor)**
(a) X, Y theory	1. Frederick Herzberg
(b) Expectancy theory	2. J Stacey Adams
(c) Two factor theory	3. Douglas McGregor
(d) Equity theory	4. Victor Vroom

Code:

	(a)	(b)	(c)	(d)
(A)	3	1	4	2
(B)	2	4	1	3
(C)	2	1	4	3
(D)	3	4	1	2

Answer: D

226. The four systems of Management in terms of Leadership styles are related to
(A) Blake and Mouton
(B) Philip Kotler
(C) Peter F. Drucker
(D) Rensis Likert
Answer: D

227. Who developed the Two-Dimensional Managerial Grid ?
(A) Blake and Mouton
(B) Howthorne
(C) McCarthy
(D) W. A. Taylor

Answer: A

228. What is the most important attribute of an effective leader?
(A)Behaviour
(B)Character
(C)Drive
(D)Influence

Answer: C

229. Match the names of the Behavioural scientists and their contributions given in the List–A and B

List–A
(a) Mayo E. and Roethlisberger F. J.
(b) Mc. Gregar D.
(c) Likert R.
(d) Kelly J.

List–B
(i) Theory X and Y
(ii) Michigan study an leadership style
(iii)Trait Theory of leadership
(iv) Hawthorne effect

	(a)	(b)	(c)	(d)
(A)	(iv)	(i)	(ii)	(iii)
(B)	(ii)	(i)	(iv)	(iii)
(C)	(iii)	(i)	(ii)	(iv)
(D)	(iv)	(i)	(iii)	(ii)

Answer: C

230. The process by which individuals attain authority over others is summarized by
(A) Leader cultural values.
(B) Leader personality.
(C) Leader styles and behaviors.
(D) Leader responsibilities.
(E) Leader power and influence.

Answer: E

Explanation: Leader power and influence summarizes the process by which individuals attain authority over others.

231. It appears that
(A) successful leaders tend to be more intelligent than followers
(B) there is no link between intelligence of the leader and success
(C) intelligence is the most important "ability" trait in leaders
(D) persons with creativity make the best leaders

Answer: A

232. Concerning leadership concepts,
(A) leader roles are unnecessary in organizations like Gore-Tex, where a self-leadership approach is used
(B) it is likely that a particular set of leader characteristics and behaviors do suit specific situations and groups
(C) it is likely that the need for leaders will decline in the 21st century due to more decentralized structures
(D) the military model of leadership will become more popular in the 21st century

Answer: B

233. Which of the following captures the specific actions that leaders take to influence others at work?
(A) Leader styles and behaviors
(B) Leader cultural values
(C) Leader personality
(D) Leader influence
(E) Leader power

Answer: A

Explanation: Leader styles and behaviors capture the specific actions that leaders take to influence others at work.

234. Match List – I with List – II. Select the correct answer from the codes given below :

List – I	List – II
a. R. Blake and J.Mouton	i. Path-goal Theory
b. Fred Fiedler	ii. Managerial grid
c. Robert House	iii. Life CycleTheory
d. P. Herseyand K. Blanchard	iv. Theory of Leadership Effectiveness

Codes :

	a	b	c	d
(A)	ii	iv	I	iii
(B)	iv	iii	ii	i
(C)	ii	iv	iii	i
(D)	I	ii	iv	iii

Answer: A

235. People of Theory of Y belongs to:
(A) They are self motivated
(B) They are lazy
(C) Work oriented & Dedicated
(D) Need close supervision

Answer: C

236. Which of the following is not the assumption of theory X ?
(A) Most people must be corrected and controlled.
(B) The average human being prefers to be directed.
(C) Most of the people do not dislike work inherently.
(D) People have relatively little ambitions and wants.

Answer: C

237. The power vested in a leader by a virtue of accepting organizational authority is known as :
(A) Legitimate Power
(B) Coercive Power
(C) Democratic Power
(D) None of the above

Answer: A

238. The concept of task - oriented and people oriented leadership was developed by :
(A) Blake and Monton
(B) John Berry
(C) Maxwell
(D) Hertzberg

Answer: A

239. The 'Tri-dimensional grid' was developed by :
(A) Fayol
(B) Gullick
(C) F. W. Taylor
(D) Reddin

Answer: D

Explanation: Tridimensional Grid: ***Reddin*** conceptualized a three-dimensional grid. It is also known as 3-D management. This leadership style borrows some of the ideas from managerial grid. Three-dimensional axes represent task-orientation, relationship-orientation and effectiveness. By adding an effectiveness dimension to the task-oriented and relationship-oriented behavior dimensions, Reddin has integrated the concept of leadership styles with the situational demand of a specific environment.

240. Autocratic leadership :
(A) Requires task completion
(B) Works with consensus of all
(C) Does not accept views and suggestions of all
(D) Demands obedience from authorities

Answer: C

Explanation: Autocratic leadership, also known as authoritarian leadership, is a leadership style characterized by individual control over all decisions and little input from group members. Autocratic leaders typically make choices based on their own ideas and judgments and rarely accept advice from followers. Autocratic leadership involves absolute, authoritarian control over a group.

241. A leader may use the following methods

a. Use criticism
b. Encourage growth
c. Set objectives
d. Give orders and directions

Which of these methods are used by a democratic leader ?

(A) (a) and (b)
(B) (c) and (d)
(C) (b) and (c)
(D) (a), (b) and (d)

Answer: C

242. In the 'Managerial grid' 9, 1 style is termed as

(A) Team Management
(B) Country Club Management
(C) Authority Obedience
(D) Improvised Management

Answer: C

243. Which of the following is not one of the ego-states of transactional analysis?

(A) Child
(B) Young
(C) Adult
(D) Parent

Answer: B

244. Match the following:

Group (A)

(a) Douglas M. Mc Gregor
(b) William Ouchi
(c) Joseph Lufth and Harry Inghams
(d) Kurt Lewin

Group(B)

(i)Johari Window
(ii) Force Field Theory
(iii) Theory 'X' and 'Y'
(iv) Theory Z

Code :

	(a)	(b)	(c)	(d)
(A)	(iii)	(ii)	(iv)	(i)
(B)	(ii)	(iii)	(i)	(iv)
(C)	(iii)	(iv)	(i)	(ii)
(D)	(iv)	(ii)	(i)	(iii)

Answer: C

245. Managers subscribing to ______ assumptions attempt to structure, control and closely supervise their employees.

(A) Theory 'X'
(B) Theory 'Y'
(C) Both Theory 'X' and Theory 'Y'
(D) Neither Theory 'X' nor Theory'Y'

Answer: A

246. According to Fiedler's Contingency Model of Leadership, which one of the following is a situational variable ?

(A) Leader – Member relationship
(B) Organisational System
(C) Degree of task structure
(D) Leader's position power

Answer: B

247. Theory X represents

(A) Democratic style of leadership
(B) Autocratic style of leadership
(C) Laissez-faire style of leadership
(D) Humanistic style of leadership

Answer: B

248. In Black and Mouton's "Managerial Grid", the 'task style' represents :

(A) High concern for people and low concern for production.
(B) High concern for people and high concern for production.
(C) Low concern for people and low concern for production.

(D) High concern for production and low concern for people.

Answer: D

249. Who had advanced the '3-D' theory of Leadership Effectiveness ?

(A) Robert Blake and Jane S. Mouton
(B) William J. Reddin
(C) Fred E. Fiedler
(D) Rensis Likert

Answer: B

250. Match the following :

Leadership Theory	Leadership Factors
(a) Contingency Theory	(i) Personal vision and energy
(b) Trait Theory	(ii) Personal drive, desire to lead, Personal integrity
(c) Charismatic Theor	(iii) Leader's Position power, task structure and leader member relations

	(a)	(b)	(c)
(A)	(i)	(iii)	(ii)
(B)	(iii)	(ii)	(i)
(C)	(ii)	(iii)	(i)
(D)	(i)	(ii)	(iii)

Answer: B

251. The Managerial Grid was given by

(A) Rensis Likert
(B) Kurt Lewin
(C) Hersey Blanchard
(D) Blake and Mouton

Answer: D

252. How many dimensions are there in Blake and Moutoni Managerial Grid ?

(A) Two (B) Three
(C) Four (D) Five

Answer: D

253. Who developed the 'Managerial Grid' Theory ?

(A) Sydney and Beatrice Webbs
(B) Robert Blake and Jane S. Mouton
(C) W.J. Reddin
(D) Rensis Likert

Answer: B

254. The concept of task oriented and people oriented leadership was developed by :

(A) John Berry
(B) Maxwell
(C) Blake and Mouton
(D) Hertzberg

Answer: C

255. Arrange the following systems in the right orderon continuum suggested by Rensis Likert

(a) Consultative
(b) Benevolent Authoritative
(c) Exploitative Authoritative
(d) Joint decision-making

(A) c, b, a, d
(B) c, a, b, d
(C) b, a, c, d
(D) c, d, b, a

Answer: A

256. The different leadership styles are :

(A) Autocratic
(B) Democratic
(C) laissez - faire
(D) All the above

Answer: D

257. The internal environment factors that influence management are:

(A) Labour
(B) Machines
(C) place
(D) All the above

Answer: D

258. A responsible leader does not limit

(A) discussions
(B) development of alternatives
(C) interactions
(D) All the above

Answer: D

259. Some of the traits of leaderships are as follows
(A) emotional stability
(B) Communication skill
(C) Knowledge of human relations
(D) All the above

Answer: D

260. Under hard boiled type of autocratic leadership, the employees tend to become
(A) qresentful
(B) uarrelsome
(C) Both
(D) None of them

Answer: C

261. Which of the following is not considered as a leadership style?
(A) Task oriented leadership style.
(B) Society oriented leadership style.
(C) Employee oriented leadership style. (D) Autocratic leadership style

Answer: B

262. In Transactional Analysis the "I am ok, you are not ok" life position is also referred to as :
(A) Bossing
(B) Avoidant
(C) Diffident
(D) Bohemian

Answer: A

263. Match List I with List II and select the correct answer using the code given below the Lists:

List- I
(Contributor)
(a) Robert Blake and Jane Mouton
(b) W.J. Reddin
(c) Rensis Likert
(d) Vroom and Yetton

List- II
(Leadership Style)
1. Four-system model
2. Normative model
3. Managerial grid
4. The 3-D theory

Code:

	a	b	c	d
(A)	3	4	1	2
(B)	3	1	4	2
(C)	2	1	4	3
(D)	2	4	1	3

Answer: A

264. Which one of the following is not a dimension of the managerial grid theory of leadership?
(A) Country club management
(B) Impoverished management
(C) Team management
(D) Entrepreneurship management

Answer: B

265. The first stage of conflict resolution is to :
(A) Analyse the problem
(B) Choose a solution
(C) Think through possible solutions
(D) Define the problem

Answer: D

266. Which term is not used in transactional analysis
(A) Ego states
(B) Life position
(C) Child states
(D) Stroking

Answer: D

267. The term 'Blind Spot' in Johari window model refers to :
(A) The self that is known to others as well as to oneself
(B) The self which is known to others but not to oneself
(C) The self which is known neither to others nor to oneself
(D) The motives, feelings etc, which are known to one's own self

Answer: B

268. Conflict is a :

(A) Natural disagreement arising between two people

(B) Disliking for each other

(C) Lack of understanding of one party

(D) Lack of understanding of the problem

Answer: A

269. The view that the conflict should be accepted and encouraged, corresponds to which of the following views :

(A) Traditional view

(B) Interactionist view

(C) Behavioural view

(D) Both (A) and (C) above

Answer: B

Explanation:

1. **Traditional view:** Conflict is dysfunctional, destructive and irrational. Usually caused by poor communication,a lack of trust, or a failure to be responsible to the needs of others.
2. **Human relations view:** Conflict is natural in groups and organizations. It may even be beneficial on occasion.
3. **Interactionist view:** Without conflict, we become static and non-responsive. Conflict keeps us viable and creative, but there are two kinds of conflict: ***Functional and dysfunctional:*** Functional conflict improves long-term group performance.

270. Which of the following is true of managers in relationship to conflict?

(A) Managers generally encourage low levels of conflict because it improves performance, up to a certain point.

(B) Managers generally ignore conflict.

(C) Managers attempt to eliminate conflict because the organization rewards them for keeping conflict out of their area of responsibility.

(D) Managers show no consistent attitude toward conflict.

Answer: C

271. Which of the following concepts are related to constructive conflict as suggested by Mary Parker Follet ?

(i) Domination

(ii) Compromise

(iii) Integration

(iv) Delegation

Select the correct answer from the codes given below :

Codes :

(A) (i), (ii)

(B) (iii), (iv)

(C) (i), (ii), (iii)

(D) (ii), (iii), (iv)

Answer: C

272. ______________ is the adverse reaction people have to excessive pressure placed on them from extraordinary demands, constraints, or opportunities.

(A) Stereotyping

(B) Stress

(C) A halo effect

(D) Creativity

Answer: B

273. Stress, in and of itself, is __________.

(A) not necessarily bad

(B) healthy in most cases

(C) harmful, especially if not managed by exercise

(D) beneficial to those who use it

Answer: A

274. ________ prevent you from doing what you desire; __________ refer to the loss of something desired.

(A) Constraints; demands

(B) Demands; constraints

(C) Fears; stressors

(D) Stressors; fears

Answer: A

275. Which of the following is true concerning stress?

(A) Stress is a static condition.

(B) Stress is a negative reaction to an outside force.
(C) Stress can be caused by change of any kind.
(D) Stress limits performance.

Answer: C

276.________ there must be uncertainty over the outcome, and the outcome must be important.
(A) For uncertainty to become fear
(B) For anxiety to become stress
(C) For potential stress to become actual stress,
(D) For anxiety to become fear

Answer: C

277. Stress symptoms can be grouped under any of the following three general categories except ____________.
(A)physiological
(B)cultural
(C)psychological
(D)behavioral

Answer: B

278. Which of the following is an example of a psychological symptom of stress?
(A)changes in metabolism
(B)increased heart and breathing rate
(C)irritability
(D)changes in productivity

Answer: C

279. Changes in eating habits are a __________ symptom of stress.
(A) physical
(B) psychological
(C) behavioral
(D) inertial

Answer: C

280. Managers need to make sure that employees' abilities ______________.
(A) match the job requirements
(B) are being maximized
(C) are not being affected by their stress
(D) are not causing them stress

Answer: A

281.______________ that increase opportunities for employees to participate in decisions and to gain social support have been found to lessen stress.
(A)Improved organizational communications
(B)Time management programs
(C)Wellness programs
(D)Job redesigns

Answer: D

282. Stress from an employee's personal life ______________.
(A) is difficult for the manager to control directly
(B) should never concern the manager
(C) indicates that the employee needs counseling
(D) always affects work behavior, so the manager should always intervene

Answer: A

283. Managers might want to offer ______________ to employees who want to talk to someone about their problems.
(A) wellness programs
(B) time management programs
(C) employee counseling
(D) performance planning programs

Answer: C

284. Find out the one which is not an element of employee empowerment :
(A) Belief system and trust
(B) Purposefulness
(C) Arbitrariness
(D) Self sufficiency or Competency

Answer: C

285. Which of the following is not a factor of emotional intelligence?
(A)Ability
(B)Reason

(C) Emotion
(D) Thinking without feeling

Answer: D

286. Employees' psychological responses to job demands that tax or exceed their capacities come under which of the following mechanisms?
(A) Job satisfaction
(B) Ability
(C) Job performance
(D) Leadership style
(E) Stress

Answer: E

Explanation: Stress reflects employees' psychological responses to job demands that tax or exceed their capacities.

287. All of these are individual mechanisms as reflected in the integrative model of organizational behavior except:
(A) Stress.
(B) Motivation.
(C) Job satisfaction.
(D) Learning.
(E) Job performance.

Answer: E

Explanation: Job performance belongs to the Individual outcomes according to the integrated model of OB.

288. Which of the following is the outcome of job satisfaction?
(A) High employee turnover
(B) High productivity
(C) Absenteeism
(D) All the above

Answer: B

289. What Suzie feels when thinking about her job and doing her day-to-day work is captured in her
(A) ability.
(B) job satisfaction.
(C) personality.
(D) decision making skills.

Answer: B

Explanation: Job satisfaction captures what employees feel when thinking about her job and doing her day-to-day work.

290. The term job satisfaction refers to :
(A) A collection of feelings that an individual has towards his/her job
(B) The degree to which an individual identifies himself/herself with job
(C) The degree to which an individual identifies himself/herself with the organization
(D) None of the above

Answer: A

291. The factors measuring the morale of the workers and ascertain whether it is increasing or diminishing can be listed as:
(A) Absenteeism
(B) Number of accidents
(C) Grievances
(D) All the above

Answer: D

292. Which of the following is a group phenomenon?
(A) Perception
(B) Attitude
(C) Morale
(D) Motivation

Answer: C

293. The different factors that affect morale are :
(A) Supervision received
(B) Nature of work
(C) Employees occupational level
(D) All the above

Answer: D

294. The factors measuring the morale of the workers and ascertain whether it is increasing or diminishing can be listed as:
(A) Absenteeism
(B) No. of accidents
(C) Grievances
(D) All the above
Answer: D

295. Any morale improvement programme of management must embrace the following rules.
(A) Respect individual
(B) Be fair and just
(C) Encourage initiative
(D) All the above
Answer: D

296. The factors measuring the morale of the workers and ascertain whether it is increasing or diminishing can be listed as
(A) Grievances
(B) Absenteeism
(C) No. of accidents
(D) All the above
Answer: D

297. The term emotion refers to:
(A) A broad range of feelings that a person experiences
(B) A broad and intense feeling that is directed at someone or something
(C) A broad range of feelings in the form of anger that a person experiences
(D) None of the above
Answer: B

298. Characteristics of all formal and informal communication are:
(A) same
(B) Unstructured
(C) Structured
(D) Different
Answer: A

299. A good communicator needs to be good at:
(A) Listening
(B) Speaking
(C) Using language
(D) Witty
Answer: C

300. Which step should a communicator take as the starting point?
(A) Select the channels of communication
(B) Set up feedback process
(C) Specify the objectives of communication
(D) Identify the tools of communication
Answer: C

301. The best way to ensure that what a person has communicated has reached I receiver is:
(A) To use simple words
(B) To communicate when there is no disturbance
(C) To communicate when the receiver is attentive
(D) To ask the receiver to tell what they have received
Answer: D

302. An effective communication does NOT require:
(A) Change in speech pattern
(B) Appropriate gestures
(C) Mastery of content
(D) Handsome personality
Answer: D

303. Communication will be effective if:
(A) It is delivered slowly and clearly
(B) It is delivered in a calm situation
(C) It reaches the receiver completely
(D) It reaches the receiver as intended by the sender
Answer: D

304. A good manager is a - communicator
(A) Poor
(B) Bad
(C) Good
(D) Least
Answer: C

305. Communication is a
(A) One way process
(B) Two way process
(C) Multi way process
(D) None of the above
Answer: B

306. Effective communication is measured through
(A) Feed Back
(B) Encoding
(C) Decoding
(D) None of the above
Answer: A

307. Communication helps to
(A) Increase productions
(B) Decrease production
(C) Increase Labor turnover
(D) None of the above
Answer: D

308. What are the basic elements of communication?
(A) Sender and receiver
(B) Message and channel of communication
(C) Response and feedback
(D) All of the above
Answer: D

309.A person who sends the message is known as
(A) Communitee
(B) Receiver
(C) Communicator
(D) None of the above
Answer: C

310. The direction in which the formal communication flows is always
(A) Upward
(B) Downward
(C) Horizontal
(D) All of these
Answer: D

311. Communication involves
(A) Information
(B) Understanding
(C) Both A and B
(D) None of the above
Answer: C

312. Grapevine is also known as
(A) Informal communication
(B) Horizontal communication
(C) Upward communication
(D) Downward communication
Answer: A

313. Communication in an organization should ideally flow
(A) From top to bottom
(B) from bottom to top
(C) Both ways
(D) None of these
Answer: C

314. Telephone, radio inter communicating system are the media used for
(A) Formal communication
(B) Downward communication
(C) Oral communication
(D) None of these
Answer: C

315. Which of the following steps would you consider first for an effective communication?
(A) Select the channel of communication
(B) Plan the evaluation procedure
(C) Specify the objectives of communication
(D) Identify various media of communication
Answer : C

316. Principles of effective communication would be
(A) clear in use of language
(B) attentive listening
(C) use of right medium
(D) All the above
Answer : D

317. Under principle of effective communication what should be fully understood by all concerned.
(A) Tasks
(B) Policies
(C) responsibilities
(D) All the above

Answer : D

318. The different types of psychological barriers to communication will be
(A) Ego
(B) status consciousness
(C) closed mind
(D) All the above

Answer: D

319. The activities of the communicator while communicating a message will include
(A) Ideation
(B) Encoding
(C) transmission
(D) All the above

Answer : D

320. Process of communication :
(A) Sender, Medium, Recipient, Feedback
(B) Sender, Feedback, Medium, Recipient
(C) Recipient, Medium, Sender, Feedback
(D) Sender, Medium, Feedback, Recipient

Answer : A

321. One of the main purposes of horizontal communication is :
(A) Problem-Solving
(B) Morale booster
(C) Give feedback to the top
(D) Provide job instructions and information

Answer : B

322. Premature evaluation takes place due to:
(A) Semantic Barriers
(B) Psychological Barriers
(C) Organizational Barriers
(D) None of the above

Answer : D

323. Which of the following is correct about 'Grapevine'?
(A) It tends to exist when members of formal group know another well.
(B) It is the result of social forces at work place.
(C) It is more common in times of high organizational excitement.
(D) All the above.

Answer : D

324. Grapevine is :
(A) Officially created
(B) Formal method of information
(C) Informal communication
(D) None of the above

Answer : C

325. Gangplank theory of communication advanced by Henry Fayol is an example of :
(A) Downward Communication
(B) Lateral Communication
(C) Upward Communication
(D) Network Communication

Answer : B

326. 'Grapevine' is a type of
(A) Written communication
(B) Formal communication
(C) Informal communication
(D) Lateral communication

Answer : C

327. Which among the following are barriers to communication?
(A) Noise
(B) time and distance
(C) Semantic barriers
(D) Wrong Medium
(E) All the above

Answer: E

328. Semantic barriers in communication occur due to :
(A) Personality problems
(B) Language problems
(C) Attitude problems

(D)All the Above

Answer : B

329. Which of the following is not a semantic barrier of communication?

(A) Faulty translation
(B) Ambiguous words
(C) Specialist's language
(D) Inattention

Answer: D

330. The definition of communication implies that

(A) communication is mostly verbal
(B) communication is mostly written
(C) most communication is in a vertical direction
(D) understanding must occur to have communication

Answer: D

331. The LEAST-used communication channel in an organization is usually

(A) upward
(B) downward
(C) diagonal
(D) horizontal

Answer: D

332. One of the most helpful mechanisms for refining a spoken or written communication is called the

(A) grapevine
(B) counseling service
(C) five C.s
(D) complaint system

Answer: C

333. Communication begins with

(A) encoding
(B) idea origination
(C) decoding
(D) channel selection

Answer: B

334. The process of any communication will include

(A) Communicator
(B) Medium
(C) message
(D) All the above

Answer: D

335. The lack of communication leads to:

(A) information gap
(B) disintegration
(C) deviation from performance
(D) All the above

Answer: D

336. What are the Communication barriers in the international environment?

(A) Loss by transmission
(B) Loss by poor retention
(C) Poor listening
(D) All the above

Answer: D

337. Objectives of communication

(i) to seek compliance and ensure uniformity in action
(ii) to meet deadlines and production targets
(iii) to disseminate information to a larger number of people, and
(iv) save cost in terms of time and money refers to :

(A) One-way communication
(B) Two-way communication
(C) Grapevine
(D) Non-verbal communication

Answer : D

338. The obstruction in communication caused due to differences in individual's interpretation of words and symbols, is known as :

(A) Psychological Barrier
(B) Social Barrier
(C) Organisational Barrier
(D) Semantic Barrier

Answer: D

339. The communication taking place among members of the same work group or among members or work groups at the same level is described as :
(A) Downward Communication
(B) Upward Communication
(C) Lateral Communication
(D) Parallel Communication

Answer: C

340. The final link in the communication process that puts the message back into the system as a check against misunderstandings is described as
(A) Decoding (B) Feedback
(C) Encoding (D) None of these

Answer: B

341. Communication can be
(A) Oral (B) Written
(C) Oral and Written (D) None of the above

Answer: C

342. Which communication component is not a paid form of communication?
(A) Advertising
(B) Sales promotion
(C) Personal selling
(D) Publicity

Answer : D

343. Gangplank theory of communication, advanced by Henri Fayol, is an example of which one of the following
(A) Vertical upward communication
(B) Vertical downward communication
(C) Lateral or horizontal communication
(D) Cyclic or circular communication

Answer : C

344. Personality is determined by:
(A) Heredity
(B) Environment
(C) Situation
(D) All the three above.

Answer: D

345. Learning means
(A) Relatively permanent change in the behavior of people
(B) Developing the skills
(C) Improving the knowledge
(D) Changing the habits

Answer: A

346. Which of the following is not Goal Conflict?
(A) Approach-Approach conflict
(B) Approach-Avoidance conflict
(C) Avoidance-Avoidance conflict
(D) Role ambiguity

Answer: D

347. Match the following Big Five Personality

I	II
a. Extroversion	1. Warm
b. Agreeableness	2. Gregarious
c. Conscientiousness	3. Stable
d. Emotional stability	4. Imaginative
e. Openness experience	5. Planful

a b c d e
(A) 2 3 1 5 4 (B) 3 1 2 4 5
(C) 2 1 5 3 4 (D) 1 3 4 5 2

Answer: C

348. Match the following

a. Maslow	1. Expectancy theory
b. Herzberg	2. ERG theory
c. Vrooms	3. Need hierarchy
d. Alderfers	4. Hygiene theory

	a	b	c	d
(A)	3	1	4	2
(B)	3	4	1	2
(C)	3	2	4	1
(D)	2	4	3	1

Answer: B

349. Consider the following statements:
Organization development is different from
1. Management development which is action oriented.
2. Operations research which is not human value oriented.

Which of the statements given above is/are correct?
(A) Only 1 (B) Only 2
(C) Both 1 and 2 (D) Neither 1 nor 2
Answer: B

350. Which of the following are the outcomes of organizational development?
1. Improvement in interpersonal skills of members
2. More organic organization
3. Resolution of conflicts through interactive methods

Select the correct answer using the code given below:
(A) 1, 2 and 3 (B) Only 1 and 2
(C) Only 2 and 3 (D) Only 1 and 3
Answer: A

351. Which one of the following is not a function of a leader in an organization?
(A) Motivating employees
(B) Fixing the remuneration package of the employees
(C) Resolving conflict
(D)Selecting the most effective communication channel
Answer: B

352. Consider the following statements:
Human diseconomies from increasing work specialization beyond a limit surface in the form of:
1. stress
2. poor quality of output
3. increased absenteeism
4. high turnover from the organization

Which of the statements given above is/are correct?
(A) 1, 2, 3 and 4 (B) Only 1 and 4
(C) Only 2 and 3 (D) Only 1
Answer: A

353. Who among the following developed the classic three- step model of organizational change?
(A) Kurt Lewin (B) H. Simon
(C) J.P. Kotter (D) L.R. Murphy
Answer: A

354. Who developed the concept that tension between worker's 'logic of sentiment' and manager's 'logic of cost and efficiency' could lead to conflict within the organization?
(A) Herbert Simon
(B) Chester Barnard
(C) Fredrick W. Taylor
(D) Elton Mayo
Answer: D

355. Match List- I (Leadership Type) with List-II (Main idea/ Model) and select the correct answer using the code given below the lists:

List -I (Leadership Type)
A. Participative
B. Contingency
C. Behavioral
D. Situational

List-II (Main idea/Model)
1. Vroom and Yettons Normative Model
2. The Managerial Grid
3. Likerts Leadership Style
4. Fiedler's Least Preferred Co-worker (LPC) Theory

Code:

	A	B	C	D
(A)	2	4	3	1
(B)	3	1	2	4
(C)	2	1	3	4
(D)	3	4	2	1

Answer: D

Directions: The following two (2) items consist of two statements, one labelled as the 'Assertion (A)' and the other as 'Reason (R).' You are to examine these two statements carefully and select the answers to these items using the codes given below:

Codes:
(A) Both A and R are individually true and R is the correct explanation of A

(B) Both A and R are individually true but R is not correct explanation of A
(C) A is true but R is false
(D) A is false but R is true

356. **Assertion (A):** Behavioral approach to leadership believes that individual's trained-in appropriate leadership would be able to lead more effectively.
Reason (R): Behaviors unlike traits can be learned.
Answer: A

357. **Assertion (A):** A bureaucrat's capacity to adapt to changing circumstances is far less than that conceived by those who drew up the organizational rules.

Reason (R) : In order to be perceived as effective, the bureaucrat behaves consistently and follows rules strictly.
Answer: A

358. Which one of the following is not included in "hygiene" factors in the Herzberg two-factor theory of motivation?
(A) Salary
(B) Working conditions
(C) Company's policy
(D) Responsibility
Answer: D

359. Consider the following statements about managerial grid in the context of leadership theories:
1. It portrays a three-dimensional view of leadership style.
2. The grid shows dominating factors in a leader's thinking in regard to getting results.
3. The grid does not show results produced.
4. The grid offers a framework for conceptualizing leadership style.

Which of the statements given above are correct?
(A) Only 1, 2 and 3 (B) Only 2, 3 and 4
(C) Only 1 and 4 (D) 1, 2, 3 and 4
Answer: D

360. Contingency approach to leadership focuses on which of the following?
I. Task requirements
2. Peers' expectations
3. Employees' expectations
4. Organizational policies

Select the correct answer using the code given below:
(A) Only l, 2 and 3 (B) Only l, 2 and 4
(C) Only 3 and 4 (D) 1, 2, 3 and 4
Answer: D

361. Consider the following statements:
1. Motivation cannot be used as a tool to arrange job relationships in organizations.
2. Individuals make conscious decisions about, their behaviour in the organization.
3. Motivating factors are related to the job content and the rewards of work performance.

Which of the statements given above are correct?
(A) Only 1 and 2 (B) Only 2 and 3
(C) Only 1 and 3 (D) 1, 2 and 3
Answer: C

362. Which one of the following is not a component of expectancy model of motivation?
(A) Positive reinforcement
(B) Valence
(C) Performance-outcome equation
(D) Effort-performance equation
Answer: A

363. Who among the following introduced the concepts and phrases— "conflict resolution" and "the task of leadership"?
(A) Henri Fayol
(B) Elton Mayo
(C) Mary Parker Follett
(D) Chester Barnard
Answer: C

****

UNIT-VII
INDUSTRIAL RELATIONS AND TRADE UNIONS

7.1. INDUSTRIAL RELATIONS (IR)-CONCEPT-SCOPE-APPROACHES-IMPORTANCE

- The term Industrial Relation is used to describe the relations between the management of a firm and its employers.
- Industrial relation is a set of phenomena, both inside and outside the workplace, concern with determining and regulating employment relationship.
- "Industrial relation is a set of functional interdependence involving historical, economic, social, psychological, demographic, technological, occupational, political and legal variables."
- **Dale Yoder:** "Industrial relation is whole field of relationship that exists because of the necessary collaboration of men and women in the employment process of an industry."
- **ILO:** "Industrial relations deal with either the relationship between the state and employers and workers organization or the relation between the occupational organizations themselves."
- **John T. Dunlop:** "Industrial societies necessarily create Industrial Relations defined as the complex of interrelations among workers, management and the government."
- If Industrial relations are good employees will be well motivated and as a result morale and productivity will be high.
- If industrial relations are poor employees will be a less motivated and productivity low with a high labor turnover.

Various Terms in Industrial Relations

- **Labour Relations:** Employment relationships and issues between groups of employees and management. Also known as management relations.
- **Collective Agreement:** Written document outlines terms and conditions of employment in a unionized workplace.
- **Employee Relations:** Usually in non-union settings.
- **Employment Relations:** Examines employment relationships in union *and* non-union workplaces.
- **Union:** A group of workers recognized by law collectively bargain terms and conditions of employment with their employer.

Factors of Industrial Relations

1. Institutional factors
2. Economic factors
3. Technological factors
4. Social and Cultural factors
5. Political factors
6. Governmental factors

Three Actors of Industrial Relations

1. Workers and their organizations
2. Employers and their organizations
3. Government

Conditions for Congenial Industrial Relations

1. Existence of strong, well organized and democratic employees unions
2. Existence of sound and organized employers unions
3. Spirit of collective bargaining and willingness to resort to voluntary arbitration
4. Maintenance of Industrial piece

Nature of Industrial Relations

1. Unitary: Emphasize on Human resource management.

- **Focus:** Strategic & integrated managerial approach to the management of people. HRM supports for achieving business aims and objectives.
- **Mechanisms**
  - o Individualism (human relations, organizational psychology)
  - o Integrating planning, monitoring and control of human resources (not just employees).
  - o Securing employee commitment or organization's aims & objectives (performance based rewards, employee involvement)

2. Marxist: Control of the labour process.

- **Focus:** The way 'capital' controls 'labour'
- **Mechanisms of management control**
  - o Scientific management or deskilling
  - o Segmentation of labour (core & periphery)
  - o Bureaucratic control (policies, procedures & rules)
  - o Responsible autonomy (self-control or adoption of management values as integral part of job.)
- **Employee response**
  - o Resistance (restrictive practices)
  - o Collectivism (joint regulation)

The approaches of Industrial Relations

- There are different types of organizations:
  1. Big organization
  2. Small organization
  3. Local or international.
- They constitute of 3 main actors:
  1. **Shareholder:** Represented by management, association of employers. Always to gain as much profit and productivity.
  2. **Employees:** Being represented by trade unions. To get good salary and good working conditions.
  3. **Government:** Being represented by specialize government agencies concern with workers, enterprise and their relationship.
- Each of the actors above always conflicting between one another in order to achieve their objectives.
- Besides the above 3 main actors, in the present context academicians have also considered another actor which can also influence the nature of IR i.e. Stakeholders.

1. Comparative approach

Importance of comparative approach

- o Inform public policy debate
- o Changing world economy
- o Development of 'fair' international employment standards

Problems of comparison

- o Lack of common terminology and definitions.
- o Differences between stated institutional framework and reality of actual practice
- o Problems of transferability
- o Convergence

Logic of industrialisation

- o All countries subject to same economic, technological and market forces
- o All need concentrated, disciplined workforce with new and changing skills
- o Similar government role in providing economic and social infrastructure for industrialisation (competing for same international investment)

Modified convergence

- o Countries at different stages of industrialisation
- o Alternative solutions to common problems
- o Regional based convergence
- o Divergence
- o Distinctive value systems and cultural features
- o Heterogeneity <u>*within*</u> national industrial relations systems (decentralisation & flexibility)
- o Different strategic choices by Government, employers and unions at macro (society) and micro (organisation) levels on nature, content and process of employment relationship
- o Political-economic framework of newer industrialised countries versus pluralistic framework of older industrialised countries.

2. System Approach

- Originated by **Dunlop**, being subjected to a variety of interpretation, uses and criticism. However they do not invalidate the systems approach but they sŭggested accommodation and Refinement.
- It is a broad based integrative model that sought to provide tools of analysis to interpret and gain understanding the widest possible range of IR facts and practices and to explain why particular rules are establish in particular IR systems and how and why they change in response to changes affecting the system.
- This model sees IR as a subsystem of society distinct from but overlapping, the economic and political subsystem.
- Actors, working within contexts (environment), developing a body of rules, held together by an ideology.
- System producing rules (IRS) and system governed by rules (production).
- Emphasis on roles rather than people.
- Importance of environmental influences.

Industrial Relations Model

1. Dunlop's Industrial Relations System Model: Four interrelated elements

1. **Actors**
   - o Specialized government agencies.
   - o Management, non-managerial employees and their representatives.
2. **Shared Ideology**

- Beliefs within the system which not only define the role of each actor or groups of actors but also define the view that they have of the role of other actors in the system. If the view compatible-stable IR system and other wise.
- Set of ideas and beliefs held by the actors
- Helps to bind or integrate the system together

3. **Contexts**
   - Influence and constraints on the decisions of the actors which emanate from other parts of society, such as technology, market, budgetary and the locus of power in the society.
4. **Rules**
   - procedural
   - substantive
   - distributive
   - The regulatory framework developed by a range of process and presented in variety of forms which expresses the terms and nature of the employment relationship.

Criticisms of the Dunlop Model

- Descriptive
- Lacks ability to predict outcomes/ relationships
- Underestimates importance of power and conflict in employment relationship
- Static.
- Cannot explain rapid decrease in unionization especially in the U.S.

2. Craig's Industrial Relations System Model

- Adds an actor: end user
- Elements from the external environment converted into outputs
- Series of conversion mechanisms
- Outputs flow back into the environment through a feedback loop

External Inputs

- Legal Subsystem
- Economics Subsystem
- Ecological Subsystem
- Political Subsystem
- Socio-cultural Subsystem

Internal Inputs

- **Goals:** Sought by actors
- **Strategies:** Processes developed and implemented to achieve goals
- **Power:** The ability to make another actor agree to your terms

Conversion Mechanisms

- Processes actors use to convert internal and external inputs into outputs
- Collective bargaining
- produces a collective agreement
- Grievances
- written complaint by employees
- Alleges collective agreement not been followed
- Day to day relations–communication

Third-party interventions

- interest arbitration
- mediation
- grievance arbitration
- conciliation
- fact-finding
- mediation/arbitration
- strikes/lockouts
- joint committees

Outputs

- Management outcomes
- Productivity, profitability
- Labour outcomes
- Equity issues, ways to achieve fairness in the workplace
- Worker perceptions
- Work climate
- Employee morale
- Organizational commitment
- Union satisfaction/commitment
- Conflict or conflict resolution

7.2. INDUSTRIAL DISPUTES-CAUSES-EFFECTS AND TRENDS

- Industrial disputes are conflicts, disorder or unrest arising between workers and employers on any ground. Such disputes finally result in strikes, lockouts and mass refusal of employees to work in the organization until the dispute is resolved.
- Industrial Disputes harm both parties' employees and employers and are always against the interest of both employees and the employers.
- **Patterson:** "Industrial strife constituent militant and organized protest against existing industrial conditions, they are symptoms of industrial unrest in the same way that boils are symptoms of disorder of body."
- **Industrial Dispute Act 1947, Sec. 2 (k):**"Industrial Dispute is any dispute or difference between the employees and employers or between employers and workmen or between workmen and workmen, which is concerned with the employment or terms of employment or with the conditions of labour of any person."
- Industrial Dispute means a conflict or unrest or dispute or any sort of difference between employees and employers which may relate with the employment or the terms of employment or working conditions.
- For a dispute to become Industrial Dispute there must be a dispute between:
    - Employers and employees
    - Employers and workmen
    - Workmen and workmen .

Principles for judging the natures of Industrial Dispute

- The dispute must affect large number of workmen
- The dispute should be taken up by the Industry Union
- The parties involved in dispute must have direct interest

- The consulted demand must become grievance
- Workmen can raise Industrial Dispute himself under Section 2A of Industrial Disputes Act - 1947

Causes of Industrial Disputes

1. Economic causes :

The economic causes will include issues relating to compensation like wages, bonus, allowances, and conditions for work, working hours, leave and holidays without pay, unjust layoffs and retrenchments.

2. Non-economic causes

- o The non economic factors will include victimization of workers, ill treatment by staff members, sympathetic strikes, political factors, indiscipline etc.
- o Pay disputes
- o Working conditions
- o Unfair dismissals
- o Promotion
- o Poor industrial relations
- o Introduction to new technology
- o Discrimination

Types of disputes

According to the Code of Industrial Relations introduced in the UK in 1972, disputes are of two kinds:

1. **Disputes of Right:** Related to the application or interpretation of an existing agreement or contract of employment.
2. **Disputes of Right:** Related to the claims by employees or proposals by a management about the terms and conditions of employment.

Organs of Industrial Peace

1. Tripartite Machinery:

- Bodies formed by the representatives of Employers, Employees and the government for consultation and discussion on issues of labour.
- The principals and policies of the tripartite body have been a machinery of consultancy at the industrial and national levels.
- The tripartite body was established to make peace and improve relations between management and unions, and maintain smooth functioning of union management relations.
- It began as a statutory organization by the recommendation of the **Whitley Commission to the ILO** in 1931.
- The tripartite body had to be sufficiently large to ensure sufficient representation of the various interests involved; encourage representatives of employers, labor and government to meet regularly; and disallow individual members from making individual contributions to meetings.
- The purpose of the tripartite body is to:
  - o Bring the aggravated parties together for mutual settlement of differences, and encourage a spirit of cooperation and goodwill.
  - o Promote uniformity in labor laws and legislation.
  - o Discuss all matters of All India importance as between employers and employees.

  - Determine a plan for settlement for all disputes.
- Tripartism is a system of labour relations in which the state, employers, and workers are autonomous yet interdependent partners, pursuing common interests and participating in decisions affecting them in a binding spirit of mutuality and reciprocity.
- This can take place at either or both macro and micro levels. Tripartite consultation is an important feature of India's industrial relations system. It was set up in india as early as 1942.
- Tripartite forums evolve norms or standards in the form of guidelines. There are number of tripartite bodies which operate at the Central and State levels.
- *The Indian Labour Conference, Standing Labour Committees, Wage Boards and Industrial Committees operate at the Central level and State Labour Advisory Boards operate at the state level.*
- All these bodies play an important role in reaching at voluntary agreements on various labour matters. Though the recommendations of these bodies are only advisory in nature they carry considerable weight with the government, workers and employers.
- The Indian Labour Conference (ILC) and the Standing Labour Committee (SLC) are two main forums for Tripartite Consultation.
- **Central and state Level tripartite bodies**
  - The Indian labour conference
  - Standing labour committee
  - Wage Board
  - Industrial committees

1.1. The Indian Labour Conference (ILC)

- Meets once in a year to promote uniformity in Labour legislations, which lays down procedures for the settlement of industrial legislation, which lays down procedures for the settlement of industrial disputes and a discussion of matters of all India importance matters which affect employers and employees alike, including matters relating to labour welfare and the morale of labour.
- Some important measures agreed to by the Indian Labour conference in past are:
  - Setting up of bipartite works committees, joint consultative and production committees.
  - Adoption by employers and unions of a voluntary code of discipline;
  - Following proper grievance and disciplinary procedures;
  - Deciding norms for fixing need based wages;
  - Rationalizing and revising wage structures of important industries through non-statutory wage boards; and
  - Encouraging voluntary arbitration for the settlement of industrial disputes.

1.2. The Standing Labour Committee(SLC)

- SLC considers all those matters referred to it by the ILC or by the central government, including the suggestions of State governments, employers and employees bearing on labour affairs.

1.3. The Industrial Committees

- This committee discuss the specific problems of industries for which they have been set up and submit their reports to the ILC, which co-ordinates their activities.
- These committees have been set up for seventeen industries, including plantations, coal mining, cotton textiles, jute, cement, etc.

1.4. The Central implementation and Evaluation Committees

- These are concern with the effective implementation of labour laws, awards, settlements, etc.

1.5. The Committee on Conventions

- This committee examines the ILO conventions and recommendations and explores the possibility or advisability or ratifying them and applying them to Indian conditions. Till 1975, 140 conventions and 148 recommendations had been ratified by India.

2. Bipartite bodies:

- With the beginning of industrialization of India, labor relations in Indian industries have also been largely influenced by Indian democracy.
- Groups like Works Committee and Management Council were established to democratize Indian industrial relations.
- The bipartite consultation machinery was established around 1920, during the time when a few joint committees were setup by the Government of India.
- These joint committees were also introduced in TISCO in Jamshedpur.

3. The Code of Discipline

- It was finalized in 1958 and applies to private and public sector industries.
- It lays down that both workers and employers should recognize their rights and responsibilities towards each other and should willingly and properly discharge their obligations to each other consequent on such recognition.
- The Code of Discipline must be laid down in consultation with those who are under its jurisdiction and are concerned with its application.
- Code of Discipline should be evaluated and appraised from time to time so as to remove anomalies. If any.
- Code of Discipline must be reasonable and simple. It should not contain rules for the sake of rules only.
- The discipline policy should lay greater emphasis on the prevention of the breach of discipline than on the administration of penalities. The approach to discipline should be positive and constructive.
- Judicious machinery preferably internal to the organisation should be provided for appeals against, and review of, all disciplinary actions.
- The management should ensure that its own conduct and policies do not encourage breach of discipline. This will promote self-discipline among the workers.
- The managers should try to remove the cause responsible for indiscipline.
- A disciplinary committee consisting of the representatives of the workers and the management should be set up to look into the cases of indiscipline and suggest remedial measures.

Objectives of Code of Discipline

- Maintain peace and order in industry.
- Promote constructive criticism at all levels of management and employment.
- Avoid work stoppage in industry.
- Secure the settlement of disputes and grievances by a mutually agreed procedure
- Avoiding litigations
- Facilitate a free growth of trade unions

- Eliminate all forms of coercion, intimidation and violations of rules and regulations governing industrial relations.

Principles of the Code of discipline

- There should be no strike or lockout without prior notice.
- No unilateral action should be taken in connection with any industrial matter.
- Employees should follow go slow tactics
- No deliberate damage should be caused to a plant or property
- Acts of violations, intimidation and coercion should not be resorted
- The existing machinery for the settlement of disputes should be utilized.
- Actions that disturb cordial relationships should be avoided.

4. Voluntary Arbitration

- Voluntary Arbitration is arbitration by the agreement of parties. It is a binding adversarial dispute resolution process in which the disputing parties choose one or more arbitrators to hear their dispute and to render a final decision or award after an expedited hearing.
- Some of the important elements in voluntary arbitration are :
    - o Voluntary submission of dispute to an arbitrator.
    - o Subsequent attendance of witnesses and investigations.
- Voluntary arbitration may be specifically needed for disputes arising under agreements.
- **Giri Approach:** The grounds on which voluntary arbitration is favoured are:
    - o It is easier and does not cause delay.
    - o It promotes goodwill and confidence between the parties to a dispute.
    - o It promotes industrial democracy, encourages collective bargaining and replaces litigation by negotiations.
    - o A settlement by arbitration is generally acceptable to the parties to a dispute, for it does not lead to any loss of personal freedom, initiative or hope and aspiration for self betterment.

5. Grievance Redressal Procedure

- Under the code of discipline, every management has to set up a grievance redressal procedure.
- As far as possible, grievances have to be settled at the lowest level; and no matter should ordinarily be taken up at more than two levels.

6. The Implementation Machinery

- The Implementation and Evaluation committee has been set up at the centre:
- To ensure a proper implementation of the code of conduct, the code of discipline, Labour laws, awards and agreements with a view to reducing at the source the main cause of industrial strife.
- To take preventive actions by settling disputes before they assume serious proportions and deal with those that have defied settlement for a long time.
- To evaluate the impact of major strikes, lockouts and disputes and fix the responsibility for them.
- To evaluate the working and implementation of important labour legislations, awards and policy decisions in order to assess the extent to which these have produced the desired results, and to suggest the measures that may be taken to effect improvements in them.

7. Workers Participation in Industry/Management

- Participative management refers to the process of involving employees or employee representatives at all levels of the decision-making process.
- *Association of Workers in decision-making process.*
- **G.D.H. Cole:** "Better participation and greater responsibility in the decision making process on the part of general workers would perhaps tend to develop in them organizational loyalty, confidence, trust, favorable attitude towards supervisors, and a sense of involvement in the organization. Schemes of worker's participation in management among other measures or industrial reform, are expected to democratize the industrial milieu, and ensure egalitarianism in the process."
- The concept of quality circle (QC) provides informal involvement of employees in the decision making and implementation process.
- **Davis:** "It is a mental and emotional involvement of a person in a group situation which encourages him to contribute to goals and share responsibilities in them."
- **Employee empowerment** is a technique of involving employees in their work through the process of inclusion.
- Empowerment encourages employees to become innovators and managers of giving them more control and autonomous decision-making capabilities.
- **An assumption of competence:** the belief that people can be trusted and therefore minimal needs for checks, controls and directives.
- Empowerment requires a situation of high trust and high competence.
- **Togetherness:** this means working in flexible teams regardless of members' status or position in the hierarchy and operating with shared goals and values.
- It creates satisfaction among workers, which in turn helps in increasing their morale.
- Without co-operation of workers industrial output cannot be increased.
- Five ethical principles identified by participative management:
  1. Morality
  2. Recognition of human dignity
  3. Loss of self respect
  4. Physical and mental problems of employees
  5. Negative consequences of hierarchical organization of work

Scope of workers' participation

1. **Social Decisions:** Hours of work, welfare measures, work rules, safety, health, sanitation and noise control.
2. **Personnel Decisions:** Recruitment and selection, promotions and transfers, grievance settlements, work distribution
3. **Economic Decisions:** Methods of manufacturing, automation, lay offs, shut-downs, mergers and acquisitions and other financial aspects.

Concept of Participation

1. Participation in decision making

- o Workers have a say in decision making.
- o More persons participate to take decisions.
- o Workers influence the process of decision making.

2. Actual decision making

- o Actual involvement in decision making.
- o Subordinates participate with superiors in decision making process.

- o Workers have considerable interest in these decisions.
- o Participation of this type is also known as joint decision making.

3. Control over decision making.

- o It refers to "Any process through which one group determines what another group or persons will do."
- o Involvement of members in the exercise of control through decision making in group meeting.
- o Subordinates are involved in determining the course of action at all the stages of decision making process.

Methods of Workers' Participation in Management

1. Board Level
2. Ownership
3. Complete Control
4. Staff Councils
5. Joint Councils
6. Collective Bargaining
7. Job Enlargement and Enrichment
8. Suggestion Schemes
9. Quality Circles
10. Empowered Teams
11. Total Quality Management
12. Financial Participation

Prerequisites of Successful Participation

1. Clearly defined and complementary Objectives
2. Free flow of information and communication
3. Representatives of workers from workers themselves
4. Outside trade union participation should be avoided
5. Workers' education and training
6. No threat by participation
7. Association at all levels of decision-making

Benefits of Participation

1. **Increased participation:** When workers are consulted on important policy decisions then they feel as part and parcel of the enterprise. This gives a sense of personal gratification to workers and they feel committed to the work and organizational goals.
2. **Growth of workers:** When workers are allowed to express their opinions in working methods then it enhances creativity among them. With their experience they try to devise better methods of performing the work. This gives an opportunity to workers for initiative and growth of work.
3. **Satisfy social & egoistic needs:** According to Maslow's theory of needs first of all physiological needs are satisfied. When workers have satisfied their basic needs, they want to satisfy social and egoistic needs. Participation of workers will give them a sense of pride and satisfaction. The desire to satisfy social and egoistic needs will also act as a motivator to workers.
4. **Acceptance of change:** Whenever a change is introduced by management there is normally a resistance from workers. When workers are a part of decisions making body and it introduces any change, it will be easily accepted by them.
5. **Better industrial relations:** Industrial relations become strained when workers and management suspect each other's intentions. This type of environment creates conflicts between the workers &

management. The participation of workers will give them a chance to understand the management's viewpoint.

6. **Greater efficiency and job satisfaction:** The importance given to workers by consulting them for various decisions will increase their efficiency and job satisfaction. There will be an atmosphere of mutual help. The improved performance of workers will give them job satisfaction also.
7. **Better understanding:** The participation of workers in organizational problems and their solutions will create an organisational balance. The discussion of workers viewpoint will help management to understand their aspiration and difficulties faced. This will create an atmosphere of understanding and mental co-operations.
8. **Solidarity among workers:** The workers will become an organized force. Since workers will be required to send their representatives for participating in various bodies they will come on a common platform.

Forms of Participation

1. **Discussions:** In this system the manager or executive called a meeting of workers and shares the information with them, whenever he feels necessary. The workers give their opinions to the problem. A sort of group discussion is held and a consensus is involved.
2. **Group decision making:** In this form of workers' participation in management, the decision making power is delegated to the group. The manager acts as a leader, a chairman but final decision made by the group will be implemented. Authority & responsibility are delegated to the group for particular managerial area. This system is also called ***democratic or participative management.***
3. **Labour management co-operation:** The representative of the management and workers sit together and discuss the issues involved and find out the suitable solutions. This type of participation may be in the form of workers committees, joint management comments etc. joint management councils relate to consultation on various matters administration of welfare measures, etc.
4. **Suggestions system:** Under this system the employees are encouraged to make suggestions for improvement. These suggestions are put before a committee of management for scrutiny. The workers giving innovating suggestions are given monetary and other rewards. Management has the benefit of getting practical suggestions from the workers and making improvements in working.
5. **Employee's representatives on board of directors:** The employee's representative is made member of board of directors. The board is supreme policy making & decision making body in an organization. The workers representative presents the workers point of view before the board of directors.

Workers Participation in Management in India

- The workers participation in management is not new even though it got encouragement only after independence.
- In 1920 Mahatma Gandhi, observed "Employees should not regard themselves as sole owners of mills and factories of which they may be legal owners. They should regard themselves trustees.

Forms of workers participation in management

1. The Works Committees
2. Joint Management Councils
3. Joint Councils
4. Shop Councils

5. Co-determination

1. The Works Committees

- The first labour management association started in 1947 with the passing Industrial Disputes Act.
- The Act provides that in the case of any industrial establishment, in which 100 or more workers are employed on any day in the preceding twelve months, the appropriate government may be general or social order require the employees to constitute in the prescribed manner a Works Committee in the establishment.
- The committee was expected to discuss matters of common interest and to maintain cordial relations between workers and employees.
- The response to works committees was encouraging in the beginning but, in spite of their large number the experience of these committees was not very fruitful.

Reasons for failure of works committees

- The workers were not satisfied with the functions assigned to the committees.
- The tendency of employers taking some matters to these committees just to bypass trade unions created a suspicion in the minds of workers leaders.
- Inter unions rivalries were also responsible for the failure of these committees.
- The casual approach of employees towards these committees made them ineffective.
- The recommendations of these committees are advisory in nature.
- The workers show less interest in the working of these committees.

2. Joint Management Councils

- Joint Management council is a voluntary body.
- Its introduction was left solely to the discretion of employers and employees.
- These councils will consist of equal number of representation of workers and management will not exceed twelve.

The criterion for selecting industrial units:

- The unit must employ at least 500 workers.
- It should have an established and representative workers union.
- The unit must be with a record of good industrial relations.

The Councils functions: The council has the right to receive information, discuss and give suggestions on general economic situation, market production, general running of the unit, etc.

- Information sharing.
- Consultative.
- Administrative.

Lacunas in the councils:

- The workers representatives were not satisfied with their role in councils.
- Management is not prepared to supply sufficient information to councils.
- The trade union leaders feel that council would weaken their hold over workers.
- The absence of representative unions made it difficult for the councils to work smoothly.

3. Shop Councils

- A new scheme for workers participation in management was adopted in October 1975.
- The scheme was voluntary in nature.
- It covered all manufacturing and mining industries employing 500 or more persons.

- The scheme provided for setting up of shops councils at the plant level.

Features of Shop Councils

- There will be a shop for each department or one council for more departments considering the number of workers employed there.
- The representatives of employees will be nominated by the management and must be from the unit concerned.
- The number of members in the council may be decided by management in consultation with recognised unions.
- All decisions of the council must be based on consensus.
- The term of shop council will be two years.
- The chairman of the council will be the nominee of management and vice-chairman shall be elected by working members amongst themselves.

Functions of Shop Councils

- Assist management in achieving monthly/yearly targets.
- Elimination of wastage and optimum utilization of machine capacity and manpower.
- To study the causes of absenteeism in the department and suggest measures to eliminate it.
- Safety measures.
- Assistance in maintaining general discipline in the department.
- Physical conditions of work such as lighting, ventilation, noise, dust, etc. reduction of fatigue.
- Welfare measures to be adopted for sufficient running of department/shop.
- Ensure proper communication between management and workers.

4. Joint Councils: Provision of a joint council is made for every unit employing 500 or more workers.

Features of Joint Councils:

- The members of the council must be actually engaged in the unit.
- The term of the council will be two years.
- The chief executive of the unit will be the chairman of and vice-chairman will be nominated by worker members.
- It shall meet at least once in a quarter.
- The decisions of the council will be based on consensus and not on voting.
- The decisions will be binding on both parties and will be implemented within one month.

Functions of Joint Councils:

- Optimum production, efficiency and function of productivity norms of man and machine for the unit as a whole.
- Functions of a shop council which has a bearing on another shop or the unit as a whole.
- Matters remaining unresolved by shop council.
- The development of skill of workmen and adequate facilities for training.
- Preparation of schedules of working hours and of holidays.
- Awarding of rewards for valuables and creative suggestions received from workers.
- Optimum use of raw materials and quality of finished products.

Reasons for the failure

- The management have been o the view that workers are not competent to take decisions.
- It was difficult for workers representatives to play the role of management and union leaders.

- o The scheme of workers participation was inspired by the government without any initiative from management.
- o The active association of union leaders with political parties was only responsible for the failure of this scheme.
- o The workers participation is mainly emphasized at top level management.
- o The workers in India do not feel motivated to participate in decision making because their lower needs too
- o Remain unsatisfied.

5. Co-determination

- Arrangement in which worker representatives are appointed to a firm's board of directors for participation in the firm's decision making process.
- Co-determination is a practice whereby the employees have a role in management of a company.
- Co-determination is a type of worker's participation in management.
- Co-determination was started in Germany in 1945.

Methods of Co-determination

1. Works councils
2. Worker's participative on the supervisory Board
3. The management Board

8. Statutory Machinery

- Statutory Machinery has been provided under the ID Act, 1947 with a view to bringing about the settlement of disputes.
- It consists of Works Committees, Conciliation officers and Boards of Conciliation, Labour Courts and Industrial Tribunals and National Tribunals.

1) Works Committee:

In establishments where hundred or more workers are employed:

a) The appropriate government may require the employer to set-up works committee.

b) It is composed of equal number of representatives of workmen and management who are chosen with consultation of the trade union.

c) Its functions are to preserve amity and establish cordial relations and to resolve differences of opinion on matters of common interest.

2) Conciliation Officer

a) The conciliation officer may be appointed by the government for specified area or specified industries.

b) Duty of conciliation officer is to mediate in and promote the settlement of industrial disputes. Where industrial dispute exists or is apprehended and relates to public utility, conciliation officer shall hold conciliation proceedings and it is mandatory. In such cases conciliation officer will investigate the dispute and induce the parties to corne to amicable settlement. However, he cannot take the decision, he has to send report of settlement to his government. If no settlement is reached then also he has to report to the government giving reasons on account of which settlement could not be reached. Conciliation officer to normally submit report within 14 days of commencement of conciliation proceedings. Duty of the conciliation officer is administrative and not judicial in nature.

If an agreement is reached by the parties, it is binding on both the parties.

3) Board of Conciliation:

The government may notify constitution of board of conciliation for promoting settlement of an industrial dispute. Its role is also consultative, like conciliation officer.

4) Court of Enquiry:

The government may constitute a court of enquiry to enquire into any matter connected with an industrial dispute. In the case of board of conciliation the object is to promote settlement of an industrial dispute. But in the case of a court of enquiry object is to enquire into and reveal the causes of an industrial dispute.

5) Voluntary Arbitration:

It is voluntary method of resolving individual disputes if dispute is not settled by negotiating parties. Here both parties are willing to go to an arbitrator of their choice and submit to his decision. Arbitrators are named by the parties in the written agreement.

The number of arbitrators can be one or even more than one. Legal sanctity to this mode of settlement of industrial disputes was given in1956 when Section lOA was introduced in Industrial Dispute Act.

6) Adjudication:

The Industrial Disputes Act provides for three-tier system of adjudication of industrial disputes. The cases either may be referred by government to court after the receipt of failure report from conciliation officer or directly by any party. Labour courts and industrial tribunal may be constituted by the state government while national tribunal is constituted by the central government.

Criticism on the working of Industrial Tribunal

- **V. V. Giri :** There have been great delays before decisions have been handed down, as a result of which both workers and employers have lost faith in its utility, this is referred as ***'Number 1 Enemy'*** of good industrial relations and the growth of collective bargaining; for he has pointed out, *justice delayed is justice denied.*
- **Industrial Truce Resolution, 1962:** Embody the principles of sound industrial practices, and lay emphasis on arbitration for the settlement of disputes.
- The association of workers with the management has been ensured in the Management Council, the shop Council and the Joint Management Council set up at the shop and department levels in a number of industries employing 500 or more workers, whether these industries are in the private or public sector.

Effects of Industrial Disputes

1. Strikes

- A strike is a very powerful weapon used by trade unions and other labor associations to get their demands accepted. It generally involves quitting of work by a group of workers for the purpose of bringing the pressure on their employer so that their demands get accepted. When workers collectively cease to work in a particular industry, they are said to be on strike.
- According to Industrial Disputes Act 1947, a strike is "a cessation of work by a body of persons employed in an industry acting in combination; or a concerted refusal of any number of persons who are or have been so employed to continue to work or to accept employment; or a refusal

under a common understanding of any number of such persons to continue to work or to accept employment".

Types of strike

1. Primary Strikes: Generally against the employer with whom the dispute exists.

- Stay away strike
- Stay-in strike or sit-down strike
- Tools -down, pen –down or mouth-shut strike
- Lightening or wildcat strike
- Token or protest strike
- Go slow
- Work to rule/Work to designation
- Picketing
- Boycott
- Gherao
- Hunger strike

2. Secondary strike: Against a third party. These strikes are sympathetic strike.

Causes of strikes

- Dissatisfaction with company policy
- Salary and incentive problems
- Increment not up to the mark
- Wrongful discharge or dismissal of workmen
- Withdrawal of any concession or privilege
- Hours of work and rest intervals
- Leaves with wages and holidays
- Bonus, profit sharing, Provident fund and gratuity
- Retrenchment of workmen and closure of establishment
- Dispute connected with minimum wages

2. Lockouts

- A lockout is a work stoppage in which an employer prevents employees from working. It is declared by employers to put pressure on their workers.
- This is different from a strike, in which employees refuse to work.
- Thus, a lockout is employers' weapon while a strike is raised on part of employees.

3. Picketing

- Picketing involves walking up and down outside the work place indicating a strike is in process.
- When workers are dissuaded from work by stationing certain men at the factory gates, such a step is known as picketing.
- Pickets are workers who are on strike that stand at the entrance to their workplace.
- It is basically a method of drawing public attention towards the fact that there is a dispute between the management and employees.

The purpose of picketing

- To stop or persuade workers not to go to work.
- To tell the public about the strike.

- To persuade workers to take their union's side.

4. Gherao

- Gherao in Hindi means to surround.
- It denotes a collective action initiated by a group of workers under which members of the management are prohibited from leaving the industrial establishment premises by workers who block the exit gates by forming human barricades.
- The workers may gherao the members of the management by blocking their exits and forcing them to stay inside their cabins.
- The main object of gherao is to inflict physical and mental torture to the person being gheraoed and hence this weapon disturbs the industrial peace to a great extent.

7.3. MEASURES FOR IMPROVING INDUSTRIAL RELATIONS

1. **Action of employee/employer in an industrial conflict**

- Getting Legal Approval.
- Before organising a strike or any other form of industrial action a trade union must follow the rules set out in the Industrial Relations Act 1990. This states that
- ***"a union cannot organise a strike or any other industrial action without getting members majority approval"***
- Taken stoppages involve employees stopping work for a short period of time to demonstrate their feeling to management
- Work to rule is where employees refuse to undertake any work outside the terms of their employment contract.
- **A go slow occurs** when employees carry out the minimum amount of work they can get away with without jeopardising their basic pay
- **All out strike**: Means employees stop working and leave the premises.

Consequences of industrial relations conflict for a business

- Reduced productivity, increased costs.
- Loss of profits.
- Damage to public image.
- Difficulty in recruiting & keeping staff.
- Wasted time and energy.

Prevention of industrial disputes

1. Labour welfare officer
2. Tripartite and Bipartite bodies
3. Standing orders
4. Grievance Procedure
5. Collective Bargaining
6. Strong trade unions
7. Labour Co-partnership and Profit sharing
8. Joint consultations

7.4. COLLECTIVE BARGAINING

- Collective bargaining is a process in which the representatives of the employer and of the employees meet and attempt to negotiate a contract governing the employer-employee union relationship.
- **Sydney &Beatrice Webb:** "Collective bargaining is a method by which trade unions protect and improve the conditions of their members working lives."

Characteristics of Collective Bargaining

- It is a group action as opposed to individual action
- It is flexible and mobile and not fixed or static
- It is a bipartite process
- It is a continuous process
- It is dynamic and not static
- Power relationship

Objectives of Collective Bargaining

- To maintain cordial relations between employer and employees by settling disputes/conflicts.
- To protect the interest of workers through collective action.
- To resolve the differences between employers and employees through voluntary negotiations.
- To avoid the need for Government intervention in matters relating to employment.
- To ensure the participation of trade unions in industry.
- To promote industrial democracy.

Types of Bargaining

1. **Conjunctive Bargaining:** The employers and employees try to maximize their respective principle "my gain is your loss and your gain is my loss."
2. **Co-operative Bargaining:** Both parties realize the importance of surviving in difficult times (like recession) and are willing to negotiate the terms of employment in a flexible way.
3. **Productivity Bargaining:** In this method worker's wages and benefits are linked to productivity. If they are able to exceed the standard productivity norms they will get substantial benefits.
4. **Composite Bargaining:** Labour bargains for wages as usual but goes a step further by demanding equity in matters relating to work, norms, employment levels, manning standards, etc.

Collective Bargaining Process

Stage-1: The negotiation stage

1. Identification of problem
2. Preparing for negotiations
3. Negotiations of agreement

Stage-2: Contract Administration

- The right of workers to bargain freely with employers is an essential element in freedom of association.
- Collective bargaining is a voluntary process through which employers and workers discuss and negotiate their relations, in particular terms and conditions of work.
- Participants include employers themselves or their organizations, and trade unions or, in their absence, representatives freely designated by the workers.

- Collective bargaining can only function effectively if it is conducted freely and in good faith by all parties. This implies:
  - o Making efforts to reach an agreement;
  - o Carrying out genuine and constructive negotiations;
  - o Avoiding unjustified delays;
  - o Respecting the agreements concluded and applying them in good faith; and
  - o Giving sufficient time for the parties to discuss and settle collective disputes.
- Bargaining in good faith aims at reaching mutually acceptable collective agreements. Where agreement is not reached, dispute settlement procedures ranging from conciliation through mediation to arbitration may be used.
- Workers' representatives should be given appropriate facilities, taking account of the needs, size, and capabilities of the enterprise involved, that will enable them to do their work effectively and allow them to perform their role without interference. Workers' representatives should be provided with information required for meaningful negotiations.
- The collective bargaining process also covers the phase before actual negotiations – information sharing, consultation, joint assessments – as well as the implementation of collective agreements.
- Collective agreements should include provisions for the settlement of disputes.
- In order to facilitate negotiations, the use of conciliation and mediation that is voluntary or established by law, may be accepted.
- On the other hand, arbitration is only legitimate if requested by both parties or required by law.

7.5. GRIEVANCE HANDLING AND DISCIPLINARY ACTION

Grievance

- **Michael J. Jucius:** "Grievance means any discontent or dissatisfaction, whether expressed or not and whether valid or not, arising out of anything connected with the company that an employee thinks, believes or even feels, is unfair, unjust or inequitable."
- As such it can be stated or unvoiced, written or oral, legitimate or ridiculous.
- If the dissatisfaction of employees' goes unattended or the conditions causing it are not corrected, the irritation is likely to increase and lead to unfavorable attitude towards the management and unhealthy relations in the organization.
- The formal mechanism for dealing with such worker's dissatisfaction is called grievance procedure.
- All companies whether unionized or not should have established and known grievance methods of processing grievances.
- The primary value of grievance procedure is that it can assist in minimizing discontent and dissatisfaction that may have adverse effects upon co-operation and productivity.
- A grievance procedure is necessary in large organization which has numerous personnel and many levels with the result that the manager is unable to keep a check on each individual, or be involved in every aspect of working of the small organization.

Steps in grievance procedure

1. Conference among the aggrieved employee, the supervisor, and the union steward.
2. Conference between middle management and middle union leadership.
3. Conference between top management and top union leadership.
4. Arbitration.
   - There may be variations in the procedures followed for resolving employee grievances.

- Variations may result from such factors as organizational or decision-making structures or size of the plant or company.
- Large organizations do tend to have formal grievance procedures involving succession of steps.

Five types of grievance systems

1. The open door policy
2. Step-review method
3. Peer-review also called the grievance committee or roundtable
4. Ombudsman and
5. Hearing officer.

Prerequisites of Grievance procedure

- Conformity with Prevailing Legislation
- Clarity
- Simplicity
- Promptness
- Training
- Follow-up

Grievance procedure

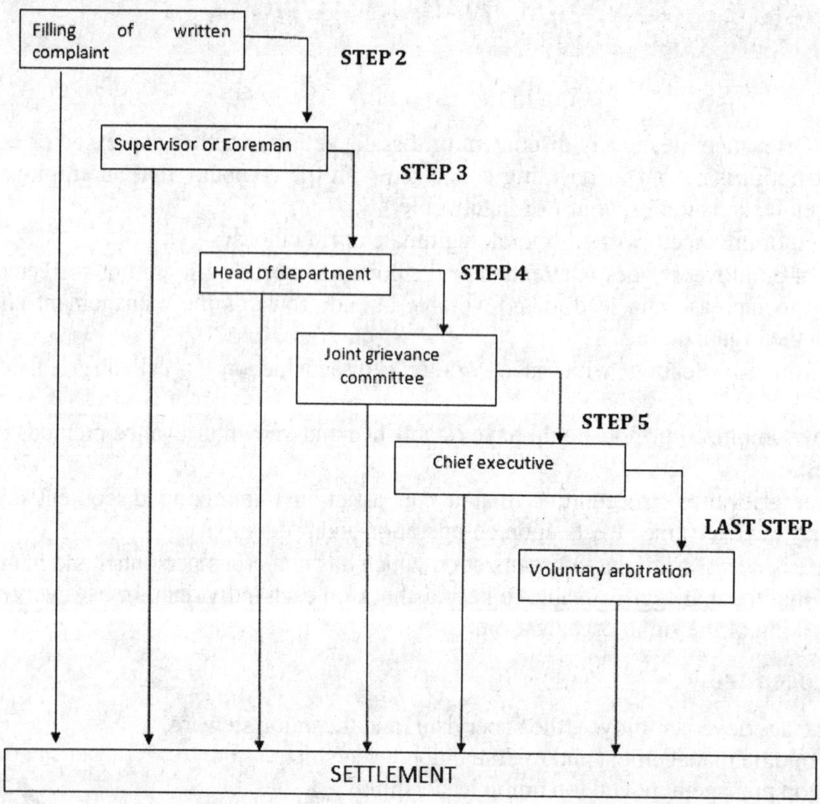

Benefits of Grievance procedure

- The grievance procedure provides a means for identifying practices, procedures, and administrative policies that are causing employee complaints so that changes can be considered.
- They reduce costly employment suits.
- A grievance procedure allows managers to establish a uniform labour policy.
- A grievance system can be a reliable mechanism to learn of, and resolve employee dissatisfaction. It can produce early settlements to disputes or provide for correction of contested employment issues.

Ways of knowing about grievance

1. **Exit interview:** The interview conducted when employees quit organizations due to dissatisfaction or better prospect elsewhere.
2. **Gripe boxes:** Boxes in which the employees can drop their anonymous complaints.
3. **Opinion Surveys:** Group meetings, periodical interviews with employees, collective bargaining sessions, etc.
4. **Open-door policies:** Some organizations extend a general invitation to their employees to informally drop in the manager's room any time and talk over their grievances.

Need for a Grievance Handling Procedure

- Without an analysis of their nature and pattern, the causes of employee dissatisfaction cannot be removed.
- The HR manager should help the top management and line managers, particularly foremen and supervisors in the formulation and implementation of the policies, programs and procedures which would best enable them to handle employee grievance.
- These policies, programs and procedures are generally known as the grievance redressal procedure.
- The grievance redressal procedure is a device by which grievances are settled, generally to the satisfaction of the trade union or employees and the management.

Essentials of Sound Grievance Handling

- Conformity with Prevailing Legislation
- Acceptability
- Clarity
- Promptness
- Simplicity
- Training
- Follow up

7.6. EMPLOYEE DISCIPLINE: NATURE-IMPORTANCE-CAUSES-FORMS

- **Richard D. Calhoon**: "Discipline is the force that prompts individuals or groups to observe rules, regulations, standards and procedures deemed necessary for an organization."
- Discipline means systematically conducting the business by the organizational members who strictly adhere to the essential rules and regulations.
- These employees/organizational members work together as a team so as to achieve organizational mission as well as vision and they truly understand that the individual and group aims and desires must be matched so as to ensure organizational success.
- A disciplined employee will be organized and an organized employee will be disciplined always.

- Employee behaviour is the base of discipline in an organization. Discipline implies confirming with the code of conduct established by the organization. Discipline in an organization ensures productivity and efficiency. It encourages harmony and co-operation among employees as well as acts as a morale booster for the employees. In absence of discipline, there will be chaos, confusion, corruption and disobedience in an organization.
- In short, discipline implies obedience, orderliness and maintenance of proper subordination among employees. Work recognition, fair and equitable treatment of employees, appropriate salary structure, effective grievance handling and job-security all contribute to organizational discipline.
- Therefore discipline means securing consistent behaviour in accordance with the accepted norms of behaviour.
- Simply stated, discipline means **orderliness**. It implies the absence of chaos, irregularity and confusion in the behaviour of workers.
- According to **Richard D Calhoon**, discipline is defined as ***"a force that prompts individuals or groups to observe the rules, regulations and procedures which are deemed to be necessary for the effective functioning of an organization."***

Nature of Discipline

According to **Megginson;** discipline involves the following three things:

1. **Self-discipline** implies that a person brings the discipline in himself with a determination to achieve the goals that he has set for himself in life.
2. **Orderly behavior** refers to discipline as a condition that must exist for an orderly behaviors in the organization.
3. **Punishment** is used to prevent indiscipline. When a worker goes astray in his conduct, he has to be punished for the same and the recurrences of it must be prevented.

Aspects of Discipline

1. Positive discipline

- Employees comply with rules not out of fear of punishment but out of an inherent desire to cooperate and achiever goals.Where the organizational climate is marked by two-way communication, clear goals, effective leadership, and adequate compensation employees need not be disciplined in a traditional way – ***constructive discipline.***
- Positive discipline involves creation of an atmosphere in the organisation whereby employees willingly conform to the established rules and regulations. Positive discipline can be achieved through rewards and effective leadership.

2. Negative Discipline

- Under negative discipline, penalties are used to force the workers to obey rules and regulations. In other words, workers try to adhere to rules and regulations out of fear of warnings, penalties and other forms of punishment. This approach to discipline is called negative or punitive approach.
- Disciplinary programme forces and constraints the employees to obey orders and function in accordance with set rules and regulations through warnings, penalties and other forms of punishment. This approach to discipline is called negative approach or corrective approach.

Essentials of a Good Disciplinary System

- Knowledge of rules

- Prompt action
- Fair action
- Well-defined procedure
- Constructive approach
- Review and revision

Principles of industrial discipline

- Discipline is intimately linked with relations within the organisation and is affected by such factors as background, social environment and emotional outlook of the workers concerned.
- Discipline is also closely related with personal feelings or sentiments.
- The sentiments are non-logical emotional factors that influence the behaviour of average worker.
- Therefore, the effective application of discipline depends primarily on understanding the behaviour of human beings and of one self.

Causes of Indiscipline

- A number of social, economic, cultural and political reasons contribute to indiscipline in an organization.
- In an organization the parties responsible for indiscipline are workers and their unions and the management.

Kinds of punishment / penalties

Minor Penalties

1. Oral Warning
2. Written Reprimand
3. Loss of Privileges
4. Fines
5. Suspension

Major Penalties

1. Withholding Increments
2. Demotion / Stopping Promotion
3. Discharge
4. Dismissal

Characteristics of a Sound Disciplinary System (Red Hot Stove Rule)

Discipline should be imposed without generating resentment. ***McGregor*** propounded the ***"red hot stove rule"*** which says that a sound and effective disciplinary system in an organization should have the following characteristics:

1. Immediate: Just as when you touch a red hot stove, the burn is immediate, similarly the penalty for violation should be immediate/ immediate disciplinary action must be taken for violation of rules.

2. Consistent: Just as a red hot stove burns everyone in same manner; likewise, there should be high consistency in a sound disciplinary system.

3.Impersonal: Just as a person is burned because he touches the red hot stove and not because of any personal feelings, likewise, impersonality should be maintained by refraining from personal or subjective feelings.

4. Prior warning and notice: Just as an individual has a warning when he moves closer to the stove that he would be burned on touching it, likewise, a sound disciplinary system should give advance warning to the employees as to the implications of not conforming to the standards of behaviour/code of conduct in an organization.

Assumption of a sound disciplinary system

1. Acquaintance/Knowledge of rules: The employees should be well aware of the desired code of conduct/ standards of behaviour in the organization. This code of discipline should be published in employee handbook.

2. Timely action: Timely enquiry should be conducted for breaking the code of conduct in an organization. The more later the enquiry is made, the more forgetful one becomes and the more he feels that punishment is not deserved.

3. Fair and just action: There should be same punishment for same offence/ misconduct. There should be no favouritism. Discipline should be uniformly enforced always.

4. Positive approach: The disciplinary system should be preventive and not punitive. Concentrate on preventing misconduct and not on imposing penalties. The employees should not only be explained the reason for actions taken against them but also how such fines and penalties can be avoided in future.

Symptoms of general indiscipline

1. Change in the normal behaviors
2. Absenteeism
3. Increased grievances
4. Lack of concern for performance
5. Go slow
6. Disorderly behaviors
7. Lack of concern for job
8. Late coming etc.

Causes of Indiscipline

1. **Unfair Management Practices:** Management sometimes indulges in unfair practices like below and these unfair management practices gradually result in indiscipline.
    - Wage discrimination
    - Non-compliance with promotional policies and transfer policies
    - Discrimination in allotment of work
    - Defective handling of grievances
    - Payment of low wages
    - Delay in payment of wages
    - Creating low quality work life etc.

2. **Absence of Effective Leadership**: Absence of effective leadership results in poor management in the areas of direction, guidance, instructions etc. This in turn, results in indiscipline.

3. **Communication Barriers:** Communication barriers and absence of humane approach on the part of superiors result in frustration and indiscipline among the workers. The management should clearly formulate the policies regarding discipline. These policies should be communicated and the policies should be consistently followed in the organizations. The management should also be empathetic towards the employees.

4. **Inadequate attention to personnel Problems**: Delay in solving personnel problems develops frustration among individual workers. The management should be proactive so that there is no discontent among the workers. It should adopt a parental attitude towards its employees. However it should be noted that no relationship can continue for long if it is one sided. What I am implying here is that the workers should also live up to their commitments. They should be reasonable in their demands.
5. **Victimization:** Victimization of subordinate also results in indiscipline. The management should not exploit the workers. It is also in the long-term interest of the management to take care of its internal customers.
6. **Absence of Code of Conduct**: This creates confusion and also provides chance for discrimination while taking disciplinary action.

Forms of indiscipline

- Inconsistent behaviour of an employee and deviation from the standard behaviour.
- Unsafe behaviour of the employee.
- Immoral action of the employee.
- When employee is abusive, disturbs the peace and is negligent towards his duties.

7.7. Misconduct

Constitutes of a misconduct

- Nature of Employment Contract
- The Nature and Meaning of Misconduct
- Legal Provisions Relating to Misconduct
- Principles of Natural Justice
- Types of Misconduct – minor /major
- Criminal Offences at Work

Investigating offences

- Suspension Pending Inquiry
- Legal Effect of Condonations
- Show Cause Letter
- Notice of Inquiry
- Procedures for Investigation

Domestic inquiry

- Procedures for Domestic Inquiry – Preparation for Inquiry
- Selection of the Inquiry Officer/Board of Inquiry
- The Role of the Inquiry Officer(s)
- Recording Proceedings
- Adducing of Evidence (Witnesses)
- The Inquiry Report: - Findings & Punishment/ Findings Review/ Types of Punishment

Disciplinary procedure

1. **Preliminary Investigation:** In first step Preliminary Investigation about misconduct carried out by the nominee of employer.

2. **Issue of charge sheet:** Once the prima facie case of misconduct is established, the management should proceed to issue a charge sheet to the employee. Charge sheet is merely a notice of the charge and provides the employee an opportunity to explain his conduct. Therefore, charge sheet is generally known as a show cause notice.
3. **Consideration of Explanation:** On getting the answer for the charge sheet served, the explanation furnished should be considered and if it is satisfactory, no disciplinary action needs to be taken. On the contrary when the management is not satisfied with the employee's explanation, it can proceed with full-fledged enquiry. However, if the worker admits the charge, the employer can warn him or award him punishment without further enquiry.
4. **Suspension pending Enquiry:** In case the charge is grave that is serious, a suspension order may be served on the employee along with the charge sheet. According to the Industrial Employment (Standing Order) Act, 1946, the suspended worker is to be paid a subsistence allowance equal to one-half of his wages for the first ninety days of suspension and three-fourths of wages for the remaining period of suspension if the delay in the completion of disciplinary proceedings is not due to the worker's conduct. What is grave will depend on the discretion of the management. It has to be decided in accordance with the Code of Discipline.
5. **Notice of enquiry:** If the explanation submitted by the employee is found unsatisfactory, the next step is to issue him a notice of holding an enquiry, giving him information as to the name of the Enquiry Officer, the date, time and venue of the enquiry as also notifying to him that he should have ready with him on the date of enquiry the witnesses that wishes to examine or any other relevant information that he may like to give.
6. **Holding of Enquiry:** An enquiry officer should be appointed to hold the enquiry and a notice to this effect should be given to the concerned worker. *Principle of natural justice must be followed.* The worker should not be denied the chance of explaining himself. The enquiry officer should give sufficient notice to the worker so that he may prepare to represent his case and make submission in his defense. The enquiry officer should proceed in a proper manner and examine witnesses. Fair opportunity should be given to the worker to cross-examine the management witnesses.
7. **Recording of Findings by the Enquiry Officer:** The Enquiry Officer should begin with recording the date of holding the enquiry, the persons present on the date of holding the enquiry, the persons present at the enquiry, a statement making reference to the charges, as per the letter of charge issued to the employee, a statement to the effect that the procedure of enquiry was explained to the charge-sheeted employee, and any other relevant statement, such as, a statement relating to a request by the charge-sheeted employee to allow an outsider union official to be present at the enquiry and the Enquiry Officer's refusal to grant such a request, whether the employee admits charges or not, etc. He should then ask the Management's representative to present the case in detail, which should be recorded.
8. **Awarding Punishment:** Disciplinary action can be taken when the misconduct of the employee is proved. While deciding the nature of disciplinary action, the employee's previous record, precedents, effects of the action on other employees, etc, have to be considered.

7.8. Trade Unions- Meaning, Objectives, functions, Theories, Structure and Importance

- Trade Union means a combination formed for the purpose of regulating the relations not only between workmen and employers but also between workmen and workmen or between employers and employers.

- **G.D.H. Cole:** "A trade union means an association of workers in one or more professions-an association is carried on mainly for the purpose of protecting and advancing the members' economic interest in connection with their daily work"
- **Indian Trade Union Act, 1926:** "Trade union as any combination whether temporary or permanent formed primarily for the purpose of regulating the relations between workmen and employer or, between workmen and workmen or, between employer and employer Or for imposing restrictive conditions on the conduct of any trade or business and include any federation of two or more trade unions."
- **Dale Yoder:** "A trade union as a continuing long term association of employees, formed and maintained for the specific purpose of advancing and protecting the interest of the members in their working relationship."
- **S.D. Punekar**: "A trade union is a continuous association of persons in the industry-whether employer or independent workers-formed primarily for the purpose of the pursuit of the interests of its members of the trade they represent."
- Trade unions are formed to protect and promote the interests of their members.
- Their primary function is to protect the interests of workers against discrimination and unfair labor practices.
- A trade union is an organized group of workers. Its main goal is to protect and advance the interests of its members
- A union often negotiates agreements with employers on pay and conditions. It may also provide legal and financial advice, sickness benefits and education facilities to its members
- Trade unions aim to represent the interests of people at work and negotiate with employers for better terms and conditions for their members
- Trade union is a body representing employee's views with their employers. Union members elect a shop steward to represent them in negotiations with the employers.
- The nature of employment organization:
  - Approaches to industrial relations
  - Unitary perspective
- **Assumptions**
  - Capitalist society
  - Integrated group of people within the work organization
  - Common values, interests and objectives
- **Nature of conflict and its resolution**
  - Irrational and aberrant (straying from the path)
  - If there is/are conflict, they are Frictional and personal
  - Coercion (force) or paternalism (limiting freedom through regulation)

History of trade union

- The first trade union was started in 1877 in Nagpur.
- It was this labour protest on an organized scale, through the support of some philanthropic personalities, that organized labour unions came to be formed
- The setting up of large-scale industrial units, created conditions of widespread use of machinery, new lines of production, and brought about changes in working and living environment of workers, and concentration of industries in large towns
- The first Factory's Act was passed in 1881. **N.M. Lokhode** was instrumental behind passing this act.
- In 1919 Madras Labour Union was the first Union in India to be formed and established by **B. P. Vadia**

- Bombay Trade Union formed in 1975 under the leadership of **Sorabjee Shapurjee Bengalee .**

Procedure of registration of trade union

- At least 7 members should be present for an application.
- It should in a prescribed form ,fees and should be registered under the Registrar of Trade Unions.
- Should be accompanied by a copy of the Rules of Trade Union
- Certificate of Registration is issued as soon as Trade Union has been duly registered under the Act.

Objectives of trade union

- Representation
- Negotiation
- Voice in decisions affecting workers
- Member services
- Education and training
- Legal assistance
- Financial discounts
- Welfare benefits

Functions of Trade unions

1. Militant functions

- To achieve higher wages and better working conditions.
- To raise the status of workers as a part of industry.
- To protect labors against victimization and injustice.

2. Fraternal functions

- To take up welfare measures for improving the morale of workers.
- To generate self confidence among workers.
- To encourage sincerity and discipline among workers.
- To provide opportunities for promotion and growth.
- To protect women workers against discrimination.

3. Social functions

- Promoting and maintaining national integration by reducing the number of industrial disputes.
- Incorporating a sense of corporate social responsibility in workers.
- Achieving industrial peace.

4. Political functions

5. Ancillary functions

- Communication
- Welfare Activities
- Education
- Research

Importance of Trade Unions

- Trade unions help in accelerated pace of economic development in many ways as follows:
- by helping in the recruitment and selection of workers.

- by inculcating discipline among the workforce
- by enabling settlement of industrial disputes in a rational manner
- by helping social adjustments. Workers have to adjust themselves to the new working conditions, the new rules and policies. Workers coming from different backgrounds may become disorganized, unsatisfied and frustrated. Unions help them in such adjustment.
- Trade Union is an important factor of the current society, as it safeguards the basic interest and needs of both the employees as well as employers, by providing better terms and conditions of employment, secured jobs, better wages, favorable working environment which in turn leads to desired profitability.

Reasons for joining a trade union

- Increased bargaining power – one voice as a representative
- Having a skilled negotiator on behalf of employees
- Greater job security if the union is powerful
- Higher standard of living for members
- Greater Bargaining Power
- Minimize Discrimination
- Sense of Participation
- Sense of Belongingness
- Platform for self expression
- Betterment of relationships

Industrial Relation Policy

- Prior to 1991, the industrial relations system in India sought to control conflicts and disputes through excessive labor legislations.
- With the coming of globalization, the 40 year old policy of protectionism proved inadequate for Indian industry to remain competitive as the lack of flexibility posed a serious threat to manufacturers because they had to compete in the international market.
- With the advent of New economic policy in1991 (liberalization, privatization, globalization) the industrial relations policy began to change.
- Now, the policy was tilted towards employers. Employers opted for workforce reduction, introduced policies of voluntary retirement schemes and flexibility in workplace also increased. Thus, globalization brought major changes in industrial relations policy in India.
- Collective bargaining in India has mostly been decentralized, but now in sectors where it was not so, are also facing pressures to follow decentralization.
- Some industries are cutting employment to a significant extent to cope with the domestic and foreign competition e.g. pharmaceuticals. On the other hand, in other industries where the demand for employment is increasing are experiencing employment growths.
- In the expansionary economy there is a clear shortage of managers and skilled labor.
- The number of local and enterprise level unions has increased and there is a significant reduction in the influence of the unions.
- Under pressure some unions and federations are putting up a united front e.g. banking.
- Another trend is that the employers have started to push for internal unions i.e. no outside affiliation.
- HR policies and forms of work are emerging that include, especially in multi-national companies, multi-skills, variable compensation, job rotation etc. These new policies are difficult to implement in place of old practices as the institutional set up still needs to be changed.
- HRM is seen as a key component of business strategy.

- Training and skill development is also receiving attention in a number of industries, especially banking and information technology.

Role of Trade Unions

- Legitimate and accepted in both economic and managerial relations
- Internal and integral to organization
- Conflict result from industrial and organizational factors.

Reasons for Joining Unions

- Compulsion
- Protection
- Social pressure
- Political beliefs
- Solidarity
- Tradition
- Pay and conditions
- Communication
- Health and safety
- Grievances, Disputes and Industrial Relations Processes
- The employee approaches his/her immediate supervisor to discuss the grievance.
- If the grievance remains unresolved, the employee next approaches the shop steward who then approaches the supervisor.
- If the matter still remains unresolved, the shop steward contacts a union organiser who negotiates with the HR manager and/or a line manager and/or an employer association representative.
- If the matter is still unresolved, it may be referred to the IRC for conciliation.

Theories of Trade Unionism

1. **Political Revolutionary Theory of Labour Movement of Marx and Engels :** This theory is based on Adam Smiths theory of labour value. Its short run purpose is to eliminate competition among labour, and the ultimate purpose is to overthrow capitalist businessman. Trade union is pure simple a class struggle, and proletarians have nothing to lose but their chains and they a world to win.
2. **Webbs Theory of Industrial Democracy :** Webb's book 'Industrial democracy' is the Bible of trade unionism. According to Webb, trade unionism is an extension of democracy from political sphere to industrial sphere. Webb agreed with Marx that trade unionism is a class struggle and modern capitalist state is a transitional phase which will lead to democratic socialism. He considered collective bargaining as the process which strengthens labour.
3. **Cole's Theory of Union Control of Industry :** Cole's views are given in his book "World of Labour" 1913. His views are somewhere in between Webb and Marx. He agrees that unionism is class struggle and the ultimate is the control of industry by labour and not revolution as predicted by Marx.
4. **Common's Environment Theory :** He was skeptical of generalisations and believed only that which could be proved by evidence. He agreed that collective bargaining was an instrument of class struggle, but he summarised that ultimately there will be partnership between employers and employees.
5. **Mitchell's Economic Protection Theory of Trade Unionism**: Mitchell, a labour leader, completely rejected individual bargaining. According to him unions afford economic protection to.

6. **Simons Theory of Monopolistic, anti-Democratic Trade Unionism :** He denounced trade unionism as monopoly founded on violence. And he claimed monopoly power has no use save abuse.

7. **Perlman's Theory of the "Scarcity Consciousness" of Manual Workers:** He rejected the idea of class consciousness as an explanation for the origin of the trade union movement but substituted it with what he called job consciousness. According to him, 'working people in reality felt an urge towards collective control of their employment opportunities, but hardly towards similar control of industry.' Perlman observed that three dominant factors emerged from the rich historical data : the capacity or incapacity of the capitalist system to survive as a ruling group in the face of revolutionary attacks (e.g., failure in Russia) the source of the anti-capitalist influences being primarily from among the intellectuals in any society. The most vital factor in the labour situation was the trade union movement. Trade unionism, which is essentially pragmatic, struggles constantly not only against the employers for an enlarged opportunity measure in income, security and liberty in the shop and industry, but struggles also, whether consciously or unconsciously, actively or passively, against the intellectual who would frame its programmes and shape its policies.

   But Perlman also felt that a theory of the labour movement should include a theory of the psychology of the labouring man. For instance, there was a historical continuity between the guilds and trade unions, through their common fundamental psychology; the psychology of seeking a livelihood in the face of limited economic opportunity. It was when manual workers became aware of a scarcity of opportunity, that they banded together into unions for the purpose of protecting their jobs and distributing employment opportunities among themselves equitably, and to subordinate the interests of the individual to the whole labour organism. Unionism was ruled thus by this fundamental scarcity consciousness (Perlman, 1970).

7. **Hoxies Functional Classification of Unionism:** He classified Unionism on the basis of their functions. His classification were Business Unionism for protecting the interest of various craftmen, "Uplift unionism" for the purpose of contributing better life such as association of sales engineers etc. "Revolutionary Unionism" which is eager to replace existing social order, "Predatory Unionism" which rests on these support of others.

8. **Tannenbaum's Theory of Man Vs. Machine:** According to him Union is formed in reaction to alienation and loss of community in an individualistic and unfeeling society. In his words, the union returns to the workers his society, which he left behind him when he migrated from a rural background to the anonymity of an urban industrial location. The union gives the worker a fellowship and a value system that he shares with others like him. Institutionally, the trade union movement is an unconscious effort to harness the drift of our time and reorganise it around the cohesive identity that men working together always achieve.

7.9. WORKPLACE RELATIONS

- Continuing high levels of unemployment, massive foreign debt, declining relative standards of living and ever-increasing competition are creating pressures for more workplace relations reform.
- Higher productivity translates into higher wages, better jobs and improved job security.
- All parties agree reform is inevitable.
- The problem is obtaining consensus about the type and degree of change necessary.
- The way people view the challenges of reform is in large part influenced by their perspective on workplace relations.

Approaches to workplace relations

- Some perceive workplace relations in terms of class conflict, others in terms of mutual cooperation and others still in terms of groups with competing interests.

- Human resource managers need to understand these varying approaches because they provide the ideological underpinning for much of the debate about workplace reform and the role of HRM.

1. Unitary approach

- Workplace conflict is seen as a temporary aberration, resulting from poor management, employees who do not fit with the organisation's culture or trade union activity.
- Trade unions are regarded as competitors for the employee's commitment and cooperation.
- The underlying assumption is that it is to the benefit of all to focus on common interests and promote harmony. Conflict in the form of strikes, therefore, is regarded as not only unnecessary, but destructive.
- Advocates of the unitary approach seek a radical overhaul of the industrial relations system. Emphasis is on direct negotiations with employees.

2. Pluralist approach

- In contrast to the unitary approach, the pluralist approach sees:
- organisations as coalitions of competing interests, where management's role is to mediate among the different interest groups
- trade unions as legitimate representatives of employee interests
- stability in workplace relations as the product of concessions and compromises between management and unions.

3. Marxist approach

- Marxists, like the pluralists, regard conflict between management and employees as inevitable.
- However, where pluralists see conflict inherent in all organisations, Marxists see if as a product of a capitalist society.
- Adversarial relations in the workplace are simply one aspect of class conflict.
- The Marxist approach thus focuses on the type of society in which an organisation exists.
- For the Marxist, therefore, all strikes are political.

4. Trade unions

- The old system of compulsory arbitration encouraged trade unionism.
- Union concerns have traditionally focused on pay rates, conditions of work and job security.
- Increasingly, however, unions are moving away from these bread and butter issues and adopting an approach of *strategic unionism* that includes industrial democracy, social welfare, training, industrial policy and taxation.
- Moreover, because most awards, determinations and industrial agreements set only minimum rates and conditions, unions also seek to negotiate above-award concessions from employers. Some unions see enterprise bargaining as being limited to just that.

Workplace-Level Grievances

- Grievances are the product of employee dissatisfaction or feelings of injustice.
- Listen carefully to what the employee says and try to distinguish between facts and feelings.
- Managers should be sure that they have all of the relevant facts.
- Avoid lengthy delays.
- Managers should also recognise that sometimes a union is placed in the awkward position of having to argue a case it does not genuinely support.
- The successful handling of grievances is related to the attitudes of the parties involved.

- Tribunal-Level Grievances
- When a grievance cannot be resolved at the workplace level, a HR manager may need to present his or her organisation's case before an industrial tribunal such as the IRC.
- HR managers must develop the skills and confidence to take (and be given) the responsibility for advocacy.

Features of Enterprise Bargaining Agreements

- Emphasis on developing a workplace culture that encourages enhanced productivity and efficiency
- Promotion of mutual discussion between employers and employees in a conflict-free environment
- A focus on customer satisfaction with an emphasis on product and service quality as a means of becoming more competitive
- An emphasis on the need to implement workplace change to ensure the survival of the enterprise by becoming internationally competitive

7.10. TRADE UNION MOVEMENT

- The trade union movement started after 1918, when the workers formed their associations to improve their conditions. It is, thus, a part of the 'labour movement', which is a much wide term.
- A trade union is an essential basis of a labour movement for without which one cannot exist, because trade unions are the principal schools in which the workers learn the lesson of self-reliance and solidarity.
- Trade Unionism in India has been the natural outcome of the modern factory system.
- The main elements in the development of trade unions of workers in every country have been more or less the same.
- The development of trade unionism in India has had a checkered history and a stormy career.

Growth of Trade union movement

1. Social Welfare Period (1875-1918)

o The development of industries led to large-scale production on the one hand and social evils like employment and exploitation of women and child labour and the deplorable workable conditions, the government's attitude of complete indifference in respect of protection of labour from such evils, on the other.

2. Early Trade Union Period (1918-1924)

o The year 1918 was an important one for the Indian trade union movement.

o The industrial unrest that grew up as a result of grave economic difficulties created by war. The rising cost of living prompted the workers to demand reasonable wages for which purpose they united to take resort to collective action.

3. Left-Wing Unionism Period (1924-1934)

o In 1924, a violent and long-drawn-out strike by unions led to the arrest, prosecution, conviction and imprisonment of many communist leaders. The rapid growth of the trade unionism was facilitated by several factors

4. Trade Union's Unity Period (1935-1938)

- In mid-thirties the state of divided labour movement was natural thought undesirable and soon after the first split, attempts at trade union unity began to be made through the efforts of the Roy Group on the basis of 'a platform of unity'.

5. Second World War Period (1939-1945)

- The Second World War, which broke out in September 1939, created new strains in the united trade union movement.
- Hence, again a rift took place in 1941 and the Radicals left the AITUC with nearly 200 unions with a membership of 3, 00,000 and formed a new central federation known as the Indian Federation of Labour.

6. The Post-Independence Period (From 1947 to-date)

- As pointed out earlier, when attempts to restructure the AITUC failed, those believing in the aims and ideals other than those of the AITUC separated from the organization and established the Indian National Trade Union Congress (INTUC) in May, 1947

7.10.1. Trade Unionism in India

Indian trade union movement can be divided into three phases.

1. Phase-I: 1850 to1900
2. Phase-II: 1900 to 1946
3. Phase-III: In 1947

Trade Union Act, 1926

- Passed on 25 March 1926
- The trade Unions Act, 1926 provides for registration of trade unions with a view to render lawful organisation of labour to enable collective bargaining. It also confers on a registered trade union certain protection and privileges.
- The Act extends to the whole of India and applies to all kinds of unions of workers and associations of employers, which aim at regularizing labor management relations. A Trade Union is a combination whether temporary or permanent, formed for regulating the relations not only between workmen and employers but also between workmen and workmen or between employers and employers.

Structure of Unions

1. Craft Unions
2. General Unions
3. Industrial Unions
4. Federation and Confederations

Major Trade unions in India

1. All India Trade Union Congress (AITUC)-1920
2. Indian National Trade Union Congress (INTUC)-1969
3. United Trade Union Congress (UTUC)-1949
4. All India Railwaymen's Federation(AIRF)-1922
5. Bharatiya Mazdoor Sangh (BMS)-1955
6. National Front of Indian Trade Unions (NFITU)
7. Hind Mazdoor Kisan Panchayat (HMKP)-1965

8. Centre of Indian Trade Unions (CITU)-1970
9. Hind Mazdoor Sabha (HMS)-1948
10. Indian Federation of Free Trade Unions (IFFTU)
11. National Labor Organization (NLO)
12. Trade Unions Co-ordination Centre (TUCC)
13. United Trade Union Congress - Lenin Sarani (UTUC - LS)

Details of some Unions in India

1. All-India Trade Union Congress (AITUC)

Origin:

- It was established in 1920 as result of a resolution passed by the organized workers of Bombay and the delegates which met I a conference on 31st October, 1920.

Objectives:

- to establish a socialist state in India;
- to socialize and nationalize means of production, distribution and exchange;
- to improve the economic and social conditions of the working class;
- to watch, promote, and further the interests, rights, and privileges of the workers in all matters relating to their employment;
- to secure and maintain for the workers the freedom of speech, freedom of press, freedom of association freedom of assembly, the right to strike, and the right to work and maintenance;
- to co-ordinate the activities of the labour unions affiliated to the AITUC;
- to abolish political or economic advantage based on caste, creed, community, race or religion;
- to secure and maintain for the workers the right to strike

Political Affiliations

- The AITUC is pro-communist. It is led by the Right **Communist Party of Inia (CPI)**. Its attitude towards the government is not entirely hostile, but of course highly critical of the government.

2. The Indian National Trade Union Congress (INTUC)

Origin:

- The INTUC came into existence on 4th May, 1948, as a result of the resolution passed on 17th November 1947, by the Central Board of the Hindustan Mazdoor Sevak Sangh, which was a labour leader on the Gandhian Philosophy of Sarvodaya

Objectives:

- To establish an order of society which is free from hindrances to an all-round development of its individual members, which fosters the growth of human personality in all its aspects, and which goes to the utmost limit in progressively eliminating social, political or economic exploitation and inequality, the profit motive in the economic activity and organization of society and the anti-social concentration of power in any form;
- to place industry under national ownership and control in a suitable form;
- to secure increasing association of workers in the administration of industry and their full participation in that control;

Political Affiliations

- On the international level, the INTUC is affiliated to the International Confederation of Free Trade Unions (ICFTU) – an organization mainly supported by the Anglo American block; while the AITUC is affiliated to the World Federation of Trade Unions (WFTU), supported by the Communist block.

3. United Trade Union Congress (UTUC)

Origin:

- Some trade union leaders of the socialist bent met together December 1948 to form a new central organization of labour, called Hind Mazdoor Sabha

Objectives:

- The objectives of the UTUC are:
- to establish a socialist society in India;
- to establish a workers' and peasants' state in India;
- to nationalize and socialize the means of production, distribution and exchange;
- to safeguard and promote the interests, rights, and privileges to the workers in all matters, social, cultural, economic and political;
- to secure and maintain workers' freedom of speech, freedom of press, freedom of association, freedom of assembly, right to strike, right to work or maintenance and the right to social security;
- to bring about unity in the trade union movement.

Political Affiliations

- The UTUC is radical, non-communist and anti-INTUC. It is led by some independent trade union leaders, the Forward Block and the Revolutionary Socialist Party.

4. Bhartiya Mazdoor Sangh (BMS)

Origin:

- This union has been the outcome of decision taken by the Jana Sangh in its Convention at Bhopal on 23rd July, 1954.

Objectives:

- to establish the Bhartiya order of classless society in which there shall be secured full employment;
- to assist workers in organizing themselves in trade unions as medium of service to the motherland irrespective of faiths and political affinities;
- the right to strike;
- to inculcate in the minds of the workers the spirit of service, co-operation and dutifulness and develop in them a sense of responsibility towards the nation in general and the industry in particular.
- The BMS is a productivity-oriented non-political trade union. Its ideological basis is the triple formula:
- nationalize the labour;
- labourise the industry;
- industrialize the nation;

5. National Front of Indian Trade Unions (NFITU)

Origin

- This union was founded in 1967, with the claim that "this trade union of India is not controlled by any of the political party, employers or government."

Objectives:

- to organize and unite trade unions with the object of building up a National Central Organisation of trade unions, independent of political parties, employers and the government, to further the cause of labour and that of national solidarity security and defence of India, and to make the working people conscious of their right as well as of obligations in all spheres of life;
- to secure to members of trade unions full facilities of recognition and effective representation of interests of workers and to ensure for the working people fair conditions of life and service and progressively to raise their social, economic and cultural state and conditions;
- to help in every possible way member trade unions in their fight to raise real wages of the workers;
- to endeavour to secure for members of affiliated trade unions adoption of progressive legislation for their welfare and to ensure the effective environment of the rights and interests of members of affiliated trade unions and for the working people in general.

6. Centre of Indian Trade Union (CITU)

Origin

- This union was formed in 1970 when as a result of the rift in the AITUC, some members of the Communist party seceded. About the objectives of the CITU, its constitution says:

Objectives:

- The CITU believes that the exploitation of the working class can be ended only by socializing all means of production, distribution and exchange and establishing a socialist state, that is, it stands for the complete emancipation of the society from all exploitation.
- The CITU fights against all encroachments on the economic and social rights of the workers and the enlargement of their rights and liberties including the right to strike, for winning, defending and extending the freedom of the democratic trade union movement.
- In the fight for the immediate interest of the working class the CITU demands: (a) nationalization of all foreign monopoly concerns who barbarously exploit the working class; (b) nationalization of all concerns owned by Indian monopolists and big industry who garner huge profits at the expenses of the workers, who exploit the people by pegging prices at a high level and who dictate the anti-labour and anti-people policies of the government.
- The CITU fights against the repressive policy of the government towards the democratic and trade union movement.

Political Affiliation of Trade Unions

1. All India Central Council of Trade Unions (Communist Party of India (Marxist-Leninist) Liberation)
2. All India Trade Union Congress (Communist Party of India)
3. All India United Trade Union Centre (Socialist Unity Centre of India (Communist))
4. Bharatiya Mazdoor Sangh (Rashtriya Swayamsevak Sangh)
5. Indian National Trade Union Congress (Indian National Congress)
6. New Trade Union Initiative (Independent from political parties, but left)
7. Centre of Indian Trade Unions (Communist Party of India (Marxist))

8. Hind Mazdoor Sabha (socialists)
9. Labour Progressive Federation (Dravida Munnetra Kazhagam)
10. Trade Union Coordination Committee (All India Forward Bloc)
11. United Trade Union Congress (Revolutionary Socialist Party)
12. Akhil Bharatiya Kamgar Sena (Akhil Bharatiya Sena)
13. All India Federation of Trade Unions (marxist-leninists)
14. Bharatiya Kamgar Sena (Shiv Sena)
15. Bharatiya Mazdoor Sabha (Provisional Central Committee, Communist Party of India (Marxist-Leninist))
16. Hind Mazdoor Kisan Panchayat (Janata Dal (United))
17. Indian Federation of Trade Unions (Communist Party of India (Marxist-Leninist) New Democracy)

7.11 INDUSTRIAL RELATIONS AND THE NEW ECONOMIC REFORM

Status of Trade Union after Globalization:

The trade union membership, activities and influence on management have been declining after globalisation.

- Proactive approach by employers
- Profit sharing and employee stock option scheme(ESOPS)
- Prevention of trade union of by employers
- Less Interest of new job entrants
- Software professionals
- Increase in educational level
- Decline in membership

7.12. OBJECTIVE QUESTIONS - ANSWER

1. Who defined Industrial Relation as a "Rule Making Process"?
(A) Robert Hoxie (B) Selig Perlman
(C) John T. Dunlop (D) Mc Kersie
Answer: C

2. Who are the three major actors of Industrial Relations?
(A) Workers (B) Employers
(C) Government (D) All the above
Answer: D

3. Which of the following factors is helpful in promoting peaceful industrial relations?
(A) Mutual understanding
(B) Freedom of expression
(C) Freedom of Association and collective Bargaining
(D) All the above
Answer: D

4. Which of the following is not true in regard to the approaches to industrial Relations ?
(A) Giri Approach
(B) Dunlop Approach
(C) Nehru Approach
(D) Gandhi Approach
Answer: C

5. "Formulation of rules and their implementation are the bread and butter of industrial relations" is commented by
(A) John T. Dunlop
(B) Alvin W. Gouldner
(C) Allan Flanders
(D) Kochan
Answer: A

6. Who said, there are three actors of industrial relations?
(A) Lester (B) Dale yoder
(C) Dunlop (D) Krikardy
Answer: C

7. Good industrial relations refer to :
(A) Absence of industrial disputes
(B) Greater use of Collective Bargaining
(C) Friendly attitude of Employer and Trade Unions
(D) All the above
Answer: D

8. Find out the approach which does not include industrial relations
(A) Psychological approach
(B) Sociological approach
(C) Human relations approach
(D) Physiological approach
Answer: D

9. Joint Consultative Board (J.C.B.) of industry and labour was set up in 1951 with the initiative of :
(A) V.V. Giri (B) G.L. Nanda
(C) Morarji Desai (D) Jagjivan Ram
Answer: B

10. Three tier framework of industrial relations was proposed by :
(A) Kochan, T.A., et. al
(B) Richardson J.H.
(C) Clark Kerr
(D) John T. Dunlop
Answer: A

11. A system of industrial relations where social and labour issues are discussed between trade unions and management at enterprise level is :
(A) Bipartism
(B) Tripartism
(C) Social dialogue
(D) None of the above
Answer: A

12. Which one is not of Michael Porters five force model of industry analysis
(A) Threat of new entrants
(B) Substitutes
(C) Intensity of rivalry among existing players
(D) Cost leadership
Answer: D

13. The relations between government and transnational corporations are divided into liberal, neo-mercantilist and neo-imperialist categories by :
(A) Richardson, J.H.
(B) Clark Kerr
(C) Kochan, T.A., et.al
(D) John T. Dunlop
Answer: C

14. Who proposed that industrial relations activities take place among three principal social partners at three levels ?
(A) John T. Dunlop
(B) Richardson, J.H.
(C) Kochan, T.A. et.al
(D) Clark Kerr
Answer: C

15. Characteristics of Industrial Relations do not include :
(A) Industrial Relations are outcome of employment relationship in an industrial enterprise.
(B) Industrial Relations promote the skills and methods of adjustment and co-operation with each other.
(C) Industrial Relations create complex rules and regulations to maintain cordial relations.
(D) Industrial Relations system creates an environment of distrust and conflict.
Answer: D

16. Who are not the Actors of Industrial Relations?
(A) Workers and their organizations
(B) Employers and their organizations
(C) Community and cultural associations
(D) Government and the role of the State
Answer: C

17. Which of the following cannot be said to be a body in the field of industrial relations?
(A) Joint Management Council
(B) Works Committee
(C) Shop Level Council
(D) Canteen Committee
Answer: D

18. Which one of the following is not a necessary condition for establishing and maintaining good industrial relations?
(A) Keep the employees informed about decision which affect their interests
(B) Payment of fair wages and adequate wage structure
(C) Maintain good relations with nearby industries
(D) Establishment of an atmosphere of participation
Answer: A

19. The scope of industrial relations does not include
(A) Employer and Employee relations
(B) Employer and Trade Union relations.
(C) Employer, Employee and Trade Union relations.
(D) Employer and Customer relations.
Answer: D

20. Who are not the actors according to Dunlop's framework of industrial relations system?
(A) Managers and their representatives
(B) Workers and their organizations
(C) Specialized government agencies
(D) Communities and their associations
Answer: D

21. Identify the correct definition of industrial relations:
(A) Relations between or among human beings
(B) Relations between employer and employees as individuals
(C) Relations between parties in an employment context
(D) Collective relationship between management and trade unions
Answer: D

22. Which of the following is not included under the concept of industrial relations?
(A) Employer - Union Relations
(B) Employer - State Relations
(C) Employer - Customer Relations
(D) Employer - Union State Relations
Answer: C

23. Who has propounded the system concept of industrial relations? Find out from the following :
(A) L. N. Allen Flander
(B) L. N. Flax
(C) John T. Dunlop
(D) Neil N. Chamberlein
Answer: C

24. The concept of industrial relations is :
(A) Static
(B) Dynamic
(C) Both Static and Dynamic
(D) None of the above
Answer: C

25. Who among the following gave a model for industrial relations?
(A) Harold J. Laski
(B) Adam Smith
(C) John T. Dunlop
(D) Heneman
Answer: C

26. Match the following :

List - I	List - II
(a) Trusteeship Theory	(i) Elton Mayo
(b) Revolutionary Theory	(ii) Labour welfare
(c) Placating Theory	(iii) Karl Marx
(d) Human Relations Theory	(iv) Gandhi

Code :

	(a)	(b)	(c)	(d)
(A)	(iv)	(iii)	(ii)	(i)
(B)	(iii)	(iv)	(i)	(ii)
(C)	(iv)	(i)	(ii)	(iii)
(D)	(i)	(iii)	(ii)	(iv)

Answer: A

27. Who observed that the respect for rules depends on the manner of their formulation?
(A)Web, S. and Web, B.
(B) Flanders, A.
(C) Durkheim, E.
(D) Gouldner, A.
Answer: C

28. The Origin, growth and development of employment's organizations in India can be identified as :
(A) Before 1933 (B) After 1933
(C) Before 1947 (D) After 1947
Answer: A

29. The concept/theory of industrial capitalism / dialectical materialism was developed by :
(A) Karl Marx
(B) Mahatma Gandhi
(C) Dunlop J. T.
(D) Thakur C. P.
Answer: A

30. TheInternational Organization of Employer's (I.O.E) with headquarters in Genevas was formulated in
(A) 1910 (B) 1920
(C) 1930 (D) 1940
Answer: B

31. Benefits (India) of globalization like sustained economic growth, free markets, economic globalization, privatisation etc., were summarised by :
(A) First National Commission on Labour
(B) Second National Commission on Labour
(C) National Labour Board
(D) International Labour Organisation
Answer: B

32. Globalization is ruthless, rootless, jobless, fruitless was stated by :
(A) U. N. O (B) U. N. D. P

(C) I. L. O (D) W. H. O.

Answer: B

33. Who said "Industrial Societies necessarily create industrial relations defined as complex of interrelations among workers, managers and governments" :

(A) John T. Dunlop
(B) P.H. Casselman
(C) I.L.O.
(D) None of the above

Answer: A

34. Fill up the blanks from one of the suitable words given in the bracket "Select the correct combination":

(i) Award,
(ii) Bi - partite Body,
(iii) Tripartite Body,
(iv) Check off,
(v) Deduction,
(vi) International Federation,
(vii) Settlement,
(viii) Consultative body

(a) The decision of Labour Court is called __________
(b) Canteen Committee is a __________
(c) Deduction of union membership fee is called __________
(d) I.L.O. is a __________

(A) (ii), (v), (vi), (viii)
(B) (viii), (iv), (ii), (i)
(C) (i), (ii), (iv), (iii)
(D) (iii), (v), (vii), (i)

Answer: C

35. Match the following

(a) ILO	(i) USSR
(b) Karl Marx	(ii) Geneva
(c) Award	(iii) Conciliation
(d) Settlement	(iv) Arbitration

(A) (a) - (i), (b) - (iii), (c) - (iv), (d) - (ii)
(B) (a) - (iv), (b) - (ii), (c) - (iii), (d) - (i)
(C) (a) - (ii), (b) - (i), (c) - (iv), (d) - (iii)
(D) (a) - (iii), (b) - (iv), (c) - (ii), (d) - (i)

Answer: C

36. Arrange the following in proper sequence :

(i) Establishment of the Indian Labour Conference
(ii) First Bombay Factory Commission
(iii) Submission of the Report of the Royal Commission on Labour
(iv) Establishment of the ILO

(A) (ii), (iv), (iii), (i)
(B) (iv), (ii), (iii), (i)
(C) (iii), (ii), (iv), (i)
(D) (i), (ii), (iii), (iv)

Answer: A

37. Arrange the following in a proper sequence according to the year in which they came into existence :

a. Indian Labour Conference
b. Defence of India Rules
c. Industrial Disputes Act
d. Scheme of Labour Management Co-operation (Joint Management Councils)
e. First National Commission on Labour
f. Workers' participation in management in Industries
g. Second National Commission on Labour

(A) a, c, d, e, f, g, b
(B) b, a, c, d, e, f, g
(C) c, d, e, f, g, a, b
(D) d, e, f, g, a, b, c

Answer: B

38. First time the May Day was celebrated in India in :

(A) 1923 (B) 1927
(C) 1935 (D) 1947

Answer: A

The first May Day celebration in India was organised in Madras by the Labour Kisan Party of Hindustan on 1 May 1923.This was also the first time the red flag was used in India.The party leader Singaravelu Chettiar made arrangements to celebrate May Day in two places in 1923.

39. The provisions regarding equal pay for equal work to men and women are provided under which of the following :
(A) Fundamental Rights
(B) Directive Principles of State Policy
(C) Preamble
(D) In all the above

Answer : B

40. There is only one source of authority – management. They own and, therefore, they control – is the argument of
(A) Pluralists
(B) Radicalists
(C) Trusteeship
(D) Unitarists

Answer : D

41. Match List – I with List – II :

List – I

a. Joint Management Council consisting of representatives of workers and management was considered by the Indian Labour Conference (ILC) in its 15th Session in the year
b. Works Committees were set-up under the Industrial Disputes Act in the year c. ILO established in the year.
c. ILO established in the year
d. First National Commission on Labour submitted its report in the year

List – II

i. 1958
ii. 1947
iii. 1919
iv. 1969

Codes :

	A	b	c	d
(A)	i	ii	iii	iv
(B)	iv	I	iii	ii
(C)	iii	I	ii	iv
(D)	ii	iv	I	ii

Answer: A

42. Which of the following trends in the employment relations in the new economic era is not correct ?
(A) Declining stability and security
(B) Declining labour intensity
(C) No shift from contract of service to contract of service
(D) Declining mutual commitment

Answer : C

43. Match the following :

List – I	List – II
a. Human Capital	i. David Mcclelland
b. Socio-Psychological Approach	ii. UNDP
c. Poverty Alleviation Approach	iii.T.W. Scultz
d. World Human Development Approach	iv. World Bank

Codes :

	a	b	c	d
(A)	ii	iv	i	iii
(B)	iii	iv	ii	i
(C)	iii	i	iv	ii
(D)	iv	ii	i	iii

Answer: C

44. A wilful disobedience of authority is called :
(A) Insubordination
(B) Indiscipline
(C) Wilful disobedience
(D) Misconduct

Answer: A

45. Which of the following is not within the scope of "Adjudication"?
(A) Conciliation
(B) Labour Court
(C) Industrial Tribunal
(D) National Tribunal

Answer: A

46. Outplacement services are provided to employees who have been :
(A) Dismissed
(B) Rendered surplus
(C) Retired
(D) Given voluntary retirement

Answer: A

47. What notice period is required for going on strike/lockout in public utility services ?
(A) One week (B) Three weeks
(C) Six weeks (D) Nine weeks
Answer: C

48. A situation where management is unable to provide employment due to non-availability of work is called :
I. Lock out
II. Lay off
III. Termination
IV. Closure
Find the correct combination according to the code.
(A) I & II (B) II & III
(C) I & III (D) II & IV
Answer: D

49. Which one of the settlement methods is not relevant here for disputes ?
(A) Collective Bargaining
(B) Compulsory Adjudication
(C) Voluntary Arbitration
(D) Reference to Civil Court
Answer: D

50. Lock out means
(A) An antithesis of strike
(B) Refusal to employ any person in employment
(C) The temporary closing of a place of employment
(D) Illegal strike
Answer: C

51. The problem of industrial discipline was debated by the Indian Labour Conference (ILC) held in India in
(A) 1948 (B) 1952
(C) 1957 (D) 1960
Answer: C

52. The outside third party who is brought into settle a dispute, and he or she has the authority to make a decision is called
(A) Government (B) An Arbitrator
(C) Union (D) Legal Expert
Answer: B

53. Changes in the population characteristics such as age, gender, marital status, income and education are the examples of
(A) Demographic characteristics
(B) Cultural characteristics
(C) Geographic characteristics
(D) None of the above
Answer: A

54. 'Rege Committee' is related to
(A) Working conditions in Indian Industry
(B) Social security in Indian Industry
(C) Individual differences in Indian Industry
(D) None of the above
Answer: A

55. The first stage of conflict resolution is to
(A) Analyze the problem
(B) Choose a solution
(C) Think through possible solutions
(D) Define the problem
Answer: D

56. Which is the correct order of settlement of industrial disputes?
a. Industrial Tribunal
b. National Tribunal
c. Conciliation
d. Labour Court
(A) c, a, d, b (B) c, d, a, b
(C) a, d, c, b (D) c, b, d, a
Answer: B

57. An enquiry that is conducted afresh because of the objections raised by alleged employee is called
(A) Domestic enquiry
(B) De-novo enquiry
(C) Ex-parte enquiry
(D) None of the above
Answer: C

58. Which of the following is a machinery for settlement of industrial disputes ?

(A) Indian Labour Conference
(B) Joint Management Council
(C) Industrial Tribunal
(D) Standing Labour Committees

Answer: C

59. Which of the following is not a machinery for settlement of industrial disputes in India?

(A) Indian Labour Conference and Standing Labour Committee
(B) Conciliation officers
(C) Labour Court
(D) National Tribunal

Answer: A

60. Which of the following is/are the methods of settlement of Industrial Disputes?

(A) Negotiation
(B) Conciliation
(C) Both A and B
(D) None of the above

Answer: B

61. Arrange the following dispute settlement methods in order of their applications :

(i) Conciliation / Mediation
(ii) Adjudication
(iii) Voluntary Arbitration
(iv) Collective Bargaining

(A)	(iv)	(i)	(iii)	(ii)
(B)	(iv)	(iii)	(ii)	(i)
(C)	(i)	(iv)	(iii)	(ii)
(D)	(i)	(iii)	(iv)	(ii)

Answer: B

62. Which one of the following methods is regarded as the most ideal for settlement of Industrial Dispute?

(A) Adjudication
(B) Mediation / Conciliation
(C) Collective Bargaining
(D) Voluntary Arbitration

Answer: C

63. Which of the following is not a machinery for settlement of industrial disputes in India ?

(A) Board of Conciliation
(B) Labour Court
(C) Collective Bargaining
(D) Industrial Tribunal

Answer: A

64. Match the following :

(a) Conciliation Machinery (i) Indian Labour Conference
(b) Consultation Machinery (ii) Industrial Tribunal
(c) Adjudication Machinery (iii) Arbitration
(d) Arbitration Machinery (iv) Board of Conciliation

	(a)	(b)	(c)	(d)
(A)	(iii)	(ii)	(i)	(iv)
(B)	(ii)	(iii)	(iv)	(i)
(C)	(iv)	(i)	(ii)	(iii)
(D)	(i)	(iv)	(iii)	(ii)

Answer: C

65. Match the following :

(Method)	**(Product)**
(a) Conciliation	(i) Report
(b) Collective Bargaining	(ii) Award
(c) Investigation	(iii) Settlement
(d) Adjudication	(iv) Agreement

Code:

	(a)	(b)	(c)	(d)
(A)	(iii)	(i)	(ii)	(iv)
(B)	(iii)	(iv)	(i)	(ii)
(C)	(ii)	(i)	(iii)	(iv)
(D)	(iv)	(iii)	(i)	(ii)

Answer: D

66. Match List-I with List-II.

List-I	**List-II**
(a) Strike	(i) The action of employer is temporarily closing down his undertaking.
(b) Lockout	(ii) Refusal of the employer to employ the workers because of coal, power and raw material.

(c) Lay-off	(iii) Temporary cessation of work by a group of employees in order to express their grievances.
(d) Closure	(iv)Permanently closing down of the establishment by the employer.

Codes :

	(a)	(b)	(c)	(d)
(A)	(iii)	(i)	(ii)	(iv)
(B)	(iii)	(ii)	(iv)	(i)
(C)	(ii)	(iii)	(i)	(iv)
(D)	(i)	(iii)	(iv)	(ii)

Answer: A

67. Which of the following is not an adjudication machinery under the Industrial Disputes Act ?
(A) Labour Court
(B) Court of Enquiry
(C) Industrial Tribunal
(D) National Tribunal
Answer: B

68. In Industrial Disputes Act, 1947; which one of the following is not an adjudication Machinery ?
(A) Labour Court
(B) Industrial Tribunal
(C) National Tribunal
(D) Court of Enquiry
Answer: D

69. Find the machinery which is not method of settlement of industrial dispute :
(A) consultation
(B) works committee
(C) conciliation
(D) Adjudication
Answer: A

70. Who considered collective bargaining as the most important concept for determining the terms and conditions of employment
(A) Sidney and Beatrice Webb
(B) Robert Hoxie
(C) John T.Dunlop
(D) Samuel Gompers
Answer: D

71. Find out the characteristics of collective bargaining which is not applicable;
(A) It is a collective process.
(B) It is a flexible process.
(C) It is not a bipartile process.
(D) It is interdisciplinary system.
Answer: C

72. Who has started that "Collective bargaining is essentially a process in which employees act as a group in seeking to shape conditions and relationships in their employment.
(A) R. F. Hoxie
(B) L. G. Reynolds
(C) Dale Yoder
(D) J. F. Richardson
Answer: C

73. Who among the following advocated the use of collective bargaining as the best method for promoting healthy labour management relations in India ?
(A) Mahatma Gandhi
(B) Guljarilal Nanda
(C) Khandubhai Desai
(D) V.V. Giri
Answer: D

74. Which part of the wages is governed by the escalatory clause in a collective bargaining agreement ?
(A) Basic Wage
(B) Dearness Allowance
(C) Wage Incentives
(D) None of the above
Answer: C

75. Which of the following countries is said to be the home of collective bargaining?
(A) United Kingdom
(B) United States of America
(C) Sweden

(D) France

Answer: A

76. Match the following :

List – I	List – II
(a) Collective Bargaining	(i) Institutions set up by the Government for fixation and revision of wages.
(b) Wage Boards	(ii) It is a procedure in which compromise is reached through balancing of opposed strengths.
(c) Wage	(iii) Remuneration paid to the clerical and managerial personnel on monthly or annual basis.
(d) Salary	(iv) Remuneration paid by the employer for the services of hourly, daily, weekly and fortnightly employees.

	(a)	(b)	(c)	(d)
(A)	(i)	(ii)	(iii)	(iv)
(B)	(iv)	(ii)	(i)	(iii)
(C)	(ii)	(iv)	(i)	(iii)
(D)	(ii)	(i)	(iv)	(iii)

Answer: D

77. The first to introduce the term collective bargaining :

(A) Sidney and Beatrice webb

(B) Samuel Gompers

(C) Clark Kerr

(D) Robert Hoxie

Answer: A

78. Grievance is

(A) A feeling of dissatisfaction.

(B) A dispute raised by a trade union.

(C) Refusal of the management of a demand.

(D) An act of indiscipline.

Answer: A

79. Which is not the characteristics of grievances?

(A) Factual (B) Fabricated

(C) Disguised (D) Imaginary

Answer: B

80. The grievance arising out of legitimate needs of employees remaining unfulfilled may be termed as :

(A) Disguised Grievance

(B) Imaginary Grievance

(C) Factual Grievance

(D) Work-Group Grievance

Answer: C

81. Consider the following punishments in disciplinary actions :

(i) Warning (ii) Demotion

(iii) Censure (iv) Dismissal

Which of the above fall under minor punishment?

(A) (i) and (ii)

(B) (i), (ii) and (iii)

(C) (i) and (iii)

(D) (i), (ii) and (iv)

Answer: C

82. Who said 'as discipline is a control of management on employee, grievance is a control of employee on management'

(A) Michael J. Jucius

(B) Richard P. Calhoon

(C) Windell French

(D) Dale Yoder

Answer: D

83. Which of the following has not been provided under the provisions of the code of discipline?
(A) Trade union recognition
(B) Unfair Labour practices
(C) Grievance handling
(D) Worker's participation in management
Answer: D

84. Consider the following punishments :
(i) Warning or censure
(ii) Demotion
(iii) Fine and withholding of increments
(iv) Discharge and dismissal
Which of the above fall under the minor punishments?
(A) (i) and (ii) (B) (i), (ii) and (iii)
(C) (i) and (iii) (D) (i), (ii) and (iv)
Answer: C

85. Which of the following is/are the essence of model grievance procedure?
(A) Settlement at the lower level
(B) Settlement as expeditiously as possible
(C) Settlement to the satisfaction of the aggrieved
(D) All the above
Answer: D

86. The Code of Discipline makes provisions for which of the following :
(A) Unfair Labour practices
(B) Grievance redressal
(C) Recognition of Trade Union
(D) All the above
Answer: D

87. If a employees have given letters, memos and documents to study the organization policy is called:
(A) Business games
(B) Role play
(C) In tray activity
(D) Case studies
Answer: C

Explanation: In-tray and case study exercises are designed to simulate a real work situation. They are a very common exercise at assessment centres.

88. An enquiry that is conducted afresh because of the objections raised by alleged employee, is called :
(A) ex-parte enquiry
(B) domestic enquiry
(C) de-novo enquiry
(D) none of the above
Answer: B

89. Arrange the sequence followed in a disciplinary procedure.
(i) Charge sheet
(ii) Reporting the misconduct
(iii) Awarding the punishment
(iv) Domestic enquiry
(A) (i), (ii), (iv), (iii)
(B) (i), (iii), (ii), (iv)
(C) (ii), (i), (iv), (iii)
(D) (ii), (iv), (i), (iii)
Answer: D

90. **Assertion (A):** Grievance and Discipline are mutually complementary control mechanisms.
Reason (R): Discipline is a control of the management on employee and Grievance is a control of the employee on the management.
(A) (A) is right but (R) is wrong
(B) Both (A) and (R) are wrong
(C) (A) is wrong and (R) is right
(D) Both (A) and (R) are right
Answer: B

91. The headquarters of Central Board for Workers' Education is located at______.
(A) New Delhi (B) Mumbai
(C) Chennai (D) Nagpur
Answer: D

92. Which of the following statements about workers' participation in Management in

India is not true ?
(A) It is a part of the 20 point Economic programme.
(B) It is provided in the Directive Principles of State Policy.
(C) It is made a Constitutional provision under the 42nd Amendment Act.
(D) It is a justiceable right of the workers.

Answer: D

93. The Scheme of Workers' Participation in Management as provided under the 20 point programme, 1975 did not provide for
(A) Shop Councils
(B) Unit Councils
(C) Joint Councils
(D)None of the above

Answer: B

94. The coverage of workers' participation under a comprehensive labour relations legislation was recommended by
(A) The First National Commission on Labour, 1969
(B) The Second National Commission on Labour,2002
(C) Participation of Workers' in Management Bill, 1990
(D) Scheme of Employees Participation in Public Sector Undertakings (1983)

Answer: A

95. Which part of the Indian Constitution bears provisions relating to workers' participation in management?
(A) The Preamble
(B) The Directive Principles of State Policy
(C) Fundamental Rights
(D) None of the above

Answer: B

96. Which one of the following is called the World Parliament of Labour ?
(A) Governing body of ILO
(B) International Labour Conference
(C) United Nations
(D) UNICEF

Answer: A

97. The scheme of workers participation in Management was introduced by Government of India in:
(A) 1965 (B) 1975
(C) 1985 (D) 1995

Answer: B

98. To which of the following the two voluntary schemes of workers' participation in management introduced in the year 1975 and 1977 do not apply :
(A) Manufacturing
(B) Mining Industries
(C) Commercial and Service Organisations
(D) Central Public Sector Undertakings

Answer: C

99. The scheme of workers' participation in management in industry in India was introduced Through:
(A) Code of Discipline in industry
(B) 20-point Economic Programme
(C) Industrial Employment (Standing Orders) Act
(D) None of the above

Answer: B

Explanation: Government of India on 30th October, 1975 announced a scheme of workers participation in management which consisted of establishment of Joint Councils and Shop council as part of its 20 point economic programs. The scheme envisages for the establishment of joint councils and shop councils in manufacturing and mining industries employing 500 or more employees in public, private and co-operative sectors. The scheme contemplated participation of workers in the decision-making process in the matters relating to production, productivity, absenteeism, safety measures, general discipline, working conditions and welfare, and overall efficiency of the shop/department.

100. The main objective of workers' participation in management is ________.

(A) To promote increased productivity for the advantage of organisation, workers and society at large
(B) To develop, enhance and utilise resources effectively
(C) To improve various skills of workers in organisation
(D) To respond to the members' demands both formally and informally

Answer: A

101. Which one of the following does not come under the schemes of workers' participation in management, 1975 & 1977 ?

(A) Joint Management Council
(B) Shop Councils
(C) Joint Councils
(D) Unit Councils

Answer: D

102. Which of the following is not a tripartite body ?

(A) Indian Labour Conference
(B) Standing Labour Committee
(C) Wage Boards
(D) Joint Management Councils

Answer: B

103. Which of the following is not a Tripartite body ?

(A) Works Committee
(B) I. L. O
(C) Indian Labour Conference
(D) Wage Boards

Answer: A

104. The first commission to recommend tripartism consultation in India was

(A) The First National Commission on Labour
(B) The Second National Commission on Labour
(C) The Royal Commission on Labour
(D) The Indian Labour Conference

Answer: C

105. Which of the following is not a tripartite body ?

(A) Indian Labour Conference
(B) Joint Management Councils
(C) Standing Labour Committee
(D) Wage Boards

Answer: C

106. Which of the following is not a voluntary tripartite body ?

(A) Indian Labour Conference
(B) Standing Labour Committee
(C) Central Advisory Board
(D) None of the above

Answer: C

107. Which of the following is not a tripartite body as created in 1942 :

(A) Indian Labour Conference
(B) Standing Labour Committee
(C) Tripartite Implementation and Evaluation Committee
(D) None of the above

Answer: A

108. Which one of the following is a tripartite body ?

(A) Works Committee
(B) Canteen Management Committee
(C) Wage Board
(D) Joint Management Council

Answer: C

109. Which of the following is not a tripartite body ?

(A) Indian Labour Conference
(B) Standing Labour Committee
(C) Wage Boards
(D) Joint Management Councils

Answer: B

110. Revolutionary theory of trade union is proposed by :

(A) Webbs (B) Hoxie

(C) Karl Marx (D) Gandhi

Answer: B

111. Theories on Trade Unionism were proposed by :
(A) Elton Mayo, Marx and Gandhi
(B) Marx, Weber and Gandhi
(C) Pearlman, Weber and Webbs
(D) Pearlman, Webbs and Marx

Answer: B

112. Which of the following is not a characteristics of Trade Union ?
(A) Is an association of employers or the employees or of the independent workers ?
(B) Is relatively a permanent combination but not temporary or casual.
(C) Is an association of workers who are engaged in not securing economic benefits for their members.
(D) Is influenced by a member of ideologies.

Answer: C

113. Who among the following defined trade unions as a continuous association of wage earners:
(A) S. D. Punekar (B) Dankert
(C) Webbs (D) V.V. Giri

Answer: C

114. Trade union means any combination formed primarily for the purpose of regulating the relations between
(A) Workmen and employers permanently
(B) Workmen and workmen permanently
(C) Workmen and employers, workmen and workmen, employers and employers temporary or permanent
(D) Workmen and employers, workmenand workmen, employers and employers permanently

Answer: C

115. Revolutionary theory of trade union was propounded by________.
(A) Webbs (B) Hoxie
(C) Karl Marx (D) Gandhi

Answer: B

116. Which of the following is not a Trade Union method as described by Webbs ?
(A) Mutual Insurance
(B) Strike
(C) Collective Bargaining
(D) Legal enactment

Answer: A

117. Which of the following systems of wage payment a trade union will advocate which may even be useful for the inefficient members ?
(A) Piece-rated wages
(B) Time-rated wages
(C) Performance-oriented wages
(D) Wages based on productivity

Answer: B

118. Match the following Theories of trade unionism with the contributors who propagated them :

Theory of Trade Unionism
(a) Industrial Democracy Theory
(b) Scarcity - consciousness Theory
(c) Socio - Psychological Theory
(d) Class collaboration and harmony Theory

Contribution
(i) M. K. Gandhi
(ii) Robert F. Hoxie
(iii) Sydney and Beatvice webbs
(iv) Selig Pearlman

	(a)	(b)	(c)	(d)
(A)	(iv)	(ii)	(iii)	(i)
(B)	(iii)	(iv)	(ii)	(i)
(C)	(i)	(iii)	(iv)	(ii)
(D)	(ii)	(i)	(iii)	(iv)

Answer: B

119. Who had propagated social engineering in industrial jurisprudence :
(A) Roscoe pound
(B) Ehilrich
(C) Both A and B
(D) None of the above
Answer: A

120. Who among the following was not a labour leader in India ?
(A) B. P. Wadia
(B) N. M. Lokhande
(C) Raja Ram Mohan Roy
(D) V. V. Giri
Answer: C

121. Which one of the following is correct so for as the definition of trade union is concerned ?
(A) Trade union is a temporary organisation
(B) Trade union is a continuous organisation
(C) Trade union is an economic organisation
(D) Trade union is a political organisation
Answer: B

122. Which among the following is not a short-term objective of trade unions?
(A) Wage increase
(B) Enhancement of dearness allowance
(C) Social Security
(D) Establishment of a Socialist Society
Answer: C

123. Which of the following is not a type of trade union ?
(A) Craft Union
(B) Stable Union
(C) Company Union
(D) Industrial Union
Answer: B

124. Trade Union movement in India emerged between
(A) 1920-1930 (B) 1850-1870
(C) 1870-1880 (D) 1930-1947
Answer: A

125. The first trade union in India was organised in :
(A) 1884 (B) 1890
(C) 1918 (D) 1920
Answer: C

126. Recognition of trade union is made by the provision of
(A) Trade Unions Act of 1926
(B) Industrial Dispute Act 1947
(C) Code of Discipline
(D) Factories Act of 1948
Answer: C

127. A Trade Union should be registered as per the law must have
(A) 20% of the workers
(B) 150 workmen
(C) Minimum 17 persons
(D) None of the above
Answer: D

128. Which is not a structure of Trade Union of Industrial Organisation ?
(A) Craft union
(B) General union
(C) Industrial union
(D) Consumers' union
Answer: D

129. Which one of the following is not an industrial relations legislation :
(A) I D Act, 1947
(B) Minimum Wages Act, 1948
(C) Trade Union Act, 1926
(D) Industrial Employment (Standing Orders) Act, 1946
Answer: B

130. The most important year in the history of Indian Trade Union Movement has been :
(A) 1920 (B) 1922
(C) 1940 (D) 1947
Answer: A

131. The founder of Ahmedabad Textile Labour Association was :
(A) V. V. Giri
(B) M. K. Gandhi
(C) B. P. Wadia
(D) N. M. Lokhande
Answer: B

132. The first union led by Maniben Kara and Kamala Sinha (two women) in India was :
(A) HMS -1948 (B) INTUC -1948
(C) AITUC -1920 (D) BMS -1954
Answer: A

133. The Bombay Mill Hands Association under the Presidentship of N.M. Lokhande which is often referred to as the starting point of the Indian Labour Movement, was established in :
(A) 1878 (B) 1879
(C) 1890 (D) 1891
Answer: C

134. Match the following :

Trade Union	**Year of establishment**
(a) INTUC	(i) 1970
(b) AITUC	(ii) 1955
(c) BMS	(iii) 1947
(d) CITU	(iv) 1920

	(a)	(b)	(c)	(d)
(A)	(iii)	(ii)	(i)	(iv)
(B)	(iii)	(iv)	(ii)	(i)
(C)	(iii)	(iv)	(i)	(ii)
(D)	(iv)	(iii)	(i)	(ii)

Answer: B

135. The First Indian Trade Union led by women was
(A) A.I.T.U.C.
(B) I.N.T.U.C.
(C) H.M.S.
(D) C.I.T.U.
Answer : C

136. Match the following trade unions according to the year of formation :

List – I	**List – II**
a. AITUC	i. 1947
b. CITU	ii. 1948
c. INTUC	iii. 1920
d. HMS	iv. 1970

Codes :

	a	b	c	d
(A)	iii	iv	i	ii
(B)	ii	iii	iv	i
(C)	iii	i	ii	iv
(D)	i	ii	iii	iv

Answer: A

137. Which one of the following Federations was organised in 1920 :
(A) INTUC (B) AITUC
(C) CITU (D) HMS
Answer: B

138. Which of the following was the first National Labour Federation organised in India ?
(A) INTUC (B) AITUC
(C) CITU (D) HMS
Answer: B

139. Among the following trade unions which one is called the first modern trade union of India?
(A) Bombay Millhands Association
(B) Kamgar Hitwardhak Sabha
(C) Madras Labour Union
(D) All India Trade Union Congress
Answer: D

140. Which of the following federations is not affiliated to any political party?
(A) INTUC (B) NFITU
(C) AITUC (D) HMS
Answer: B

141. Arrange the events in Indian Trade Unionism in the order in which they have occurred from earliest to the latest :
(a) Formation of CITU

(b) Formation of UTUC
(c) Formation of AITUC
(d) Formation of INTUC

(A)	(c)	(d)	(b)	(a)
(B)	(d)	(b)	(a)	(c)
(C)	(a)	(c)	(d)	(b)
(D)	(b)	(a)	(c)	(d)

Answer: A

142. Match the trade union leaders associated with the trade unions :

(a) Madras Labour Union (i)V.V. Giri
(b) Ahmedabad Textile Labour Association (ii) A.R. Ramanujam
(c) All India Railwaymen's Federation (iii)Mahatma Gandhi
(d)Indian National Trade Union Congress (iv) B.P. Wadia

	(a)	(b)	(c)	(d)
(A)	(iii)	(iv)	(ii)	(i)
(B)	(ii)	(i)	(iii)	(iv)
(C)	(i)	(ii)	(iv)	(iii)
(D)	(iv)	(iii)	(i)	(ii)

Answer: D

143. UTUC was formed in the year :
(A) 1949 (B) 1984
(C)1920 (D) 1947

Answer: A

144. Who is the President of INTUC?
(A) Sanjeeva Reddy
(B) Dutta Samanth
(C) Sitaram Etchuri
(D) S. R. Kulkarni

Answer: A

145. BMS is affiliated to one of the following political parties :
(A) Indian National Congress
(B) Bharteeya Janata Party
(C) Communist Party of India (Marxists)
(D) Bahujan Samaj Party

Answer: B

146. The founder of Textile Labour Association was__________ .
(A) V. V. Giri
(B) Gulzarilal Nanda
(C) Mohandas Karamchand Gandhi
(D) Jaya Prakash Narayan

Answer: C

147. The oldest trade union in the country is__________.
(A) INTUC
(B) AITUC
(C) CITU
(D) HMS

Answer: B

148. Match the following :

(a) Madras Labour Union (i) 1890
(b) Ahmedabad Textile Labour Association (ii) 1909
(c) Bombay Mill Hands Association (iii) 1917
(d) Kamgar Hitwardhan Sabha (iv) 1920

Codes :

	(a)	(b)	(c)	(d)
(A)	(iv)	(iii)	(ii)	(i)
(B)	(iii)	(iv)	(i)	(ii)
(C)	(ii)	(i)	(iii)	(iv)
(D)	(i)	(ii)	(iv)	(iii)

Answer: B

149. INTUC, AITUC, HMS and UTUC adopted the code of conduct for Trade Union Rivalry in the year
(A) 1948 (B) 1958
(C) 1968 (D) 1978

Answer: B

150. Who among the following was the First Trade Union Leader in India ?
(A) N.M. Lokhande (B) B.P. Wadia
(C) G.L. Nanda (D) M.K. Gandhi

Answer: B

151. Match the following :

Trade Union Federation	Year of Formation
(a) AITUC	(i) 1947
(b) CITU	(ii) 1948
(c) INTUC	(iii) 1920
(d) HMS	(iv) 1970

Codes :

	(a)	(b)	(c)	(d)
(A)	(iv)	(iii)	(i)	(ii)
(B)	(iii)	(i)	(iv)	(ii)
(C)	(iii)	(iv)	(i)	(ii)
(D)	(ii)	(iii)	(iv)	(i)

Answer: C

152. Which of the following provides for recognition of trade unions in India?
(A) Inter-Union Code of Conduct
(B) Code of Discipline in Industry
(C) Code of Efficiency and Welfare
(D) Code of Ethics

Answer: B

153. According to the Trade Unions Act, 1926 a minor member of the union :
(A) Can be elected as Office-bearer
(B) Can be elected as Office-bearer for one term
(C) Cannot be a member of the registered union
(D) Cannot be elected as Office-bearer of the registered trade union

Answer: D

154. Which of the following cannot be regarded as a union security measure ?
(A) Closed-shop agreement
(B) Union-shop agreement
(C) Check-off
(D) Open-shop agreement

Answer: C

155. Intra-Union rivalry means :
(A) Rivalry between unions
(B) Rivalry within the same union
(C) Rivalry between unions and management
(D) Rivalry between unions and government

Answer: A

156. The code of discipline implemented by the central Government was :
(A) Voluntary in nature
(B) Compulsory in nature
(C) Partly voluntary and partly compulsory
(D) None of the above

Answer: C

157. The primary source of income for the union is :
(A) Membership subscription
(B) Donations
(C) Sale of periodicals
(D) Other sources

Answer: A

158. Who among the following will not be regarded as an outsider in trade union ?
(A) Political leader
(B) Persons working in other industry
(C) Lawyers
(D) Ex – employees

Answer: B

159. The provision regarding political fund under the trade union Act, 1926 is :
(A) Creation of political fund is compulsory
(B) It is optional
(C) It is partly compulsory and partly voluntary
(D) None of the above

Answer : B

Explanation: *Constitution of a separate fund for political purposes:*(1) A registered Trade Union may constitute a separate fund, from contributions separately levied for or made to that fund, from which payments may be made, for the promotion of the civic and political interests of its members, in furtherance of any of the objects specified in sub-section (2).

160. Which of the following is not a part of the structure of Trade Union in India ?
(A) Craft Union
(B) Industrial Union
(C) Company Union
(D) Federations

Answer: A

Explanation: Industrial unionism contrasts with craft unionism, which organizes workers along lines of their specific trades, i.e., workers using the same kind of tools, or doing the same kind of work with approximately the same level of skill, even if this leads to multiple union locals (with different contracts, and different expiration dates) in the same workplace.

161. The basic function of trade union is
(A) To protect and promote the interest of the workers.
(B) Acquiring the control of industry by workers.
(C) Imbibing sincerity and discipline in workers.
(D) To provide cultural and recreational facilities.

Answer: A

162. Which of the following aims to check inter and intra union rivalry in India ?
(A) The Trade Union Act
(B) The Code of Discipline in Industry
(C) The Inter Union Code of Conduct.
(D) All the above

Answer: C

163. Which of the following is not a type of labour legislation?
(A) Protective
(B) Regulative
(C) Social Security
(D) Social Legislation

Answer: D

164. A list of Unfair Labour Practices on the part of Trade Unions and Employers was inserted in
(A) Trade Union Act, 1926
(B) The Factories' Act, 1948
(C) The Industrial Disputes Act, 1947
(D) None of the above

Answer: A

165. Which of the following contributes in promoting healthy industrial relations in an organization ?
(A) Compulsory Arbitration
(B) Adjudication
(C) Collective Bargaining
(D) Voluntary Arbitration

Answer: C

166. In which of the following an Individual Dispute cannot take the form of Industrial Dispute without the help of the Trade Union ?
(A) Termination
(B) Dismissal / Discharge
(C) Retrenchment
(D) Promotion

Answer: D

167. Which of the following directly aims to control inter and intra–union rivalry in India ?
(A) The Industrial Dispute Act, 1947
(B) Code of Discipline in Industry
(C) Inter-Union Code of Conduct
(D) Trade Unions Act, 1926

Answer: C

168. Which of the following is not regarded as Trade Union Weapon ?
(A) Strike (B) Check-off
(C) Picketing (D) Boycott

Answer: B

169. Which of the following is not long term objective of Trade Union ?
(A) Establishment of Socialist Society
(B) Nationalisation of Industries

(C) Parliament of Proletariate
(D) Higher Wages and Short hours of work

Answer: D

170. Which of the following can be said to be the first Trade Union in India?
(A) Amalgamated Society of Railway Servants of India and Burma
(B) Kamgar Hitvardhak Sabha
(C) Madras Labour Union
(D) Bombay Millhand's Association

Answer: D

1. Bombay Millhand's Association formed in 1890.
2. The Amalgamated Society of railway servants of India and Burma formed in 1897
3. The Kamgar Hitwardhak Sabha Bombay formed in 1910.
4. Madras Labour Union-1918: Along with V. Kalyanasundaram Mudaliar, Wadia founded the Madras Labour Union, one of India's first organised labour unions.

171. Which of the following cannot be said to be the short-term objective of trade unions?
(A) Higher wages
(B) Shorter Hours of work
(C) Establishment of Socialist society
(D) Better conditions of Employment

Answer: C

172. Arrange the following in the order of their coverage from lower to higher :
(a) Regional Union
(b) Craft Union
(c) Industrial Union
(d) Confederation
(e) Federation

(A) a, b, c, d, e (B) b, c, a, e, d
(C) c, b, a, d, c (D) d, a, b, c, e

Answer: B

173. A Trade Union means "An association of workers in one or more professions carried on mainly for the purpose of protecting and advancing the members' economic interest in connection with their daily work". Identify the author :
(A) Sidney and Beatrice Webb
(B) J. Cunnison
(C) G.D.H. Cole
(D) Clyde E. Dankert

Answer: A

174. A union may claim recognition for an industry in a local area, if it has membership of
(A) 10% of the workers in that industry.
(B) 15% of the workers in that area.
(C) 25% of the workers of that industry in that area.
(D) 30% of the workers in similar industry.

Answer: C

175. Who among the following advocated the Trusteeship Theory of Trade Union ?
(A) N.M. Lokhande (B) B.P. Wadia
(C) G.L. Nanda (D) M.K. Gandhi

Answer: D

176. Inter and intra-union rivalry in Trade Unions is reduced by
(A) The provisions of the Industrial Disputes Act 1947
(B) By voluntary tripartite code of inter-union rivalry – 1957
(C) By bipartite mutual agreement at the industry level
(D) Above all

Answer: B

177. 'Employment Injury' means personal injury to an employee caused by accident or occupational disease arising out of and in the course of employment being an insurable employment if the accident occurs or occupational disease is contracted only within territorial limits of

India and not outside India. This statement is
(A) correct.
(B) incorrect.
(C) true only in case of occupational injury.
(D) true only in case of accident.

Answer: B

178. Sequence the following as per the chronological order :
(i) Formation of ILO
(ii) Moore Report
(iii) AITUC
(iv) INTUC
(v) First World War
(A) (ii), (v), (i), (iii), (iv)
(B) (v), (iv), (i), (ii), (iii)
(C) (iii), (ii), (iv), (v), (i)
(D) (iv), (iii), (ii), (i), (v)

Answer: A

179. Which of the following is method of Union recognition ?
(A) Secret Ballot
(B) Membership Verification
(C) Check-off System
(D) All the above

Answer: D

180. Workers do join Trade Unions : Find out the incorrect reason out of the following :
(A) To attain economic security
(B) To improve bargaining power
(C) To ventílate their grievancies
(D) To satisfy their family needs

Answer: D

181. Match the following :

List – I (Unions)	List – II (Functions)
a. Craft Union	i. Associations of workers or different categories
b. General Union	ii. Based on craft non – managerial personnel
c. Industrial Union	iii. Either unionization of the same industry or different industry.
d. Federation	iv. Unionisation of workers any region or any job occupation

Codes :

	a	b	c	d
(A)	ii	iv	i	iii
(B)	ii	i	iii	iv
(C)	iv	i	ii	iii
(D)	i	ii	iii	iv

Answer: A

182. Who identified the types of unions as business, predatory, dependent and friendly?
(A) Roberts, B.C. (B) Robert F. Hoxie
(C) Kirkaldy, H.S. (D) Perlman Selig

Answer: B

183. Trade Union *cannot* represent legally if it is :
(A) not registered
(B) not recognized
(C) led by political leader
(D) working for multiple industries

Answer: A

184. Match the following :

(a) Check-off system	(i) Registered trade union
(b) Report	(ii) Arbitration
(c) Award	(iii) Union subscription
(d) Political fund	(iv) Conciliation

	(a)	(b)	(c)	(d)
(A)	(iv)	(iii)	(iv)	(i)
(B)	(iii)	(iv)	(i)	(ii)
(C)	(iii)	(iv)	(ii)	(i)
(D)	(ii)	(iii)	(iv)	(i)

Answer: C

185. As per the rights of the registered trade unions, account books can be inspected :
(A) Only by the trade union members of the concerned union

(B) Only by the office bearers of the concerned unions
(C) Members and office bearers of the trade union at such time as provided in the rules
(D) Members of any trade union

Answer: C

186. Which of the following codes aims to check the problem of trade union rivalries in India?
(A) Code of discipline in industry
(B) Inter-union code of conduct
(C) Code of efficiency and welfare
(D) None of the above

Answer: A

187. As a result of the New Economic Policy which of the following has been badly affected ?
(A) Trade Unions
(B) Collective Bargaining
(C) Strikes
(D) All the above

Answer: A

188. Where the recruitment happens through the compulsory intervention of trade unions, the system is called
(A) Closed shop
(B) Union shop
(C) Open shop
(D) None of the above

Answer: A

189. Match the following :

Trade Union	Political Affiliation	
(a) INTUC	(i)	Congress (I)
(b) AITUC	(ii)	CPI (M)
(c) CITU	(iii)	CPI
(d) BMS	(iv)	BJP

Code :

	(a)	(b)	(c)	(d)
(A)	(iv)	(iii)	(ii)	(i)
(B)	(i)	(ii)	(iii)	(iv)
(C)	(i)	(iii)	(ii)	(iv)
(D)	(i)	(iv)	(iii)	(ii)

Answer: C

190. Which of the following are not significant causal factors for grievances?
(A) Wages, working conditions and supervision
(B) Management policies, practices and maladjustment of employees
(C) Both (A) and (B) above
(D) None of the above

Answer: D

191. The Central Trade Union AITUC is associated with :
(A) Bharatiya Janta Party
(B) Congress Party of India
(C) Communist Party of India (Marxist)
(D) Communist Party of India

Answer: D

192. Match the following :

Trade Union	Year of Establishment
I. INTUC	i. 1920
II. AITUC	ii. 1970
III. CITU	iii. 1947
IV. BMS	iv. 1954

(A) I - iv, II - iii, III - ii, IV - i
(B) I - i, II - ii, III - iii, IV - iv
(C) I - iv, II - i, III - iii, IV - ii
(D) I - iii, II - i, III - ii, IV – iv

Answer: D

193. The Central Trade Union CITU is associated with :
(A) Congress Party of India
(B) Communist party of India Marxist
(C) Communist Party of India
(D) Shiv Sena

Answer: B

194. "Hind Mazdoor Sabha" established in which year?
(A) 1940 (B) 1942
(C) 1948 (D) 1952

Answer: C

195. Negotiation of labour contract by Union and Management is referred to as
(A) Industrial Relations

(B) Trade Union
(C) Consumerism
(D) Collective Bargaining
Answer: D

196. Which among the following is odd one?
(A) BMS (B) FICCI
(C) AITUC (D) INTUC
Answer: B

197. Match the following :

List – A	List – B
(i) Indian Trade Union Act	(a) 1923
(ii) Industrial Dispute Act	(b) 1926
(iii) The Workmen's Compensation Act	(c) 1948
(iv) The Employees' State Insurance Act	(d) 1947

Codes :

	(i)	(ii)	(iii)	(iv)
(A)	(b)	(d)	(a)	(c)
(B)	(b)	(c)	(d)	(a)
(C)	(b)	(d)	(c)	(a)
(D)	(a)	(c)	(b)	(d)

Answer: A

198. Which of the following is not the principle of Trade Unionism ?
(A) Unity is Strength
(B) Equal Pay for equal work
(C) Security of service
(D) Right to lock out
Answer: D

199. A system in which Unions and Management negotiate with each other to develop the work rules, under which Union members will work for a stipulated period of time, is referred to as
(A) Man Power Planning
(B) Career Planning
(C) Collective Bargaining
(D) Training and Development
Answer: C

200. Under Worker's Participation Scheme
(A) Workers participate in decision making process
(B) Workers get more benefits
(C) Workers increase productivity
(D) Workers decide their work themselves
Answer: A

201. Collective Bargaining is
(A) one party process
(B) two party process
(C) multi party process
(D) none of the above
Answer: B

202. Identify the one that is not a function of Industrial Relations
(A) Establishment of Workers and Managers Communication
(B) Establishment of Employees and Management rapport
(C) Ensure Trade Union Creative contribution
(D) To Improve Workers Strength
Answer: D

203. Match the following

a. Strike	1. Employer
b. Lock out	2. Arbitrator
c. Adjudication	3. Employee
d. Arbitration	4. Courts

a b c d
(A) 3 2 4 1 (B) 3 1 4 2
(C) 3 4 1 2 (D) 3 1 2 4
Answer: B

****

UNIT-VIII
LABOUR (EMPLOYEE) WELFARE AND SOCIAL SECURITY MEASURES

8.1. LABOUR WELFARE - CONCEPT-SCOPE-CHARACTERISTICS - THEORIES - IMPORTANCE

- **Oxford dictionary:** "Labour welfare is efforts to make life worth living for workmen."
- The need for providing such services and facilities arise from the social responsibility of industries, a desire for upholding democratic values and a concern for employees.
- Welfare includes anything that is done for the comfort and improvement of employees and is provided over and above the wages.
- Welfare helps in keeping the morale and motivation of the employees high so as to retain the employees for longer duration.
- The welfare measures need not be in monetary terms only but in any kind/forms. Employee welfare includes monitoring of working conditions, creation of industrial harmony through infrastructure for health, industrial relations and insurance against disease, accident and unemployment for the workers and their families.
- Labor welfare entails all those activities of employer, which are directed towards providing the employees with certain facilities and services in addition to wages or salaries.
- Labour welfare implies providing better work conditions for example, proper lighting, cleanliness, low noise, etc. and amenities viz. recreation, housing, education, etc.
- **Arthur James Todd**: "Labour welfare means anything done for the comfort and improvement, intellectual and social, of the employees over and above the wages paid which is not a necessity of the Industry."

  Industrial Labour Organisation (ILO): "Labour welfare may be understood and including such services facilities and amenities which may be established in vicinity of undertaking to perform their work in healthy and congenial environment and to avail of facilities which improve their health and bring high morale."
- **S.T. Edwards (1953):** "One can buy a man's time, his physical presence at a particular space, even a few muscular movements, but enthusiasm, initiative, loyalty and devotion to duty cannot be bought. They will have to be created through right employer-employee relations, provision of constructive opportunities for satisfying the major motivating desires of human action."
- ***In 1931 the Royal Commission on Labour*** stressed the need of labour welfare primarily because of the harsh treatment meted out to the workers.
- **Constitutional provision:**

  "**Article 42:** The state shall make provision for securing just and humane conditions of work."

  "**Article 43:** The state shall endeavor to secure by suitable legislation or economic organization or in any other way, to all workers agricultural, industrial or otherwise, a living wage, conditions of work ensuring a decent standard of life and full enjoyment of leisure and social and cultural opportunities."

Concept and Scope of Labour welfare

- The concept of 'Labour welfare' is flexible and elastic and differs widely with times, regions, industry, country, social values and customs, the degree of industrialization, the general social economic development of people and political ideologies prevailing at particular moments.
- **The Committee on Labour Welfare (1969)**: "Such facilities and amenities as adequate canteens, rest and recreation facilities, sanitary and medical facilities arrangements for travel to and from and for accommodation of workers employed at a distance from their homes, and such other services, amenities and facilities including social security measures as contribute to conditions under which workers are employed."
- **The second report of the ILO:** "Labour welfare as, such services and amenities which may be established in or in the vicinity of undertakings to enable the persons employed in them to perform their work in healthy, congenial surroundings and such amenities conducive to good health, and high morale."

Types of Labour welfare services

- **The International Labour Organisation (ILO) Regional Conference**: Described welfare to mean "such services, facilities and amenities, which may be established outside or in the vicinity of undertakings to enable the persons employed therein to work in healthy and congenial surroundings and to provide them with amenities conducive to good health and high morale".
- **The Report of the Committee on Labour Welfare (1969)** :Labour welfare includes "such services, facilities, sanitary and medical facilities, arrangements for travel to and from work and for the accommodation of workers employed at a distance from their homes, and such other services, amenities and facilities, including social security measures as contribute to improve the conditions under which workers are employed"
- In other words, labour welfare services include all extramural and intramural welfare work, statutory and non-statutory welfare facilities undertaken by the employers, government, trade unions or voluntary agencies.
- They also include social security - measures which contribute to workers welfare such as insurance, provident fund, gratuity, maternity benefits, workmen's compensations, retirement benefits, etc.
- ***The International Labour Organization in 1963 had divided*** **welfare services** ***into two types:***
  1. **Intramural services:** *Welfare* within the precincts of an establishment (Medical aid, Creches, Canteens, Safety, Health, Counseling,etc.)
  2. **Extramural services:** Non-statutory *welfare* measures voluntarily provided outside the factory (Education, Housing, Transport, Recreation etc.)

Characteristics of labour welfare

- The work which is usually undertaken within the premises or in the vicinity of the industrial undertakings for the benefit of the employees and the members of their family and this generally includes those items of welfare which are over and above what is provided by statutory provisions and what the employees expect as a result of a contract of employment from the employers.
- These facilities may either be provided voluntarily by the progressive and enlightened employers of their own, out of their realization of social responsibility towards labour or the statutory laws may compel them to make provision for these facilities or these may be taken up by the govt. or the trade unions.
- As far as the statutory measures to safeguard the welfare of factory workers are concerned, the beginning of the same was made with the passing of the ***Factories Act in 1881*** as a result of the joint efforts of the philanthropist and social workers and Lancashire manufacturers in Britain. This

Act applied to manufacturing establishments using mechanical power and employing 100 or more persons.

- The Act regulated the employment of child labour below 7 years and provided for 9 hours a day as the maximum working hours for children in the age group of 7 to 12 years, an interval of 1 hour for rest and a weekly holiday.
- The Act also contained provisions relating to safety and inspection of factories.
- Later on, this Act was amended several times gradually expanding its scope to cover more and more persons within its ambit (by way of reducing the limit in terms of number of persons) and welfare measures, finally culminating in the Factories Act, 1948 (Which came into force on 1st April, 1949) which is in existence even today with some notable amendments introduced in 1954, 1976 and 1987.

Theories of Labour Welfare

- The form of labor welfare activities is flexible, elastic and differs from time to time, region to region, industry to industry and country to country depending upon the value system, level of education, social customs, degree of industrialization and general standard of the socio-economic development of the nation.
- Seven theories constituting the conceptual frame work of labour welfare activities are the following:

1. The policing theory of labour welfare

- The policing theory is based on assumption that Human Being is so much selfish and always tries for own benefits whether on the cost of others welfare. Any of the employers will not work for the welfare of employees until he is forced to do so.
- This theory is based on the contention that a minimum standard of welfare is necessary for workers.
- The assumption on which the theory is based is the without compulsion, supervision and fear of punishment, no employer will provide even the barest minimum of welfare facilities for workers this theory is based on the assumption that man is selfish and self –centered, and always tries to achieve his own ends, even at the cost of the welfare of others.
- This is based on the contention that a minimum standard of welfare is necessary for labourers. Here the assumption is that without policing, that is, without compulsion, employers do not provide even the minimum facilities for workers.
- According to this theory, owners and managers of industrial undertakings get many opportunities for exploitation of labour. Hence, the state has to intervene to provide minimum standard of welfare to the working class.

2. The religious theory of labour welfare

- This is based on the concept that man is essentially "a religious animal." Even today, many acts of man are related to religious sentiments and beliefs. These religious feelings sometimes prompt an employer to take up welfare activities in the expectation of future emancipation either in this life or after it.
- The theory views were an essentially religious. Religious feelings are what sometimes prompt employers to take up welfare activities in the belief of benefits either in his life or in support after life.
- Any good work is considered an investment, because both the benefactor and the beneficiary are benefited by the good work done by the benefactor.

- This theory does not take into consideration that the workers are not beneficiaries but rightful claimants to a part of the gains derived by their labour.

3. The philanthropic theory of labour welfare

- Philanthropy is the inclination to do or practice of doing well to ones fellow men.
- Man is basically self centered and acts of these kinds stem from personal motivation, when some employers take compassion on their fellowmen, they may undertake labor welfare measures for their workers.
- This theory is based on man's love for mankind. Philanthropy means "Loving mankind." Man is believed to have an instinctive urge by which he strives to remove the suffering of others and promote their well-being.
- In fact, the labour welfare movement began in the early years of the industrial revolution with the support of philanthropists.

4. The paternalistic or trusteeship theory of labour welfare

- In this theory it is held that the industrialists or employers hold the total industrial estate, properties and profits accruing form them in trust for the workmen, for him, and for society.
- It assumes that the workmen are like minors and are not able to look after their own interests that they are ignorant because of lack of education. Employers therefore have the moral responsibility to look after the interests of their wards, who are the workers.
- In other words, the employer should hold the industrial assets for himself, for the benefit of his workers, and also for society.
- The main emphasis of this theory is that employers should provide funds on an ongoing basis for the well-being of their employees.

5. The placating theory of labour welfare

- As labour groups are becoming better organized and are becoming demanding and militant, being more conscious of their rights and privileges that even before, their demand for higher wages and better standards increases.
- The placing theory advocates timely and periodical acts of labour welfare to appease the workers.
- This theory is based on the fact that the labour groups are becoming demanding and militant and are more conscious of their rights and privileges than ever before. Their demand for higher wages and better standards of living cannot be ignored. According to this theory, timely and periodical acts of labour welfare can appease the workers. They are some kind of pacifiers which come with a friendly gesture.

6. The public relations theory of labour welfare

- This theory provides the basis for an atmosphere of goodwill between labour and management, and also between management and the public, labour welfare programmes under this theory, work as a sort of an advertisement and help an organization to project its good image and build up and promote good and healthy public relations.
- The labour welfare movements may be utilized to improve relations between management and labour.
- An advertisement or an exhibition of alobour welfare programme may help the management projects a good image of the company.

7. The functional theory of labour welfare

- The concept behind this theory is that a happy and healthy person is a better, more productive worker.
- Here, welfare is used as a means to secure, preserve and develop the efficiency and productivity of labour. As discussed earlier, the approach to any solutions, especially as that as between the workers and the management should be dialogue and an understanding of one another's viewpoint. Once agreement has been reached, compliance by both parties can be assured to a very great extent.
- This also called the ***efficiency theory***.
- This theory is a reflection of contemporary support for labour welfare.
- It can work well if both the parties have an identical aim in view; that is, higher production through better welfare.
- This will encourage labour's partcipation in welfare programmes.

8.2. STATUTORY AND NON STATUTORY LABOUR WELFARE

8.2.1 Statutory welfare schemes

1. **Drinking Water:** At all the working places including dock areas, safe hygienic drinking water points are provided.
2. **Latrines and Urinals:** A sufficient number of latrines and urinals must be provided in a neat and clean condition.
3. **Spittoons:** In every work place, such as ware houses, store places, in the dock area and office premises where employees/workers are deployed, spittoons are provided in convenient places and same are maintained in a hygienic condition.
4. **Lighting:** At all the working places in the dock area, sufficient lights are provided for working safely during the night shift.
5. **Ventilation:** For the circulation of fresh air, and maintaining the normal temperatures sufficient number of ventilators are provided in dock area, where workers are required to work in three shifts, such as ware houses, and office premises in dock area.
6. **Washing places:** Adequate washing places such as bathrooms, wash basins with tap and tap on the stand pipe are provided in the port area in the vicinity of the work places.
7. **First-aid appliances and Ambulance room:** Adequate first-aid boxes are provided on the working places in the dock area & port premises and same are accessible. First-aid treatments are readily available during the working hours to the workers at the working places and the ambulance is also provided with the full equipment and qualified nursing staff.
8. **Changing rooms:** Adequate changing rooms are provided to the male and female workers separately to change their cloth in the dock area and office premises. Adequate lockers are also provided to the workers to keep their cloth and belongings, etc.
9. **Rest rooms:** Adequate no. of rest rooms are provided in the dock area to the workers with provisions of drinking water, wash basins, toilets, bathrooms, etc. for those who are working in the night shift.
10. **Canteens:** The canteens are provided in the dock area and other places of working for giving nutritious valued food to the dock workers
11. **Hospital/Medical facility:** Apart from medical officers, the hospital is enriched with qualified and experienced nursing personnel and other paramedical staff.

8.2.2. Non statutory Labour welfare schemes

- Educational facilities
- Recreation facilities
- Transport facilities
- Family planning
- Comparative credit societies
- Consumers comparative stores and fair price shop
- Distress relief and cash benefits

8.3. LAWS RELATING TO LABOUR WELFARE

- Generally, the labour welfare services are divided into two groups:-
- Welfare within the precincts of an establishment - It includes medical aid, creches, canteens, supply of clean drinking water, health services, uniforms and protective clothing, rest shelters, etc. It is the employer's responsibility to provide these facilities to his/ her employees and several legislations have been enacted to set certain minimum standards for provision of these facilities.
- Welfare outside the establishment - It includes social insurance measures like gratuity,pension fund, provident fund,etc; educational facilities; housing facilities; recreational facilities; workers' cooperatives; vocational training, etc.
- In order to extend a measure of social assistance to workers in the unorganised sector, the concept of 'Labour Welfare Fund' was evolved. Accordingly, five welfare funds have been set up under the Ministry of Labour and Employment to provide housing, medical care, educational and recreational facilities to workers employed in beedi industry, certain non-coal mines and cine workers. These funds are financed out of the proceeds of cess levied under respective Cess/Fund Acts. The various legislation so enacted include:-

▪ **The Mica Mines Labour Welfare Fund Act, 1946**: It was enacted to provide for constitution of a fund for financing the activities which promote welfare of labour employed in the mica mining industry.
▪ **The Limestone and Dolomite Mines Labour Welfare Fund Act, 1972** :It was enacted to provide for the levy and collection of a cess on limestone and dolomite for financing the activities which promote the welfare of persons employed in the limestone and dolomite mines.
▪ **The Iron Ore Mines, Manganese Ore Mines & Chrome Ore Mines Labour Welfare Fund Act, 1976:**It was enacted to provide for financing the activities which promote the welfare of persons employed in the iron ore mines, manganese ore mines and chrome ore mines.
▪ **The Beedi Workers Welfare Fund Act, 1976**:It was enacted to provide for financing the measures which promote the welfare of persons engaged in beedi establishments.; and
▪ **The Cine Workers Welfare Fund Act, 1981**: It was enacted to provide for financing the activities which promote the welfare of certain cine-workers.
▪ They also look after the welfare and redressal of grievances of the workers, administration of Welfare Schemes and advise the managements on various Labour Matters including constitution of bilateral committees, such as, **Shop Councils, Works Committees etc.**
▪ The scheme of Welfare Funds is outside the framework of specific employer and employee relationship, in as much as the resources are raised by the Government on a non-contributory basis and delivery of welfare services affected without linkage to individual worker's contribution.
▪ To advise the Central Government on matters related to administration of the above Funds, tripartite Central Advisory Committees have been set up under the respective Welfare Fund Acts. These Committees are headed by Union Labour & Employment Minister.

8.3.1. Welfare Provisions Under Various Acts

1. The Factories Act, 1948

- This Act, as amended by the latest amendment in the year, 1987 makes elaborate provisions in relation to health, safety, and welfare of workers, provisions regarding working hours including weekly hours, daily hours, weekly holidays, regarding employment of young persons, annual leaves with wages and provision regarding employment of women and young persons.
- Under the Chapter on Welfare, provisions have been made in connection with washing facilities in the factories, facilities for storing and drying clothing, facilities for sitting for all workers obliged to work in a standing position in order that they may take advantage of any opportunities for rest which may occur in the course of their work. The Act also provides under the same chapter for first aid appliances to be maintained in every factory and for an ambulance room of the prescribed size in case of those factories wherein more than 500 workmen are ordinarily employed.
- The State Governments have been empowered to make rules requiring that in any specified factory wherein more than two hundred fifty workers are ordinarily employed, a canteen or canteens shall be provided and maintained fro the use of workers.
- The Act further provides for shelters, rest rooms and lunchrooms in every factory employing 150 workmen or more.
- In case of factory employing more than 30 women workers a crèche is to be maintained for the use of their children below 6 years of age.
- Finally the Act makes provision for the employment of ***Welfare Officer*** in factories ordinarily employing more than 500 workmen.

2. The Mines act, 1952

1. Creches, if there are 50 or more women are employed.
2. Shelter for taking food and rest if 150 or more workers are employed.
3. Canteen, if employing 250 or more workers
4. First-aid boxes and first-aid rooms in mines employing more than 150 workers.
5. Bathrooms with shower, sanitary latrines and lockers for men and women workers.

3. The Plantation labour Act, 1951

1. Canteens, if 150 or more workers are employed.
2. Creches in plantation employing 50 or more women workers.
3. Recreational facilities for workers and their children.
4. Educational arrangement in the estate if there are 25 or more children of workers, between the age of 6 and 12.
5. Housing facilities for every workers.

4. The Motor transport workers Act, 1961

1. Canteen, if employing 100 or more workers.
2. First-aid equipment in each transport vehicle.
3. Rest rooms should be cleaned, ventilated and properly lighted.
4. Uniforms, raincoats to drivers and conductors
5. Medical facilities.
6. First-aid boxes.

5. The contract labour (regulation and abolition) Act, 1970

1. Canteen, if employing 100 or more workers.
2. Restrooms or other suitable alternative accomodation if contract labour is required to halt at night.
3. Wholesome drinking water, sufficient number of latrines and urinals and washing facilities.
4. First-aid boxes.

6. The merchant shipping Act, 1958

1. Crew Accommodation
2. Supply of sufficient drinking water
3. Supply of medicines and medical stores and provisions of surgical and medical advice etc.
4. Proper weights and measures on board and grant of relief to distressed seamen abroad a ship
5. A qualified medical officer on board.
6. Establishment of hostels, clubs, canteens and libraries.
7. Appointment of a seamen's welfare officer at such ports in or outside India as the government may consider necessary.
8. Educational facilities.

7. Dock workers (safety, health and welfare) scheme, 1961

- The above stated scheme is framed under the Dock Workers (Regulation of Employment) Act,1948.
- Amenities provided in the port premises include provision of urinals and latrines, drinking water, washing facilities, bathing facilities, canteens, rest shelters and first-aid boxes. In addition to these provisions, other welfare measures provided are – housing, schools, educational facilities, grant of scholarship, libraries, sports and recreation and fair price shops.

8. Inter-State Migrant Workmen (Regulation of Employment and Conditions of Service) Act, 1979.

1. Regular payment of wages (at least minimum wages to be paid).
2. Equal pay for equal work irrespective of sex.
3. Suitable conditions of work.
4. Suitable residential accommodation.
5. Medical facilities, free of charges
6. Protective clothing to workmen.

8.4. AGENCIES OF LABOUR WELFARE: STATE, TRADE UNION, VOLUNTARY AGENCIES AND EMPLOYER

Workers education in India

- Government of India set up in **1958** a semi-autonomous body called the Central Board of Workers Education (**CBWE**).
- CBWE has its **head office at Nagpur.**
- INTUC-run Ambedkar Institute of Labour Studies, Bombay.
- Maniben Kara Institute of HMS, Bombay.
- Indian institute of labour of NFITU, Calcutta.
- Vishwakarma Labour institute of BMS.
- Michael John Centre of Research and Human Resource Development of the Tata Workers Union.

- Vasavada Labour Institute of NLO, Ahmedabad.
- Mahatma Gandhi Labour institute, Ahmedabad.
- 1966: Central Labour institute, Bombay.
- V. V. Giri Labour institute, New Delhi.

8.5. INTERNATIONAL LABOUR ORGANIZATION (ILO)

- International labour Organization (ILO) formed on 19th April 1919.
- Headquarters of ILO situated at **Geneva**.
- The ILO is the international organization responsible for drawing up and overseeing international labour standards.
- The ILO established the Geneva-based International Institute for Labour Studies in 1960 and the International Training Centre in Turin in 1965. The Organization won the Nobel Peace Prize on its 50th anniversary in 1969.
- Union based on respect for Convention No. 87 on freedom of association, which Poland had ratified in 1957.
- On 4 March 1999, Juan Somavia of Chile took over as Director General. He emphasizes the importance of making decent work a strategic international goal and promoting a fair globalization.
- He also underlines work as an instrument of poverty alleviation and ILO's role in helping to achieve the Millennium Development Goals, including cutting world poverty in half by 2015.
- It is the only ***'tripartite'*** United Nations agency that brings together representatives of governments, employers and workers to jointly shape policies and programmes promoting Decent Work for all.
- This unique arrangement gives the ILO an edge in incorporating ***'real world'*** knowledge about employment and work.
- Objectives of ILO are known as ***Declaration of Philadelphia.***

Director-General of ILO :

- A Director-General is elected every five years by the Governing Body.
- Subject to the instructions of the Governing Body, the Director-General is responsible for the efficient conduct of the International Labour Office and other duties as may be assigned.

1. 1 October 2012 to till date: Guy Ryder
2. 1999-2012:Juan Somavia, Chile
3. 1989-1999:Michel Hansenne, Belgium
4. 1974-1989:Francis Blanchard, France
5. 1970-1973:Clarence Wilfred Jenks, UK
6. 1948-1970:David A. Morse, US
7. 1941-1948:Edward Phelan, Ireland
8. 1939-1941:John G. Winant, US
9. 1932-1938:Harold Butler, UK
10. 1919-1932:Albert Thomas, France

ILO Centers and Institutes

1. **International Institute for Labour Studies , Geneva**
2. **International Training Centre of the ILO**: In 1965, the ILO established its training arm in Turin, Italy, to assist countries in their social and economic development through training.
3. **The Inter-American Centre for Knowledge Development in Vocational Training**
4. **International Occupational Safety and Health Information Centre (CIS)**
   a. CIS is the knowledge management arm of Safe work of the International Labour Organization (ILO).
   b. Its goal is to ensure that workers and everyone concerned with their protection have access to the facts they need to prevent occupational injuries and diseases.
   c. CIS was founded in 1959 as a joint Endeavour of the ILO, the International Social Security Association (ISSA), the European Coal and Steel Community (one of the predecessors of the European Union) and occupational safety and health institutions in 11 European countries.

Three principle organs of ILO

1. **The International labour Conference:**
   - Tripartite in composition and meets at least once in a year.
   - The first International Labour Conference held in Washington in October 1919 adopted six International Labour Conventions, which dealt with hours of work in industry, unemployment, and maternity protection, night work for women, minimum age and night work for young persons in industry.
2. **The Governing body:** It is a tripartite body consisting of 56 members of which 28 represent governments, 14 Employers and 14 Workers. The period of office of this boby is 3 years.
3. **International labour Office**
   - Head office: Geneva
   - The Director General is chief executive of this office appointed by the governing body for 10 years.

8.6. SOCIAL SECURITY

- A comprehensive social security was introduced in Germany.
- **Lord Beveridge:** Social Security "is an attack on five giants viz.,want, disease,ignorance, squalorand idleness."This concept is related to social justice and equality.
- **ILO:** Social Security as, "the security that society furnishes, through appropriate organization again certain risks to whichits members are exposed..Social security is designed to prevent and cure disease, to support when people are unable to earn and restore to gainful employment."
- **Social Assistance:** ILO defines Social assistance as, "a service or scheme which provides benefits to persons of small means as of right in amount sufficient to meet minimum standards of need and financed from taxation."Thus social assistance is the obligation of the community or the Government.
- **Social Insurance:** ***William Beveridge*** defines Social Insurance as, "the giving in return for contribution, benefits up to subsistence level, as of right and without meanstests, so that an individual may build freely upon it. Thus Social Insurance implies that it is compulsory."
- In socialist countries the vowed goal is complete protection to every citizen from ***the cradle to grave.***
- According to the social security convention (No.102) adopted by the ILO in 1952, following are the nine components of social security:
  - Medical Care

- Sickness Benefit
- Unemployment Benefit
- Old-age Benefit
- Employment Injury Benefit
- Family Benefit
- Maternity Benefit
- Invalidity Benefit
- Survivor's Benefit

International Standards of Social Security

- Compulsory participation
- Government sponsorship
- Contributory finance
- Eligibility derived from contributions
- Benefits prescribed in law
- Benefits not directly related to contributions.

Social Security Laws and Acts

- The Workmen's Compensation Act, 1923
- The Employees' State Insurance Act, 1948
- The Employees' Provident Fund and Miscellaneous Provisions Act, 1952
- The Maternity Benefit Act, 1961
- The Payment of Gratuity Act, 1952

Types of Social Security and Welfare Programmes

1. For employment security
2. For health protection
3. For old and retirement
4. For personnel identification, participation and stimulation

Classification of Fringe Benefits: Robert H. Hoge

1. Payment for time not worked

- Sick leave with pay
- Vacation pay
- Paid rest and relief time
- Paid lunch periods
- Grievance time
- Bargaining time
- Travel time

2. Extra Pay for time worked

- Premium pay
- Incentive bonus
- Shift premium
- Old age insurance
- Profit sharing and unemployment compensation
- Christmas bonus
- Diwali or Pooja bonus

- Food cost subsidy
- Housing subsidy
- Recreation

Health and Safety

Industrial Health: In an industrial plant, the health of the employees working there plays a vital role in the production.

Physical Health: Bad health of employees increases absenteeism of employees and hence, affects the production process. On the other hand, healthy employees help in increasing the production.

Mental Health: These days the mental health of employees has become a matter of concern for the employees.

Noise Control: These days noise from the machineries has increased problems like hearing impairment among the employees. Hormonal imbalance, changes in blood circulation, dizziness, increase in respiratory rate, heartburn, sleep disturbance and fatigue, also occur because of noise.

Work Stress: The factors that cause stress can be physical, psychological and behavioral. These factors are called stressors. Stress can be positive or negative.

Industrial Accident

- An industrial accident may be defined as 'an occurrence which interferes with the orderly progress of work in an industrial establishment.'
- According to the Factories Act, industrial accident is " an occurrence in an industrial establishment causing bodily injury to a person which makes him unfit to resume his duties in the next 48 hours".

Accident Prevention: According to the National Safety Council USA, accident prevention depends on three E's:

1. Engineering – the job should be engineered for safety.
2. Employees – employees should be educated in safe procedure and
3. Enforcing safety – safety rules should be properly enforced.

Occupational Diseases

- Occupational diseases are the result of constant exposure to the influence of toxic substances of micro-organisms, of air-borne contaminants and stress – producing elements.
- Provisions under the Factories Act 1948: The Factories Act 1948 provides for health safety and welfare.
- **Health:** The Act provides detailed instructions on cleanliness, disposal of wastage, ventilation, lighting, over-crowding, etc.
- **Safety:** Prevention of accidents in an objective which requires no expansion. This is one area in which there is complete identity of employer – employee interests.
- The employee does not want to be injured and the employer does not want to incur the cost of injuring him.

8.7. OBJECTIVE QUESTIONS - ANSWER

1. Which of the following statements is not true in explaining the concept and scope of labour welfare?
   (A) Labour welfare has no roots in social work.
   (B) Long Arm of the job and social invasion of workplace' concepts, explain the mutuality between intramural and extra-mural labour welfare
   (C) Labour welfare is a social concept.
   (D) Corporate social responsibility is an extended concept of welfare.

Answer: A

2. Who is the champion of the 'Welfare movement' propagated in mid 19th century ?
   (A) Frederick Winslow Taylor
   (B) Andrew Ure
   (C) Sheebhom Rownlvee
   (D) Robert Owners

Answer: D

3. Welfare is considered as
   (A) Total Concept
   (B) Social Concept
   (C) Relative Concept
   (D) All the above

Answer: D

4. Which of the following experiments is associated with the welfare movement ?
   (A) Hawthorne Experiment
   (B) New Lanark Experiment
   (C) Ahmedabad Experiment
   (D) None of the above

Answer: B

5. The seven approaches to philosophy or theory of labour welfare were first identified by
   (A) K.N. Vaid
   (B) M.V. Moorthy
   (C) A.M. Sharma
   (D) I.D. Punekar

Answer: B

6. Who considered 'want', 'ignorance', 'squalor', 'idleness' and 'disease' as five giants on the road to social security ?
   (A) V.V. Giri
   (B) M.V. Moorthy
   (C) Lord Beveridge
   (D) Pal Chu

Answer: C

7. The success of welfare work depends on six basic principles was advocated by
   (A) S. D. Punekar
   (B) D. Paul Choudhury
   (C) A. M. Sharma
   (D) M. V. Moorthy

Answer: D

8. The father of the Employees State Insurance Scheme in India is :
   (A) B.P. Wadia
   (B) B.P. Adarkar
   (C) V.V. Giri
   (D) N.M. Lokhande

Answer: B

9. Robert Owen, the founder of 'Welfare Movement' conducted which of the following experiments ?
   (A) New Lanark Experiment
   (B) Hawthorne Experiment
   (C) Experiment on Illumination
   (D) None of the above

Answer: A

10. Trusteeship theory of labour welfare was propounded by
    (A) G. L. Nanda
    (B) Mahatma Gandhi
    (C) Indira Gandhi
    (D) None of the above

Answer: B

11. Minimum conditions of welfare is explained by
    (A) Dr. Aykroid's formula

(B) Subsistence Theory
(C) Both (A) and (B)
(D) None of the above

Answer: C

12. Which of the following is not a principle of Labour Welfare ?
(A) The Principle of Uniformity
(B) The Principle of Co-ordination and Integration
(C) The principle of Association
(D) The Principle of Timeliness

Answer: A

13. Match the following :

List – I (Theme)

a. The labour welfare philosophy is meant for guarding the interests of labour against the exploitation of employers.
b. The labour welfare philosophy exposes the cause of empathic considerations by the employer of employee well being
c. The employer has to set out a portion of the profits for the benefit of the employees
d. Labour Welfare is provided for pacifying the agitating working class

List – II(Theory)

i. Trusteeship Theory
ii. Placating Theory
iii. Policing Theory
iv. Philanthropic Theory

Codes :

	a	b	c	d
(A)	ii	iv	iii	i
(B)	iii	iv	i	ii
(C)	iii	i	ii	iv
(D)	iv	ii	iii	i

Answer: B

14. Which of the following are not the theories of Labour Welfare ?
(A) Policing Theory and Placating Theory
(B) Religious Theory and Trusteeship Theory
(C) Functional Theory and Public Relations Theory
(D) Subsistence Theory and Residual Claimant Theory

Answer: D

15. "Welfare work is a means of securing, preserving and increasing the efficiency of labour" is the theme of
(A) Paternalistic Theory
(B) Religious Theory
(C) Functional Theory
(D) Placating Theory

Answer: C

16. The central theme of paternalistic theory of labour welfare is :
(A) Welfare enhances workers' efficiency
(B) Employees are treated as the guardians of the industrial property
(C) Workers are treated as members of the industrial family
(D) Welfare is a kind of investment

Answer: B

17. Who is called as the father of Labour Welfare Movement ?
(A) Frederick Herzberg
(B) Robert Owen
(C) F.W. Taylor
(D) Charles Babbage

Answer: B

18. The welfare is a state of living of an individual or a group in desirable relation to the total environment , animate and inanimate , according to :
(A) K. N. Vaid (B) A. M. Sharma
(C) M. V. Moorthy (D)S.D. Punekar

Answer: C

19. 'Trusteeship theory' of labour welfare was proposed by :
(A) M. K. Gandhi
(B) V. V. Giri
(C) Bal Gangadhar Tilak
(D) Jawaharlal Nehru

Answer: A

20. The concept of the stewardship of one's possessions to increase wealth, using one's
talent and displaying the surplus in public causes was emphasized by :
(A) Conflict Theory of Karl Marx
(B) Trusteeship Theory of Mahatma Gandhi
(C) Rational Theory of Robert Hoxie
(D) Behavioural Theory of Max Weber

Answer: B

21. Match the following
(a) Policing theory
(i) Labour welfare work is taken up in a spirit of atonement
(b) Religious theory
(ii) Passing the laws and strictly implementing them to ascertain that welfare measures are provided
(c) Functional theory
(iii) Welfare work is a means of securing,preserving and increasing efficiency means of securing their cooperation
(d) Placating theory
(iv) Workers are becoming conscious of their rights and welfare work is the best means of securing their cooperation

	(a)	(b)	(c)	(d)
(A)	(ii)	(i)	(iv)	(iii)
(B)	(ii)	(i)	(iii)	(iv)
(C)	(i)	(iii)	(iv)	(ii)
(D)	(iii)	(iv)	(ii)	(i)

Answer: A

22. Welfare programmes undertaken outside the organisation are called :
(A) Statutory welfare programme
(B) Intra mural welfare programmes
(C) Extra mural welfare programmes
(D) Non statutory welfare programmes

Answer: C

23. Which of the following is not a principle of labour welfare ?
(A) Policing Theory of Labour Welfare
(B) Religious Theory of Labour Welfare
(C) The Philanthropic Theory of Labour Welfare
(D) Productivity Theory of Labour Welfare

Answer: D

24. Sequence the following developments by their period of occurrence from earliest to the latest :
(i) The Labour Investigation Committee
(ii) The Whitley Commission
(iii) The Enactment of Factories Act
(iv) The 1st National Commission on Labour

(A)	(ii)	(i)	(iii)	(iv)
(B)	(ii)	(iii)	(iv)	(i)
(C)	(i)	(ii)	(iv)	(iii)
(D)	(iv)	(ii)	(iii)	(i)

Answer: A

25. Which of the following statements relating to Welfare Officer is not true
(A) The provision of Welfare Officer is given in both the Factories Act, 1948 and the Mines Act, 1952.
(B) Welfare Officer's duties and responsibilities are defined and prescribed in the legislation.
(C) Welfare Officer's appointment is tagged to the provision of minimum workforce employed in an organisation
(D) The Welfare Officer's role was designed as a 'Third force'.

Answer: B

26. Match the following :

(a) Royal Commission on	(i) 1937 Labour
(b) Bombay Textile Labour	(ii) 1946 Enquiry committee
(c) Second Labour	(iii)1929 Ministers' Conference
(d) Labour Investigation	(iv)2002 Committee
(e) Second National	(v)1941 Commission on Labour

	(a)	(b)	(c)	(d)	(e)
(A)	(ii)	(i)	(iii)	(iv)	(v)
(B)	(iii)	(ii)	(i)	(v)	(iv)
(C)	(iii)	(v)	(iv)	(i)	(ii)
(D)	(iii)	(i)	(v)	(ii)	(iv)

Answer: D

27. Assertion (A) : Intra-mural and extra-mural welfare are mutually complimentary.

Reason (R) : The work-life balances need to be ensured in order to get the best output from an employee.

(A) Assertion is wrong but Reason is logical.
(B) Both Assertion and Reason are wrong.
(C) Assertion and Reason are right.
(D) The Assertion is right but Reason is wrong.

Answer: C

28. Which of the following is not included under intra-mural labour welfare facilities

(A) Latrines and Urinals
(B) Washing Facilities
(C) Creches
(D) Housing Facilities

Answer: D

29. Classification of labour welfare facilities under (a) Extra-mural and (b) Intra-mural was done by :

(A) I.L.O.
(B) The Study Group constituted by the Govt. of India in 1959
(C) Indian Labour Conference
(D) National Commission on Labour, 1969

Answer: A

30. Which of the following cannot be regarded as an organisation in the field of Labour Welfare :

(A) Central Board of Workers' Education
(B) Consumer Courts
(C) Workmen's compensation commissioner
(D) Employees' State Insurance Corporation

Answer: B

31. Choose the appropriate answer from the option given below : In India, Labour Welfare work of trade unions is ________

(A) Not developed at all
(B) Developed to some extent
(C) Fully developed
(D) Highly developed

Answer: B

32. Which of the following cannot be said to be an extra-mural welfare facility ?

(A) Sports
(B) Hospital
(C) Transport facility
(D) Canteens and First Aid Boxes

Answer: D

33. Which of the following is not an agency of providing labour welfare ?

(A) State
(B) Employer
(C) Trade Unions
(D) Customers

Answer: D

34. Which of the following is not a statutory welfare facility under the Factories Act, 1948 ?

(A) Canteen
(B) Sports facility
(C) Creche
(D) First-Aid Appliances

Answer: B

35. Under which part of the Indian Constitution necessity of more labour welfare is emphasised :

(A) Fundamental Rights
(B) Directive Principles of State Policy
(C) Both under Fundamental Rights and Directive Principles of State Policy
(D) None of the above

Answer: B

36. Match the following :

Contributors	Contribution
(a) Robert Owen	(i) Social Security
(b) Mahatma Gandhi	(ii) Employee State Insurance
(c) Beveridge	(iii) Welfare Movement
(d) Adarkar	(iv) Trusteeship Theory

Code:

	(a)	(b)	(c)	(d)
(A)	(iii)	(i)	(ii)	(iv)
(B)	(iii)	(iv)	(i)	(ii)
(C)	(ii)	(iii)	(i)	(iv)
(D)	(iii)	(ii)	(iv)	(i)

Answer: B

37. Sequence the following from the earliest to the latest :

(i) Gajendragadkar Commission
(ii) First Factory Commission
(iii) Whitely Commission
(iv) Rege Committee

Codes :

(A)	(ii)	(iii)	(iv)	(i)
(B)	(iii)	(ii)	(i)	(iv)
(C)	(ii)	(iv)	(iii)	(i)
(D)	(iii)	(i)	(ii)	(iv)

Answer: A

38. Match the following :

Commission/Committee	Year
(a) First Factory Commission	(i) 1946
(b) Royal Commission on Labour	(ii) 1969
(c) Labour Investigation Committee	(iii) 1931
(d) First National Labour Commission	(iv) 1875

	(a)	(b)	(c)	(d)
(A)	(i)	(iii)	(iv)	(ii)
(B)	(iv)	(ii)	(iii)	(i)
(C)	(iv)	(iii)	(i)	(ii)
(D)	(ii)	(i)	(iii)	(iv)

Answer: C

39. Sequence the following offices from latest to earliest in their emergence.

(a) Labour Officer
(b) Safety Officer
(c) Personnel Officer
(d) Welfare Officer

(A)	(b)	(c)	(d)	(a)
(B)	(a)	(c)	(d)	(b)
(C)	(c)	(b)	(a)	(d)
(D)	(a)	(d)	(c)	(b)

Answer: D

40. Which of the following is a non-statutory welfare facility ?

(A) Welfare Officer
(B) Creche
(C) Transport facility
(D) Canteen

Answer: C

41. Who opined that the "Labour Welfare officer should not merely remain looking after the interests of the management , but also consider they are custodians of the rights and privileges of the workers ?

(A) G. L. Nanda
(B) V. V. Giri
(C) Morarji Desai
(D) M. K. Gandhi

Answer: B

42. Match the following :

Welfare funds

(a) Coal Mines Welfare Fund Act.
(b) The Mica Mines Welfare Fund Act.
(c) The Iron Ore Mines Labour Welfare Fund Act.
(d) The Lime Stone And Dolomite Mines Labour

Years

(i) 1973
(ii) 1961
(iii) 1946
(iii) 1947

Welfare Fund Act

	(a)	(b)	(c)	(d)
(A)	(ii)	(iii)	(i)	(iv)

(B) (iv) (ii) (iii) (i)
(C) (ii) (iv) (i) (iii)
(D) (iv) (iii) (ii) (i)

Answer: D

43. Which of the following recommended to the Government of India to consider making social security as a fundamental human right ?
(A) The Labour Investigation Committee
(B) The Royal Commission on Labour
(C) The First National Commission on Labour
(D) The second National Commission on Labour

Answer: D

44. Which of the following cannot be regarded as a statutory welfare facility for factory workers?
(A) Canteen
(B) Housing
(C) Shelter, Rest rooms and Lunch rooms
(D) First Aid Box

Answer: B

45. Who among the following is not included in labour force ?
(A) Persons below 15 years of age
(B) Housewives and pensioners
(C) Mentally Disabled
(D) All the Above

Answer: D

46. The scope of state regulation of wages in the present scenario in India particularly , in the organized sector is :
(A) Increasing
(B) Decreasing
(C) Irrelevant
(D) None of the above

Answer: B

47. The ongoing industrialisation in the country is contributing to which type of unemployment?
(A) Cyclical Unemployment
(B) Frictional Unemployment
(C) Seasonal Unemployment
(D) Technological Unemployment

Answer: D

48. The programmes generally providing benefits for meeting the minimum needs of persons of small means are called
(A) Social Insurance
(B) Social Assistance
(C) Mutual Aid
(D) None of the above

Answer: B

49. Which of the following cannot be regarded as extra mural labour welfare facility ?
(A) Canteen
(B) Housing
(C) Hospital
(D) Playground

Answer: A

50. Who among the following is not regarded as welfare agency for factory workers ?
(A) Employer
(B) Trade Unions
(C) N.G.Os
(D) State and Central Government

Answer: C

51. There shall be delegation of authority in the welfare fields, either by election to committees, or by proper nomination, according to
(A) Principle of Timeliness
(B) Principle of Accountability
(C) Principle of Evaluation and Assessment
(D) Principle of Responsibility

Answer: D

52. The need for imparting necessary education to workers in India had been emphasised first by :
(A) The Royal Commission on Labour
(B) The Indian Industrial Commission

(C) The Labour Investigation Committee
(D) None of the above

Answer: A

53. Which of the following is an agency for providing labour welfare facilities in Factories ?
(A) Management (B) Trade Union
(C) Government (D) NGO

Answer: A

54. Which of the following is not included under intra-mural labour welfare facilities ?
(A) Canteen
(B) Crèche
(C) Hospitals
(D) Shelter, Rest rooms

Answer: C

55. One first aid box must be provided for every
(A) 150 workers (B) 200 workers
(C) 250 workers (D) 300 workers

Answer: A

56. The author of the book 'Principles of Labour Welfare' is :
(A) K. N. Vaid
(B) M. V. Murthy
(C) S. C. Pant
(D) T. N. Bhagoliwal

Answer: B

57. Which of the following is not a labour welfare agency ?
(A) Bharat Sewak Samaj
(B) Harijan Sewak Sangh
(C) Central Social Welfare Board
(D) Standing Labour Committee

Answer: D

58. Which of the following is not an intra-mural labour welfare measure ?
(A) Canteen
(B) Creche
(C) Rest room, shelter and lunch room
(D) Housing and hospital facility

Answer: D

59. Which of the following does not affect the supply of labour ?
(A) Population
(B) Strike
(C) Labour force participation
(D) Mobility of labour

Answer: C

60. "A desirable state of existence comprehending physical, mental, moral and emotional health or well being" is the theme of which concept of Labour Welfare ?
(A) Social Concept
(B) Total Concept
(C) Relative Concept
(D) Positive Concept

Answer: B

61. Assertion (A) : Labour Welfare is relative to time and space.
Reason (R) : It shall be universal and perpetual.
(A) Assertion and Reason are right.
(B) Assertion is wrong and Reason is right.
(C) Both Assertion and Reason are wrong.
(D) Assertion is right but its explanation given in Reason is wrong.

Answer: D

62. "Labour is not a commodity" – is the assertion made by
(A) the Declaration of Philadelphia adopted by 26th session of ILO
(B) the Magna Carta
(C) the Constitution of India
(D) the International Labour Conference

Answer: A

63. Match the following :

Concept	Propagators
a. Industrial Democracy	i. Karl Marx
b. Industrial Citizenship	ii. Robert Owen
c. Class Conflict	iii. Peter F. Drucker
d. Welfare Movement	iv. Sydney & Beatrize Webbs

Codes :

	a	b	c	d
(A)	iii	i	ii	iv
(B)	iv	iii	i	ii
(C)	ii	i	iv	iii
(D)	ii	iv	i	iii

Answer: B

64. Assertion (A) : Industrial Labour in India has been migratory.

Reason (R) : Driving force in migration comes almost entirely from one end of the channel, that is the village end.

(A) Both (A) and (R) are wrong.
(B) (A) is wrong and (R) is right.
(C) (A) is right and (R) also is right.
(D) (A) is right and (R) is wrong.

Answer: C

65. Which of the following is not a method of social security ?

(A) Social Assistance
(B) Social Action
(C) Social Insurance
(D) Mutual Assistance

Answer: B

66. Who has given the concept of 'Core competence' ?

(A) Sumantra Ghosal & C.A. Bartlett
(B) T. Deal and A. Kennedy
(C) C.K. Prahalad and G. Hamel
(D) C.A. Forehand and B. Von Gilnev

Answer: C

67. The Central Social Welfare Board was established by :

(A) Parliamentary enactment
(B) Resolution of Cabinet
(C) Registration under company Act,1956
(D) The order of the President

Answer: C

68. The interaction between Government and NGOs in India mostly relates to

(i) Policies and legislation related to disadvantaged sections.
(ii) Economic policies
(iii) Operational collaboration for programmes with or without Government funding.
(iv) Peaceful protest movement of people in which NGOs are involved.

Select the correct answer from the codes given below :

Codes :

(A) (i), (ii)
(B) (i), (ii), (iv)
(C) (i), (iii), (iv)
(D) (iii), (iv)

Answer: C

69. The term 'Social Justice' is originally based on the teachings of

(A) St. Thomas Aquinas
(B) Karl Marx
(C) John Rawls
(D) B.R. Ambedkar

Answer: A

70. "Creating jobs, guaranteeing rights at work, extending social protection and promoting social dialogue" are contents of which of the following programmes of ILO ?

(A) Human Rights
(B) Decent Work
(C) International Programme on the Elimination of Child Labour
(D) INDUS Child Labour Project

Answer: B

71. ILO was formed in the year

(A) 1919 (B) 1947
(C) 1951 (D) 1926

Answer: A

72. "Creating jobs, guaranteeing rights at work, extending social protection and promoting social dialogue" are

contents of which of the following programmes of ILO ?
(A) Human Rights
(B) Decent Work
(C) International Programme on the Elimination of Child Labour
(D) INDUS Child Labour Project

Answer: B

73. The constitution of India upholds the principle 'Freedom of Association' as a fundamental right enunciated by I. L. O. convention in
(A) Article 20(C) (B) Article 19(C)
(C) Article 24(C) (D) Article 18(C)

Answer: B

74. Which ILO convention is concerned with equal remuneration for equal work' ?
(A) Convention No. 98
(B) Convention No. 99
(C) Convention No. 100
(D) Convention No. 101

Answer: C

75. The international labour code consists of :
(A) The conventions and Recommendations of I. L. O
(B) The proposals submitted by the member countries
(C) The opinions of the U. N. O
(D) All the above.

Answer: A

76. The number of bipartite committees as provided under the factories Act, 1948 :
(A) 1 (B) 2
(C) 3 (D) 4

Answer: A

77. Which of the following statements relating to I.L.O. is not true ?
(A) I.L.O. is a tripartite body.
(B) I.L.O. has a standing labour committee.
(C) I.L.O. believes not only in people at work but also their development.
(D) I.L.O. recommendations are compulsorily binding in nature.

Answer: D

78. The primary function of I.L.O. is to formulate the international labour standards in the shape of
(A) Conventions only
(B) Recommendations only
(C) Both (A) and (B)
(D) None of the above

Answer: C

79. Which of the following statements about I.L.O. is not true?
(A) I.L.O is a tripartite body.
(B) I.L.O was established in 1919.
(C) I.L.O passes only recommendations.
(D) I.L.O conventions are mandatory for those countries which ratify them.

Answer: C

80. India ratified I.L.O. Convention No. 144 on tripartite consultation among government, employer's and worker's representatives in :
(A) 1968 (B) 1958
(C) 1978 (D) 1988

Answer: C

81. The code of discipline was ratified by the Indian Labour Conference to ensure discipline in industry. Identify the year of ratification out of the following :
(A) 1957 (B) 1958
(C) 1942 (D) 1962

Answer: B

82. In which year the formation of the National Renewal Fund to protect the interest of the workers was announced :
(A) 1956 (B) 1991
(C) 1969 (D) 1992

Answer : B

83. The code of discipline in industry was adopted by the Indian labour conference (tripantite) in

(A) 1948 (B) 1958
(C) 1968 (D) 1950

Answer: B

84. Arrange the following in the order they appeared. Use the codes given below :

a. First Labour Legislation
b. I. L. O.
c. Indian Constitution
d. E. S. I. Corporation

(A) (iv) (ii) (iii) (i)
(B) (i) (ii) (iii) (iv)
(C) (ii) (i) (iv) (iii)
(D) (i) (ii) (iv) (iii)

Answer: B

85. Ravindra Verma was the Chairman of

(A) Royal Commission on Labour
(B) First National Commission on Labour
(C) Second National Commission on Labour
(D) Labour Investigation Committee

Answer: C

86. The Tripartite Declaration of Principles concerning MNEs and social policy enunciated by ILO was in

(A) 1976 (B) 1977
(C) 1978 (D) 1979

Answer: B

87. The Chairman of the Second National Commission on Labour was

(A) Gajendra Gadkar
(B) Ravindra Verma
(C) George Fernandes
(D) Vallabh Bhai Patel

Answer: B

88. Find out the origin of the statement in a socialist democracy labour is a partner in the common task of development, should participate in it with enthusiasm.

(A) Constitution of India
(B) Directive principles of State Policy
(C) Industrial Policy Resolution 1956
(D) Royal Commission on Labour

Answer: C

89. The goal of I LO is

(A) creation of jobs for men and women
(B) not just creation of jobs but the creation of jobs of acceptable quality
(C) not overcoming under employment
(D) not to provide freedom of choice in employment

Answer: B

90. ILO was formed in the year :

(A) 1919 (B) 1947
(C) 1951 (D) 1926

Answer: A

91. The basic postulates on which the ILO standards lie are

(A) Labour is not a commodity
(B) Freedom of expression and of association are essential to sustained progress
(C) Poverty anywhere constitutes danger to prosperity everywhere
(D) All the above

Answer: D

92. The establishment of Indian Labour Conference and Standing Labour Committee in India was on the pattern of

(A) ILO
(B) Report of Royal Commission on Labour
(C) Both (A) and (B)
(D) None of the above

Answer: C

93. Plenary labour conference was initial name of which of the following organization?

(A) ILO
(B) Standing labour committee
(C) Indian labour conference
(D) International labour conference

Answer: A

94. Which of the following has done considerable work in the field of labour welfare ?

(A) CARE (B) WHO
(C) ILO (D) UNICEF

Answer: C

95. What is the full form of RMMS?

(A) Retired Mill Mazdoor Seva
(B) Rashtriya Mill Mazdoor Seva
(C) Rashtriya Mill Mazdoor Sangh
(D) Retired Mill Mazdoor Sangh

Answer: C

96. Employee stock option plan (ESOP)aims at :

(A) Only as an incentive to employee
(B) Only for employee retention
(C) Both (A) and (B)
(D) None of the above

Answer: C

97. The basic postulates on which the ILO standards lie are

(A) Labour is not a commodity
(B) Freedom of expression and of association are essential to sustained progress
(C) Poverty anywhere constitutes danger to prosperity everywhere
(D) All the above

Answer: D

98. ILO stands for:-

(A) International Labour Office
(B) International Labour Order
(C) International Labour Organization
(D) International Labour Audit

Answer: C

99. The leading social insurance program is:

(A) unemployment insurance.
(B) social security for retirees.
(C) Medicare.
(D) public assistance programs such as food stamps.

Answer: B

100. Most social welfare programs are:

(A) uniform throughout the states.
(B) widely supported by Americans.
(C) run jointly by federal and state governments.
(D) managed entirely by the federal government.

Answer: C

101. Who is the father of labour welfare movement in India?

(A)N.M.Joshi
(B) Narayan Meghaji Lokhande
(C) M.K.Gandhi
(D) Robert Owen

Answer: (B)

102. Who is the father of labour welfare movement in world?

(A) N.M.Joshi
(B) Narayan Meghaji Lokhande
(C) M.K.Gandhi
(D) Robert Owen

Answer: (D)

*****

UNIT-IX
LABOUR LEGISLATION

9.1. LABOUR LEGISLATION –NATURE-NEED-OBJECTIVE-PRINCIPLE

- Labour Legislation includes all the laws which have been enacted to deal with employment and non-employment, wages, working conditions, industrial relations, social security and welfare of persons employed in industries. Also refers to all laws of the government to provide social and economic security to the workers.
- The aim of labour legislation is to reduce production losses due to industrial disputes and to ensure timely payment of wages and statutory amenities to workers.

Nature of Labour Legislation

1. Products of Industrial Revolution
2. Regards Individual as a worker
3. Deals with Problems of Labour
4. It is Role- Relation
5. Regulates Conditions of Labour

Need for Labour Legislation

1. **Weak Labour Organizations:** Now as the payment of wages, lay off, dismissal, retrenchments etc, are all governed by the legislations, economic insecurity of workers is removed to great extent.
2. **Occupational Insecurity:**
   - o The workers in many organizations, did not get the amount in case of accidents, deaths etc. As a result, the workers faced occupational insecurity.
   - o Benefits such as Occupational Act, Employees State Insurance Act, etc. have been statutorily given to the employees.
3. **Hazardous Working Conditions**
   - o Workers health and safety is always in danger due to harmful working condition in some factories.
   - o The Factories Act, contains a number of provisions relating to health, safety and welfare of workers.
4. **Law And Order**
   - o Labour legislation is also necessary in order to maintain law and order situation and national security of the country.
   - o The idea of welfare state is embodied in the directive principles of the constitution and for that reason various labour laws have been enacted to protect the sections of the society.
5. **Achieving Socio-economic Progress:** Labour legislation is one of the most progressive and dynamic instruments for achieving socio- economic progress.

Objectives of Labour Legislation

- To protect the workers from profit seeking exploiters/industrialist.
- To ensure that the service conditions should be clearly spelt out by the employer to the employee.
- To improve and regulate the working conditions of workers employed in different factories and establishments.
- To make statutory provision for the regular trainings of a certain number of apprentices in different trades.
- To ensure that the employees are paid their wages on fixed dates and there should be no deduction made from the wages.
- To promote industrial relations and industrial peace between employers and employees.
- To preserve the health, safety and welfare of workers.
- To protect the interest of women and children working in the factories.
- To maintain the dignity of employees in their organizations.
- The objectives of labour legislations are two-fold:
  1. Preservation of the health, safety and welfare of workers; and
  2. Maintenance of good relations between employers and employees.

Principles of labour legislation

1. **Social Justice:** In modern industrial set-up, workers are unable to protect their interest therefore the State has to intervene to help them by granting them freedom of association, the power of collective bargaining and by providing for mediation or arbitration in the case of industrial conflict.
2. **Social Equity:** Legislation based on this principle provides for achievement of definite standards of the working population in terms of living, position, etc. in society.
3. **National Economy:** Ensure normal growth of industry for the benefit of the nation as a whole and satisfy the physical and intellectual needs of the citizens. Also ensure the growth of industrial efficiency such as to adjust the wage system with a view to increase the productivity and prosperity of the workers.
4. **International Uniformity**: Securing minimum standards for the working population- worldwide on a uniform basis in respect of all labour matters has been the main objective of ILO. To this end, conventions are passed at the conferences of ILO. As a member of the ILO, adopting these conventions would require appropriate legislation to be brought about. The influence of international labour conventions has been significant in shaping the course of labour legislation in India.

9.2.LABOUR JURISDICTION: STATE Vs CENTRAL

- Under the Constitution of India, Labour is a subject in the Concurrent List where both the Central & State Governments are competent to enact legislation subject to certain matters being reserved for the Centre.

Constitutional Status

Union List	Concurrent List
Entry No. 55 : Regulation of labour and safety in mines and oil fields	Entry No. 22: Trade Unions; industrial and labour disputes.
Entry No. 61: Industrial disputes concerning Union employees	Entry No.23: Social Security and insurance, employment and unemployment.
Entry No.65: Union agencies and institutions for "Vocational training etc."	Entry No. 24: Welfare of about including conditions of work, provident funds, employers 'invalidity and old age pension and maternity benefit.

- Matters relating to Social Security are Directive Principles of State Policy and the subjects in the Concurrent List. The following social security issues are mentioned in the Concurrent List (List III in the Seventh Schedule of the Constitution of India).

Part III Fundamental Rights:

Article-16: Equality of opportunity in matters of public employment:

(1) There shall be equality of opportunity for all citizens in matters relating to employment or appointment to any office under the State.

(2) No citizen shall, on grounds only of religion, race, caste, sex, descent, place of birth, residence or any of them, be ineligible for, or discriminated against in respect of, any employment or office under the State.

(3) Nothing in this article shall prevent Parliament from making any law prescribing, in regard to a class or classes of employment or appointment to an office under the Government of, or any local or other authority within, a State or Union territory, any requirement as to residence within that State or Union territory prior to such employment or appointment.

(4A) Nothing in this article shall prevent the State from making any provision for reservation in matters of promotion to any class or classes of posts in the services under the State in favour of the Scheduled Castes and the Scheduled Tribes which, in the opinion of the State, are not adequately represented in the services under the State.

(4B) Nothing in this article shall prevent the State from considering any unfilled vacancies of a year which are reserved for being filled up in that year in accordance with any provision for reservation made under clause (4) or clause (4A) as a separate class of vacancies to be filled up in any succeeding year or years and such class of vacancies shall not be considered together with the vacancies of the year in which they are being filled up for determining the ceiling of fifty per cent reservation on total number of vacancies of that year.

(5) Nothing in this article shall affect the operation of any law which provides that the incumbent of an office in connection with the affairs of any religious or denominational institution or any member of the governing body thereof shall be a person professing a particular religion or belonging to a particular denomination.

Article-24: Prohibition of employment of children in factories:

No child below the age of fourteen years shall be employed to work in any factory or mine or engaged in any other hazardous employment.

Part- IV: Directive Principles of State Policy

- **Article-39: Equal pay for equal work for both men and women:** Article 39 of the Constitution envisages that the State shall direct its policy, among other things, towards securing that there is equal pay for equal work for both men and women.
- **Article-41: Right to work, to education and to public assistance in certain cases:** The State shall, within the limits of its economic capacity and development, make effective provision for securing the right to work, to education and to public assistance in cases of unemployment, old age, sickness and disablement, and in other cases of undeserved want.
- **Article 42: Provision for just and humane conditions of work and maternity relief:** The State shall make provision for securing just and humane conditions of work and for maternity relief.
- **Article 43: Living wage, etc., for workers:** The State shall Endeavour to secure, by suitable legislation or economic organization or in any other way, to all workers, agricultural, industrial or otherwise, work, a living wage, conditions of work ensuring a decent standard of life and full enjoyment of leisure and social and cultural opportunities and, in particular, the State shall endeavour to promote cottage industries on an individual or co-operative basis in rural areas.
- **Article 43A: Participation of workers in management of industries:** The State shall take steps, by suitable legislation or in any other way, to secure the participation of workers in the management of undertakings, establishments or other organisations engaged in any industry.

Labour Policy of India

- Labour policy in India has been evolving in response to specific needs of the situation to suit requirements of planned economic development and social justice and has two-fold objectives, viz., maintaining industrial peace and promoting the welfare of labour.

Highlights of Labour Policy

- Creative measures to attract public and private investment.
- Creating new jobs
- New Social security schemes for workers in the unorganised sector.
- Social security cards for workers.
- Unified and beneficial management of funds of Welfare Boards.
- Reprioritization of allocation of funds to benefit vulnerable workers.
- Model employee-employer relationships.
- Long term settlements based on productivity.
- Vital industries and establishments declared as `public utilities`.
- Special conciliation mechanism for projects with investments of Rs.150 crores or more.
- Industrial Relations committees in more sectors.
- Labour Law reforms in tune with the times. Empowered body of experts to suggest required changes.
- Statutory amendments for expediting and streamlining the mechanism of Labour Judiciary.
- Amendments to Industrial Disputes Act in tune with the times.
- Efficient functioning of Labour Department.
- More labour sectors under Minimum Wages Act.
- Child labour act to be aggressively enforced.
- Modern medical facilities for workers.
- Rehabilitation packages for displaced workers.

- Restructuring in functioning of employment exchanges.
- Revamping of curriculum and course content in industrial training.
- Joint cell of labour department and industries department to study changes in laws and rules.

9.3. IMPACT OF ILO ON LABOUR LEGISLATION

- The ILO was set up in the year 1919, with an aim to improve the conditions of labours around the world.
- The success of labour legislations must be attributing to the ILO, as the guidelines issued by the ILO formed the principle on which these legislations were drawn.
- The ILO did have a great impact on the labour laws in India. Many new laws were enacted to incorporate the guidelines of the ILO.
- The Setting of ILO also saw the amendment of Factories Act, 1881. All these amended and enacted legislations make provisions for the general welfare and protection of interest of the labours in India.
- The positive influence of ILO was seen in the form of recognition of many new kinds of rights that were not available to the labour class, but were made available post creation of ILO.
- The impact of ILO on India is felt in the following fields:

1. **Labour Legislation**: Until 1919, there were no important labour legislations in India but, with the establishment of ILO and Indians uninterrupted association with these organizations, coupled with trade union pressure in the country, has greatly influenced labour legislation.
2. **Technical Assistance:** The ILO has been providing technical assistance in implementing various social security measures in programs designed to explore workers education, including vocational training and in improving employment service.
3. **Social Security:** The ILO assigned technical expertise to advise on the implementation of social security legislation such as Employees State Insurance Act of 1948.
4. **Vocational Training:** Technical assistance in the fields of vocational training began in 1950 and has since covered various aspects of the programs. During this period, ILO assisted in formulating suitable syllabuses for different grades of workers in different trades and thereby helped to improve the standards of vocational training in India.
5. **Training within the Industry:** ILO experts helped in training large number of persons in India to ensure systematic introduction of the training within the program in interested mills.
6. **Employment Service:** The ILO provided experts to assist the authorities to improve employment service. They assisted in organizing pilot projects for collecting exhaustive data on labour market and in classification of industrial occupation on the basis of ILO's international standards classification for further research and analysis in India.
7. **Productivity**: The ILO experts have been collaborating with their Indian counter parts in the study of the problems connected with productivity since 1952.The recommendations given by them led to the establishment of the national productivity center.
   - The Factories Act 1881 is the basis of all labour and industrial laws of the country. It contained provisions for even working hours for men and women, minimum age for employment of children.
   - After the formation of ILO in 1919, this act was amended, which made provisions for safety, health and hygiene of the workers. It also made special provision for women and juvenile workers (i.e. labour above the age of 16 but less than 18).It also prohibited child labour.

- Under the Mines Act 1923, which applies to workers employed in mines, the hours of work for the persons employed on the surface are limited to ten per day and fifty four per week. The periods of work including rest interval should not be more than 12 hours in a day. For the workers working underground, the working hours per day is nine. The Act does not contain provisions for overtime. No worker is to work in a mine for more than six days a week. The Act does not provide for wages for the weekly rest day.
- The Government of India set up an enquiry committee in 1926 to ascertain the loophole for irregularity of payment of wages to industrial workers.
- **The Royal Commission on Labour** considered the reports and suggestions and recommended for enactment relating to payment of wages.
- It aimed (a) At disbursement of actual wages to workers within the prescribed period and (b) To ensure that the employees get their full wages without any deduction. The object of the Act obviously was to provide a cheap and speedy remedy for employees to recover the wages due to them.
- **The Weekly holidays Act, 1942**: Prescribes one paid holiday a week for persons employed in any shop, restaurant or theater. The government is empowered to grant additional half- day holiday with pay in a week.
- **The Industrial Dispute Act, 1947**: Provided for establishment of industrial tribunal by the appropriate government in British India. It established a full- fledged industrial tribunal for adjudication of industrial disputes for the first time.
- **The Industrial Employment (Standing Orders) Act, 1946 :** Defined the terms of employment of workmen in the form of standing orders.
- **The Merchant Shipping Act, 1923**: Provided for agreement between a seaman and the master of the ship regarding the terms of service.

Impact of ILO Conventions on Labour Laws

- Conventions are international treaties and are instruments, which create legally binding obligations on the countries that ratify (accept) them. Recommendations are non- binding and set out guidelines orienting national policies and actions.
- ILO through its conventions and recommendations helps nations to draw their own set of labour laws for the better treatment of the working class and the preservation of their rights.
- India was the founding member of ILO. The ILO instruments have provided guidelines and useful framework for the evolution of legislative and administrative measures for the protection and advancement of the interest of labour in India.
- Ratification of a convention imposes legally binding obligations on the country concerned; therefore India has been very careful in ratifying conventions. India has always made it a practice to ratify conventions when it is fully satisfied that its laws and practices are in conformity with the relevant ILO convention. So far, India has ratified 39 conventions of the ILO.
- There are eight core conventions of the ILO (also called fundamental / human rights conventions). They are as follows:
- The first four conventions have been ratified by India.

1. Forced Labour Convention (No.29)
2. Abolition of forced Labour Convention. (No.105)
3. Equal Remuneration Convention. (No. 100)
4. Discrimination (Employment Occupation) Convention (No.111),
5. Freedom of Association and Protection of Right to Organized Convention (No.87),

6. Right to Organize and Collective Bargaining Convention (No.98),
7. Minimum Age Convention.(No.138)
8. Worst Forms of Child Labour Convention.(No.182)

Growth of Labour Legislation in India

- In India the plantation industry in Assam was the first to attract the legislation.
- A number of acts were passed from 1863 onwards to regulate the recruitments.
- These legislations protected more interests of the employers than safeguarding the interest of the workers.
- The Factories Act was passed in 1881 and the Mines Act in1901.
- The most important act that was passed to protect the interest of the workers was the Workmen's Compensation Act, 1923.

9.4. TYPES OF LABOUR LEGISLATIONS

1. Protective Labour Legislations:

- The legislations whose primary purpose is to protect minimum labour standards and improve working conditions are protective labour legislations.
- Legislations laying down the minimum labour standards in the areas of work, safety, employment of children and women and also the manner of wage payment come under this category.
- The Indian labour laws under this category are:
    1. The Factories Act, 1948
    2. The Mines Act, 1952
    3. The Plantation Labour Act, 1951
    4. The Motor Transport Workers Act, 1961
    5. The Payment of Wages Act, 1936
    6. The Minimum Wages Act, 1948
    7. The Child Labour (Prohibition and regulation) Act, 1986 and
    8. Contract Labour (Regulation and Abolition) Act, 1970.

2. Regulative Legislations :

- The legislations whose primary purpose is to regulate the relations between employers and employees and to provide for methods and manners for settling industrial disputes are Regulative Legislations.
- These laws also regulate the relationships between workers and trade unions, the rights and obligations of the organizations of employers and workers, as well as their mutual relationships.
- The laws under this category are as follows:

1. The Trade Unions Act, 1926
2. The Industrial Disputes Act, 1947, and
3. The Industrial Employment (Standing Orders) Act, 1946

3. Social Security Legislations :

- The Legislations which intend to provide social security benefits to the workmen during certain contingencies of life are Social Security Legislations.
- Though these legislations may cover other classes of citizens also, their primary goal has been to protect the workers.

- The laws under this category are as follows:

1. The Workmen's Compensation Act, 1923
2. The Employees State Insurance Act, 1948
3. The Coal Mines Provident Fund and Miscellaneous Provisions Act, 1948
4. The Employees Provident Funds and Miscellaneous Provisions Act, 1952
5. The Maternity Benefit Act, 1961, and
6. The Payment of Gratuity Act, 1972.

4. Welfare Legislations:

- The aim of welfare legislations is to promote the general welfare of the workers and improve their living conditions.
- Such laws carry the term "Welfare" in their titles.
- All of these laws provide for the funds which is spent on improving the general welfare of workers including housing, medical, educational and recreational facilities.
- The Laws under this category are as follows:

1. Mica Mines Labour Welfare Fund Act, 1946
2. Iron Ore Mines, Manganese Ore Mines and Chrome Ore Mines labour Welfare Fund Act, 1976 and
3. Beedi Workers Welfare Fund Act, 1976.

9.4.1. The Factories Act, 1948

Introduction

- In India the first Factories Act was passed in **1881**.
- This Act was basically designed to protect children and to provide measures for health and safety of the workers.
- This law was applicable to only those factories, which employed 100 or more workers.
- In **1891** another factories Act was passed which extended to the factories employing 50 or more workers.
- The Factories Act, 1948 came into force on the 1st day of April, 1949 and extends across entire length and breadth of India.
- It was extended to Dadra & Nagar Haveli, Pondicherry in 1963, to Goa in 1965 and to the State of Jammu & Kashmir in 1970.
- ***The Factories Act was amended in 1949, 1950, 1954, 1956, 1976 and 1989.***

Objective

- The Act has been enacted primarily with the object of protecting workers employed in factories against industrial and occupational hazards. For that purpose, it seeks to impose upon the owner or the occupier certain obligations to protect the workers and to secure for them employment in conditions conductive to their health and safety.

Applicability

- At any place wherein manufacturing process is carried on with or without the aid of power or is so ordinarily carried on, not withstanding that:

- o The number of persons employed therein is less than ten, if working with the aid of power and less than twenty if working without the aid of power, or
- o The persons working therein are not employed by the owner thereof but are working with the permission of, or under agreement with, such owner.

Definition of "Factory" (Sec. 2(m))

- "Factory" is defined in Section 2(m) of the Act. It means any premises including the precincts thereof:
  - i. Wherein ten or more workers are working, or were working on any day of the preceding twelve months, and in any part of which a manufacturing process is being carried on with the aid of power, or is ordinarily so carried on; or
  - ii. Wherein twenty or more workers are working, or were working on any day of the preceding twelve months, and in any part of which a manufacturing process is being carried on without the aid of power, or is ordinarily so carried on;
- But does not include a mine subject to the operation of the Mines Act, 1952 or a mobile unit belonging to the Armed forces of the Union, a railway running shed or a hotel, restaurant or eating place.

The following have held to be a factory:

i. Salt works
ii. A shed for ginning and pressing of cotton
iii. A Bidi making shed
iv. A Railway Workshop
v. Composing work for Letter Press Printing
vi. Saw Mills
vii. Place for preparation of foodstuff and other eatables

Important terms

1. **Adult:** Person who has completed his eighteenth year of age.
2. **Adolescent :** A person who has completed his fifteenth year of age but has not completed his eighteenth year;
3. **Calendar year:** The period of twelve months beginning with the first day of January in any year.
4. **Child:** A person who has not completed his fifteenth year of age.
5. **Competent person:** In relation to any provision of this Act, means a person or an institution recognized as such by the Chief Inspector for the purposes.

Registration & Renewal of Factories (Secs. 6)

To be granted by Chief Inspector of Factories on submission of prescribed form, fee and plan.

Health of workers (Sec. 11 to 20)

- **Cleanliness:** Disposal of wastes and effluents.
- Ventilation and temperature, dust and fume.
- Overcrowding, Artificial humidification, Lighting.
- Drinking water, Spittoons.

Safety Measures (Sec.21 to 41)

- Fencing of machinery
- Work on near machinery in motion.
- Employment prohibition of young person's on dangerous machines.
- Striking gear and devices for cutting off power.
- Self-acting machines.
- Casing of new machinery.
- Prohibition of employment of women and children near cotton-openers.
- Hoists and lifts.

Welfare Measures (Sec.42to 50)

- Washing facilities
- Facilities for storing and drying clothing
- Facilities for sitting
- **First-aid appliances**: One first aid box not less than one for every 150 workers.
- **Canteens:** When there are 250 or more workers.
- **Shelters**, rest rooms and lunch rooms when there are 150 or more workers.
- **Crèches** when there are 30 or more women workers.
- **Welfare officer** when there are 500 or more workers.

Working Hours, Spread Over & Overtime of Adults (Secs. 51, 54 to 56, 59 & 60)

- Weekly hours not more than 48.
- Daily hours, not more than 9 hours.
- Intervals for rest at least ½ hour on working for 5 hours.
- Spread over not more than 10½ hours.
- Overlapping of shifts are prohibited.
- Extra wages for overtime double than normal rate of wages.
- Restrictions on employment of women before 6AM and beyond 7 PM.

Employment of Young Persons (Secs. 51, 54 to 56, 59 & 60)

- Prohibition of employment of young children e.g. 14 years.
- Non-adult workers to carry tokens e.g. certificate of fitness.
- Working hours for children not more than 4 ½ hrs. and not permitted to work during night shift.

Annual Leave with Wages (Secs.79)

- A worker having worked for 240 days @ one day for every 20 days and for a child one day for working of 15 days.
- Accumulation of leave for 30 days.

Offences and Penalties

Offence	Penalties
For contravention of the Provisions of the Act or Rules	Imprisonment upto 2 years or fine upto Rs.1,00,000 or both
On Continuation of contravention	Rs.1000 per day
On contravention of Chapter IV pertaining to	Not less than Rs.25000 in case of death.

safety or dangerous operations.	Not less than Rs.5000 in case of serious injuries.
Subsequent contravention of some provisions	Imprisonment upto 3 years or fine not less than Rs.10,000 which may extend to Rs.2,00,000.
Obstructing Inspectors	Imprisonment upto 6 months or fine upto Rs.10,000 or both.
Wrongful disclosing result pertaining to results of analysis.	Imprisonment upto 6 months or fine upto Rs.10,000 or both.
For contravention of the provisions of Sec.41B, 41C and 41H pertaining to compulsory disclosure of information by occupier, specific responsibility of occupier or right of workers to work imminent danger.	Imprisonment upto 7 years with fine upto Rs.2,00,000 and on continuation fine @ Rs.5,000 per day. Imprisonment of 10 years when contravention continues.

9.4.2. Employee State Insurance (ESI) Act, 1948

Objective

- To secure sickness, maternity, "employment injury", disablement and medical benefits to employees of factories and establishments and dependents' benefits to the dependents of such employees.

Applicability

- All factories including factories belonging to the Government other than seasonal factories.
- It is extended in area-wise to factories using power and employing 10 or more persons and to non-power using manufacturing units and establishments employing 20 or more person upto Rs.7500/- per month w.e.f. 1.4.2004.
- It has also been extended upon shops, hotels, restaurants, roads motor transport undertakings, equipment maintenance staff in the hospitals.

Coverage of employees

- Drawing wages upto Rs.10000/- per month engaged either directly or through contractor.

Contribution

1. **Employer:** 4.75 % of salary (total monthly wages).
2. **Employee:** 1.75% of salary (total monthly wages).

Contribution period

- 1st April to 30th September and
- 1st October to 31st March.

Time & Method for payment of Contribution

- Both the employer's and the Employees' contribution are to paid in cash or by cheque , into the State Bank of India or any other bank authorized by the ESI Corporation, by filling in a prescribed

Challan in quadruplicate within 21 days following the end of the calendar month in which the contribution falls due.

- The Bank will retain two copies of the Challan and return other two to the employer, one for submitting to the Regional office of the corporation and the other for the record of the employer.

Procedure for Registration

- The employer of a factory or an establishment desirous of registering it under the Act has to send to the Regional Office within 15 days from the Act becomes applicable to it a Declaration of Registration in the prescribed form.
- Upon receipt of the Declaration of Registration the Regional Office shall if satisfied that the factory or the establishment is covered by the Act, allot to it a Code Number and thereupon the factory or the establishment shall stand registered under the Act.

Benefits under the ESI, Act

1. Sickness benefit :

- Insured employees are entitled to receive for the period of his sickness as the daily "standard benefit rate".
    - o Minimum 78 days of the corresponding contribution is must.
    - o Benefit is not available for the first 2 days of sickness.
    - o Maximum period for benefit is 91 days in one year.
- **Standard benefit rate:** The daily rate which sickness benefit is payable to an insured employee during the period of his sickness.
    - o Lowest rate is Rs. 14/-
    - o Highest rate is Rs. 195/-

2. Maternity benefit

- Confinement, miscarriage or medical termination of pregnancy, Sickness arising out of pregnancy, confinement, premature birth of child or miscarriage or medical termination of pregnancy.
- Minimum 80 days in the immediately preceding two consecutive contribution periods is must.
- Maximum period for benefit is 91 days in one year.

3. Disablement benefit

- Permanent disablement, whether total or partial, as a result of an employment injury (personal injury caused by an accident arising out of and in the course of employment).
- Benefit for the whole of life.

4. Dependents' benefit

- When an insured employee dies as a result of an employment injury, his widow and children and in case the employee does not leave behind him a widow or children, his other dependants, are entitled to receive periodical payments.

5. Medical benefit

- Sickness of Insured employee or (where medical benefits is extended to his family) a member of his family.

- Available to the employee during any period for which contributions are paid in respect of him or in which he can claim sickness benefit.

6. Funeral expenses

- In case of death of an insured employee, the eldest surviving member of his family, and if the employee had no family or was not living with his family at the time of his death, then the person who actually incurs expenditure on the funeral of the employee, is entitled to receive the a payment called "funeral expenses".
- Maximum permissible amount of such payment is Rs. 2500/-

Benefits cannot be combined

- An employee is not entitled to receive two benefits at the same time. That means he cannot receive for the same period.
  - o Both sickness benefit and maternity benefit; or
  - o Both sickness benefit and disablement benefit for temporary disablement; or
  - o Both maternity benefit and disablement benefit for temporary disablement.

Offences and Penalties

- Different punishment have been prescribed for different types of offences in terms of Section 85:
  - o Six months imprisonment and fine Rs.5000,
  - o One year imprisonment and fine and 85-A: (five years imprisonment and not less to 2 years) and 85-C(2) of the ESI Act, which are self explanatory.
- Besides these provisions, action also can be taken under section 406 of the IPC in cases where an employer deducts contributions from the wages of his employees but does not pay the same to the corporation which amounts to criminal breach of trust.

Revision w.e.f. 01.12.2007

- The daily rates of sickness benefit as given under rules 55 has been increased by 20 per cent.
- Daily rates of disability benefits have been increased to 50 per cent form 40 per cent.
- Daily rates of dependent's benefit have been increased to 50 per cent from 40 per cent.
- Funeral expenses given under rule 59 has been increased to Rs. 3,000/- from Rs. 2,500/-

9.4.3. Workmen compensation Act, 1923

Objective

- The Act provides for payment of compensation to the worker injured during the course of employment or contracted by any occupational disease peculiar to that employment
- Act extends to the whole of India.
- **Sec.4: The amount of compensation** for accidents resulting in death, an amount equal to fifty per cent of the monthly wages of the deceased workman multiplied by the relevant factor; or an amount of eighty thousand rupees, whichever is more for permanent total disablement, an amount equal to sixty per cent of the monthly wages of the injured workman multiplied by the relevant factor, or an amount of ninety thousand rupees, whichever is more.

The maximum compensation as per workmen compensation Amendment Act, 2000

- Fatal Injury - Rs.4,57,080
- Permanent Total Disablement - Rs.5,48,496
- Permanent Partial Disablement - According to incapacity caused
- Temporary Disablement - Rs. 2000 per month upto a period of 5 years

Applicability (Sec.1)**:** All over India

Coverage of Workmen

All workers irrespective of their status or salaries either directly or through contractor or a person recruited to work abroad. Sec.1 (3)

Employer's liability to pay compensation to a workman

On death or personal injury resulting into total or partial disablement or occupational disease caused to a workman arising out of and during the course of employment.(Sec.3)

Amount of compensation (Sec. 4)

- Where death of a workman results from the injury.
- An amount equal to fifty per cent of the monthly wages of the deceased workman multiplied by the relevant factor on an amount of eighty thousand rupees, whichever is more.
- Where permanent total disablement results from the injury.
- An amount equal to sixty per cent of the monthly wages of the injured workman multiplied by the relevant factor or an amount of ninety thousand rupees, whichever is more.

Procedure for calculation:

- Higher the age – Lower the compensation
- Relevant factor specified in second column of Schedule IV giving slabs depending upon the age of the concerned workman.
- Example: In case of death.
- Wages Rs.3000 PM and Age 23 years
- Factor as schedule IV Rs.19.95
- Amount of compensation Rs.329935
- In case of total disablement Rs.395910.

When an employee is not liable for compensation (Sec. 3(a) & (b))

- In respect of any injury which does result in the total or partial disablement of the workman for a period exceeding three days.
- In respect of any injury, not resulting in death or permanent total disablement caused by an accident which is directly attributable to:
  - The workman having been at the time thereof under the influence of drink or drugs, or
  - Willful disobedience of the workman to an order expressly given, or to a rule expressly framed, for the purpose of securing the safety of workmen, or
  - Willful removal or disregard by the workman of any safety guard or other device which he knew to have been provided for the purpose of securing the safety of workman.

Wages (Sec. 4)

When the monthly wages are more than Rs.4000 per month it will be deemed Rs.4000.
Notice of Accident (Sec. 10): As soon as Practicable

Report of accident (Sec.10B)

- Report of fatal Accident and Serious Injury within 7 days to the Commissioner (not application when ESI Act applies).
  Bar upon contracting out (Sec.14)
- Any workman relinquishing his right for personal injury not permissible.

Penalty (Sec.4A)

- In case of default by employer: 50% of the compensation amount + interest to be paid to the workman or his dependents as the case may be.
- Deposit of Compensation: Within one month with the Compensation Commissioner

Latest amendment

- Workmen's Compensation Act is now Employees Compensation Act, 1923 and the definition of employee includes clerical employees & casual employees also.
- The minimum compensation limits on no-fault basis are increased to Rs.1,20,000 & 1,40,000 (erstwhile limits being Rs. 80,000 & 90,000).
- Under the maximum compensation limit, the monthly wage limit of Rs.4,000 is removed, hence, the maximum compensation can go upto 50% of total monthly wages now, irrespective of limits [now a new ceiling of Rs.8000 is introduced.
- Funeral expenses limit extended to Rs.5000 (from Rs.2,500)
- The employee shall be reimbursed the actual (full) medical expenditure incurred by him for treatment of injuries caused during the course of employment.
- Time limit for disposal of cases relating to compensation introduced: The Commissioner shall dispose of the matter relating to compensation within 3 months of reference.

Definition (Sec.2) "Employee" means a person, who is:

(i) a railway servant as defined in clause (34) of section 2 of the Railways Act, 1989 (24 of 1989), not permanently employed in any administrative district or sub-divisional office of a railway and not employed in any such capacity as is specified in Schedule II; or

(ii) (a) a master, seaman or other members of the crew of a ship, (b) a captain or other member of the crew of an aircraft, (c) a person recruited as driver, helper, mechanic, cleaner or in any other capacity in connection with a motor vehicle.(d) a person recruited for work abroad by a company, and who is employed outside India in any such capacity as is specified in Schedule II and the ship, aircraft or motor vehicle, or company, as the case may be, is registered in India; or

(iii) employed in any such capacity as is specified in Schedule II, whether the contract of employment was made before or after the passing of this Act and whether such contract is expressed or implied, oral or in writing; but does not include any person working in the capacity of a member of the Armed Forces of the Union; and any reference to any employee who has been" injured shall, where the employee is dead, include a reference to his dependants or any of them.

9.4.4. Maternity Benefit Act, 1961

Objective

- To protect the dignity of motherhood and the dignity of a new person's birth by providing for full and healthy maintenance of the woman and her child at this important time when she is not working.

Coverage of the Act

- Upon all women employees either employed directly or through contractor except domestic women employees employed in mines, factories, plantations and also in other establishments if the State Government so decides. Therefore, if the State Government decides to apply this Act to women employees in shops and commercial establishments, they also will get the benefit of this Act. Bihar, Punjab Haryana, West Bengal, U.P., Orissa and Andhra have done so.

Conditions for eligibility of benefits (Sec. 5.)

- Women indulging temporary of unmarried are eligible for maternity benefit when she is expecting a child and has worked for her employer for at least 80 days in the 12 months immediately proceeding the date of her expected delivery
- Ten weeks before the date of her expected delivery, she may ask the employer to give her light work for a month. At that time she should produce a certificate that she is pregnant.
- She should give written notice to the employer about seven weeks before the date of her delivery that she will be absent for six weeks before and after her delivery. She should also name the person to whom payment will be made in case she can not take it herself.
- She should take the payment for the first six weeks before she goes on leave.
- She will get payment for the six weeks after child-birth within 48 hours of giving proof that she has had a child.
- She will be entitled to two nursing breaks of fifteen minutes each in the course of her daily work till her child is fifteen months old.
- Her employer cannot discharge her or change her conditions of service while she is on maternity leave.

Cash Benefits

- Leave with average pay for six weeks before the delivery.
- Leave with average pay for six weeks after the delivery.
- A medical bonus of Rs.25 if the employer does not provide free medical care to the woman.
- An additional leave with pay up to one month if the woman shows proof of illness due to the pregnancy, delivery, miscarriage, or premature birth.
- In case of miscarriage, six weeks leave with average pay from the date of miscarriage.
- Medical bonus of Rs. 250 if no prenatal confinement and post natal care is provided by employer free of charge.

Non Cash Benefits/Privilege

- Light work for ten weeks (six weeks plus one month) before the date of her expected delivery, if she asks for it.
- Two nursing breaks in the course of her daily work until the child is 15 months old.

- No discharge or dismissal while she is on maternity leave.
- No change to her disadvantage in any of the conditions of her employment while on maternity leave.
- Pregnant women discharged or dismissed may still claim maternity benefit from the employer.
- **Exception :** Women dismissed for gross misconduct lose their right under the Act for Maternity Benefit

Leave for Miscarriage & Tubectomy Operation

- Leave with wages at the rate of maternity benefit, for a period of six weeks immediately following the day of her miscarriage or her medical termination of pregnancy.
- Entitled to leave with wages at the rate of maternity benefit for a period of two weeks immediately following the day of her tubectomy operation.

Leave for illness arising out of pregnancy (Sec.10)

- A woman suffering from illness arising out of pregnancy, delivery, premature birth of child (Miscarriage, medical termination of pregnancy or tubectomy operation) be entitled, in addition to the period of absence allowed to her leave with wages at the rate of maternity benefit for a maximum period of one month.

Prohibition of dismissal during absence of pregnancy

- Discharge or dismissal of a woman employed during or on account of such absence or to give notice or discharge or dismissal on such a day that the notice will expire during such absence or to very her disadvantage.
- Discharge or dismissal during or on account of such absence or to give notice of discharge or dismissal on such a day that the notice will expire during such absence, or to vary to her disadvantage any of the conditions of her service.
- At the time during her pregnancy, if the woman but for such discharge or dismissal would have been entitled to maternity benefit or medical bonus, etc.
- Not barred in case of dismissal for cross misconduct. Sec.

Forfeiture of maternity benefit (Sec. 18)

- If permitted by her employer to absent herself under the provisions of section 6 for any period during such authorized absence, she shall forfeit her claim to the maternity benefit for such period.
- For discharging or dismissing such a woman during or on account of her absence from work, the employer shall be punishable with imprisonment which shall not be less than 3 months, but it will extend to one year and will find, but not exceeding Rs.5,000.

Failure to Display Extract of Act

- Imprisonment may extend to one year or fine.
- Prohibition from dismissal for absence during pregnancy. However, for Misconducts, forfeiting of Maternity Benefit and Medical bonus permissible.

9.4.5. The Trade Union Act, 1926

Objective

- To provide the registration of Trade Union and in certain respects to define the law relating to registered Trade Unions.

Registration of trade Union(Sec. 5)

- Any 7 or more members of a trade union may, by subscribing their names to the rules of the trade union and its compliance.
- There should be at least 10%, or 100 of the workmen, whichever is less, engaged or employed in the establishment or industry with which it is connected.
- It has on the date of making application not less than 7 persons as its members, who are workmen engaged or employed in the establishment or industry with which it is connected.
- Prescribed form with following details:
  1. Names, occupations and address of the members' place of work.
  2. Address of its head office; and
  3. Names, ages, addresses and occupations of its office bearers.

Minimum requirements for membership of trade union registration (Sec. 9A)

- Not less than 10%, or 100 of the workmen, whichever is less, subject to a minimum of 7, engaged or employed in an establishments etc.

Cancellation of registration (Sec. 10)

- If the certificate has been obtained by fraud or mistake or it has ceased to exist or has willfully contravened any provision of this Act.
- If it ceases to have the requisite number of members.

Criminal conspiracy in trade disputes (Sec. 17)

- No office bearer or member of a registered trade union shall be liable to punishment under sub section (2) of conspiracy u/s 120B of IPC in respect of any agreement made between the members for the purpose of furthering any such object of the Trade Union.

Disqualification of office bearers of Trade Union (Sec. 21-A)

- If one has not attained the age of 18 years.
- Conviction for an offence involving moral turpitude. Not applicable when 5 years have elapsed.

Returns (Sec. 28)

- Annually to the Registrar, on or before such date as may be prescribed, a general statement, audited in the prescribed manner, of all receipts and expenditure of every registered Trade Union during the year ending on the 31st December.

Offences and Penalties

Penalties	Offence	Punishment
U/S 31	• For making false entry in or any omission in general statement required for sending returns. • For making false entry in the form.	• Fine upto Rs.500. On continuing default, additional fault, Rs.5 for each week (not exceeding Rs.50). • Fine upto Rs.500.
U/S 32	Supplying false information regarding Trade Union	Fine upto Rs.200.

Trade Unions (Amendment) Act, 2001

- Requirement of 10% or 100 workmen (whichever is less) employed in an establishment or industry with a minimum of 7 workmen as members for being eligible for registration as workers' trade union in place of only 7 persons provided for earlier, and subsequent maintenance of this membership after registration.
- Election of members of executive and office-bearers at an interval of not more than 3 years.
- Prescribing minimum subscriptions for rural, unorganized, and other workers.
- Designation of appellate courts.
- Limiting the proportion of outsiders to 1/3rd of the total number of office-bearers or 5, whichever is less, generally 50% in the organized sector; and
- Debarring members of Council of Ministers or persons holding office of profit in the Union or State (excluding those persons who are employed in an establishment or industry with which the trade union is connected) from membership of the executive or other office-bearer of a registered trade union.

9.4.6. Industrial Employment (Standing order)Act, 1946

Objective

- To require employers to define the conditions of work.
- To bring about uniformity in terms and conditions of employment.
- To minimize industrial conflicts.
- To foster harmonious relations between employers and employees.
- To provide statutory sanctity and importance to standing orders.

Applicability of the Act (Sec. 1)

- Every industrial establishment wherein 100 or more (in many States it is 50 or more).
- Any industry covered by Bombay Industrial Relations Act, 1946.
- Industrial establishment covered by M.P. Industrial Employment(Standing Orders) Act, 1961.

Matters to be provided in Standing orders(Secs.2(g), 3(2) and Rule 2A)

- Classification of workmen, e.g., whether permanent, temporary, apprentices, probationers, or badlis.
- Manner of intimating to workmen periods and hours of work, holidays, pay-days and wage rates.
- Shift working. Attendance and late coming.
- Conditions of procedure in applying for and the authority which may grant, leave and holidays.

- Requirement to enter premises by certain gates, and liability to search.
- Closing and re-opening of sections of the industrial establishments, and temporary stoppages of work and the right and liabilities of the employer and workmen arising therefrom.
- Termination of employment, and the notice thereof to be given by employer and workmen.
- Suspension or dismissal for misconduct, and acts or omissions which constitute misconduct.
- Means of redressal for workmen against unfair treatment or wrongful exactions by the employer or his agents or servants.

Additional Matters

- **Service Record**: Matters relating to service card, token tickets, certification of service, change of residential address of workers and record of age Confirmation Age of retirement Transfer Medical aid in case of Accident Medical Examination Secrecy Exclusive service.

Conditions for Certification of Standing Orders

- Every matter to be set out as per Schedule and Rule 2A.
- The standing orders to be in conformity with the provisions of the Act.

Submissions of Draft Standing Orders (Sec.3)

- Within six months from the date when the Act becomes applicable to an industrial establishment. Five copies of the draft Standing Orders are to be submitted to the Certifying Officer under the Act.

Procedure for Certification of Standing Orders (Sec.5)

- Certifying Officer to forward a copy of draft standing orders to the trade union or in the absence of union, to the workmen of the industry. The trade union or the other representatives, as the case may be, are to be heard.

Date of Operation of Standing Orders (Sec.7)

- On the date of expiry of 30 days from certification or on the expiry of 7 days from authentication of Standing Orders.

Posting of Standing Orders (Sec. 9)

- The text of the standing orders as finally certified shall prominently be posted in English or in the language understood by majority of workmen on special board at or near the entrance for majority of workers.

Temporary application of Model Standing Orders (Sec.12-A)

- Temporary application of model standing orders shall be deemed to be adopted till the submitted standing orders are certified.

Payment of Subsistence Allowance to the Suspended Workers (Sec.10-A)

- At the rate of fifty percent of the wages which the workman was entitled to immediately proceeding the date of such suspension, for the first ninety days of suspension.
- At the rate of seventy-five percent of such wages for the remaining period of suspension if the delay in the completion of disciplinary proceedings against such workman is not directly attributable to the conduct such workman.

Penalties

- Failure of employer to submit draft Standing Orders fine of Rs.5000 and Rs.200 for every day on continuation of offence.
- Fine of Rs.100 on contravention and on continuation of offence Rs.25 for every day.

9.4.7. Industrial Disputes Act,1947

Objective

- Provisions for investigation and settlement of industrial disputes and for certain other purposes.

Important Clarifications (Secs.7, 7A & 7B)

1. **Industry:** Industry has attained wider meaning than defined except for domestic employment, covers from barber shops to big steel companies. Sec.2(I)
2. **Works Committee:** Joint Committee with equal number of employers and employees' representatives for discussion of certain common problems. (Sec.3)
3. **Conciliation:** An attempt by a third party in helping to settle the disputes (Sec.4)
4. **Adjudication:** Labour Court, Industrial Tribunal or National Tribunal to hear and decide the dispute.

Power of Labour Court to give Appropriate Relief (Sec.11A)

- Labour Court/Industrial Tribunal can modify the punishment of dismissal or discharge of workmen and give appropriate relief including reinstatement.

Persons Bound by Settlement

- When in the course of conciliation proceedings etc., all persons working or joining subsequently.
- Otherwise than in course of settlement upon the parties to the settlement. (Sec.18)

Notice of Change (Sec.9A)

- 21 days by an employer to workmen about changing the conditions of service as provided in 4th Schedule.

Prohibition of Strikes & Lock Outs

- Without giving to the employer notice of strike, as hereinafter provided, within six weeks before striking.
- Within fourteen days of giving such notice.
- Before the expiry of the date of strike specified in any such notice as aforesaid.
- During the pendency of any conciliation proceedings before a conciliation officer and seven days after the conclusion of such proceedings.
- During the pendency of conciliation proceedings before a Board and seven days after the conclusion of such proceedings.
- During the pendency of proceedings before a Labour Court, Tribunal or National Tribunal and two months, after the conclusion of such proceedings.
- During the pendency of arbitration proceedings before an arbitrator and two months after the conclusion of such proceedings, where a notification has been issued under Sub-Section(3A) of section 10A

- During any period in which a settlement or award is in operation, in respect of any of the matters covered by the settlement or award. (Sec.22&23)

Period of Operation of Settlements and Awards

- A settlement for a period as agreed by the parties, or
- Period of six months on signing of settlement.
- An award for one year after its enforcement. (Sec.19)

Lay off & Payment of Compensation – Conditions for Laying off(Sec.25-C)

- Failure, refusal or inability of an employer to provide work due to:
  - o Shortage of coal, power or raw material.
  - o Accumulation of stocks.
  - o Breakdown of machinery.
  - o Natural calamity.

Retrenchment of Workmen Compensation & Conditions

- Workman must have worked for 240 days.
- Retrenchment compensation @ 15 days wages for every completed year to be calculated at last drawn wages
- One month's notice or wages in lieu thereof.
- Reasons for retrenchment
- Complying with principle of 'last come first go'.
- Sending Form P to Labour Authorities.

Prior Permission by the Government for Retrenchment (Sec.25-N)

- When there are more than 100 (in UP 300 or more) workmen during preceding 12 months.
- Three months' notice or wages thereto.
- Compensation @ 15 days' wages.

Conditions of service etc. to remain unchanged under certain circumstances during pendency of proceedings (Sec.33)

- Not to alter to the prejudice of workmen concerned the condition of service.
- To seek Express permission of the concerned authority by paying one month's wages on dismissal, discharge or punish a protected workman connected with the dispute.
- To seek approval of the authority by paying one month's wages before altering condition of service, dismissing or discharging or punishing a workman.

Closure of an Undertaking

- 60 days' notice to the labour authorities for intended closure in Form QA. Sec.25FFA
- Prior permission atleast 90 days before in Form O by the Government when there are 100 or more workmen during preceding 12 months (in UP 300 or more workmen) (Sec.25-O)

Prohibition of unfair labour practice either by employer or workman or a trade union as stipulated in fifth schedule

- Both the employer and the Union can be punished. Sec.25-T

Conditions of service etc. to remain unchanged under certain circumstances during pendency of proceedings

- Not to alter to the prejudice of workmen concerned the condition of service.
- To seek Express permission of the concerned authority by paying one month's wages on dismissal, discharge or punish a protected workman connected with the dispute.
- To seek approval of the authority by paying one month's wages before altering condition of service, dismissing or discharging or punishing a workman. (Sec.33)

Prior Permission for Lay off

- When there are more than 100 workmen during proceeding 12 months.Sec.25-M
- Lay off Compensation
- Payment of wages except for intervening weekly holiday compensation 50% of total or basic wages and DA for a period of lay off upto maximum 45 days in a year. Sec.25-C
- Right of a Workman during Pendency of Proceedings in High Court
- Employer to pay last drawn wages to reinstated workman when proceedings challenging the award of his reinstatement are pending in the higher Courts. (Sec.17B)

Schedule in ID Act- 1947.

- Schedule-I- Industries which may be declared as public utility services.
- Schedule-II & III - Labour Courts and Industrial Tribunals.
- Schedule-IV - Conditions of service for change of which notice is to be given.
- Schedule-V - Unfair labour practices.

Offences and Penalties

Penalties	Offence	Punishment
Sec.25-U	Committing unfair labour practices	Imprisonment of upto 6 months or with fine upto Rs.3,000.
Sec.26	Illegal strike and lock-ourts	Imprisonment upto one month or with fine upto Rs.50(Rs.1000 for lock-out) or with both.
Sec.27	Instigation etc. for illegal strike or lock-outs.	
Sec.28	Giving financial aid to illegal strikes and lock-outs.	Imprisonment upto 6 months or with fine upto Rs.1,000
Sec.29	Breach of settlement or award	
Sec.30	Disclosing confidential information pertaining to Sec.21	Imprisonment upto 6 months or with fine.On continuity of offence fine uptoRs.200 per day
Sec.31A	Closure without 60 days' notice	

	under Sec.25 FFA	
	Contravention of Sec.33 pertaining to change of conditions of	Imprisonment upto 6 months or with fine upto Rs.1,000
	Service during pendency of dispute etc.	Imprisonment upto 6 months or with fine upto Rs.5,000
Sec.31	When no penally is provided for contravention	Imprisonment upto 6 months or fine upto Rs.1,000. Fine upto Rs.100

Recent Amendments

- In the amendment to the Industrial Disputes Act, wherein the definition of a workman now includes a supervisor drawing a salary upto Rs. 10,000 p.m. and any person performing supervisory functions but being paid below Rs. 10,000 p.m. would be treated as workmen.
- In Maharashtra, where such workmen get protection of the MRTU & PULP Act, it means that termination of the supervisors can also become an industrial dispute and they would be workmen for all practical purposes. This is an important change, though many supervisors are paid in excess of Rs. 10,000/- this change is worthy of notice. The import of some of the amendments are below:
  (i) The definition of 'Appropriate Government'. Has been amplified.
  (ii) While The definition of workmen remains the same, section 2(s)(iv)has been amended to exclude a person who is employed in a Supervisory capacity draws wages exceeding Rs.10,000/- per month from the definition of 'workmen'. Earlier the wage limit was Rs.1600/- per month in other states and Rs. 6,500 in Maharashtra.
  The rest of the definition (i.e., or exercises, either by the nature of the duties attached to the office or by reason of the powers vested in him, function mainly of a managerial nature) remains unchanged.
  (iii) A grievance redressal machinery in an establishment having 20 or more workmen with one stage appeal to the employer has been provided.
  (iv) In cases of retrenchment, discharge, dismissal or termination of services, the workman can directly apply to Labour Courts/Tribunals after expiry of 45 days from the date he has made the application for reinstatement to the conciliation officer. The outer limit to approach the Labour Court or the Industrial Tribunal is 3 years from the date of the dispute, termination, retrenchment etc.

9.4.8. The Payment of Wages Act, 1936

Objective

- To regulate the payment of wages of certain classes of employed persons

Applicability of Act

- Factory industrial Establishment
- Tramway service or motor transport service engaged in carrying passengers or good or both by road for hire or reward, Air transport service Dock, Wharf or Jetty, Inland vessel, mechanically propelled, Mine, quarry or oil-field Plantation, Workshop or other establishment etc.

Coverage of Employees

- Drawing average wage upto Rs.6500 pm as amended w.e.f. 6.9.2005.

Wages to be paid in current coins or currency notes(Sec. 6)

- All wages shall be paid in current coins or currency notes or in both.
- After obtaining the authorization, either by cheque or by crediting the wages in employee's bank Account

Time of payment of wages (Sec. 5)

- The wages of every person employed be paid.
- When less than 1000 persons are employed shall be paid before the expiry of the 7th day of the following month.
- When more than 1000 workers, before the expiry of the 10th day of the following month.

Deduction made from wages (Sec. 7)

- Deductions such as, fine, deduction for amenities and services supplied by the employer, advances paid, over payment of wages, loan, granted for house-building or other purposes, income tax payable, in pursuance of the order of the Court, PF contributions, cooperative societies, premium for Life Insurance, contribution to any fund constituted by employer or a trade union, recovery of losses, ESI contributions etc.

Deduction for damage or loss (Sec.10)

- For default or negligence of an employee resulting into loss, show cause notice has to be given to the employee.

Deduction for absence from duties for unauthorised absence (Sec. 9)

- Absence for whole or any part of the day. If 10 or more persons absent without reasonable cause, deduction of wages upto 8 days.

Fines as prescribed (Sec.8)

- Not to imposed unless the employer is given an opportunity to show cause
- To record in the register

Deductions for service rendered (Sec.11)

- When accommodation amenity or service has been accepted by the employee.

Offences and Penalties

Offences	Penalties
On contravention of S.5 (except sub-sec.4), S.7, S.8 (except Ss.8), S.9, S.10 (except Ss.2) and Secs.11 to 13.	• Fine not less than Rs.1000 which may extend to Rs.5000. • On subsequent conviction fine not less than Rs.5000, may extend to Rs.10,000. On contravention S.4, S.5(4), S6, S.8(8), S.10(2) or S.25 fine not less than Rs.1000. –

	may extend to Rs.5000. On subsequent • On conviction fine not less.
For failing to maintain registers or records; or • Wilfully refusing or without lawful excuse neglecting to furnish information or return; or • Wilfully furnishing or causing to be furnished any information or return which he knows to be false or • Refusing to answer or wilfully giving a false answer to any question necessary for obtaining any information required to be furnished under this Act.	Fine which shall not be less than Rs.1000 but may extend to Rs.5000 – On record conviction fine not less than Rs.5000, may extend to Rs.10,000. • For second or subsequent conviction, fine not less than Rs.5000 but may extend to Rs.10,000
• Wilfully obstructing an Inspector in the discharge of his duties under this Act; or • Refusing or wilfully neglecting to afford an Inspector any reasonable facility for making any entry, inspection etc. • Wilfully refusing to produce on the demand of an inspector any register or other document kept in pursuance of this Act; or preventing any person for appearance etc.	Fine not less than Rs.1000 extendable Upto Rs.5000 – On subsequent conviction fine not less than Rs.5000 – may extent to Rs.10,000
• On conviction for any offence and again guilty of Contravention of same provision. • Failing or neglecting to pay wages to any employee	• Imprisonment not less than one month extendable upto six months and fine not less than Rs.2000 extendable upto Rs.15000. • Additional fine upto Rs.100 for each day.

9.4.9. Workmen's Compensation Act, 1923

Objectives

- Aims to provide workmen and/or their dependents some relief in case of accidents arising out of and in the course of employment and causing either death or disablement of workmen.

Coverage of Workmen (Sec. 1(3))

- All workers irrespective of their status or salaries either directly or through contractor or a person recruited to work abroad.
- All over India(Sec.1)

Employer's liability to pay compensation to a workman (Sec.3)

- On death or personal injury resulting into total or partial disablement or occupational disease caused to a workman arising out of and during the course of employment.

Amount of compensation

- Where death of a workman results from the injury: An amount equal to fifty per cent of the monthly wages of the deceased workman multiplied by the relevant factor on an amount of eighty thousand rupees, whichever is more.
- Where permanent total disablement results from the injury: An amount equal to sixty per cent of the monthly wages of the injured workman multiplied by the relevant factor or an amount of ninety thousand rupees, whichever is more

Procedure for calculation:

- Higher the age – Lower the compensation (Sec. 4)
- Relevant factor specified in second column of Schedule IV giving slabs depending upon the age of the concerned workman.
- **Example:** In case of death.
- The workman having been at the time thereof under the influence of drink or drugs, or
- Wages Rs.3000 PM and Age 23 years
- Factor as schedule IV Rs.19.95
- Amount of compensation Rs.329935
- In case of total disablement Rs.395910.

When an employee is not liable for compensation (Sec.3(a) & (b))

- In respect of any injury which does result in the total or partial disablement of the workman for a period exceeding three days.
- In respect of any injury, not resulting in death or permanent total disablement caused by an accident which is directly attributable to:
  - Willful disobedience of the workman to an order expressly given, or to a rule expressly framed, for the purpose of securing the safety of workmen, or
  - Willful removal or disregard by the workman of any safety guard or other device which he knew to have been provided for the purpose of securing the safety of workman.

Wages (Sec.4)

- When the monthly wages are more than Rs.4000 per month it will be deemed Rs.4000.

Notice Accident (Sec. 10): As soon as Practicable

- **Report of accident:** Report of fatal Accident and Serious Injury within 7 days to the Commissioner (not application when ESI Act applies).

Bar upon contracting out (Sec.14)

- Any workman relinquishing his right for personal injury not permissible.

Deduction (sec 7 to 13)

- Deductions for absence from duty

- Deductions for damage or loss
- Deductions for services rendered.
- Deductions for recovery of advances
- Deductions for recovery of loans
- Deductions for payments to co-operative societies and insurance schemes

Penalty (Sec. 4A)

- In case of default by employer: 50% of the compensation amount + interest to be paid to the workman or his dependents as the case may be.
- Deposit of Compensation: Within one month with the Compensation Commissioner.

9.4.10. The Minimum Wages Act, 1948

Objective

- To provide for fixing minimum rates of wages in certain employments.

Fixation of Minimum Rates of Wages

- The appropriate government to fix minimum rates of wages. The employees employed in para 1 or B of Schedule either at 2 or either part of notification u/s 27.
- To make review at such intervals not exceeding five years the minimum rates or so fixed and revised the minimum rates.
- **Government can also fix Minimum Wages** (Sec. 3): For Time work, Piece work at piece rate, Piece work for the purpose of securing to such employees on a time work basis, Overtime work done by employees for piece work or time rate workers.

Minimum Rates of Wages(Sec. 4)

- Such as Basic rates of wages etc.
- Variable DA and Value of other concessions etc.

Procedure for fixing and revising Minimum Rates of Wages(Sec. 5)

- Appointing Committee issue of Notification etc.

Fixing Hours for Normal Working (Sec. 13)

- Shall constitute a normal working day inclusive of one or more specified intervals.
- To provide for a day of rest in every period of seven days with remuneration.
- To provide for payment for work on a day of rest at a rate not less than the overtime rate.

Overtime (Sec. 5)

- To be fixed by the hour, by the day or by such a longer wage-period works on any day in excess of the number of hours constituting normal working day.
- Payment for every hour or for part of an hour so worked in excess at the overtime rate double of the ordinary rate of (1½ times or for agriculture labour)

Composition of Committee (Sec. 9)

- Representation of employer and employee in schedule employer in equal number and independent persons not exceeding 1/3 rd or its total number one such person to be appointed by the Chairman.

Payment of Minimum Rates of Wages (Sec.12)

- Employer to pay to every employee engated in schedule employment at a rate not less than minimum rates of wages as fixed by Notification by not making deduction other than prescribed.

Wages of workers who works for less than normal working days (Sec.15)

- Save as otherwise hereinafter provided, be entitled to receive wages in respect of work done by him on that day as if he had worked for a full normal working day.

Wages for two class of work (Sec. 16)

- Where an employee does two or more classes of work to each of which a different minimum rate of wages is applicable, wages at not less than the minimum rate in respect of each such class.

Maintenance of registers and records

- Register of Fines – Form I Rule 21(4)
- Annual Returns – Form III Rule 21 (4-A)
- Register for Overtime – Form IV Rule 25
- Register of Wages–Form X, Wages slip–Form XI, Muster Roll–Form V Rule 26
- Representation of register – for three year Rule 26-A Sec. 18

Minimum time rate wages for piece work (Sec. 17)

- Not less than minimum rates wages as fixed.

Claims by employees (Sec. 16)

- To be filed by before authority constituted under the Act within 6 months.
- Compensation upto 10 times on under or non-payment of wages

Offences and Penalties

Penalties	Offence	Punishment
Sec. 20	For paying less than minimum rates of wages	Imprisonment upto 6 months or with fine upto Rs.500/-
	For contravention of any provisions pertaining to fixing hours for normal working day etc.	Imprisonment upto 6 months or with fine upto Rs.500/-

9.4.11. Payment of Bonus Act, 1965

Objective

- An act to prevent "sweated labour and exploitation of labour"

Applicability of Act

- Every factory where in 10 or more persons are employed with the aid of power or
- An establishment in which 20 or more persons are employed without the aid of power on any day during an accounting year.
- **Establishment:** Establishment includes Departments, undertakings and branches, etc.
- **Separate establishment**: If profit and loss accounts are prepared and maintained in respect of any such department or undertaking or branch, then such department or undertaking or branch is treated as a separate establishment.

Computation of available surplus (Sec.5)

- Income tax and direct taxes as payable.
- Depreciation as per section 32 of Income Tax Act.
- Development rebate, investment or development allowance.

Components of Bonus

- Salary or wages includes dearness allowance but no other allowances e.g. over-time, house rent, incentive or commission.

Disqualification & Deduction of Bonus (Sec. 9 & 18)

- On dismissal of an employee for Fraud; or riotous or violent behaviour while on the premises of the establishment; or theft, misappropriation or sabotage of any property of the establishment or Misconduct of causing financial loss to the Employer to the extent that bonus can be deducted for that year.

Eligible Employees

- Employees drawing wages upto Rs.3500 per month or less.
- For calculation purposes Rs.2500 per month maximum will be taken even if an employee is drawing upto Rs.3500 per month.
- Note: The proposal to enhance the existing ceiling of Rs.3500 is under active consideration by the Govt.

Computation of gross profit (Sec.4)

- For banking company, as per First Schedule.
- Others, as per Second Schedule

Eligibility of Bonus (Sec. 8)

- An employee will be entitled only when he has worked for 30 working days in that year.

Payment of Minimum Bonus (Sec.10)

- 8.33% of the salary or Rs.100 (on completion of 5 years after 1 st Accounting year even if there is no profit)
- **Time Limit for Payment of Bonus(Sec.19):** Within 8 months from the close of accounting y ear

Set-off and Set-on of allocable surplus (Sec. 15) :

1. Where for any accounting year, the allocable surplus exceeds the amount of maximum bonus payable to the employees in the establishment under sec.11,then the excess shall, subject to a limit of 20 percent of the total salary or a wage of the employees employed in the establishment in that accounting year, be carried forward for being set on in the succeeding accounting year and so on up to an inclusive of the 4th accounting year to be utilized for the purpose of payment of bonus in the fourth schedule.
2. Where for any accounting year, there is no available surplus or allocable surplus in respect of that year falls short of the amount of minimum bonus payable to the employees in establishment under sec.10, and there is no amount or sufficient amount carried forward and set on under sub-sec.(1) which could be utilized for the purpose of payment of the minimum bonus, then, such minimum amount or the deficiency, as case may be, shall be carried forward for being set off in the succeeding accounting year and so on up to and inclusive of the forth accounting year in the manner illustrated in the forth schedule.
3. The principle of set on and set off as illustrated in the forth schedule shall apply to all other cases not coved by sub-sec.(1) or sub-sec. (2) for the purpose of payment of bonus under this act.
4. Where in any accounting year any amount has been carried forward and set on or set off under this section, then in calculating bonus for the succeeding accounting year, the amount of set on or set off carried forward from the earliest accounting year shall first be taken into account.

Maintenance of Registers and Records

- A register showing the computation of the allocable surplus referred to in clause (4) of section 2, in form A.
- A register showing the set-on and set-off of the allocable surplus, under section 15, in form B
- A register showing the details of the amount of bonus due to each of the employees, the deductions under section 17 and 18 and the amount actually disbursed, in form C.
- Act not applicable to certain employees of LIC, General Insurance, Dock Yards, Red Cross, Universities & Educational Institutions, Chambers of Commerce, Social Welfare Institutions, Building Contractors, etc. (Sec.32.)

Penalty (Sec.28)

- For contravention of any provision of the Act or the Rule
- Upto 6 months or with fine upto Rs.1000.

9.4.12. The Equal Remuneration Act, 1976

- Act provides for the payment of equal remuneration to men and women.
- Extends to the whole of India
- *Act makes it obligatory on the part of employer to pay equal remuneration to men and women workers for same work or work of a similar nature.*
- In order to make the wages equal, prevailing wages shall not be reduced but the higher rate shall be maintained.
- No discrimination while making recruitment for the same work or work of a similar nature, except where the employment of women in such work is prohibited or restricted by or under any law for the time being in force.
- No discrimination in any condition of service subsequent to recruitment such as promotions, training or transfer.

9.4.13. Payment of Gratuity Act, 1972

Objective

- To provide for a scheme for the payment of gratuity to employees engaged in factories, mines, oilfields, plantations, ports, railway companies, shops or other establishments and for matters connected therewith or incidental thereto.

Applicability (Sec. 2(s))

- Every factory, mine, oil field, plantation, port, railways, company, shop, establishment or educational institutions employing 10 or more employees

Calculation (Sec.1):

- Seasonal employee @ 7 days' wages for every completed year of service.
- **Wages for Calculation** (Sec.1):@ 15 days' wages for every completed year as if the month comprises of 26 days at the last drawn wages.
- **Calculation Piece-rated employee:** @ 15 days wages for every completed year on an average of 3 months' wages.
- **Qualifying period:** On rendering of 5 years' service, either termination, resignation or retirement.(Sec.2(e))
- **Employee:** All employees irrespective of status or salary
- **Entitlement:** On completion of five years' service except in case of death or disablement.
- **Display of Notice:** On conspicuous place at the main entrance in English language or the language understood by majority of employees of the factory, etc.(Sec.6)
- **Nomination:** To be obtained by employer after expiry of one year's service, in Form 'F' (Sec. 4(3))
- **Maximum Ceiling:** Rs.3,50,000
- **Mode of payment:** Cash or, if so desired, by Bank Draft or Cheque.

Penalties

- Imprisonment for 6 months or fine upto Rs.10,000 for avoiding to make payment by making false state-ment or representa -tion.
- Imprisonment not less than 3 months and upto one year with fine on default in comply-ing with the provisions of Act or Rules.
  Recovery of Gratuity: To apply within 30 days in Form I when not paid within 30 days Sec. 4 (6)

Forfeiture of Gratuity

- On termination of an employee for moral turpitude or riotous or disorderly behaviour.
- Wholly or partially for wilfully causing loss, destruction of property etc. (Sec. 13)
  Protection of Gratuity: Can't be attached in execution of any decree.

Payment of gratuity

- Gratuity shall be payable to an employee on the termination of his employment after he has rendered continuous service for more than five years,-
  - (a)on his superannuation, or

- o (b)on his retirement of resignation, or
- o (c)on his death or disablement due to accident or disease:

Latest amendments

- Under the gratuity Act, the ceiling of Rs.3.5 lakhs has been increased to Rs.10,00,000/- with effect from 24.05.2010.

9.4.14. Employees' Provident Funds & Miscellaneous Provisions Act, 1952

Objective

- The Employee's provident funds and miscellaneous provisions act, 1952 is enacted to provide a kind of social security to the industrial workers.
- The Act mainly provides retirement or old age benefits, such as Provident Fund, Superannuation Pension, Invalidation Pension, Family Pension and Deposit Linked Insurance.

Applicability

- Every establishment which is factory engaged in any industry specified in Schedule 1 and in which 20 or more persons are employed.
- Any other establishment employing 20 or more persons which Central Government may, by notification, specify in this behalf.
- Any establishment employing even less than 20 persons can be covered voluntarily u/s 1(4) of the Act.
- **Eligibility**: Any person who is employed for work of an establishment or employed through contractor in or in connection with the work of an establishment.

Clarification about Contribution

- After revision in wage ceiling from Rs.5000 to Rs.6500 w.e.f. 1.6.2001 per month, the government will continue to contribute 1.16% upto the actual wage of maximum Rs.6500 per month towards Employees' Pension Scheme.
- The employer's share in the Pension Scheme will be Rs.541 w.e.f. 1.6.2001.
- Under Employees' Deposit-Linked Insurance Scheme the contribution @ 0.50% is required to be paid upto a maximum limit of Rs.6500.
- The employer also will pay administrative charges @ 0.01% on maximum limit of Rs.6500 whereas an exempted establishment will pay inspection charges @ 0.005% on the total wages paid.
- The above clarification is given by taking wages upto a maximum of Rs.6500 towards wage (basic+ DA).
- Since an excluded employee i.e. drawing wages more than Rs.6500 can also become member of the fund and the Schemes on joint request and if, for instance, such an employee is getting Rs.10, 000 per month, his share towards provident fund contribution will be Rs.1200 e.g. 12% and employer's share towards provident fund contribution will be Rs.659 and Rs.541 towards Employees' Pension Fund.

Payment of Contribution

- The employer shall pay the contribution payable to the EPF, DLI and Employees' Pension Fund in respect of the member of the Employees' Pension Fund employed by him directly by or through a contractor.
- It shall be the responsibility of the principal employer to pay the contributions payable to the EPF, DLI and Employees' Pension Fund by himself in respect of the employees directly employed by him and also in respect of the employees directly employed by him and also in respect of the employees employed by or through a contractor.

Benefits

- Employees covered enjoy a benefit of Social Security in the form of an unattachable and unwithdrawable (except in severely restricted circumstances like buying house, marriage/education, etc.) financial nest egg to which employees and employers contribute equally throughout the covered persons' employment.
- This sum is payable normally on retirement or death. Other Benefits include Employees' Pension Scheme and Employees' Deposit Linked Insurance Scheme.

Rates of Contribution

Scheme	Employee's	Employer's	Central Govt's
Provident Fund Scheme	12%	Amount > 8.33% (in case where contribution is 12% of 10%) 10% (in case of certain Establishments as per details given earlier)	NIL
Insurance Scheme	NIL	0.5	NIL
Pension Scheme	NIL	8.33% (Diverted out of Provident Fund)	1.16%

Damages

- Less than 2 months ....@ 17% per annum
- Two months and above but less than upto four months ....@22% per annum
- Four months and above but less than upto six months ....@ 27% per annum
- Six months and above

Penal Provision

- Liable to be arrested without warrant being a cognisable offence.
- Defaults by employer in paying contributions or inspection/administrative charges attract imprisonment upto 3 years and fines upto Rs.10,000 (S.14).
- For any retrospective application, all dues have to be paid by employer with damages upto 100% of arrears.

Latest amendments

There is a proposal to raise the PF limits for coverage to Rs. 10,000 from the current Rs. 6,500 p.m.

9.4.15. Apprentices Act, 1961

Objective

- Promotion of new manpower at skills. Improvement/refinement of old skills through theoretical and practical training in number of trades and occupation.

Applicability of the Act (Sec. 1):

- Areas and industries as notified by the Central Government.
- **Apprenticeship Advisor (Sec. 2(b)):** Central Apprenticeship Advisor – when appointed by Central Government.
- **Industry (Sec. 2(k)):** Industry means any industry, or business or in which any trade, occupation or subject/field in engineering or technology or any vocational course may be specified as a designated trade.

Qualification for being trained as an Apprentice (Sec. 3)

- A person cannot be an apprentice in any designated trade unless He is not more than 14 years of age; He satisfies such standard of education and physical fitness as may be prescribed.

Contract of Apprenticeship (Sec. 4):

- To contain such terms and conditions as may be agreed to by the apprentice, or his guardian (in case he is a minor) and employers.

Conditions for Notation of Contract of Apprenticeship (Sec. 5)

- There exists an apprenticeship contract.
- The employer is unable to fulfil his obligation.
- The approval of the Apprenticeship Advisor is obtained.
- Agreement must be registered with the Apprenticeship Advisor.
- **Period of Apprenticeship**: Training to be Determined by the National Council

Obligations of employers (Sec.11)

- To Provide the apprentice with the training in his trade.
- To ensure that a person duly qualified is placed in charge of the training of the apprentice.
- To carry out contractual obligations.

Termination of Apprenticeship (Sec. 6)

- On the expiry of the period of Apprenticeship training.
- On the application by either of the parties to the contract to the Apprenticeship Advisor.

Payment to Apprentices(Sec. 6)

- The employer to pay such stipend at a rate of not less than the prescribed minimum rate as may be specified.

Obligations of Apprentice

- To learn his trade conscientiously, diligently.
- To attend practical and instructional classes regularly.
- To carry out all lawful orders.
- To carry out his contractual obligations.
  - **Health safety & Welfare measures for Apprentices:** As per Factories Act or Mines Act as the case may be when undergoing training.
  - **Hours of work**
    - 42 to 48 in a week while on theoretical training.
    - 42 in a week while on basic training.
    - 42 to 45 in a week in second year of training.
    - As per other workers (in the third year).
    - Not allowed to work between 10 PM to 4 AM unless approved by Apprenticeship Advisor.

Employer's liability to pay compensation for injury(Sec. 16): As per provisions of Workmen's Compensation Act.

Leave and Holidays (Sec. 15)

- Casual leave for the maximum period of 12 days in a year.
- Medical leave for the maximum period of 15 days and the accumulated leave up to 40 days in a year.
- Extraordinary leave up to a maximum period of 10 days in a year.

Offences & Punishment

- Imprisonment of a term up to 6 months or with fine when employer:
  (i) engages as an apprentice a person who is not qualified for being so engaged or
  (ii) fails to carry out the terms and conditions of a contract of apprenticeship, or
  (iii) contravenes the provisions of the Act relating to the number of apprentices which he is required to engage under those provisions.

9.4.16. The Mines Act, 1952

The Welfare Provisions

1. Creches, if there are 50 or more women are employed.
2. Shelter for taking food and rest if 150 or more workers are employed.
3. Canteen, if employing 250 or more workers
4. First-aid boxes and first-aid rooms in mines employing more than 150 workers.
5. Bathrooms with shower, sanitary latrines and lockers for men and women workers.

9.4.17. The Plantation Labour Act, 1951

Welfare amenities

1. Canteens, if 150 or more workers are employed.
2. Creches in plantation employing 50 or more women workers.

3. Recreational facilities for workers and their children.
4. Educational arrangement in the estate if there are 25 or more children of workers, between the age of 6 and 12..
5. Housing facilities for every workers.

9.4.18. The Motor transport workers Act, 1961

Welfare facilities

1. Canteen, if employing 100 or more workers.
2. First-aid equipment in each transport vehicle.
3. Rest rooms should be cleaned, ventilated and properly lighted.
4. Uniforms, raincoats to drivers and conductors
5. Medical facilities.
6. First-aid boxes.

9.4.19. The Contract Labour (regulation and abolition) Act, 1970

Welfare measures

1. Canteen, if employing 100 or more workers.
2. Restrooms or other suitable alternative accomodation if contract labour is required to halt at night.
3. Wholesome drinking water, sufficient number of latrines and urinals and washing facilities.
4. First-aid boxes.

9.4.20. The Merchant Shipping Act, 1958

Welfare facilities

1. Crew Accommodation
2. Supply of sufficient drinking water
3. Supply of medicines and medical stores and provisions of surgical and medical advice etc.
4. Proper weights and measures on board and grant of relief to distressed seamen abroad a ship
5. A qualified medical officer on board.
6. Establishment of hostels, clubs, canteens and libraries.
7. Appointment of a seamen's welfare officer at such ports in or outside India as the government may consider necessary.
8. Educational facilities.

9.4.21. Dock Workers (safety, health and welfare) Scheme, 1961

- The above stated scheme is framed under the Dock Workers (Regulation of Employment) Act,1948.
- Amenities provided in the port premises include provision of urinals and latrines, drinking water, washing facilities, bathing facilities, canteens, rest shelters and first-aid boxes. In addition to these provisions, other welfare measures provided are – housing, schools, educational facilities, grant of scholarship, libraries, sports and recreation and fair price shops.

9.4.22. Inter-State Migrant Workmen (Regulation of Employment and Conditions of Service) Act, 1979

The inter-state migrant workmen are entitled to get the following facilities:
1. Regular payment of wages (at least minimum wages to be paid).
2. Equal pay for equal work irrespective of sex.
3. Suitable conditions of work.
4. Suitable residential accommodation.
5. Medical facilities, free of charges
6. Protective clothing to workmen.

9.5. OBJECTIVE QUESTION - ANSWER

1. Which of the following is not a principle of labour legislation :
(A) Principle of social justice
(B) Principle of natural justice
(C) Principle of international uniformity
(D) Principle of national justice

Answer: D

2. Which of the following is not a type of labour legislation?
(A) Protective Legislation
(B) International Labour Legislation
(C) Regulative Labour Legislation
(D) Welfare Legislation

Answer: A

3. Which of the following is not a principle of labour legislations?
(A) Principle of Social Justice
(B) Principle of Economic Equality
(C) Principle of Social Welfare
(D) Principle of International Uniformity

Answer: B

4. Which of the following statements is / are true ?
(a) Labour Legislation is part of Social legislation.
(b) Social Legislation is part of Labour Legislation.
(c) Government is the regulatory authority in case of Social Legislation and Labour Legislation.
(d) Civil Law judgement is based on earlier judgements and labour law judgement is based on workers welfare.

(A) All the statements are true.
(B) (b) is true.
(C) (d) is true.
(D) (a), (c) and (d) are true.

Answer: D

5. Which of the following Articles of the Indian Constitution envisages that the state shall direct its policy, among other things, towards securing that there is equal pay for equal work for both men and women?
(A) Article 37 (B) Article 38
(C) Article 39 (D) Article 40

Answer: C

6. Which of the following statements is / are true ?
(a) Labour Legislation is part of Social legislation.
(b) Social Legislation is part of Labour Legislation.
(c) Government is the regulatory authority in case of Social Legislation and Labour Legislation.
(d) Civil Law judgement is based on earlier judgements and labour law judgement is based on workers welfare.

(A) All the statements are true.
(B) (b) is true.
(C) (d) is true.
(D) (a), (c) and (d) are true.

Answer: D

7. The article in Indian Constitution that imposes prohibition on traffic in human beings, beggar and other similar forms of forced labour is
(A) Article 19 (B) Article 23
(C) Article 32 (D) Article 45
Answer: B

8. Which of the following is not a principle of Labour Legislation?
(A)Social Justice
(B)Social Equity
(C)International Uniformity
(D)Human Rights
Answer: D

9. The principle of "natural justice" means :
(A) Nobody should be condemned without being heard.
(B) Person should not be punished twice for one offence.
(C) There should not be equitability in handling cases of misconduct.
(D) All the above.
Answer: A
Explanation: The opportunity to be heard by an impartial decision maker is at the heart of the rules of natural justice and procedural fairness.

10. Which of the following is not a type of labour legislation?
(A)Ameliorative legislation
(B)Protective legislation
(C)Social Security legislation
(D)Regulative legislation
Answer: A

11. Which of the following is not a statutory welfare measure under the Factories Act, 1948?
(A) Canteen
(B)Creche
(C)Worker's Cooperatives
(D)First Aid
Answer: C

12. As per the Factories' Act, 1948, a crèche will be provided in Factories where more than
(A) 30 unmarried women are employed
(B) 30 married women are employed
(C) 30 women are employed
(D) None of the above
Answer: C

13. Under the Factories Act no worker is permitted to work for more than _____ hours in a day
(A) 8 (B) 9
(C) 10 (D) 24
Answer: B

14. Under the Factories Act, white washing of the factory building should be carried out in every _______ months
(A) 12 (B) 24
(C) 26 (D) 14
Answer: D

15. An adult worker under the Factories Act is eligible for leave with wages @ I day for every_________ days worked during the preceding year
(A) 50 (B) 20
(C) 15 (D) 240
Answer: B

16. Repainting or re varnishing under the Factories Act is required to be carried out in every _______ years
(A) 5 (B) 10
(C) 3 (D) 1
Answer: A

17. Continuous Service under major labour legislations means _____________
(A) work of 240 days if work is above the ground and 190 days if work is below the ground
(B) work of 240 days
(C) work of 180 days
(D) work of 160 days
Answer: A

18. Subsistence Allowance @ __________ shall be paid if suspension extends to a period beyond 90 days
(A) 50% (B) 75%
(C) 90% (D) 100%

Answer: B

19. According to the Factories' Act, 1948 crèche must be provided in a factory if there are
(A) 10 or more women workers
(B) 20 or more women workers
(C) 25 or more women workers
(D) 30 or more women workers

Answer: D

20. Ambulance room shall be provided if
(A) 30 womens workers are employed under Maternity Benefit Act, 1965.
(B) Creche is provided under the Factories Act, 1948.
(C) 500 workers are employed in the factory under the Factories Act, 1948.
(D) The Workmens' Compensation Act, 1923 is applicable to the factory.

Answer: C

21. Out of the following which is not a manufacturing process
(A) Finished goods and packing there of
(B) The making of bidis
(C) Stitching old gunny bags and making them fit for use.
(D) Pumping of water from a tubewell

Answer: A

22. The occupier of a factory is required to send a written notice to the Chief inspector of Factories at least-
(A) 7 Days before he beings to occupy or use the premises as a factory.
(B) 15 Days before he beings to occupy or use the premises as a factory.
(C) 21 Days before he beings to occupy or use the premises as a factory.
(D) 10 Days before he beings to occupy or use the premises as a factory.

Answer: B

23. The first factory commission was appointed in
(A) 1875 (B) 1881
(C) 1885 (D) 1895

Answer: A

24. Which of the following legislations was amended to incorporate a separate chapter on safety for hazardous occupations as a result of Bhopal Gas Leakage?
(A) Mines Act
(B) Factories' Act
(C) Plantation Labour Act
(D) Shops and Commercial Establishment Act

Answer: B

25. Appointment of welfare officer is a statutory requirement according to
(A) Factories Act, 1948
(B) Industrial Disputes Act, 1947
(C) Trade Union Act, 1926
(D) Workmen's Compensation Act, 1923

Answer: A

26. The Chapter on "Annual Leave with wages" is provided under the
(A) Payment of Wages Act, 1936
(B) Minimum Wages Act, 1948
(C) Factories Act, 1948
(D) The E.S.I. Act , 1948

Answer: C

27. Employer is required to provide a canteen if there are______ .
(A) More than 500 workers
(B) More than 400 workers
(C) More than 250 workers
(D) More than 150 workers

Answer: C

28. Which among the following Acts contains the provisions relating to hours of work of women workers ?
(A) The Employees State Insurance Act, 1948
(B) The Factories Act, 1948
(C) The Maternity Benefit Act, 1961
(D) The Workmens' Compensation Act, 1923

Answer: B

29. At least one labour welfare officer must be appointed in a factory wherein ________or more workers are ordinarily employed.
(A) 50 (B) 100
(C) 300 (D) 500

Answer: D

30. Young persons under the Factories Act, 1948 :
(A) Cannot be employed at all on dangerous machines
(B) Can be employed if given full instruction or sufficient training or under the adequate supervision of knowedgeable and experienced person
(C) Can be employed
(D) None of the above

Answer: B

31. Which of the following is a statutory welfare facility under the Factories Act, 1948 ?
(A) Games and Sports
(B) Housing Facilities
(C) Transport Facilities
(D) None of the above

Answer: D

32. Among the following which cannot be said to be a statutory labour welfare facility under the factories Act, 1948 ?
(A) Canteen (B) Fist Aid Box
(C) Creche (D) Housing

Answer: D

33. The provisions of 'leave with wages' are found under :
(A) ESI Act
(B) Factories Act
(C) Workmen's Compensation Act
(D) Maternity Benefit Act

Answer: B

34. In case of fatal accident if the commissioner serves notice to the employer based on his source
(a) the employer can neglect the notice.
(b) if the employer thinks liable, he shall make the deposit within sixty days of the service of notice.
(c) if the employer thinks liable, he shall make the deposit within thirty days of the service of notice.
(d) if the employer is not liable, he shall in his statement indicate the grounds on which he disclaims liability.
(A) All statements are correct.
(B) All statements are incorrect.
(C) Only (a) and (d) are correct.
(D) Only (c) and (d) are correct.

Answer: D

35. The maximum daily hours of work in a day with normal wage allowed in factories is :
(A) 11 hours (B) 10 hours
(C) 9 hours (D) 8 hours

Answer: C

36. To avoid over crowding the space provided for each worker under the Factories Act, 1948 is
(A) 12 cubic metres for factories built before 1948 and 14.2 cubic meters for those built after 1948
(B) 10 cubic metres for factories built before 1948 and 14.2 cubic meters for those built after 1948
(C) 9.9 cubic metres for factories built before 1948 and 14.2 cubic meters for those built after 1948
(D) 9.9 cubic meters for factories built before 1948 and 14.4 cubic meters for those built after 1948.

Answer: C

37. The constitution of site appraisal committees is under the :
(A) Factories Act, 1948
(B) Contract labour (Regulation and Abolition) Act, 1970
(C) Maternity Benefit Act, 1965
(D) Employees State Insurance Act, 1948

Answer: A

38. Under the Factories Act, 1948 the working hours of 8 per day and 48 per week.
(A) Include spread over
(B) Are minimum working hours
(C) Include rest interval period
(D) Do not include rest interval period

Answer: D

39. Which of the following is true ?
(A) Labour officer is appointed under section 49 of the Factories Act, 1948
(B) Welfare officer is appointed under section 49 of the Factories Act, 1948
(C) Safety officer is appointed only if the workers are more than 1000
(D) None of the above is true

Answer: B

40. Under the Factories Act, 1948 every worker who has worked for a period of ....or more in a factory during a calendar year shall be allowed during the subsequent calendar year, leave with wages.
(A) Full one year (B) 365 days
(C) 250 days (D) 240 days

Answer: D

41. For which of the following there is no provision under the Factories Act, 1948 ?
(A) Canteen Managing Committee
(B) Safety Officer
(C) Site Appraisal Committee
(D) Welfare Committee

Answer: C

42. The period of work of an adult worker in a factory including intervals cannot be more than:
(A) 8.2 hours (B) 10.2 hours
(C) 8 hours (D) 9 hours

Answer: D

43. According to the Factories' Act, 1948, which of the following is correct ?
(A) 8 hours a day and 48 hours a week
(B) 9 hours a day and 54 hours a week
(C) 9 hours a day and 48 hours a week
(D) 8 hours a day and 56 hours a week

Answer: C

44. The first Factories Act was enacted in
(A) 1881 (B) 1895
(C) 1897 (D) 1885

Answer: A

45. Who is an adult as per Factories Act, 1948?
(A)Who has completed 18 years of age
(B) who is less than 18 years
(C) who is more than 14 years
(D) who is more than 15 years

Answer: A

46. A person who has ultimate control over the affairs of the factory under Factories Act,1948 is called as ________
(A) Occupier
(B) Manager
(C) Chairman
(D) Managing Director

Answer: A

47. The space for every worker employed in the Factory after the commencement of Factories Act, 1948 should be ________ Cubic Meters.
(A) 9.9 (B) 10.2
(C) 14.2 (D) 13.2

Answer: C

48. The provision for cooling water during hot weather should be made by the organization if it employees _______ or more employees.
(A) 200 (B) 250
(C) 300 (D) 150

Answer: B

49. Who is an Adolescent as per Factories Act, 1948?
(A) Who has completed 17 years of age
(B) who is less than 18 years
(C) who has completed 15 years but less than18 years.
(D) None of these

Answer: C

50. Which one of the following is not a welfare provision under Factories Act, 1948
(A) Canteen (B) Creches
(C) First Aid (D) Drinking water.
Answer: D

51. First Aid Boxes is to be provided for ______ persons.
(A) 125 (B) 135
(C) 150 (D) 160
Answer: C

52. Safety Officers are to be appointed if Organisation is engaging ______ or more employees.
(A) 1000 (B) 2000
(C) 500 (D) 750
Answer: A

53. Canteen is to be provided if engaging employees more than ______
(A) 250 (B) 230
(C) 300 (D) 275
Answer: A

54. Leave with wages is allowed for employees if they work for ______ days in a month
(A) 15 (B) 25
(C) 20 (D) 28
Answer: C

55. Welfare Officers are to be appointed if organization is engaging ______ or more employees.
(A) 500 (B) 250
(C) 600 (D) 750
Answer: A

56. The Ambulance Room is to be provided if engaging employees more than______
(A) 400 (B) 350
(C) 500 (D) 450
Answer: C

57. Crèches is to be provided if ______ or more lady employees are engaged.
(A) 25 (B) 32
(C) 30 (D) 50
Answer: C

58. An adult worker can upto ____ hrs in aday as per factories Act, 1948
(A) 8 (B) 9
(C) 10 (D) 12
Answer: B

59. Obligations of Workers under the Factories Act 1947 was discussed in section-----
(A) 78 (B) 101
(C) 111 (D) 99
Answer: C

60. The term Sabbatical is connected with
(A) Paid leave for study
(B) Paternity leave
(C) Maternity leave
(D) Quarantine leave
Answer: A

61. Section 49 of the Factories Act 1947Says about
(A) Welfare officer (B) Canteen
(C) Rest room (D) Crèche
Answer: A

62. Section 2 (K)of the Factories Act 1947says about
(A) Manufacturing Process
(B) Factory
(C) Worker
(D) None of these
Answer: A

63. If the factory employs more than 1000workers, they should appoint qualified------------- to carry out the prescribed duties
(A) Safety Officer
(B) Welfare officer
(C) Security officer
(D) None of these
Answer: A

64. For contravention of provisions of Factories Act or Rules, the occupier shall liable for punishment up to
(A) 2 years or fine up to Rs.1,00,000 or both
(B) 6 months or fine upto 10, 000 or both
(C) 3 three years or fine 10, 000 or both
(D) None of these

Answer: A

65. Manager of every factory should sent aannual report to the Inspectorate of factories containing details like numbers of workers employed , leave with wages, safety officers, ambulance room, canteen, shelter, accidents in form no --- on or before 31 st January
(A) Form No: 22 (B) Form No: 21
(C) Form No: 25 A (D) Form No: 25 B

Answer: A

66. Who is responsible for payment to a person employed by him in a Factory under the Payment of wages Act 1936
(A) Accounts Manager
(B) HR manager
(C) Manager
(D) Owner

Answer: C

Explanation: Manager of a factory nominated under the section 7 (f) of Factories Act, 1948.

67. The applicant / occupier who propose to start the factory should submit the______
(A) Form No.1 (B) Form No.2
(C) Form No. 2A (D) Form No.1 A

Answer: B

68. The license fee can be paid to get a license for a factory maximum upto:
(A) One Year only
(B) Two Years only
(C) Three Years only
(D) Five years only.

Answer: D

69. The occupier has to submit the document on or before------- of every year to renewal of a license for a factory.
(A) 31st October
(B) 31st December
(C) 31st March
(D) None of the above.

Answer: A

70. Section 41- G of the Factories Act1948 says about
(A) Fencing of machineries
(B) Facing of machineries
(C) Work on near machinery in motion
(D) Workers participation in safety mgt.

Answer: D

71. The renewal application for a license submitted after December 31st of the every year shall paid the fine amount.
(A) 10 % of the license fee
(B) 20% of the license fee
(C) 30 % of the license fee
(D) None of these.

Answer: B

72. The Section 20 of the Factories act discusses about
(A) Drinking Water
(B) Lighting
(C) Spittoons
(D) Latrines and Urinals

Answer: C

73. The employment of young person on dangerous machines shall be prohibited the section -------- of Factories Act.1947.
(A) Section 21 (B) Section 22
(C) Section 23 (D) Section 24

Answer: C

74. The occupier shall be punishable with imprisonment extend to -------- months or fine ---------or both for using false certificate of fitness.
(A) two months, 1000 rupees
(B) one year, 2000 rupees
(C) six months, 1000 rupees
(D) one month, 5000 rupees

Answer: C

75. Where ------------or more workers are employed in a factory, then there shall be a Safety Committee in the factory.
(A) 100 or more workers
(B) 150 or more workers
(C) 200 or more workers
(D) 250 or more workers
Answer: D

76. Under the Section 41.A. of the Factories Act , the Site Appraisal Committee shall be constituted once in ---------- year under the chairmanship of Chief Inspector of Factories.
(A) Once in 5 Year (B) Once in 2 Year
(C) Once in 3 Year (D) Once in a Year.
Answer: A

77. The occupier shall liable for punishment imprisonment for term of ------------ or fine------------or both for failure to comply with the provisions of Factories Act.
(A) 2 years, fine Rs. One Lakh.
(B) One Year, fine Rs, 10,000
(C) Six months, fine Rs. 50,000
(D) One year, fine 1, 00,000
Answer: A

78. The workers shall be provided with minimum -------- litres of water for everyday under the Factories Act.
(A) 2 litres (B) 4.5 litres
(C) 3 litres (D) 5 litres.
Answer: B

79. To close down a factory, the occupier has to give ------- days notice to the authorities.
(A) 30 Days (B) 60 Days
(C) 90 Days (D) 14 Days
Answer: B

80. By an Amendment Act of 1987 in Factories Act 1948, who is to appointed as an occupier?
(A) Manager
(B) General Manager
(C) Human Resource Manager
(D) Board of Directors
Answer: D

81. A weekly holiday was introduced in the Factories for the first time in the year------.
(A) 1948 (B) 1931
(C) 1926 (D) 1923
Answer: D

82. The expression of "Time card" in Form No.25. shall be substituted as "Service card" by an amendment in the Factories Act from the year.
(A) 1984 (B) 2005
(C) 2004 (D) 1981
Answer: B

83. Under the Section 41.A. of the Factories Act , the Site Appraisal Committee shall be constituted once in ---------- year under the chairmanship of Chief Inspector of Factories.
(A) Once in 5 Year (B) Once in 2 Year
(C) Once in 3 Year (D) Once in a Year.
Answer: A

84. Ambulance room shall be provided if
(A) 30 womens workers are employed under Maternity Benefit Act, 1965.
(B) Creche is provided under the Factories Act, 1948.
(C) 500 workers are employed in the factory under the Factories Act, 1948.
(D) The Workmens' Compensation Act, 1923 is applicable to the factory.
Answer: C

85. The first factory commission was appointed in
(A) 1875 (B) 1881
(C) 1885 (D) 1895
Answer: A

86. In a factory, where more than ________ women workers are ordinarily employed creche facility has to be provided.
(A) 20 (B) 30
(C) 40 (D) 50
Answer: B

87. Labour Welfare facilities were incorporated in which legislation?
(A) MRTP Act
(B) Essential Commodities Act
(C) Consumer Protection Act
(D) Factories Act
Answer: D

88. Which of the following benefits is not found under the Employees' State Insurance Act, 1948?
(A) Sickness Benefit
(B) Maternity Benefit
(C) Children's Allowance
(D) Dependent's Benefit
Answer: C

89. Employees who are drawing salary not more than __________ are covered under the Employees State Insurance Act, 1948.
(A) Rs10000 (B) Rs 7500
(C) Rs 6500 (D) Rs 3500
Answer: A

90. ______________ absolves the employer's liability under the Maternity Benefit Act and Workmen's Compensation Act.
(A) Employees Provident Fund Act
(B) IndustrialEmployment (Standing Order) Act
(C) Employees State Insurance Act
(D) Industrial Disputes Act
Answer: C

91. Employees' share of contribution under the ESI Act is _______
(A) 12% (B) 8.33%
(C) 1.75 % (D) 4.75%
Answer: C

92. The employer's share of contribution under the ESI Act is _____
(A) 12% (B) 8.33%
(C) 1.75 % (D) 4.75%
Answer: D

93. Employees who are getting a daily average wages up to ________ are exempted from contributing employees' share of ESI contribution.
(A) Rs 70 (B) Rs 50
(C) Rs 100 (D) Rs 384.60
Answer: A

94. Under ESI Act, 1948 a member of the Corporation, Standing Committee or the Medical Council shall cease to be a member of the body if he fails to attend
(A) two consecutive meetings
(B) three meetings intermittently
(C) three consecutive meetings
(D) four consecutive meetings
Answer: C

95. The scope and coverage of which of the following legislations was recently extended to cover workers drawing wages upto 15,000 per month ?
(A) Maternity Benefit Act
(B) Industrial Disputes Act
(C) E.S.I. Act
(D) Shops and Establishments Act
Answer: C
Explanation: Employee' means any person employed for wages in or in connection with work of a factory or establishment to which the ESI Act applies. Employees drawing wages up to Rs. 15,000 per month can be presently covered under the ESI Act scheme [Section 2(9)].

96. Which of the following is based on contributory principle?
(A) Maternity Benefit Act, 1961
(B) E.S.I. Act, 1948
(C) Workmen's Compensation Act, 1923
(D) Old Age Pension Scheme
Answer: B

97. Who is an 'exempted employee' under the Employee's state Insurance Act, 1948 ?
(A) Employee who is minor
(B) Employee who is not liable under the Act to pay the employee's contribution
(C) Minor employee who is not liable under the Act to pay the employee's contribution
(D) None of the above
Answer: B

98. The unemployment insurance benefit was included in the ESI Act since
(A) 1975 (B) 1985
(C) 1995 (D) 2005

Answer: D

Explanation: Rajiv Gandhi Shramik Kalyan Yojana: This scheme of Unemployment allowance was introduced w.e.f. 01-04-2005. An Insured Person who become unemployed after being insured three or more years, due to closure of factory/establishment, retrenchment or permanent invalidity are entitled to :

- Unemployment Allowance equal to 50% of wage for a maximum period of upto one year.
- Medical care for self and family from ESI Hospitals/Dispensaries during the period IP receives unemployment allowance.
- Vocational Training provided for upgrading skills - Expenditure on fee/travelling allowance borne by ESIC.

99. 'According to the employees' state insurance Act 1948, the wage ceiling is :
(A) Rs 7500/- (B) Rs 8000/-
(C) Rs 9000/- (D) Rs 10000/-

Answer: D

100. The administration of the ESI Act, 1948 is done by which of the following machinery ?
(A) ESI Corporation
(B) Standing Committee
(C) Medical Benefit Council
(D) All the above

Answer: A

101. The employee State Insurance Act was enacted the basis of which committee's report?
(A) B. R. Ambedkar Committee
(B) B. P. Adarkar Committee
(C) Royal Commission on Labour
(D) Labour Investigation Committee

Answer: B

102. 'Unemployment allowance' payable is stated in
(A) Employee State Insurance Act,1948
(B) Unorganised Sector Workers Social Security Act, 2005
(C) Factories Act, 1948
(D) None of the above

Answer: A

103. Funeral Expenses, Rehabilitation Allowances, Vocational Rehabilitation, old age medicare and medical bonus are provided under which of the following social security legislations in India ?
(A)Workmens' Compensation Act, 1923
(B)ESI Act, 1948
(C)Maternity Benefit Act, 1961
(D)Payment of Gratuity Act, 1972

Answer: B

104. Which of the following benefits are provided under the ESI Act, 1948 ?
(A) Sickness benefit
(B) Maternity benefit
(C) Disablement benefit
(D) Unemployment benefit
(E) All the above

Answer: E

105. For which of the following social security legislations, there has been created a central enforcement machinery ?
(A) Maternity Benefit Act
(B) Employees' State Insurance Act
(C) Workmen's Compensation Act
(D) Payment of Gratuity Act

Answer: B

106. Which of the following is not a benefit under the Employees State Insurance Act, 1948 ?
(A) Sickness and Maternity Benefit
(B) Disablement and Dependents' Benefit
(C) Medical Benefit and Funeral Assistance
(D) Child Allowance and Unemployment Benefit

Answer: D

107. What is the content of the Schedule I of the ESI Act, 1948 ?
(A) List of injuries deemed to result in permanent total disablement.
(B) List of injuries deemed to result in permanent partial disablement.
(C) List of occupational diseases.
(D) None of the above
Answer: D

108. The term 'wages' under the Employees' State insurance Act, 1948 does not include-
(A)Incentives
(B)Over time wages
(C)Travelling allowance
(D)Any other additional remuneration
Answer: C

109. The ESI Corporation to function efficiently has been provided with two wings namely ------------ and Medical Benefit Council.
(A) Standing Committee
(B) Steering Committee
(C) Core Committee
(D) Review Committee
Answer: A

110. The rate of contribution toward the Employees State Insurance Funds of employees wages by the employers and employee respectively-------
(A) 4.75% and 1.75%
(B) 12% and 2%
(C) 12% and 12%
(D) 1.75% and 4.75%
Answer: A

111. The minimum amount of compensation in case of permanent total disablement is -
(A) Rs. 1,00,000
(B) Rs. 90,000
(C) Rs. 80,000
(D) Rs. 70,000
Answer: B

112. Under the Workmens' Compensation Act, 1923, the Commissioner for Workmen's Compensation shall not entertain any claim unless it is preferred before him on the occurrence of the accident, with-
(A) 1 Week (B) 6 months
(C) 1 Year (D) 2 Years
Answer: D

113. The employer is required to send a report to the commissioner for employee's compensation with------ days of the death or serious injury of the employees:
(A) 7 (B) 10
(C) 15 (D) 30
Answer: A

114. The terms 'arising out of employment' and 'during and in the course of employment' have been used in
(A) Maternity Benefit Act, 1961
(B) Payment of Gratuity Act, 1972
(C) Workmen's Compensation Act, 1923 (Employees' Compensation Act, 1923)
(D) Employees Provident Fund (and Miscellaneous Provisions) Act, 1952
Answer: C

115. Under Workmen's Compensation Act, 1923
(A) individual manager subordinate to an employer cannot act as managing agent.
(B) managing agent includes an individual manager subordinate to an employer.
(C) only employer can act as managing agent.
(D) the appropriate government shall appoint managing agent.
Answer: D

116. The Workmen's Compensation Act, 1923, the Maternity Benefit Act, 1965 and the Employees State Insurance Act, 1948
(A) together can be applicable.
(B) the Maternity Benefit Act and the Employees State Insurance Act can be applicable at a time.

(C) the Workmen's Compensation Act and the Employees State Insurance Act can be applicable at a time.
(D) if the Workmen's Compensation Act and the Maternity Benefit Act are applicable, the Employees State Insurance Act is not applicable.

Answer: D

117. After the enactment of the Workmen's Compensation Act, 1923 a contract has been made under which a workman relinquishes any right of compensation from the employer for personal injury arising out of or in the course of the employment, what will be the fate of the contract?
(A) The contract shall be null and void
(B) The contract shall remain in operation
(C) The Act is silent on this matter
(D) None of the above

Answer: B

118. Which of the following is not a disqualifying condition for receiving compensation under the Workmen's Compensation Act, 1923 ?
(A) Under the influence of drinks and drugs
(B) Wilful disregard of safety rules
(C) Not completed two years of continuous service
(D) Wilful disregard of safety devices

Answer: B

119. A worker has instituted a claim for compensation in respect of an injury before a Workmen's compensation Commissioner and now he wants to institute a suit in a civil court for the same injury. Which of the following will be the correct in this regard ?
(A) He can institute a suit in the civil court
(B) He cannot institute a suit in the civil court as he has taken the claim to the commissioner
(C) The suit can be taken to both simultaneously
(D) None of the above

Answer: B

120. Which of the following is correct?
(A) Maternity Benefit Act, 1961 is a scheme of social assistance
(B) Maternity Benefit Act is a scheme of social insurance
(C) It is an example of both social insurance and social assistance
(D) None of the above

Answer: C

121. The women employees are now entitled to maternity leave according to Maternity Benefit Act, 1961 for a period of
(A) 12 weeks (B) 100 days
(C) 180 days (D) 150 days

Answer: A

122. Which of the following legislations is not based on the provisions given under the Directive Principles of State Policy in Indian Constitution ?
(A) Maternity Benefit Act, 1961
(B) Equal Remuneration Act, 1976
(C) Child Labour Act, 1986
(D) Payment of Bonus Act, 1965

Answer: A

123. In order to be eligible for maternity benefit under the Maternity Benefit Act, 1961, a woman worker should have worked for not less than________ days in the 12 months immediately preceding the date of delivery
(A) 160 (B) 240
(C) 30 (D) 150

Answer: A

124. Under the Maternity Benefit Act, a woman worker is eligible for ______ weeks leave with wages
(A) 6 (B) 24
(C) 15 (D) 12

Answer : D

125. In case of miscarriage, a woman worker shall be allowed______ weeks leave with wages
(A) 12 (B) 6
(C) 4 (D) 24

Answer: B

126. Every woman entitled for maternity benefit under the Maternity Benefit Act, 1961 shall also be entitled to receive from the employer a medical bonus of :

(A)Rs. 25/- (B) Rs. 50/-
(C)Rs. 250/- (D) Rs. 500/-

Answer: C

Explanation: Payment of medical bonus: Every woman entitled to maternity benefit under this Act shall also be entitled to receive from her employer a medical bonus of Rs. 250/-, if no pre-natal confinement and post-natal care is provided for by the employer free of charge.

127. The maternity leave period with full wage is

(A) six months (B) twelve weeks
(C)four months (D) sixteen weeks

Answer: B

Explanation: The maximum period for which any woman shall be entitled to maternity benefit shall be twelve weeks of which not more than six weeks shall precede the date of her ex delivery.

128. Maternity Benefit Act, 1961 provides maternity benefit to women employees for a total period of :

(A) 8 weeks (B) 10 weeks
(C) 12 weeks (D) 16 weeks

Answer: C

129. Not more than 50% of members of the office bears of Trade union can be outsiders, as per provisions of legislations.

(A) Industrial Dispute Act
(B) Trade Union Act
(C) Mines Act
(D) ESI Act

Answer: B

130. The minimum no. of workers required to register a Trade Union under the Trade Unions Act, 1926 is ________

(A) 10%
(B) 50%
(C) 33 %
(D) 10% or 100 whichever is less

Answer: D

131. A person is qualified to be chosen as a member of the executive or any other office bearer of the registered trade union if he attained the age of

(A) Fifteen years
(B) Eighteen years
(C) Twenty one years
(D) Twenty five years

Answer: B

132. The registered trade union can collect political fund from its members as a

(A) general fund
(B) cannot collect political fund
(C) separate fund from the interested members
(D) only from political parties

Answer: C

133. Which of the following statements is correct for the Trade Unions Act, 1926 ?

(A) It provides only for registration of Trade Unions.
(C) It provides only for recognition of Trade Unions.
(D) It provides both for registration and recognition of Trade Unions.
(E) None of the above

Answer: C

134. Assertion (A) : At least seven persons can apply to the Registrar for registration of their trade union.

Reason (R) : The Trade Unions Act,1926 makes registration of trade unions compulsory so that the trade union is recognized as a bargaining agent.

(A) (A) is correct, but (R) is wrong.
(B) Both (A) and (R) are correct.
(C) Both (A) and (R) are wrong.
(D) (A) is wrong, but (R) is correct.

Answer: B

135. As per the Trade Unions Act, 1926, the proportion of outsiders as office bearers of registered trade union is :

(A) Up to 25%
(B) Up to 50%
(C) More than 50%
(D) No mention in the Trade Union Act, 1926

Answer: B

136. Union office bearer of a registered union may be :
(A) Protected workman under the ID Act, 1947
(B) Protected workman under the Trade Unions Act, 1926
(C) Protected employee under the Industrial Employment (Standing Orders) Act, 1946
(D) None of the above

Answer: D

137. The provision regarding recognition of trade union in India is given under :
(A) ID Act, 1947
(B) Trade Union Act, 1926
(C) Code of Discipline in Industry
(D) Inter - union code of conduct

Answer: B

138. As per the Trade Unions Act, 1926 what is the minimum trade union membership fee to be paid by a member in a factory ?
(A) 25 paise per month
(B) 1 rupee per annum
(C) 3 rupees per annum
(D) 12 rupees per annum

Answer: B

139. The minimum required membership for registration of a trade union according to the Trade Unions Act, 1926 is :
(A) not less than 7 members
(B) not less than 10% of the total workmen or 100 whichever is less
(C) not less than 10% or 100 of the workmen engaged in the industry or establishment with a minimum of 7
(D) None of the above

Answer: A

140. An application has been made by a union of 10,000 workers for registration to the Registrar of Trade Unions. More than half of the total number of workers (6000) who made the application, have ceased to be the members of the union before registration. What will happen to the registration of that union ?
(A) Since 4000 workers are still there, the union will be registered by the registrar
(B) The application will be rejected
(C) The Trade Union Act, 1926 is silent on this subject
(D) None of the above

Answer: A

141. Which of the following has not been provided under the Trade Unions Act, 1926 ?
(A) Provision regarding trade union recognition
(B) Collective Bargaining
(C) Unfair Labour Practices
(D) All of the above

Answer: D

142. Which of the following statements relating to the Trade Unions Act is correct?
(A) A registered trade union cannot constitute a separate fund for political purposes
(B) Any person who has attained the age of fourteen years may be a member of a registered trade union
(C) A person who has not attained the age of eighteen years shall be disqualified for being chosen as an office-bearer a union
(D) The general fund of a union cannot be spent for payment of salaries to office-bearers of the union

Answer: C

143. Which of the following statements relating to the Trade Unions (Amendment) Act, 2001 is not correct?
(A) The Act came into force in the year 2002

(B) The Act limits the proportion of outsiders to 1/3rd of the total number of office bearers or 5, whichever is less generally.
(C) A person who is a member of the Council of Ministers in a State can become an office bearer of a union
(D) Election of office-bearer of a union should be held at an interval of three years.

Answer: C

144. Which of the following is not a part of the Trade unions Act, 1926 ?
(A) Registration of trade unions
(B) Rights and Liabilities of Registered Trade unions
(C) Cancellation of Registration
(D) Recognition of Trade union

Answer: D

145. What is the minimum number of members required for registration of a trade union ?
(A) Seven members
(B) 100 members
(C) 100 or 10% but not less than seven
(D) None of the above

Answer: A

146. The provisions of constituting a political fund is given under which of the following legislations?
(A) Industrial Disputes Act, 1947
(B) Trade Unions Act, 1926
(C) Employees Provident Funds Act, 1952
(D) Industrial Employment (Standing Order's) Act, 1946

Answer: A

147. Which of the following is correct with regard to termination of an award ?
(A) After completing the tenure.
(B) After giving a notice by any one of the parties.
(C) After lapse of two months from the date a notice is given by any of the parties.
(D) None of the above.

Answer: C

148. The following persons are constructed as insider of a registered trade union.
(A) Honorary member from the other organization.
(B) Honorary member from other profession.
(C) Politician who guides the registered trade union.
(D) retired and retrenched members of the trade union.

Answer: D

149. Recognition of the trade union in industry under the code of discipline was developed in the year
(A) 1952 (B) 1957
(C) 1958 (D) 1962

Answer: B

150. Union Security is related with :
(A) Union democracy
(B) Industrial democracy
(C) Living wage
(D) Union shop and closed shop

Answer: A

151. As a result of the New Economic Policy in India, for which of the following legislations there is a growing demand from employers for a change ?
(A) Maternity Benefit Act, 1961
(B) Trade Unions Act, 1926
(C) Industrial Disputes Act, 1947
(D) E.S.I. Act, 1948

Answer: B

152. The following persons are constructed as insider of a registered trade union.
(A) Honorary member from the other organization.
(B) Honorary member from other profession.
(C) Politician who guides the registered trade union.
(D) retired and retrenched members of the trade union.

Answer: D

153. A trade union after registration acquires the following characteristics:-
a) It has perpetual succession and a common seal
b) It has no power to contract
c) It has no power to acquire and hold both the movable and immovable property
d) If can by the name under which it is registered sue or be sued
(A) d & b (B) a & b
(C) a & d (D) c & d
Answer: C

154. The Industrial Employment (standing orders) Act, 1946 applies to every establishment employing
(A) 100 workmen
(B) 150 workmen
(C) 150 workmen on any day preceding 12 months
(D) 150 workmen on any day preceding 12 months and the government can order by application to establishments employing less than 100.
Answer: D

155. Certification of Standing Orders under the Industrial Employment (Standing Orders) Act, 1946 is mandatory where ________ workers are employed
(A) 500 (B) 1000
(C) 250 (D) 100
Answer: D

156. The Industrial Employment (Standing Orders) Act was enacted in the year :
(A) 1946 (B) 1947
(C) 1948 (D) 1950
Answer: A

157. The Industrial Employment (Standing Orders) Act, 1946 is applicable to every establishment wherein ________ workmen are employed.
(A) 50 (B) 70
(C) 80 (D) 100
Answer: D

158. Who among the following has been authorized to certify standing orders. under Industrial Employment (standing order's) Act, 1946 ?
(A) Labour Inspector
(B) Labour Commissioner
(C) Chief Inspector of Factories
(D) Certifying officers
Answer: D

159. Standing orders will, unless an appeal is preferred, come into operation on the expiry of :
(A) 20 days (B) 30 days
(C) 45 days (D) 60 days
Answer: B

160. Draft standing orders are to be submitted within
(A) Two years from the date on which the Act is applicable in five copies.
(B) One year from the date on which the Act is applicable in five copies
(C) Six months from the date on which the Act is applicable in five copies
(D) Six months from the date on which the act is applicable in ten copies
Answer: C

161. An employer has submitted draft standing orders to certifying officer for certification. Mean while which of the following will be applicable :
(A) Nothing will be applicable there
(B) Certified standing orders of any other similar organization
(C) Model standing orders
(D) None of the above
Answer: C

162. An employer insists to include certain subjects in his draft standing orders for certification by the certifying officer, which are neither covered by any item of the

schedule nor by the model standing orders
(A) He can do so
(B) He cannot do so
(C) The Act is silent about it
(D) None of the above
Answer: A

163. An employer has submitted Draft Standing Orders to the certifying officer for certification. Which of the following will apply till the final certified standing orders become enforceable ?
(A) Nothing will apply
(B) Model Standing Orders
(C) Certified Standing Order of similar organization in that locality
(D) It will be decided by the employer.
Answer: B

164. Which act requires employers in industrial establishments to define the conditions of employment ?
(A) The Factories Act, 1948
(B) The Industrial Disputes Act,1947
(C) The Industrial Employment (standing orders) Act, 1946
(D) The Trade Union Act, 1926
Answer: C

165. The industrial establishments covered by the Industrial Employment Act, 1946 include:-
a) Oil-fields
b) Mines
c) Schools
d) Workshops
(A) a & c (B) a, b & d
(C) c (D) c & d
Answer: B

166. Which Act provides for the appointment of conciliation officers and adjudication authorities ?
(A) The Factories Act, 1948
(B) The Industrial Disputes Act,1947
(C) The Trade Unions Act, 1926
(D) None of the above
Answer: B

167. 'Award' under Industrial Disputes Act,1947 is
(a) not interim determination of labour court
(b) not arbitration award under Section 10A
(c) not final determination of labour court
(d) not final determination of arbitration award under section10A
(A) All statements are true.
(B) (a) and (d) are true.
(C) (b) is true.
(D) All statements are wrong.
Answer: D

168. The dispute of individual workman is deemed to be industrial dispute if the dispute or difference is connected with or arising out of the following where no other workman nor any union of workman is a party to the dispute.
(A) Grievance of an individual workman.
(B) Discharge of an individual workman.
(C) Dismissal of an individual workman.
(D) Discharge, dismissal, retrenchment or otherwise termination of services of an individual workman.
Answer: D

169. "Model Grievance Procedure" is given in the
(A) Industrial Disputes Act
(B) Employee State Insurance Act
(C) Industrial Employment (standing orders) Act
(D) Code of Discipline
Answer: D

170. What is the limit of the salary of the supervisor to be covered under the I.D. Act, 1947 ?
(A) Rs.1200 per month
(B) Rs.1600 per month
(C) Rs.2500 per month
(D) Rs.3500 per month
Answer: A

171. Which of the following is not a machinery under the Industrial Disputes Act, 1947 ?
(A) Works Committee
(B) Conciliation Officer and Board of Conciliation
(C) Labour Court and Industrial Tribunal
(D) Labour Appellate Tribunal
Answer: D

172. Which of the following legislation cannot be included under the category of protective labour legislations?
(A) Factories Act, 1948
(B) Minimum Wages Act, 1948
(C) Mines Act, 1952
(D) Industrial Disputes Act, 1947
Answer: D

173. As per Industrial Disputes Act, 1947 works committee is constituted if there are
(A) 100 workers
(B) 50 workers
(C) 80 workers
(D) None of the above
Answer: A

174. Which of the following legislations makes Provision of 240 days of service equivalent to one year continuous service ?
(A) The Payment of Wages Act
(B) The E.S.I. Act
(C) The Industrial Disputes Act
(D) The Minimum Wages Act
Answer: C

175. Special provisions relating to lay - off retrenchment and closure will apply where not less than :
(A) 50 Workmen were employed
(B) 100 Workmen were employed
(C) 300 Workmen were employed
(D) 500 Workmen were employed
Answer: A

176. Which of the following in valid under the industrial disputes Act 1947 with regard to Arbitration Award :
(A) It shall become enforceable on the expiry of 30 days from the date of its publication
(B) It shall not become enforceable on the expiry of 30 days from the date of its publication
(C) Partly A and partly B
(D) The Act is silent about it.
Answer: A

177. The provision of "Protected Workmen" is given under :
(A) Factories' Act, 1948
(B) Mines Act, 1952
(C) Industrial Disputes Act, 1947
(D) Payment of Bonus Act, 1965
Answer: C

178. In which of the following legislations there are provisions of compulsory mediation and collective bargaining ?
(A) Industrial Disputes Act, 1947
(B) Trade Unions Act, 1926
(C) Industrial Employment (Standing Orders) Act, 1946
(D) None of the above
Answer: A

179. Which schedule of the Industrial Disputes Act, 1947 deals with Unfair Labour Practices ?
(A) Second Schedule
(B) Third Schedule
(C) Fourth Schedule
(D) Fifth Schedule
Answer: D

180. Which of the following is not a duty of a conciliation Officer?
(A) To induce parties to come to a fair and amicable decision on the matters in dispute.
(B) To act as a mediator
(C) To promote settlement of disputes
(D) To act as adjudicator
Answer: D

181. Temporary closing down the undertaking with the intention of forcing workers to accept the demands of employers is called________ .

(A) Lockout (B) Layoff
(C) Strike (D) Retrenchment

Answer: A

182. Which schedule of the Industrial Disputes Act, 1947 gives the list of public utility services ?

(A) First Schedule
(B) Second Schedule
(C) Third Schedule
(D) Fourth Schedule

Answer: A

183. Arrange the following dispute settlement machineries in the order in which they are Given in the Industrial Disputes Act.

(a) Industrial Tribunal
(b) National Tribunal
(c) Works Committee
(d) Labour Court
(e) Court of Inquiry
(f) Board of Conciliation
(g) Conciliation Office

(A) (d) (e) (f) (g) (a) (b) (c)
(B) (c) (g) (f) (e) (d) (a) (b)
(C) (b) (c) (d) (e) (f) (g) (a)
(D) (g) (a) (b) (c) (d) (e) (f)

Answer: B

184. The right to strike and lock-out were recognised in India indirectly under the provision of :

(A) The Industrial Disputes Act 1947
(B) The British Industrial Trade Dispute Act 1929
(C) The Indian Trade Union Act 1926
(D) None of the above

Answer: A

185. Unfair Labour Practices are listed in

(A) the Factories Act, 1948.
(B) the Industrial Employment (Standing Orders) Act, 1946.
(C) the Industrial Disputes Act, 1947.
(D) the Trade Unions Act, 1926.

Answer: C

186. List of unfair labour practices on the part of the trade unions and employers was included in

(A) Factories Act
(B) Industrial Dispute Act
(C) Trade union Act
(D) None of the above

Answer: B

187. Grievance Handing Machinery is given in

(A) Industrial Disputes Act
(B) Factories Act
(C) Both (A) and (B)
(D) None of the above

Answer: A

188. Match the following schedules under the ID Act 1947

(a) Schedule-I	(i) Conditions of service for change of which notice is to be given
(b) Schedule-II & III	(ii) Labour Courts and Industrial Tribunals
(c) Schedule-IV	(iii) Industries which may be declared as public utility services
(d) Schedule-V	(iv) Unfair labour practices

Code:

	(a)	(b)	(c)	(d)
(A)	(iv)	(iii)	(ii)	(i)
(B)	(ii)	(iii)	(i)	(iv)
(C)	(iii)	(ii)	(i)	(iv)
(D)	(iv)	(ii)	(iii)	(i)

Answer: C

189. Put the following in the right sequence as stated in I.D. Act, 1947.

(a) Enquiry Report
(b) Award
(c) Memorandum of settlement
(d) Penalties

(A) (c), (a), (b), (d)
(B) (a), (b), (c), (d)
(C) (b), (a), (d), (c)
(D) (d), (c), (b), (a)

Answer: A

190. Conditions of service of the workmen remain unchanged :
(A) during pendency of industrial dispute before conciliations, labour court and tribunals
(B) during pendency of industrial dispute before conciliation, arbitration and adjudication
(C) during pendency of industrial dispute before conciliation, arbitration and adjudication unless written permission is obtained by the employer
(D) can be changed by the employer on his own will at any time

Answer: A

191. Disputes relating to retrenchment of workmen and closure of establishment come under the purview of :
(A)Schedule I of I.D. Act, 1947
(B)Schedule II of I.D. Act, 1947
(C)Schedule III of I.D. Act, 1947
(D)None of the above

Answer: D

192. An individual workman can raise an industrial dispute in case of :
(A)Retrenchment
(B)Dismissal
(C)Discharge
(D)All the above

Answer: D

193. Match the following :

List - I	List - II
(a) Two or more members	(i) Board of Conciliation
(b) Chairman and two or four members	(ii) Works Committee
(c)One member	(iii) Labour Court
(d) Number of workmen representatives	(iv) Court of Enquiry not less than management representatives

Code :

	(a)	(b)	(c)	(d)
(A)	(iv)	(iii)	(ii)	(i)
(B)	(iv)	(i)	(iii)	(ii)
(C)	(iii)	(i)	(iv)	(ii)
(D)	(ii)	(iii)	(iv)	(i)

Answer: C

194. According to the industrial disputes Act, 1947 which of the following is not a public utility service?
(A) Hotel and Restaurants
(B) Railways
(C) Post, Telegraph and telephone services
(D) Industry Supplying water, light and power to the public

Answer: D

195. Which of the following is not a settlement machinery under the Industrial Disputes Act 1947 ?
(A) Conciliation Officer, Board of Conciliation
(B) Labour Court
(C) Industrial Tribunal
(D) Indian Labour Conference and Standing Labour Committee

Answer: D

196. The detailed provisions regarding unfair Labour Practices have been given under which of the following schedules under the Industrial Disputes Act, 1947 :
(A)Schedule I and II
(B) Schedule III
(C)Schedule IV
(D)Schedule V

Answer: D

197. Which of the following is a function of conciliation officer?
(A)To investigate
(B)To Arbitrate
(C)To Promote Settlement
(D)To Mediate

Answer: A

Explanation: Section 12 of I.D. Act 1947 provides duties of conciliation officers. A conciliation officer is required to investigate without delay the industrial disputes and make efforts to settlement thereof and for the purpose of bringing about a settlement of the dispute he may do all such things as he deems fit for the purpose of bringing parties to come to a fair and amicable settlement of the disputes.

198. Which of the following statements is not true ?
(A) Conciliation process results into a settlement
(B) Adjudication process results into an award
(C) Court of enquiry results into a report
(D) There is no time limit for submission of the report by the court of enquiry

Answer: D

199. As per the Industrial dispute Act. 1947 the constitution of works committee is mandatory if the number of workers are :
(A)200 or more (B) 100 or more
(C)300 or more (D) None of the above

Answer: B

200. Temporary cessation of work by a group of workers is called :
(A)Strike (B) Gherao
(C)Lockout (D) None of the above

Answer: A

201. The inability of an employer to provide employment due to shortage of power, rawmaterial and breakdown of machinery is called ________.
(A)Retrenchment (B) Lockout
(C)Lay off (D) None of the above

Answer: C

202. The provision of Grievance settlement Authority is provided in which of the following Acts ?
(A) The industrial employment (standing orders) Act
(B) The Factories Act
(C) The Industrial Disputes Act
(D) The Trade Unions Act

Answer: C

203. Adjudication machineries under the Industrial Disputes Act, 1947 shall submit their award in case of an individual workman within a period of
(A)One year (B) Two years
(C)Three years (D) Three months

Answer: D

204. Which of the following cannot be said to be a public utility service under the Industrial Disputes Act, 1947 ?
(A) Railways/Airlines
(B) Post, telegraph and telephone service
(C) Automobile Industry/Jute and Cotton industries
(D) Undertakings related to power, electricity and water supply

Answer: C

205. Which of the following machineries have been provided by The Industrial Disputes Act for settlement of disputes between the employee and the employer?
(A)Conciliation
(B)Arbitration
(C)Adjudication
(D)All of the above

Answer: D

206. If the money is due from the employer under the settlement or award, the workman or his assignee can make an application to the appropriate government for the recovery within the period given below.
(A) One year.
(B) One year and also after the said period of the appropriate government is satisfied that the applicant has sufficient cause for not making the application within one year.
(C) Two years.
(D) Three years.

Answer: B

207. From the date on which the Industrial Employment (Standing Orders) Act, 1948 becomes applicable to an industrial establishment an employed is required to

submit to the certifying officer the draft standing orders.
(A) Within 3 months
(B) Within 6 months
(C) Within a months
(D) Immediately on receipt
Answer: B

208. The employer of an establishment to which the Industrial Employment (Standing Orders) Act, 1948 applies shall submit to the certifying officer draft standing orders propose by him for adaptation in the establishment within-
(A) 6 months (B) 4 months
(C) 30 Days (D) 2 Months
Answer: A

209. Which Act provides for the appointment of conciliation officers and adjudication authorities ?
(A) The Factories Act, 1948
(B) The Industrial Disputes Act,1947
(C) The Trade Unions Act, 1926
(D) None of the above
Answer: B

210. Prior intimation to the appropriate Govt to lay off, retrench or close down an establishment is required under the Industrial Disputes Act, 1947 where there are ________ workers
(A) 100 (B) 1000
(C) 50 (D) 500
Answer: C

211. Prior permission from the appropriate Govt to lay off, retrench or close down an establishment is required under the Industrial Disputes Act where there are ________ workers
(A) 100 (B) 1000
(C) 50 (D) 500
Answer: A

212. Forming of a Works Committee under the Industrial Disputes Act, is mandatory where the no. employees is ________
(A) 1000 (B) 100
(C) 500 (D) 250
Answer: B

213. Lay off compensation is to be paid @ ________ of average wages
(A) 15 days (B) 50%
(C) 60% (D) 75 %
Answer: B

214. Any amount due from an employer under settlement or award can be recovered following the procedures laid down in ________
(A) The Standing Orders
(B) Section 15 of the Payment of Wages Act
(C) Minimum Wages Act
(D) Section 33-C of the Industrial Dispute Act
Answer: D

215. The object of retrenchment compensation is :-
a) To give the retrenched workmen some employment
b) To soften the rigour of hardship
c) To give partial protection to the retrenched employee and his family to enable them to tide over the hard period of unemployment
d) To provide education to the retrenched workmen
(A) b & c (B) a & d
(C) a & b (D) a & c
Answer: A

216. The Industrial Disputes Bill was introduced in the Central Legislative assembly on:-
a) 8th October 1950
b) 9th March 1946
c) 8th October 1946
d) 10th May 1950
(A) c (B) a & b
(C) a & c (D) a, b & d
Answer: A

217. A situation where management is unable to provide employment due to non availability of work is called :

(A) Lock out (B) Lay off
(C) Termination (D) Closure

Answer: B

218. Which of the following is related with "change in conditions of service" of a worker ?

(A) Section 9A of the ID Act
(B) Section 9B of the ID Act
(C) Section 3 of the ID Act
(D) Section 25 of the ID Act

Answer: A

219. Referring a dispute to an agreed third party for setlement or advice without the force of litigation or resort to law is known as :

(A) Adjudication (B) Arbitration
(C) Conciliation (D) All of the above

Answer: B

220. (1) In a particular case, after setting aside the order of dismissal, whether a workman should be reinstated or paid compensation is within the judicial discretion of a Sessions Court or Tribunal
(2) In a particular case, after setting aside the order of dismissal, whether a workman should be reinstated or paid compensation is within the judicial discretion of a High Court or Tribunal
(3) In a particular case, after setting aside the order of dismissal, whether a workman should be reinstated or paid compensation is within the judicial discretion of a Labour Court or Tribunal
Which statement is correct?

(A) Statement (1) (B) Statement (2)
(C) Statement (3) (D) All of the above

Answer: C

221. Some of the following are held not to be unavoidable circumstances beyond the control of the employer. They are:-

a) Closure due to financial impossibility to carry out the business
b) Non-availability of orders for supply of goods
c) Non-cooperation from workmen
d) Disinterest of the employer in continuing business

(A) a & d (B) a, b & c
(C) c & d (D) All of the above

Answer: B

222. (1) A Industrial Tribunal shall consist of one person only to be appointed by the Central Government
(2) A National Tribunal shall consist of two persons only to be appointed by the Central Government
(3) A National Tribunal shall consist of one person only to be appointed by the State Government
(4) A National Tribunal shall consist of one person only to be appointed by the Central Government
Which statement is correct?

(A) Statement (4) (B) Statement (3)
(C) Statement (1) (D) Statement

Answer: A

223. (1) Conciliation proceedings before a Board are similar in nature to those before a Conciliation Officer
(2) Conciliation proceedings before a Board are opposite in nature to those before a Conciliation Officer
Which statement is correct?

(A) Statement (1)
(B) Statement (2)
(C) Both statements are correct
(D) Both statements are incorrect

Answer: A

224. __________ is temporarily closing down the undertaking with the intention of forcing workers to accept the demands of employer.

(A) Lay-off (B) Retrenchment
(C) Lock out (D) Termination

Answer: C

225. Which of the following method has not been given a statutory form in India?

(A) Conciliation
(B) Mediation
(C) Voluntary Arbitration
(D) Adjudication

Answer: B

226. A wage period shall not exceed :
(A) Forty days
(B) One week
(C) One month
(D) Thirty - five days

Answer: C

227. Which of the following is not an authorized deduction under the Payment of Wages Act, 1936 ?
(A) Fines
(B) Income-tax
(C) Contributions for LIC premiums
(D) Deductions made for payment of debt to money lender

Answer: D

228. Under the Payment of Wages Act, 1936 payment of wages of establishments employing not more than 1000 employees shall be paid within ______ of the wage month
(A) 10th day (B) 7th day
(C) 2nd day (D) 15th day

Answer: B

229. Under the Payment of Wages Act, payment of wages of establishments employing not less than 1000 employees shall be paid within ________ of the wage month
(A) 7th day (B) 15th day
(C) 2nd day (D) 10th day

Answer: D

230. As per the payment of wages Act, 1936 no fine shall be imposed on any employed person who is under the age of :
(A) 14 years (B) 15 years
(C) 16 years (D) 18 years

Answer: B

231. A wage period shall not exceed :
(A) Forty days
(B) One month
(C) One week
(D) Thirty five days

Answer: B

232. Which of the following statements relating to the Payment of Wages Act is not correct ?
(A) The Act was enacted in 1936
(B) Under this Act payment of wages cannot be made fortnightly
(C) The Act has provision for authorised deductions from wages
(D) Under this Act, the definition of 'Employed Person' includes the legal representative of a deceased employee

Answer: B

233. Under the payment of wages Act, 1936 no fine can be recovered after the expiry of______ days from the day on which it was imposed.
(A) 15 days (B) 30 days
(C) 60 days (D) 90 days

Answer: D

234. Wage Board is a ______
(A) Bipartite body
(B) Tripartite body
(C) Both (A) and (B)
(D) None of the above

Answer: B

235. Which of the following is not an authorised deduction under the payment of wages Act, 1936 ?
(A) Recovery of advances
(B) Absence from duty
(C) Life Insurance premium
(D) Payment to cooperative societies not approved by state governments.

Answer: D

236. If deduction is made contrary to the provisions of the Payment of Wages Act, 1936 the aggrieved employee can write to the inspector appointed under the Act within the time period given below from the date on which the deduction from

wages was made or the date on which the payment of wages is due
(A) Two years (B) One year
(C) Twelve weeks (D) Six weeks

Answer: C

237. Under the Payment of Wages Act, 1936 the maximum limit on deductions should not ordinarily cross
(A) 50 percent generally and 65 percent in case of payments due to the cooperatives
(B) 60 percent generally and 75 percent in case of payments due to the cooperatives
(C) 50 percent generally and 75 percent in case of payments due to the cooperatives
(D) 40 percent generally and 75 percent in case of payments due to the cooperatives

Answer: C

238. Which of the following statements is wrong ?
(A) Wages are fixed through collective bargaining
(B) Wages are fixed by the trade unions.
(C) Wages are fixed under the Minimum Wages Act, 1948
(D) Wages are fixed through the awards

Answer: D

239. Which of the following is/are authorised deducation(s) under the Payment of Wages Act, 1936.
(A) Fine
(B) Contribution towards E.S.I. Fund
(C) Contribution towards Provident Fund
(D) All the above.

Answer: D

240. The wage period as provided under the Payment of Wages Act, 1936 should not be more than
(A)30 days (B) 31 days
(C)1 month (D)None of the above

Answer: C

241. Which among the following comes under the category of economic legislations ?
(A) The Industrial Disputes Act, 1947
(B) The Payment of Wages Act, 1936
(C) Workmens' Compensation Act, 1923
(D) The Apprentices Act, 1961

Answer: B

242. According to the workmen's compensation Act, 1923 for calculating the compensation the maximum salary slab amount , the management can consider is :
(A) Rs 2000/- (B) Rs 3000/-
(C) Rs 4000/- (D) Rs 5000/-

Answer: C

243. The workmen's compensation Act came into force on the following date:
(A) 1st July, 1924
(B) 1st July, 1923
(C) 1st January, 1924
(D) 1st January, 1923

Answer: A

244. In which of the following years was the Workmen's Compensation Act introduced?
(A)1924 (B) 1923
(C) 1948 (D) 1927

Answer: B

245. The Minimum Wages Act, 1948 has:
(A) One schedule covering different types of industries.
(B) One schedule covering different types of industries, shops and establishments.
(C) One schedule covering shops and establishments.
(D) Two schedules covering industrial establishments and agriculture.

Answer: D

246. Which of the following bodies is provided under the Minimum Wages Act, 1948?
(A) Standing Labour Committee
(B) Shop Level Council
(C) Advisory Board
(D) Joint Management Council

Answer: C

Explanation: Advisory Board.- For the purpose of co-ordinating the work of advising the appropriate Government generally in the matter of fixing and revising minimum rates of wages, the appropriate Government shall appoint an Advisory Board.

247. Minimum Wages Act, 1948 aims to
(A) maintain purchasing power of wages.
(B) encourage workers to produce more.
(C) check exploitation of labour by employer.
(D) pay workers according to their work.
Answer: C

248. Statutory Minimum wage is fixed under
(A) Payment of Wages Act, 1936
(B) Equal Remuneration Act, 1976
(C) Workmen's Compensation Act, 1923
(D) Minimum Wages Act, 1948
Answer: D

249. Under the Minimum Wages Act, 1948 the appropriate government shall fix the minimum rates of wages payable to the employees employed in an employment specified in
(A) Schedule I part I
(B) Schedule I part II
(C) Schedule I, Part I, II and the employments and added under section 27
(D) Schedule I and II
Answer: C

250. Central Advisory Board under the Minimum Wages Act, 1948 is constituted to :
(A) To advise the employers for payment of minimum wages as fixed under this Act.
(B) Co-ordinate the work of committees and sub-committees
(C) Co-ordinate the work of advisory boards
(D) None of the above
Answer: A

251. About which of the following there is no provision under Minimum Wages Act, 1948 ?
(A) Minimum Wage Committee
(B) Minimum Wages Advisory Board
(C) Fair Wage Committee
(D) Central Advisory Board
Answer: C

252. Which of the following statements relating to the Minimum Wages Act, 1948 is not correct ?
(A) The Act lays down for fixation of a minimum time rate of wages.
(B) The Act has only one Schedule.
(C) Minimum rates of wages cannot be fixed by a State Government
(D) Under the Act, different minimum rates of wages may be fixed for different localities.
Answer: D

253. Which of the following statements is correct ?
(A) Minimum wage provides only the basic requirements of life.
(B) Minimum Wages Act is applicable in all organisations.
(C) Minimum wage is fixed by the employer
(D) None of the above
Answer: B

254. Under the Minimum Wages Act, 1948 which of the following has/have been provided for fixation of minimum wages?
(A) Wage Boards
(B) Awards of Labour Court
(C) Notification method and Committee method
(D) None of the above
Answer: C

255. The wages under the Minimum Wages Act, 1948 shall include ____________
(A) CTC

(B) A basic rate of wages and dearness allowance variable according to cost of living
(C) Basic rate of wages, DA, HRA and CCA
(D) A consolidated amount decided by the employer

Answer: B

256. Which of the following stands for bonus in the context of Indian situation?
(A) Profit sharing
(B) Deferred wage
(C) Incentive
(D) None of the above

Answer: C

257. An employee is eligible to get bonus under the Payment of Bonus Act, 1965 if he had worked for not less than ________ days in the preceding year
(A) 30 (B) 240
(C) 160 (D) 190

Answer: A

258. An employee whose salary does not exceed ___________ is eligible for Bonus under the Payment of Bonus Act.
(A) Rs 3500 (B) Rs 2500
(C) Rs 6500 (D) Rs 10000

Answer: D

259. The statutory minimum bonus is ________
(A) 8.33% (B) 10%
(C) 24% (D) 20%

Answer: A

260. Maximum bonus under the Payment of Bonus Act is _______
(A) 8.33% (B) 10%
(C) 24% (D) 20%

Answer: D

261. Under the payment of Bonus Act, 1965, the gross profits derived by an employer from an establishment in respect of any accounting year shall be computed
(A) In case of Banking Company according to schedule II and in any other case schedule I.
(B) In case of Banking Company according to schedule I and in any other case schedule II.
(C) In case of Banking Company and in any other case schedule I.
(D) In case of Banking Company and in any other case schedule II.

Answer: B

262. The ceiling on wage or salary for calculation of Bonus under the Payment of Bonus Act 1965 is
(A) Rs.2,500 (B) Rs. 3,500
(C) Rs. 4,500 (D) Rs. 6,500

Answer: B

263. Under the Payment of Bonus Act, 1965 any employee who has worked for not less than______ working days in a year is entitled to payment of bonus by his employer.
(A) 5 (B) 10
(C) 20 (D) 30

Answer: D

264. The Payment of Bonus Act, 1965 is applicable to an employee who draws wage or salary of
(A) Rs.3500 in case of apprentice
(B) Rs. 5000 in case of apprentice and employee
(C) Rs. 7500 in case of employee only
(D) Rs.10000 in case of employee only

Answer: D

265. Bonus is calculated from :
(A) Gross profits
(B) Available surplus
(C) Allocable surplus
(D) None of the above

Answer: B

266. Bonus is paid from :
(A) Gross profit
(B) Available surplus
(C) Allocable surplus

(D) None of the above

Answer: B

267. Within how many months from the date of closing of the Accounting year bonus must be paid by the employer under the Payment of Bonus Act, 1965 :
(A) 7 months (B) 8 months
(C) 9 months (D) 10 months

Answer: B

268. As per the Payment of Bonus Act, 1965 every employee shall be entitled to be paid by his employer, Bonus, provided he has worked in the establishment for not less than :
(A) 20 working days (B) 30 working days
(C) 60 working days (D) 180 working days

Answer: B

269. Which of the following is not regarded as a wage legislation ?
(A) Payment of Wages Act, 1936
(B) Minimum Wages Act, 1948
(C) Payment of Bonus Act, 1965
(D) Equal Remuneration Act, 1976

Answer: C

270. Under the Equal Remuneration Act, 1976 remuneration means
(A) Basic wage only
(B) Basic wage and dearness allowance
(C) Basic wage and emoluments what soever payable
(D) None of the above

Answer: C

271. Equal Remuneration Act, 1976 was enacted to check –
(A) Occupational wage differentials.
(B) Geographical wage differentials.
(C) Wage differential based on sex.
(D) Inter-industry wage differentials.

Answer: C

272. The Equal Remuneration Act was enacted in the year ________.
(A)1972 (B) 1974
(C)1976 (D) 1977

Answer: C

273. An 'Advisory Committee' to increase employment opportunities for women is required to be constituted under which of the following Acts ?
(A) The Equal Remuneration Act
(B) The Industrial Disputes Act
(C) The Minimum Wages Act
(D) None of the above

Answer: A

274. Equal Remuneration Act, 1976 was mainly enacted to check
(A) Child Exploitation
(B) Men Exploitation
(C) Women Exploitation
(D) All the above

Answer: C

275. Advisory committee under the Equal Remuneration Act, 1976 shall consists of :
(A) 10 persons of which one - third shall be women
(B) 10 persons of which one half shall be women
(C) Not less than 10 persons of which one half shall be women
(D) None of the above

Answer: C

276. The Equal Remuneration Act, 1976, aims to do away with which of the following types of wage differential :
(A) Occupational wage - differential
(B) Industrial Wage Differential
(C) Wage Differential on the basis of sex
(D) Geographical Wage Differential

Answer: C

Which of the following wage differentials in India has been controlled by the enactment of the Equal Remuneration Act, 1976 ?
(A) Occupational Wage Differentials
(B) Geographical Wage Differentials
(C) Wage differentials according to sex
(D) Industrial Wage Differential

Answer: C

277. The Equal Remuneration Act, 1976 provides :
(A) Equal Remuneration to men and women
(B) Equal Remuneration to men and women and helps to remove discrimination in recruitment
(C) Equal Remuneration to men and women for same work and helps to remove discrimination while recruiting men and women
(D) None of the above

Answer: C

278. The provisions regarding equal pay for equal work to men and women are provided under which of the following :
(A) Fundamental Rights
(B) Directive Principles of State Policy
(C) Preamble
(D) All the above

Answer: B

279. Which act prohibits discrimination in fixing salary to men and women engaged in the work of similar nature:
(A) Minimum Wages Act, 1948
(B) Payment of Wages Act, 1936
(C) Payment of Subsistence Allowance Act
(D) Equal Remuneration Act, 1976

Answer: D

280. Under the Payment of Gratuity Act, 1972 the maximum gratuity payable is
(A) Rs. 10 lakhs (B) Rs. 8 lakhs
(C) Rs. 5 lakhs (D) Rs. 3.5 lakhs

Answer: A

281. Consumer price index' is taken into account in connection with which of the following:
(A) Payment of Bonus Act, 1965
(B) Maternity Benefit Act, 1961
(C) Workmen's Compensation Act, 1923
(D) Payment of Gratuity Act, 1972

Answer: D

282. In order to be eligible for Gratuity under the Payment of Gratuity Act, 1972, an employee should have a minimum continuous service of ________
(A) 10 years (B) 5 years
(C) 7 years (D) 3 years

Answer: B

283. Under the Payment of Gratuity Act, the rate of gratuity is ________ salary for every completed year of service
(A) 20 days (B) 30days
(C) 15 days (D) 2 months

Answer: C

284. A news paper employee is eligible for gratuity if he has ______ years continuous years of service
(A) 10 (B) 5
(C) 7 (D) 3

Answer: D

285. Gratuity is calculated treating a month as having the following days :
(A) 25 (B) 26
(C) 30 (D) 31

Answer: B

286. The name of which of the following legislation has been recently changed :
(A) Minimum Wages Act, 1948
(B) Maternity Benefit Act, 1961
(C) Workmen's Compensation Act, 1923
(D) Payment of Gratuity Act, 1972

Answer: D

287. Employees Provident Fund and Miscellaneous Provisions Act, 1952 is applied to establishments employing not less than _______
(A) 10 employees (B) 20 employees
(C) 50 employees (D) 100 employees

Answer: B

288. An employee whose salary at the time of joining does not exceed ________ shall become a member of the provident fund under the Act.
(A) Rs 10000 (B) Rs7500
(C) Rs 6500 (D) Rs 5000

Answer: C

289. Employees' share of provident fund contribution is ________

(A) 12 % (B) 8.33%
(C) 1.75 % (D) 4.75%

Answer: A

290. Employer's share of contribution to the provident fund is ________

(A) 8.33% (B) 12%
(C) 3.67 % (D) 4.75 %

Answer: C

291. Employer's contribution to Employees Pension Scheme is ________

(A) 8.33% (B) 12%
(C) 3.67 % (D) 4.75 %

Answer: A

292. Employer's contribution to Employees' Deposit Linked Insurance is ________

(A) 3.67 % (B) 1.1 %
(C) 0.5 % (D) 0.05 %

Answer: C

293. Employment Exchanges (Compulsory Notification of Vacancies) Act, 1959 and Apprenticeship Act, 1961 represent which of the following types of labour legislations ?

(A) Protective Legislation
(B) Regulative Legislation
(C) Social Security Legislation
(D) None of the above

Answer: B

294. Under which Act 'housing' is a statutory provision ?

(A) The Factories Act
(B) The Mines Act
(C) The Port and Dock Workers (Regulation of Employment) Act
(D) The Plantation Labour Act

Answer: D

295. Housing is a statutory welfare programme under________.

(A) Factories Act
(B) Plantations Labour Act
(C) Industrial Disputes Act
(D) Trade Unions Act

Answer: B

296. Housing is a statutory welfare under which of the following Acts?

(A) Factories' Act
(B) Mines Act
(C) Shops and Commercial Establishment Act
(D) Plantation Labour Act

Answer: D

297. Under Plantation Labour Act, 1951 a Welfare Officer is required to be appointed where the no. of workers is________

(A) 100 (B) 300
(C) 500 (D) 1000

Answer: B

298. Under Plantation Labour Act, crèche is to be set up where ________ women workers are employed or the no. of children of women workers exceeds ______

(A) 50 and 20 (B) 30 and 20
(C) 50 and 30 (D) 30 and 5

Answer: A

299. Under Plantation Labour Act, canteen is compulsory where ________ workers are working

(A) 100 (B) 250
(C) 500 (D) 150

Answer: D

300. Which of the following legislations does not contain labour welfare provisions ?

(A) Industrial Disputes Act, 1947
(B) Mines Act, 1952
(C) Plantation Labour Act, 1951
(D) Factories Act, 1948

Answer: A

301. Who among the following was the chairman of the Second National Commission on Labour ?

(A) Ravindra Verma
(B) Gajendra Ghadkar
(C) Indira Gandhi
(D) Lalbahadur Shastri

Answer: A

302. Match the following :

Enactment

i. Industrial employment Standing orders Act
ii. Industrial Disputes Act
iii. Factories Act
iv. Trade Unions Act

Year

(i) 1948 (ii) 1926
(iii) 1947 (iv) 1946

	(a)	(b)	(c)	(d)
(A)	(iii)	(ii)	(iv)	(i)
(B)	(iv)	(ii)	(i)	(iii)
(C)	(ii)	(i)	(iv)	(iii)
(D)	(iv)	(iii)	(i)	(ii)

Answer: D

303. In USA ,the Labour Management Relations Act (Taft Hartley Act) was enacted in:

(A) 1937 (B) 1947
(C) 1957 (D) 1967

Answer: B

304. Arrange the following in right sequence :

(a) Payment of Wages Act
(b)Trade Disputes Act
(c) Second Factories Act
(d) Workmen's Compensation Act

(A) (a), (b), (c), (d)
(B) (d), (c), (b), (a)
(C) (c), (d), (b), (a)
(D) (d), (c), (a), (b)

Answer: C

Explanation: The Trade Disputes and Trade Unions Act- 1927.
Workmen's Compensation Act-1923
Payment of Wages Act-1936
Second Factories Act-1891

305. Match the following :

(a) Discipline — (i) Payment of Wages Act, 1936
(b) Regulation of employee-employer — (ii) Industrial Employment relations (Standing Orders), Act 1946
(c) Wage revision — (iii) Industrial Disputes Act, 1947
(d) Mode and time of Payment of Wages — (iv) Minimum Wages Act, 1948

	(a)	(b)	(c)	(d)
(A)	(ii)	(iii)	(iv)	(i)
(B)	(i)	(ii)	(iv)	(iii)
(C)	(ii)	(iv)	(i)	(iii)
(D)	(iii)	(ii)	(iv)	(i)

Answer: A

306. Match the following :

List - I	List - II
(a) Protected workman	(i) Industrial Employment (Standing orders) Act, 1946
(b) Immunity from civil suit	(ii) Maternity Benefit Act, 1961
(c) Subsistence Allowance	(iii) Industrial Disputes Act, 1947
(d) Medical Bonus	(iv) Trade Union Act, 1926

Code:

	(a)	(b)	(c)	(d)
(A)	(iii)	(iv)	(i)	(ii)
(B)	(iv)	(i)	(ii)	(iii)
(C)	(ii)	(i)	(iii)	(iv)
(D)	(i)	(iii)	(iv)	(ii)

Answer: A

307. Which of the following is not a social security legislation ?

(A) Workmen's Compensation Act
(B) ESI Act
(C) Employee's Pension Scheme
(D) Maternity Benefit Act

Answer: C

308. Match the year in which these Acts were promulgated.

Group A	Group B
(a) The Payment of Wages Act	(i) 1948
(b) The Minimum Wages Act	(ii) 1976
(c) The Payment of Bonus Act	(iii) 1936
(d) The Equal Remuneration Act	(iv) 1965

	(a)	(b)	(c)	(d)
(A)	(i)	(iv)	(iii)	(ii)
(B)	(ii)	(iv)	(i)	(iii)
(C)	(iii)	(i)	(iv)	(ii)
(D)	(i)	(ii)	(iii)	(iv)

Answer: C

309. Match the years of enactment with appropriate Act.

(a) The Trade Union Act
(b) The Bombay Industrial Disputes Act
(c) The Workmen's Compensation Act
(d) The Factories Act

Years

(i) 1948 (ii) 1923
(iii) 1926 (iv) 1938

	(a)	(b)	(c)	(d)
(A)	(iii)	(iv)	(ii)	(i)
(B)	(iv)	(iii)	(i)	(ii)
(C)	(i)	(ii)	(iii)	(iv)
(D)	(ii)	(i)	(iv)	(iii)

Answer: A

310. Sequence the following in the order of the year in which they came into being from earliest to the latest :

(a) The Workmen's Compensation Act
(b) The Maternity Benefit Act
(c) The Employees State Insurance Act
(d) Establishment of the ILO

(A) (c) (d) (a) (b)
(B) (c) (a) (d) (b)
(C) (a) (c) (b) (d)
(D) (c) (b) (d) (a)

Answer: B

311. Match the following :

Group - A

i. Comprehensive Social Security
ii. Post-natal Benefit
iii. Welfare Officer
iv. Theory of Notional Extension

Group – B

(i) The Factories Act
(ii) The Workmen's Compensation Act
(iii) The ESI Act
(iv) The Maternity Benefit Act

	(a)	(b)	(c)	(d)
(A)	(iii)	(ii)	(iv)	(i)
(B)	(ii)	(i)	(iii)	(iv)
(C)	(iii)	(iv)	(i)	(ii)
(D)	(iii)	(i)	(iv)	(ii)

Answer: C

312. The doctrine of 'contributory negligence' and 'assumed risks' are associated with which of the following benefits extended to workers.

(A) Workmen's Compensation
(B) Safety under the Factories Act
(C) ESI Benefit
(D) All the above

Answer: D

313. Sequence the following Acts in order of their year of enactment from earliest to latest :

(a) The Equal Remuneration Act
(b) The Trade Union Act
(c) The Payment of Wages Act
(d) The Payment of Bonus Act

(A) (b) (d) (c) (a)
(B) (d) (b) (a) (c)
(C) (b) (c) (d) (a)
(D) (c) (b) (d) (a)

Answer: C

314. Match the following :

Group - A

(a) Provision of Controlled Industry
(b) Principle of 'Set on' and 'Set off'
(c) Recovery of loans
(d) Payment by kind

Group – B

(i) The Payment of Wages Act
(ii) The Minimum Wages Act
(iii) The Industrial Disputes Act
(iv) Payment of Bonus Act

	(a)	(b)	(c)	(d)
(A)	(ii)	(i)	(iii)	(iv)
(B)	(iii)	(i)	(iv)	(ii)
(C)	(iv)	(ii)	(iii)	(i)
(D)	(iii)	(iv)	(i)	(ii)

Answer: D

315. Arrange the following Acts in the order they were enacted. Use the codes given below :

(i) Workmen's Compensation Act
(ii) Maternity Benefit Act
(iii) Factories Act
(iv) Equal Remuneration Act

(A) (i) (iii) (ii) (iv)

(B) (i) (iv) (iii) (ii)
(C) (ii) (iii) (iv) (i)
(D) (iv) (ii) (iii) (i)

Answer: A

316. Which of the following is not correct ?
(A) Both the Central and State Governments can enact labour laws
(B) Only the Central Government can enact labour laws
(C) Only the State Government can enact labour laws
(D) None of them can enact labour laws

Answer: D

317. Which of the following statements is wrong ?
(A) Part IV of the Indian Constitution deals with the Directive Principles of State Policy
(B) Employees State Insurance Act was enacted in the year 1948
(C) Factories Act, 1948 comes under the category of Social Security Legislations
(D) Social Assistance is contributory in nature

Answer: A

318. Which of the following statements is not correct ?
(A) The basic objective of labour laws is to protect interest of both parties in industry
(B) Labour laws protect only the interest of working class
(C) Labour laws control the behaviour of both the parties in industry
(D) Labour laws protect the interest of employers only

Answer: A

319. Which of the following is correctly matched ?
(A) Indian Constitution : Equal Remuneration Act, 1976
(B) Dependant Benefit : Maternity Benefit Act, 1961
(C) Hours of Work Convention : Workmens' Compensation Act, 1923
(D) Chief Inspector of Factories : E.S.I. Act, 1948

Answer: D

320. Which of the following is not correctly matched ?
(A) Workmens' Compensation : Employees' State Insurance Corporation Act, 1923
(B) Employees' State Insurance : Partial disablement Act, 1948
(C) International Labour : Social Justice organisation
(D) Factories Act, 1948 : Hazardous occupation

Answer: A

321. **Assertion - (A) :** Development of Labour Legislation after Independence is welfare oriented.
Reason - (R) : Development of Labour Legislation after Independence gives more protection to national economy.
(A) Both (A) and (R) are true
(B) Both (A) and (R) are false
(C) (A) is true but (R) is false
(D) (A) is false but (R) is true

Answer: A

322. Which of the following Legislations took into account the provision 81A of the Defense of India Rules?
(A) Trade Union Act, 1926
(B) Industrial Disputes Act, 1947
(C) Industrial Employment(Standing Orders) Act, 1946
(D) All the above

Answer: D

323. Match the following :
List – I
a. Principle of Protection and Welfare
b. Principle of Social Justice
c. Principle of Regulation
d. Principle of Social Security
List – II
i. The Trade Union Act, 1926
ii. Robert Owen

iii. Payment of Gratuity Act
iv. The Philadelphia Charter

Codes :

	a	b	c	d
(A)	ii	iv	i	iii
(B)	ii	iv	iii	i
(C)	iv	ii	iv	i
(D)	iv	iii	i	ii

Answer: A

324. Which of the following cannot be said to be a labour legislation ?
(A) Industrial Employment (Standing Orders) Act, 1946
(B) Payment of Bonus Act, 1965
(C) Protection of Civil Rights Act,1955
(D) Trade Unions Act, 1926

Answer: C

325. Workers' facilitation centres shall be set up by the facilitating agency under the
(A) Payment of Bonus Act, 1965
(B) Equal Remuneration Act, 1976
(C) Factories Act, 1948
(D) The unorganized sector workers' Social Security Act, 2005

Answer: D

326. As per the Contract labour (Regulation and abolition) Act, 1970 and the central rule, in case the work is completed before the expiry of the wage period, final payment shall be made within:
(A) 24 Hours of the least working day
(B) 48 Hours of the last working day
(C) 7 Days of the working day
(D) 3 Days of the last working day

Answer: B

327. The article in Indian Constitution that imposes prohibition on traffic in human beings, beggar and other similar forms of forced labour is
(A) Article 19 (B) Article 23
(C) Article 32 (D) Article 45

Answer: B

328. If the money is due from the employer under the settlement or award, the workman or his assignee can make an application to the appropriate government for the recovery within the period given below.
(A) One year.
(B) One year and also after the said period of the appropriate government is satisfied that the applicant has sufficient cause for not making the application within one year.
(C) Two years.
(D) Three years.

Answer: B

329. If there is willful removal or disregard by the workman of any safety guard or other device which he knew to have been provided for the purpose of securing safety of workman,
(A) Employer is liable to pay compensation
(B) Employer is not liable to pay compensation
(C) Appropriate government is liable to pay compensation
(D) The Trade Union is liable to pay compensation

Answer: B

****

UNIT-X
BOOKS AND AUTHORS

10.1. BOOKS AND AUTHORS

1. Scientific Management: **Frederick Taylor.**
2. Shop Management (1903): **Fredrick Taylor.**
3. Principle of Scientific Management (1911): **Fredrick Taylor.**
4. The One Best Way: Frederick Winslow Taylor and the Enigma of Efficiency: **Robert Kanigel.**
5. The Downfall of Money: Germany's Hyperinflation and the Destruction of the Middle Class: **Frederick Taylor.**
6. Primer of Scientific Management: **Frank Bunker Gilbreth.**
7. Cheaper by the Dozen: **Frank B. Gilbreth and Ernestine Gilbreth Carey** .
8. Applied Motion Study: A Collection of Papers On the Efficient Method to Industrial Preparedness: **Frank Bunker Gilbreth and Lillian Moller Gilbreth.**
9. Field System: **Frank Bunker Gilbreth.**
10. Fatigue Study, the Elimination of Humanity's Greatest Unnecessary Waste; a First Step in Motion Study: **Frank Bunker Gilbreth and Lillian Moller Gilbreth.**
11. Organizing for Work: **Henry Laurence Gantt** .
12. Investigating an Industry: A Scientific Diagnosis of the Diseases of Management: **William Kent and Henry Laurence Gantt.**
13. Work, Wages, and Profits: Their Influence on the Cost of Living: **Henry Laurence Gantt.**
14. Economy and Society: **Max Weber.**
15. The Protestant Ethic and the Spirit of Capitalism: **Max Weber.**
16. The Theory of Social and Economic Organization: **Max Weber, A. M. Henderson and Talcott Parsons**
17. Max Weber: A Critical Introduction: **Kieran Allen.**
18. The Foundation of the Juridico-Political: Concept Formation in Hans Kelsen and Max Weber: **Ian Bryan, Peter Langford and John McGarry**
19. Modernity and Politics in the Work of Max Weber: **Charles Turner.**
20. Max Weber in Politics and Social Thought: From Charisma to Canonization **: Joshua Derman.**

21. Marx, Marginalism and Modern Sociology: From Adam Smith to Max Weber (Contemporary Social Theory) :**Simon Clarke.**
22. Max Weber on Economy and Society (Routledge Revivals) : **Robert Holton and Bryan S. Turner**
23. Max Weber and the Idea of Economic Sociology**: Richard Swedberg.**
24. Max Weber's "Economy and Society": A Critical Companion**: Charles Camic, Philip S. Gorski and David M. Trubek.**
25. Protestantism and the Rise of Capitalism**: Max Weber**
26. Toward a Psychology of Being : **Abraham H. Maslow**
27. Maslow on Management**: Abraham H. Maslow**
28. Motivacion Y Personalidad :**Abraham H. Maslow**
29. Business and Society: Corporate Strategy, Public Policy, Ethics:**Keith Davis, William C. Frederick .**
30. The Human Problems of an Industrial Civilization: **Elton Mayo**
31. Administration Industrielle Generale: **Henry Fayol**
32. General and Industrial Management**: Henri Fayol and Irwin Gray**
33. Mintzberg on Management: Inside our Strange World of Organizations: **Henry Mintzberg.**
34. Managing (Financial Times Series) : **Henry Mintzberg**
35. The Nature of Managerial Work**: Henry Mintzberg**
36. Tracking Strategies: Toward a General Theory : **Henry Mintzberg**
37. Strategy Safari: The Complete Guide Through the Wilds of Strategic Management :**Henry Mintzberg, Prof Bruce Ahlstrand and Joseph B. Lampel.**
38. Managers Not MBAs: A Hard Look at the Soft Practice of Managing and Management Development: **Henry Mintzberg**
39. Strategy Bites Back**: Henry Mintzberg, Prof Bruce Ahlstrand and Joseph B. Lampel**
40. The Structuring of Organizations: A Synthesis of Research :**Henry Mintzberg**
41. Management - it's Not What You Think**: Henry Mintzberg, Prof Bruce Ahlstrand and Joseph B. Lampel.**
42. The Strategy Process: Concepts, Contexts, Cases : **Henry Mintzberg and Prof Sumantra Ghoshal .**
43. Simply Managing: What Managers Do and Can Do Better**: Henry Mintzberg**
44. Why I Hate Flying: Tales for the Tormented Traveler: Tales for the Tormented Traveller: **Henry Mintzberg.**
45. The Rise and Fall of Strategic Planning**: Henry Mintzberg**

46. Directivos, No MBAs :**Henry Mintzberg and Isabel Murillo Fort**
47. Management: A System of Contingency Analysis of Managerial Functions: **Koontz, H. and C. O'Donnell.**
48. Innovation and Entrepreneurship: **Peter Drucker.**
49. The Effective Executive:**Peter F. Drucker .**
50. Management Challenges for the 21st Century**: Peter F. Drucker**
51. Managing People and Organizations: Peter Drucker's Legacy:**Guido Stein**
52. Post-Capitalist Society : **Peter F. Drucker**
53. "The Practice of Management **:Peter Drucker**
54. "The Balanced Scorecard : Translating Strategy into Action": **Robert S. Kaplan and David P. Norton.**
55. The future of industrial man: **Peter Drucker**
56. The age of discontinuity: **Peter Drucker**
57. Drucker on Asia: **Peter Drucker.**
58. The human organization: Its management and value: **Rensis Likert**
59. The Fortune at the Bottom of the Pyramid: Eradicating Poverty Through Profits: **C.K. Prahalad .**
60. The Future of Competition: Co-Creating Unique Value With Customers : **C.K. Prahalad and Venkat Ramaswamy .**
61. Competing for the Future : **Gary Hamel and C.K. Prahalad**
62. The Fifth Discipline: The art and practice of the learning organization: **Peter M. Senge.**
63. Presence: Exploring Profound Change in People, Organizations and Society**: Peter M. Senge, Joseph Jaworski, C. Otto Scharmer and Betty Sue Flowers**
64. The Fifth Discipline Field book: Strategies for Building a Learning Organization :**Peter M. Senge and et al.**
65. Games People Play: **Eric Berne.**
66. Human Behaviour at work: **Keith Davis**
67. Full employment in free society: **William Beveridge.**
68. Bureaucrazy: **M.K. Kaw**
69. Principles of Labour Welfare : **M. V. Murthy**
70. Future Shock: **Alvin Toffler.**
71. Revolutionary Wealth: **Alvin Toffler and his wife Heidi Toffler.**
72. The World Is Flat: A Brief History of the Twenty-First Century: **Thomas Friedman**

73. In Search of Excellence: **Tom Peters and Robert H. Waterman, Jr.**

74. Management and Worker: **F.J. Roethlisberger.**

75. Labour Welfare Trade Unionism And Industrial Relations: **Punekar S D, Deodhar S B, Sankaran Saraswathi.**

76. Management white-collar relations: **S. D. Punekar, Manorama G. Savur.**

77. Industrial peace in India: the problem and its solution: **S. D. Punekar**

78. Industrial Democracy: **Kshetra Mohan Sahoo**

79. Labour welfare in *India*: **K. N. Vaid**

80. Indian Labour Problems: **S. C. Pant**

81. Economics of Labour and Industrial Relations: **T.N. *Bhagoliwal***

82. Industrial relations: **T. N. Bhagoliwal**

83. Economics of Labour and Social Welfare: An Authoritative Account :**T. N. Bhagoliwal**

84. **P. Subba Rao (2012):** *Essentials of Human Resource and Industrial Relations Text, Cases and Games,* Himalaya Publishing House -5th Revised edition.

85. **P. Subba Rao (2012) :** *Personnel and Human Resource Management,* Himalaya Publishing House -4th Revised edition.

86. **Garry Dessler and Biju Varkkey (2009) :** *Human Resource Management,* Pearson Prentice Hall -11th edition.

87. **Garry Dessler and Biju Varkkey (2009) :** *Human Resource Management,* Pearson Prentice Hall -11th edition.

88. **Raymond A.Noe, John R. Hollenbeck, Barry Gerhat and Pratik M. Wright (2007) :** *Fundamentals of Human Resource Management,* Tata McGraw-Hill Publishing- 2nd edition.

89. **David A. Decenzo and Stephen P. Robbins (2001) :** *Human Resource Management,* John Wiley & Sons, Inc -6th edition.

90. **Harold Koontz and Heinz Weihrich (2004) :** *Essentials of Management,* Tata McGraw-Hill Publishing- 6th edition.

91. **Ruddar Datt and K.P.M. Sundharam (2004) :** *Indian Economy* S.Chand-49th Revised edition.

92. **John W. Newstrom and Keith Davis (1997) :** *Organizational Behaviour: Human Behaviour at work,* Tata McGraw-Hill Publishing- 10th edition.

93. **Suja R.Nair (2010) :** *Organizational Behaviour : Text and Cases,* Himalaya Publishing House -1st edition.

94. **C.B.Mamoria :** *Personnel Management(Management of Human Resources)(1997),* Himalaya Publishing House -12th edition.

95. **S.C.Srivastava:** *Industrial Relations and Labour Laws(2004),*Vikas publishing House Pvt.Ltd.-4th revised edition.

96. **Wendell L. French and Cecil H.Bell, Jr :** *Organization Development(2006),*Prentice –Hall of India Pvt .Ltd-6th edition.

97. **Durga Das Basu:** *Introduction to the constitution of India(2006),*Wadhwa Nagpur-19th edition.

98. P. C. Tripathi: *Personnel Management and Industrial Relations(1998) ,Sultan Chand and Sons* -13th Revised edition.

99. Aswathappa, K. (2005) : *Human Resource and Personnel Management Text and Cases,* 4th edition.

100. ICFAI Center for Management Research, *"Introduction to Human Resource Management, 2004.*

10.2. OBJECTIVE QUESTION - ANSWER

1. The Book "Human Behaviour at work" was written by :
(A)McGregor
(B)Abraham Maslow
(C)Herzberg
(D)Keith Davis

Answer: D

2. Henry Fayol authored the book:
(A) The making of scientific management
(B) General and industrial management
(C)The philosophy of management
(D) Innovation and Entrepreneurship

Answer: B

3. Who is the author of Book "The philosophy of management".
(A) F. W. Taylor
(B) Henry Fayol
(C) Oliver Sheldon
(D) Elton Mayo

Answer: C

4. Who is the author of Book "The making of scientific management".
(A) F.W.Taylor
(B) Henry Fayol
(C) Urwick and Breach
(D) Elton Mayo

Answer: C

5. Who is the author of book "Administration Industrielle Generale"?
(A) Frank and Lillian Gilbreth
(B) Henri Fayol
(C) Peter Drucker
(D) Max Weber

Answer: B

6. Who is the author of Book "The system age(1974)".
(A) Ackoff
(B) Henry Fayol
(C) Oliver Sheldon
(D) Elton Mayo

Answer: A

7. The Book "Human Behaviour at work" was written by :
(A) McGregor
(B) Abraham Maslow
(C) Herzberg
(D) Keith Davis

Answer: D

8. Who is the author of book "General & Industrial Administration"?
(A) Edwin B. Flippo
(B) Henri Fayol
(C) Keith Davis
(D) Max Weber

Answer: B

9. Match the following :

Name of the Book

(a) Human side of Enterprise
(b) Management and Worker
(c) Social Problems of an Industrial Civilisation
(d) The Human Organization

Authors

(i) F.J. Roethlisberger
(ii) Elton Mayo
(iii) Rensis Likert
(iv) Douglas McGregor

	(a)	(b)	(c)	(d)
(A)	(iv)	(i)	(ii)	(iii)
(B)	(iv)	(iii)	(i)	(ii)
(C)	(iii)	(i)	(iii)	(iv)
(D)	(ii)	(iii)	(iv)	(i)

Answer: A

10. Who is the author of the book "Fifth Discipline the Art and Practice of the Learning Organization"?
(A) Peter Clark
(B) Peter Segne
(C) Peter F. Drucker
(D) Tom Peters

Answer: B

11. Match the following authors with the books they have authored.

(Authors)	**(Books)**
(a) Elton Mayo	(i) The Practice of Management
(b) Douglas Mc Gregor	(ii) The human problems of industrial civilisation
(c) Rensis Likert	(iii) The human side of enterprise
(d) Peter F. Drucker	(iv) The human Organization

Code:

	(a)	(b)	(c)	(d)
(A)	(ii)	(iv)	(iii)	(i)
(B)	(ii)	(iii)	(iv)	(i)
(C)	(iii)	(ii)	(iv)	(i)
(D)	(iv)	(ii)	(iii)	(i)

Answer: B

12. Who is the author of the book "Full employment in free society" which is a treatise on social security
(A) A. C. Pigou
(B) Ricardo
(C) William Beveridge
(D) None of the above

Answer: C

13. Match List – I with List – II. Select the correct answer from the codes given below :

List – I (Author)	**List – II (Types of Leadership)**
a. Mooney and Reiley	1. Institutionalists, Specialists, Hybrids
b. Etzioni	2. Titular leaders, Controllers, true organizers
c. Marwick	3. Officials, Informal and formal leaders
d. Gowldner	4. Locals and Cosmopolitans

Codes :

	a	b	c	d
(A)	1	3	4	2
(B)	2	3	1	4
(C)	2	4	1	3
(D)	4	2	3	1

Answer: B

14. Match the following :

Name of the Book

(a) Management and Worker
(b) The Human Side of Enterprise
(c) The New Patterns of Management
(d) The Human Problems of Industrial Civilization.

Author

(i) Rensis Likert
(ii) Elton Mayo
(iii) Roethlisberger and Dickson
(v) Douglas McGregor

Codes :

	(a)	(b)	(c)	(d)
(A)	(ii)	(iv)	(iii)	(i)
(B)	(iii)	(ii)	(iv)	(i)
(C)	(i)	(iii)	(ii)	(iv)
(D)	(iii)	(iv)	(i)	(ii)

Answer : D

15. Match List – I with List – II. Select the correct answer from the codes given follow :

List – I (Definitions) **List – II (Authors)**

1. Henry Fayol a. An employee should receive orders from one superior only.
2. Pfiffner and Presthus leader.
b. A man cannot serve two masters.
3. Dimock and Dimock c. Every member of an organization should report to one and only one.
4. Gullick and Urwick
d. Each employee should have only one boss.

Codes :

	A	b	c	d
(A)	1	4	2	3
(B)	1	3	2	4
(C)	2	3	4	1
(D)	3	2	4	1

Answer: A

16. Who is the author of the book titled 'Bureaucrazy' ?
(A) Michael Crozier
(B) M.K. Kaw
(C) P.N. Haxer
(D) Veerappa Moily

Answer: B

17. Match the following managerial activities with the managerial functions :

(Books)	**(Authors)**
(a) Shop Management	(i) Elton Mayo
(b) Management and worker	(ii) Douglas Mc Gregor
(c) Social Problems of Industrial Civilization	(iii) F.W. Taylor
(d) Human side of Enterprise	(iv) F. J. Roethlisberger

Code:

	(a)	(b)	(c)	(d)
(A)	(ii)	(i)	(iv)	(iii)
(B)	(iii)	(ii)	(i)	(iv)
(C)	(iii)	(iv)	(i)	(ii)
(D)	(ii)	(iv)	(iii)	(i)

Answer : C

18. Match the following :

Books and Concepts	**Authors**
a. Games People Play	i. Eric Bernie
b. I am OK you are OK	ii. Kurt Lewin
c. Johari Window	iii. Thomas A. Harris
d. Force Field Analysis	iv. Joseph Lufth & Harry Inghams

Codes :

	a	b	c	d
(A)	ii	i	iv	iii
(B)	i	iii	iv	ii
(C)	iv	ii	iii	i
(D)	iii	i	ii	iv

Answer: B

19. Match the following :

List – I	**List – II**
(Authors)	**(Books)**
a. Tom Peters & Waterman	i. The Future Shock
b. Thomas Friedman	ii. The Revolutionary Wealth
c. Alvin Tofler	iii. The World is flat
d. Heidi & Alvin Tofler	iv. In search of Excellence

Codes:

	a	b	c	d
(A)	iv	ii	iii	i
(B)	i	iv	ii	iii
(C)	iv	iii	i	ii
(D)	iii	iv	ii	i

Answer : C

20. The author of the book 'Principles of Labour Welfare' is :

(A) K. N. Vaid
(B) M. V. Murthy
(C) S. C. Pant
(D) T. N. Bhagoliwal

Answer: B

****

QUESTION PAPER

1. UGC-NET-LABOUR WELFARE AND INDUSTRIAL RELATIONS

1. Which of the following principles of management was not given by Fayol ?
(A) Unity of direction
(B) Subordination of individual interest to common interest
(C) Stability of tenure
(D) Standardisation

2. Arrange different phases of Hawthorne experimentsin their right sequence :
a. Relay assembly test room experiments
b. Bank wiring observation test
c. Illumination experiment
d. Personal counseling
e. Mass interviewing programme
(A) a, b, c, d, e
(B) c, a, e, b, d
(C) c, b, e, a, d
(D) e, d, c, b, a

3. Delphi technique is used in
(A) Organising
(B) Operating
(C) Staffing
(D) Forecasting

4. Narrow span of control results into
(A) Tall structure
(B) Flat structure
(C) Mechanistic structure
(D) All the above

5. Which of the following is correct about 'Grapevine'?
(A) It tends to exist when members of formal group know another well.
(B) It is the result of social forces at work place.
(C) It is more common in times of high organizational excitement.
(D) All the above.

6. The following concept is developed on unitarism, individualism, commitment and strategic alignment.
(A) Personnel Management
(B) Human Resource Management
(C) Industrial Relations
(D) Personnel Administration

7. Human Resource Planning include
(A) Scenario planning
(B) Action planning
(C) Demand and Supply forecasts
(D) All the above

8. Which one is not a part of recruitment process ?
(A) Determining requirements
(B) Planning recruitment campaign
(C) Attracting candidates
(D) Selecting candidates

9. Which one is not a non-quantitative job evaluation method ?
(A) Ranking method
(B) Grading method
(C) Point rating method
(D) Job-classification method

10. Consider the following punishments in disciplinary actions :
(i) Warning (ii) Demotion
(iii) Censure (iv) Dismissal
Which of the above fall under minor punishment ?
(A) (i) and (ii)

(B) (i), (ii) and (iii)
(C) (i) and (iii)
(D) (i), (ii) and (iv)

11. Which of the following factors are included in the calculation of human development index ?
(A) Life expectancy
(B) Adult literacy
(C) Decent standard of living
(D) All the above

12. Who is not associated with development of human development index ?
(A) Mahabub-ul-Haq
(B) Manmohan Singh
(C) Meghnad Desai
(D) Sudhir Anand

13. The sequence of human resource development activities according to Leonard Nadler are
(A) Education, training and development
(B) Development, training and education
(C) Training, education and development
(D) Training, development and education

14. Who introduced the concept of quality circles in India ?
(A) P. V. Rao
(B) Udai Pareek
(C) Dharani P. Sinha
(D) S. R. Udpa

15. Which of the following is the correct sequence of training evaluation ?
(A) Reaction, learning, behaviour and results
(B) Learning, reaction, behaviour and results
(C) Learning, behaviour, reaction and results
(D) Reaction, learning, results and behaviour

16. Which of the following is the outcome of job satisfaction ?
(A) High employee turnover
(B) High productivity
(C) Absenteeism
(D) All the above

17. Under Alderfer's ERG theory, the three core needs are
(A) Emotional, Relational, and Growth
(B) Emotional, Rational and Growth
(C) Existence, Reliability and Gain
(D) Existence, Relatedness and Growth

18. The group to which a person would like to belong is known as
(A) Primary Group
(B) Membership Group
(C) Reference Group
(D) None of the above

19. The Managerial Grid was given by
(A) Rensis Likert
(B) Kurt Lewin
(C) Hersey Blanchard
(D) Blake and Mouton

20. Arrange the following stages of group dynamics in right sequence :
a. Norming
b. Performing
c. Storming
d. Forming
(A) d, c, a, b (B) a, b, c, d
(C) d, c, b, a (D) c, d, b, a

21. Identify the correct definition of industrial relations :
(A) Relations between or among human beings
(B) Relations between employer and employees as individuals
(C) Relations between parties in an employment context
(D) Collective relationship between management and trade unions

22. Who has propounded the system concept of industrial relations ? Find out from the following :
(A) L. N. Allen Flander
(B) L. N. Flax
(C) John T. Dunlop

(D) Neil N. Chamberlein

23. Which is the correct order of settlement of industrial disputes ?
    a. Industrial Tribunal
    b. National Tribunal
    c. Conciliation
    d. Labour Court

(A) c, a, d, b (B) c, d, a, b
(C) a, d, c, b (D) c, b, d, a

24. Which of the following is not a Tripartite body ?
    (A) Works Committee
    (B) I. L. O
    (C) Indian Labour Conference
    (D) Wage Boards

25. The code of discipline was ratified by the Indian Labour Conference to ensure discipline in industry. Identify the year of ratification out of the following :
    (A) 1957 (B) 1958
    (C) 1942 (D) 1962

26. Which of the following is not a characteristics of Trade Union ?
    (A) Is an association of employers or the employees or of the independent workers ?
    (B) Is relatively a permanent combination but not temporary or casual.
    (C) Is an association of workers who are engaged in not securing economic benefits for their members.
    (D) Is influenced by a member of ideologies.

27. Recognition of trade union is made by the provision of
    (A) Trade Unions Act of 1926
    (B) Industrial Dispute Act 1947
    (C) Code of Discipline
    (D) Factories Act of 1948

28. Which is not a structure of Trade Union of Industrial Organisation ?
    (A) Craft union
    (B) General union
    (C) Industrial union
    (D) Consumers' union

29. A Trade Union should be registered as per the law must have
    (A) 20% of the workers
    (B) 150 workmen
    (C) Minimum 17 persons
    (D) None of the above

30. The founder of Ahmedabad Textile Labour Association was
    (A) V. V. Giri (B) M. K. Gandhi
    (C) B. P. Wadia (D) N. M. Lokhande

31. If there is wilful removal or disregard by the workman of any safety guard or other device which he knew to have been provided for the purpose of securing safety of workman,
    (A) Employer is liable to pay compensation
    (B) Employer is not liable to pay compensation
    (C) Appropriate government is liable to pay compensation
    (D) The Trade Union is liable to pay compensation

32. In case of fatal accident if the commissioner serves notice to the employer based on his source
    (a) the employer can neglect the notice.
    (b) if the employer thinks liable, he shall make the deposit within sixty days of the service of notice.
    (c) if the employer thinks liable, he shall make the deposit within thirty days of the service of notice.
    (d) if the employer is not liable, he shall in his statement indicate the grounds on which he disclaims liability.
    (A) All statements are correct.
    (B) All statements are incorrect.
    (C) Only (a) and (d) are correct.
    (D) Only (c) and (d) are correct.

33. The maternity leave period with full wage is

(A) six months
(B) twelve weeks
(C) four months
(D) sixteen weeks

34. Match the following :

(a)	Royal Commission on	(i) 1937 Labour
(b)	Bombay Textile Labour committee	(ii) 1946 Enquiry
(c)	Second Labour	(iii) 1929 Ministers' Conference
(d)	Labour Investigation Committee	(iv) 2002
(e)	Second National	(v) 1941 Commission on Labour

	(a)	(b)	(c)	(d)	(e)
(A)	(ii)	(i)	(iii)	(iv)	(v)
(B)	(iii)	(ii)	(i)	(v)	(iv)
(C)	(iii)	(v)	(iv)	(i)	(ii)
(D)	(iii)	(i)	(v)	(ii)	(iv)

35. The goal of I LO is
(A) creation of jobs for men and women
(B) not just creation of jobs but the creation of jobs of acceptable quality
(C) not overcoming under employment
(D) not to provide freedom of choice in employment

36. The Payment of Bonus Act, 1965 is applicable to an employee who draws wage or salary of
(A) Rs. 3500 in case of apprentice
(B) Rs. 5000 in case of apprentice and employee
(C) Rs. 7500 in case of employee only
(D) Rs. 10,000 in case of employee only

37. Unfair Labour Practices are listed in
(A) the Factories Act, 1948.
(B) the Industrial Employment (Standing Orders) Act, 1946.
(C) the Industrial Disputes Act, 1947.
(D) the Trade Unions Act, 1926.

38. The Minimum Wages Act, 1948 has
(A) one schedule covering different types of industries.
(B) one schedule covering different types of industries, shops and establishments.
(C) one schedule covering shops and establishments.
(D) two schedules covering industrial establishments and agriculture.

39. If deduction is made contrary to the provisions of the Payment of Wages Act, 1936 the aggrieved employee can write to the inspector appointed under the Act within the time period given below from the date on which the deduction from wages was made or the date on which the payment of wages is due
(A) two years
(B) one year
(C) twelve weeks
(D) six weeks

40. The maximum daily hours of work in a day with normal wage allowed in factories is
(A) 11 hours
(B) 10 hours
(C) 9 hours
(D) 8 hours

41. Assertion (A) : Intra-mural and extra-mural welfare are mutually complimentary.
Reason (R) : The work-life balances need to be ensured in order to get the best output from an employee.
(A) Assertion is wrong but Reason is logical.
(B) Both Assertion and Reason are wrong.
(C) Assertion and Reason are right.
(D) The Assertion is right but Reason is wrong.

42. Which of the following statements is not true in explaining the concept and scope of labour welfare ?
(A) Labour welfare has no roots in social work.

(B) Long Arm of the job and social invasion of workplace' concepts, explain the mutuality between intramural and extra-mural labour welfare
(C) Labour welfare is a social concept.
(D) Corporate social responsibility is an extended concept of welfare.

43. Who is the champion of the 'Welfare movement' propagated in mid 19th century ?
(A) Frederick Winslow Taylor
(B) Andrew Ure
(C) Sheebhom Rownlvee
(D) Robert Owners

44. Sequence the following developments by their period of occurrence from earliest to the latest :
(i) The Labour Investigation Committee
(ii) The Whitley Commission
(iii) The Enactment of Factories Act
(iv) The 1st National Commission on Labour

(A)	(ii)	(i)	(iii)	(iv)
(B)	(ii)	(iii)	(iv)	(i)
(C)	(i)	(ii)	(iv)	(iii)
(D)	(iv)	(ii)	(iii)	(i)

45. Which of the following statements relating to Welfare Officer is not true
(A) The provision of Welfare Officer is given in both the Factories Act, 1948 and the Mines Act, 1952.
(B) Welfare Officer's duties and responsibilities are defined and prescribed in the legislation.
(C) Welfare Officer's appointment is tagged to the provision of minimum workforce employed in an organisation
(D) The Welfare Officer's role was designed as a 'Third force'.

46. Which of the following statements about characteristics of labour is not true ?
(A) Labour is a perishable commodity.
(B) Labour cannot be separated from the person.
(C) Workers have no reserve price.
(D) Labour is as flexible and mobile as capital.

47. Which of the following statements about labour market is not true ?

(A) Labour market like commodity market is analyzed by supply, demand and price equilibrium.
(B) Labour Market is relatively more local than commodity market.
(C) Unlike a commodity market, the relationship between a buyer and seller in a labour market is not temporary.
(D) Monopoly in the labour market is high.

48. Money Wage is otherwise called as
(A) Real wage
(B) Living wage
(C) Nominal wage
(D) Fair wage

49. Wage Boards set right
(A) Inter-regional differentials
(B) Inter-sectoral differentials
(C) Intra-industry differentials
(D) Inter-industry differentials

50. Which of the following is not a determinant of wages ?
(A) Prevailing wages
(B) Bargaining strength of Unions
(C) Job Evaluation
(D) Performance Appraisal

ANSWER KEYS

Q01 D	Q02 B	Q03 D	Q04 A	Q05 D	Q06 B	Q07 D	Q08 D	Q09 C	Q10 C
Q11 D	Q12 B	Q13 C	Q14 D	Q15 A	Q16 B	Q17 D	Q18 C	Q19 D	Q20 A
Q21 D	Q22 C	Q23 B	Q24 A	Q25 B	Q26 C	Q27 C	Q28 D	Q29 D	Q30 B
Q31 B	Q32 D	Q33 A	Q34 D	Q35 B	Q36 D	Q37 C	Q38 D	Q39 C	Q40 C
Q41 C	Q42 A	Q43 D	Q44 A	Q45 B	Q46 D	Q47 D	Q48 C	Q49 C	Q50 D

2. UGC-NET-PAPER-III_LABOUR WELFARE AND INDUSTRIAL RELATIONS

1. Match the following :

List-I

(a) F. J. Roethlisberger& Dickson
(b) Elton Mayo
(c) Douglas Mc Gregor
(d) Rensis Likert

List-II

(i) New Patterns of Management
(ii) The Human side of enterprise
(iii) The Management and Worker
(iv) The Human problems of industrial civilization

Codes :

	(a)	(b)	(c)	(d)
(A)	(ii)	(iv)	(i)	(iii)
(B)	(iii)	(iv)	(ii)	(i)
(C)	(iv)	(iii)	(i)	(ii)
(D)	(ii)	(iii)	(iv)	(i)

2. Who is associated with The 'illumination experiment' of The Hawthorne experiment
(A) Elton Mayo
(B) George A. Pennock
(C) F. J. Roethlisberger
(D) None of the above

3. The paper "Engineer as Economist", which influence F. W.Taylor to develop his Scientific Management Principles authored by
(A) Charles A. Babbage
(B) Henry Gnatt
(C) Henry R. Towne
(D) Louis D. Brandies

4. The systematic process of making job evaluation determinations about a job based upon its content and the way is which it actually functions within the organization is called :
(A) Job Determination
(B) Job Analysis
(C) Job Evaluation
(D) Job Grading

5. Sensitivity training is also known as
(A) X- group training
(B) Y – group training
(C) t – group training
(D) Core group training

6. In which public sector organization quality circles was first introduced in India.
(A) Hindustan Aeronautics Ltd.
(B) Bharath Earth Movers Ltd.
(C) Bharath Heavy ElectricalsLtd.
(D) Hindustan Machine Tools Ltd.

7. Which is not the characteristics of grievances ?
(A) Factual
(B) Fabricated
(C) Disguised
(D) Imaginary

8. Match the following :

Enactment

(a) Industrial employment Standing orders Act
(b) Industrial Disputs Act
(c) Factories Act
(d) Trade Unions Act

Year

(i) 1948 (ii) 1926
(iii) 1947 (iv) 1946

	(a)	(b)	(c)	(d)
(A)	(iii)	(ii)	(iv)	(i)
(B)	(iv)	(ii)	(i)	(iii)
(C)	(ii)	(i)	(iv)	(iii)
(D)	(iv)	(iii)	(i)	(ii)

9. List of unfair labour practices on the part of the trade unions and employers was included in
(A) Factories Act
(B) Industrial Dispute Act
(C) Trade union Act
(D) None of the above

10. Not more than 50% of members of the office bears of Trade union can be outsiders, as per provisions of legislations.
(A) Industrial Dispute Act
(B) Trade Union Act
(C) Mines Act
(D) ESI Act

11. Who coined the term Scientific Management ?
(A) Louis D. Brandies
(B) F. W. Taylor
(C) Douglas Mc Gregor
(D) None of the above

12. Who propagated the quality of work life as a descending participation mechanism ?
(A) Frederick Herzberg
(B) Eric Tryst
(C) A. K. Rice
(D) John T. Dunlop

13. Statutory Minimum wage is fixed under
(A) Payment of Wages Act, 1936
(B) Equal Remuneration Act, 1976
(C) Workmen's Compensation Act, 1923
(D) Minimum Wages Act, 1948

14. The employee State Insurance Act was enacted the basis of which committee's report?
(A) B. R. Ambedkar Committee
(B) B. P. Adarkar Committee
(C) Royal Commission on Labour
(D) Labour Investigation Committee

15. Who is the author of the book "Fifth Discipline the Art and Practice of the Learning Organization" ?
(A) Peter Clark
(B) Peter Segne
(C) Peter F. Drucker
(D) Tom Peters

16. Who has advanced the single loop and double loop learning models ?
(A) Albert Bandura
(B) Robert Blake
(C) Robert Katz
(D) Chris Argyris

17. "Creating jobs, guaranteeing rights at work,extending social protection and promoting social dialogue" are contents of which of the following programmes of ILO ?
(A) Human Rights
(B) Decent Work
(C) International Programme on the Elimination of Child Labour
(D) INDUS Child Labour Project

18. In which company 'Six Sigma' was first experimented ?
(A) Toyota (B) Motorola
(C) Sony (D) Ford

19. The philosophy of 'never-ending improvement' in total quality management is called
(A) Kanaban
(B) Business Process Re-engineering
(C) Benchmarking
(D) Kaizan

20. Who has given the 'Balance Score Card' as a measurement based performance management strategy ?
(A) Robert S. Kaplan and David P.Norton
(B) Hammel and Prahallad
(C) Stablein and Nord
(D) Pascale and Athos

21. Who had advanced the 'Business Process Reengineering' concept ?
(A) K. Pang and N. Oliver
(B) R. Stablein and W. Nord
(C) Micheal Hammer and James Champy
(D) M. Mandenhall and U.Oddon

22. Which of the following statements is not true about the five disciplines identified by Peter Senge ?
(A) Personal Mastery in the first discipline
(B) Mental models is not included in the five disciplines
(C) Building shared vision is a part of the five disciplines
(D) System thinking is the last discipline

23. Who has started that "Collective bargaining is essentially a process inwhich employees act as a group in seeking to shape conditions an relationships in their employment.
(A) R. F. Hoxie
(B) L. G. Reynolds
(C) Dale Yoder
(D) J. F. Richardson

24. In which year the formation of the National Renewal Fund to protect the interest of the workers was announced :
(A) 1956 (B) 1991
(C) 1969 (D) 1992

25. Identify the factors which donot help organization in dealing with knowledge management
(A) Improve the returns
(B) Improve competency
(C) Do not exploit opportunity
(D) Great value for core business

26. Who are not the actors according to Dunlop's framework of industrial relations system ?
(A) Managers and their representatives
(B) Workers and their organizations
(C) Specialized government agencies
(D) Communities and their associations

27. According to whom 'Conflict is necessary but it can be and needs to be managed and resolved'.
(A) Unitarists
(B) Pluralists
(C) Classicalists
(D) Modernists

28. Who observed that the respect for rules depends on the manner of their formulation?
(A) Web, S. and Web, B.
(B) Flanders, A.
(C) Durkheim, E.
(D) Gouldner, A.

29. The concept/theory of industrial capitalism / dialectical materialism was developed by :
(A) Karl Marx
(B) Mahatma Gandhi
(C) Dunlop J. T.
(D) Thakur C. P.

30. Benefits (India) of globalization like sustained economic growth, free markets, economic globalization, privatisation etc., were summarised by :
(A) First National Commission on Labour
(B) Second National Commission on Labour
(C) National Labour Board
(D) International Labour Organisation

31. Globalization is ruthless, rootless, jobless, fruitless was stated by :
(A) U. N. O (B) U. N. D. P
(C) I. L. O (D) W. H. O

32. The Origin, growth and development of employment's organizations in India can be identified as :
(A) Before 1933
(B) After 1933
(C) Before 1947
(D) After 1947

33. The International Organization of Employer's (I.O.E) with headquarters in Genevas was formulated in
(A) 1910 (B) 1920
(C) 1930 (D) 1940

34. Trade Union movement in India emerged between
(A) 1920-1930 (B) 1850-1870
(C) 1870-1880 (D) 1930-1947

35. The code of discipline in industry was adopted by the Indian labour conference (tripantite) in
(A) 1948 (B) 1958
(C) 1968 (D) 1950

36. The constitution of India upholds the principle 'Freedom of Association' as a fundamental right enunciated by I. L. O. convention in
(A) Article 20(C) (B) Article 19(C)
(C) Article 24(C) (D) Article 18(C)

37. Training refers to
(A) An act of increasing the knowledge and skill of an employee for doing a particular job
(B) A short term educational process and utilizing systematic and organized procedure by which employees learn technical knowledge and skills for a definite purpose.
(C) It bridges the differences between job requirements and employee's present specifications
(D) All of the above

38. Which of the following is not an objectives of sensitivity training ?
(A) Awareness of behavioural pattern of oneself and others
(B) Increased openness and greater concern for others
(C) Increased tolerance and less ethnic prejudice
(D) Potentialities for the next level job

39. Match the following with List-A to

List-A **List-B**
(a) Job Rotation (i) The trainer appraises the performance of the trainee,provides feedback information and orrectsthe trainee
(b) Job Instruction (ii) The movement of the trainee from one job to another
(c) Vestible training (iii) Simulation of actual work conditions in a class room
(d) Programmed Instruction (iv) The subject matter to be learned is presented in a services of carefully planned sequential units.

	(a)	(b)	(c)	(d)
(A)	(iv)	(iii)	(ii)	(i)
(B)	(ii)	(i)	(iii)	(iv)
(C)	(iii)	(iv)	(ii)	(i)
(D)	(i)	(ii)	(iii)	(iv)

40. Off the job training does not include :
(A) Role playing
(B) Lecture method
(C) Coaching
(D) Conference or discussion

41. Arrange thefollowing steps of training procedure in proper sequence
a. Preparing the trainee
b. Preparing the instructor
c. Presenting the operation
d. Getting ready to teach
e. Tryout the trainee's performance

f. Follow up

(A) a, b, c, d, e, f
(B) b, a, d, c, e, f
(C) f, e, d, c, a, b
(D) a, d, c, e, b, f

42. Which of the following is not correct about Organisation Development ?
(A) It is not a top management led and supported process.
(B) It is a process ofplanned change.
(C) It is an ongoing collaborative management of organization culture
(D) It is a problem solving process.

43. Who has given the concept of OCTAPACE culture
(A) Dharni P. Sinha
(B) T. V. Rao
(C) D. M. Pestonjee
(D) Udai Pareek

44. The components of Marvin Weisbord's six box model are
(A) Purposes, structure, rewards, mechanisms, relationships and leadership
(B) Processes, structure, resources, mechanisms, relationships and leadership
(C) Performance, structure, rewards, machines,relationships and leadership
(D) Purposes, structure, resources, machines, relationships and leadership

45. Action research, as a methodology for behavioural science was proposed by
(A) Wendell L. French
(B) P. F. Drucker
(C) Kurt Lewin
(D) Reddin

46. The process of comparing work and service methods against the best practices and outcomes in industry is known as
(A) Benchmarking
(B) Kaizens
(C) Quality Circles
(D) None of the above

47. In a learning organisation
(A) Vision is provided by top management
(B) Conflicts are resolved through power and hierarchical influence
(C) Formulation and implementation of ideas takes place at all levels of organisation
(D) All the above

48. When an organization outsources the responsibilities for the end-to-end delivery of the recruitment/selection process covering all vacancies is
(A) Recruitment process and screening
(B) Business process and screening
(C) Knowledge process and screening
(D) All the above

49. Lean production aims at :
(A) Continuous improvement
(B) Aim at zero defects
(C) Just-in-time inventory system
(D) All of the above

50. Which one of the following is not a decision role identified by Henry Mintzberg
(A) The spokesperson role
(B) The Entrepreneurial role
(C) The Disturbance handler role
(D) The Resource allocator role

51. Which one is not of Michael Porters five force model of industry analysis
(A) Threat of new entrants
(B) Substitutes
(C) Intensity of rivalry among existing players
(D) Cost leadership

52. Which one is not a part of Mc Kinsy's 7's' framework ?
(A) Systems
(B) Strategy
(C) Standards
(D) Style

53. The change in specialization and integration in organization context is called :
(A) Co-ordination
(B) Co-operation
(C) Organizational restructuring
(D) Feedback

54. Which one is a part of performance measurement ?
(A) Trait (B) Behaviour
(C) Outcome (D) All the above

55. Which of the following is a single use plan ?
(A) Budget (B) Rule
(C) Procedure (D) Policy

56. The basic role of policy is
(A) To provide guidelines for action
(B) To set procedures
(C) To give direction for motivation
(D) To prescribe methods

57. Grievance Handing Machinery is given in
(A) Industrial Disputes Act
(B) Factories Act
(C) Both (A) and (B)
(D) None of the above

58. Who has given the 'expectancy theory' of Motivation ?
(A) Abraham Maslow
(B) Victor Vroom
(C) Frederick Herzberg
(D) Clayton Adler

59. The categories of human process, technostructural, human resources management and strategic applications are related to :
(A) Change management
(B) O. D. application
(C) Training
(D) Action research

60. The constitution of site appraisal committees is under the :
(A) Factories Act, 1948
(B) Contract labour (Regulation and Abolition) Act, 1970
(C) Maternity Benefit Act, 1965
(D) Employees State Insurance Act, 1948

61. Under the Minimum Wages Act, 1948 the appropriate government shall fix the minimum rates of wages payable to the employees employed in an employment specified in
(A) Schedule I part I
(B) Schedule I part II
(C) Schedule I, Part I, II and the employments and added under section 27
(D) Schedule I and II

62. Under the Equal Remuneration Act, 1976 remuneration means
(A) Basic wage only
(B) Basic wage and dearness allowance
(C) Basic wage and emoluments what soever payable
(D) None of the above

63. Under the Payment of Wages Act, 1936 the maximum limit on deductions should not ordinarily cross
(A) 50 percent generally and 65 percent in case of payments due to the cooperatives
(B) 60 percent generally and 75 percent in case of payments due to the cooperatives

(C) 50 percent generally and 75 percent in case of payments due to the cooperatives
(D) 40 percent generally and 75 percent in case of payments due to the cooperatives

64. Draft standing orders are to be submitted within
(A) Two years from the date on which the Act is applicable in five copies.
(B) One year from the date on which the Act is applicable in five copies
(C) Six months from the date on which the Act is applicable in five copies
(D) Six months from the date on which the act is applicable in ten copies

65. Under the Payment of Gratuity Act, 1972 the maximum gratuity payable is
(A)Rs. 10 lakhs (B) Rs. 8 lakhs
(C) Rs. 5 lakhs (D) Rs. 3.5 lakhs

66. To avoid over crowding thespace provided for each worker under the Factories Act, 1948 is
(A) 12 cubic metres for factories built before 1948 and 14.2 cubic meters for those built after 1948
(B) 10 cubic metres for factories builtbefore 1948 and 14.2 cubic meters for those built after 1948
(C) 9.9 cubic metres for factories built before 1948 and 14.2 cubic meters for those built after 1948
(D) 9.9 cubic meters for factories built before 1948 and 14.4 cubic meters for those built after 1948.

67. Who is an 'exempted employee' under the Employee's state Insurance Act, 1948 ?
(A) Employee who is minor
(B) Employee who is not liable under the Act to pay the employee's contribution
(C) Minor employee who isnot liable under the Act to pay the employee's contribution
(D) None of the above

68. 'Unemployment allowance' payable is stated in
(A) Employee State Insurance Act, 1948
(B) Unorganised Sector Workers Social Security Act, 2005
(C) Factories Act, 1948
(D) None of the above

69. Trade union means any combination formed primarily for the purpose of regulating the relations between
(A) Workmen and employers permanently
(B) Workmen and workmen permanently
(C) Workmen and employers, workmen and workmen, employers and employers temporary or permanent
(D) Workmen and employers, workmen and workmen, employers and employers permanently

70. Under the Factories Act, 1948 the working hours of 8 per day and 48 per week
(A) include spread over.
(B) are minimum working hours
(C) include rest interval period.
(D) do not include rest interval period.

71. Match the following schedules under the I. D. Act, 1947

(a) I schedule	(i) conditions of service for change of which notice is to be given
(b) II and IIIschedules	(ii) Labour courts

	and Industrial Tribunals
(c) IV schedule	(iii) Industries which may be declared as public utility services
(d) V schedule	(iv) Unfair labour practices

	(a)	(b)	(c)	(d)
(A)	(iv)	(iii)	(ii)	(i)
(B)	(ii)	(iii)	(i)	(iv)
(C)	(iii)	(ii)	(i)	(iv)
(D)	(iv)	(ii)	(iii)	(i)

72. In USA, the Labour Management Relations Act (Taft Hartley Act) was enacted in :
(A) 1937 (B) 1947
(C) 1957 (D) 1967

73. Recognition of the trade union in industry under the code of discipline was developed in the year
(A) 1952 (B) 1957
(C) 1958 (D) 1962

74. Who considered collective bargaining as the most important concept for determining the terms and conditions of employment
(A) Sidney and Beatrice Webb
(B) Robert Hoxie
(C) John T. Dunlop
(D) Samuel Gompers

75. Where the recruitment happens through the compulsory intervention of trade unions, the system is called:
(A) Closed shop
(B) Union shop
(C) Open shop
(D) None of the above

ANSWER KEYS

Q01 B	Q02 B	Q03 C	Q04 C	Q05 C	Q06 C	Q07 B	Q08 D	Q09 B	Q10 B
Q11 B	Q12 B	Q13 D	Q14 B	Q15 B	Q16 D	Q17 B	Q18 B	Q19 D	Q20 A
Q21 C	Q22 B	Q23 C	Q24 B	Q25 C	Q26 D	Q27 A	Q28 C	Q29 A	Q30 B
Q31 B	Q32 A	Q33 B	Q34 A	Q35 B	Q36 B	Q37 D	Q38 D	Q39 B	Q40 C
Q41 B	Q42 A	Q43 D	Q44 A	Q45 C	Q46 A	Q47 C	Q48 D	Q49 D	Q50 A
Q51 D	Q52 C	Q53 C	Q54 D	Q55 A	Q56 A	Q57 A	Q58 B	Q59 B	Q60 A
Q61 C	Q62 C	Q63 C	Q64 C	Q65 A	Q66 C	Q67 B	Q68 A	Q69 C	Q70 D
Q71 C	Q72 B	Q73 B	Q74 D	Q75 A					

3. UGC-NET-PAPER-II_LABOUR WELFARE AND INDUSTRIAL RELATIONS

1. Match the following :

Thinker Management Principle

a. F.W. Taylor	i. Authority and Responsibility
b. Henri Fayol	ii. Hierarchy
c. Weber	iii. Separation of planning from doing
d. Elton Mayo	iv. Human Relations Approach

Codes :

	a	b	c	d
(A)	iii	i	iv	ii
(B)	iii	iv	i	ii
(C)	iii	i	ii	iv
(D)	iii	ii	i	iv

2. Which of the following is the major element of planning process ?
   (A) Developing leadership abilities
   (B) Selecting right people
   (C) Perception of opportunities
   (D) Motivating people

3. Which principle of management is violated by matrix organization structure ?
   (A) Division of Labour
   (B) Unity of Direction
   (C) Unity of Command
   (D) None of the above

4. Which of the following involves careful analysis of inputs and corrective actions before operation is completed ?
   (A) Feed forward control
   (B) Concurrent control
   (C) Feedback control
   (D) All the above

5. Which of the following is not a semantic barrier of communication ?
   (A) Faulty translation
   (B) Ambiguous words
   (C) Specialist's language
   (D) Inattention

6. People should be regarded as assets rather than variable costs was emphasised in
   (A) Personnel Management
   (B) Human Resource Management
   (C) Personnel Administration
   (D) Public Administration

7. The classical theorists favoured organisation based on
   (A) Civilian model
   (B) Strategic model
   (C) Military model
   (D) None of the above

8. Job analysis includes :
   (A) Job description and job enlargement
   (B) Job enlargement and job enrichment
   (C) Job description and job specification
   (D) All of the above

9. A test which measures, what it is intended to measure is
   (A) Reliable test
   (B) Standardised test
   (C) Objective test
   (D) Valid test

10. An enquiry that is conducted afresh because of the objections raised by alleged employee is called
   (A) Domestic enquiry
   (B) De-novo enquiry
   (C) Ex-parte enquiry
   (D) None of the above

11. The concept of HRD scorecard was introduced in India by
(A) Udai Pareek
(B) Rao and Pareek
(C) T.V. Rao
(D) Arun Honappa

12. Performance appraisal by all the following parties is called 360^0 performance appraisal :
(A) Supervisors and Peers
(B) Subordinates and Employees themselves
(C) Users of Service and Consultants
(D) All the above

13. The following is the right process of training :
(A) Instructional design, validation, need analysis, implementation and evaluation
(B) Need analysis, instructional design, validation, implementation and evaluation
(C) Need analysis, validation, instructional design, implementation and evaluation
(D) Instructional design, need analysis, implementation, validation and evaluation

14. Fish bone analysis as a tool of quality circle was advanced by
(A) Edward Deming
(B) Joseph Juran
(C) Kouru Ishi Kawa
(D) Phillip Crosby

15. Match the following :

Books and Concepts	Authors
a. Games People Play	i. Eric Bernie
b. I am OK you are OK	ii. Kurt Lewin
c. Johari Window	iii. Thomas A.Harris
d. Force Field Analysis	iv. Joseph Lufth & Harry Inghams

Codes :

	a	b	c	d
(A)	ii	i	iv	iii
(B)	i	iii	iv	ii
(C)	iv	ii	iii	i
(D)	iii	i	ii	iv

16. Which of the following decreases group cohesiveness ?
(A) Agreement on group goals
(B) Frequency of interaction
(C) Large group size
(D) All the above

17. Managers subscribing to ______ assumptions attempt to structure, control and closely supervise their employees.
(A) Theory 'X'
(B) Theory 'Y'
(C) Both Theory 'X' and Theory 'Y'
(D) Neither Theory 'X' nor Theory'Y'

18. According to Fiedler's Contingency Model of Leadership, which one of the following is a situational variable ?
(A) Leader – Member relationship
(B) Organisational System
(C) Degree of task structure
(D) Leader's position power

19. The right sequence of steps in Kurt Lewin's change procedure is
(A) Unfreezing – Moving – Freezing
(B) Moving – Unfreezing – Freezing
(C) Unfreezing – Freezing – Moving
(D) Freezing – Moving – Unfreezing

20. Which of the following is not a traditional method of organizational development ?
(A) Survey feedback
(B) Sensitivity training
(C) Process consultation
(D) Managerial grid

21. Characteristics of Industrial Relations do not include :

(A) Industrial Relations are outcome of employment relationship in an industrial enterprise.
(B) Industrial Relations promote the skills and methods of adjustment and co-operation with each other.
(C) Industrial Relations create complex rules and regulations to maintain cordial relations.
(D) Industrial Relations system creates an environment of distrust and conflict.

22. Who are not the Actors of Industrial Relations ?
(A) Workers and their organizations
(B) Employers and their organisations
(C) Community and cultural associations
(D) Government and the role of the State

23. Which of the following is a machinery for settlement of industrial disputes ?
(A) Indian Labour Conference
(B) Joint Management Council
(C) Industrial Tribunal
(D) Standing Labour Committees

24. Match List – I with List – II :

List – I

a. Joint Management Council consisting of representatives of workers and management was considered by the Indian Labour Conference (ILC) in its 15th Session in the year
b. Works Committees were set-up under the Industrial Disputes Act in the year
c. ILO established in the year
d. First National Commission on Labour submitted its report in the year

List – II

i. 1958
ii. 1947
iii. 1919
iv. 1969

Codes :

	a	b	c	d
(A)	i	ii	iii	iv
(B)	iv	i	iii	ii
(C)	iii	i	ii	iv
(D)	ii	iv	i	ii

25. Which of the following trends in the employment relations in the new economic era is not correct ?
(A) Declining stability and security
(B) Declining labour intensity
(C) No shift from contract of service to contract of service
(D) Declining mutual commitment

26. A Trade Union means "An association of workers in one or more professions carried on mainly for the purpose of protecting and advancing the members' economic interest in connection with their daily work". Identify the author :
(A) Sidney and Beatrice Webb
(B) J. Cunnison
(C) G.D.H. Cole
(D) Clyde E. Dankert

27. A union may claim recognition for an industry in a local area, if it has membership of
(A) 10% of the workers in that industry.
(B) 15% of the workers in that area.
(C) 25% of the workers of that industry in that area.
(D) 30% of the workers in similar industry.

28. Who among the following advocated the Trusteeship Theory of Trade Union ?
(A) N.M. Lokhande
(B) B.P. Wadia
(C) G.L. Nanda
(D) M.K. Gandhi

29. Inter and intra-union rivalry in Trade Unions is reduced by
(A) The provisions of the Industrial Disputes Act 1947

(B) By voluntary tripartite code of inter-union rivalry – 1957
(C) By bipartite mutual agreement at the industry level
(D) Above all

30. Match the following trade unions according to the year of formation :

List – I	List – II
a. AITUC	i. 1947
b. CITU	ii. 1948
c. INTUC	iii. 1920
d. HMS	iv. 1970

Codes :

	a	b	c	d
(A)	iii	iv	i	ii
(B)	ii	iii	iv	i
(C)	iii	i	ii	iv
(D)	i	ii	iii	v

31. 'Employment Injury' means personal injury to an employee caused by accident or occupational disease arising out of and in the course of employment being an insurable employment if the accident occurs or occupational disease is contracted only within territorial limits of India and not outside India. The above statement is
(A) correct.
(B) incorrect.
(C) true only in case of occupational injury.
(D) true only in case of accident.

32. Under ESI Act, 1948 a member of the Corporation, Standing Committee or the Medical Council shall cease to be a member of the body if he fails to attend
(A) two consecutive meetings
(B) three meetings intermittently
(C) three consecutive meetings
(D) four consecutive meetings

33. Under Workmen's Compensation Act,1923
(A) individual manager subordinate to an employer cannot act as managing agent.
(B) managing agent includes an individual manager subordinate to an employer.
(C) only employer can act as managing agent.
(D) the appropriate government shall appoint managing agent.

34. The Workmen's Compensation Act, 1923, the Maternity Benefit Act, 1965 and the Employees State Insurance Act, 1948
(A)together can be applicable.
(B) the Maternity Benefit Act and the Employees State Insurance Act can be applicable at a time.
(C) the Workmen's Compensation Act and the Employees State Insurance Act can be applicable at a time.
(D) if the Workmen's Compensation Act and the Maternity Benefit Act are applicable, the Employees State Insurance Act is not applicable.

35. What is the content of the Schedule I of the ESI Act, 1948 ?
(A) List of injuries deemed to result in permanent total disablement.
(B) List of injuries deemed to result in permanent partial disablement.
(C) List of occupational diseases.
(D) None of the above

36. A person is qualified to be chosen as a member of the executive or any other office bearer of the registered trade union if he attained the age of
(A) Fifteen years
(B) Eighteen years
(C) Twenty one years
(D) Twenty five years

37. The registered trade union can collect political fund from its members as a
(A) general fund
(B) cannot collect political fund
(C) separate fund from the interested members
(D) only from political parties

38. 'Award' under Industrial Disputes Act, 1947 is
(a) not interim determination of labour court
(b) not arbitration award under Section 10A
(c) not final determination of labour court
(d) not final determination of arbitration award under section 10A
(A) All statements are true.
(B) (a) and (d) are true.
(C) (b) is true.
(D) All statements are wrong.

39. The dispute of individual workman is deemed to be industrial dispute if the dispute or difference is connected with or arising out of the following where no other workman nor any union of workman is a party to the dispute.
(A) Grievance of an individual workman.
(B) Discharge of an individual workman.
(C) Dismissal of an individual workman.
(D) Discharge, dismissal, retrenchment or otherwise termination of services of an individual workman.

40. The ceiling on wage or salary for calculation of Bonus under the Payment of Bonus Act 1965 is:
(A) Rs. 2,500 (B) Rs. 3,500
(C) Rs.4,500 (D) Rs. 6,500

41. "A desirable state of existence comprehending physical, mental, moral and emotional health or well being" is the theme of which concept of Labour Welfare ?
(A) Social Concept
(B) Total Concept
(C) Relative Concept
(D) Positive Concept

42. **Assertion (A) :** Labour Welfare is relative to time and space.
Reason (R) : It shall be universal and perpetual.
(A) Assertion and Reason are right.
(B) Assertion is wrong and Reason is right.
(C) Both Assertion and Reason are wrong.
(D) Assertion is right but its explanation given in Reason is wrong.

43. Minimum conditions of welfare is explained by
(A) Dr. Aykroid's formula
(B) Subsistence Theory
(C) Both (A) and (B)
(D) None of the above

44. Which of the following is not a principle of Labour Welfare ?
(A) The Principle of Uniformity
(B) The Principle of Co-ordination and Integration
(C) The principle of Association
(D) The Principle of Timeliness

45. Match the following :
List – I
(Theme)
a. The labour welfare philosophy is meant for guarding the interests of labour against the exploitation of employers.
b. The labour welfare philosophy exposes the cause of empathic considerations by the employer of employee well being
c. The employer has to set out a portion of the profits for the benefit of the employees

d. Labour Welfare is provided for pacifying the agitating working class

List – II
(Theory)
i. Trusteeship Theory
ii. Placating Theory
iii. Policing Theory
iv. Philanthropic Theory

Codes :

	a	b	c	d
(A)	ii	iv	iii	i
(B)	iii	iv	i	ii
(C)	iii	i	ii	iv
(D)	iv	ii	iii	i

46. "Labour is not a commodity" – is the assertion made by
(A) the Declaration of Philadelphia adopted by 26th session of ILO
(B) the Magna Carta
(C) the Constitution of India
(D) the International Labour Conference

47. Match the following :

Concept	**Propagators**
a. Industrial Democracy	i. Karl Marx
b. Industrial Citizenship	ii. Robert Owen
c. Class Conflict	iii. Peter F. Drucker
d. Welfare Movement	iv. Sydney & Beatrice Webbs

Codes :

	a	b	c	d
(A)	iii	i	ii	iv
(B)	iv	iii	i	ii
(C)	ii	i	iv	iii
(D)	ii	iv	i	iii

48. **Assertion (A) :** Industrial Labour in India has been migratory.
Reason (R) : Driving force in migration comes almost entirely from one end of the channel, that is the village end.
(A) Both (A) and (R) are wrong.
(B) (A) is wrong and (R) is right.
(C) (A) is right and (R) also is right.
(D) (A) is right and (R) is wrong.

49. Match the following :

Theory of wages	**Propagators**
a. Wage Fund Theory	i. John Bates Clark
b. Marginal Productivity Theory	ii. John Davidson
c. Bargaining Theory	iii. John Stuart Mill
d. Investment Theory	iv. Gilelman

Codes :

	a	b	c	d
(A)	ii	iv	i	iii
(B)	iii	i	ii	iv
(C)	iv	ii	iii	i
(D)	i	iii	ii	iv

50. The "Marginal Discounted Product of Labour" as a modified version of Marginal productivity Theory was advanced by
(A) Taussig
(B) Kalecki
(C) Ricardo
(D) Adam smith

ANSWER KEYS

Q01 C	Q02 C	Q03 C	Q04 A	Q05 D	Q06 B	Q07 C	Q08 C	Q09 D	Q10 B
Q11 C	Q12 D	Q13 B	Q14 C	Q15 B	Q16 C	Q17 A	Q18 B	Q19 A	Q20 C
Q21 D	Q22 C	Q23 C	Q24 A	Q25 C	Q26 A	Q27 C	Q28 D	Q29 B	Q30 A
Q31 B	Q32 C	Q33 D	Q34 D	Q35 D	Q36 B	Q37 C	Q38 D	Q39 D	Q40 B
Q41 B	Q42 D	Q43 C	Q44 A	Q45 B	Q46 A	Q47 B	Q48 C	Q49 B	Q50 A

4. UGC-NET-Paper-III_LABOUR WELFARE AND INDUSTRIAL RELATIONS

1. Match the following:

List – I	**List – II**
(Contributions)	(Propagators)
a. Ivan Pavlov	i. Social Learning Thoery
b. B.F. Skinner	ii. S-O-B-C.Model
c. Albert Bandura	iii.Classical Conditioning
d. Freud Luthans	iv. Operant Conditioning

Codes :

	a	b	c	d
(A)	i	iii	iv	ii
(B)	ii	iv	iii	i
(C)	iii	iv	i	ii
(D)	iv	ii	iii	i

2. 'Case of Schimdt' is associated with which School of Management thought ?
   (A) Human Relations School
   (B) Behavioural School
   (C) Systems Approach
   (D) Scientific Management
3. Arrange the following systems in the right order on the managerial style continuum suggested by Rensis Likert
   (a) Consultative
   (b) Benevolent Authoritative
   (c) Exploitative Authoritative
   (d) Joint decision-making
   (A) c, b, a, d (B) c, a, b, d
   (C) b, a, c, d (D) c, d, b, a
4. Performance Appraisal is a primary human resource management process that links employees and organizations and provides input for other processes through these means :
   (A) Identification, measurement, management.
   (B) Assessment, direction, development.
   (C) Recruitment, Selection, on boarding.
   (D) Skill, effort, responsibility.
5. The amount sufficient to enable a worker to live in reasonable comfort, having regard to all obligations to which an average worker would ordinarily be subject to
   (A) Minimum Wage
   (B) Fair Wage
   (C) Living Wage
   (D) Nominal Wage
6. Technique of drawing conclusions from a candidate's hand writing about future performance in a role is

(A) Graphology
(B) Physiognomy
(C) Phrenology
(D) Astronomy

7. Which of the following is method of Union recognition ?
(A) Secret Ballot
(B) Membership Verification
(C) Check-off System
(D) All the above

8. Find out the approach which does not include industrial relations
(A) Psychological approach
(B) Sociological approach
(C) Human relations approach
(D) Physiological approach

9. Workers do join Trade Unions : Find out the incorrect reason out of the following :
(A) To attain economic security
(B) To improve bargaining power
(C) To ventilate their grievancies
(D) To satisfy their family needs

10. Match the following :

List – I (Unions)	**List – II (Functions)**
a. Craft Union	i. Associations of workers or different categories
b. General Union	ii. Based on craft non-managerial personnel
c. Industrial Union	iii. Either unionization of the same industry or different industry.
d. Federation	iv. Unionisation of workers any region or any job occupation

Codes :

	a	b	c	d
(A)	ii	iv	i	iii
(B)	ii	i	iii	iv
(C)	iv	i	ii	iii
(D)	i	ii	iii I	v

11. Who coined the term 'informal sector'?
(A) Keith Davis
(B) Amartya Sen
(C) Mahabub Ul Haq
(D) Keith Hart

12. Reducing the number of employees at operational level and reorganizing the work system in order to attain greater productivity.
(A) Downsizing
(B) Manpower inventory
(C) Manpower forecasting
(D) All the above

13. Which of the following is not a method of social security ?
(A) Social Assistance
(B) Social Action
(C) Social Insurance
(D) Mutual Assistance

14. Which of the following statements about workers' participation in Management in India is not true ?
(A) It is a part of the 20 point Economic programme.
(B) It is provided in the Directive Principles of State Policy.
(C) It is made a Constitutional provision under the 42nd Amendment Act.
(D) It is a justiceable right of the workers.

15. Who has given the concept of 'Core competence' ?
(A) Sumantra Ghosal & C.A. Bartlett
(B) T. Deal and A. Kennedy
(C) C.K. Prahalad and G. Hamel
(D) C.A. Forehand and B. Von Gilnev

16. Who has advanced the Goal setting theory of Performance Management ?
(A) E.A. Locke & Gary Lutham
(B) F. Trompenaavs and Charles Hamp
(C) R. Tung and Arthur Anderson
(D) J. C. Usunier and P.N. Gharvi

17. Match the following :

List – I (Authors)	List – II (Books)
a. Tom Peters & Waterman	i. The Future Shock
b. Thomas Friedman	ii. The Revolutionary Wealth
c. Alvin Tofler	iii. The World is flat
d. Heidi & Alvin Tofler	iv. In search of Excellence

Codes :

	a	b	c	d
(A)	iv	ii	iii	i
(B)	i	iv	ii	iii
(C)	iv	iii	i	ii
(D)	iii	iv	ii	i

18. Who has advance the PDCA cycle of Quality Management ?
(A) Joseph M. Juran
(B) W. Edwards Deming
(C) Kaoru Ishikawa
(D) Phillip Crosby

19. Which of the following statements about I.L.O. is not true ?
(A) I.L.O is a tripartite body.
(B) I.L.O was established in 1919.
(C) I.L.O passes only recommendations.
(D) I.L.O conventions are mandatory for those countries which ratify them.

20. Match the following contributions to TQM with the contributors :

List – I (Contributors)	List – II (Contributions)
a. Walter A.Shewart	i. Concept of Internal Customer
b. Joseph M.Juran	ii. Product Design Quality
c. Kaoru Ishikawa	iii. Statistical control charts
d. Genichi Taguchi	iv. Quality as 'fitness for use'

Codes :

	a	b	c	d
(A)	ii	i	iii	iv
(B)	iv	iii	i	ii
(C)	ii	iii	i	iv
(D)	iii	iv	i	ii

21. Power distance, uncertainty avoidance, individualism and masculinity as dimensions of cross–cultural comparative model is given by
(A) Kluckhohn & Strodthbeck
(B) Geert Hofstede
(C) Andres Lauvent
(D) Hall and Trompenaar

22. Which of the following organizations are world oriented ?
(A) Geocentric
(B) Polycentric
(C) Regiocentric
(D) Ethnocentric

23. Find out the characteristics of collective bargaining which is not applicable;
(A) It is a collective process.
(B) It is a flexible process.
(C) It is not a bipartile process.
(D) It is interdisciplinary system.

24. Find out the one which is not an element of employee empowerment :
(A) Belief system and trust
(B) Purposefulness
(C) Arbitrariness
(D) Self sufficiency or Competency

25. Which of the following is not a factor of emotional intelligence ?
(A) Ability
(B) Reason
(C) Emotion
(D) Thinking without feeling

26. Find out the origin of the statement in a socialist democracy labour is a partner in the common task of development, should participate in it with enthusiasm.

(A) Constitution of India
(B) Directive principles of State Policy
(C) Industrial Policy Resolution 1956
(D) Royal Commission on Labour

27. The First Indian Trade Union led by women was
(A) A.I.T.U.C.
(B) I.N.T.U.C.
(C) H.M.S.
(D) C.I.T.U.

28. The first commission to recommend tripartism consultation in India was
(A) The First National Commission on Labour
(B) The Second National Commission on Labour
(C) The Royal Commission on Labour
(D) The Indian Labour Conference

29. India ratified I.L.O. Convention No. 144 on tripartite consultation among government, employer's and worker's representatives in :
(A) 1968 (B) 1958
(C) 1978 (D) 1988

30. A Joint Consultative Board (J.C.B.) of industry and labour was set up in 1951 with the initiative of :
(A) V.V. Giri
(B) G.L. Nanda
(C) Morarji Desai
(D) Jagjivan Ram

31. Three tier framework of industrial relations was proposed by :
(A) Kochan, T.A., et. Al
(B) Richardson J.H.
(C) Clark Kerr
(D) John T. Dunlop

32. A system of industrial relations where social and labour issues are discussed between trade unions and management at enterprise level is :
(A) Bipartism
(B) Tripartism
(C) Social dialogue
(D) None of the above

33. The relations between government and transnational corporations are divided into liberal, neo-mercantilist and neoimperialist categories by :
(A) Richardson, J.H.
(B) Clark Kerr
(C) Kochan, T.A., et.al
(D) John T. Dunlop

34. Which act requires employers in industrial establishments to define the conditions of employment ?
(A) The Factories Act, 1948
(B) The Industrial Disputes Act,1947
(C) The Industrial Employment (standing orders) Act, 1946
(D) The Trade Union Act, 1926

35. Who identified the types of unions as business, predatory, dependent and friendly ?
(A) Roberts, B.C.
(B) Robert F. Hoxie
(C) Kirkaldy, H.S.
(D) Perlman Selig

36. Who proposed that industrial relations activities take place among three principal social partners at three levels ?
(A) John T. Dunlop
(B) Richardson, J.H.
(C) Kochan, T.A. et.al
(D) Clark Kerr

37. Arrange the following steps involved in establishing a career development system in proper sequence :
(a) Vision
(b) Needs

(c) Action plan
(d) Results
(A) d, c, b, a (B) b, a, c, d
(C) b, d, a, c (D) c, a, b, d

38. Human values in regard to Management Development do not include
(A) Dignity and forgiveness
(B) Arrogance and anger
(C) Gratitude and gentleness
(D) Humility and Honesty

39. Management development is concerned with learning of
(A) Mechanical skills
(B) Specific job skills
(C) Conceptual and creative skills
(D) All the above

40. According to Robert L. Katz, the right sequence of relative importance of various managerial skills from top to bottom is
(a) technical
(b) human
(c) conceptual
(A) c, b, a (B) a, b, c
(C) c, a, b (D) b, c, a

41. The concept of management by objectives was given by
(A) Peter F. Drucker
(B) Luther Gulick
(C) Rensis Likert
(D) Blake and Mouton

42. OCTAPACE culture means:
(A) Openness-cooperation-Truth-Authenticity-Proaction-Autonomy-Collaboration-Experimentation
(B) Openness-Confrontation-Trust-Autonomy-Proaction-Authority-Collaboration-Experimentation
(C) Openness-Confrontation-Trust-Authority-Proaction-Autonomy-cooperation-Experimentation
(D) Openness-Confrontation-Trust-Authenticity-Proaction-Autonomy-Collaboration-Experimentation

43. Empowerment means authority to make decisions in ones area of operation
(A) by taking approval from the senior
(B) without having to get approval from anyone else
(C) without caring for the consequences
(D) All the above

44. Self perceived talents, motives and values that influence career of an individual are known as
(A) career anchors
(B) career plans
(C) career aims
(D) none of the above

45. Who has advanced the Bottom of the Pyramid concept ?
(A) Garry Dessler
(B) Peter Drucker
(C) C.K. Prahlad
(D) Michael Porter

46. Which one is not a general conceplt of T.Q.M. ?
(A) Continuous Improvement
(B) Team Work
(C) Strategy
(D) Quality Education

47. Which one of the following is not an interpersonal role identified by Henry Mintzberg ?
(A) The Figure head role
(B) The Leader role
(C) The Liason role
(D) The Resource – allocator role

48. Which one is part of Michael Porter's generic strategies ?
(A) Cost leadership strategy
(B) Focus strategy

(C) Differentiation strategy
(D) All the above

49. Which one is not a part of M.C. Kinsy's 7's frame work ?
(A) Standards
(B) Structure
(C) Skills
(D) Strategy

50. A corporate wide pay plan that uses a structured formula to allocate a portion of annual company profits to employees is known as :
(A) Gain sharing
(B) Profit sharing
(C) ESOPS sharing
(D) All of the above

51. Who has called the POSDCORB a 'folklore' ?
(A) Michael Armstrong
(B) Michael Poole
(C) Rosemary Stewart
(D) Henry Mirzberg

52. Who has called the scientific management a 'rabble hypothesis'?
(A) Peter F. Drucker
(B) Elton Mayo
(C) Douglas McGregor
(D) None of the above

53. 'Red hot stove' rule of disciplinary action was suggested by
(A) Douglas Mc Gregor
(B) Dale Yader
(C) Richard P. Calhoon
(D) Fred Luthans

54. "Model Grievance Procedure" is given in the
(A) Industrial Disputes Act
(B) Employee State Insurance Act
(C) Industrial Employment (standingorders) Act
(D) Code of Discipline

55. Which of the following is a reason for supporting a wider span of control ?
(A) To reduce opportunities for delegations
(B) To have tighter control within the organisation
(C) To increase contact between managers and employees
(D) To reduce a process of delaying

56. A manager may delegate any of the following except
(A) Authority
(B) Work load
(C) Responsibility
(D) None of the above

57. Which of the following is Herzberg's hygine factors ?
(A) Recognition at work place
(B) Reasonable salary
(C) Responsibility for work
(D) Sense of achievement

58. During whose prime ministership the New Economic Policy was introduced in India ?
(A) Indira Gandhi
(B) Rajiv Gandhi
(C) P.V. Narasimha Rao
(D) A.B. Vajpayee

59. Arrange the needs in the order given by Abraham Maslow in his need hierarchy theory of motivation.
(a) Esteem need
(b) Self-actualization need
(c) Physiological need
(d) Safety needs
(e) Social needs
(A) d, a, c, b, e (B) c, d, e, a, b
(C) a, d, c, b, e (D) c, e, d, a, b

60. What is the limit of the salary of the supervisor to be covered under the I.D. Act, 1947 ?
(A)Rs. 1200 per month
(B) Rs.1600 per month
(C) Rs. 2500 per month
(D) Rs. 3500 per month

61. Match the following :
List – I
a. Principle of Protection and Welfare
b. Principle of Social Justice
c. Principle of Regulation
d. Principle of Social Security
List – II
i. The Trade Union Act, 1926
ii. Robert Owen
iii.Payment of Gratuity Act
iv. The Philadelphia Charter
Codes :

	a	b	c	d
(A)	ii	iv	i	iii
(B)	ii	iv	iii	i
(C)	iv	ii	iv	i
(D)	iv	iii	i	ii

62. The basic postulates on which the ILO standards lie are
(A) Labour is not a commodity
(B) Freedom of expression and of association are essential to sustained progress
(C) Poverty anywhere constitutes danger to prosperity everywhere
(D) All the above

63. Which of the following statements is / are true ?
(a) Labour Legislation is part of Social legislation.
(b) Social Legislation is part of Labour Legislation.
(c) Government is the regulatory authority in case of Social Legislation and Labour Legislation.
(d) Civil Law judgement is based on earlier judgements and labour law judgement is based on workers welfare.
(A) All the statements are true.
(B) (b) is true.
(C) (d) is true.
(D) (a), (c) and (d) are true.

64. The article in Indian Constitution that imposes prohibition on traffic in human beings, beggar and other similar forms of forced labour is:
(A) Article 19 (B) Article 23
(C) Article 32 (D) Article 45

65. The Industrial Employment (standing orders) Act, 1946 applies to every establishment employing
(A) 100 workmen
(B) 150 workmen
(C) 150 workmen on any day preceeding 12 months
(D) 150 workmen on any day preceeding 12 months and the government can order by application to establishments employing less than 100.

66. The following persons are constructed as insider of a registered trade union.
(A) Honorary member from the other organization.
(B) Honorary member from other profession.
(C) Politician who guides the registered trade union.
(D) retired and retrenched members of the trade union.

67. Workers' facilitation centres shall be set up by the facilitating agency under the
(A) Payment of Bonus Act, 1965
(B) Equal Remuneration Act, 1976
(C) Factories Act, 1948

(D) The unorganized sector workers' Social Security Act, 2005

68. If the money is due from the employer under the settlement or award, the workman or his assignee can make an application to the appropriate government for the recovery within the period given below.
(A) One year.
(B) One year and also after the said period of the appropriate government is satisfied that the applicant has sufficient cause for not making the application within one year.
(C) Two years.
(D) Three years.

69. Ambulance room shall be provided if
(A) 30 womens workers are employed under Maternity Benefit Act, 1965.
(B) Creche is provided under the Factories Act, 1948.
(C) 500 workers are employed in the factory under the Factories Act, 1948.
(D) The Workmens' Compensation Act, 1923 is applicable to the factory.

70. The first factory commission was appointed in
(A) 1875 (B) 1881
(C) 1885 (D) 1895

71. Under the payment of Bonus Act, 1965, the gross profits derived by an employer from an establishment in respect of any accounting year shall be computed
(A) In case of Banking Company according to schedule II and in any other case schedule I.
(B) In case of Banking Company according to schedule I and in any other case schedule II.
(C) In case of Banking Company and in any other case schedule I.
(D) In case of Banking Company and in any other case schedule II.

72. Which Act provides for the appointment of conciliation officers and adjudication authorities ?
(A) The Factories Act, 1948
(B) The Industrial Disputes Act,1947
(C) The Trade Unions Act, 1926
(D) None of the above

73. The first to introduce the term collective bargaining :
(A) Sidney and Beatrice webb
(B) Samuel Gompers
(C) Clark Kerr
(D) Robert Hoxie

74. Find the machinery which is not method of settlement of industrial dispute :
(A) consultation
(B) works committee
(C) conciliation
(D) Adjudication

75. Match the following :

List – I	**List – II**
a. Human Capital Approach	i. David Mcclelland
b. Socio-PsychologicalApproach	ii. UNDP
c. Poverty Alleviation Approach	iii.T.W. Scultz
d. World Human Development Approach	iv. World Bank

Codes :

	a	b	c	d
(A)	ii	iv	i	iii
(B)	iii	iv	ii	i
(C)	iii	i	iv	ii
(D)	iv	ii	i	iii

ANSWER KEYS

Q01 C	Q02 D	Q03 A	Q04 A	Q05 A	Q06 A	Q07 D	Q08 D	Q09 D	Q10 A
Q11 D	Q12 A	Q13 B	Q14 D	Q15 C	Q16 A	Q17 C	Q18 B	Q19 C	Q20 D
Q21 B	Q22 A	Q23 C	Q24 C	Q25 D	Q26 C	Q27 C	Q28 C	Q29 C	Q30 B
Q31 A	Q32 A	Q33 C	Q34 C	Q35 B	Q36 C	Q37 B	Q38 B	Q39 C	Q40 A
Q41 A	Q42 D	Q43 B	Q44 A	Q45 C	Q46 C	Q47 D	Q48 D	Q49 A	Q50 B
Q51 D	Q52 B	Q53 A	Q54 D	Q55 C	Q56 C	Q57 B	Q58 C	Q59 B	Q60 D
Q61 A	Q62 D	Q63 D	Q64 B	Q65 D	Q66 D	Q67 D	Q68 B	Q69 C	Q70 A
Q71 B	Q72 B	Q73 A	Q74 A	Q75 C					

HIGHLIGHTS

- **Frederick Taylor:** Father of scientific management.
- **Henry Fayol:** Father of Administrative management or Father of Modern Operational Management Theory.
- **Gang plank: Henry Fayol-** A Gang Plank is a temporary arrangement between two different points to facilitate quick & easy communication.
- **Max Weber:** Father of Bureaucracy
- **Robert Owen:** Father of Personnel management
- **Elton Mayo:** Father of Human relation movement
- **Luther Gullick:** POSDCORB
- **Newman and Summer:** POLC
- **POCCC:** Henry Fayol
- **POSDC:** Koontz and O'Donnell
- **Roethlisberger and Dickson**: Management and Worker
- **Douglas McGregor:** The Human Side of Enterprise
- **Rensis Likert:** The New Patterns of Management
- **Elton Mayo:**The Human Problems of Industrial Civilization
- **Elton Mayo:** IRMB.
- **William J. Reddin:** 3-D theory of Leadership Effectiveness.
- **Kelly J.**: Trait theory of leadership
- **Dale Yoder:** Trade union as a continuous long term association of employees.
- **Robert Hoxie:** Revolutionary Theory of Trade union.
- **John Dunlop:** Industrial Relation is rule making process.
- **Robert Owen:** The New Lenark experiment(Welfare)
- **Sydey Webb and Betrice Webb:** Collective Bargaining
- **V. M. Moorthy:** The seven approaches to philosophy or theory of labour welfare.
- **Lord Beveridge:** Want, Ignorance, Squalor, Idleness, Disease as good as the road to social security.
- **Eric Tryst:** Work linked democracy.
- **Kurt Lewin:** Action Research.
- **T.V. Rao:** Father of Indian HRD.
- **ILO:** 1919-Tripartite body- Geveva
- **Dunlop:** System approach of management.
- **Taiichi Ohno:** KANBAN: Just in time: Downward communication
- **First National Commission on Labour:**1969-Dr.P.Gajendragadkar(Chairman)
- **Second National Commission on Labour:**1998-2002-Dr.Ravindra Varma(Chairman)
- **Peter Drucker:** Management by Objective(MBO)
- **W. Edward Deming:** Quality Circle
- **S. R. Udpa:** In 1981, BHEL-First implementation of Quality Circle in India.
- **B. P. Wadia:** First trade union leader in India(Madras)
- **First Factory commission:** 1875

- **Royal Commission on Labour:** 1931
- **Labour investigation committee:** 1946
- Bonus is calculated from available surplus.
- **CBWE:** 1958-Nagpur.
- **IIWE:** 1970
- **Grapevine:** Informal Communication.
- **Delphi technique:** Forecasting

Performance Appraisal Error:

- o Halo effect
- o Contrast error
- o Recency bias
- o Leniency bias
- o Severity bias
- o Self serving bias

Motivation theories

1. **Content theories:** Focus on profiling the needs that people seek to fulfill.
   1) Maslow's Hierarchy of needs theory.
   2) Herzberg's Two factor theory
   3) Alderfer's ERG theory
   4) Mc Clelland Achievement theory

2. **Process theories:** Focus on people's thought or cognitive processes. Emphasize controlling behavior by manipulating its consequences.
   1) Goal Setting theory
   2) Vroom's Expectancy theory
   3) Porters Performance satisfaction model
   4) Adams Equity theory

Theories of Learning

- **Ivan pavlov:** Classical conditioning
- **B. F. Skinner:** Operant conditioning
- **Albert Bandura:** Social learning model
- **Edward Tolman:** Cognitive framework

ID Act, 1947:

- o **Works Committee:** Equal number of employers and employees.
- o **Conciliation: Settlement-** An attempt by a third party in helping to settle the dispute.
- o **Adjudication: Award-** Labour court, Industrial tribunal or National tribunal to hear and decide the dispute.
- o **Court of Enquiry:** Report
- o **Labour Court, Industrial tribunal and National tribunal**
- o **Schedule-I:** Industries which may be declared to be Public Utility Services.
- o **Schedule-II:** Matters within the jurisdiction of Labour Courts
- o **Schedule-III:** Matters within the jurisdiction of Industrial Tribunals

- **Schedule-IV:** Conditions of Service for Change of which Notice is to be given
- **Schedule-V:** Unfair Labour Practices

Factories Act, 1948:

- **Sec.49:** Welfare officer for more than 500 workers.
- **Sec.40B:** Safety officer for more than 1000 workers.
- **Creches:** For more than 30 womens
- **Canteen:** For more than 250 workers.
- **First Aid Box:** One for every 150 workers
- Ambulance:
- **Shelter, Lunch room, Rest room:** More than 150 workers

Trade Union

- **Webbs:** Industrial Democracy
- **Robert Hoxie:** Social-Psychological approach
- **Hoxie:** Functional Classification of Unionism
- **Karl Marx:** Classical society approach
- **Mahatma Gandhi:** Sarvodaya approach, Class collaboration and Harmony theory
- **Frank Tannenbanum:** Sociological approach
- **Kerr, Dunlop:** Protest approach.
- **Pearlman:** Scarcity-Consciousness theory
- **Cole:** Theory of Union Control of Industry
- **Marx and Engels:** Political Revolutionary Theory of Labour Movement
- **Common:** Environment Theory
- **Mitchell:** Economic Protection Theory of Trade Unionism
- **Simons**: Theory of Monopolistic, anti-Democratic Trade Unionism
- **Tannenbaum:** Theory of Man Vs. Machine

Trade Union Formation :

- **Madras Labour Union**-1918-B.P.Wadia
- **AITUC**-1920-Communist Party
- **INTUC**-1947-Congress party-A. R. Ramanujan
- **HMS**-1948-Socialist Party
- **UTUC**-1949
- **BMS-1955**-BJP-Dattopantji Thengdi
- **All India Railwayman's Federations**-President (V. V. Giri)
- **Ahmedabad Textile Labour Association:** Mahatma Gandhi

Welfare Theories :

- **Trustiship theory:** M. K. Gandhi
- **Revolutionary Theory:** Karl Marx
- **Human relation theory: Elton Mayo**

Theory of Wages:

- **Equity theory:** J. Stacky Adams
- **Purchasing power theory**: A. C. Pigou

- **Demand and Supply theory:** Alfred Marshal
- **Exploitation Theory:** Karl Marx
- **Subsistence theory:** Adam Smith and David Recardo
- **Wage Fund Theory:** John Stuart Mill
- **Marginal Productivity theory:** J.B.Clark
- **Residual Claimant theory:** Francis A.Walker
- **Bargaining theory:** John Davidson

Johari Window: Joseph Luft and harry Inghams

	Known to self	Not known to self
Known to others	Arena	Blind Spot
Not Known to Others	Façade	Unknown

*****

BIBLIOGRAPHY

- P. Subba Rao(2012): *Essentials of Human Resource and Industrial Relations Text, Cases and Games,* Himalaya Publishing House -5th Revised edition.
- P. Subba Rao(2012): *Personnel and Human Resource Management,* Himalaya Publishing House -4th Revised edition.
- Garry Dessler and Biju Varkkey(2009): *Human Resource Management,* Pearson Prentice Hall -11th edition.
- Garry Dessler and Biju Varkkey(2009): *Human Resource Management,* Pearson Prentice Hall -11th edition.
- Raymond A.Noe, John R. Hollenbeck, Barry Gerhat and Pratik M. Wright(2007):*Fundamentals of Human Resource Management,* Tata McGraw-Hill Publishing- 2nd edition.
- David A. Decenzo and Stephen P. Robbins (2001): *Human Resource Management,* John Wiley & Sons, Inc -6th edition.
- Harold Koontz and Heinz Weihrich (2004):*Essentials of Management,* Tata McGraw-Hill Publishing- 6th edition.
- Ruddar Datt and K.P.M. Sundharam(2004):*Indian Economy* S.Chand-49th Revised edition.
- John W. Newstrom and Keith Davis(1997):*Organizational Behaviour: Human Behaviour at work,* Tata McGraw-Hill Publishing- 10th edition.
- Suja R.Nair(2010):*Organizational Behaviour: Text and Cases,* Himalaya Publishing House - 1st edition.
- C.B.Mamoria: *Personnel Management(Management of Human Resources)(1997),* Himalaya Publishing House -12th edition.
- S.C.Srivastava: *Industrial Relations and Labour Laws(2004),*Vikas publishing House Pvt.Ltd.-4th revised edition.
- Wendell L. French and Cecil H.Bell, Jr:*Organization Development(2006),*Prentice –Hall of India Pvt .Ltd-6th edition.
- Durga Das Basu: *Introduction to the constitution of India(2006),*Wadhwa Nagpur-19th edition.
- P.C.tripathi: *Personnel Management and Industrial Relations(1998) ,Sultan Chand and Sons* -13th Revised edition.
- Aswathappa, K. (2005): *Human Resource and Personnel Management Text and Cases,* 4th edition
- ICFAI Center for Management Research, *"Introduction to Human Resource Management, 2004.*

****